纪念改革开放40周年
庆祝中华人民共和国成立70周年

中国城市发展报告

（2018/2019）

主　办

中　国　市　长　协　会

承　办

国际欧亚科学院中国科学中心

《中国城市发展报告》编委会　编

中国城市出版社

图书在版编目（CIP）数据

中国城市发展报告（2018/2019）/《中国城市发展报告》编委会编．—北京：中国城市出版社，2019.9

ISBN 978-7-5074-3190-2

Ⅰ．①中…　Ⅱ．①中…　Ⅲ．①城市经济—经济发展—研究报告—中国—2018-2019　Ⅳ．①F299.21

中国版本图书馆 CIP 数据核字（2019）第 158178 号

责任编辑：徐昌强　陈夕涛　陈小娟
责任校对：张惠雯

中国城市发展报告（2018/2019）
主办
中国市长协会
承办
国际欧亚科学院中国科学中心
《中国城市发展报告》编委会　编
*
中国城市出版社出版、发行（北京海淀三里河路 9 号）
各地新华书店、建筑书店经销
逸品书装设计制版
北京圣夫亚美印刷有限公司印刷
*
开本：880 × 1230 毫米　1/16　印张：28½　插页：1　字数：666 千字
2019 年 9 月第一版　　2019 年 9 月第一次印刷
定价：**398.00** 元
ISBN 978-7-5074-3190-2
（904173）

《中国城市发展报告（2018/2019）》
机构组成名单

协办单位：（排名不分先后）

中国城市规划设计研究院

清华大学建筑学院

中国城市科学研究会

中国城市规划学会

中国城市经济学会

中山大学城市与区域研究中心

中国科学院地理科学与资源研究所

国家遥感应用工程技术研究中心

广东工业大学

《中国城市发展报告（2018/2019）》工作委员会

主任委员：王长远

委　　员：林家宁　方兆瑞　　赵旺华

序　一

蒋正華

（第九届、十届全国人大常委会副委员长、国际欧亚科学院执行院长、
国际欧亚科学院中国科学中心主席）

2018 年是全面贯彻习近平新时代中国特色社会主义思想和党的十九大精神的开局之年，同时也恰逢中国改革开放 40 周年。面对世界经济复苏乏力、局部冲突和动荡频发，全球性问题加剧，以及美国挑起的中美贸易战的外部环境，面对我国经济发展进入新常态等一系列深刻变化，全党和全国人民在以习近平同志为核心的党中央坚强领导下，紧紧围绕统筹推进“五位一体”总体布局和协调推进“四个全面”战略布局，坚持以人民为中心的发展思想，坚持稳中求进工作总基调，坚持新发展理念，坚持推进高质量发展，砥砺前行，开拓进取，取得了改革开放的社会主义现代化建设的伟大成就。

过去的一年，还有一件规划界议论和盼望已久的大事——《关于建立国土空间规划体系并监督实施的若干意见》（以下简称《若干意见》），经 2019 年 1 月 23 日中央全面深化改革委员会第六次会议审议通过后，于 2019 年 5 月 23 日由中共中央、国务院正式发布。紧接着，自然资源部为贯彻落实《若干意见》，又印发了《关于全面开展国土空间规划工作的通知》（自然资发〔01987〕号）。这两个文件的出台，为实现“多规合一”和强化国土空间规划对各专项工作的指导约束作用提供了根本遵循方针。

国土空间规划是国家空间发展的指南、可持续发展的空间蓝图，是各类开发保护建设活动的基本依据。党中央、国务院高度重视国土空间规划，习近平总书记曾对此作过多次指示。2014 年 2 月，习近平总书记在北京考察时强调，“考察一个城市首先看规划，规划科学是最大的效益，规划失误是最大的浪费，规划折腾是最大的忌讳”。归纳起来，《若干意见》具有以下四大特点：一是明确要求将主体功能区规划、土地利用规划、城乡规划等空间规划融合为统一的国土空间规划，实现“多规合一”。二是要强化底线约束，立足于资源赋予环境承载能力，划定生态保护红线，永久基本农田保护红线、城镇开发边界以及各类海域保护线，作为调整经济结构、规划产业发展布局，推进城镇化不可逾越的红线。三是强调国土空间规划编制要体现战略性，提高科学性，强化权威性，加强协调性，注重可操作性，国土空

间开发保护实现更高质量、更有效率、更加公平、更可持续目标。四是建立包括国家、省、市县、乡镇四级以及总体规划、详细规划和相关专项规划在内的国土空间规划体系。明确各类规划的编制重点、审批权限，以及实施与监管机制。

本年度《中国城市发展报告》，围绕改革开放40年和新中国成立70周年以及国土空间规划体系改革三大重点，聚焦于改革开放40年来中国城市与城市科学发展、香港与澳门回归、智慧城市、从珠三角到粤港澳大湾区规划，以及中央有关建立国土空间规划体系和全面开展国土空间规划工作的官方与民间专家学者的解读。为此，我们邀请了一些著名院士专家和退休领导作为特邀作者各自撰写某一方面专题，其中包括：中国科学院、中国工程院两院院士、著名人居环境科学家、清华大学吴良镛教授；中国工程院原副院长、光纤传送网与宽带信息网专家邬贺铨院士；中国工程院院士、计算机专家李国杰教授；住房和城乡建设部原副部长、国务院参事、城市规划与建设管理专家仇保兴教授；北京航空航天大学党委书记、移动通信专家曹淑敏教授；原澳门大学校长赵伟教授，以及作为中国改革开放先行探索城市、深圳市委原书记厉有为同志等，我们对他们辛勤的付出谨表示衷心的感谢！

《中国城市发展报告（2018/2019）》仍坚持“中国城市编年史”的基本定位，通过记载、分析、研究全国各类城市本年底的热点问题与最新进展，为决策者、管理者、研究者及社会各界提供参考，并努力体现权威性、综合性和前瞻性。该报告仍延续以往的体例结构，分综论篇、论坛篇、观察篇、专题篇、案例篇及附录篇，全书共收录论文28篇，另附2018年中国城市发展大事记以及城市基本统计数据与城市政策法规文件索引等，力图从不同视角和方面较全面地反映中国城市发展、规划、建设及管理等方面所取得的成绩和存在的问题。与以往几年相比，选题内容有所拓展，特别是以往相对显得有些单薄的论坛篇得到明显加强，文体形式也更具多样性，但由于受编者专业和水平所限，疏漏与不当之处在所难免，敬请读者批评指正。

2019年6月

序　二

（中国市长协会副会长，住房和城乡建设部原副部长）

新中国成立70年来，取得了举世瞩目的伟大成就，社会生产力、综合国力实现了历史性跨越，城镇化进程波澜壮阔，城乡面貌发生了翻天覆地的变化，人民的生活水平显著提高。中国特色社会主义进入新时代，中国经济由高速增长阶段转向高质量发展阶段，城市发展作为经济社会发展的重要组成部分，也进入高质量发展阶段。新时代，我国城市工作要以习近平新时代中国特色社会主义思想为指导，把握我国社会主要矛盾的深刻变化，贯彻创新、协调、绿色、开放、共享的发展理念，坚持以人民为中心的发展思想，满足人民日益增长的美好生活需要，转变城市发展方式，完善城市治理体系，提高城市治理能力，着力解决城市发展中的突出矛盾和问题，不断提升城市环境质量、人民生活质量和城市竞争力，走出一条中国特色的城市发展道路。

住房和城乡建设事业在改革大潮中不断发展前进，群众居住条件显著改善，城市基础设施建设步伐加快，城市承载能力不断提高，生态环境明显改善，为经济社会持续健康发展做出了积极贡献。我们要继续坚持新发展理念，坚定不移推进住房和城乡建设事业高质量发展，做好关系人民群众切身利益的工作：

一是以稳地价稳房价稳预期为目标，促进房地产市场平稳健康发展。坚持房子是用来住的、不是用来炒的定位，着力建立和完善房地产市场平稳健康发展的长效机制，防范化解房地产市场风险。坚持因城施策、分类指导，夯实城市主体责任，加强市场监测和评价考核，切实把稳地价稳房价稳预期的责任落到实处。继续保持调控政策的连续性稳定性，加强房地产市场供需双向调节，改善住房供应结构，支持合理自住需求，坚决遏制投机炒房，强化舆论引导和预期管理，确保市场稳定。加大房地产市场监管力度，继续深入开展打击侵害群众利益的违法违规行为治理房地产乱象专项行动。

二是以加快解决中低收入群体住房困难为中心任务，健全城镇住房保障体系。坚持以政府为主提供基本保障，完善住房保障政策制度，多渠道满足住房困难群众基本住房需要。要完善土地、财税、信贷等支持政策，支持人口流入量大的一线、二线城市和其他热点城市，降低准入门槛，增加公租房有效供应，因地制宜发展共有产权住房。坚持既尽力而为，又量力而行，继续推进棚户区改造，严格把握棚改范围和标准，重点改造老城区内脏乱差的棚户区和国有工矿区、林区、垦区棚户区，加大配套基础设施建设。大力培育发展住房租赁市场，以解决新市民住房问题为主要出发点，补齐租赁住房短板。租赁住房建设要充分考虑产业发展、生活配套等因素，合理布局、科学选址，解决新市民的住房需求。

三是以完善城市基础设施为重点，着力提升城市承载力和系统化水平。用统筹系统的方法加强城市基础设施建设，推进海绵城市建设，加大城市黑臭水体治理和排水防涝设施补短板工作力度。按照垃圾分类的总体原则，加快城镇生活垃圾无害化处理设施建设。继续因地制宜推进地下综合管廊建设。强化城市市政公用设施安全管理，加强城镇供排水、供气、供热、道路桥梁、环卫设施和城市公园等风险排查和隐患治理，切实保障安全运行。

四是以贯彻新发展理念为引领，努力消除“城市病”隐患。切实把新发展理念贯穿到城市建设全过程，加快转变城市发展方式，着力治理“城市病”，促进城市高质量发展。推进绿色城市建设，持续开展生态修复城市修补，系统性修复城市水系统、绿地系统等生态环境，完善城市功能，增强城市宜居性。推进智慧城市建设，充分运用物联网、云计算、大数据、人工智能等现代技术，提高城市信息化、智能化管理水平。推进人文城市建设，保护和传承城市历史文化，贯彻“适用、经济、绿色、美观”的建筑方针，治理贪大、媚洋、求怪等乱象，彰显城市特色和活力。

五是以集中力量解决群众关注的民生实事为着力点，提升城市品质。运用“美好环境与幸福生活共同缔造”的理念和方法，推进老旧小区改造，重点解决供水、供电、供气等问题，促进解决二次供水、停车难问题。打造“15 分钟城市居民活动圈”，逐步完善社区及周边区域的综合服务设施，拓展公共活动空间，让群众生活更加舒适、便利。加强城市管理统筹协调，搭建城市综合管理服务平台，提升城市精细化管理水平，切实增强群众的获得感幸福感。

中国市长协会自 1991 年经国务院批准成立以来，得到了党中央、国务院的高度重视和市长们的大力支持。本着“为城市发展服务，为市长工作服务”的宗旨，协会围绕研究城市问题，促进城市交流，提高城市治理水平以及发展城市经济，面向城市和市长开展了一系列工作，受到了广泛拥戴。新时代、新形势、新任务对我们提出了新的更高要求，协会要认真贯彻落实十九大和中央城市工作会议精神，开拓创新，扎实工作，推动协会工作迈上新台阶。

《中国城市发展报告（2018/2019）》汇集了城市建设管理观念创新、政策创新、制度创新、技术创新的积极探索和宝贵经验，对推进城市绿色、低碳、可持续发展，构建人与自然和谐共处的城市家园，提供了有益借鉴，相信读者会从中受益。

2019 年 6 月

目　录

综论篇

论坛篇

观察篇

专题篇

案例篇

附录篇

综论篇

2018 年中国城市发展综述

春华秋实，岁物丰成。全国人民在前进路上奋力奔跑，年年的收获都丰满而充实。

2018 年，我国的国内生产总值总量突破 90 万亿元，再登新台阶。城镇调查失业率稳定在 5% 左右的较低水平。全国又有 1 000 万以上农村贫困人口摆脱贫困。各项民生事业加快发展，城乡人居环境和居民生活水平又有新的提高。

2018 年，党和国家机构进行了系统性、整体性、重构性的改革，推出 100 多项重要改革举措。京津冀协同发展、长江经济带发展和长三角区域一体化发展、粤港澳大湾区建设等国家战略稳步实施。中国制造、中国创造、中国建造共同发力：嫦娥四号探测器成功发射，第二艘航母出海试航，国产大型水陆两栖飞机水上首飞，北斗导航向全球组网迈出坚实一步。

2018 年，庆祝改革开放 40 周年大会于 12 月 18 日在北京人民大会堂隆重举行。中共中央、国务院颁布“关于表彰改革开放杰出贡献人员的决定”，授予 100 名同志改革先锋称号，颁授改革先锋奖章。96 岁高龄的吴良镛先生以“人居环境科学的创建者”的贡献接受了党和国家“改革先锋”的表彰。中国的人居环境科学理论与实践，成为改革开放 40 周年的标志性成果之一。

一、城镇化与城市发展

（一）城乡经济发展概况

2018 年，面对复杂严峻的国际环境和艰巨繁重的改革发展稳定任务，在以习近平总书记为核心的党中央坚强领导下，我国城乡各地深入贯彻新发展理念，落实高质量发展要求，深化改革扩大开放，经济运行总体平稳、稳中有进。

国家统计局初步核算，2018 年国内生产总值比上年增长 6.6%。其中，第一产业增长 3.5%，第二产业增长 5.8%，第三产业增长 7.6%。一、二、三产业比重为：7.2∶40.7∶52.2，全年最终消费支出对国内生产总值增长的贡献率为 76.2%，资本形成总额的贡献率为 32.4%，货物和服务净出口的贡献率为 −8.6%。全国人均国内生产总值64 644元，比上年增长 6.1%。全员劳动生产率为107 327元/人，比上年提高 6.6%。年末全国居民拥有私人轿车12 589万辆，比上年增长 10.3%。

2018 年，全国居民人均可支配收入28 228元，实际增长 6.5%。按常住地分，城镇居民人均可支配收入39 251元，实际增长 5.6%；农村居民人均可支配收入14 617元，实际增长 6.6%。城乡居民人均收入倍差 2.69，比上年缩小 0.02 个百分点。全国居民人均消费支出19 853元，恩格尔系数为 28.4%，比上年下降 0.9 个百分点，其中城镇为 27.7%，农村为 30.1%。居民消费价格比上年上涨 2.1%。全国农民工总量28 836万人，其中，外出农民工17 266万人，本地农民工11 570万人，农民工人均月收入3 721元。

2018 年年末，中国大陆总人口139 538万人，比上年末增加 530 万人，其中城镇常住人口83 137万人，占总人口比重（常住人口城镇化率）为 59.58%，比上年末提高 1.06 个百分点。户籍人口城镇化率为 43.37%，比上年末提高 1.02 个百分点。全年出生人口1 523万人，出生率为 10.94‰；死亡人口 993 万人，死亡率为 7.13‰；自然增长率为 3.81‰。全国人户分离的人口 2.86 亿人，其中流动人口 2.41 亿人。年末全国就业人员77 586万人，其中城镇就业人员43 419万人。城镇新增就业1 361万人，年末城镇登记失业率为 3.8%，下降 0.1 个百分点。

全年房地产开发投资120 264亿元，房屋新开工面积209 342万平方米，商品房销售面积171 654万平方米，其中住宅147 929万平方米。年末商品房待售面积52 414万平方米，比上年末减少6 510万平方米。棚户区住房改造开工 626 万套，基本建成 511 万套。全国农村地区危房改造 190 万户，其中建档立卡贫困户危房改造 157 万户。

（二）市级行政区划调整与新区设立

据民政部最新统计，2018 年末全国有设市城市 672 个；其中直辖市 4 个，副省级市（中央计划单列）15 个，地级市 278 个，县级市 375 个；县（旗）合计 1 505 个，建制镇21 297个，乡 10 253 个，街道办事处 8 393 个，村委会 54.2 万个，居委会 10.8 万个。

2018 年内，全国设市城市建制的调整变动如下：

国务院批复山东省人民政府，同意撤销地级莱芜市，将其所辖区域划归济南市管辖。设立济南市莱芜区，以原莱芜市莱城区的行政区域为莱芜区的行政区域；设立济南市钢城区，以原莱芜市钢城区的行政区域为钢城区的行政区域。

根据国务院批复，山西省长治市撤销潞城市，设立长治市潞城区。

经国务院批准，山西省撤销怀仁县，设立县级怀仁市；陕西省撤销彬县，设立县级彬州市；青海省撤销茫崖行政委员会和冷湖行政委员会，设立县级茫崖市；江苏省撤销海安县，设立县级海安市；黑龙江省撤销漠河县，设立县级漠河市；湖北省撤销京山县，设立县级京山市；河北省撤销滦县，设立县级滦州市；安徽省撤销潜山县，设立县级潜山市；山东省撤销邹平县，设立县级邹平市；广西壮族自治区撤销荔浦县，设立县级荔浦市；贵州省撤销兴仁县，设立县级兴仁市；云南省撤销水富县，设立县级水富市；甘肃省撤销华亭县，设立县级华亭市。

国务院批复科技部、甘肃省人民政府、浙江省人民政府、新疆维吾尔自治区人民政府、新疆生产建设兵团：同意兰州、白银、宁波、温州、乌鲁木齐、昌吉、石河子等高新技术产业开发区建设国家自主创新示范区。国务院批复山西省人民政府、广西壮族自治区人民政府、广东省人民政府和科技部、同意太原市、桂林市、深圳市等建设国家可持续发展议程创新示范区。

国务院批复湖北省、江西省、广东省、云南省、安徽省、湖南省和重庆市人民政府：同意将荆州、黄石大冶湖、潜江、九江共青城、宜春丰城、湛江、茂名、楚雄、淮南、怀化、荣昌、永川等高新技术产业园区升级为国家高新技术产业开发区，实行现行的国家高新技术产业开发区的政策。这 12 个高新技术产业开发区升级后的规划面积合计 91.841 平方公里。

国务院批复海南省人民政府和商务部：同意设立中国（海南）自由贸易试验区。中国（海南）自由贸易试验区实施范围为海南岛全岛。相关土地、海域开发利用要严格遵守国家法律法规和海南省“多规合一”总体规划，并符合节约集约用地用海的有关要求。涉及无居民海岛的，要严格按照《中华人民共和国海岛保护法》等有关规定办理。

国务院批复同意将河北省蔚县列为国家历史文化名城。至 2018 年末，全国共有国家历史文化名城 134 个。

（三）城市（城区）建设

据住房和城乡建设部统计，2017 年年末，全国设市城市 661 个，城市城区户籍人口 4.1 亿人，暂住人口 0.82 亿人，建成区面积 5.62 万平方公里。

2017 年，全国城市市政公用设施固定资产投资完成19 328亿元，比上年增长 10.7%，占同期全社会固定资产投资总额的 3.01%。其中，道路桥梁、轨道交通、园林绿化投资分别占城市市政公用设施固定资产投资的 36.2%、26.1% 和 9.1%。

2017 年，全国城市用水人口 4.83 亿人，人均日生活用水量 179 升，用水普及率 98.30%；用气人口 4.73 亿人，燃气普及率 96.14%；集中供热面积 83.1 亿平方米；城市道路长度 39.8 万公里，人均城市道路面积 16.05 平方米。全国城市新建地下综合管廊2 429公里。全国城市共有污水处理厂2 209座，污水处理厂集中处理率 91.98%；市政再生水日生产能力3 588万立方米，再生水利用量 71.3 亿立方米。全国城市共有生活垃圾无害化处理场（厂）1013 座，城市生活垃圾无害化处理率 97.74%；城市道路清扫保洁面积 84.2 亿平方米，机械清扫率 65.0%；全年清运生活垃圾、粪便 2.15 亿吨。城市建成区绿地率 37.11%，人均公园绿地面积 14.01 平方米。2017 年年末，全国共有 247 处国家级风景名胜区，风景名胜区面积合计 10.9 万平方公里，其中可游览面积 5.0 万平方公里，全年接待游人 11.7 亿人次。国家投资 82.1 亿元用于风景名胜区的维护和建设。

2017 年，在生态环境部监测的 338 个城市中，环境空气质量达标的城市占 29.3%；未达标的城市占 70.7%。新环境空气质量标准第一阶段实施监测的 74 个城市平均优良天数比例为 72.7%，比 2016 年下降 1.5 个百分点；平均超标天数比例为 27.3%。细颗粒物（$PM_{2.5}$）平均浓度比 2016 年下降 6.0%。474 个城市（区、县）开展了降水监测，降水 pH 年均值低于 5.6 的酸雨城市比例为 18.8%；酸雨频率平均为 10.8%，比 2016 年下降 1.9 个百分点。

据交通运输部统计，2017年年末全国拥有公共汽电车65.12万辆，其中BRT车辆8 802辆。全国有32个城市开通了轨道交通，拥有轨道交通车站3040个，运营车辆28 125辆。拥有巡游出租车139.58万辆，拥有城市客运轮渡264艘。全国拥有公共汽电车运营线路56 786条，运营线路总长度106.9万公里，其中，公交专用车道10 914.5公里，BRT线路长度3 424.5公里。轨道交通运营线路149条，运营线路总长度4 484.2公里。城市客运轮渡运营航线92条，运营航线总长度434.9公里。全年完成城市客运量1 272.15亿人，其中，公共汽电车完成722.87亿人（含BRT客运量21.96亿人次），轨道交通完成183.05亿人，巡游出租车完成365.40亿人。城市客运系统完成的客运量构成为：公共汽电车56.82%、轨道交通14.39%、出租汽车28.72%、客运轮渡0.07%。

2017年年末，全国50个城市在建轨道交通，线路长度4914公里。

（四）县城建设

2017年，根据全国1 526个县汇总，年末县城户籍人口1.39亿人，暂住人口0.17亿人，建成区面积19 854平方公里。全国县城完成市政公用设施固定资产投资3 634.2亿元，其中：道路桥梁、排水和污水处理、市容和环境卫生分别占县城市政公用设施固定资产投资的44.1%、12.6%和17.4%。

2017年，全国县城用水人口1.45亿人，用水普及率92.9%，人均日生活用水量120.2升；用气人口1.27亿人，燃气普及率81.35%；集中供热面积14.63亿平方米；县城道路总长度14.1万公里，人均城市道路面积17.18平方米。县城共有污水处理厂1572座，污水处理厂集中处理率88.9%。共有生活垃圾无害化处理场（厂）1300座，日处理能力20.5万吨，生活垃圾无害化处理率91.0%；全年清运生活垃圾6747万吨。县城建成区绿地率30.74%，人均公园绿地面积11.86平方米。

（五）村镇建设

据住房和城乡建设部对国内1.81万个建制镇、1.03万个乡和244.9万个村庄进行统计汇总：2017年年末，全国村镇户籍总人口9.36亿人，其中建制镇建成区1.55亿人，乡建成区0.25亿人，村庄7.56亿人。建制镇建成区面积392.6万公顷，乡建成区63.38万公顷。

2017年，全国村镇建设总投资17 231亿元，其中住宅建设投资9 155亿元，市政公用设施建设投资4 571亿元。年末，全国村镇实有住宅建筑面积308亿平方米；按户籍人口统计，人均住宅建筑面积32.91平方米。

2017年，全国建制镇建成区用水普及率88.1%，人均日生活用水量109.5升，人均公园绿地面积3.1平方米。乡建成区用水普及率78.8%，人均日生活用水量104.3升，人均公园绿地面积1.65平方米。在建制镇和乡的建成区内，年末实有道路长度40.1万公里，排水管道长度18.3万公里，公共厕所15.28万座。

二、国家机构改革与统一规划体系

根据中共十九届三中全会通过的《深化党和国家机构改革方案》，第十三届全国人民代表大会第一次会议于 2018 年 3 月 17 日批准了《国务院机构改革方案》。会议强调，国务院要坚持党中央集中统一领导，精心组织，周密部署，确保完成国务院机构改革任务。实施机构改革方案需要制定或修改法律的，要及时启动相关程序，依法提请全国人民代表大会常务委员会审议。

（一）《深化党和国家机构改革方案》

深化党和国家机构改革是推进国家治理体系和治理能力现代化的一场深刻变革，是关系党和国家事业全局的重大政治任务。深化改革的八个方面是：深化党中央机构改革，深化全国人大机构改革，深化国务院机构改革，深化全国政协机构改革，深化行政执法体制改革，深化跨军地改革，深化群团组织改革，深化地方机构改革。

《深化党和国家机构改革方案》要求，中央和国家机关机构改革要在 2018 年年底前落实到位。省级党政机构改革方案要在 2018 年 9 月底前报党中央审批，在 2018 年年底前机构调整基本到位。省以下党政机构改革，由省级党委统一领导，在 2018 年年底前报党中央备案。所有地方机构改革任务在 2019 年 3 月底前基本完成。

（二）《国务院机构改革方案》

深化国务院机构改革，要着眼于转变政府职能，坚决破除制约使市场在资源配置中起决定性作用、更好发挥政府作用的体制机制弊端，围绕推动高质量发展，建设现代化经济体系，加强和完善政府经济调节、市场监管、社会管理、公共服务、生态环境保护职能，结合新的时代条件和实践要求，着力推进重点领域和关键环节的机构职能优化和调整，构建起职责明确、依法行政的政府治理体系，提高政府执行力，建设人民满意的服务型政府。改革的具体方案为：

（1）关于国务院组成部门调整，包括：组建自然资源部，组建生态环境部，组建农业农村部，组建文化和旅游部，组建国家卫生健康委员会，组建退役军人事务部，组建应急管理部，重新组建科学技术部，重新组建司法部，优化水利部职责，优化审计署职责，监察部和国家预防腐败局并入新组建的国家监察委员会。改革后，除国务院办公厅外，国务院设置组成部门 26 个。

（2）关于国务院其他机构调整，包括：组建国家市场监督管理总局，组建国家广播电视总局，组建中国银行保险监督管理委员会，组建国家国际发展合作署，组建国家医疗保障局，组建国家粮食和物资储备局，组建国家移民管理局，组建国家林业和草原局，重新组建国家知识产权局，调整全国社会保障基金理事会隶属关系，改革国税地税征管体制。国务院组成部门以外的国务院所属机构的调整和设置，将由新组成的国务院审查批准。

(三) 统一规划体系

2018 年 11 月 18 日，中共中央、国务院发布《关于统一规划体系更好发挥国家发展规划战略导向作用的意见》(以下简称《意见》)。

以规划引领经济社会发展，是党治国理政的重要方式，是中国特色社会主义发展模式的重要体现。科学编制并有效实施国家发展规划，阐明建设社会主义现代化强国奋斗目标在规划期内的战略部署和具体安排，引导公共资源配置方向，规范市场主体行为，有利于保持国家战略连续性稳定性，集中力量办大事，确保一张蓝图绘到底。

《意见》要求，坚持下位规划服从上位规划、下级规划服务上级规划、等位规划相互协调，建立以国家发展规划为统领，以空间规划为基础，以专项规划、区域规划为支撑，由国家、省、市县各级规划共同组成，定位准确、边界清晰、功能互补、统一衔接的国家规划体系。

1. 明确规划功能定位

国家发展规划，即中华人民共和国国民经济和社会发展五年规划纲要，是社会主义现代化战略在规划期内的阶段性部署和安排，主要是阐明国家战略意图、明确政府工作重点、引导规范市场主体行为，是经济社会发展的宏伟蓝图，是全国各族人民共同的行动纲领，是政府履行经济调节、市场监管、社会管理、公共服务、生态环境保护职能的重要依据。

国家级专项规划是指导特定领域发展、布局重大工程项目、合理配置公共资源、引导社会资本投向、制定相关政策的重要依据。国家级区域规划是指导特定区域发展和制定相关政策的重要依据。

国家级空间规划以空间治理和空间结构优化为主要内容，是实施国土空间用途管制和生态保护修复的重要依据。

2. 理顺规划关系

国家发展规划根据党中央关于制定国民经济和社会发展五年规划的建议，由国务院组织编制，经全国人民代表大会审查批准，居于规划体系最上位，是其他各级各类规划的总遵循。

国家级专项规划、区域规划、空间规划，均须依据国家发展规划编制。国家级专项规划要细化落实国家发展规划对特定领域提出的战略任务，由国务院有关部门编制，其中国家级重点专项规划报国务院审批，党中央有明确要求的除外。国家级区域规划要细化落实国家发展规划对特定区域提出的战略任务，由国务院有关部门编制，报国务院审批。国家级空间规划要细化落实国家发展规划提出的国土空间开发保护要求，由国务院有关部门编制，报国务院审批。国家级专项规划、区域规划、空间规划，规划期与国家发展规划不一致的，应根据同期国家发展规划的战略安排对规划目标任务适时进行调整或修编。国家级空间规划对国家级专项规划具有空间性指导和约束作用。

(四) 组建自然资源部

国家高度重视生态文明建设，提出要牢固树立尊重自然、顺应自然、保护自然的理念，坚持绿水青山就是金山银山，加快形成人与自然和谐发展的现代化建设新格局，开创社会主义生态文明新时代。为统一行使全民所有自然资源资产所有者职责，统一行使所有国土空间用途管制和生态保护修复职责，着力解决自然资源所有者不到位、空间规划重叠等问题，《国务院机构改革方案》明确，将国土资源部的职责，国家发展和改革委员会的组织编制主体功能区规划职责，住房和城乡建设部的城乡规划管理职责，水利部的水资源调查和确权登记管理职责，农业部的草原资源调查和确权登记管理职责，国家林业局的森林、湿地等资源调查和确权登记管理职责，国家海洋局的职责，国家测绘地理信息局的职责整合，组建自然资源部，作为国务院组成部门。自然资源部对外保留国家海洋局牌子。

2018 年 8 月 1 日，中共中央办公厅、国务院办公厅印发《自然资源部职能配置、内设机构和人员编制规定》。在国土空间领域，自然资源部内设机构的职责包括：

（1）国土空间规划局。拟订国土空间规划相关政策，承担建立空间规划体系工作并监督实施。组织编制全国国土空间规划和相关专项规划并监督实施。承担报国务院审批的地方国土空间规划的审核、报批工作，指导和审核涉及国土空间开发利用的国家重大专项规划。开展国土空间开发适宜性评价，建立国土空间规划实施监测、评估和预警体系。

（2）国土空间用途管制司。拟订国土空间用途管制制度规范和技术标准。提出土地、海洋年度利用计划并组织实施。组织拟订耕地、林地、草地、湿地、海域、海岛等国土空间用途转用政策，指导建设项目用地预审工作。承担报国务院审批的各类土地用途转用的审核、报批工作。拟订开展城乡规划管理等用途管制政策并监督实施。

（3）国土空间生态修复司。承担国土空间生态修复政策研究工作，拟订国土空间生态修复规划。承担国土空间综合整治、土地整理复垦、矿山地质环境恢复治理、海洋生态、海域海岸带和海岛修复等工作。承担生态保护补偿相关工作。指导地方国土空间生态修复工作。

三、脱贫攻坚战三年行动

党的十八大以来，全国农村贫困人口累计减少 8239 万人，贫困发生率累计下降 8.5 个百分点，贫困地区农村居民收入增长幅度高于全国农村平均水平。中央政府确定的脱贫攻坚战三年行动基本要求和核心指标是，到 2020 年要稳定实现农村贫困人口不愁吃、不愁穿（两不愁），义务教育、基本医疗、住房安全有保障（三保障）。2018 年，各地区各部门认真贯彻精准扶贫方略，扎实推进脱贫攻坚，脱贫攻坚战三年行动实现良好开局。

（一）全国农村贫困人口减少 1386 万人

据国家统计局全国农村贫困监测调查，按照每人每年 2300 元（2010 年不变价）的现行国家农村贫困标准计算，2018 年年末农村贫困人口 1660 万人，比上年末减少 1386 万人；贫困发生率 1.7%，比上年下降 1.4 个百分点。2018 年预计有 280 个左右贫困县摘帽。

（二）贫困地区农村居民人均可支配收入增速继续高于全国农村

工资性和转移性收入是贫困地区农村居民增收的主要来源。2018 年，贫困地区农村居民人均可支配收入 10 371 元，比上年增加 994 元，扣除价格因素，实际增长 8.3%，实际增速高于全国农村增速 1.7 个百分点，圆满完成增长幅度高于全国增速的年度目标任务。

深度贫困地区农村居民人均可支配收入增速高于贫困地区增速 0.1 个百分点。深度贫困地区农村居民人均可支配收入 9 668 元，比上年增加 935 元，名义增长 10.7%。

（三）《关于打赢脱贫攻坚战三年行动的指导意见》

根据各地区各部门贯彻落实中共中央、国务院《关于打赢脱贫攻坚战的决定》的进展和实践中存在的突出问题，2018 年 6 月 15 日，中共中央、国务院发布《关于打赢脱贫攻坚战三年行动的指导意见》。

（1）指导思想。聚焦深度贫困地区和特殊贫困群体，突出问题导向，优化政策供给，下足绣花功夫，着力激发贫困人口内生动力，着力夯实贫困人口稳定脱贫基础，着力加强扶贫领域作风建设，切实提高贫困人口获得感，确保到 2020 年贫困地区和贫困群众同全国一道进入全面小康社会，为实施乡村振兴战略打好基础。

（2）任务目标。到 2020 年，巩固脱贫成果，通过发展生产脱贫一批，易地搬迁脱贫一批，生态补偿脱贫一批，发展教育脱贫一批，社会保障兜底一批，因地制宜综合施策，确保现行标准下农村贫困人口实现脱贫，消除绝对贫困；确保贫困县全部摘帽，解决区域性整体贫困。实现贫困地区农民人均可支配收入增长幅度高于全国平均水平。实现贫困地区基本公共服务主要领域指标接近全国平均水平。集中连片特困地区和革命老区、民族地区、边疆地区发展环境明显改善，深度贫困地区如期完成全面脱贫任务。

（3）工作要求。坚持严格执行现行扶贫标准。确保贫困人口不愁吃、不愁穿；保障贫困家庭孩子接受九年义务教育，确保有学上、上得起学；保障贫困人口基本医疗需求，确保大病和慢性病得到有效救治和保障；保障贫困人口基本居住条件，确保住上安全住房。要量力而行，既不能降低标准，也不能擅自拔高标准、提不切实际的目标，避免陷入“福利陷阱”，防止产生贫困村和非贫困村、贫困户和非贫困户待遇的“悬崖效应”，留下后遗症。

（四）脱贫攻坚形势依然严峻

全国人大常委会专题调研组在近期的《关于脱贫攻坚工作情况的调研报告》中指出：随着脱贫攻坚逐步向纵深推进，深度贫困问题凸显，攻坚难度递增，工作中还存在一些不容忽视的实际困难和突出问题。

（1）截至 2018 年年底，全国还有约 400 个贫困县，近 3 万个贫困村。且尚未脱贫人口中，长期患病者、残疾人、孤寡老人等特殊困难群体和自身发展动力不足的贫困人口比例高，且越往后比例会越高，这部分人中很多需要依靠财政兜底才能实现稳定脱贫，保障性扶贫特别是财政兜底的压力越来越大。

（2）各省区普遍存在产业扶贫项目单一、同质化的现象，后续发展面临较大的市场风险。健康扶贫政策仍需完善，各地普遍反映慢性病家庭医生签约服务政策落实不到位、管理不规范，签约医生以村医为主，多流于形式，不少地方反映医疗托底政策在实践中出现了不同程度的过度医疗现象。住房安全方面，一些易地扶贫搬迁项目重搬迁轻扶持，配套产业和促进就业没跟上，后续脱贫缺乏支撑。各地不同程度地存在易地扶贫搬迁入住滞后，搬迁入住进度和竣工进度不相匹配的问题。

（3）各地普遍反映，当前的扶贫政策都是真金白银，对贫困地区和贫困人口给的越来越多，帮的越来越实，但相比之下，如何激发脱贫攻坚的内生动力仍是亟须补齐的短板。一些贫困群众主动致富意愿不强，过度依赖帮扶政策，个别贫困群众甚至存在“你不帮，我不动”现象。同时，脱贫攻坚工作中的形式主义、官僚主义、弄虚作假、急躁和厌战情绪以及消极腐败现象等仍有存在，各省区仍不同程度地存在算账脱贫、突击脱贫甚至虚假脱贫现象。

（4）贫困地区摘帽退出后仍将长期处于经济欠发达、发展相对落后的状况，持续稳定增收基础仍很薄弱，自我发展能力不强。从长远看，不解决长效机制的问题，不走出良性发展的路子，贫困地区和贫困人口返贫的压力仍将长期存在。

四、区域协调发展新机制

区域协调发展是新时代国家重大战略之一。党的十八大以来，各地区各部门围绕促进区域协调发展与正确处理政府和市场关系，在建立健全区域合作机制、区域互助机制、区际利益补偿机制等方面进行积极探索并取得一定成效。但与此同时，我国区域发展差距依然较大，区域分化现象逐渐显现，无序开发与恶性竞争仍然存在，区域发展不平衡不充分问题依然比较突出。为破除地区之间利益藩篱和政策壁垒，全面落实区域协调发展战略各项任务，促进区域协调发展向更高水平和更高质量迈进，中共中央、国务院于 2018 年 11 月 18 日发布《关于建立更加有效的区域协调发展新机制的意见》。

（一）区域战略统筹机制

以“一带一路”建设助推沿海、内陆、沿边地区协同开放，以国际经济合作走廊为主骨架加强重大基础设施互联互通，构建统筹国内国际、协调国内东中西和南北方的区域发展新格局。以疏解北京非首都功能为“牛鼻子”推动京津冀协同发展，调整区域经济结构和空间结构，推动河北雄安新区和北京城市副中心建设，探索超大城市、特大城市等人口经济密集地区有序疏解功能、有效治理“大城市病”的优化开发模式。充分发挥长江经济带横跨东中西三大板块的区位优势，以共抓大保护、不搞大开发为导向，以生态优先、绿色发展为引领，依托长江黄金水道，推动长江上中下游地区协调发展和沿江地区高质量发展。建立以中心城市引领城市群发展、城市群带动区域发展新模式，推动区域板块之间融合互动发展。同时，要加强国家各重大战略的协调对接，推动各区域合作联动。

（二）市场一体化发展机制

实施全国统一的市场准入负面清单制度，消除歧视性、隐蔽性的区域市场准入限制。加快深化农村土地制度改革，推动建立城乡统一的建设用地市场，进一步完善承包地所有权、承包权、经营权三权分置制度，探索宅基地所有权、资格权、使用权三权分置改革。探索建立规划制度统一、发展模式共推、治理方式一致、区域市场联动的区域市场一体化发展新机制，促进形成全国统一大市场。进一步完善自然资源资产有偿使用制度，构建统一的自然资源资产交易平台。

（三）区域合作机制

深化京津冀地区、长江经济带、粤港澳大湾区等合作，提升合作层次和水平。积极探索建立城市群协调治理模式，鼓励成立多种形式的城市联盟。加快推进长江经济带、珠江—西江经济带、淮河生态经济带、汉江生态经济带等重点流域经济带上下游间合作发展。建立健全上下游毗邻省市规划对接机制，协调解决地区间合作发展重大问题。支持晋陕豫黄河金三角、粤桂、湘赣、川渝等省际交界地区合作发展，探索建立统一规划、统一管理、合作共建、利益共享的合作新机制。以“一带一路”建设为重点，实行更加积极主动的开放战略，推动构建互利共赢的国际区域合作新机制。推进重点开发开放试验区建设，支持边境经济合作区发展，稳步建设跨境经济合作区，更好发挥境外产能合作园区、经贸合作区的带动作用。

（四）区际利益补偿机制

贯彻绿水青山就是金山银山的重要理念和山水林田湖草是生命共同体的系统思想，按照区际公平、权责对等、试点先行、分步推进的原则，不断完善横向生态补偿机制。研究制定粮食主产区与主销区开展产销合作的具体办法，鼓励粮食主销区通过在主产区建设加工园区、建立优质商品粮基地和建立产销区储备合作机制以及提供资金、人才、技术服务支持等方式开展产销协作。围绕煤炭、石油、天然气、水能、风能、太阳能以及其他矿产等重要资源，坚持市场导向和政府调控相结合，加快完善有利于资源集约节约利用和可持续发展的资源价格形成机制，确保资源价格能够涵盖开采成本以及生态修复和环境治理等成本。

（五）区域发展保障机制

加强区域规划编制前期研究，完善区域规划编制、审批和实施工作程序，实行区域规划编制审批计划管理制度，进一步健全区域规划实施机制，加强中期评估和后评估，形成科学合理、管理严格、指导有力的区域规划体系。围绕缩小区域发展差距、区域一体化、资源环境协调等重点领域，建立区域协调发展评价指标体系，科学客观评价区域发展的协调性，为区域政策制定和调整提供参考。研究论证促进区域协调发展的法规制度，明确区域协调发展的内涵、战略重点和方向，健全区域政策制定、实施、监督、评价机制，明确有关部门在区域协调发展中的职责，明确地方政府在推进区域协调发展中的责任和义务，发挥社会组织、研究机构、企业在促进区域协调发展中的作用。

五、努力实现更高质量的发展

习近平总书记指出，高质量发展是体现新发展理念的发展，突出高质量发展导向，就是要坚持稳中求进，在稳的前提下，有所进取、以进求稳，更好满足人民群众多样化、多层次、多方面的需求。前进道路上，我们必须围绕解决好人民日益增长的美好生活需要和不平衡不充分的发展之间的矛盾这个社会主要矛盾，坚决贯彻创新、协调、绿色、开放、共享的发展理念，努力实现更高质量、更有效率、更加公平、更可持续的发展。

（一）打造推动高质量发展的全国样板

2018 年 12 月 25 日，国务院发布了关于河北雄安新区总体规划（2018—2035 年）的批复，原则同意《河北雄安新区总体规划（2018—2035 年）》，拉开了雄安新区开发建设的序幕。《规划》按照高质量发展要求，牢牢把握北京非首都功能疏解集中承载地这个初心，坚持世界眼光、国际标准、中国特色、高点定位，坚持生态优先、绿色发展，坚持以人民为中心、注重保障和改善民生，坚持保护弘扬中华优秀传统文化、延续历史文脉，对于高起点规划高标准建设雄安新区、创造“雄安质量”、建设“廉洁雄安”、打造推动高质量发展的全国样板、建设现代化经济体系的新引擎具有重要意义。

按照《河北雄安新区规划纲要》设定的建设目标，到本世纪中叶，雄安新区将全面建成高质量高水平的社会主义现代化城市，成为京津冀世界级城市群的重要一极。集中承接北京非首都功能成效显著，为解决“大城市病”问题提供中国方案。新区各项经济社会发展指标达到国际领先水平，治理体系和治理能力实现现代化，成为新时代高质量发展的全国样板。

2019 年年初，习近平总书记在主持召开京津冀协同发展座谈会时再次强调，建设雄安新区是千年大计。新区首先就要新在规划、建设的理念上，要体现出前瞻性、引领性。要全面贯彻新发展理念，坚持高质量发展要求，努力创造新时代高质量发展的标杆。

（二）特色小镇和特色小城镇高质量发展

特色小镇和特色小城镇是新型城镇化与乡村振兴的重要结合点，也是促进经济高质量发展的重要平台。国家发展改革委等部门印发《关于加快美丽特色小（城）镇建设的指导意见》《关于规范推进特色小镇和特色小城镇建设的若干意见》，引导特色小镇和特色小城镇发展取得一定成效，概念不清、盲目发展及房地产化苗头得到一定程度的纠正。为进一步巩固纠偏成果、有力有序有效推动高质量发展，国家发展改革委办公厅于 2018 年 8 月 30 日发布《关于建立特色小镇和特色小城镇高质量发展机制的通知》。要求如下：

（1）基本原则。坚持产业立镇。坚持规范发展。坚持典型引路。坚持优化服务。立足各地区发展阶段，遵循经济规律和城镇化规律，实事求是、因地制宜、量力而行，使特色小镇和特色小城镇建设成为市场主导、自然发展的过程。

（2）明确典型特色小镇条件。基本条件是：立足一定资源禀赋或产业基础，区别于行政建制镇和产业园区，利用3平方公里左右国土空间（其中建设用地1平方公里左右），在差异定位和领域细分中构建小镇大产业，集聚高端要素和特色产业，兼具特色文化、特色生态和特色建筑等鲜明魅力，打造高效创业圈、宜居生活圈、繁荣商业圈、美丽生态圈，形成产业特而强、功能聚而合、形态小而美、机制新而活的创新创业平台。

（3）明确典型特色小城镇条件。基本条件是：立足工业化城镇化发展阶段和发展潜力，打造特色鲜明的产业形态、便捷完善的设施服务、和谐宜居的美丽环境、底蕴深厚的传统文化、精简高效的体制机制，实现特色支柱产业在镇域经济中占主体地位、在国内国际市场占一定份额，拥有一批知名品牌和企业，镇区常住人口达到一定规模，带动乡村振兴能力较强，形成具有核心竞争力的行政建制镇排头兵和经济发达镇升级版。

（4）探索差异化多样化经验。鼓励各地区挖掘多种类型小镇案例，避免模式雷同、难以推广。立足不同产业门类，挖掘先进制造类、农业田园类及信息、科创、金融、教育、商贸、文旅、体育等现代服务类案例。立足不同地理区位，挖掘“市郊镇”“市中镇”“园中镇”“镇中镇”等特色小镇案例，以及卫星型、专业型等特色小城镇案例。立足不同运行模式，挖掘在机制政策创新、政企合作、投融资模式等方面的先进经验。

（三）社会领域公共服务补短板强弱项提质量的行动方案

近年来，我国的社会领域公共服务投入不断加大，设施条件不断改善，但相对于群众多层次多样化需求，仍然存在供给不足、质量不高、发展不均衡等突出问题，托幼、上学、就医、养老等方面的服务质量和水平与群众期待还有不小差距。为加大力度推动社会领域公共服务补短板、强弱项、提质量，促进形成强大国内市场，2019年1月23日，国家发展改革委、中央宣传部等十八部门联合印发《加大力度推动社会领域公共服务补短板强弱项提质量，促进形成强大国内市场的行动方案》。

1. 主要目标

到2020年，公共服务供给结构更加合理，社会力量参与更加积极，实施保障机制更加完善，服务质量与水平不断提升，公共服务对保障民生、促进就业、扩大消费的作用不断增强，基本实现基本公共服务能力全覆盖、质量全达标、标准全落实、保障应担尽担，实现非基本公共服务付费可享有、价格可承受、质量有保障、安全有监管。其中，教育现代化取得重要进展，劳动年龄人口平均受教育年限达到10.8年；覆盖城乡的基本医疗卫生制度基本建立，人均预期寿命提高到77.3岁；以居家为基础、社区为依托、机构为补充、医养相结合的养老服务体系更加完善，养老床位中护理型床位比例不低于30%；婴幼儿照护服务的政策法规和标准规范体系初步建立；现代公共文化服务体系基本建成，文化产业成为国民经济支柱性产业；旅游经济稳步增长，对国民经济的综合贡献度达到12%；群众身体素质稳步增强，人均体育场地面积达到1.8平方米；家政培训标准化程度进一步提升，行业规范化建设进一步巩固。

到 2022 年，公共服务供给更加充足、资源布局不断优化、体制机制日趋完备、人才队伍发展壮大、服务质量明显提高，覆盖全民、普惠共享、城乡一体的基本公共服务体系不断健全，就近就便、高效快捷、便民利民的公共服务体验不断改善，政府保障基本、社会积极参与、全民共建共享的公共服务格局不断完善，社会关注的民生热点难点问题得到有效缓解，多样化可选择的公共服务资源更加丰富，潜力巨大的国内市场需求得到满足，广大群众的获得感、幸福感、安全感不断提升。

2. 行动任务

在补齐基本公共服务短板、加快实现基本公共服务均等化方面包括：推进义务教育均衡发展，提升贫困地区县域医疗卫生服务能力，加强妇幼健康服务体系建设，提高医学应急救援和传染病等防治能力，健全基本养老服务体系，加强社会福利服务体系建设，提升公共就业创业服务水平，推动基本公共文化服务均等化，推动公共体育设施建设和开放，健全完善残疾人公共服务体系。

在补强非基本公共服务弱项、着力增强人民群众公共服务供给方面包括：增加托育服务有效供给，扩大城乡普惠性学前教育资源，促进社会办医加快发展，全面放开养老服务市场，加强老年人健康服务体系建设，推进家政培训和就业服务，推广城乡社区助餐服务，加强优秀传统文化保护传承利用，完善重点地区旅游基础设施，加快有线电视网络整合发展和互联互通，加快发展体育健身休闲运动和竞赛表演业。

在充分发挥有效市场和有为政府作用、提升公共服务质量水平方面包括：提升教育服务内涵质量，均衡发展优质医疗资源，提升养老服务质量，提高公共文化服务效能，加快智慧广电发展，推进多种旅游业态发展。

（四）城市高质量发展的工程建设标准

我国已形成具有中国特色的工程建设标准体系。国务院《深化标准化工作改革方案》确定改革总体目标为：建立政府主导制定的标准与市场自主制定的标准协同发展、协调配套的新型标准体系，健全统一协调、运行高效、政府与市场共治的标准化管理体制，让标准成为对质量的“硬约束”，推动中国经济迈向中高端水平。同时，明确提出培育发展团体标准、放开搞活企业标准、提高标准国际化水平的重大改革举措。

2018 年 10 月至 11 月，中国城市规划学会首批团体标准《小城镇空间特色塑造指南》《建设工程规划电子报批数据标准》发布。这些团体标准针对当前发展需要和问题，及时、快速提出公用准则，与国家规范形成互补，以解决具体问题为目的，由社会自愿采用。

2018 年 12 月 6 日，住房和城乡建设部在南宁市举办“推动城市高质量发展系列标准发布”活动，旨在适应中国经济由高速增长阶段转向高质量发展阶段的新要求，以高标准支撑和引导我国城市建设、工程建设高质量发展。发布的标准涵盖促进城市绿色发展、保障城市安全运行、建设和谐宜居城市 3 个方面，包括《海绵城市建设评价标准》《绿色建筑评价标准》《城市综合防灾规划标准》《城市排水工程规划规范》《城镇内涝防治技术规范》《城市居住区规划设计标准》《城市综合交通体系规划标准》等。

据报道，在住房和城乡建设领域，迄今为止已发布356项工程建设国家标准，765项城乡规划、房屋建筑、市政工程行业的工程建设行业标准。各省（自治区、直辖市）已发布工程建设地方标准4 468项。

六、建设可持续的韧性城市

（一）2018年世界城市日

2018年2月9日，新当选联合国人居署执行主任的马来西亚规划师麦慕娜·莫哈德·谢里夫在吉隆坡宣布，2018年世界城市日的主题是：“建设可持续的韧性城市”(Building Sustainable and Resilient Cities)。

10月31日，联合国秘书长古特雷斯发表“世界城市日致辞”。他说：《2030年可持续发展议程》、关于气候变化的《巴黎协定》《仙台减少灾害风险框架》和《新城市议程》共同提供了一个可持续的韧性世界路线图。我们的城市如何发展，将对实现我们希望的未来产生重大影响。

古特雷斯指出：今天的世界上，每周就有140万人迁到城市，这种快速的城市化使地方的承载负荷不断加重，使自然灾害和人为灾害的风险增大。但是，危险并非必然变成灾难，个中答案在于如何提升抵御经济危机和风暴、洪水、地震、火灾、流行病的能力。

现在，世界各地的城市都在采取行动，增强自身的韧性和可持续性。在曼谷，已经建造了巨大的地下储水设施，以应对有所增加的洪水风险，并为干旱时期蓄水。在基多，当地政府改造或保护了2 000多平方公里土地，以加强防洪，减少土壤侵蚀，保护城市的淡水供应和生物多样性。在约翰内斯堡，城市让居民参与改善公共空间的努力，使公共空间能够安全地用于娱乐、体育、社区活动和免费医疗等服务。

古特雷斯呼吁：在世界城市日，让我们以这些实例为启迪，共同努力建设能为所有人提供安全和机遇的可持续的韧性城市。

（二）世界城市日中国主场

2018年世界城市日的中国主场活动，由住房和城乡建设部、江苏省人民政府与联合国人居署共同在徐州市举办。中国主场围绕城市日年度主题，重点交流和展示世界各地在城市可持续发展、防灾抗灾、绿色建筑、建设海绵城市、绿色城市和韧性城市方面的创新做法，探讨如何进一步落实联合国《新城市议程》，推动国际合作与交流。主场活动包括世界城市日主题论坛、市长对话、专家对话、城市可持续发展实践展、发布《上海手册——21世纪城市可持续发展指南·2018年度报告》中文版，以及相关配套活动等。有关国家和地区政府部门负责人、国内外城市市长、国际组织代表、城市规划建设管理专家学者等约400人参会。

中国主场活动配合世界城市日“建设可持续韧性城市”的主题，发布了“城市绿色发展徐州倡议”：

（1）携手推动城市生态文明建设。城市应当秉持“绿水青山就是金山银山”的理念，构筑尊崇自然、绿色发展的生态体系，合力建设清洁美丽的城市家园；处理好生态环境保护和经济发展的关系，加强新旧动能转换，促进城市发展方式的转变。

（2）全面加强城市生态修复。老工业基地和资源枯竭型城市应着力生态修复和城市修补，将包袱当作资源来转化，把“生态疮疤”打造成为“城市亮点”；深入开展城市污染综合治理，加强固体废物科学化、资源化处置利用。

（3）共同探索城市转型之路。城市应准确把握自身发展阶段性特征，积极构建绿色低碳可持续发展新格局：加快推动产业结构、能源结构、运输结构绿色转型，努力打造现代绿色产业体系；树立绿色生活新理念，倡导绿色消费、绿色出行、绿色居住，培养形成绿色生活习惯。

（三）建设可持续和韧性城市的徐州案例

徐州市位于江苏省北部、苏鲁豫皖四省交界处，是有 2600 年建城史的历史文化名城、全国重要的综合性交通枢纽和淮海经济区中心城市，2018 年全市常住人口 880 万人。徐州市产业转型、生态修复、棚户区改造和固体废弃物的管理所取得的显著成绩与经验，可在全国范围推广示范。

（1）产业转型。徐州是我国煤炭工业的起源地之一，已形成以煤炭、钢铁、水泥、化工为主导的重工业体系。在高质量发展的新要求下，徐州先后关闭矿井 14 对，压减煤炭产能 1062 万吨、钢铁产能 163 万吨，提前 3 年完成江苏省煤炭去产能任务。

徐州紧紧围绕“调高、调轻、调优、调强”的产业发展导向，积极构建“6＋6”现代工业产业新体系。以装备制造、食品及农副产品加工等 6 个传统优势产业为主体，通过科技创新提升传统产业的竞争力。以新能源、新材料等 6 个战略性新兴产业为先导，出台装备与智能制造、新能源、集成电路与 ICT、生物医药四大新兴主导产业实施方案，制定特色产业基地发展实施意见。2018 年，全市规模以上工业实现高新技术产业产值占比为 38.3%。

（2）生态修复。“进了徐州城，先喝二两土”，“晴天一身土、雨天一身泥”，这些都曾是徐州的真实写照，作为传统老工业城市，徐州长期形成的资源高消耗、环境高污染的产业结构，使得空气、水体污染严重，生态欠账包袱沉重。

近年来，徐州整治采煤塌陷地 19.72 万亩，全市 42 处采石宕口被修复。全市林木覆盖率达 30.1%，城市建成区绿化覆盖率 43.8%，人均公园绿地面积 15.7 平方米，三类以上水体占比达 79.2%，先后获得国家生态园林城市、国家卫生城市、国家环保模范城市、国家森林城市等称号，完成了由“一城煤灰半城土”向“一城青山半城湖”的华丽转身。

（3）棚户区改造。徐州根据城市建设规划和棚户区的实际情况，坚持尊重民意、量力而行的原则，大力开展棚户区、城中村改造，实施了历史上规模最大、惠及群众最多的保障房建设工程。

全市已实施棚户区改造超过1亿平方米，52.6万户居民受益。其中主城区改造3872万平方米，30万户居民实现了出棚入楼、安居乐业，彻底解决了吃水难、如厕难、进出难等诸多问题。徐州在棚改中采取了“三项特殊政策”：其一，对棚户区征迁中符合经济适用房条件的直接安排经济适用房；其二，对双特困户和符合廉租房条件的直接采取廉租房安置，交纳政策性房租；其三，对经济困难、补不起差价的，实行共有产权安置，10年内被征迁群众可按房屋征迁时的价格购买剩余产权。

（4）固废管理。多年来，徐州对城市垃圾等固体废弃物的治理措施相对滞后，区域生态环境受到较大损害，“垃圾靠风刮、污水靠蒸发”的现象普遍。城市固废产出量大、回收量小、利用率低的问题凸显，固废处理能力不足与人民对美好生活环境的期待之间的矛盾日益突出。

徐州市政府认识到垃圾治理的重要性，制定了把城市当家园来建设、把家园当公园来打造，突出垃圾治理的工作主线，围绕科学分类、针对性治理、资源化利用的思路，探索推行居民生活垃圾分类可持续运行模式路径，通过开展智能化管控、网络化收运、循环化利用、集中化处置，创造了城市固废管理的徐州经验。

2018年10月1日，肯尼亚共和国政府在联合国内罗毕办事处暨联合国人居署总部所在地主办了世界人居日全球庆典。中国江苏省徐州市因通过废弃物智慧管理，全面整体推进生态修复的优异成绩，获得2018年联合国人居奖。

七、结语

奋斗创造历史，实干成就未来。回顾改革开放40年的历程，中国人民用几十年时间走过了发达国家历经几百年的工业化、城市化道路，创造出举世瞩目的中国奇迹，谱写了一曲感天动地、气壮山河的奋斗赞歌。

2019年，我们将迎来中华人民共和国70周年华诞。从创建新中国到跨入新世纪，从站上新起点到进入新时代，70年披荆斩棘，70年风雨兼程。70年一路走来，中国人民自力更生、艰苦奋斗，不管风吹浪打，胜似闲庭信步。

2019年，是决胜第一个百年奋斗目标的关键之年。在新的征程上，既有新的发展机遇，也有新的风险挑战。我们要以新时代中国特色社会主义思想为指导，全面贯彻落实中共十九大精神，坚持新发展理念，坚持推进高质量发展，不断提高人民群众获得感、幸福感、安全感，保持经济持续健康发展和社会大局稳定，为全面建成小康社会收官打下决定性基础，以优异成绩庆祝中华人民共和国成立70周年。

（作者：毛其智，清华大学教授，国际欧亚科学院院士）

An Introduction of Urban Development in China: 2018

The age is rich with flowers in spring and fruits in autumn. The Chinese people are forging ahead on the way forward, and the harvest every year is full and solid.

In 2018, China's gross domestic product (GDP) exceeded 90 trillion yuan, a new record high. The urban registered unemployment rate stabilized at a relatively low level of about 5 per cent. More than 10 million rural low-income people were lifted out of poverty across the country. The people's livelihood causes sped up in development. And there were new improvement in the living environment of urban and rural areas and the living standards.

In 2018, the Party and state institutions carried out systematic, holistic and restructured reforms, launching more than 100 important reform measures. The coordinated development of the Beijing-Tianjin-Hebei region, the development of the Yangtze River economic belt and the integrated development of the Yangtze River Delta, the construction of Guangdong-Hong Kong-Macau Greater Bay Area and other national strategies were steadily implemented. Made in China, created in China, and built in China were prompted together: Chang'e-4 lunar probe was successfully launched, the second aircraft carrier went to sea for trial voyage, the domestic large-scale amphibious aircraft flew on the water for the first time, and Beidou Navigation took a solid step towards global networking.

On December 18, 2018, a grand gathering was solemnly held at the Great Hall of the People in Beijing to celebrate the 40th anniversary of reform and opening up. The Communist Party of China Central Committee and the State Council promulgated a decision to "honor people of outstanding contributions to reform and opening up," awarding 100 people the title of "pioneer in reform" and conferring them with medals. Mr. Wu Liangyong, 96 years old, was commended as a "pioneer of reform" by the Party and the state for his contribution as "the founder of science of human settlements". The theory and practice of science of human settlements in China has become one of the iconic achievements of the 40th anniversary of reform and opening up.

Ⅰ. Urbanization and Urban Development

(Ⅰ) General situation of urban and rural economic development

In 2018, facing the complicated and severe international environment as well as the daunting and heavy tasks of reform, development and stability, the Chinese people, under the strong leadership of the CPC Central Committee with General Secretary Xi Jinping as the core, implemented the new concept of development, fulfilled the requirements for high-quality development, deepened reform and expanded opening up in all parts of the motherland. The overall economic operation remained stable and steady.

According to the preliminary estimation of the National Bureau of Statistics, the GDP increased by 6.6% in 2018 over the previous year. Among them, the primary industry grew by 3.5%, the secondary industry by 5.8%, and the tertiary industry by 7.6%. The proportion of the three industries was 7.2:40.7:52.2. The contribution of the final consumer expenditure of the year to the GDP growth was 76.2%. The contribution of the gross capital formation was 32.4%. The contribution of net exports of goods and services was -8.6%. The country's per capita GDP was 64 644 yuan, an increase of 6.1% over the previous year. The overall labor productivity was 107 327 yuan per person, an increase of 6.6%. At the end of the year, residents owned 125.89 million private cars, an increase of 10.3% over the previous year.

In 2018, the per capita disposable income of residents nationwide was 28 228 yuan, an increase of 6.5% in real terms. Divided by the place of residence, the per capita disposable income of urban residents was 39 251 yuan, an actual increase of 5.6%; and the per capita disposable income of rural residents was 14 617 yuan, an actual growth of 6.6%. The difference of per capita income between urban and rural residents was 2.69, 0.02% smaller than that of the previous year. The per capita consumer expenditure of the whole country was 19 853 yuan, and the Engel coefficient was 28.4%, down 0.9 percentage points from the previous year. It was separated into 27.7% in cities and 30.1% in rural areas. The consumer prices rose 2.1% from the previous year. The total number of migrant workers in the country was 288.36 million, of which 172.66 million worked in other cities, while 115.7 million worked in the local places. The per capita monthly income of migrant workers was 3 721 yuan.

By the end of 2018, the total number of Chinese population at the mainland reached 1 395.38 million, an increase of 5.30 million over the previous year. Among them, the urban permanent residents numbered 831.37 million, accounting for 59.58 percent of the total population, 1.06 percentage points higher than the end of 2017. The urbanization rate of the household registered population was 43.37%, 1.02 percentage points higher than the end of the previous year. There were 15. 23 million births in the whole year, with a birth rate of 10. 94‰. There were 9. 93 million deaths, with a mortality rate of 7. 13‰. The natural growth rate was 3. 81‰. There were 286 million people with actual residences separated from their registered residences in the country, including 241 million migrant population. At the end of the year, there were 775. 86 million employed people across the country, of whom 434. 19 million were employed in cities and towns, and 13. 61 million new jobs were created. The registered unemployment rate in urban areas was 3. 8% at the end of the year, down 0. 1 percentage points.

In 2018, the investment in real estate development was 12. 0264 trillion yuan. Floor space of buildings newly started amounted to 2. 09342 billion square meters. The sales area of commercialized buildings was 1. 71654 billion square meters, including 1. 47929 billion square meters of residences. The floor space of commercial buildings for sale was 524. 14 million square meters, 65. 1 million square meters less than the end of the previous year. In 2018, some 6. 26 million housing units were started to be rebuilt in shantytown nationwide. The number of housing units rebuilt in shantytown was 5. 11 million. There were 1. 9 million dangerous houses reconstructed in rural areas, of which 1. 57 million were registered low-income families.

(Ⅱ) Adjustment of municipal administrative areas and establishment of new areas

According to the latest statistics of the Ministry of Civil Affairs, there were 672 cities in the country at the end of 2018. They were separated into four municipalities directly under the Central Government, 15 sub-provincial cities (specifically designated in the state plan), 278 prefecture-level cities and 375 county-level cities. There were 1 505 counties and banners, 21 297 administrative towns, 10 253 townships, 8 393 sub-district offices, 542 000 village committees and 108 000 neighborhood committees.

In 2018, the organizational system of the country's cities was adjusted and changed as follows:

The State Council approved the People's Government of Shandong Province to cancel the prefecture-level Laiwu City and transfer the area under its jurisdiction to Jinan City; set up Laiwu District of Jinan City, taking the administrative area of the former Laicheng District of Laiwu City as the administrative area of Laiwu District; set up the Gangcheng District of Jinan City, taking the administrative area of the former Gangcheng District of Laiwu City as the administrative area of Gangcheng District.

According to the official reply of the State Council, Lucheng City under Changzhi City of Shanxi Province was canceled, replaced by Lucheng District of Changzhi City.

With the approval of the State Council, Shanxi Province canceled Huairen County and established county-level Huairen City; Shaanxi Province canceled Binxian County and set up county-level Binzhou City; Qinghai Province canceled the Mangya Administrative Committee and

Lenghu Administrative Committee, and established county-level Mangya City; Jiangsu Province canceled Hai'an County and established county-level Hai'an City; Heilongjiang Province canceled Mohe County and set up county-level Mohe City; Hubei Province canceled Jingshan County and established county-level Jingshan City; Hebei Province canceled Luanxian County and established county-level Luanzhou City; Anhui Province canceled Qianshan County and set up county-level Qianshan City; Shandong Province canceled Zouping County and set up county-level Zouping City; Guangxi Zhuang Autonomous Region canceled Lipu County and set up county-level Lipu City; Guizhou Province canceled Xingren County and set up county-level Xingren City; Yunnan Province canceled Shuifu County and established county-level Shuifu City; Gansu Province canceled Huating County and set up county-level Huating City.

The State Council gave a reply to the Ministry of Science and Technology, People's Government of Gansu Province, People's Government of Zhejiang Province, People's Government of Xinjiang Uygur Autonomous Region, and Xinjiang Production and Construction Corps, agreeing to develop the National Independent Innovation Demonstration Zones in the existed high-tech industrial development zones of Lanzhou, Baiyin, Ningbo, Wenzhou, Urumqi, Changji and Shihezi. The State Council gave a reply to the People's Government of Shanxi Province, the People's Government of Guangxi Zhuang Autonomous Region, the People's Government of Guangdong Province and the Ministry of Science and Technology, agreeing to develop the National Sustainable Development Agenda Innovation Demonstration Zone in Taiyuan, Guilin and Shenzhen cities.

The State Council gave a reply to the people's governments of Hubei, Jiangxi, Guangdong, Yunnan, Anhui and Hunan provinces and Chongqing municipality, agreeing to upgrade the high-tech industrial parks of Jingzhou, Huangshi Dayehu, Qianjiang, Jiujiang Gongqingcheng, Yichun Fengcheng, Zhanjiang, Maoming, Chuxiong, Huainan, Huaihua, Rongchang and Yongchuan into national high-tech industrial development zones, implementing the current policy of the national high-tech industrial development zone. The planned areas of these 12 high-tech industrial development zones, after upgrading, will total 91. 841 square kilometers.

The State Council gave a reply to the Hainan Provincial People's Government and the Ministry of Commerce, approving the establishment of the China (Hainan) Free Trade Pilot Zone. The scope of the pilot zone covers the whole Hainan Island. The development and utilization of land and sea areas should strictly abide by the national laws and regulations and the "multiple plans in one" master plan of Hainan Province, and meet the requirements of optimal and intensive use of the land and sea. Where an uninhabited island is involved, it shall be handled in strict accordance with relevant provisions of the Island Protection Law of the People's Republic of China.

The State Council approved to list Yuxian County of Hebei Province as a national famous historical and cultural city. By the end of 2018, there were 134 national famous historical and cultural cities.

(Ⅲ) Urban (urban district) construction

According to the statistics of the Ministry of Housing and Urban-Rural Development, China had 661 cities by the end of 2017, with a registered population of 410 million and a temporary population of 82 million in these urban areas. The urban built-up areas amounted to 56 200 square kilometers.

In 2017, investment in fixed assets of urban municipal utilities in China amounted to 1. 9328 trillion yuan, an increase of 10. 7% over the previous year, accounting for 3. 01% of the total investment of fixed assets in the same period. In breakdown, the investment in road and bridge, rail transit and landscaping accounted for 36. 2%, 26. 1% and 9. 1% of the fixed assets investment of urban municipal utilities respectively.

In 2017, the urban population with access to water was 483 million, with per capita daily household water consumption of 179 liters, water access rate was 98. 30%; the population with to gas was 473 million and the gas access rate was 96. 14%; the central heating area was 8. 31 billion square meters; the length of urban roads was 398 000 kilometers, with per capita urban road area of 16. 05 square meters. A total of 2 429 kilometers of underground utility tunnels were newly built in the whole country. There were 2 209 sewage treatment plants in the country, with a 91. 98% of centralized treatment rate. The daily production capacity of municipal recycled water was 35. 88 million cubic meters, with 7. 13 billion cubic meters of reclaimed water utilized yearly. There were 1 013 harmless treatment plants of household waste with 97. 74% municipal solid waste harmlessly treated. A total of 8. 42 billion square meters of urban roads were cleaned, with 65. 0% under mechanical sweeping rate. In the whole year, 215 million tons of household waste and feces were cleared and transported. The green land rate of urban built-up areas was 37. 11%, and the per capita park green space area was 14. 01 square meters. At the end of 2017, there were 247 national scenic spots across the country, covering a total area of 109 thousand square kilometers, of which 50 thousand square kilometers were available to visitors, receiving 1. 17 billion visits throughout the year. The country invested 8. 21 billion yuan for the maintenance and construction of the scenic spots.

In 2017, total 338 cities monitored by the Ministry of Ecological Environment, the 29. 3% of those cities met the environmental air quality standard, and 70. 7% of them failed. For 74 cities monitored in the first phase of the new ambient air quality standard, average excellent days was 72. 7% and 1. 5 percentage points lower than in 2016. The average number of days exceeding the standard was 27. 3%. The average concentration of fine particulate matters (PM2. 5) decreased by 6. 0% compared with 2016. The precipitation monitoring was carried out in 474 cities (districts and counties). The proportion of acid rain cities with an annual average precipitation pH of less than

5.6% was 18.8%. The frequency of acid rain averaged 10.8%, down 1.9 percentage points from 2016.

According to the Ministry of Transport statistics, by the end of 2017, there were 651 200 buses and trams nationwide, of which 8 802 were BRT vehicles. A total of 32 cities opened rail transit, with 3 040 rail transit stations and 28 125 vehicles. There were 1.3958 million taxis and 264 urban passenger ferries. There were 56 786 bus and tram lines in the country, with a total length of 1.069 million kilometers. Among them, the bus lanes reached 10 914.5 kilometers, and BRT lines were 3 424.5 kilometers. There were 149 rail transit lines with a total length of 4 484.2 km. There were 92 urban passenger ferry operation routes, with a total length of 434.9 km. In the year, there were total of 127.215 billion passenger trips in urban areas, of which 72.287 billion trips were made with bus and tram (including 2.196 billion trips with BRT), 18.305 billion trips with the rail transit, and 36.54 billion trips with taxi. The composition of passengers transported by the urban passenger transport system was: bus 56.82%, rail transit 14.39%, taxi 28.72%, and passenger ferries 0.07%.

By the end of 2017, rail transit facilities were under construction in 50 cities across the country with a total line length of 4 914 kilometers.

(Ⅳ) Construction of county seats

Statistics from 1 526 counties across the country showed that by the end of 2017, the registered population of these county seats was 139 million, the temporary resident population was 17 million, and the built-up areas of county seats were 19 854 square kilometers. A total of 363.42 billion yuan were poured as fixed assets investment for public utilities construction in county seats. Among them, the road and bridge, drainage and sewage treatment, townscape and environmental sanitation accounted for 44.1%, 12.6% and 17.4% of the fixed assets investment of public utilities respectively.

In 2017, the population of county seats who access to water was 145 million, with water access rate of 92.9%. The per capita daily domestic water consumption was 120.2 liters. The gas access population was 127 million, with a gas access rate of 81.35%. The central heating areas were 1.463 billion square meters. The total length of road in county seats was 141 000 kilometers, with per capita urban road areas of 17.18 square meters. There were 1 572 sewage treatment plants in the counties, and a centralized treatment rate was 88.9%. There were 1 300 harmless treatment plants of domestic waste, with a daily treatment capacity of 205 000 tons and the harmless disposal rate of 91.0%. A total of 67.47 million tons of domestic waste were cleared and transported throughout the year. The green space rate of built-up areas was 30.74%, and the per capita green area was 11.86 square meters.

(Ⅴ) Construction of towns and villages

According to the statistics of the Ministry of Housing and Urban-Rural Development, collected from 18 100 towns, 10 300 townships and 2.449 million villages, by the end of 2017, the registered population of villages and towns reached 936 million. They were separated into 155 million population in towns, 25 million in townships, and 756 million in villages. The built-up areas of towns were 3.926 million hectares, and those of built-up townships were 633 800 hectares.

In 2017, a total of 1.7231 trillion yuan was invested in village and town construction nationwide, of which 915.5 billion yuan was put in residential construction, and 457.1 billion yuan in public utilities construction. At the end of the year, there were 30.8 billion square meters of residential buildings in villages and towns throughout the country. The per capita residential building area was 32.91 square meters, according to the household registration population statistics.

In 2017, the water access rate in the built-up towns of the country was 88.1%. The per capita daily domestic water consumption was 109.5 liters, and the per capita park green space area was 3.1 square meters. The water access rate in built-up townships was 78.8%. The per capita daily domestic water consumption was 104.3 liters, and the per capita park green area was 1.65 square meters. In the built-up areas of towns and townships, there were 401 000 kilometers of roads, 183 000 kilometers of drainage pipes and 152 800 public toilets at the end of the year.

Ⅱ. Reform of State Institutions and Unified Planning System

According to the Plan for Deepening the Reform of Party and State Institutions adopted by the Third Plenary Session of the 19th CPC Central Committee, the first session of the 13th National People's Congress approved The State Council Institutional Reform Plan on March 17, 2018. The Congress emphasized that the State Council should adhere to the centralized and unified leadership of the Central Committee of the CPC, carefully organize and make a well-planned deployment to ensure completing the task of institutional reform of the State Council. If it is necessary to formulate or amend laws to implement the institutional reform plan, the relevant procedures shall be initiated in a timely manner, and submitted to the Standing Committee of the National People's Congress for deliberation in accordance with the law.

(Ⅰ) Plan for Deepening Institutional Reform of the Party and State

Deepening institutional reform of the Party and the country is a profound change to promote the modernization of the state governance system and ability. It is a major political task related to the overall situation of the cause of the Party and the country. It is carried out in eight aspects: deepening the institutional reform of the Party Central Committee, deepening the institutional reform of the National People's Congress, deepening the institutional reform of the State Council, deepening the institutional reform of the National Committee of the Chinese People's Political Consultative Conference, deepening the reform of the administrative law enforcement system, deepen the cross-military-civilian reform, deepening the reform of the mass organizations, and deepening the reform of local institutions.

The plan requires the reform of the central and state organs should be put in place by the end of 2018. The reform plan of the provincial Party and government institutions should be submitted to the Party Central Committee for approval by the end of September 2018, and the adjustment of the institutions is basically in place by the end of 2018. The reform of Party and government institutions below the provincial level shall be led by provincial Party committee and reported to the Party Central Committee for the record by the end of 2018. All local institutional reforms should be basically completed by the end of March 2019.

(Ⅱ) Institutional Reform Scheme of the State Council

To deepen the institutional reform of the State Council, we should focus on changing the functions of the government. We should resolutely break the restrictions and disadvantages of the institutional mechanism to make the market play a decisive role in the allocation of resources, and give a better play to the role of the government. Centering on promoting high-quality development and building a modern economic system, we should strengthen and improve the functions of the government in economic regulation, market supervision, social management, public service and ecological environment protection. In the light of the new era conditions and practical requirements, we should focus on promoting the optimization and adjustment of the institutional functions in key areas and crucial links, and construct a government governance system with clear responsibility and administration by law, so as to improve the executive ability of the government and build a service-oriented government to satisfaction of the people. The specific program of reform is:

(1) Adjustment of constituent departments of the State Council, including the establishment of the Ministry of Natural Resources, Ministry of Ecology and Environment, Ministry of Agriculture and Rural Affairs, Ministry of Culture and Tourism, National Health Commission, Ministry of Veterans Affairs, and Ministry of Emergency Management; reestablishment of the Ministry of Science and Technology and Ministry of Justice; optimization of the responsibilities of the Ministry of Water Resources and National Audit Office. The Ministry of Supervision and the National Bureau for Prevention of Corruption are incorporated into the newly established National Supervisory Commission. After the reform, in addition to the General Office of the State Council,

the State Council is constituted of 26 departments.

(2) Adjustment of other institutions under the State Council, including the establishment of the State Administration for Market Regulation, National Radio and Television Administration, China Banking and Insurance Regulatory Commission, China International Development Cooperation Agency, National Healthcare Security Administration, National Food and Strategic Reserves Administration, State Immigration Administration, National Forestry and Grassland Administration; reestablishment of the National Intellectual Property Administration. It also adjusted the administrative subordination of the National Council for Social Security Fund, and reformed the national tax and local tax collection and management systems. The adjustment and establishment of the institutions under the State Council other than the constituent departments of the State Council will be examined and approved by the newly formed State Council.

(Ⅲ) Unifying the planning system

On November 18, 2018, the CPC Central Committee and the State Council issued the Opinions on Unifying the Planning System to Better Play the Strategic Guiding Role of the National Development Planning.

Leading economic and social development with planning is an important way for the Party to govern the country. It is also an important embodiment of the development mode of socialism with Chinese characteristics. By scientifically formulating and effectively implementing the .national development plan, clarifying the strategic deployments and specific arrangements for the goal of building a modern socialist country during the planning period, guiding the direction of public resource allocation, and standardizing the behavior of market subjects, the mechanism is conducive to maintaining the continuity and stability of the national strategy, focusing on major events, and ensuring that a blueprint is drawn to the end.

The opinions stipulate that the lower level planning shall be subject to the upper level planning, the subordinate planning shall serve the superior planning, and the planning at equal status shall be coordinated with each other. It calls for the establishment of a unified and coherent national planning system that is guided by the national development planning, based on the spatial planning, supported by special planning and regional planning, and composed of plans at the national, provincial, municipal and county levels, featuring accurate positioning, clear boundaries and complementary functions.

(1) Clarify planning function positioning

National development planning, i. e. , the outline of the five-year plan for the national economic and social development of the People's Republic of China, is the phased deployment and arrangement of the socialist modernization strategy during the planning period. The main purpose is to clarify the national strategic intention, define the priorities of the government work, and guide and standardize the behaviors of market entities. It is the grand blueprint of economic and social development, the common action program of the people of all ethnic groups, and the important basis for the government to perform the functions of economic regulation, market supervision, social management, public service and ecological environment protection.

National special planning is an important basis for guiding the development of specific fields, laying out major engineering projects, making rational allocation of public resources, guiding social capital investment, and formulating relevant policies. National level regional planning is an important basis to guide the development of specific regions and formulate related policies.

National spatial planning takes spatial governance and spatial structure optimization as the main contents. It is an important basis for the implementation of national territorial space use control and ecological protection and restoration.

(2) Straighten out planning relationship

The national development plan is organized and formulated by the State Council in accordance with the suggestions of the CPC Central Committee on the formulation of the five-year plan for national economic and social development. Examined and approved by the National People's Congress, it is at the top of the planning system and shall be followed in the formulation of all kinds of planning at all levels.

National special planning, regional planning and spatial planning shall all be formulated on the basis of the national development plan. National special planning is formulated by relevant departments of the State Council, implementing in details the strategic tasks put forward in the national development plan for specific areas. Among them, national key special plans are submitted to the State Council for examination and approval, with the exception of those explicitly required by the CPC Central Committee. State-level regional planning, which implements in details the strategic tasks put forward for specific regions in the national development plan, is formulated by relevant departments of the State Council and submitted to the State Council for examination and approval. National spatial planning, implementing in detail the requirements for national territory space development and protection proposed in the national development plan, is formulated by relevant departments of the State Council and submitted to the State Council for examination and approval. In case the national special planning, regional planning and spatial planning are formulated inconsistent with the national development plan, the planning objectives and tasks shall be adjusted or revised in due course in accordance with the strategic arrangements of the national development plan for the same period. The national spatial planning has the guidance and restraint function to the national special planning in terms of space affairs.

(Ⅳ) Establishing Ministry of Natural Resources

China attaches great importance to the construction of ecological civilization. It has put forward the idea to firmly establish the concept of respecting nature, complying with nature and protecting nature. It has insisted that lucid waters and lush mountains are invaluable assets. It should speed up the formation of a new pattern of modernization construction featuring harmonious development of man and nature, and create a new era of socialist ecological civilization. To uniformly exercise the responsibilities of owner of all natural resources assets for the whole people, uniformly exercise all duties of territorial space use control and ecological protection and restoration, and work hard to solve the problems of inadequate ownership of natural resources and overlapping spatial planning, the Organizational Reform Plan of the State Council clearly states to establish the Ministry of Natural Resources as a constituent department of the State Council. The ministry has integrated the responsibilities of the Ministry of Land and Resources, the planning responsibilities of the main functional zones of the National Development and Reform Commission, the urban and rural planning and management responsibilities of the Ministry of Housing and Urban-Rural Construction, the responsibilities of water resources investigation and confirmation registration management of the Ministry of Water Resources, the responsibilities of grassland resources investigation and confirmation registration management of the Ministry of Agriculture, the responsibilities of forest and wetland resources investigation and registration management of the State Forestry Administration, the duties of the State Oceanic Administration, and the duties of the State Surveying and Mapping Geographic Information Administration. The Ministry of Natural Resources retains the brand of the State Oceanic Administration for external communication.

On August 1, 2018, the General Office of the CPC Central Committee and the General Office of the State Council issued the Provisions on the Functional Allocation, Internal Establishment and Staffing of the Ministry of Natural Resources. In the field of territorial space, the internal bodies of the ministry shoulder the responsibilities as follows:

(1) Territory Spatial Planning Bureau. It develops the policies of territory spatial planning, and is responsible for establishing the spatial planning system and supervising the implementation. It organizes and compiles national territory spatial planning and related special plans and supervises the implementation, undertakes the examination and approval of local territory planning submitted to the State Council for examination and approval, guides and examines major national special plans involving the development and utilization of the territorial space. It carries out territorial space development suitability evaluation, establishes territory spatial planning implementation monitoring, evaluation and early warning system.

(2) Department of Territorial Space Application Control. It formulates norms and technical standards for the territorial space use control system, puts forward the annual use plans of land and ocean and organizes and implements them, organizes the development of the policies on the use and conversion of territorial space, including cultivated land, forest land, grassland, wetland,

sea area, and island, and guides the preliminary examination of land use for construction projects. It undertakes the examination and approval of all kinds of land use and conversion submitted to the State Council for examination and approval, formulates and supervises the implementation of policies for the control of urban and rural planning and management.

(3) Department of Territorial Space Ecological Rehabilitation. It undertakes the research of territorial space ecological restoration policies, formulates territorial space ecological restoration plans, undertakes comprehensive renovation of territorial space, land consolidation and reclamation, mine geological environment restoration and treatment, marine ecology, coastal zones and island restoration, undertakes related works of ecological protection and compensation, and guides the territorial space ecological restoration in the local level.

Ⅲ. Three-Year Actions for Poverty Alleviation

Since the 18th National Congress of the CPC, the total number of rural poor people has decreased by 82. 39 million, the incidence of poverty has fallen by 8. 5 percentage points, and the incomes of rural residents in the poor areas have grown higher than the national average level. The basic requirements and core targets of the three-year action to get rid of poverty and fight against poverty set by the central government are that by 2020, China should steadily realize that the rural poor do not worry about food and clothing, and are guaranteed in compulsory education, basic medical care, and housing security. In 2018, all regions and departments conscientiously implemented the strategy of accurate poverty alleviation, earnestly promoted poverty alleviation and tackling key problems, and achieved a good start to the three-year campaign of getting rid of poverty.

(Ⅰ) Rural poor population reduced by 13. 86 million

According to the national rural poverty monitoring survey conducted by the National Bureau of Statistics, there were total 16. 6 million poor people in rural areas at the end of 2018, 13. 86 million fewer than at the end of the previous year; and the incidence of poverty was 1. 7% , 1. 4 percentage points lower than the previous year, calculated on the basis of the current national rural poverty standard of 2 300 yuan per person per year (constant price in 2010) . In 2018, about 280 poor counties are expected to be removed from the list.

(Ⅱ) Per capita disposable incomes growth rate of rural residents in poverty-stricken areas continue to be higher than average of rural areas

Wages and transfer incomes are the main sources of the income increase for rural residents in poverty-stricken areas. In 2018, the per capita disposable income of rural residents in poverty-stricken areas was 10 371yuan, an increase of 994 yuan over the previous year. After deducting the price factor, the real growth rate was 8.3%, 1.7 percentage points higher than the national rural growth rate, successfully completing the annual target of higher growth rate than the national average.

The growth rate of per capita disposable income of rural residents in deep poverty areas was 0.1 percentage points higher than that in poverty-stricken areas. The per capita disposable income of rural residents in deep poverty areas was 9 668 yuan, an increase of 935 yuan, or 10.7% in nominal terms, over the previous year.

(Ⅲ) Guidance for Three-Year Actions to Win the Battle of Against Poverty

According to the progress and prominent problems in all regions and departments in the implementation of the Decision of the CPC Central Committee and the State Council on Winning the Battle of Against Poverty, the CPC Central Committee and the State Council issued the Guiding Opinions on the Three-Year Action to Win the Battle of Against Poverty on June 15, 2018.

(1) Guiding ideology. Focus on the deep poverty areas and special poor groups, highlight problem orientation, optimize policy supply, devote time and energy, stimulate the internal motivation of the poor people, and consolidate the foundation for the stable lifting of the poor out of poverty. make great efforts to strengthen the work style in the field of poverty alleviation, effectively improve the sense of gains of the poor, ensure that by 2020, the poor areas and poor people, together with the whole country, will enter a well-off society in an all-round way, and lay a solid foundation for the implementation of the strategy of rural revitalization.

(2) Mission objectives. By 2020, China will consolidate the achievements of poverty eradication. Through helping people to get rid of poverty via the development of production, relocation, ecological compensation, development of education, social security, and comprehensive measures according to local conditions, we will ensure that the rural poor under the current standard are lifted out of poverty to eradication absolute poverty. We will ensure that all poor counties take off their hats and solve regional poverty as a whole. We will realize the growth rate of per capita disposable income of farmers in poor areas is higher than the national average, and indicators in the main areas of basic public services in poor areas are close to the national average. The development environment of concentrated destitute areas, old revolutionary base areas, ethnic minority areas and border areas will be improved obviously, and the task of comprehensively out of poverty will be completed on schedule in deep poverty areas.

(3) Working requirements. We will adhere to strict implementation of the current poverty alleviation standards, ensure that the poor do not worry about food and clothing, children from poor families receive nine-year compulsory education, get well-educated and can afford to go to

school, the poor enjoy basic medical care, have access to effective treatment and protection of serious and chronic diseases, basic living conditions, and live in safe houses. We will act according to our ability, neither lower the standard, nor raise the standard without authorization, and raise unrealistic goals. We will avoid falling into the "welfare trap", and prevent the "cliff effect" of the treatment of poor and non-poor villages, poor and non-poor households, leaving after effects.

(Ⅳ) Situation Still Grim for Poverty Alleviation

The special research group of the Standing Committee of the National People's Congress pointed out in its recent "Investigation Report on Tackling Key Problems in Poverty Alleviation" that with the gradual progress in depth in tackling poverty, the problem of deep poverty has become prominent, and it has become even harder to tackle key problems. There are still some practical difficulties and problems that cannot be ignored in the work.

(1) By the end of 2018, there were about 400 poor counties and nearly 30 000 poor villages in the country. And among the people who have not yet been lifted out of poverty, the proportion of people with special difficulties, such as those who have been ill for a long time, those with disabilities, and the elderly of no family, and the poor population with insufficient motivation for their own development is high, and the proportion will be even higher in the future. Many of these people need to rely on the last line of financial support to achieve stable poverty eradication. The pressure of guaranteed poverty alleviation, especially the last line of financial support, is increasing.

(2) There is a common phenomenon of single and homogeneous industrial poverty alleviation projects in various provinces and autonomous regions. The follow-up development faces greater market risk. The health poverty alleviation policy still needs to be improved. It is generally acknowledged that in various localities, the policy of signing services for family doctors with chronic diseases is not in place and the management is not standardized. The contracted doctors are mainly village doctors, and most of them are mere formalities. It is shown in many places that the policy of base line medical service has ended in excessive medical treatment to varying degrees in practice. In terms of housing security, some relocation projects for poverty alleviation focus on relocation and neglect support. The supporting industries and promotion of employment have not kept pace, and poverty alleviation is lack of follow-up support. There is a lag in moving in the relocation of poverty alleviation to varying degrees in various localities. The progress of relocation does not match the progress of completion.

(3) It is generally reflected that in various localities, the current poverty alleviation policies are all real money, and that more and more are given to the poor areas and the poor people, with earnest help. But by contrast, how to stimulate the intrinsic motivation to get rid of poverty

remains deficient that needs to be made up. Some poor people are weak in taking the initiative to become rich. They rely too much on the support policy. And some poor people go so far as "If you don't help, I won't take action". At the same time, formalism, bureaucracy, fraud, impatience and weariness and corruption still exist in the work of lifting out poverty and tackling key problems. There are still varying degrees of settling accounts to get rid of poverty, getting out of poverty in a raid, or even false lifting out of poverty in various provinces and autonomous regions.

(4) After taking off the hats of poverty, the poor areas will still be underdeveloped for a long time, their development is relatively backward, the foundation of sustainable and stable income increase is still very weak, and the ability of self-development is not strong. In the long run, if we cannot solve the long-term mechanism and take the path of benign development, the pressure on poor areas and the poor population to return to poverty will still exist for a long time.

Ⅳ. New Mechanism for Regional Coordinated Development

Regional coordinated development is one of the major national strategies in the new era. Since the 18th National Congress of the Communist Party of China, all regions and departments have actively explored and achieved some results in establishing and improving regional cooperation mechanism, regional mutual assistance mechanism, and inter-regional benefit compensation mechanism, around promoting regional coordinated development and correctly handling government and market relations. However, the regional development gap in China remains large, regional differentiation is gradually emerging, disorderly development and vicious competition still exist, and unbalanced and inadequate regional development is still prominent. To remove the interest barriers and policy barriers between regions, fully implement the tasks of the regional coordinated development strategy, and promote regional coordinated development to a higher level and in a higher quality, the CPC Central Committee and the State Council issued the Opinions on the Establishment of a New Mechanism for More Effective Regional Coordinated Development on November 18, 2018.

(Ⅰ) Regional strategic coordination mechanism

Promoting the coordinated opening up of the coastal, inland and border areas with the Belt and Road construction, and strengthening the connectivity of major infrastructure with the corridor for international economic cooperation as the main skeleton, China will constructs a new pattern of regional development that coordinates the domestic and the international, harmonizes the east, central and west and the north and south of the country. It will promote the coordinated development of the Beijing-Tianjin-Hebei region by taking the "nose of an ox", which is to ease the "non-capital" function of Beijing. It will adjust the regional economic structure and spatial structure to promote the construction of Xiongan New Area in Hebei Province and the Sub-Center of Beijing, explore the optimal development modes of orderly easing the functions of population-intensive areas such as super-cities and mega-cities, and effectively managing the "big city diseases". It will give full play to the regional advantages of the Yangtze River economic belt across the three major sectors of the East, the Central and the West, take joint protection rather than large-scale development as the guide, follow the tenet of ecological priority and green development, and rely on the golden waterway of the Yangtze River to promote coordinated development of the upper, middle and lower reaches and the high-quality development of the areas along the River. It will establish a new model of leading the development of urban agglomeration with central cities, driving regional development by urban agglomeration, and promoting the integration and interactive development of regional boards. Meanwhile, it is necessary to strengthen the coordination and docking of major national strategies and promote the linkage of regional cooperation.

(Ⅱ) Market integration development mechanism

China will implement a unified national negative list system for market access and eliminate discriminatory and hidden restrictions on regional market access. It will speed up deepening the reform of the rural land system, promote the establishment of a unified market for construction land in urban and rural areas, further improve the system of separating the ownership of contracted land, the right to contract land and the right to operate land, and explore the reform of the split of the ownership, qualification and use right of the homestead. It will explore the establishment of a new mechanism of regional market integration with a unified planning system, common development model, consistent governance mode and regional market linkage, so as to promote the formation of a unified national market. It will further improve the paid use system of natural resources assets and build a unified natural resources asset trading platform.

(Ⅲ) Regional cooperation mechanism

China will deepen the cooperation of the Beijing-Tianjin-Hebei region, the Yangtze River economic belt, and Guangdong-Hong Kong-Macao Greater Bay Area, and upgrade the level of cooperation. It will actively explore the establishment of a coordinated governance model for urban agglomerations and encourage the establishment of various forms of urban coalitions. It will speed up the cooperative development between the upper and lower reaches of key river basin economic belts, including the Yangtze River Economic Belt, the Pearl River-Xijiang Economic Belt, the Huaihe River Ecological Economic Belt, and the Hanjiang River Ecological Economic Belt. It will establish and improve the mechanism of docking planning of neighboring provinces and municipalities in the upstream and downstream areas, coordinate to solve major problems of inter-regional cooperation and development. It will support the cooperation and development in the border areas between provinces, including the Golden Triangle of the Yellow River in Shanxi, Shaanxi and Henan, the Guangdong-Guangxi border, the Hunan-Jiangxi border and the Sichuan-Chongqing border, and explore the establishment of a new cooperative mechanism of unified planning, unified management, cooperative joint construction and benefit-sharing. It will focus on the Belt and Road construction, implement a more proactive strategy of opening up, and promote the construction of a new mechanism for mutually beneficial and win-win international regional cooperation. It will promote the construction of key development and open-up pilot zones, support the development of border economic cooperation zones, steadily build cross-border economic cooperation zones, and give better play to the driving role of overseas capacity cooperation parks and economic and trade cooperation zones.

(Ⅳ) Inter-regional interest compensation mechanism

China will carry out the important idea that "lucid waters and lush mountains are invaluable assets" and the systematic thought that "mountain, river, forest, field, lake and grass" are the community of lives. It will constantly improve the horizontal ecological compensation mechanism according to the principle of regional fairness, equal rights and responsibilities, pilot projects first, and step by step advance. It will study and formulate specific measures for carrying out production and marketing cooperation between the main grain producing areas and the main marketing areas, and encourage the main grain marketing areas to carry out production and marketing cooperation through the construction of processing parks in the main production areas, the establishment of high-quality commodity grain bases and the establishment of reserve cooperation mechanisms in production and marketing areas, as well as providing funding, talent, technical service support. In the light of the important resource such as coal, oil, natural gas, hydro-energy, wind energy, solar energy, and other mineral resources, it will adhere to the combination of market orientation and government regulation, and speed up the resource price formation mechanism which is conducive to the intensive and economical utilization of resources and sustainable development, ensuring that resource prices cover the costs of mining costs, eco-remediation and environmental governance.

(Ⅴ) Regional development guarantee mechanism

China will strengthen the preliminary study of regional planning, improve the working procedures of regional planning, examination, approval and implementation, implement the management system of regional planning examination and approval plan, further improve the implementation mechanism of regional planning, and strengthen the mid-term evaluation and post-evaluation, to form a scientific and reasonable regional planning system with strict management and strong guidance. Focusing on narrowing the regional development gap, regional integration, resources and environment coordination and other key areas, it will set up a regional coordination and development evaluation index system, and scientifically and objectively evaluate the coordination of regional development, and provide a reference for the development and adjustment of regional policy. It will study and demonstrate the legal system to promote the coordinated development of regions, clarify the connotation, strategic focus and direction of the coordinated development of regions, and improve the mechanism of regional policy formulation, implementation, supervision and evaluation, clarify the responsibilities of the relevant departments in the coordinated development of regions, and clarify the responsibilities and obligations of the local governments in promoting the coordinated development of regions, and play the role of social organizations, research institutions and enterprises in promoting regional coordination and development.

V. Strive to Achieve Higher Quality Development

General Secretary Xi Jinping has pointed out that high-quality development is a development that embodies the concept of new development. Highlighting the orientation of high quality development is to adhere to the steady pursuit of progress. On the premise of maintaining stability, we will make progress, and seek stability with advance, to better meet the needs of the people's diverse, multi-layer and multi-aspect needs. On the way forward, we must focus on solving the main contradiction of society, which is the contradiction between the growing needs of the people for a better life and unbalanced and inadequate development, and resolutely implement the concept of innovation, coordination, green, openness, and sharing for development, and strive to achieve higher quality, more efficient, fairer and more sustainable development.

(I) Building a national model for high quality development

On December 25, 2018, the State Council issued a reply on the Master Plan of Xiongan New Area of Hebei Province (2018-2035). It agreed in principle the master plan, which unveiled the prelude to the development and construction of Xiongan New Area. In accordance with the requirements of high quality development, the master plan firmly grasps the original orientation as a carrier of Beijing's non-capital functions. It adheres to the world vision, international standards, Chinese characteristics, high positioning. It adheres to ecological priority, green development, putting people first, paying attention to ensuring and improving people's livelihood, persisting in protecting and carrying forward the excellent traditional culture of China, and continuing the historical context. All these are of great significance to build Xiongan New Area with high starting point planning and high standards, create "Xiongan quality", build "clean Xiongan", construct a national model for high quality development, and build a new engine of the modern economic system.

In accordance with the construction objectives set in the Outline of Planning for Xiongan New Area of Hebei Province, by the middle of this century, Xiongan New Area will be built into a high-quality and high-level socialist modern city, and become an important pole of Beijing-Tianjin-Hebei world-class urban agglomeration. It has achieved remarkable results in undertaking Beijing's non-capital functions, providing a Chinese solution for solving the "big city disease" problem. All the indicators of economic and social development in the New Area have reached the international leading level. The governance system and ability have been modernized, to become a national model for high-quality development in the new era.

In the beginning of 2019, Xi Jinping stressed once again when chairing a meeting on coordinated development of the Beijing-Tianjin-Hebei region, that the building of the Xiongan New Area is a millennium project of vital and lasting importance. The New Area should be new in the concept of planning and construction. It should be forward-looking and leading, fully implement the new concept of development, adhere to the high-quality development requirements, and strive to create the benchmark of high-quality development in the new era.

(Ⅱ) Characteristic small towns and administrative towns' high-quality development

The characteristic small towns and administrative towns are important combination of the new urbanization and rural revitalization, and important platform to promote the high quality development of the economy. The Guiding Opinions on Speeding Up the Construction of Beautiful Characteristic Small Towns (Administrative Towns) and the Opinions on Standardizing and Promoting the Construction of Characteristic Small Towns and Administrative Towns, issued by the National Development and Reform Commission, have achieved certain results in guiding the development of characteristic small towns and administrative towns. They have corrected the problems of unclear concept, blind development and real estate oriented development to a certain extent. To further consolidate the achievements of rectifying deviation and effectively promote high-quality development in an orderly manner, the General Office of the NDRC released the Circular on the Establishment of High quality Development Mechanism for Characteristic Small Towns and Administrative Towns on August 30, 2018. The requirements are as follows:

(1) Basic principle. Insist on building towns with industries, standardized development, guiding with typical cases, and optimized services. Based on the development stages of various regions, we should follow the laws of economy and urbanization, seek truth from facts, adapt measures to local conditions, and act according to our ability, to make the construction of characteristic small towns and administrative towns a market-based process of natural development.

(2) Identify conditions of characteristic small towns. The basic conditions: Based on certain resource endowment or industrial base, different from administrative towns and industrial parks, construct the big industry of the town with differential orientation and segmented domain in an area of about three square kilometers (including about one square kilometers construction land), gathering high-end elements and characteristic industries, featuring characteristic culture, ecology and architecture, to build an efficient start-up circle, a livable circle, a prosperous business circle and a beautiful ecosystem, and establish a platform for innovation and entrepreneurship that has a unique and strong industry, multiple functions, small and beautiful form, and a new and flexible mechanism.

(3) Identify conditions of characteristic administrative towns. The basic conditions: Based on the development stage and potential of industrialization and urbanization, create a distinctive industrial form, convenient and complete facilities services, a harmonious and livable beautiful environment, a profound traditional culture, and a streamlined, efficient institutional mechanism, enable characteristic pillar industry to dominate the town economy and seize certain shares in the domestic and international markets, possess a number of well-known brands and enterprises. The resident population in the town has reached a certain scale. Possess strong ability to drive the rural revitalization. Develop into a pacesetter of administrative towns with core competitiveness, an upgraded version of economically developed towns.

(4) Explore the experience of diversified development. Encourage to seek a variety of town cases, avoiding similar patterns as it is hard to popularize. Based on different industrial sectors, search for modern service cases, such as advanced manufacturing sector, agricultural and pastoral sector, information, scientific innovation, finance, education, commerce, culture and sports. Based on different geographical locations, sort out cases of characteristic towns, such as "suburban town", "urban town", "park town" and "town in town", as well as "satellite town" and "specialized town". Based on various operation modes, to find out advanced experience in mechanism and policy innovation, government-enterprise cooperation, investment and financing mode.

(Ⅲ) Action plan for improving quality of social public services

In recent years, China has been intensifying investment in public services in the social field, and continuously improved the facilities and conditions. However, compared with the multi-level diversified demands of the masses, there are still some problems, such as insufficient supply, low quality, and unbalanced development. There is still a big gap between the service quality and level of attending kindergarten and schools, seeking medical treatment and providing for the aged and people's expectations. To promote public service in the social field, make up the short board and weakness, improve the quality, and promote the formation of a strong domestic market, on

January 23, 2019, 18 central government departments, including the National Development and Reform Commission and Publicity Department of the CPC Central Committee, jointly issued the Action Plan to Strengthen Efforts to Improve the Quality of Public Services in the Social Field and Promote the Formation of a Strong Domestic Market.

(1) Main objectives

By 2020, the public service supply structure will be more reasonable, the social forces will be more active in participation, the implementation guarantee mechanism will be more perfect, and the quality and level of services will continue to be improved. Public services will play a greater role in ensuring people's livelihood, promoting employment and expanding consumption. China will basically achieve full coverage of the basic public service capacity, meet the full standards of quality, fully implement the standards and ensure guarantee. It will make non-basic public services available for payment, featuring affordable prices, guaranteed quality, and regulated safety. Among them, important progress will be made in the modernization of education, and the average number of years of education of the working-age population will reach 10. 8 years. The basic medical and health system covering urban and rural areas will be basically established, and the average life expectancy will be raised to 77. 3 years. The elderly care service system, based on homes, supported by the community and supplemented by institutions, combined with medical and nursing care, will be more perfect, and the proportion of nursing beds for the aged will be no less than 30%. The policies, regulations and standard specification system of infant care service will be basically established. The modern public cultural service system will be basically built, and the cultural industry will become a pillar industry of the national economy. The tourism economy will grow steadily, making 12% comprehensive contribution to the national economy. The physical quality of the masses will be steadily enhanced, with a per capita sports venue area of 1. 8 square meters. Housekeeping training will be further standardized, and the industry standardization will be further consolidated.

By 2022, the supply of public service will be more sufficient, the resource layout will be continuously optimized, and the institutional mechanism will be increasingly complete. The talent team will keep expanding, and the service quality will be improved obviously. The basic public service system covering the whole people, with inclusive sharing, and urban-rural integration, will be steadily improved. The public service experience, which is close, convenient and efficient for the people, will be constantly improving. The public service pattern, basically covered by the government, with active social participation, and construction and sharing by the whole people, will be constantly improved. The most concerned, difficult problems on people's livelihood will be effectively relieved. The diversified, optional public service resources will be even richer. The domestic market demands with great potential will be met, and the people's sense of obtaining, happiness and security will be constantly improved.

(2) Action tasks

Efforts to make up for the weakness of basic public services and speed up the equalization of basic public services include promoting balanced development of the compulsory education, improving the health service ability of counties in poor areas, strengthening the construction of the health service system for the women and children, improving the prevention and control ability of medical emergency rescue and infectious diseases, improving the basic aged people service system, strengthening the construction of the social welfare service system, improving the service level of public employment and entrepreneurship, promoting the equalization of basic public cultural services, promoting the construction and opening of public sports facilities, and improving the public service system of the disabled.

Efforts to strengthen the weaknesses of non-basic public services and enhance the supply of public services to people include increasing the effective supply of nurseries services, expanding resources for inclusive pre-school education in urban and rural areas, promoting the accelerated development of social medical services, fully liberalizing the market for old-age care, strengthening the construction of the health service system for the elderly, promoting the housekeeping training and the employment service, popularizing community dinner service in urban and rural areas, strengthening the protection, inheritance and utilization of excellent traditional culture, improving tourism infrastructure in key areas, speeding up the integration, development and interconnection of cable television networks, and accelerating the development of sports, fitness, leisure sports and competitive performance industries.

Efforts to give full play to the roles of effective market, responsible government, and improve the quality of public services include improving the content and quality of educational services, balancing the development of high-quality medical resources, improving the quality of old-age services, elevating the efficiency of public cultural services, speeding up the development of intelligent radio and television, and promoting the development of a variety of tourism industries.

(Ⅳ) Engineering construction standards for high-quality urban development

China has built up a standard system of engineering construction with Chinese characteristics. The Reform Plan for Deepening Standardization Work of the State Council has identified the overall objectives of the reform as: establish a new standard system for coordinated development and harmony between the standards led by the government and standards independently formulated by the market, improve the standardized management system of unified coordination, efficient operation and co-governance of the government and the market, let the standard become a "hard constraint" on quality, and push the Chinese economy to march to the middle and high level. At the same time, it clearly puts forward some major reform measures to cultivate and develop the social organization standards, liberalize and invigorate the enterprise standards, and improve the level of internationalization of standards.

From October to November 2018, China Urban Planning Society released the first social organization standards, including the Small Town Spatial Characteristic Guideline, and the Data Standards for Electronic Approval of Construction Project Planning. In view of the current development needs and problems, these social organization standards put forward public norms in a timely and rapid manner, complementing with national norms. They are adopted voluntarily by the society for the purpose of solving specific problems.

On December 6, 2018, the Ministry of Housing and Urban-Rural Development held an activity in the city of Nanning, releasing a series of standards promoting high-quality urban development. It aimed to adapt to the new requirements of China's economy from high-speed growth to high-quality development, support and guide the urban construction in China with high standards and project construction high-quality development. The issued standards covered three aspects, which were to promote the green city development, ensuring the safe city operation, and build harmonious and livable cities. They included Assessment Standard for Sponge City, Assessment Standard of Green Building, Provisions for Standard of Urban Planning on Comprehensive Disaster Resistance and Prevention, Code for Urban Wastewater and Stormwater Engineering Planning, Technical Code for Urban Flooding Prevention and Control, Standard for Urban Residential Area Planning and Design, Standard for City Comprehensive Transport System Planning.

It is reported that in the fields of housing and urban-rural development, China has so far released 356 national standards for engineering construction and 765 standards for urban-rural planning, housing construction and municipal engineering. The provinces (autonomous regions, municipalities) have also issued 4 468 local standards for engineering construction.

Ⅵ. Building Sustainable Resilient Cities

(Ⅰ) World Cities Day 2018

On February 9, 2018, Maimunnah Moh'd Sharif, a Malaysian planner newly elected as the Executive Director of UN-habitat, announced in Kuala Lumpur that the theme of the World Cities Day 2018 was "Building Sustainable and Resilient Cities".

On October 31, António Guterres, Secretary-General of the United Nations, delivered a message on the World Cities Day. He said: The 2030 Agenda for Sustainable Development, the Paris Agreement on climate change, the Sendai Framework for Disaster Risk Reduction and the New Urban Agenda together provided a roadmap for more sustainable resilient world. How our cities develop will have significant implication for realizing the future we want.

Guterres pointed out that in today's world, every week, 1.4 million people move to cities. Such rapid urbanization can strain local capacities, contributing to increased risk from natural and human made disasters. But hazards do not need to become disasters. The answer is to build resilience—to storms, floods, earthquakes, fires, pandemics and economic crises.

Cities around the world are already acting to increase resilience and sustainability. Bangkok has built vast underground water storage facilities to cope with increased flood risk and save water for drier periods. In Quito, the local government has reclaimed or protected more than 200 000 hectares of land to boost flood protection, reduce erosion and safeguard the city's freshwater supply and biodiversity. And in Johannesburg, the city is involving residents in efforts to improve public spaces so they can be safely used for recreation, sports, community events and services such as free medical care.

Guterres said that "On the World Cities Day, let us be inspired by these examples. Let us work together to build sustainable and resilient cities that provide safety and opportunities for all."

(Ⅱ) World City Day China observance

The World Cities Day 2018 China observance was co-organized by the Ministry of Housing and Urban-Rural Development, Jiangsu Provincial People's Government and UN-habitat in Xuzhou City. Focusing on the annual theme of the World Cities Day, the China observance gave priorities to the exchanges and demonstration of the innovative practices in urban sustainable development, disaster prevention and resilience, green buildings, spongy cities, green cities and resilient cities around the world. They also explored how to further implement the New Urban Agenda of the United Nations and promote international cooperation and exchanges. The China observance included the World Cities Day thematic forum, mayor dialogue, expert dialogue, urban sustainable development practice exhibition, release of the Chinese version of Shanghai Manual—21 World Cities Sustainable Development Guide 2018 Annual Report, as well as related supporting activities. They were attended by about 400 persons, including heads of national and regional government departments, mayors at home and abroad, representatives of international organizations and experts and scholars in urban planning and construction management.

In line with the theme of The World Cities Day, "Building Sustainable and Resilient Cities", the China observance issued the Xuzhou Initiative for Urban Green Development:

(1) Work hand in hand to promote the construction of urban ecological civilization. Cities should adhere to the concept that "lucid waters and lush mountains are invaluable assets", build an ecological system that respects nature and green development, and work together to build a clean and beautiful urban homestead. We should well deal with the relationship between ecological environment protection and economic development, strengthen the conversion of old and new driving forces, and promote the transformation of urban development mode.

(2) Comprehensively strengthen urban ecological restoration. Old industrial bases and resource-exhausted cities should focus on ecological restoration and urban repair, transform the burdens as resources, and turn the "ecological scars" into "bright spots of the city." They should carry out comprehensive treatment of urban pollution and strengthen the scientific disposal and utilization of solid waste.

(3) Jointly explore the pathway of urban transformation. Cities should accurately grasp the characteristics of their own development stages and actively construct a new pattern of green, low carbon and sustainable development: Speed up green transformation of the industrial structure, energy structure and transportation structure, and strive to build a modern green industrial system. Set up a new concept of green life, advocate green consumption, green travel, green living, cultivate and form green living habits.

(Ⅲ) Xuzhou case of building sustainable and resilient cities

Xuzhou, located in northern Jiangsu Province and the junction of the four provinces of Jiangsu, Shandong, Henan, and Anhui, is a historical and cultural city with a history of 2 600 years. It is an important comprehensive transport hub of the country and a central city of the Huaihai Economic Zone. In 2018, the city's permanent residents were 8.8 million. Xuzhou has achieved remarkable results and experiences in industrial transformation, ecological restoration, shantytown redevelopment and solid waste management, which are popularized throughout the country.

(1) Industrial transformation. Xuzhou, one of the birthplaces of coal industry in China, has formed a heavy industry system dominated by coal, steel, cement and chemical industry. Under the new requirements of high quality development, the city has closed 14 pairs of mines, reduced coal production capacity of 10.62 million tons, iron and steel capacity of 1.63 million tons, completing the task of cutting coal production overcapacity three years ahead of schedule in Jiangsu Province.

Xuzhou has closely followed the industrial development orientation to make adjustment to seek the "high, light, optimized and strong", and actively constructed the "6 + 6" modern industrial system. It has focused on the six traditional superior industries, such as equipment manufacturing, food and agricultural and sideline product processing, as the main body to enhance the competitiveness of traditional industries through scientific and technological innovation. Guided by six strategic emerging industries, such as new energy and new materials, it has put forward implementation plans for the four emerging industries of equipment and intelligent manufacturing, new energy, integrated circuit and ICT, biomedicine, and formulated plans on the development of characteristic industrial bases. In 2018, the output values of high-tech industry enterprises above the scale totaled 38.3% in the city.

(2) Ecological restoration. "I'm treated with two cups of mud after entering Xuzhou city". "In a sunny day, I'm covered with soil, and in a rainy day, I'm covered with mud". These were the true portrayals of Xuzhou in the past. As a traditional old industrial city, Xuzhou developed an industrial structure with high consumption of resources and high environmental pollution over the years, which led to serious air and water pollution, and heavy burden of ecological arrears.

In recent years, Xuzhou has renovated 197 200 mu of coal mining subsidence, and 42 quarrying caves in the city have been repaired. The forest coverage rate of the city is 30.1%, the greening coverage of urban built-up areas is 43.8%, the per capita park green space area is 15.7 square meters, and the quality of water bodies above three categories is 79.2%. It has won honorary titles of national ecological garden city, national health city, national environmental protection model city, and national forest city, completing the gorgeous turn from "a city of coal ash and half dust" to "a city of green mountains and half lake".

(3) Redevelopment of shanty town. According to the actual situation of urban construction planning and shantytowns, Xuzhou adheres to the principle of respecting public opinion and doing what it can, and vigorously carries out the redevelopment of shantytowns and villages in cities. It has implemented the affordable housing construction project, which is the largest in history and benefits the largest number of people.

The city has reconstructed shantytowns of more than 100 million square meters, benefiting 526 000 households. This includes 38.72 million square meters in the main urban areas, where 300 000 residents have moved out of sheds into apartment buildings, solving all sorts of daily necessity problems. The city has adopted "three special policies" in shantytown redevelopment: First, arrange those meeting economically affordable housing conditions directly to such houses in the expropriation and relocation of shantytowns; Second, arrange the "double special needy households" and those meeting the conditions of low-rent housing directly to low-rent housing resettlement, who would pay policy rent. Third, allow those in economic difficulties, who cannot afford to make up for the house price difference, to have joint property rights in the resettlement, and ensure they could buy back the whole property rights within 10 years at the price of housing requisition.

(4) Solid waste management. Over the years, Xuzhou lagged behind in the treatment of solid waste, such as municipal solid waste, and the regional ecological environment was greatly damaged. It was a common scene to see "garbage blown away by wind and sewage evaporated by the sun". The city suffered heavily from the solid waste, which had large output, small recovery and low utilization rate. The contradiction between the lack of solid waste treatment capacity and people's expectations for a better living environment became increasingly prominent.

The Xuzhou Municipal Government has recognized the importance of garbage control. It has formulated the main line of work to build the city as a home, to build the home as a park, and to highlight the garbage treatment. It has explored the ways to carry out sustainable operation mode of household waste classification around the thoughts of scientific classification, targeted management and resource utilization, Through developing intelligent management and control, network collection and transportation, recycling utilization, and centralized disposal, it has created the Xuzhou experience of urban solid waste management.

On October 1, 2018, the Government of the Republic of Kenya hosted the global celebration of World Human Settlements Day at the United Nations Office at Nairobi and the headquarters of UN-habitat. Xuzhou City of Jiangsu Province, China won the UN-Habitat Scroll of Honour Award 2018 for its outstanding achievements in promoting ecological restoration in an all-round way through intelligence management of waste.

Ⅶ. Conclusion

In struggle, we create history. With solid work, we achieve the future. Looking back to the 40-year course of reform and opening-up, we have noted that the Chinese people have gone through the road of industrialization and urbanization in several decades that the developed countries had experienced over centuries. They have created a Chinese miracle that attracts the attention of the world, and composed a chant of life that moves the world, full of power and grandeur.

In 2019, we will celebrate the 70th anniversary of the founding of the People's Republic of China. From creating the New China to entering the new century, from standing on a new starting point to embracing a new era, the Chinese people have blazed a trail regardless of hardship over the past 70 years. They have been self-reliance and hard struggle. Though beaten by wind and waves, they have marched forward in confidence.

In 2019, we have entered a key year to win the first centenary goal of the struggle. In the new journey, there are both new development opportunities and new risks and challenges. We should follow the guidance of the thought of socialism with Chinese characteristics in a new era, fully implement the spirit of the 19th CPC National Congress, adhere to the new concept of development, persist in promoting high-quality development, constantly improve the people's sense of achievement, happiness, and sense of security, maintain sustained and healthy economic development and social stability, lay a decisive foundation for building a well-off society in an all-round way, and celebrate the 70th anniversary of the founding of the People's Republic of China with outstanding achievements.

Author: Mao Qizhi, Professor of Tsinghua University, Academician of International Eurasian Academy of Sciences

2018年中国城市发展十大事件

一、我国隆重纪念改革开放40周年

2018年是我国改革开放的第40个年头，40年来，我国经济社会发展取得了举世瞩目的历史性成就，实现了前所未有的历史性变革。2018年，我国举行了隆重的纪念活动，庆祝改革开放40周年。

2018年11月13日，“伟大的变革——庆祝改革开放40周年大型展览”在国家博物馆开幕，展览以坚持和发展中国特色社会主义为主题，紧扣改革开放40年历程，紧扣改革开放的历史纵深感、群众获得感、发展成就感，设计了伟大的变革、壮美篇章、关键抉择、历史巨变、大国气象、面向未来六个主题内容展区，运用历史图片、文字视频、实物场景、沙盘模型、互动体验等多种手段和元素，充分展示了改革开放的光辉历程、伟大成就、宝贵经验。展览自开幕以来吸引了全国各地大量的参观者，截至2018年12月31日，参观人数累计达230万人次，日均4.7万人次。

2018年12月18日，庆祝改革开放40周年大会在北京人民大会堂隆重举行。习近平在大会上发表了重要讲话。习近平从理论创新、经济建设、政治建设、文化建设、社会建设、生态文明建设、国防和军队建设、祖国统一、外交工作、党的建设等方面总结了我国改革开放的伟大成就。

理论创新方面，勇于推进理论创新、实践创新、制度创新、文化创新以及各方面创新，形成了中国特色社会主义道路、理论、制度、文化。经济建设方面，我国已成为世界第二大经济体、制造业第一大国、货物贸易第一大国、商品消费第二大国、外资流入第二大国，我国外汇储备连续多年位居世界第一。政治建设方面，党和国家领导体制日益完善，全面依法治国深入推进，中国特色社会主义法律体系日益健全，人民当家作主的制度保障和法治保障更加有力。文化建设方面，爱国主义、集体主义、社会主义精神广为弘扬，文化艺术日益繁荣，网信事业快速发展，全民族理想信念和文化自信不断增强，国家文化软实力和中华文化影响力大幅提升。社会建设方面，全国居民人均可支配收入大幅增加，贫困人口急剧减少，教育事业全面发展，建成了包括养老、医疗、低保、住房在内的世界最大的社会保障体系。生态文明建设方面，生态文明制度体系加快形成，节能减排取得重大进展，重大生态保护和修复工程进展顺利，生态环境治理明显加强。国防和军队建设方面，武器装备取得历史性突破，治军方式发生根本性转变，革命化现代化正规化水平显著提高。祖国统一方面，相继恢复对香港、澳门行使主权，牢牢掌握两岸关系发展主导权和主动权。外交工作方面，始终坚持独立自主的和平外交政策，为世界和平与发展不断贡献中国智慧、中国方案、中国力量。党的建设方面，积极应对在长期执政和改革开放条件下党面临的各种风险考验，积极探索共产党执政规律、社会主义建设规律、人类社会发展规律，坚持党要管党、从严治党，反腐败斗争取得压倒性胜利。

习近平指出，改革开放 40 年积累的宝贵经验是党和人民弥足珍贵的精神财富，对新时代坚持和发展中国特色社会主义有着极为重要的指导意义，必须倍加珍惜、长期坚持，在实践中不断丰富和发展。一是必须坚持党对一切工作的领导，不断加强和改善党的领导。二是必须坚持以人民为中心，不断实现人民对美好生活的向往。三是必须坚持马克思主义指导地位，不断推进实践基础上的理论创新。四是必须坚持走中国特色社会主义道路，不断坚持和发展中国特色社会主义。五是必须坚持完善和发展中国特色社会主义制度，不断发挥和增强我国制度优势。六是必须坚持以发展为第一要务，不断增强我国综合国力。七是必须坚持扩大开放，不断推动共建人类命运共同体。八是必须坚持全面从严治党，不断提高党的创造力、凝聚力、战斗力。九是必须坚持辩证唯物主义和历史唯物主义世界观和方法论，坚持问题导向，正确处理改革发展稳定的关系。

习近平强调，全党全国各族人民要更加紧密地团结在党中央周围，高举中国特色社会主义伟大旗帜，不忘初心，牢记使命，将改革开放进行到底，不断实现人民对美好生活的向往，在新时代创造中华民族新的更大奇迹，创造让世界刮目相看的新的更大奇迹。

在庆祝改革开放 40 周年之际，中共中央、国务院颁布“关于表彰改革开放杰出贡献人员的决定”，授予 100 名同志改革先锋称号，颁授改革先锋奖章。96 岁高龄的吴良镛先生以“人居环境科学的创建者”的贡献接受了党和国家“改革先锋”的表彰。

（资料来源：新华网、光明网、人民日报）

“十八大”以来我国全面深化改革开放大事记

2013 年 11 月，党的十八届三中全会审议通过《中共中央关于全面深化改革若干重大问题的决定》，提出了全面深化改革的指导思想、目标任务、重大原则，描绘了全面深化改革的新蓝图、新愿景、新目标。

2013 年 12 月，中共中央政治局召开会议，决定成立中央全面深化改革领导小组，负责改革总体设计、统筹协调、整体推进、督促落实。

2014 年 1 月，习近平总书记主持召开中央全面深化改革领导小组第一次会议，成立了经济体制和生态文明体制改革、民主法制领域改革、文化体制改革、社会体制改革、党的建设制度改革、纪律检查体制改革 6 个专项小组。

2014年7月，国务院公布《关于进一步推进户籍制度改革的意见》，取消“农业”和“非农业”户口性质的区别，建立城乡统一的户口登记制度，根据城市类型实施差别化落户政策。

2015年4月，中共中央、国务院印发《关于加快推进生态文明建设的意见》，明确了生态文明建设的总体要求、主要目标、重点任务等。同年9月，《生态文明体制改革总体方案》发布。

2015年8月，中共中央、国务院印发《关于深化国有企业改革的指导意见》。以此为统领，陆续出台了有关国有企业分类、发展混合所有制经济、完善国资监管体制、防止国有资产流失、完善法人治理结构等多个配套文件。

2016年11月，中共中央办公厅印发《关于在北京市、山西省、浙江省开展国家监察体制改革试点方案》，部署在3个省（市）设立省、市、县三级监察委员会。同年12月25日，十二届全国人大常委会第二十五次会议通过关于在北京市、山西省、浙江省开展国家监察体制改革试点工作的决定。

2016年11月，《中共中央国务院关于完善产权保护制度依法保护产权的意见》（以下简称《意见》）公布。这是我国首次以中央名义出台产权保护的顶层设计，《意见》在多处对于公众关心的土地与房屋财产问题，作了说明和安排。

2016年12月，中共中央、国务院印发《关于深入推进农业供给侧结构性改革　加快培育农业农村发展新动能的若干意见》。文件提出，把农业农村工作的重心转移到推进农业供给侧结构性改革上来。加大农村改革力度，激活农业农村内生发展动力。

2017年7月，全国金融工作会议举行。习近平总书记强调，要加强党对金融工作的领导，紧紧围绕服务实体经济、防控金融风险、深化金融改革3项任务，会议决定设立国务院金融稳定发展委员会。

2017年10月，习近平总书记在十九大报告中指出，坚持全面深化改革。全面深化改革总目标是完善和发展中国特色社会主义制度、推进国家治理体系和治理能力现代化。

2018年1月，中共中央、国务院印发《关于实施乡村振兴战略的意见》，描绘了加快推进农业农村现代化，走中国特色社会主义乡村振兴道路的政策蓝图。

2018年2月，中共十九届三中全会通过《关于深化党和国家机构改革的决定》和《深化党和国家机构改革方案》，决定组建中央全面依法治国委员会、中央审计委员会等机构。3月17日，第十三届全国人大一次会议批准国务院机构改革方案。

2018年11月，首届中国国际进口博览会在上海举行。习近平出席开幕式并在发表主旨演讲时宣布：增设中国上海自由贸易试验区的新片区、在上海证券交易所设立科创板并试点注册制、支持长江三角洲区域一体化发展并上升为国家战略。

2018年12月，庆祝改革开放40周年大会在北京人民大会堂隆重举行。中共中央总书记、国家主席、中央军委主席习近平在大会上发表重要讲话。

（资料来源：人民网、新华网）

二、国务院批复河北雄安新区总体规划

2018 年 2 月 22 日，习近平总书记主持召开中央政治局常务委员会会议，听取雄安新区规划编制情况汇报。会议认为，雄安新区规划和建设要全面贯彻党的十九大精神，以习近平新时代中国特色社会主义思想为指导，坚持世界眼光、国际标准、中国特色、高点定位。要贯彻高质量发展要求，创造“雄安质量”，在推动高质量发展方面成为全国的一个样板。

2018 年 4 月 14 日，中共中央、国务院批复同意《河北雄安新区规划纲要》。批复指出，要以《雄安规划纲要》为指导，推动雄安新区实现更高水平、更有效率、更加公平、更可持续发展，建设成为绿色生态宜居新城区、创新驱动发展引领区、协调发展示范区、开放发展先行区，努力打造贯彻落实新发展理念的创新发展示范区。开展规划建设时，应依据以下具体原则：要科学构建城市空间布局，实行组团式发展；要合理确定城市规模，蓝绿空间占比要稳定在 70%，远景开发强度控制在 30%；要有序承接北京非首都功能疏解，积极稳妥有序承接符合雄安新区定位和发展需要的高校、医疗机构、企业总部、金融机构、事业单位等；要实现城市智慧化管理，构建汇聚城市数据和统筹管理运营的智能城市信息管理中枢，建设多级网络衔接的市政综合管廊系统；要营造优质绿色生态环境，实现雄安新区森林覆盖率达到 40%，起步区绿化覆盖率达到 50%；要实施创新驱动发展，高起点布局高端高新产业，建立以企业为主体、市场为导向、产学研深度融合的技术创新体系；要建设宜居宜业城市，落实职住平衡要求，形成多层级、全覆盖、人性化的基本公共服务网络；要打造改革开放新高地，探索新时代推动高质量发展、建设现代化经济体系的新路径；要塑造新时代城市特色风貌，体现中华传统经典建筑元素，彰显地域文化特色；要保障城市安全运行，以城市安全运行、灾害预防、公共安全、综合应急等体系建设为重点，构建城市安全和应急防灾体系；要统筹区域协调发展，加强同北京、天津、石家庄、保定等城市的融合发展，与北京中心城区、北京城市副中心合理分工，实现错位发展。

2018 年 12 月 25 日，国务院批复同意《河北雄安新区总体规划（2018—2035 年）》。批复指出，总体规划要优化国土空间开发保护格局，坚持以资源环境承载能力为刚性约束条件，统筹生产、生活、生态三大空间，形成“一淀、三带、九片、多廊”的生态空间结构。要打造优美自然生态环境，强化白洋淀生态整体修复和环境系统治理，推动区域环境协同治理。要推进城乡融合发展，形成“一主、五辅、多节点”的城乡空间布局，集中建设起步区，率先开发启动区，集约发展外围组团，稳步推进新型城镇化，实施乡村振兴战略。要塑造新区风貌特色，打造蓝绿交织、清新明亮、疏密有度、城淀相映的总体景观风貌，合理保护和利用雄安新区历史文化遗产。要打造宜居宜业环境，构建多层次、全覆盖、人性化的基本公共服务网络，建立多主体供给、多渠道保障、租购并举的住房制度和房地产市场平稳健康发展长效机制。要构建现代综合交通体系，加快建立连接雄安新区与京津及周边其他城市、北京大兴国际机场之间的轨道和公路交通网络，完善雄安新区与外部连通的高速公路、干线公路网，综合布局各类城市交通设施。要建设绿色低碳之城，确立水资源开发利用红

线，建设海绵城市，优化能源结构，提高绿色建筑、节能相关标准，构建先进的垃圾处理系统，合理布局地下基础设施网络。要建设国际一流的创新型城市，建设实体经济、科技创新、现代金融、人力资源协同发展的现代产业体系，强化知识产权保护及综合运用。要创建数字智能之城，建设宽带、融合、安全、泛在的通信网络和智能多源感知体系，构建城市网络安全保障体系，建立城市智能运行模式和智能治理体系。

国务院批复河北雄安新区总体规划，标志着雄安新区进入大规模发展建设的新阶段。雄安新区的高质量发展建设，对承接北京非首都功能、探索人口密集地区优化开发模式、调整优化京津冀空间结构、培育推动高质量发展和建设现代化经济体系的新引擎，具有重大现实意义和深远历史意义。

（资料来源：中国政府网、新华网）

三、国务院批准设立海南自由贸易试验区

2018 年 4 月 13 日，中共中央总书记、国家主席习近平出席海南建省办经济特区 30 周年大会并发表重要讲话，宣布建设海南自由贸易试验区和中国特色自由贸易港。

习近平指出，海南是我国最大的经济特区，地理位置独特，拥有全国最好的生态环境，同时又是相对独立的地理单元，具有成为全国改革开放试验田的独特优势。海南全岛建设自由贸易试验区，要以制度创新为核心，赋予更大改革自主权，支持海南大胆试、大胆闯、自主改，加快形成法治化、国际化、便利化的营商环境和公平开放统一高效的市场环境；要更大力度转变政府职能，深化简政放权、放管结合、优化服务改革，全面提升政府治理能力；要实行高水平的贸易和投资自由化便利化政策，对外资全面实行准入前国民待遇加负面清单管理制度，围绕种业、医疗、教育、体育、电信、互联网、文化、维修、金融、航运等重点领域，深化现代农业、高新技术产业、现代服务业对外开放，推动服务贸易加快发展，保护外商投资合法权益，推进航运逐步开放。海南建设自由贸易港要体现中国特色，符合中国国情，符合海南发展定位，学习借鉴国际自由贸易港的先进经营方式、管理方法。

2018 年 4 月 14 日，国务院发布《中共中央国务院关于支持海南全面深化改革开放的指导意见》（以下简称《意见》）。《意见》提出，到 2020 年，自由贸易试验区建设取得重要进展，国际开放度显著提高；到 2025 年自由贸易港制度初步建立，营商环境达到国内一流水平；到 2035 年，自由贸易港的制度体系和运作模式更加成熟，营商环境跻身全球前列；到本世纪中叶，率先实现社会主义现代化，形成高度市场化、国际化、法治化、现代化的制度体系，成为综合竞争力和文化影响力领先的地区。《意见》明确，将按照先行先试、风险可控、分步推进、突出特色的原则，分两步在海南推动形成全面开放新格局：第一步是在海南全境建设自由贸易试验区，赋予其现行自由贸易试验区试点政策；第二步是探索实行符合海南发展定位的自由贸易港政策。

2018 年 10 月 16 日，国务院印发《中国（海南）自由贸易试验区总体方案》（以下简称《方案》）。《方案》提出，到 2020 年，自贸试验区建设取得重要进展，努力建成投资贸易便

利、法治环境规范、金融服务完善、监管安全高效、生态环境质量一流、辐射带动作用突出的高标准高质量自贸试验区，为逐步探索、稳步推进海南自由贸易港建设，分步骤、分阶段建立自由贸易港政策体系打好坚实基础。

《方案》明确自贸试验区的实施范围为海南岛全岛，并以现有自贸试验区试点任务为基础，明确了海南自贸试验区在加快构建开放型经济新体制、加快服务业创新发展、加快政府职能转变等方面开展改革试点，并加强重大风险防控体系和机制建设。具体包括，加快构建开放型经济新体制，要大幅放宽外资市场准入、提升贸易便利化水平、创新贸易综合监管模式、推动贸易转型升级、加快金融开放创新、加强“一带一路”国际合作。加快服务业创新发展，要推动现代服务业集聚发展、提升国际航运能力、提升高端旅游服务能力、加大科技国际合作力度。加快政府职能转变，要深化机构和行政体制改革、打造国际一流营商环境、深入推进行政管理职能与流程优化、全面推行“互联网+政务服务”模式、完善知识产权保护和运用体系、提高外国人才工作便利度。加强重大风险防控体系和机制建设，要建立健全事中事后监管制度、建立健全贸易风险防控体系、建立健全金融风险防控体系、加强口岸风险防控。

（资料来源：新华网）

四、国家出台《深化党和国家机构改革方案》

2018 年 3 月 17 日，第十三届全国人民代表大会第一次会议审议批准了国务院机构改革方案。《深化党和国家机构改革方案》包括八个方面：深化党中央机构改革、深化全国人大机构改革、深化国务院机构改革、深化全国政协机构改革、深化行政执法体制改革、深化跨军地改革、深化群团组织改革、深化地方机构改革。

深化党中央机构改革主要包括：组建国家监察委员会，同中央纪律检查委员会合署办公，履行纪检、监察两项职责，实行一套工作机构、两个机关名称；组建中央全面依法治国委员会；组建中央审计委员会；中央全面深化改革领导小组、中央网络安全和信息化领导小组、中央财经领导小组、中央外事工作领导小组改为委员会；组建中央教育工作领导小组；组建中央和国家机关工作委员会；组建新的中央党校（国家行政学院），实行一个机构两块牌子，作为党中央直属事业单位；组建中央党史和文献研究院，不再保留中央党史研究室、中央文献研究室、中央编译局；中央组织部统一管理中央机构编制委员会办公室，统一管理公务员工作；中央宣传部统一管理新闻出版工作，统一管理电影工作；中央统战部统一领导国家民族事务委员会，统一管理宗教工作，统一管理侨务工作；优化中央网络安全和信息化委员会办公室职责；不再设立中央维护海洋权益工作领导小组；不再设立中央社会治安综合治理委员会及其办公室；不再设立中央维护稳定工作领导小组及其办公室；将中央防范和处理邪教问题领导小组及其办公室职责划归中央政法委员会、公安部。

深化全国人大机构改革包括：组建全国人大社会建设委员会；全国人大内务司法委员会更名为全国人大监察和司法委员会；全国人大法律委员会更名为全国人大宪法和法律委

员会。

深化国务院机构改革包括：组建自然资源部，不再保留国土资源部、国家海洋局、国家测绘地理信息局；组建生态环境部，不再保留环境保护部；组建农业农村部，不再保留农业部；组建文化和旅游部，不再保留文化部、国家旅游局；组建国家卫生健康委员会；组建退役军人事务部；组建应急管理部，不再保留国家安全生产监督管理总局；重新组建科学技术部；重新组建司法部，不再保留国务院法制办公室；优化审计署职责；组建国家市场监督管理总局，不再保留国家工商行政管理总局、国家质量监督检验检疫总局、国家食品药品监督管理总局；组建国家广播电视总局，不再保留国家新闻出版广电总局；组建中央广播电视总台，撤销中央电视台（中国国际电视台）、中央人民广播电台、中国国际广播电台建制；组建中国银行保险监督管理委员会；组建国家国际发展合作署，作为国务院直属机构；组建国家医疗保障局；组建国家粮食和物资储备局；组建国家移民管理局；组建国家林业和草原局；重新组建国家知识产权局；国务院三峡工程建设委员会及其办公室、国务院南水北调工程建设委员会及其办公室并入水利部；调整全国社会保障基金理事会隶属关系；改革国税地税征管体制。

深化全国政协机构改革包括：组建全国政协农业和农村委员会；全国政协文史和学习委员会更名为全国政协文化文史和学习委员会；全国政协教科文卫体委员会更名为全国政协教科卫体委员会。

深化行政执法体制改革包括：整合组建市场监管综合执法队伍；整合组建生态环境保护综合执法队伍；整合组建文化市场综合执法队伍；整合组建交通运输综合执法队伍；整合组建农业综合执法队伍。

深化跨军地改革包括：公安边防部队改制；公安消防部队改制；公安警卫部队改制；海警队伍转隶武警部队；武警部队不再领导管理武警黄金、森林、水电部队；武警部队不再承担海关执勤任务。

深化群团组织改革强调，要认真落实党中央关于群团改革的决策部署，健全党委统一领导群团工作的制度，紧紧围绕保持和增强政治性、先进性、群众性这条主线，强化问题意识，以更大力度、更实举措推进改革。

深化地方机构改革强调，要全面贯彻落实党中央关于深化党和国家机构改革的决策部署，坚持加强党的全面领导，坚持省市县统筹、党政群统筹，根据各层级党委和政府的主要职责，合理调整和设置机构，理顺权责关系，改革方案按程序报批后组织实施。

推进国家治理体系和治理能力现代化，是一项复杂的系统工程，深化党和国家机构改革是推进国家治理体系和治理能力现代化的一场深刻变革，此次党和国家机构改革，有利于构建系统完备、科学规范、运行有效的制度体系，充分发挥我国社会主义制度优越性，为党和国家事业取得历史性成就、发生历史性变革提供了有力保障。

（资料来源：新华网、人民网）

国务院机构改革回顾

1981年以来，国务院机构进行了7次改革，逐步建立起具有我国特点的国家机构职能体系。

第一次：减少职数、年轻化

1982年，我国自上而下地展开了各级机构改革，明确规定各级各部门领导班子的职数、年龄和文化结构，减少副职，提高素质。国务院部委、直属机构、办事机构从100个减为61个，编制从5.1万人减为3万人。

第二次：转变职能

1988年机构改革首次提出转变政府职能是机构改革的关键，强调政府的经济管理部门要从直接管理为主转变为间接管理为主。改革的重点是与经济体制改革关系密切的经济管理部门，如撤销国家计委和国家经委，组建新的国家计委；撤销煤炭工业部、石油工业部、核工业部，组建能源部；撤销国家机械工业委员会和电子工业部，成立机械电子工业部；撤销国家计量局和国家标准局及国家经委质量局，设立国家技术监督局。经此次改革，国务院部委数量由45个减为41个，直属机构从22个减为19个，人员编制减少9700多人。

第三次：统筹党政机构

1993年机构改革是在确立社会主义市场经济体制的背景下进行的，核心任务是建立起适应市场经济体制的行政管理体制。根据改革方案，中纪委机关和监察部合署办公，这是统筹党政机构设置的重要方式之一。改革后，国务院组成部门41个，直属机构和办事机构18个，比改革前减少27个，人员减少20%。

第四次：政企分开

1998年机构改革结束了专业经济部门直接管理企业，政府职能转变有了重大进展，撤销了几乎所有的工业专业经济部门：电力工业部、煤炭工业部、冶金工业部、机械工业部、电子工业部、化学工业部、地质矿产部、林业部、中国轻工业总会、中国纺织总会。改革后除国务院办公厅外，国务院组成部门由原有的40个减少到29个，直属机构15个，办事机构6个。

第五次：透明高效、“计划”消失

2003年机构改革是在加入WTO的背景下进行的。改革的重点是，深化国有资产管理体制改革，完善宏观调控体系，健全金融监管体制，继续推进流通体制改革，加强食品安全和安全生产监管体制建设。为此，分别建立国资委、银监会，组建商务部、国家食品药品监督管理局，调整国家安全生产监督管理局为国家直属机构。这次改革后，形成了行政机关决策、执行、监督的相互协调。国务院组成部门变为28个。

第六次：大部制

2008年机构改革首次明确提出“大部门制”，旨在探索实行职能有机统一的大部门体制。合理配置宏观调控部门职能，加强能源环境管理机构，整合完善工业和信息化、交通运输行业管理体制，以改善民生为重点加强与整合社会管理和公共服务部门，进一步转变政府职能和理顺部门职责关系。国务院组成部门调整为27个，改革调整变动的机构15个，正部级机构减少4个。

第七次：打通职能、科学合并、捋顺关系

2018年机构改革着眼于转变政府职能，坚决破除制约使市场在资源配置中起决定性作用、更好发挥政府作用的体制机制弊端，围绕推动高质量发展，建设现代化经济体系，加强和完善政府经济调节、市场监管、社会管理、公共服务、生态环境保护职能，结合新的时代条件和实践要求，着力推进重点领域和关键环节的机构职能优化和调整，构建起职责明确、依法行政的政府治理体系，提高政府执行力，建设人民满意的服务型政府。国务院组成部门调整为26个。

（资料来源：新华社）

五、我国举办首届中国国际进口博览会

2018年11月5日至10日，首届中国国际进口博览会（以下简称进博会）在上海举行。作为世界上第一个以进口为主题的大型国家级展会，进博会包括展会和论坛两个部分。展会即国家贸易投资综合展（简称国家展）和企业商业展（简称企业展），论坛即虹桥国际经贸论坛。首届进博会以“新时代，共享未来”为主题，吸引172个国家、地区和国际组织参会，3600多家企业参展，超过40万名境内外采购商到会洽谈采购，展览总面积达30万平方米。

中国国家主席习近平出席开幕式并发表题为《共建创新包容的开放型世界经济》的主旨演讲。习近平指出，中国国际进口博览会是迄今为止世界上第一个以进口为主题的国家级展会，是国际贸易发展史上一大创举。这体现了中国支持多边贸易体制、推动发展自由贸易的一贯立场，是中国推动建设开放型世界经济、支持经济全球化的实际行动。当今世界正在经历新一轮大发展大变革大调整。经济全球化是不可逆转的历史大势。面对世界经济格局的深刻变化，各国都应该拿出更大勇气，积极推动开放合作，实现共同发展。各国应该坚持开放融通，拓展互利合作空间；坚持开放的政策取向，共同建设开放型世界经济；加强宏观经济政策协调，合力促进世界经济增长；推动构建公正、合理、透明的国际经贸规则体系，促进全球经济进一步开放、交流、融合。

习近平指出，改革开放40年来，中国人民自力更生、发奋图强、砥砺前行，依靠自己的辛勤和汗水书写了国家和民族发展的壮丽史诗。中国坚持打开国门搞建设。开放已经成为当代中国的鲜明标识。中国不断扩大对外开放，不仅发展了自己，也造福了世界。中国将坚定不移奉行互利共赢的开放战略，将始终是全球共同开放的重要推动者、世界经济增长的稳定动力源、各国拓展商机的活力大市场、全球治理改革的积极贡献者。为进一步扩大开放，中国将在以下几方面加大推进力度：第一，激发进口潜力。中国将进一步降低关税，提升通关便利化水平，削减进口环节制度性成本，加快跨境电子商务等新业态新模式发展。第二，持续放宽市场准入。中国已经进一步精简了外商投资准入负面清单，减少投资限制，提升投资自由化水平，正在稳步扩大金融业开放。第三，营造国际一流营商环境。中国将加快出台外商投资法规，完善公开、透明的涉外法律体系，全面深入实施准入前国民待遇加负面清单管理制度。第四，打造对外开放新高地。中国将支持自由贸易试验区深化改革创新，抓紧研究提出海南分步骤、分阶段建设自由贸易港政策和制度体系，加快探索建设中国特色自由贸

易港进程。第五，推动多边和双边合作深入发展。中国一贯主张，坚定维护世界贸易组织规则，支持对世界贸易组织进行必要改革，共同捍卫多边贸易体制。

截至 11 月 10 日中午 12 时，首届进博会累计进场达 80 万人，交易采购按一年计，累计意向成交 578.3 亿美元，其中，智能及高端装备展区成交额达到 164.6 亿美元，食品及农产品展区成交 126.8 亿美元，汽车展区成交 119.9 亿美元，医疗器械及医药保健展区成交 57.6 亿美元，消费电子及家电展区成交 43.3 亿美元，服装服饰及日用消费品展区成交 33.7 亿美元，服务贸易展区成交 32.4 亿美元。首届进博会取得了圆满成功。

（资料来源：人民网、《人民日报》）

中国政府主导型展会概览表

序号	展会名称	创办时间	主办单位	举办地	定位
1	中国出口商品交易会（广交会）	1957 年	中华人民共和国商务部、广东省人民政府	广州	综合性国际贸易盛会，进出口双向交易平台
2	中国华东进出口商品交易会（华交会）	1991 年	中华人民共和国商务部（支持），上海、江苏、浙江、安徽、福建、江西、山东、南京、宁波 9 省市商务部门	上海	区域性国际经贸盛会，华东进出口商品交易平台
3	中国义乌国际小商品博览会（义博会）	1995 年	中华人民共和国商务部、浙江省人民政府、中国国际贸易促进委员会、中国轻工业联合会、中国商业联合会	义乌	日用消费品类国际性展会
4	中国国际投资贸易洽谈会（投洽会）	1997 年	中华人民共和国商务部	厦门	以促进双向投资为目的的国际投资促进活动
5	中国国际高新技术成果交易会（高交会）	1999 年	中华人民共和国商务部、科学技术部、工业和信息化部、国家发展和改革委员会、教育部、人力资源和社会保障部、国家知识产权局、中国科学院、中国工程院、深圳市人民政府	深圳	中国高新技术领域对外开放的重要窗口和高新技术产业化的高端平台
6	中国国际工业博览会（工博会）	1999 年	中华人民共和国工业和信息化部、国家发展和改革委员会、商务部、科学技术部、中国科学院、中国工程院、中国国际贸易促进委员会、联合国工业发展组织、上海市人民政府	上海	以装备制造业为展示交易主体的国际工业品牌展
7	中国国际装备制造业博览会（中国制博会）	2002 年	中华人民共和国商务部、国家发展和改革委、科学技术部、国务院振兴东北办、中国国际贸易促进委员会、辽宁省人民政府	沈阳	国际装备制造业集成品展示、信息交流、贸易订货、投资洽谈和技术合作平台
8	中国国际农产品交易会（农交会）	2003 年	中华人民共和国农业农村部	昆明、北京、长沙等	国内外农业企业、政府官员、农产品经销商广泛交流与合作平台
9	中国—东盟博览会（东博会）	2004 年	中国和东盟 10 国经贸主管部门及东盟秘书处	南宁	中国—东盟自由贸易区经贸合作平台，国家级、国际性经贸交流盛会
10	中国国际中小企业博览会（中博会）	2004 年	中国工业和信息化部、国家工商行政管理总局、广东省人民政府	广州	国内外中小企业展示、交易、交流、合作的平台
11	中国（深圳）国际文化产业博览交易会（文博会）	2004 年	中华人民共和国文化部、国家广播电影电视总局、中华人民共和国新闻出版总署、广东省人民政府、深圳市人民政府	深圳	国家级综合性的文化产业博览交易会，中国文化产品与项目交易平台

续表

序号	展会名称	创办时间	主办单位	举办地	定位
12	中国—东北亚博览会（原中国吉林·东北亚投资贸易博览会）	2005年	中华人民共和国商务部、国家发展和改革委员会、吉林省人民政府	长春	中国与东北亚国家商品展洽、投资洽谈平台，以推动中国与东北亚国家经贸往来和区域合作为目的的综合性展会
13	中国中部投资贸易博览会	2006年	中华人民共和国商务部、税务总局、工商行政管理总局、广播电影电视总局、国家旅游局、中国国际贸易促进会、中华全国工商联合会、中国工业经济联合会，山西、安徽、江西、河南、湖北、湖南六省人民政府	长沙、郑州、武汉等	推动中部六省扩大对外开放和加强区域及国际交流合作的重要平台
14	中国（北京）国际服务贸易交易会（京交会）	2012年	中华人民共和国商务部、北京市人民政府	北京	全球服务贸易行业领域的专题展示、高峰论坛、交易洽谈平台
15	中国国际进口博览会（进博会）	2018年	中华人民共和国商务部、上海市人民政府	上海	以进口为主题的大型国家级展会

（资料来源：人民网、中国政府网）

六、重大交通设施建设助推粤港澳大湾区发展

2017年7月1日，香港特别行政区行政长官林郑月娥、澳门特别行政区行政长官崔世安、国家发展改革委主任何立峰、广东省省长马兴瑞在香港共同签署了《深化粤港澳合作推进大湾区建设框架协议》。大湾区建设将推进基础设施互联互通，强化内地与港澳交通联系，构建高效便捷的现代综合交通运输体系。发挥香港作为国际航运中心优势，带动大湾区其他城市共建世界级港口群和空港群，优化高速公路、铁路、城市轨道交通网络布局，推动各种运输方式综合衔接、一体高效。强化城市内外交通建设，便捷城际交通，共同推进包括港珠澳大桥、广深港高铁、粤澳新通道等区域重点项目建设，打造便捷区域内交通圈。

2018年8月16日，广深港高铁香港段试营运工作顺利完成，9月23日，广深港高铁香港段通车。广深港高铁香港段是中国广深港高速铁路位于香港的部分，连接长达25 000公里的国家高铁网络。起于香港西九龙填海区香港西九龙站，止于香港与深圳的边境，总长26公里。建成后中国内地上海、石家庄、郑州、武汉、长沙、杭州、南昌、福州、厦门、汕头、贵阳、桂林、昆明等城市共44座车站与香港西九龙站间开行高速列车，其中福田站至香港西九龙站行车时间由原来的45分钟缩短至14分钟，广州南站至香港西九龙站行车时间由2小时缩短到47分钟，北京西站至香港西九龙站最快行车时间8小时58分。截至11月29日，广深港高铁香港段总乘客量超过340万人次，平均每日乘客量超过5万人次。

2018年10月23日，港珠澳大桥开通仪式在广东珠海举行，习近平出席仪式并宣布大桥正式开通，10月24日上午9时大桥正式通车。港珠澳大桥是国家高速公路网规划中珠江三角洲地区环线的组成部分和跨越伶仃洋海域的关键性工程，是连接珠江东西两岸新的公路运输通道。大桥东接香港特别行政区，西接广东省（珠海市）和澳门特别行政区，由香港口

岸至珠澳口岸全长 41.6 公里，是世界上最长桥隧组合的跨海通道。采用双向六车道技术标准，设计速度 100km/h。港珠澳大桥于 2011 年 1 月开工，于 2017 年 12 月 31 日基本建成。建成后往来珠海与葵青货柜码头的行车时间由约 3.5 小时缩减至约 75 分钟，往来珠海与香港国际机场的行车时间由约 4 小时缩减至约 45 分钟，珠三角西部纳入香港 3 小时车程可达范围内。大桥通车最初几天，每日客流量均超过 3 万人次，其中 10 月 28 日高峰时段每小时客流量达到3 500人次。

交通基础设施建设，是粤港澳大湾区建设的重要载体和主要内容。目前，粤港澳大湾区海陆空对外通道已基本成网，客运、货运总量占全国比重均超过 35%，有条件形成功能完备、及时可靠、通关便利、流转顺畅、经济高效、海陆空并进的联通“一带一路”的门户和枢纽，从而促进粤港澳大湾区物流、资金流、人流和信息流等生产要素的自由流动，提高区域内资源配置的效益和竞争力，助推粤港澳大湾区提速发展。

（资料来源：新华网、中国新闻网）

七、《中华人民共和国电子商务法》发布实施

伴随着电子商务的迅猛发展，电子商务市场秩序、管理体制等方面存在的矛盾和问题逐渐凸显，为保障电子商务各方主体权益，鼓励、支持、促进电子商务发展和创新，迫切需要电子商务立法。2018 年 8 月 31 日，第十三届全国人大常委会第五次会议表决通过了《中华人民共和国电子商务法》，自 2019 年 1 月 1 日起施行。

《电子商务法》分总则、电子商务经营者、电子商务合同的订立与履行、电子商务争议解决、电子商务促进、法律责任和附则，共七章八十九条。重点包括：

《电子商务法》调整对象。电子商务是通过互联网等信息网络销售商品或者提供服务的经营活动。法律、行政法规对销售商品或者提供服务有规定的，适用其规定；金融类产品和服务，利用信息网络提供新闻信息、音视频节目、出版以及文化产品等内容方面的服务，不适用本法。

电子商务经营主体。电子商务经营者是通过互联网等信息网络从事销售商品或者提供服务的经营活动的自然人、法人和非法人组织，包括电子商务平台经营者、平台内经营者以及通过自建网站、其他网络服务销售商品或者提供服务的电子商务经营者。其中，《电子商务法》单独对电子商务平台经营者作出明确规定，主要包括：应当要求申请进入平台销售商品或者提供服务的经营者提交其身份、地址、联系方式、行政许可等真实信息，进行核验、登记；应当采取技术措施和其他必要措施保证其网络安全、稳定运行；应当遵循公开、公平、公正的原则，制定平台服务协议和交易规则；应当记录、保存平台上发布的商品和服务信息、交易信息，并确保信息的完整性、保密性、可用性；应当建立健全信用评价制度，公示信用评价规则；应当建立知识产权保护规则，与知识产权权利人加强合作，依法保护知识产权。

电子商务合同。该章节内容主要有电子合同、快递物流和电子支付。关于电子合同，

《电子商务法》在现有法律规定的基础上规定了电子商务当事人行为能力推定规则、电子合同的订立等内容。关于快递物流，《电子商务法》明确了商品交付时间，规范了电子商务寄递过程中的环保和服务问题。关于电子支付，《电子商务法》规定了电子支付服务提供者和接受者的法定权利义务，对于支付确认、错误支付、非授权支付等作出规定。

电子商务争议解决。为了更加有利于电子商务发展和消费者权益保护，《电子商务法》对商品、服务质量担保机制以及投诉、举报机制等内容作了相关规定。对于电子商务争议的解决，《电子商务法》规定，电子商务争议可以通过协商和解，请求消费者组织、行业协会或者其他依法成立的调解组织调解，向有关部门投诉，提请仲裁，或者提起诉讼等方式解决；在电子商务争议处理中，电子商务经营者应当提供原始合同和交易记录；电子商务平台经营者可以建立争议在线解决机制，制定并公示争议解决规则，根据自愿原则，公平、公正地解决当事人的争议。

电子商务促进。《电子商务法》作出一系列规定促进电子商务的发展，包括将电子商务发展纳入国民经济和社会发展规划，支持、推动绿色包装、仓储、运输，推动电子商务基础设施和物流网络建设等。对于跨境电子商务，《电子商务法》作了专门规定，包括国家促进跨境电子商务发展，建立健全适应跨境电子商务特点的管理制度，提高跨境电子商务各环节便利化水平等。

《电子商务法》的颁布和实施是我国电子商务发展史上的一个里程碑，能够在我国电子商务行业的发展过程中起到规范和促进的双重效果。有利于形成更加规范的电子商务服务体系、更加公开透明的电子商务经营环境，此外，《电子商务法》将有效遏制电子商务经营者的不诚信经营行为，规范电子商务经营者对其用户个人信息的收集、使用行为，逐步遏制互联网领域的垄断竞争，从而促进良好的电子商务市场秩序的形成，促进电子商务管理体制的完善，使得电子商务得到高质量发展和不断创新。

（资料来源：中国人大网、新华网）

中国电子商务发展大事记

1997 年，中国化工信息网正式在互联网上提供服务，开拓了网络化工的先河，是全国第一个介入行业网站服务的国有机构。

1998 年 10 月，美商网（又名“相逢中国”）获多家美国知名 VC 千万美元投资，是最早进入中国 B2B 电子商务市场的海外网站，开创全球 B2B 电子商务先河。12 月，阿里巴巴正式在开曼群岛注册成立，1999 年 3 月其子公司阿里巴巴中国在我国杭州创建。

1999 年 9 月，招商银行率先在国内全面启动“一网通”网上银行服务，并经央行批准成为国内首个开展网上个人银行业务的商业银行。

2000 年 4 月，于 1992 年成立的慧聪国际推出了慧聪商务网，即现在的慧聪网；5 月，卓越网成立，为我国早期 B2C 网站之一。

2001年7月9日，中国人民银行颁布《网上银行业务管理暂行办法》。

2002年7月3日，国家信息化领导小组第二次会议召开，审议通过了《国民经济和社会发展第十个五年计划信息化重点专项规划》《关于我国电子政务建设的指导意见》和《振兴软件产业行动纲要》。

2003年5月，阿里巴巴集团投资1亿元人民币成立淘宝网，进军C2C。10月，阿里巴巴推出"支付宝"，致力于为网络交易用户提供基于第三方的在线支付服务，正式进军电子支付领域。

2004年1月，京东涉足电子商务领域，京东多媒体网正式开通，启用域名。8月，亚马逊以7500万美元协议收购卓越网，并更名为卓越亚马逊。

2005年1月，国务院办公厅发布《关于加快电子商务发展的若干意见》。4月1日，《电子签名法》正式施行，是中国信息化领域的第一部法律。

2006年12月15日，电子商务领军企业网盛科技登陆深圳中小企业板，标志着A股"中国互联网第一股"诞生。

2007年3月6日，商务部发布了《中华人民共和国商务部关于网上交易的指导意见（暂行）》。6月1日，国家发展改革委、国务院信息化工作办公室联合发布《电子商务发展"十一五"规划》，这是我国第一个国家级的电子商务发展规划。11月6日，阿里巴巴网络有限公司（1688-HK）成功在香港主板上市，融资16.9亿美元，创全球互联网企业融资额第二大纪录。12月17日，国家商务信息化主管部门商务部，公布了《商务部关于促进电子商务规范发展的意见》。

2008年4月24日，商务部起草了《电子商务模式规范》和《网络购物服务规范》。中国电子商务B2B市场交易额达到3万亿元；网购交易额也首次突破千亿元，达到1500亿元。

2009年5月1日起，由中国国际经济贸易仲裁委员会颁布的《中国国际经济贸易仲裁委员会网上仲裁规则》正式施行。6月，银联支付与B2C企业当当网签订合作协议，首度进入电子商务支付领域，与在线第三方支付市场领导支付宝形成了正面竞争。

2010年1月，苏宁电器旗下电子商务平台苏宁易购网正式上线。3月，《政府工作报告》首次明确提出大力扶持电子商务。11月，国美正式进军电子商务领域。12月8日，当当网在美国成功上市，融资2.72亿美元。2010年，包括团购在内的电子商务掀起史无前例的高潮。

2012年1月，淘宝商城宣布更改中文名为天猫，加强其平台的定位。2月，八部委下发通知，在22个城市开展网络（电子）发表应用试点。3月，工信部发布《电子商务"十二五"发展规划》。11月，天猫与淘宝两家网购单日纪录再次被刷新，天猫为132亿元、淘宝59亿元，合计191亿元。

2013年5月28日，阿里巴巴集团、银泰集团联合复星集团、富春控股、三通一达（申通、圆通、中通、韵达）等共同组建菜鸟网络科技有限公司。6月，阿里巴巴推出"余额宝"增值服务产品。8月，微信5.0版中出现"微信支付"，开始做移动B2C生意，为移动互联网的电商化提供了更加宽广的想象空间。12月27号，全国人大财经委在人民大会堂召开电子商务法起草组成立暨第一次全体会议，正式启动电子商务法立法工作。

2014年2月，工商总局公布《网络交易管理办法》，明确网络商品经营者和有关服务经营者应承担的义务。3月22日，携程被披露用户信息泄漏，电子商务数据安全意识被关注，电子商务立法进程加速的呼声再次升高。9月19日，阿里巴巴在纽约证券交易所挂牌上市。11月19日，首届世界互联网大会在乌镇开幕。

2015 年 6 月 20 日，国务院办公厅发布了《关于促进跨境电子商务健康快速发展的指导意见》。

2016 年 10 月 11 日，顺丰控股借壳鼎泰新材登陆 A 股市场。12 月 25 日，十二届全国人大常委会第二十五次会议举行分组会，审议电子商务法草案。

2017 年 4 月 8 日，财政部联合海关总署和国家税务总局共同推出《关于跨境电子商务零售进口税收政策的通知》。10 月 31 日，十二届全国人大常委会第三十次会议对电子商务法草案进行了再次审议。

2018 年 7 月 26 日，拼多多正式在纽交所挂牌上市。8 月 31 日，中华人民共和国第十三届全国人民代表大会常务委员会第五次会议通过《中华人民共和国电子商务法》，于 2019 年 1 月 1 日起施行。

（资料来源：中国经济网）

八、中办国办印发《关于推进城市安全发展的意见》

随着我国城市化进程明显加快，城市人口、功能和规模不断扩大，发展方式、产业结构和区域布局发生了深刻变化，新材料、新能源、新工艺广泛应用，新产业、新业态、新领域大量涌现，城市运行系统日益复杂，安全风险不断增大。为强化城市运行安全保障，有效防范事故发生，2018 年 1 月，中共中央办公厅、国务院办公厅印发《关于推进城市安全发展的意见》（以下简称《意见》）。

《意见》指出，到 2020 年，城市安全发展取得明显进展，建成一批与全面建成小康社会目标相适应的安全发展示范城市。在深入推进示范创建的基础上，到 2035 年，城市安全发展体系更加完善，安全文明程度显著提升，建成与基本实现社会主义现代化相适应的安全发展城市。持续推进形成系统性、现代化的城市安全保障体系，加快建成以中心城区为基础，带动周边、辐射县乡、惠及民生的安全发展型城市，为把我国建成富强、民主、文明、和谐、美丽的社会主义现代化强国提供坚实稳固的安全保障。

为实现推进城市安全发展的总体目标，《意见》从城市安全源头治理、城市安全防控机制、城市安全监管效能、城市安全保障能力以及推动方式五方面提出具体要求。

要加强城市安全源头治理。科学制定规划，加强建设项目实施前的评估论证工作；完善安全法规和标准，加强体现安全生产区域特点的地方性法规建设，完善城市高层建筑和大型综合体等设施的技术标准；加强基础设施安全管理，包括有序推进城市地下管网依据规划采取综合管廊模式进行建设，强化与市政设施配套的安全设施建设，加强消防站点、水源等消防安全设施建设和维护，加快推进城区铁路平交道口立交化改造，加强城市交通基础设施建设，加强城市棚户区、城中村和危房改造过程中的安全监督管理；加快重点产业安全改造升级，包括完善高危行业企业退城入园、搬迁改造和退出转产扶持奖励政策，制定中心城区安全生产禁止和限制类产业目录，加强矿产资源型城市塌（沉）陷区治理，加快推进城镇人口密集区不符合安全和卫生防护距离要求的危险化学品生产、储存企业就地改造达标、搬迁进入规范化工园区或依法关闭退出，引导企业集聚发展安全产业，大力推进企业安全生产标准化建设。

要健全城市安全防控机制。强化安全风险管控，包括对城市安全风险进行全面辨识评估，编制城市安全风险白皮书，研究制定重大安全风险"一票否决"的具体情形和管理办法，对重点人员密集场所、安全风险较高的大型群众性活动开展安全风险评估；深化隐患排查治理，包括制定城市安全隐患排查治理规范，进一步完善城市重大危险源辨识、申报、登记、监管制度等；提升应急管理和救援能力，包括完善事故应急救援预案，建立完善应急避难场所等。

要提升城市安全监管效能。落实安全生产责任，包括完善党政同责、一岗双责、齐抓共管、失职追责的安全生产责任体系；完善安全监管体制，包括加强负有安全生产监督管理职责部门之间的工作衔接，合理调整执法队伍种类和结构，明确健全经济技术开发区、工业园区、港区、风景名胜区等各类功能区的安全生产监督管理机构；增强监管执法能力，包括加强安全生产监管执法机构规范化、标准化、信息化建设；严格规范监管执法，完善执法人员岗位责任制和考核机制。

要强化城市安全保障能力。健全社会化服务体系，制定完善政府购买安全生产服务指导目录，大力实施安全生产责任保险，加快推进安全信用体系建设，完善城市社区安全网格化工作体系；强化安全科技创新和应用，加大城市安全运行设施资金投入，加强城市安全监管信息化建设，深入推进城市生命线工程建设；提升市民安全素质和技能，建立完善安全生产和职业健康相关法律法规、标准的查询、解读、公众互动交流信息平台。

要加强统筹推动。强化组织领导，城市安全发展工作由国务院安全生产委员会统一组织，各省（自治区、直辖市）党委和政府要切实加强领导；强化协同联动，把城市安全发展纳入安全生产工作巡查和考核的重要内容，鼓励引导社会化服务机构、公益组织和志愿者参与推进城市安全发展。

《意见》是转型期城市安全发展的指导性文件，为推进城市安全发展、强化城市运行安全保障提供了较好的遵循和指导，能够促进建立以安全生产为基础的综合性、全方位、系统化的城市安全发展体系，全面提高城市安全保障水平，有效防范和坚决遏制重特大安全事故发生，为人民群众营造安居乐业、幸福安康的生产生活环境。

（资料来源：新华网）

全国城市公共安全感指数排行榜

城市	城市公共安全感指数	排名	城市	城市公共安全感指数	排名
拉萨	0.5350	1	合肥	0.4760	17
西宁	0.5192	2	贵阳	0.4703	18
杭州	0.5052	3	济南	0.4670	19
福州	0.5034	4	北京	0.4653	20
广州	0.5007	5	沈阳	0.4634	21
银川	0.4976	6	长春	0.4629	22
昆明	0.4955	7	重庆	0.4597	23
长沙	0.4912	8	上海	0.4532	24
武汉	0.4903	9	石家庄	0.4477	25
天津	0.4892	10	哈尔滨	0.4466	26
西安	0.4875	11	呼和浩特	0.4383	27
海口	0.4873	12	南昌	0.4328	28
郑州	0.4869	13	南宁	0.4296	29
南京	0.4823	14	太原	0.4261	30
成都	0.4793	15	乌鲁木齐	0.4096	31
兰州	0.4767	16			

(资料来源:《公共安全感蓝皮书:中国城市公共安全感调查报告(2018)》(社会科学文献出版社,2018.12))

九、中共中央国务院决定“统一规划体系”

2018年9月20日,国家主席习近平主持召开中央全面深化改革委员会第四次会议,会议审议通过了《关于统一规划体系更好发挥国家发展规划战略导向作用的意见》(以下简称《意见》)。《意见》提出几个方面的具体要求:

要明确规划功能定位,理顺规划关系。国家发展规划是社会主义现代化战略在规划期内的阶段性部署和安排,主要是阐明国家战略意图、明确政府工作重点、引导规范市场主体行为,是经济社会发展的宏伟蓝图,是全国各族人民共同的行动纲领,是政府履行经济调节、市场监管、社会管理、公共服务、生态环境保护职能的重要依据。国家级专项规划是指导特定领域发展、布局重大工程项目、合理配置公共资源、引导社会资本投向、制定相关政策的重要依据。国家级区域规划是指导特定区域发展和制定相关政策的重要依据。国家级空间规划以空间治理和空间结构优化为主要内容,是实施国土空间用途管制和生态保护修复的重要依据。

要统一规划体系,形成规划合力。建立以国家发展规划为统领,以空间规划为基础,以专项规划、区域规划为支撑,由国家、省、市县各级规划共同组成,定位准确、边界清晰、功能互补、统一衔接的国家规划体系。一是要强化国家发展规划的统领作用，提高国家发展规划的战略性、宏观性、政策性，发挥国家发展规划统筹重大战略和重大举措时空安排功能，明确空间战略格局、空间结构优化方向以及重大生产力布局安排，为国家级空间规划留出接口。二是要强化空间规划的基础作用，聚焦空间开发强度管控和主要控制线落地，整合形成“多规合一”的空间规划，强化国家级空间规划在空间开发保护方面的基础和平台功能。三是要强化专项规划和区域规划的支撑作用，国家级专项规划要围绕国家发展规划在特定领域提出的重点任务，制定细化落实的时间表和路线图，国家级区域规划以贯彻实施重大区域战略、协调解决跨行政区重大问题为重点，指导特定区域协调协同发展，省级规划、市县级规划既要加强与国家级专项规划、区域规划、空间规划的衔接，又要因地制宜，符合地方实际，突出地方特色。

要统筹规划管理，加强规划衔接协调。建立健全目录清单、编制备案、衔接协调等规划管理制度，有效解决规划数量过多、质量不高、衔接不充分、交叉重叠等问题。一是要建立健全规划编制目录清单管理制度。二是要强化规划衔接协调，建立健全规划衔接协调机制，明确衔接原则和重点，规范衔接程序，确保各级各类规划协调一致。三是要发挥规划管理信息平台作用，建设国家规划综合管理信息平台，推动规划基础信息互联互通和归集共享。

要规范规划编制程序，提高规划质量。创新规划理念、规范编制程序，提高规划编制科学化、民主化、法治化、规范化水平，确保规划实用管用。一是要明确规划编制的基本遵循，以习近平新时代中国特色社会主义思想为指导，紧紧围绕建设社会主义现代化强国的宏伟目标，坚持以人民为中心的发展思想，坚持目标导向和问题导向相统一。二是要深化重大问题研究论证，拓展规划前期研究广度和深度，深入研究国民经济和社会发展全局性、前瞻性、关键性、深层次重大问题，科学研判发展趋势和阶段性特征，准确把握突出短板和发展方向，加强规划内容多角度论证和多方案比选。三是要创新规划编制方式方法，坚持开门编制规划，提高规划编制的透明度和社会参与度，综合运用大数据、云计算等现代信息技术，创新规划编制手段。四是要严格规划编制程序，建立健全规划起草、衔接、论证、审批、发布等制度。

《意见》是对于我国未来一定时期内规划体系建设、规划编制及规划实施的纲领性文件，为新时代规划编制指明了方向。科学编制并有效实施国家发展规划，阐明建设社会主义现代化强国奋斗目标在规划期内的战略部署和具体安排，引导公共资源配置方向，规范市场主体行为，有利于保持国家战略的连续性和稳定性，集中力量办大事，确保一张蓝图绘到底。

（资料来源：新华网）

改革开放40年来城乡规划大事记

1978年3月，第三次全国城市工作会议形成文件《中共中央关于加强城市建设工作的意见》，提出“城市中的各项建设，都应按照城市总体规划进行安排，服从城市有关部门的统一管理”。

1979年5月，国家成立直属国务院领导的城市建设总局，指导和组织城市规划工作，参与经济建设的区域规划工作，为城市规划改革创造了制度保障。

1980年10月，召开全国城市规划工作会议，会议提出“正确认识城市规划的地位和作用，明确城市发展的指导方针，根据城市特点确定城市性质，尽快建立我国的城市规划法制”等十个方面的工作要求，首次提出土地有偿使用的建议。

1981年末，在国家基本建设委员会内设立国土局。1981年11月，北京市政府决定成立北京市规划委员会，加强对首都规划的引导与管理。

1982年5月，组建城乡建设环境保护部（下设城市规划局），形成了规划、国土、环保和建设“四位一体”的统一管理体制。

1984年1月，《城市规划条例》颁布施行，初步建立起我国城市规划的法律体系，明确了建设项目的规划许可证和竣工验收等各项基本制度。7月，经国务院同意，城市规划局改由城乡建设环境保护部与国家计委双重领导。

1986年3月，国家土地管理局成立，国土管理职能从城乡建设环境系统分出。

1988年5月，通过《关于国务院机构改革方案的决定》，撤销“城乡建设环境保护部”，设立“建设部”。并把国家计委主管的基本建设方面的勘察设计、建筑施工、标准定额工作及其机构划归“建设部”。

1989年12月，《城市规划法》颁布并于1990年4月起施行，是我国第一部关于城市规划的法律，标志着城市规划工作全面走上了制度化轨道。

1991年，建设部颁布《城市规划编制办法》，正式列入控制性详细规划。同年建设部和国家计委共同发布《建设项目选址规划管理办法》。

1992年，建设部发布《城市国有土地使用权出让转让规划管理办法》，提出“城市规划区内城市国有土地使用权出让、转让必须符合城市规划”，控制性详细规划内容作为规划设计条件及附图纳入到城市国有土地使用权出让、转让合同。

1993年，中国城市规划协会在国家民政部登记注册成立，业务主管部门为建设部，是城市规划行业全国性社会团体。

1994年，《城镇体系规划编制办法》《风景名胜区建设管理条例》和《村镇规划标准》同年发布并实施。

1996年5月，国务院发布《关于加强城市规划工作的通知》，将城市规划明确为指导城市合理发展，建设和管理城市的重要依据和手段，并对城市土地及空间资源的调控起到作用。

1999年，颁布《注册城市规划师执业资格制度暂行规定》《注册城市规划师执业资格认定办法》，城市规划的执业资格认证逐步建立并完善。

2000年，国务院办公厅发出《关于加强和改进城乡规划工作的通知》，对各项规划的编制与审批工作、城市总体规划修改认定制度和备案制度、城乡规划的实施管理、城乡规划的监督检查制度等，提出指导要求。

2002 年，建设部发布《近期建设规划工作暂行办法》《城市规划强制性内容暂行规定》，对城市规划在近期实施和强制性内容的管理发挥作用。国务院下发《国务院关于加强城乡规划监督管理的通知》，加强城乡规划监督管理。

2005 年，党的十六届五中全会召开，报告提出建设社会主义新农村。

2006年，国务院审议通过《风景名胜区条例》(2006年12月 1 日施行)。建设部审议通过《城市蓝线管理办法》《城市黄线管理办法》，自 2006 年 3 月 1 起施行。

2008 年 1 月，《中华人民共和国城乡规划法》开始实施，确立城镇体系规划、城市（镇）总体规划、乡规划和村庄规划被纳入统一的城乡规划体系。

2009 年，国务院公布《汶川地震灾后恢复重建条例》，这是我国首个专门针对一个地方地震灾后恢复重建的条例，将灾后恢复重建工作纳入法制化轨道。

2010 年，国务院印发《全国主体功能区规划》，将国土空间划分为优化开发区域、重点开发区域、限制开发区域和禁止开发区域。住房城乡建设部审议通过《城市、镇控制性详细规划编制审批办法》，自 2011 年 1 月 1 日起施行；通过《省域城镇体系规划编制审批办法》，自 2010 年 7 月 1 日起施行。

2012 年，住房城乡建设部审议通过《城乡规划编制单位资质管理规定》，自 2012 年 9 月 1 日起施行。

2014 年，国家发展改革委、国土资源部、环保部、住房城乡建设部联合下发《关于开展市县“多规合一”试点工作的通知》，确定了 28 个“多规合一”市县试点单位，其中地级市 6 个，县级市（县）22 个。中共中央、国务院发布《国家新型城镇化规划（2014—2020 年）》，明确未来城镇化的发展路径、主要目标和战略任务，统筹相关领域制度和政策创新。

2015 年，中共中央、国务院印发《关于加快推进生态文明建设的意见》和《生态文明体制改革总体方案》，形成了推进生态文明建设、完善生态文明体制的纲领性架构。

2016 年 2 月，中共中央国务院《关于进一步加强城市规划建设管理工作的若干意见》发布，勾画了“十三五”乃至更长时间中国城市发展的“路线图”。10 月，住房城乡建设部公布了第一批中国特色小镇名单，国家发展改革委发布《关于加快美丽特色小（城）镇建设的指导意见》。

2017 年 1 月，中共中央办公厅、国务院办公厅印发了《省级空间规划试点方案》，首次划定了城镇、农业、生态“三类空间”。4 月，中共中央、国务院印发通知，决定设立河北雄安新区。

2018 年 3 月，根据第十三届全国人民代表大会第一次会议批准的国务院机构改革方案，将住房和城乡建设部的城乡规划管理职责整合，组建自然资源部。9 月，中共中央、国务院印发了《乡村振兴战略规划（2018—2022 年）》。12 月，国务院批复同意《河北雄安新区总体规划（2018—2035 年）》。

（资料来源：中国城市规划网）

十、国家推进长江经济带绿色发展

长江经济带面积约205万平方公里，占全国的21%，人口和经济总量均超过全国的40%，生态地位重要、综合实力较强、发展潜力巨大。针对长江经济带发展面临的生态环境状况形势严峻、长江水道存在瓶颈制约、区域发展不平衡问题突出、产业转型升级任务艰巨、区域合作机制尚不健全等困难和问题，党中央、国务院于2016年对推动长江经济带发展作出重大决策部署，明确提出生态优先、绿色发展的战略定位，要求共抓大保护，不搞大开发。

2018年4月26日，习近平在武汉主持召开深入推动长江经济带发展座谈会并发表重要讲话。习近平强调，总体上看，实施长江经济带发展战略要加大力度。必须从中华民族长远利益考虑，把修复长江生态环境摆在压倒性位置，共抓大保护、不搞大开发，努力把长江经济带建设成为生态更优美、交通更顺畅、经济更协调、市场更统一、机制更科学的黄金经济带，探索出一条生态优先、绿色发展新路子。

习近平明确提出了推动长江经济带发展需要正确把握的五个关系。第一，正确把握整体推进和重点突破的关系，全面做好长江生态环境保护修复工作。要从生态系统整体性和长江流域系统性着眼，实现整体推进和重点突破相统一。第二，正确把握生态环境保护和经济发展的关系，探索协同推进生态优先和绿色发展新路子。生态环境保护和经济发展是辩证统一的关系，生态环境保护的成败取决于经济结构和经济发展方式，要坚持在发展中保护、在保护中发展。第三，正确把握总体谋划和久久为功的关系，坚定不移将一张蓝图干到底。要做好顶层设计，深入推进《长江经济带发展规划纲要》贯彻落实，组织开展《规划纲要》中期评估，按照新形势新要求调整完善规划内容。第四，正确把握破除旧动能和培育新动能的关系，推动长江经济带建设现代化经济体系。要扎实推进供给侧结构性改革，建设现代化经济体系，积极稳妥腾退化解旧动能，破除无效供给，为新动能发展创造条件、留出空间。第五，正确把握自身发展和协同发展的关系，努力将长江经济带打造成为有机融合的高效经济体。长江经济带作为流域经济，要运用系统论的方法，正确把握自身发展和协同发展的关系，长江经济带的各个地区、每个城市在各自发展过程中一定要从整体出发，实现错位发展、协调发展、有机融合，形成整体合力。

9月25日，国家发展改革委、水利部、自然资源部、国家林业和草原局联合印发了《关于加快推进长江两岸造林绿化的指导意见》，意见提出，到2020年，全面实现长江两岸宜林地植树造林，整体提升绿化质量，基本建成沿江绿化带；到2025年，长江两岸造林绿化全面完成，实现应绿尽绿，森林质量明显提升，沿江生态防护体系基本完善，连续完整、结构稳定的森林生态系统初步形成，岸绿景美、绵延万里的沿江美丽生态带基本建成。

10月26日，国家发展改革委、生态环境部、农业农村部、住房城乡建设部、水利部会同有关部门印发了《关于加快推进长江经济带农业面源污染治理的指导意见》。意见提出，到2020年，长江经济带农业农村面源污染得到有效治理，种养业布局进一步优化，农业农村废弃物资源化利用水平明显提高，绿色发展取得积极成效，对流域水质的污染显著降低。

12 月 31 日，生态环境部、国家发展改革委下发《关于印发〈长江保护修复攻坚战行动计划〉的通知》。提出到 2020 年底，长江流域水质优良（达到或优于Ⅲ类）的国控断面比例达到 85% 以上，丧失使用功能（劣于Ⅴ类）的国控断面比例低于 2%；长江经济带地级及以上城市建成区黑臭水体控制比例达 90% 以上；地级及以上城市集中式饮用水水源水质达到或优于Ⅲ类比例高于 97%。

推动长江经济带发展是党中央作出的重大决策，是关系国家发展全局的重大战略。长江经济带的绿色发展是社会主义生态文明建设的样板工程，有利于全面建成水脉畅通、功能完备的长江全流域黄金水道，建立创新型现代产业体系，形成上中下游一体化发展格局。对于实现“两个一百年”奋斗目标和中华民族伟大复兴的中国梦，具有重大现实意义和深远历史意义。

（资料来源：新华网、中国网、人民网）

（作者：邵益生，中国城市规划设计研究院研究员，国际欧亚科学院院士；周长青，中国城市规划设计研究院水务院水务发展研究所所长，教授级高工）

2018年中国城市经济发展概述

2018年年底，中国改革开放整整走过了40年。经过40年发展，我国城市经济取得了长足进步，带动我国由一个以农村经济为主的国家变为一个以城市经济为主的国家。

一、城市经济发展现状

（一）城市经济规模快速扩张

近年来，高新科技快速崛起促使新兴产业和经济新业态不断涌现，极大地推动了城市经济发展。2018年国内生产总值达到90万亿元，比上年增长6.6%，在经济下行压力大的条件下取得了较好的业绩。城市经济的各个方面都发生了巨大变化：2018年社会消费品零售总额38.1万亿元，比上年增长了4.02%，其中，城镇消费品零售额32.6亿元，比上年增长8.8%。全国居民人均消费支出19 853元，城镇居民人均消费支出26 112元，增长6.8%，全国居民恩格尔系数为28.4%，比上年下降0.9个百分点，其中城镇为27.7%，农村为30.1%。1978—2018年，城镇居民人均可支配收入由343.4元增加至2018年的39 251元，增加了114.3倍[①]。（表1、图1）

表1　2018年城市经济发展主要经济指标增长情况

（单位:%）

	GDP	城镇常住人口	城镇就业人员	城镇居民人均可支配收入	城镇居民人均消费支出	城镇固定资产投资
较2017年环比增速	8.85	2.20	2.25	7.84	6.82	0.63
近五年平均增速	8.63	2.60	2.57	8.20	7.15	7.84

资料来源：国家统计局编．《中国统计年鉴2014—2018》，《2013、2014、2015、2016、2017、2018年国民经济和社会发展统计公报》。

① 国家统计局，2018年国民经济和社会发展统计公报。

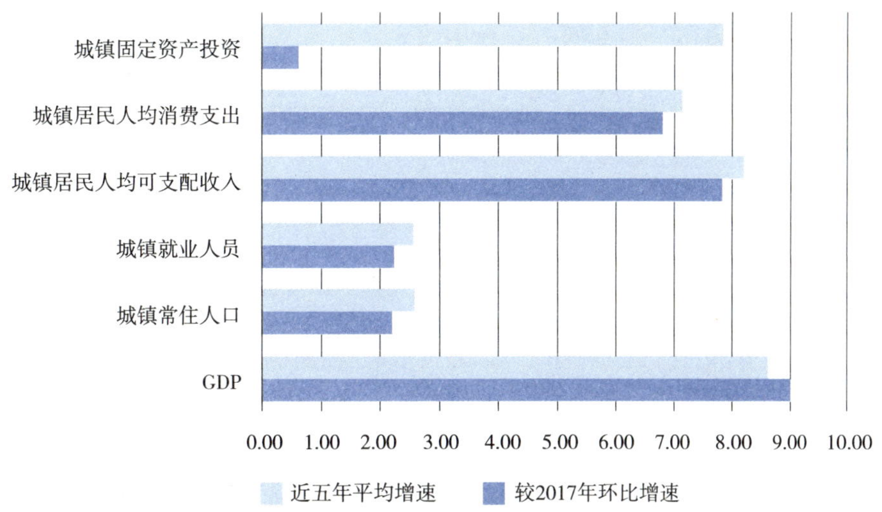

图 1 2018 年城市经济发展主要经济指标增长情况示意图

资料来源：国家统计局编．《中国统计年鉴 2014—2018》，《2013、2014、2015、2016、2017、2018 年国民经济和社会发展统计公报》。

（二）城市产业结构不断优化和提升

1. 城市产业结构日趋优化

2018 年三次产业结构比为 7:41:52，国内生产总值在较快上涨的同时，第三产业产值比重不断提升，产业结构愈发合理。（图 2）

供给侧结构性改革深入推进。2018 年，“三去一补”取得明显的成效，全国工业产能利用率为 76.5%。年末商品房待售面积52 414万平方米，比上年末减少6 510万平方米。年末规模以上工业企业资产负债率为 56.5%，比上年末下降 0.5 个百分点。全年生态保护和环境治理投资、农业固定资产投资（不含农户）分别比上年增长 43.0% 和 15.4%。

2. 城市新兴产业稳步增长

战略性新兴产业成为我国城市经济稳步增长的重要力量。战略性新兴产业具有知识密集型、物质资源消耗少、成长潜力大、综合效益好的特点，包括 9 大领域：新一代信息技术产业、高端装备制造产业、新材料产业、生物产业、新能源产业、新能源汽车产业、节能环保产业、数字创意产业、现代服务业。

新一代信息技术产业对城市经济转型升级和高质量发展具有引领作用，为制造强国和网络强国建设提供了坚实基础。2018 年，全国软件和信息技术服务业规模以上企业 3.78 万家，比上年增加 2881 家；累计完成软件业务收入 63 061 亿元，同比增长 14.2%；实现利润总额 8 079 亿元，同比增长 9.7%；从业人员为 643 万人，比上年增加 25 万人，同比增长 4.2%；实现出口 554.5 亿美元，同比增长 0.8%，占全行业业务收入的 6% 左右。

文化创意产业蓬勃发展，正在向国民经济支柱产业迈进。互联网新业态的快速发展改变了文化产业发格局，2018 年共有北京、江西、湖北、甘肃 4 个省（直辖市）发布了本地文

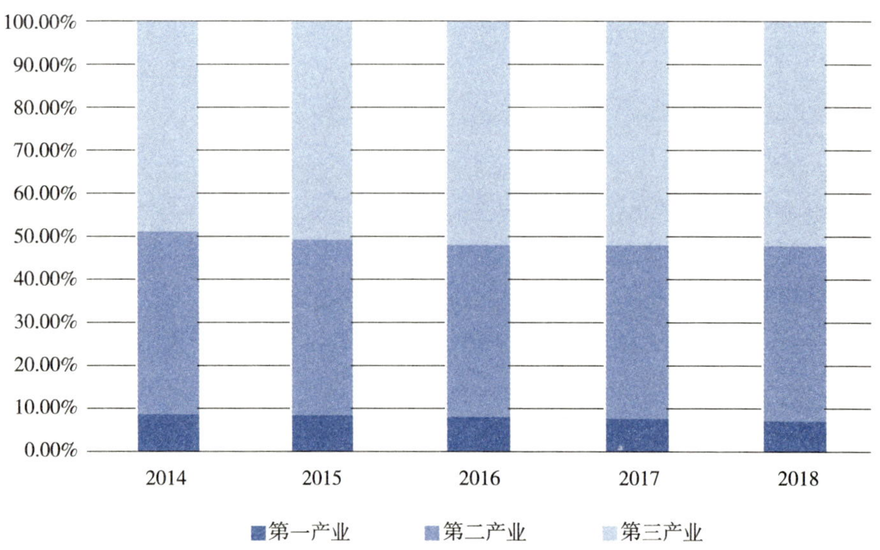

图 2　2014—2018 年产业结构变动图

资料来源：国家统计局编.《中国统计年鉴 2014—2018》，《2018 年国民经济和社会发展统计公报》。

化产业发展的纲领性文件，数字文化产业迎来发展高峰，直播、短视频应用迅速下沉至三四线城市，VR、AR、全息投影等技术更广泛地应用在博物馆展览、旅游、影视、游戏等领域，加强了文化呈现形式的互动性和趣味性。

先进制造业快速发展。制造业是强国之基、富国之本。2018 年工信部赛迪研究院发布了中国先进制造业城市发展指数 50 强榜单，中国先进制造业城市发展指数呈现东强西弱，由沿海向中西部地区逐渐降低，由集群中心城市向周边扩散的分布态势。上海、深圳、广州、北京与苏州排名前五强，入围城市数量最多的省份是江苏（10 个），其次依次为浙江（8 个）、广东（7 个）、山东（5 个）、福建（3 个）。

3. 创新驱动作用愈加明显

2018 年，全年国家重点研发计划共安排 1052 个项目，国家科技重大专项共安排 563 个课题，国家自然科学基金共资助 44 504 个项目。全年境内外专利申请 432.3 万件，比上年增长 16.9%；授予专利权 244.7 万件，增长 33.3%；PCT 专利申请受理量为 5.5 万件。共签订技术合同 41.2 万项，技术合同成交金额 17 697 亿元。2018 年科技创造了多项奇迹，我国首艘国产航母完成海试、多颗北斗卫星相继发射、港珠澳大桥正式通车等。

2018 年规模以上工业中，战略性新兴产业增加值比上年增长 8.9%。高技术制造业增加值增长 11.7%，占规模以上工业增加值的比重为 13.9%。装备制造业增加值增长 8.1%，占规模以上工业增加值的比重为 32.9%。全年规模以上服务业中，战略性新兴服务业营业收入比上年增长 14.6%。全年高技术产业投资比上年增长 14.9%，工业技术改造投资增长 12.8%。

（三）城市基础设施明显改善

随着改革开放的推进和现代化步伐的加快，城市基础设施建设和市政公用事业设施建设日益受到重视，市政公用设施承载能力提高，服务功能加强，为外来投资和城市聚集辐射功能创造了良好的环境条件，为城市的进一步发展增添了后劲。（表 2）

表 2　近五年城市基础设施变化

	旅客周转量（亿人公里）	货运量（亿吨）	民用汽车总计（万辆）	邮政业务总量（亿元）	电信业务总量（亿元）	能源消费总量（亿吨标准煤）
2014	28 647. 13	4 167 296	14 598. 11	3 696. 08	18 138. 33	425 806
2015	30 058. 9	4 175 886	16 284. 45	5 078. 72	23 346. 3	429 905
2016	31 258. 46	4 386 763	18 574. 54	7 397. 24	15 616. 95	435 818. 63
2017	32 812. 8	4 804 850	20 906. 67	9 763. 71	27 596. 74	449 000
2018	34 213. 5	5 146 000	23 122	12 345	65 556	464 000

资料来源：国家统计局编．《中国统计年鉴 2014—2018》，《2018 年国民经济和社会发展统计公报》。

1. 城市交通基础设施建设取得巨大进展

2018 年，货物运输总量为 515 亿吨，货物运输周转量205 452亿吨公里，规模以上港口完成货物吞吐量 133 亿吨，规模以上港口集装箱吞吐量24 955万标准箱。年末全国民用汽车保有量24 028万辆，民用轿车保有量13 451万辆。铁路运行方面，“八纵八横”高铁网建设全面展开，十余条铁路新线相继开通，中国铁路运营里程突破 13 万公里，发送旅客 33. 7 亿人次，是欧洲总人口的 4. 5 倍，接近世界总人口的一半；货物发送量达 40. 22 吨，稳居世界第一。

城市轨道交通蓬勃发展。随着我国城市化进程的推进，城市轨道交通建设也迎来了高速发展时期，并逐渐形成网络规模效应。截至 2017 年年底，中国城市轨道开通线路 165 条，运营长度达到 5 033 公里，其中，地铁 3 384 公里，占比 77. 2%。从布局来讲，北上广深占全国通车里程的 60%，北京和上海就占到 40%。（图 3）

城市航空客运量的变化反映了地方经济的发展情况。2018 年，我国航空旅客运输量 6. 1 亿人次，同比增长 10. 9%。北京首都国际机场旅客吞吐量突破 1 亿人次，全国千万级机场达 37 个。东南沿海经济发达地区的泉州晋江、南通兴东、揭阳潮汕、常州奔牛和徐州观音以及中部地区宜昌三峡的城市机场 2018 年航空客运人次保持了 30% 以上增长，且都达到 250 万人次以上。中西部仍是未来机场基建重点。（图 4）

2. 城市通信建设水平显著提高

通信方面，2018 年完成邮政行业业务总量 12 345 亿元，电信业务总量 65 556 亿元，电信业新增移动电话交换机容量 17 267 万户，达到 259 453 万户。年末全国电话用户总数 174 835万户，移动电话普及率上升至 112. 2 部/百人。固定互联网宽带接入用户 40 738 万户，移动宽带用户 130 565 万户，移动互联网用户接入流量 711 亿 GB。此外，货运量、旅客

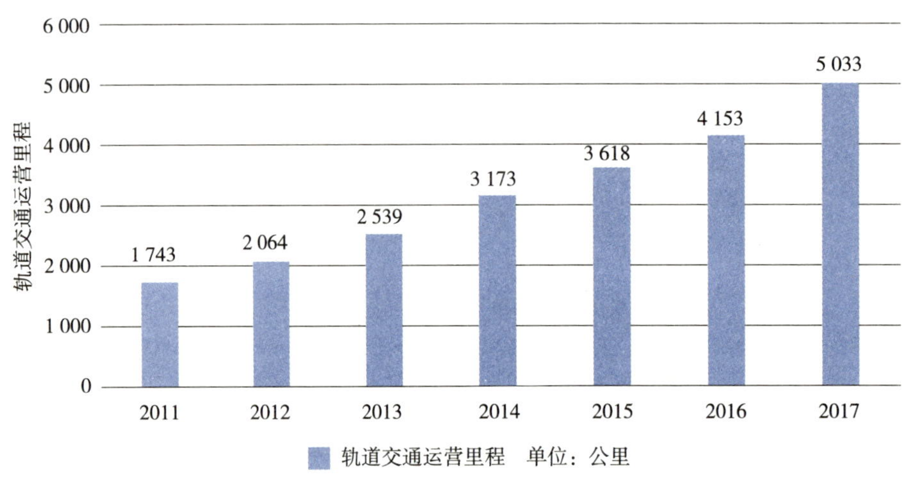

图3 2011—2017年我国城市轨道交通运营里程

数据来源：城市轨道交通协会。

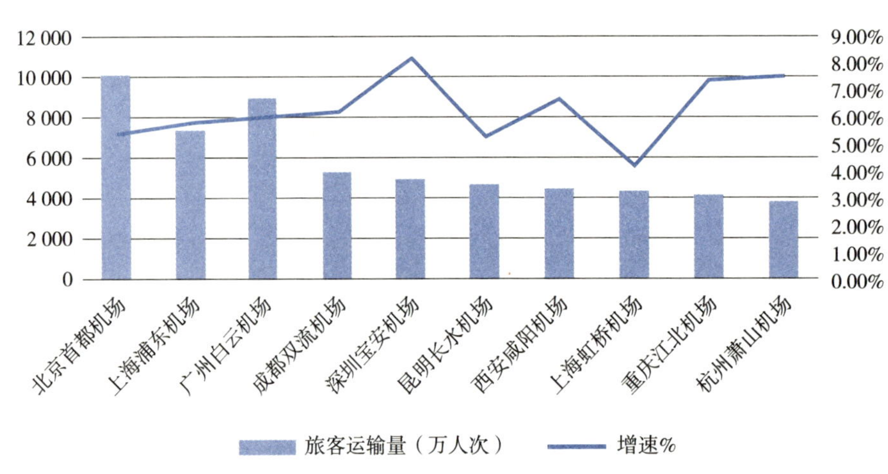

图4 2018年国内排名前十机场客运量及增速

数据来源：民航资源网

周转量、能源消耗总量均有所改善。

3. 城市能源效率不断提升

随着产业结构调整，单位产值能耗呈下降趋势。2018年初步核算，重点耗能工业企业单位烧碱综合能耗下降0.5%，单位合成氨综合能耗下降0.7%，吨钢综合能耗下降3.3%，单位铜冶炼综合能耗下降4.7%，每千瓦时火力发电标准煤耗下降0.7%。全国来看，2018年万元GDP能耗同比下降3.1%。

4. 绿色城市建设成效显著

绿色发展是高质量发展的必由之路。2018年国土绿化公报显示，全国共完成造林707.4万公顷，森林抚育851.7万公顷，治理退化草原666万公顷以上。全国乡村绿化覆盖率达到20%，城市建城区绿化率达37.9%，城市人均绿地面积达14.1平方米。新增国家森林城市29个，全国国家森林城市达166个。(图5)

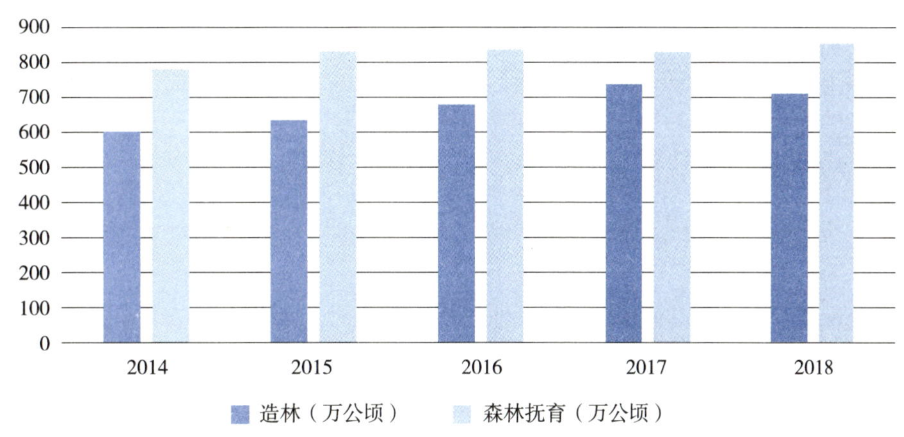

图 5　2014—2018 年全国造林面积和森林抚育面积统计

数据来源：国家林草局

空气质量持续改善。2018 年，全国 338 个地级及以上城市中有 121 个城市空气质量达标，占 35.8%；全年优良天数比率 79.3%，重度及以上污染天数比率降为 2.2%。京津冀及周边地区、长三角地区 $PM_{2.5}$浓度同比分别下降 11.8%、10.2%。2018 年 1—12 月，169 个重点城市空气质量排名 1～5 位的城市是：海口、黄山、舟山、拉萨、丽水；排名后 5 位（169～165）的城市是：临汾、石家庄、邢台、唐山、邯郸。海南、西安等省市开始推进受损山体修复、水环境治理、防治大气污染等工作，西安荣获“2018 绿色发展示范城市”称号。

（四）城市化水平进一步提高

《2018 年国民经济和社会发展统计公报》显示，年末全国大陆总人口 139 538 万人，比上年末增加 530 万人，其中城镇常住人口 83 137 万人，占总人口的比重（常住人口城镇化率）为 59.58%，比上年末提高 1.06 个百分点。户籍人口城镇化率为 43.37%，比上年末提高 1.02 个百分点，城镇化水平进一步提升。此外，各省市的城市化水平变动较大，总体呈现较高的发展状态。中国各省市的城市化水平都有不同程度的显著提高，2017 年所有省份的城市化水平均超过 30%，北京、天津、上海的城市化水平已超过 80%。（图 6、图 7）

城市化推进过程中，城市人口不断增加，城乡差距仍不断扩大。2018 年，全国就业人员 77 586 万人，其中城镇就业人员 43 419 万人，占总就业人数的 56%，城镇登记失业率为 3.8%，下降 0.1 个百分点。全国农民工总量 28 836 万人，比上年增长 0.6%。2016—2018 年全国居民人均可支配收入稳步增长（图 8），农村居民收支增速快于城镇。就各省市城乡人均可支配收入情况来看，上海和北京作为经济最发达的直辖市，城镇居民人均可支配收入高居前列，上海农村居民人均可支配收入同样高居第一，是唯一突破 3 万元的省市，浙江农村居民人均可支配收入比北京高近千元，城乡收入比只有 2.04。天津的城乡收入差距全国最小，其次是浙江、黑龙江、吉林。从全国范围来看，西部地区由于受地理环境限制，农业不发达，城乡收入差距普遍较大。（图 9）

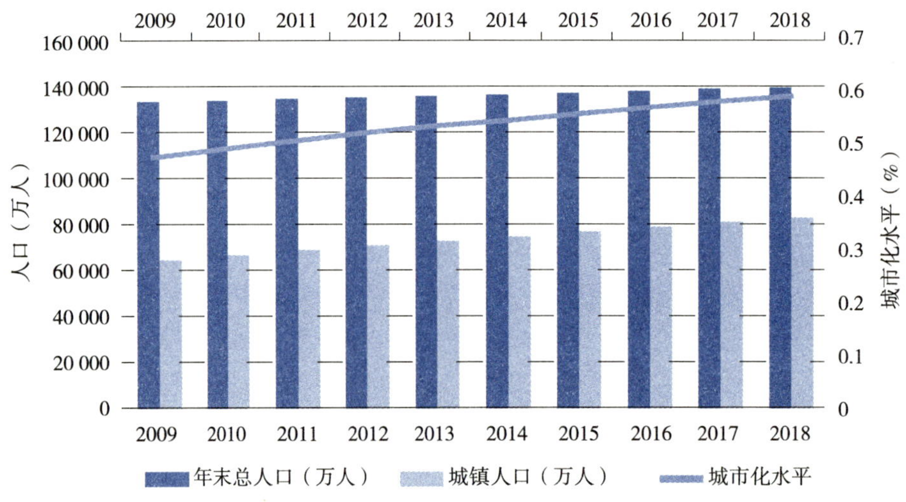

图6　2009 年以来中国城市化水平的变动

资料来源：国家统计局编.《中国统计年鉴 2010—2018》,《2018 年国民经济和社会发展统计公报》。

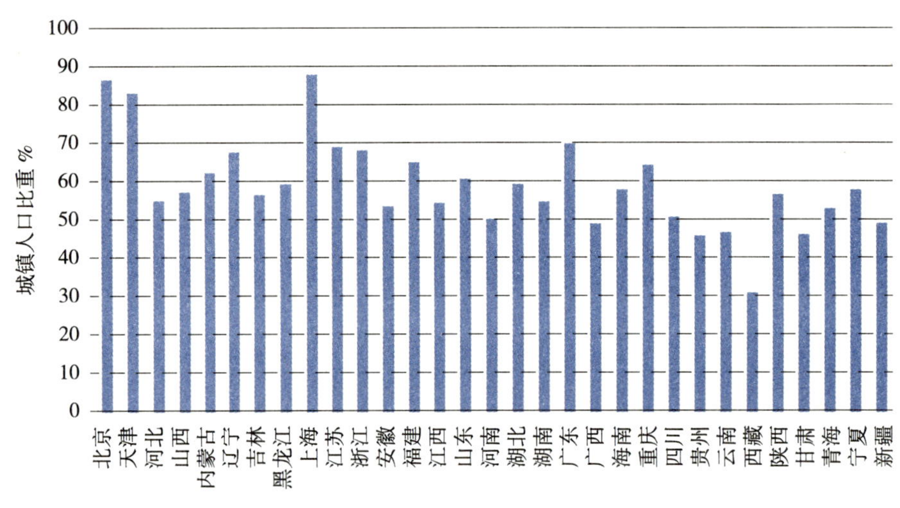

图7　2017 年中国各省市城市化水平

资料来源：国家统计局编.《中国统计年鉴》(2018 年)

（五）城市规模体系日益完善

我国城市发展体系逐渐走向成熟。以特大城市发展为引领的、城市群为主体发展的新格局日益显现。从微观的角度来看，我国城市内部已形成中心城区、近郊区以及远郊县组合的空间结构层次。从宏观格局看，联系日益密切的城市群成为主导城市经济发展的新驱动方式。

首先，中国城市体系日趋合理，中心城市作用发挥显著。截至 2017 年年底，全国共有建制市 661 个，其中直辖市 4 个，地级市 294 个，县级市 363 个；东部地区 212 个，占

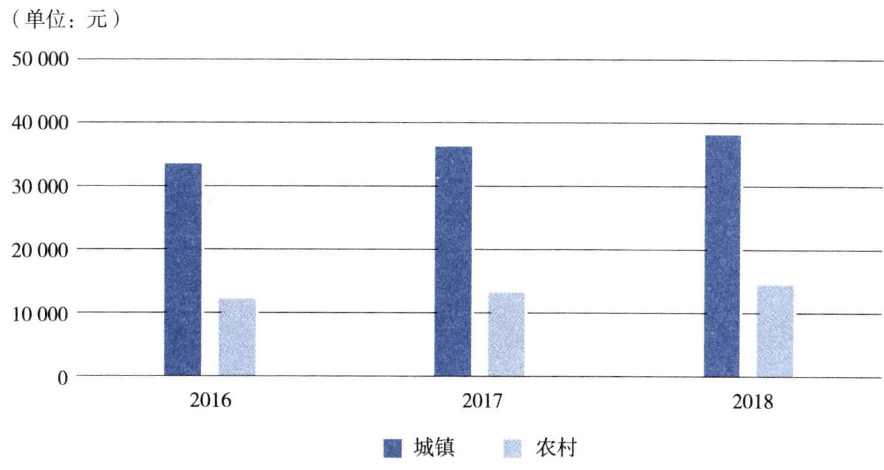

图 8　2016—2018 年城乡人均可支配收入

资料来源：国家统计局编．《中国统计年鉴 2017—2018》，《2018 年国民经济和社会发展统计公报》。

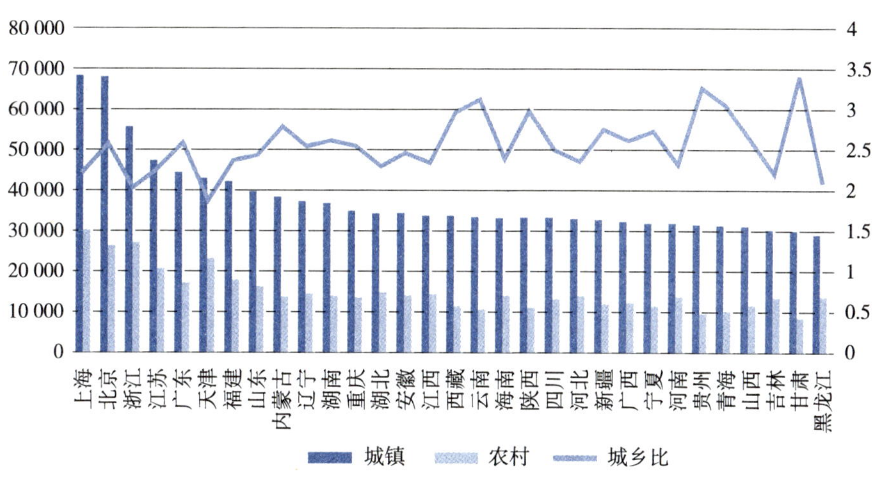

图 9　2018 年城市及农村人均可支配收入及城乡之比

资料来源：各省《2018 年国民经济和社会发展统计公报》。

32.07%；中部地区 170 个，占 25.72%；西部地区 190 个，占 28.74%；东北地区 89 个，占 13.46%（表 3）。2017 年中国城市建成区面积56 225.4平方公里，较 1999 年的21 524.5平方公里，增长了 161.2%（图 10）。中国作为全球第二大经济体，拥有北京、上海、广州、深圳等新兴世界级城市，同时也拥有一批以重庆、成都、天津、武汉、南京等为代表、已经在世界城市体系中崭露头角、影响力超越了其所在区域的国家中心城市。

表 3　中国城市规模体系构成

	2008	2013	2017
全部城市个数	655	658	661
地级市个数	283	286	294
县级市个数	368	368	363
城区面积(平方公里)	178 110. 3	183 416. 1	198 357. 2
建成区面积(平方公里)	36 295. 3	47 855. 3	56 225. 4

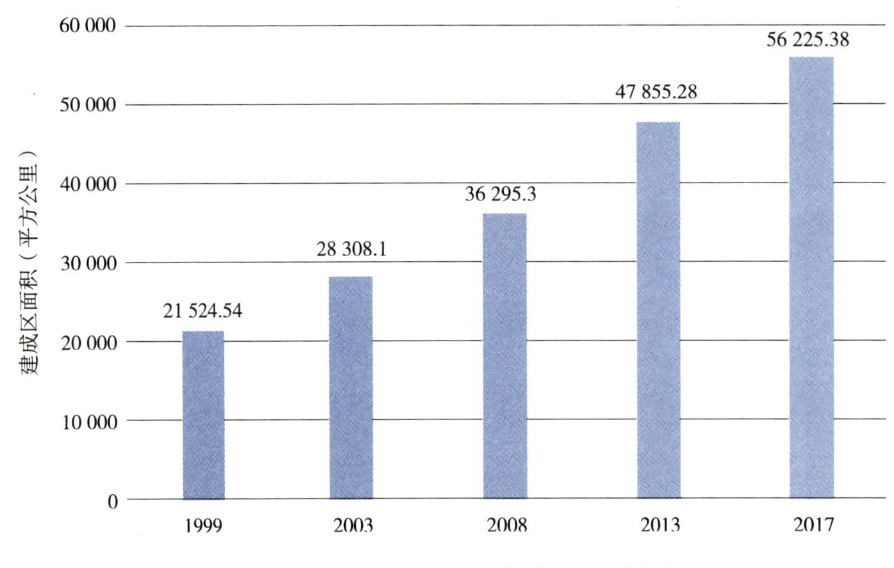

图 10　1999—2017 年城市建成区面积的变化

资料来源：国家统计局编.《中国统计年鉴 2010—2018》

其次，中国城市群蓬勃发展，空间分布趋向合理。一直以来我国政策非常重视城市群的培育。2015 年国家发展改革委提出要明确不同城市群的发展目标、开发方向和城市的功能定位，重点建设国家的五大国家级城市群，强调互联互通和协同发展；“十三五”规划纲要提出要加大城市群建设步伐，将建设 19 大城市群，旨在利用城市群带动区域的经济增长，缩小区域差距。截至 2018 年，我国的国家级城市群共有 9 个，包括长三角城市群、长江中游城市群、成渝城市群、哈长城市群、中原城市群、关中平原城市群、呼包鄂榆城市群、兰西城市群、北部湾城市群，京津冀和珠三角则显示待批复。长江三角洲城市群是当前中国城市化程度最高、经济发展程度最高的世界级的城市群；粤港澳大湾区是我国改革开放的前沿以及经济增长的重要引擎；京津冀城市群协同发展能力增强，核心与周边城市发展持续受益。

最后，滨海城市群（带）地位愈加凸显。凭借 13% 的国土面积，聚集了全国 50% 的人口，并创造了 60% 的国内生产总值，长三角、珠三角和环渤海为代表的滨海城市群已成为具有强大辐射力与影响力的区域发展的引领中心。粤港澳大湾区是继美国纽约湾区和旧金山湾区、日本东京湾区的世界第四大湾区，总面积 5.6 万平方公里，总人口超过 7000 万人，2018 年大湾区的经济总量已经达到 1.6 万亿美元，是我国经济最为发达、机制体制最为活跃的地区。

二、城市经济发展新形态

（一）智慧城市建设全面推进

智慧城市就是利用新一代信息技术促进城市发展智慧化，是城市发展的新模式，也是未来城市的新形态。从 2012 开始，我国先后推出数百个智慧城市建设试点，全国 100% 的副省级以上城市，包括 76% 以上的地级城市和 32% 的县级市，总计大约 500 座城市已经明确提出或正在建设智慧城市。但整体来看，目前都处于初级建设阶段。在 5G 网络技术支撑下，智慧城市将由单一的、碎片化的建设阶段步入系统全面推进的新阶段，进入迅猛发展的快车道。一些城市也做好了迎接新型智慧城市建设的准备。例如，2018 年深圳市人民政府印发《新型智慧城市建设总体方案的通知》，厦门市发布了《厦门市新一代人工智能产业发展行动计划（2019—2021）》，全面推进智慧城市建设，优化城市管理与服务。

（二）新区成为城市经济高质量发展的重要载体

新区建设成为经济高质量发展的重要主体。《关于促进国家级新区健康发展的指导意见》提出，国家级新区是由国务院批准设立，承担国家重大发展和改革开放战略任务的综合功能区。出于区域经济平衡发展考量，着眼于产城融合，人口与产业协同集聚，新区在区域经济发展过程中发挥增长极的引领作用。当前我国有 19 个新区正在积极落实发展规划，2017 年，18 个国家级新区（不含雄安新区）地区生产总值总和接近 4 万亿元，约占全国总量的 5%，其中有 11 个国家级新区的地区生产总值超过千亿规模。

两年来，河北雄安新区的建设取得重大进展，承接北京非首都功能的一批重点项目和重大工程启动，市民服务中心投入使用，实现全过程数字化管控；骨干交通路网建设加紧推进；水电气等基础设施、地下管廊等建设准备工作有序展开。教育、卫生等方面积极对接，新区本级注册登记的 2 585 家企业大多来自北京，首批入驻市民服务中心的 26 家高端高新企业 90% 来自北京。新区发展具有全面深化改革扩大开放的引领示范作用。

值得注意的是，2013 年 9 月我国第一个贸易试验区——中国（上海）自由贸易试验区成立，迄今为止，国务院批准成立的自由贸易区有中国（广东）自由贸易试验区、中国（福建）自由贸易试验区、中国（天津）自由贸易试验区、中国（辽宁）自由贸易试验区、中国（浙江）自由贸易试验区、中国（河南）自由贸易试验区、中国（湖北）自由贸易试验区、中国（重庆）自由贸易试验区、中国（四川）自由贸易试验区、中国（陕西）自由贸易试验区、中国（海南）自由贸易试验区——从沿海到内陆，从“一枝独秀”到形成“雁阵效应”，并与“一带一路”建设、自贸协定谈判等国际区域合作相互配合，中国自由贸易试验区在不断拓展、扩围、升级。

（三）综合管廊、海绵城市建设初见成效

海绵城市的建设强调优先使用绿色措施来解决城市问题，实现城市绿色可持续发展；“综合管廊”建设则是拓展综合利用地下空间布局管道，缓解城市地面空间压力，增加城市承载能力的绿色措施。我国政府高度重视综合管廊和海绵城市的建设，2015 年起，财政部、住房和城乡建设部、水利部在全国择优选取了 25 个地下综合管廊试点城市和 30 个海绵城市建设试点城市。4 月 2 日公布第一批试点城市名单：迁安、白城、镇江、嘉兴、池州、厦门、萍乡、济南、鹤壁、武汉、常德、南宁、重庆、遂宁、贵安新区和西咸新区；2016 年 4 月 27 日，公布第二批试点城市名单：北京、天津、大连、上海、宁波、福州、青岛、珠海、深圳、三亚、玉溪、庆阳、西宁和固原市。

自 2015 年启动地下综合管廊和海绵城市建设试点以来，截至 2018 年 9 月，我国地下综合管廊试点项目已开工建设 738 公里，完成投资约 400 亿元；海绵城市建设试点项目已建设面积 420 平方公里，完成投资约 544 亿元。

目前，海绵城市的建设已经取得了阶段性成果，比如北京市通过对环路下凹式立交桥区进行改造有效缓解了城市内涝灾害；遂宁市对老旧小区进行“海绵化”改造来控制小区内涝积水点；承德市通过采用调蓄、生态净化灯“海绵化”措施，解决了水体黑臭问题，较大改善河道生态环境，与此同时，带来了周边土地的升值。

我们对综合管廊与海绵城市的建设还处于探索阶段，通过试点城市总结成功经验，对于推广和全面落实建设具有重要意义。

（四）国家“三大战略”塑造城市经济发展新格局

当前国家全力推进“一带一路”倡议、京津冀协同发展、长江经济带发展“三大战略”，以此为引领正在形成轴带贯通的、要素自由流动的、产业发达分工合作的城市发展新体系新格局。

“一带一路”涉及 18 个重点省份，2018 年对沿线国家进出口总额为 83 657 亿元，在对外开放水平显著提高的同时，省份与城市之间的沟通与联系日益密切，生产要素流动更加充分与活跃。京津冀发展战略实施四年多，北京、天津、河北实现九条城际铁路开通、河北省通用机场超 30 个、教育资源共享、河北省三地实现异地就医直接结算、三地城市轨道交通一体化进程也在同步加速，“京津冀”发展战略对该区域城市发展与布局影响直接而有力。长江经济带覆盖中国 11 个省市、110 个地级以上城市，以约 20% 的国土面积支撑起超过全国 45% 的经济总量，涵养了 40% 以上的中国人口。

中国城市经济的空间形式在巨变之中，在由分散式到集群式，趋向湾区式、圈带式、流域式，未来将形成以特大城市（国家中心城市）、区域中心城市为节点的城市群带经济一体化发展模式。

三、城市经济发展存在的主要问题

（一）发展不充分不均衡的问题还较严峻

不平衡主要体现在以下几个方面：首先，在城乡融合、城乡一体化的过程中，二元结构始终存在。2017 年城镇居民人均可支配收入为 39 251 元，农村居民人均可支配收入为14 617 元，城乡收入比 2.69:1；其次，区域之间发展不平衡。2018 年北京和上海人均 GDP 分别为 2.11 万美元、2.04 万美元，其他发达省份如天津、江苏、浙江人均 GDP 在 1.5 万美元到 2 万美元之间，中西部欠发达省份如贵州、西藏、云南、甘肃等人均 GDP 均在 8 000 美元以下，东西极值差（北京 21 108 美元、甘肃 4 756 美元）4.44 倍；即使区域内部发展差距也较大，如珠三角与粤西粤东人均 GDP 发展差距在 3 倍以上。最后，经济内部结构不平衡。突出表现在收入分配结构、产业结构、投资消费结构等方面。

不充分主要体现以下两个方面：一是创新不充分。研发投入不高，2018 年中国的 R&D 投入占 GDP 的比重为 2.18%，进入创新型国家行列。但与美国、欧盟和日本等发达国家相比，仍需要不懈努力。目前中国的科技进步贡献率为 39%，而发达的创新型国家在 70% 以上。我国自主创新能力整体较弱，对国外先进技术的依赖性强，创新主体动力不足，创新政策体系亟待建立。二是改革不充分。营造公平竞争的市场环境、完善产权制度、规范市场秩序、增强政府宏观调控能力、加强国企改革激发市场主体活力等，仍是社会主义市场经济体制改革的重点。

（二）城市经济总体质量依然偏低

“我国经济已由高速增长阶段转向高质量发展阶段。”追求经济发展高质量，要改变以往注重经济增长速度与数量的惯性思维，更关注经济、社会、生态的协调发展，将人民的幸福感与安全感放在更加重要的位置。高质量发展的内涵应该包括更依靠创新驱动、更高的生产效率、更高的经济效益、更合理的资源配置、更优化的经济结构、更加注重消费对经济发展的基础性作用、更小的贫富差距、更注重幸福导向、更加注重防范金融风险、更绿色环保的发展方式等。

在经济发展转型阶段，我国城市经济发展需要更加关注高效、生态、均衡、优化等内容。然而，从人民幸福感的角度，人均收入的增长仍然低于 GDP 增速，仍然面临住房压力、出行拥堵、食品安全威胁等问题，当下我国高质量发展要求突出解决环境污染问题、产品质量不高问题和民生短板问题等。

（三）城市经济可持续发展能力偏弱

以往我国依靠资源、劳动力要素等低成本的投入，粗放式的增长模式虽然带来了经济的高速增长，但是也带来了严重的生态污染、环境破坏，发展的持续性明显减弱。目前，我国大部分城市缺水，饮用水源污染严重；垃圾无害化处理率很低；城市基础设施建设与当地资源环境的匹配度差，尤其是都市区等人口产业密集地区，更受到环境与生态条件的制约。

很多城市的发展往往由于路径依赖陷入“刚性专业化”的“低端锁定”陷阱。比如山西、东北三省等资源型城市，长期严重依赖重工业与资源初级产业；再比如珠三角地区主要承担价值链中游的加工、装配、制造等环节活动，高附加值环节不占据优势。由于长期以来过分依赖低生产要素成本优势，缺少战略眼光与可持续发展的思维，因而处于价值链低端且对全球价值链的治理者产生强烈的依赖关系，形成低端锁定效应。

（四）新动能亟待培育

新时代的到来，中国城市经济发展的增长动力、需求特征、供给条件、风险状况、竞争环境以及政府与市场的关系等，也都发生了不同于以往的深刻变化，中国将进入发展方式转变、经济结构调整、长期保持中高速发展的“经济新常态”。世界经济的深度调整和变革，也将进一步倒逼中国城市经济发展模式的全面转型，不同于以往高投资、高增长、高加工贸易出口的发展模式，扩大内需、提高创新能力、实现经济发展动能转换是我们面临的促进经济发展方式转变的新机遇，需要依靠科技创新为城市经济发展注入新的动力。从城市“抢人大战”即可看出转型发展新的端倪。

四、未来发展展望

（一）数字经济和共享经济加速推进

进入21世纪以来，数字经济在传统经济的低迷中表现出旺盛的生命力，在整个世界经济构成中的比重持续上升，已经成为世界生产方式变革的重要驱动力量。物联网、大数据、人工智能等新兴技术飞速发展，能源、材料、制造等技术也取得了重大突破——在新一轮产业革命的背景下，传统产业与新技术融合如电子商务、现代物流、互联网金融等，使得传统产业重新焕发活力；新技术也催生了新产业、新产品、新业态、新模式，引领着未来发展的潮流。共享经济是基于移动互联网技术成熟产生的，其核心意义在于将过剩资源进行重新配置，实现资源共享和利润共享。互联网的繁荣给传统企业带来了巨大冲击，低成本地将现有资源利用起来，提高效率，对于提高企业竞争力甚至于生存能力都是至关重要的。

新时代背景下，充分认识新一轮技术革命带来的机遇与挑战，加快技术创新，促进新旧动能转换，走新型工业化道路，对提升城市竞争力具有重要的意义。

（二）智慧城市发展将进一步繁荣

智慧城市让城市中各个功能彼此协调运作，智慧城市是以智慧技术高度集成、智慧产业高度发展、智慧服务高效便民为主要特征的城市发展模式，其本质是更加透彻的感知、更加广泛的联接、更加集中和更有深度的计算，为城市植入智慧的基因。城市建设与数字经济、共享经济相融合所打造的就是智慧城市，随着数字经济、共享经济渗透人们生活的方方面面，走智慧型城市化之路，积极推动城市信息化，完善智慧型产业体系。

（三）城市群成为经济发展新空间载体

随着互联网、高速交通、智能城市、共享经济的发展，城市群带成为一种实现经济、管理高效的新模式。在国家重大方针战略如“一带一路”“三纵五横”大通道建设的影响下，我国城市群、都市圈的建设发展将拉开序幕。自贸区在我国的城市群建设中起着开放发展、经济引领作用；长江经济带、海峡经济圈、大湾区将是城市群活跃的热点区域。可以预见，未来我国城市经济主要集聚在城市群、都市圈（带）、大湾区。

（四）新交通方式将重塑城市发展新格局

随着我国城市化进程的持续推进，高铁、地铁、轻轨等轨道交通进入高速发展时期，网络规模效应开始形成；民航事业持续发展，以交通方式为媒介的人流、物流、信息流相互贯通，深刻影响着城市空间格局。如高铁的开通，不仅对于沿线地区的投资、发展有良好的带动作用，更突出了枢纽城市的集聚力和竞争力，吸引人口向其集聚，高铁的开通可以为城市赋能，也为产业的转移、承接、升级创造了条件。根据我国的中长期规划，合肥、长沙、北京、武汉、重庆、南京、西安等城市交通优势将得到强化，这意味着这些城市作为枢纽与节点城市，将会有更强的集聚力与竞争力，会成为区域的中心城市，影响城市集群的形成。

（作者：付晓东，中国人民大学应用经济学院教授；刘治彦，中国社科院城市发展与环境研究所研究员）*

参考文献

[1] 刘治彦，付晓东．中国城市经济发展评价与展望［J］．城市发展研究，2010（8）：37－44.

[2] 王茂林．新中国城市经济 50 年［M］．北京：经济管理出版社，2000.

[3] 高波．新常态下中国经济增长的动力和逻辑［J］．南京大学学报（哲学·人文科学·社会科学），2016（5）：31－42.

[4] 黄剑，黄卫平．中国经济“新常态”下的创新驱动与转型调整［J］．江淮论坛，2015（12）：40－47.

* 感谢以下两位研究生：王谦、王静田

2018 年中国城市住房发展概述

2018 年，中美贸易摩擦持续升级，为防范系统性金融风险，中央在房地产市场调控方面继续坚持房住不炒，对房价调控从年中“坚决遏制房价上涨”到年末转向“稳地价、稳房价、稳预期”，并提出夯实城市政府主体责任，因城施策、分类指导。居民长期以来对房价上涨持有的强烈预期在 2018 年发生明显转变，上半年市场形势依然火爆的二三四线城市于年中开始冷却。2018 年，住房制度改革继续深化，中央和地方在住房保障和人才住房的供给机制上做出诸多探索。一方面继续实施新的三年棚改攻坚计划，并强调根据新的房地产形势，因地制宜调整货币化安置政策；另一方面，针对夹心层需求，以共有产权住房作为配售型保障性住房的代表，在各地深入推广试点。在保障弱势群体的同时，各地也将支持创新和吸引人才作为提升城市竞争力的核心抓手，积极探索住房供给制度的政策创新，降低安居成本，吸引人才安居就业。

一、房地产后半年显著降温，市场调控“稳”字当头

（一）宏观经济环境与政策影响叠加，房价上涨预期转变

2018 年，在外部不确定性与内部经济向高质量发展转型面临阵痛的双重作用下，我国经济面临着空前严峻的挑战。首先，中美贸易摩擦持续升级和国际贸易纠纷频出造成外部环境不确定性增大。3 月 22 日，美国总统特朗普宣布计划对中国 600 亿美元的商品加征关税，并表示将限制中国企业对美投资并购。4 月 3 日，美国正式提出对中国 500 亿美元的商品加征 25% 的关税。7 月 10 日，美国政府公布进一步对华加征关税清单，拟对约 2 000 亿美元中国产品加征 10% 的关税。在贸易摩擦不断升级的情况下，人民币汇率一度快速贬值，企业及投资者对市场的信心减弱。其次，国内方面，民营企业经营成本、融资压力、债务风险全面上升，部分民营企业举步维艰。2018 年全年 GDP 增速 6.6%，创逾 10 年新低。6 月末，广义货币（M2）同比增长 8%，创该数据有统计以来最低纪录[①]。在经历短暂回升后，M2 同比增速在 10 月末、11 月末再次刷新最低纪录。1—8 月全国固定资产投资同比增 5.3%，

① 资料来源：界面新闻 https://www.jiemian.com/article/2727810_qq.html.

创该数据有统计以来最低纪录[①]。在基建补短板、地方专项债加速发行的背景下，第四季度投资增速有所回升，但总体仍显疲软。11 月末，狭义货币（M1）同比增长 1.5%，创历史次低纪录[②]。11 月，社会消费品零售总额同比增长 8.1%，创 2003 年 6 月以来新低[③]。在经济增速放缓和未来发展不确定性增大的环境下，我国居民在投资和消费领域持更加谨慎的态度，长期以来我国居民持有的房价上涨的强烈预期发生明显转变。

（二）市场形势年中急转，从二三四线城市依然火爆到开始冷却

2018 年全年商品住房销售面积与 2017 年基本持平（2017 年 144 789 万平方米，2018 年 147 929 万平方米），销售价格较 2017 年有明显提升（2017 年 7 614 元/平方米，2018 年 8 544元/平方米）[④]。具体而言，2018 年商品房销售面积、销售金额增速自年初以来逐月下滑，至年中受企业集中备案和业绩冲刺等因素影响，小幅拉升；而步入下半年以来，随着热门城市“四限”政策效应的逐步显现，加之经济下行压力、中美贸易战等诸多外部因素影响，商品房成交规模也随之持续降低。整体来看，商品房全年成交呈现出“先升后降”的趋势，在 5 月、6 月形成小高峰，热点二线城市“万人摇号，一房难求”，但 8 月之后市场明显转冷，“日光盘”不再，项目去化率显著下调[⑤]。（图 1）

具体来看，上半年，以省会城市为代表的二线城市纷纷为争夺人才出台一系列优惠政策，通过降低落户门槛吸引大学毕业生和外来人口，造成房地产市场销售更加火爆。例如，西安放开落户条件后 2018 年新晋落户 75 万人[⑥]，带来购房需求迅速攀升。天津“海河英才计划”实施两周因落户人数超出预期而被紧急叫停，但也带动了房地产成交量猛增。此外，南京、武汉、长沙、成都等也相继放松落户条件，直接加剧了房价上涨预期。

三季度开始房价走势出现明显变化。根据中国指数院百城房价监测，9 月百城样本城市中 18 个城市出现新房价格环比下跌，数量明显增加。11 月，百城房价单月环比涨幅为 0.27%，涨幅明显回落，更是有 31 个样本城市出现新房价格下跌。从各级城市来看，三四线城市房地产市场降温最明显。2018 年 1—11 月三四线城市房价累计上涨 8.25%，较去年同期收窄 3.38 个百分点，累计涨幅收窄幅度各线城市中最显著，11 月，有 21 个三四线城市价格环比下跌。2018 年 1—11 月，三四线城市商品住房成交面积同比下降约 3.5%，超六成城市成交同比下降[⑦]。

---

① 资料来源：华尔街见闻 https://wallstreetcn.com/articles/3406715.

② 资料来源：新浪财经 http://finance.sina.com.cn/stock/hkstock/ggscyd/2018-12-11/doc-ihmutuec8232268.shtml.

③ 资料来源：国家统计局。

④ 资料来源：国家统计局 2017 年和 2018 年全国房地产开发和销售情况。

⑤ 资料来源：易居研究院 http://www.cricchina.com/research/Details/8201.

⑥ 资料来源：易居研究院 http://www.cricchina.com/research/Details/8201.

⑦ 资料来源：中国房地产 2018 年市场总结，中国指数研究院。

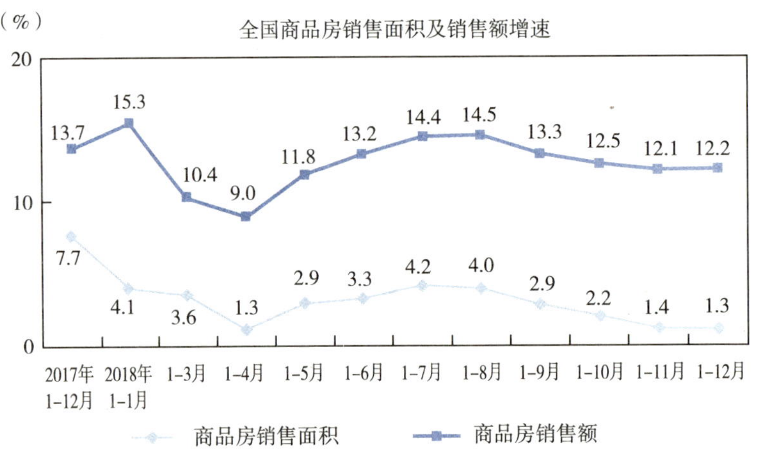

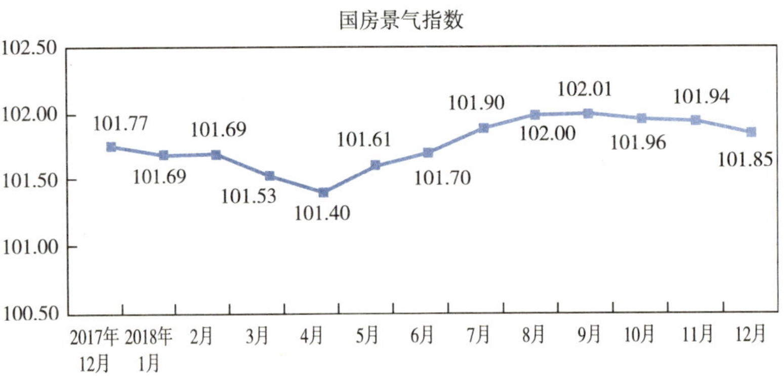

图 1　2018 年全国商品房销售情况

数据来源：国家统计局

（三）房地产调控从坚决遏制房价上涨转向稳地价、稳房价、稳预期，城市政府主体责任加强

2018 年中央对房地产市场调控政策在大方向上仍坚持房住不炒的重要原则，7 月 31 日召开的中共中央政治局会议中明确提出“坚决遏制房价上涨”，体现了党和国家对楼市调控的坚定决心和巨大力度。下半年，由于中美贸易摩擦导致经济增长预期不稳定，且在上半年严格的调控政策下，房地产市场显著降温，在 12 月 24 日召开的全国住房和城乡建设工作会议上，住房城乡建设部提出要以稳地价、稳房价、稳预期为目标，防止房地产市场大起大落。房地产长效机制建设加快，强调因城施策，进一步强化城市政府主体责任。

3 月，两会政府工作报告重申“房住不炒”，提出要“落实地方主体责任，继续实行差别化调控，建立健全长效机制，促进房地产市场平稳健康发展。支持居民自住购房需求，培育住房租赁市场，发展共有产权住房。加快建立多主体供给、多渠道保障、租购并举的住房制度，让广大人民群众早日实现安居宜居”。

7 月，中共中央政治局会议将解决好房地产市场问题作为六大任务之一，对于房价的措辞更加严厉，从“遏制房价过快上涨”升级为“坚决遏制房价上涨”。具体调控手段仍然强调坚持因城施策，促进供求平衡，合理引导预期，整治市场秩序，加快建立促进房地产市场平稳健康发展的长效机制。“坚决遏制房价上涨”体现了中央维护房地产市场秩序的决心。

8 月，为落实中央精神，住房城乡建设部在辽宁沈阳召开部分城市房地产工作座谈会，对地方政府提出两大要求：一是加快制定住房发展规划；二是坚决遏制投机炒房，并引入问责机制，对工作不力、市场波动大、未能实现调控目标的城市坚决问责。城市政府层面积极响应中央调控要求。7 月 31 日，深圳发布一线楼市最严新政，涉及暂停公司买房、公寓限售 5 年、新供应土地上公寓只租不售、住宅限售 3 年等内容。8 月 8 日，成都、杭州相继跟进发布楼市新规，重点打击投机炒房行为，整顿房地产违法乱象。8 月之后，热点城市房价过快上涨的局面基本被遏制，多数城市房价涨幅趋于平缓，部分城市房价更是由上涨转向下行，市场观望情绪浓厚。

12 月，中央经济工作会议继续坚持“房住不炒”，重申要构建房地产市场健康发展长效机制，因城施策、分类指导，夯实城市政府主体责任。12 月 24 日，全国住房和城乡建设工作会议上，住房城乡建设部提出 2019 年要以稳地价、稳房价、稳预期为目标，强调不能大起大落，要保持平稳，体现了中央调控政策导向从遏制房价上涨转变为防止房价大涨和大跌。截至年底，全国热点城市房价过快上涨势头得到遏制，市场预期已发生重大变化，更强调因城施策、分类指导，城市政府承担主体责任，也被赋予了更大的自主弹性调控空间。12 月 18 日，山东省菏泽市率先取消限售，被认为是城市政府履行主体责任确保实现稳房价目标的信号。此外，广州、武汉、南宁等部分城市局部放松限价，部分房价下行压力大的城市下调房贷利率上浮比例。预计 2019 年中央将把更多的政策自主权下放给城市政府，各城市根据实际情况进行有针对性的房地产调控政策调整，以实现保持房地产市场平稳发展的目标。（图 2）

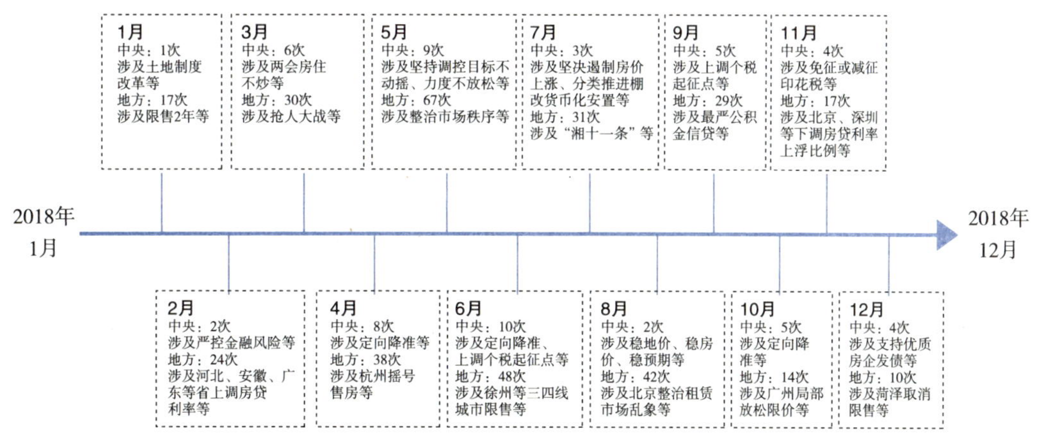

图 2　2018 年历月中央及地方房地产调控政策频次及内容①

① 根据克尔瑞发布的“2018 房地产市场总结展望（政策篇）”整理形成。

（四）房地产市场整顿力度加大，租赁市场违法违规行为受到重点整治

2018 年国家对房地产市场整顿力度空前加大。6 月底七部委在 30 城联合开展治理楼市乱象专项行动。7 月底住房城乡建设部公布 20 家违法违规房企及中介黑名单，直指哄抬房价、“黑中介”、捂盘惜售、虚假宣传等房地产市场乱象。租赁市场乱象问题成为本轮房地产整顿的重点工作。

针对频繁出现的利用租客信用套取资金、再用该资金哄抬租金价格收房等租赁市场不规范行为，北京、上海和西安等城市对“租金贷”启动调查，多地发文暂停“租金贷”。北京银行、建设银行、平安银行等金融机构也均暂停租房贷款业务。9 月 30 日，上海市金融服务办公室发布《关于暂停本市小额贷款公司融资担保公司与代理经租企业合作开展个人“租金贷”业务的通知》，要求上海市小额贷款公司、融资担保公司立即暂停与代理经租企业合作开展个人“租金贷”业务。与此同时，各区主管部门要结合 2018 年度现场检查，对辖区内小额贷款公司、融资担保公司开展个人“租金贷”业务情况进行排查。同日，上海市住建委发布《关于进一步规范本市代理经租企业及个人“租金贷”相关业务的通知》，要求代理经租企业不得与未经国家金融监管部门批准设立、无金融许可证的机构合作开展个人“租金贷”及相关业务。代理经租企业不得强制或诱骗租客使用个人“租金贷”产品，不得在签约前收取定金或设置其他条件，不得收取与个人“租金贷”业务相关的其他费用。个人“租金贷”贷款合同和住房租赁合同应当分别签署，有关住房租赁租金贷款的内容不得出现在住房租赁合同中。9 月 28 日，南京市房屋租赁管理办公室首次发布的“房屋租赁风险提示”指出，个别中介机构和住房租赁企业故意隐瞒贷款事实，引导、诱骗或强制租房人办理租金贷，导致租房人“被贷款”，面临贷款合同不易撤销、退租时难以退贷、贷款逾期失信等多重风险。9 月 19 日，广州相关部门联合发布的《广州住房租赁行业倡议书》指出，住房租赁企业不诱导、引导和强迫承租人参与任何有金融风险的行为；不用承租人或出租人资金建立资金池；不截留租金、挪作他用以及期限错配；不在未经承租人同意的情况下或采取虚假宣传等方式诱导承租人签订贷款合同；不未经监管部门批准从事发放贷款业务；不以住房租赁名义从事非法集资活动。

2018 年，因行业成本、竞争环境、扩张速度发生明显变化，长租市场状况频出，暴露出长租公寓企业无证经营和超范围经营现象突出、“高杠杆”金融风险、装修污染问题、产权关系错综复杂甚至属于违建、消防隐患突出、运营服务费标准混乱等问题。行业问题的集中爆发倒逼监管政策出台，各地政府相继出台了多项长租行业规范细则。10 月，浙江省出台《关于促进长租公寓市场平稳健康有序发展的指导意见》，确立了定期通告租金收付情况、落实租赁住房安全责任、落实租赁住房空气质量合格责任、建立租金价格分类管控制度等十个方面内容。北京市工商局联合北京市住建委开展为期半年的房地产经纪机构专项整治工作，对拖延支付租客租金、押金，发布虚假广告等长租公寓运营商行为进行严打。

二、优化住房保障机制，试点推进房源类型与管理服务新方式

（一）因地制宜推进棚改，针对性调整货币化安置政策

近年来，我国持续推进棚户区改造工作，继“十二五”保障性安居工程大规模推进之后，国务院又提出了2015—2017年的棚改三年计划①，并在2017年提前、超额完成改造任务。2017年5月，李克强总理在国务院常务会议上再次提出继续实施2018—2020年的三年棚改攻坚计划，计划再改造各类棚户区1 500万套，并在2018年政府工作报告中，明确提出全年新开工棚改580万套的目标计划，实际改造620多万套②。自2011年算起，全国棚户区改造合计开工已达4 500万套以上，显著改善了原棚户区居民的生活居住条件，也有效带动了投资、消费和去库存。

自2015年起，国家大力推进棚改货币化安置：2014年货币化安置比例仅有9%，而在2017年这一比例已高达60%③。从地方样本来看，2017年上半年，江苏22个县（市、区）棚改货币化安置比例已达到100%④。在推动棚改工作的同时，高比例的货币化安置政策逐渐显示出了一些弊端：在供给没有增加的情况下，大量货币刺激和推动了需求，使得棚改量较大的三四线城市库存迅速消化，但同时也大幅推高了房价。与此同时，货币化安置的成本也水涨船高，在新开工数量大致相当的情况下，棚改总投资额随货币化安置比例提升而快速增加，据相关市场机构测算，2017年货币化安置单套成本已经高达实物安置的160%⑤。当前，全国百城库存已经跌回到2012年水平⑥，棚改货币化对商品房销售的拉动作用也出现了边际弱化现象，货币化安置在一定程度上已经完成促进“去库存”的历史使命。基于当前的房地产形势，为严控三四线城市市场风险，棚改货币化安置的方式势必需要有所调整。

事实上，早在2017年8月，住房和城乡建设部等六部委就联合发文⑦要求“商品住宅消化周期15个月以下市县，应控制货币化安置比例，提高实物安置比例”；同年年底，住房

---

① 国务院《关于进一步做好城镇棚户区和城乡危房改造及配套基础设施建设有关工作的意见》。

② 2019年政府工作报告。

③ 2014年全国棚改货币化安置率为9.0%；而到了2015、2016年，这一比率上升至29.9%、48.5%。——人民网：http://paper.people.com.cn/mszk/html/2018-10/29/content_1889820.htm。民生证券发布《棚改对地产销售和投资的量化分析》报告预测，全国棚改的货币化安置比例2017年有望达到60%。——每日经济新闻 http://www.nbd.com.cn/articles/2018-03-05/1196317.html.

④ 中国政府网：http://www.gov.cn/shuju/2017-07/10/content_5209238.htm.

⑤ 2015—2017年分别为1.18万亿、1.48万亿和1.84万亿。据恒大研究院测算，2015年货币化安置单套成本，是实物安置的107%，而随着房价（特别是三四线城市）快速上涨，这一比例在2016年和2017年分别上升至135%和160%。——任泽平：棚改货币化即将落幕，去库存任务完成。https://news.fang.com/open/29073214.html.

⑥ 根据易居房地产研究院发布的数据，百城住宅库存总量为42708万平方米，环比减少1.6%，同比减少8.2%。综合历史数据，当前百城库存规模已经跌回到2012年3月的水平。

⑦《关于申报2018年棚户区改造计划任务的通知》。

和城乡建设部会同国开行、农发行发文①："对商品住房库存不足、房价上涨压力较大的城市，棚改专项贷款不支持仍采取货币化安置的2018年新开工项目。"2018年6月，国开行在年度报告中提到"严控库存不足地区的棚改货币化安置比例"，新增棚改专项贷款审批趋于收紧。同年7月12日，住房和城乡建设部相关负责人②表示要因地制宜推进棚改货币化安置："商品住房库存不足、房价上涨压力较大的地方，应有针对性地及时调整棚改安置政策，采取新建棚改安置房的方式；商品住房库存量较大的地方，可以继续推进棚改货币化安置"，要求各地"坚持既尽力而为、又量力而行的原则，切实评估论证财政承受能力，不搞一刀切、不层层下指标、不盲目举债铺摊子，进一步合理界定和把握棚改的标准和范围，重点攻坚改造老城区内脏乱差的棚户区和国有工矿、林区、垦区棚户区。"在年底建设工作会上，住房和城乡建设部也再次强调"进一步合理界定和把握棚改范围及标准，有针对性的调整完善棚改货币化安置政策"。未来，棚改工作仍将扎实推进，但大量三四线城市以货币化为主的安置模式将有序退出和转换，棚改范围也将进一步聚焦。

多地明确表示，将减少货币化安置的比例，取消对于货币化安置的奖励补贴③

山东首次取消货币化安置奖励，不再鼓励货币化补贴；湖南则提出，商品住房库存不足、房价上涨压力较大的市县，要及时取消棚户区改造货币安置优惠政策。江西省也强调因地制宜实施棚改货币化安置，住房供需矛盾突出的市县应加大实物安置住房建设力度。广东则提出，控制棚改成本，实现收支平衡，因地制宜推进棚改货币化安置。

（二）提升管理服务水平，试点推行政府购买公租房管理运营服务

"十二五"以来，国家大力推进保障性安居工程建设，极大提升了公租房的供给规模。截至2018年11月，全国公租房已累计分配1 493万套，惠及3 700万困难群众④。然而，随着大量公租房建成和交付使用，承租人以低价承租，再以高价转租的案例层出不穷。如2018年9月，北京曝出多个公租房小区部分公租房存在被转租、经营的乱象。这其中暴露的也是公租房运营管理中专业人员不足、服务水平不高、管理不规范等问题。管理乱象的出现也进一步要求，未来我国公租房的工作重心，由单纯的规模增长逐步向优化管理转变。

基于这一背景，住房和城乡建设部开始着力于优化公租房管理服务。在2018年9月，住房和城乡建设部、财政部联合印发《推行政府购买公租房运营管理服务的试点方案》，确定在浙江、安徽、山东、湖北、广西、四川、云南、陕西8个省（自治区），开展政府购买

① 《关于进一步加强棚户区改造项目和资金管理的通知》。

② http：//politics. people. com. cn/n1/2018/0712/c1001 – 30144219. html.

③ http：//k. sina. com. cn/article_ 2603857891_ 9b33b7e302000diqh. html.

④ 2018年王蒙徽部长在全国住房和城乡建设工作会议上的讲话。

公租房运营管理服务的试点，政府购买服务内容主要包括入住和退出管理事项、租金收缴和房屋使用管理事项、维修养护事项以及综合管理事项四大类。同时，国家要求试点市县在12 月底上报实施方案。

（三）持续优化保障方式，深入推进共有产权住房试点

2017 年 9 月，住房和城乡建设部发文明确支持北京市、上海市深化发展共有产权住房试点工作。两市都制定完善了相关管理办法，在建设模式、产权划分、使用管理等方面形成了一定经验。截至 2018 年年底，北京市已供应共有产权住房 5.3 万套，上海市签约近 9.8 万户①。

在京、沪率先示范的基础上，其他省市也开始陆续加入试点探索。2018 年 6 月，广东省住房和城乡建设厅印发《关于开展共有产权住房政策探索试点的通知》，提出在广州、深圳、珠海、佛山、茂名 5 个城市先行探索试点共有产权住房政策，试点时限为 1 年。

对比京、沪、广三地的政策，可见各地试点政策仍存在较大的差异。首先是对房源性质的考虑有所不同：因为北京共有产权住房源自原来的自住型商品房，所以北京将其定义为“政策性商品房”而非保障性住房。在准入准出标准方面，上海最严格，除了住房困难还要求户口年限和收入，而后续购房会要求腾退共有产权住房。而北京在产权交易上最为严格，形成封闭管理，购房人既不能自购全部产权也不能通过上市交易将住房转化为商品房性质。总体来看，北京的封闭内循环模式可以保障房源储备的稳定，最大程度限制牟利空间，但同时缺乏“转正”机会，限制了住房的价值释放，会一定程度地影响购房积极性，从而影响政策的可持续性以及平抑房价的作用。而过高的土地楼面价和限制严格的售价，也造成房企望而却步。

此外，北京也积极推进土地供应制度上的创新。一方面，北京一直鼓励国有企业利用自有用地建设保障性住房。2017 年年底，北京首次推出怀柔和大兴的两宗国企自有用地，用于建设共有产权房，这既可以拓宽保障房建设渠道，又可以促进国企盘活自身闲置土地，从而实现双赢。另一方面，北京也积极探索农村土地制度改革，在 2018 年 12 月，首次挂牌集体土地共有产权房三宗用地，这进一步为保障性住房建设开辟了土地供应新渠道，同时，也是推进农村集体经营性建设用地出让、租赁、入股与国有土地“同等入市、同权同价”的有益尝试。

在各地因城施策，试点推进如火如荼的基础上，仍需要进一步总结其中的经验和问题，在产权管理制度、土地供应渠道等方面深入研究、深化改革。坚持因地制宜，并重点指引人口流入量大，房价较高，住房困难群体数量较多的大中城市发展共有产权住房，更好地解决“夹心层”的住房需求。（表 1）

---

① 2018 年王蒙徽部长在全国住房和城乡建设工作会议上的讲话。

表 1　试点省市关于共有产权住房的管理制度

	北京①	上海②	广东③
房源性质	政策性商品住房	保障性住房	纳入城镇保障性安居工程(保障性住房)
供给对象	符合本市住房限购条件且家庭成员在本市均无住房	具有本市城镇常住户口达到规定年限,且户口在提出申请所在地达到规定年限; 住房面积低于规定限额; 可支配收入和财产低于规定限额	符合规定条件的城镇无房家庭,具体各地制定
产权份额	购房人产权份额,参照项目销售均价占同地段、同品质普通商品住房价格的比例确定	购房人产权份额,参照共有产权保障住房所在项目的销售基准价格占相邻地段、相近品质商品住房价格的比例	实际出资价格占评估价格④的比例 原则上不低于 50%
购买限制	每户家庭仅一套	仅限一套	每户家庭仅一套
腾退要求	文件中不明确	5 年内购买商品房或户口迁出的需要腾退并由指定机构回购	文件中不明确
面积标准	中小套型为主		$90m^2$ 以下为主
产权转让	满 5 年的,可按市场价格转让所购房屋产权份额。转让对象应为其他符合共有产权住房购买条件的家庭。 不满 5 年不得转让,如需转让由代持机构回购继续作为共有产权住房使用	满 5 年后,共有产权保障住房可以上市转让或者购买政府产权份额,转为商品房	10 年及以上可一次性增购全部产权,转为商品房; 5 年以上可由代持机构安排转让给符合条件的其他申请人; 不满 5 年不得转让,如需转让需要缴纳全部增值收益
用地方式	采取“限房价、竞地价”“综合招标”等多种出让方式		划拨或招拍挂
房源筹集		单独选址、集中建设和在商品住宅建设项目中配建,收购存量房源	政府集中新建、“限房价竞地价”交开发商集中新建;“竞配建”交开发商配建;收购市场商品房房源;盘活存量保障房

三、创新住房供应体系，探索人才安居扶持

(一) 海南省人才住房新政

当前，支持创新和吸引人才已经成为各地提升城市竞争力的核心抓手。各类城市纷纷探索住房供给和支持上的政策创新，降低安居成本，吸引人才安居就业。

2018 年 6 月，海南出台《关于引进人才住房保障的指导意见》，以期为海南自由贸易试验区和中国特色自由贸易港建设提供强有力的人才支撑和智力保障。海南人才住房建设实施

① 北京住建委网站:http://www.bjjs.gov.cn/bjjs/xxgk/ztzl/gycqzf/zcfg23/432910/index.shtml.

② 上海市共有产权保障住房管理办法。

③ 广东省住房和城乡建设厅关于《关于推进共有产权住房发展的指导意见(征求意见稿)》。

④ 参考同地段、同品质商品住房确定评估价。一房一价。

“定区域”：重点选在主城区、产业园区等人才就业集中的区域；“定对象”：对确定的引进人才实行分类保障，高端人才提供人才公寓，其他人才发放租赁和购房补贴；采取“限地价、竞房价”方式，降低人才住房建设成本；通过“限转让年限”，遏制投机炒房行为。

海南人才住房保障政策

1. 人才公寓

面向引进的大师级人才、杰出人才、领军人才供应，每人限供一套。面积标准分别为：200 平方米、180 平方米、150 平方米。人才公寓 8 年免收租金，人才全职工作满 5 年由政府无偿赠与 80% 产权，满 8 年无偿赠与 100% 产权。

2. 住房租赁补贴和购房补贴

面向 50 岁以下拔尖人才和其他类高层次人才（急需紧缺的可适当放宽年龄限制），40 岁以下全日制硕士毕业生，35 岁以下全日制本科毕业生和具有中级专业技术职称的人才。

住房租赁补贴累计发放不超过 36 个月，补贴指导标准为每月 5 000 元、3 000 元、2 000 元、1 500元。购房补贴累计发放不超过 3 年，补贴指导标准为每年 6 万元、3.6 万元、2.4 万元、1.8 万元。已领取购房补贴的，不再发放住房租赁补贴。领取购房补贴前，已领取住房租赁补贴的，应扣除已领取的住房租赁补贴。

资料来源：海南省《关于引进人才住房保障的指导意见》

（二）北京市人才住房新政

2018 年 7 月，北京发布《关于优化住房支持政策服务保障人才发展的意见》，提出，以配租公共租赁住房为主，配售共有产权住房、发放人才租房补贴为辅，对符合条件的人才给予住房支持。在支持对象上，提出由各区、园区根据差异化的需求类型自行确定；在保障面积上，提出可根据人才需求适当提高成套公租房面积；并要求共有产权住房内部封闭管理，循环使用。

北京市人才住房保障政策

支持对象由各区拟定。同时要求在本区认定的单位就业或签约达到一定年限，各区认定的行业或单位应符合首都城市战略定位。人才需要以单位名义申请。

1. 公租房

要求在本市无房，或在本市有住房但距离工作单位超过一定距离。

2. 共有产权住房

符合本市共有产权住房申请条件。

购房人取得不动产权证未满5年，因特殊原因确需转让的，由代持机构按规定价格回购。购房人取得不动产权证满5年的，可通过市级交换服务平台面向本区或园区符合购买条件的人才家庭出售。房屋产权性质仍为“共有产权住房”，产权份额比例不变。

3. 人才租房补贴及购房支持

各区人民政府可结合实际制定人才租房补贴标准。

经市级人才主管部门备案引进的非京籍优秀人才及境外个人（含港澳台居民），家庭成员在本市均无住房的，可以购买用于自住的普通商品房，也可申请购买一套共有产权住房。（突破当前的北京非户籍限购政策）

资料来源：北京《关于优化住房支持政策服务保障人才发展的意见》

（三）深圳市人才住房新政

作为改革先锋的深圳，早在2011年、2015年先后出台过两版《深圳市人才安居暂行办法》。2018年8月，深圳市发布《关于深化住房制度改革 加快建立多主体供给多渠道保障租购并举的住房供应与保障体系的意见》，意见提出了未来住房供应的类型和比例，尤其是创新性的首次将政策支持性住房（人才住房和安居型商品房）明确写入供应体系。未来政策支持住房在全部住房供给中的比例将高达40%，成为深圳住房供给体系中的核心组成。加上占比达20%的公租房，深圳未来的住房供给结构将由市场为主转向政府支持和保障为主。而因为这一结构性的变化，深圳方案又被媒体评价为“二次房改”。这一方案最大的亮点，就是通过完善人才安居政策体系，以货币补贴、租售人才住房、免租入住等多种方式，有效解决各类人才的住房困难。

深圳人才安居政策

1. 人才住房（占住房供应总量的20%左右）

对象宽泛：重点面向符合条件的企事业经营管理、专业技术、高技能、社会工作、党政等方面人才供应。包括全日制本科及以上学历、属于符合深圳产业发展需要的技师（国家职业资格二级及以上）、列入深圳市人力资源保障部门发布的紧缺专业人才目录，且与本市用人单位签订聘用合同或服务协议的各类人才等。

有条件供给：购买了市场商品住房（包括在本市拥有任何形式住房）、在本市享受过购房优惠政策、在申请受理日之前一定年限内在本市转让过自有住房等，均不可以申请购买人才住房。封闭流转期间，如另行购买市场商品住房，应当面向其他符合申购条件的对象转让，或由政府按规定回购。

租购灵活：可租可售；探索先租后购、以租抵购制度，工作满一定年限、取得本市户籍且符合相关规定的人才，可申请购买人才住房；符合条件的高层次人才，可以申请在一定年限内免租入住相应面积标准的住房，同时在深全职工作满5年以上、符合条件的可以按优惠政策购买人才住房或者申请获赠住房产权。

限制面积：建筑面积以小于 90 平方米为主

优惠价格：租金、售价分别为届时同地段市场商品住房租金、售价的 60% 左右。对符合条件的高层次人才实行更加优惠的政策。

流转封闭：一定年限内实行封闭流转。封闭流转期间，因另购市场商品住房等法定事由或自身原因需要转让的，应当面向其他符合申购条件的对象转让，或由政府按规定回购。自购房之日起累计在深缴纳社保满 15 年，或者年满 60 周岁且购房满 10 年，符合规定条件的，可以进入市场流转，但要向政府缴纳一定比例的增值收益。

2. 货币补贴

面向符合条件的人才发放人才安居补贴、实施购房贷款贴息。

资料来源：深圳市《关于深化住房制度改革　加快建立多主体供给多渠道保障租购并举的住房供应与保障体系的意见》

可以看到，各地在人才住房的供给上，普遍采用实物保障和货币补贴相结合的方式。在实物保障上，充分体现了租售并举的方式，有专列人才住房类型的，也有统筹使用现有保障性住房的。针对“自住”需求，各地普遍在准入退出机制上考虑了在本地无房、没有购房记录等限制性条件，同时通过封闭管理，遏制配售型住房的牟利空间。可以预见，为了更好地吸引和保障人才安居，人才住房将成为各地住房供给重点创新和突破的方向。

（作者：卢华翔，中国城市规划设计研究院住房与住区所所长，教授级高级城市规划师；高恒，中国城市规划设计研究院住房与住区所城市规划师；张璐，中国城市规划设计研究院住房与住区所高级城市规划师）

2018 年中国城市交通进展

2018 年，随着新型城镇化战略的深入实施，我国城市群交通系统加快布局，区域重大交通基础设施规划建设取得显著进展。城市交通发展进一步聚焦社会和民生重大需求，服务意识、风险防范意识在城市交通规划、建设、管理中得到高度关注，促进了城市交通与城市融合互动发展。共享交通的负面效应开始显现，保障出行安全成为政府市场监管的重点。总体上，区域交通与城市交通仍处于转型发展之中，城市轨道交通规划建设持续推进但审批更加严格，地方停车立法取得突破。政策体系和管理机制持续完善，为构建可持续的综合交通体系建立了良好的发展基础。

一、城市群与区域交通

（一）加快区域交通设施建设

为了进一步增强基础设施对促进城乡和区域协调发展的支撑作用，10 月 11 日国务院办公厅印发了《关于保持基础设施领域补短板力度的指导意见》（国办发〔2018〕101 号），坚持以供给侧改革为主线，进一步完善基础设施和公共服务，推进京津冀、长三角、粤港澳大湾区等地区城际铁路规划建设，加快启动一批国家高速公路网待贯通路段项目和对“一带一路”建设、京津冀协同发展、长江经济带发展、粤港澳大湾区建设等重大战略有重要支撑作用的地方高速公路项目等。在区域交通设施建设中，城际铁路依然是热点之一。2018 年，国家发展改革委先后批复了新建北京至雄安城际铁路调整可研报告、海峡西岸城市群粤东地区城际铁路网规划、广西北部湾经济区城际铁路建设规划（2019—2023 年）、江苏省沿江城市群城际铁路建设规划（2019—2025 年）等（表 1）。

2018 年，京津冀、长三角、粤港澳大湾区重大交通基础设施建设取得显著进展。北京至雄安城际铁路和雄安站开工建设，雄安站规划引入北京至商丘高铁、京雄城际、津雄城际等 5 条线路，预计 2020 年建成通车。北京大兴国际机场、延崇高速公路、京雄高速公路加快建设，以高铁、城际铁路为骨架的京津冀综合运输网络正快速形成，有力地支撑了京津冀协同发展和雄安新区建设。长三角铁路建设快速推进，商合杭、连淮扬镇、徐宿淮盐、连徐、苏南沿江等高铁正在建设。截至 2018 年年底，长三角高速铁路里程达 4171 千米，连通了上海、江苏、浙江、安徽三省一市的 34 个地级以上城市。港珠澳大桥于 10 月 24 日建成通车，港珠澳大桥集桥、隧、岛为一体，全长 55 千米，是连接中国大陆、香港、澳门的陆路交通“超级工程”。跨越珠江口的深中大桥也正在建设中，全长 24 千米，预计 2024 年建成通车，届时将形成连接珠江口两岸、促进粤港澳大湾区产业协同发展的第二条交通大通道。

表 1　城际铁路规划批复概况表

名称	工程概况
北京至雄安城际铁路	新建正线 92.4 千米，共设 5 座车站。设计速度目标值：350 千米/小时（李营至北京新机场段 250 千米/小时）。规划远景年输送能力：单向 5 000 万人/年
粤东地区城际铁路	远期规划总里程 460 千米，形成“一线两环两射线”为骨架的城际铁路网络。近期规划建设“一线一环一射线”，即汕尾—汕头—饶平、汕头—潮州东—潮汕—潮汕机场—汕头、潮汕机场—揭阳南城际铁路，总里程 320 千米
广西北部湾经济区城际铁路	构建覆盖广西北部湾经济区的铁路客运网络，南宁至北部湾经济区节点城市 1 小时左右到达，基本覆盖区域 50 万人口城市。近期规划建设南宁—横县—玉林、南宁—崇左城际铁路，总里程 325 千米
江苏省沿江城市群城际铁路	规划形成区域城际铁路主骨架，以及南京都市圈和苏锡常都市圈城际铁路网，基本实现对 20 万人口以上城市的覆盖。近期规划建设南京至淮安、南京至宣城等城际铁路项目，总里程约 1 063 千米，其中江苏段 980 千米，安徽段 83 千米

（注：根据国家发展改革委相关批复文件整理）

近年来，为了完善区域综合交通运输体系，促进产业升级，培育新的经济增长点，通用机场规划建设加快，但也存在功能定位模糊、规划布局不合理等问题。8 月 14 日，为科学有序推进通用机场规划建设，国家发展改革委、民航局印发了《关于促进通用机场有序发展的意见》（发改基础〔2018〕1164 号）。要求科学编制通用机场布局规划，加强与全国民用运输机场布局规划衔接，按照安全、经济、实用、绿色的原则，突出重点、量力而行，分类分级规划布局通用机场。优先在中西部地区推进以通用航空短途运输为主的通用机场建设。在京津冀、长三角、珠三角等城镇化和市场需求较高的地区布局综合性通用机场，疏解枢纽机场非核心业务，提供个性化、高效率的出行服务，并鼓励以社会公共服务为主的通用机场建设。

（二）完善城市群交通系统布局

雄安新区是党中央深入推进京津冀协同发展的重大决策部署。4 月 14 日，中共中央、国务院批复了《河北雄安新区规划纲要》，12 月 25 日，国务院批复了《河北雄安新区总体规划（2018—2035 年）》（国函〔2018〕159 号），要求雄安新区加强同北京、天津、石家庄、保定等城市的融合发展，按照网络化布局、智能化管理、一体化服务的要求，构建现代综合交通体系，综合布局各类城市交通设施。加快建立连接雄安新区与京津及周边其他城市、北京新机场之间的轨道和公路交通网络，完善雄安新区与外部连通的高速公路、干线公路网，实现多种交通方式顺畅换乘和无缝衔接，打造便捷、安全、绿色、智能的交通系统。

2018 年，关中平原城市群、呼包鄂榆城市群、兰州—西宁城市群等新一批区域发展规划先后获得批复，为城市群综合交通网络布局和重大交通基础设施建设明确了方向（表2）。关中平原城市群发展规划提出了构建“四纵四横”的对外运输大通道，加快城际铁路、省级高速公路、国省干线建设，强化一体衔接的综合交通枢纽功能，提升综合运输服务能力和水平等规划举措。呼包鄂榆城市群发展规划在提升城市群内部联通水平、畅通对外陆路交通通道、打造综合航空运输体系、加快综合交通枢纽建设等方面部署了交通基础设施重点项目。兰州—西宁城市群发展规划重点强化了城市群内综合运输网络和综合交通枢纽建设，推进不同运输方式间的客票一体联程和不同城市间的一卡互通、公共交通一卡互通，提升交通运输服务水平。

表2 关中平原、呼包鄂榆、兰州—西宁三城市群交通基础设施重点项目

	关中平原城市群
铁路	高速铁路。建设西安—银川、西安—延安—包头、西安—安康—重庆、西安—武汉等高速铁路。 普速铁路干线。建设蒙西至华中地区铁路煤运通道，规划宝鸡至中卫铁路扩能、西安至平凉铁路扩能、平凉—庆阳—黄陵、天水—哈达铺、西安枢纽货运第二双线等。 城际铁路。建设西安北—咸阳机场、阎良—咸阳机场、西安—韩城、西安—法门寺等城际铁路。 轨道交通。完善西安地铁线网，适时启动新一轮城市轨道交通建设规划研究。
公路	国家高速公路。建设坪坎—汉中、宝鸡—坪坎、湫坡头(陕甘界)—旬邑、陕甘界—陇县、旬邑—凤翔、合阳—铜川、蒲城—黄龙、青兰高速(长治—临汾)，以及京昆等国家高速公路交通繁忙路段扩容改造。 地方高速公路。建设一批对促进区域互联互通具有重要意义的地方高速公路。
民航	运输机场。实施西安咸阳国际机场三期扩建工程，增建跑道，扩建航站楼和站坪，完善配套服务设施，主动引入公路、高速铁路、城铁、地铁等交通方式；推进宝鸡、天水、平凉等支线机场项目前期工作，力争形成“干支结合”的机场体系。 通用机场。加快建设一批通用机场和低空飞行服务站等配套设施，发展低空旅游、飞行培训等通航业务，培育2~3家骨干通用航空企业。
客货运枢纽	西安综合客运枢纽。建设西安咸阳国际机场东航站楼、西安火车站、西安文景路、西安南站(三星)等综合客运枢纽，西安城西、西安国际港务区、西安航天基地、蓝田、凤翔等一级客运枢纽，周至城东、临潼等二级客运枢纽。规划建设西安东站、新西安南站综合客运枢纽。 西安综合货运枢纽。建设西咸快递分拨中心、西安国际港务区公路港、西咸空港等综合货运枢纽，西安草滩、西安泾河等一级枢纽站。 区域综合交通枢纽。积极建设宝鸡眉县、渭南、运城、临汾、天水、平凉等一批区域性交通枢纽。
“交通+”新设施	研究启动依托太白高速连接线、沿黄公路等项目的交通旅游融合发展示范工程、秦岭和渭北旅游轨道示范工程、动货物流工程、无人机物流工程、信息智能化工程等。
	呼包鄂榆城市群
铁路	建设呼和浩特—准格尔—鄂尔多斯等铁路和准格尔—朔州、蒙西—华中等大能力货运铁路，以及神木—瓦塘等普通铁路；规划建设新上海庙—定边铁路；扩能改造包头—白云鄂博、大同—准格尔等铁路。
公路	规划建设保德—榆林、呼和浩特—朔州、赛罕塔拉—二连浩特等高速公路；加快推进包茂高速扩建。
航空	规划建设府谷、定边等支线机场和一批通用机场。
综合交通枢纽	在呼和浩特、包头、鄂尔多斯、榆林、绥德、神木、定边等市(县)建设一批客运枢纽、物流园区、集装箱中转站、物流公铁联运中心等。
	兰州—西宁城市群
铁路	稳妥推进兰州—中卫、西宁—成都、兰州—合作、兰州—张掖铁路三四线等铁路建设，规划研究西宁—玉树—昌都、定西—平凉、环县—海源、红会—同心铁路。
公路	有序推进G6、G30等国家高速公路繁忙路段扩容改造，G1816乌玛高速公路兰州新区—兰州段(中通道)和景泰—中川机场段、G75兰海高速公路渭源—武都段、G0612东延至乐都、G0611同仁—塞尔龙等国家高速公路新建项目。

续表

兰州—西宁城市群	
枢纽	机场枢纽。重点推进兰州中川国际机场三期改扩建工程、西宁机场三期扩建工程,新建临夏、定西、青海湖等支线机场以及一批通用机场。 铁路枢纽。新建曹家堡综合交通枢纽,完善兰州站、兰州西站、西宁站、西宁(货)区段站。 公路枢纽。兰州、西宁、海东等地新建一批客运站和综合客运枢纽。

(摘自:关中平原城市群发展规划、呼包鄂榆城市群发展规划、兰州—西宁城市群发展规划)

(三)推动高铁站周边区域开发

高铁站是区域与城市衔接的重要节点,随着我国高铁的快速发展,高铁站远离城市中心区、周边区域综合配套设施不完善、与城市生活和产业融合不紧密等问题也越来越凸显。在城市群发展的大背景下,如何依托高铁站推进周边区域开发建设并与城市相融合,已经成为城市与区域协同发展、优化城市空间结构、高铁建设与城市发展良性互动的不可回避的重大问题。4 月 24 日,国家发展改革委、自然资源部、住房城乡建设部、中铁总公司印发了《关于推进高铁站周边区域合理开发建设的指导意见》(发改基础〔2018〕514 号),要求着力解决个别地方高铁车站周边开发建设初期规模过大、功能定位偏高、发展模式较单一、对人口和产业吸引力不够等突出问题。

意见提出,要坚持规划引领,结合城市功能提升和结构布局优化做好车站周边综合开发,合理确定车站周边开发建设的功能定位、规模和边界,做好规划预留和控制,按照规划规范有序推进开发建设。深入研究论证高铁车站与城市发展衔接问题,新建铁路选线应尽量减少对城市的分割,新建车站选址尽可能在中心城区或靠近城市建成区,确保人民群众乘坐高铁出行便利。高铁车站周边开发建设要坚决防控单纯房地产化倾向,突出产城融合、站城一体,与城市建成区合理分工,在城市功能布局、综合交通运输体系建设、基础设施共建共享等方面同步规划、协调推进,加强新建高铁车站城市公共交通配套线路和换乘设施建设。在开发建设时序方面,意见也明确提出要量力而行,尽力而为,严禁借高铁车站周边开发建设名义盲目搞城市扩张。中小城市不宜过高预估高铁带动作用,避免照搬照抄大城市开发经验,硬造特色、盲目造城。在创新开发建设体制机制方面,应进一步理顺政府与市场关系,充分发挥市场对资源配置的决定性作用,理清权责关系,完善综合开发、运营管理及收益分配机制,形成促进发展的多种合力。

二、城市交通与出行服务

(一)发展低碳环保交通工具

近年来,在供给侧结构性改革的大背景下,城市交通转型发展趋势明显,低碳交通、绿色出行成为城市交通发展的主导方向。2018 年,国家颁布了多项政策和行动计划,加快推广新能源交通工具。

在国务院发布的《打赢蓝天保卫战三年行动计划》（国发〔2018〕22号）中，为大幅减少主要大气污染物排放总量、明显改善环境空气质量、明显增强人民的蓝天幸福感，提出了发展绿色交通体系，并部署了相应的行动计划。主要包括：推广新能源汽车，加快推进城市建成区新增和更新的公交、环卫、邮政、出租、通勤、轻型物流配送车辆使用新能源或清洁能源汽车，重点区域使用比例达到80%，2020年年底前重点区域的直辖市、省会城市、计划单列市建成区公交车全部更换为新能源汽车。在物流园、产业园、工业园、大型商业购物中心、农贸批发市场等物流集散地建设集中式充电桩和快速充电桩，为承担物流配送的新能源车辆在城市通行提供便利。同时，大力淘汰老旧车辆，推广使用达到国六排放标准的燃气车辆，对符合条件的新能源汽车免征车辆购置税。要求2020年年底前，京津冀及周边地区、汾渭平原淘汰国三及以下排放标准营运中型和重型柴油货车100万辆以上。2019年7月1日起，重点区域、珠三角地区、成渝地区提前实施国六排放标准。

国务院办公厅印发的《完善促进消费体制机制实施方案（2018—2020年）》（国办发〔2018〕93号），也把促进汽车消费优化升级作为促进消费的重要举措，继续实施新能源汽车车辆购置税优惠政策，完善新能源汽车积分管理制度，落实好乘用车企业平均燃料消耗量与新能源汽车积分并行管理办法，研究建立碳配额交易制度。

新能源汽车充电设施建设落地难、运行效率低等仍是制约新能源汽车发展的短板。为加快推进充电基础设施规划建设，全面提升新能源汽车充电保障能力，11月9日，国家发展改革委、国家能源局、工信部、财政部印发了《提升新能源汽车充电保障能力行动计划》（发改能源〔2018〕1698号），力争用3年时间，通过重点任务的实施，进一步优化充电基础设施发展环境和产业格局。在优化充电设施规划布局重点任务中，提出要及时滚动编制纳入城乡整体规划的充电设施建设专项规划，细化充电基础设施的用地政策，保证公交车、出租车、物流车、分时租赁车、共享汽车等运营类新能源汽车充电设施的建设用地，以及有明确需求的其他新能源车辆的充电专用场地。针对老旧、电力增容困难且有充电需求的居民区，提出要在周边合理范围内科学规划公共充电设施建设用地。进一步落实简化规划审批要求，重点加快居民自有停车库、停车位建桩，企事业单位既有停车位建桩，以及运营商在城市公共停车场建桩的推进速度。行动计划对供电保障也提出了明确的要求，如针对老旧居民区电力容量不够等问题，要引导电动汽车低谷充电，挖掘现有电网设备利用潜力，千方百计满足“一车一桩”接电需求。

（二）加强城市轨道交通建设管理

近年来，我国城市轨道交通规划建设速度加快，不少城市把城市轨道交通建设作为引导城市空间结构优化、缓解城市交通拥堵的重要对策加以实施，取得了明显的成效。但也有部分城市存在需求不足、急于建设、过度超前等问题，加大了地方债务负担和社会经济风险。为此，国务院办公厅于6月28日印发了《关于进一步加强城市轨道交通规划建设管理的意见》（国办发〔2018〕52号），这是继《国务院办公厅关于加强城市快速轨道交通建设管理的通知》（国办发〔2003〕81 号）印发以来，再一次对城市轨道交通规划建设进行调整。意见强化了严控地方政府债务风险的要求，明确了“量力而行，有序推进”“因地制宜，经济适用”“衔接协调，集约高效”“严控风险，持续发展”的原则，要求确保城市轨道交通发展规模与实际需求相匹配、建设节奏与支撑能力相适应。进一步严格了建设申报条件，规定“地铁主要服务于城市中心城区和城市总体规划确定的重点地区，申报建设地铁的城市一般公共财政预算收入应在 300 亿元以上，地区生产总值在 3 000 亿元以上，市区常住人口在 300 万人以上。引导轻轨有序发展，申报建设轻轨的城市一般公共财政预算收入应在 150 亿元以上，地区生产总值在1 500亿元以上，市区常住人口在 150 万人以上。拟建地铁、轻轨线路初期客运强度分别不低于每日每公里 0.7 万人次、0.4 万人次，远期客流规模分别达到单向高峰小时 3 万人次以上、1 万人次以上”。同时，强化了建设规划的导向和约束作用，针对各城市建设中经常修改调整工程建设项目的现象，意见规定“已经国家批准的城市轨道交通建设规划应严格执行，原则上不得变更，规划实施期限不得随意压缩。在规划实施过程中，因城市规划、工程条件、交通枢纽布局变化等因素影响，城市轨道交通线路功能定位、基本走向、系统制式等发生重大变化的，或线路里程、地下线路长度、直接工程投资（扣除物价上涨因素）等较建设规划增幅超过 20% 的，应按相关规定履行建设规划调整程序”。意见的出台，进一步优化完善了我国城市轨道交通规划建设的管理机制。

2018 年，国家发展改革委先后批复了苏州市城市轨道交通第三期建设规划（2018—2023 年）、重庆市城市轨道交通第三期建设规划（2018—2023 年）、杭州市城市轨道交通第三期建设规划（2017—2022 年）调整、济南市城市轨道交通第一期建设规划（2015—2019 年）调整、长春市城市轨道交通第三期建设规划（2019—2024 年）、武汉市城市轨道交通第四期建设规划（2019—2024 年）、上海市城市轨道交通第三期建设规划（2018—2023 年），为上述城市未来几年的城市轨道交通建设奠定了规划基础（表 3）。

表 3　2018 年城市轨道交通建设规划概况

城　市	建设项目
苏州市城市轨道交通第三期建设规划（2018—2023 年）	6 号线、7 号线、8 号线、S1 线
重庆市城市轨道交通第三期建设规划（2018—2023 年）	新增 4 号线二期、5 号线北延伸和 5A 线，优化调整 4 号线一期、6 号线支线二期、10 号线 3
杭州市城市轨道交通第三期建设规划（2017—2022 年）调整	3 号线一期工程主线调整为吴山前村站至星桥路站，5 号线二期工程调整为中央公园站至老余杭站，新增机场轨道快线，其余项目按原批复执行
济南市城市轨道交通第一期建设规划（2015—2019 年）调整	R2 线一期工程调整为王府庄站至彭家庄站，其余项目按原批复执行
长春市城市轨道交通第三期建设规划（2019—2024 年）	2 号线东延、3 号线南延、4 号线南延、5 号线一期、6 号线、7 号线一期、空港线一期工程
武汉市城市轨道交通第四期建设规划（2019—2024 年）	12 号线、6 号线二期、8 号线三期、11 号线三期（武昌段首开段、新汉阳火车站段和葛店段）、7 号线北延线、16 号线、19 号线、新港线
上海市城市轨道交通第三期建设规划（2018—2023 年）	19 号线、20 号线一期、21 号线一期、23 号线一期、13 号线西延伸线、1 号线西延伸线及机场联络线、嘉闵线、崇明线

（注：根据国家发展改革委相关批复文件整理）

随着我国城市轨道交通运营里程迅速增加、线网规模不断扩大，城市轨道交通安全运行压力风险也随之增大。为此，3 月 7 日，国务院办公厅印发了《关于保障城市轨道交通安全运行的意见》（国办发〔2018〕13 号），要求以切实保障城市轨道交通安全运行为目标，完善体制机制，健全法规标准，创新管理制度，强化技术支撑，夯实安全基础，提升服务品质，增强安全防范治理能力。在健全管理体制机制方面，界定了国家相关部委、省人民政府的职责，并按照属地管理原则明确了城市人民政府对辖区内城市轨道交通安全运行负总责。同时，在完善法规标准体系、有序统筹规划建设运营、加强运营安全管理、强化公共安全防范、提升应急处置能力等方面，提出了全面系统的对策和措施。

2018 年，城市轨道交通运行管理法规进一步完善，交通运输部发布了《城市轨道交通运营管理规定》（交通运输部令 2018 年第 8 号），明确了城市轨道交通试运行、初期运营、正式运营等建设与运营交接界面的工作内容和办理程序，界定了相关部门和单位的工作职责和义务。根据国家部门管理职责调整，住房城乡建设部废止了 2005 年发布的《城市轨道交通运营管理办法》（建设部令第 140 号）。

（三）完善停车管理法规

停车难依然是城市面临的突出问题。积极推动停车设施建设作为释放内需潜力、保障和改善民生的重要举措，在《完善促进消费体制机制实施方案（2018—2020 年）》（国办发〔2018〕93 号）中得到进一步落实，方案提出要综合运用发行城市停车场建设专项债券、调整完善车辆购置税分配政策等措施，加大停车设施建设资金支持力度。

2018 年，加强停车设施建设和管理被纳入众多城市的政府工作任务和计划。停车法规建设取得较大进展，沈阳等城市将停车管理条例纳入立法计划，北京、广州先后出台了停车管理条例。

3 月 30 日，北京市人大常委会发布了《北京市机动车停车条例》（以下简称《停车条例》），于 5 月 1 日起实施。《停车条例》规定，机动车停车坚持有偿使用、共享利用、严格执法、社会共治，将停车纳入城市综合交通体系，综合运用法律、经济、行政、科技等方法，严格控制首都功能核心区、北京城市副中心机动车保有量。在停车泊位供给方面，实行分类分区定位、差别供给，适度满足居住停车需求，从严控制出行停车需求。新增停车泊位以配套建设为主，临时设置、独立建设、驻车换乘建设等方式为补充。《停车条例》规定了机动车停车设施专项规划的编制主体、编制内容和实施管理等，确立了配建停车泊位的动态调整机制及建设要求，明确了各类停车设施的属性、建设和管理主体。要求市交通行政主管部门建立停车综合管理服务系统，对停车泊位进行统一编码管理。《停车条例》明确了不同停车设施的定价要求，驻车换乘停车设施和道路停车实行政府定价，道路停车收费应当按照中心城区高于外围区域、重点区域高于非重点区域、拥堵时段高于空闲时段的原则确定，并根据高于周边非道路停车收费价格的原则动态调节。其他停车设施实行市场调节价，但调整居住小区内业主共有的停车泊位的收费价格时，应当经专有部分占建筑物总面积过半数的业主且占总人数过半数的业主同意。针对居住区停车，《停车条例》要求逐步建立居住停车区域认证机制，停车人在划定的居住停车范围内停车，可以按照居住停车价格付费。另外，《停车条例》也规定了停车经营、违法停放等方面的内容。

4 月 20 日，广州市人大常委会发布了《广州市停车场条例》（以下简称《停车场条例》），并于 10 月 1 日起实施。《停车场条例》适用于公共停车场、专用停车场、临时停车场和城市道路临时泊位，对市相关部门的管理职责做出了明确的界定，要求市交通行政主管部门组织编制停车场专项规划，建立全市统一的停车信息管理系统。《停车场条例》规定了停放服务收费分别实行市场调节价、政府指导价或者政府定价管理，按照城市中心区域高于外围区域、重点区域高于非重点区域、拥堵时段高于空闲时段的原则，对实行政府指导价、政府定价管理的停车场制定差别化的收费标准，对城市道路临时泊位制定累进式加价的阶梯式收费标准。《停车场条例》明确了支持和鼓励社会力量投资建设公共停车场的方式，以及配建停车位指标的调整程序和要求，鼓励单位或者个人利用待建土地、存量建设用地等场所设置临时停车场。另外，《停车场条例》在停车设施建设标准、运营管理等方面也给出了具体的要求。

（四）改善弱势群体出行服务

为弱势群体特别是老年人、残疾人出行提供方便，是推进基本公共服务均等化的重要任务。1 月 8 日，交通运输部、住房城乡建设部等七部门联合印发《关于进一步加强和改善老年人残疾人出行服务的实施意见》，致力于加快无障碍交通基础设施建设和改造，鼓励推广应用无障碍出行新技术、新设备，加强和改善老年人、残疾人出行服务，保障老年人、残疾人出行权益。意见要求，到 2020 年，新建或改扩建的铁路客运站、城市轨道交通车站等交通场站无障碍设施实现全覆盖，鼓励具备条件的城市新增公交车辆优先选择低地板公交车，500 万人口以上城市新增公交车辆全部实现低地板化。到 2035 年，基本建成覆盖全面、无缝衔接、安全舒适的无障碍出行服务体系。为了实现上述发展目标，意见在加快无障碍交通基础设施建设和改造、提升出行服务品质、优化出行政策体系等方面做出了系统性部署。要求创新服务模式，保障安全出行。具备条件的地区，要在交通枢纽等人流密集场所为老年人、残疾人设立优先无障碍购票窗口、专用等候区域和绿色通道，在交通枢纽和交通工具上提供便于老年和残疾乘客识别的语音报站和电子报站服务，完善站场、枢纽、车辆设施的盲文标志标识配置、残疾人通讯系统、语音导航和导盲系统建设，为老年人、残疾人提供多样化、便利化的无障碍出行信息服务。有条件的地区开行服务老年人、残疾人的康复巴士。建立完善无障碍交通设施安全检查制度，及时发现安全隐患，妥善处理，为老年人、残疾人提供安全可靠的无障碍出行服务。

（五）健全城市快递物流体系

近年来，城市快递物流业迅速发展，成为城市社会活动的重要组成部分。2018 年，为了推动相关设施建设，加强监督管理，国家及相关部门出台了多项政策文件，着力营造促进和规范城市快递、城市物流健康发展的政策环境及管理机制。

3月2日，《快递暂行条例》（国务院令第697号）发布，并于2018年5月1日起实施。条例要求县级以上地方人民政府应将快递业发展纳入本级国民经济和社会发展规划，在城乡规划和土地利用总体规划中统筹考虑快件大型集散、分拣等基础设施用地的需要。国家引导和推动快递业与铁路、公路、水路、民航等行业的标准对接，支持在大型车站、码头、机场等交通枢纽配套建设快件运输通道和接驳场所，对快递服务车辆加强统一编号和标识管理。10月22日，交通运输部发布《快递业务经营许可管理办法》（部长令2018年第23号），完善了快递业务市场的管理制度。

《关于推进电子商务与快递物流协同发展的意见》（国办发〔2018〕1号）明确要求强化制度创新和规划引领，健全完善促进快递物流发展的政策环境和基础设施。意见界定了智能快件箱、快递末端综合服务场所的公共属性，要求为专业化、公共化、平台化、集约化的快递末端网点提供用地保障等配套政策，将智能快件箱、快递末端综合服务场所纳入公共服务设施相关规划。在不改变用地主体、规划条件的前提下，利用存量房产和土地资源建设电子商务快递物流项目的，可在5年内保持土地原用途和权利类型不变。要求完善城市配送车辆通行管理政策，合理确定通行区域和时段，对快递服务车辆等城市配送车辆给予通行便利，鼓励快递物流领域加快推广使用新能源汽车和满足更高排放标准的燃油汽车。将推广智能快件箱纳入便民服务、民生工程等项目，加快社区、高等院校、商务中心、地铁站周边等末端节点布局。

9月17日，国务院办公厅印发《推进运输结构调整三年行动计划（2018—2020年）》（国办发〔2018〕91号），推进城市绿色货运配送示范工程，引导特大城市群和区域中心城市规划建设绿色货运配送网络，完善干支衔接型物流园区（货运枢纽）和城市配送网络节点及配送车辆停靠装卸配套设施建设。鼓励邮政快递企业、城市配送企业创新统一配送、集中配送、共同配送、夜间配送等集约化运输组织模式。提出充分发挥铁路既有站场资源优势，打造“轨道+仓储配送”的铁路城市物流配送新模式。到2020年，在全国建成100个左右的城市绿色货运配送示范项目，城市建成区新增、更新轻型物流配送车辆中新能源车辆和达到国六排放标准清洁能源车辆的比例超过50%，重点区域达到80%，在有条件的地区建立新能源城市配送车辆运营补贴机制，降低使用成本。交通运输部办公厅、公安部办公厅、商务部办公厅联合发布通知，公布了天津、石家庄、邯郸、衡水、鄂尔多斯、苏州、厦门、青岛、许昌、安阳、襄阳、十堰、长沙、广州、深圳、成都、泸州、铜仁、兰州、银川、太原、大同22个城市为绿色货运配送示范工程创建城市，要求上述城市完善示范工程创建实施方案、推进落实示范工程工作任务、加大示范工程支持力度、强化示范工程建设绩效考核。

三、共享交通与交通安全

（一）建立共享交通监管机制

2018年，共享单车、网约车、汽车共享等共享交通服务质量下降、安全隐患增多等问题凸显，资本驱动的共享交通市场重组加快，用户押金退回难成为社会的焦点。如何加强共享交通市场监管、强化运营企业的主体责任、规范经营服务行为，成为共享交通能否持续健康发展的重大问题。

针对共享经济发展的突出问题，国家发展改革委办公厅、中央网信办秘书局、工信部办公厅印发《关于做好引导和规范共享经济健康良性发展有关工作的通知》（发改办高技〔2018〕586号），要求严格压实平台企业主体责任，切实保证消费者人身和财产安全，加强消费者权益保护。审慎出台新的市场准入政策，依法依规落实相关领域的资质准入要求，严肃处理违法违规经营行为。对于使用公共资源的共享经济业态，统筹考虑市场需求、城市承载能力等因素，科学设定总量规模。严厉打击以“发展共享经济”为幌子，从事非法集资、窃取用户隐私、危害国家安全等违法犯罪行为。通知中的各项要求，同样也是共享交通普遍存在并亟待解决的突出问题。

共享交通信息和规范运营成为主管部门市场监管的重点。交通运输部办公厅印发《网络预约出租汽车监管信息交互平台运行管理办法》，要求各城市交通运输主管部门应通过网约车监管信息交互平台及时录入网约车平台公司、车辆、驾驶员相关许可信息，将运政信息系统与网约车监管信息交互平台对接，实时传输更新相关许可信息。在交通运输部办公厅、公安部办公厅印发的《关于切实做好出租汽车驾驶员背景核查与监管等有关工作的通知》中，也要求各地出租汽车行政主管部门将持证出租汽车驾驶员信息提供同级公安机关，推动出租汽车驾驶员有关信息系统与公安机关人口信息、车辆驾驶人违法记录信息、暴力犯罪信息实现联通共享，加强事中事后监管，保障乘客出行安全和合法权益。

交通运输部办公厅、中央网信办秘书局、工信部办公厅、公安部办公厅、中国人民银行办公厅、国家税务总局办公厅、国家市场监督管理总局办公厅联合印发《关于加强网络预约出租汽车行业事中事后联合监管有关工作的通知》，要求各级交通运输、网信、通信、公安、人民银行、税务、工商和市场监管等部门建立健全联合监管工作机制，密切协调配合，强化信息数据共享，加强对网约车平台公司有关经营行为的监管。并明晰了监管处置流程和应急处置机制。

（二）建设交通诚信体系

2018年，铁路、民航都出了“霸座”的现象，强行阻止列车关门的事件也时有发生，引发了全社会的热议和抨击。为了防范这类事件再次发生，国家开始重视交通诚信体系建设，并将各种失信行为纳入其中，构建“一处失信、处处受限”的信用惩戒大格局。

8月8日，国家发展改革委办公厅、交通运输部办公厅、公安部办公厅印发《关于开展交通出行领域严重失信行为专项治理工作的通知》（发改办运行〔2018〕958号），要求加大对交通领域各种失信行为的治理力度，开展失信专项治理，对存量失信行为进行整治，督促具有严重失信行为的主体完成信用修复。深入推进交通出行领域信用体系建设，强化信用监管，进一步引导规范客运服务提供者和出行者的行为，营造诚信经营、优质服务的市场环境，增强文明出行的意识，提高全社会的诚信意识和信用水平。交通运输部印发《出租汽车服务质量信誉考核办法》，分别对巡游出租车、网约出租车制定了相应的考核办法，进一步完善了出租汽车信用管理体系。

国家发展改革委陆续印发了《关于在一定期限内适当限制特定严重失信人乘坐火车推动社会信用体系建设的意见》（发改财金〔2018〕384号）、《关于在一定期限内适当限制特定严重失信人乘坐民用航空器推动社会信用体系建设的意见》（发改财金〔2018〕385号）和《关于落实在一定期限内适当限制特定严重失信人乘坐火车、民用航空器有关工作的通知》（发改办财金〔2018〕794号），要求将交通领域和其他领域的严重失信人纳入全国信用信息共享平台，并在一定周期内限制其乘坐火车和飞机。2018年我国新增限制乘坐火车、飞机的严重失信人6 908余人，其中交通失信人占98.14%[①]。

（三）强化交通出行安全保障

建立安全、方便的交通环境是现代化城市管理的重要内容。中共中央办公厅、国务院办公厅在《关于推进城市安全发展的意见》中明确提出，全面提高城市安全保障水平，有效防范和坚决遏制重特大安全事故发生，为人民群众营造安居乐业、幸福安康的生产生活环境。在城市交通方面，强调要加强城市交通等基础设施建设、运营过程中的安全监督管理，加快推进城区铁路平交道口立交化改造，加快消除人员密集区域铁路平交道口。加强城市交通基础设施建设，优化城市路网和交通组织，科学规范设置道路交通安全设施，完善行人过街安全设施。加强城市隧道、桥梁、易积水路段等道路交通安全隐患点段排查治理，保障道路安全通行条件。建立道路交通等部门公共数据资源开放共享机制，加快实现城市安全管理的系统化、智能化。

近年来，智能网联汽车等技术发展迅速，北京、上海等城市陆续启动了智能汽车测试区建设，为智能汽车和相关技术测试验证提供开放的道路空间。在开放道路空间开展技术验证和测试，存在着严重的交通隐患和管理难点。为了规范智能网联汽车道路测试管理，4月3日，工信部、公安部、交通运输部印发了《智能网联汽车道路测试管理规范（试行）》，界定了测试主体、测试驾驶人及测试车辆，明确了测试申请及审核程序，规定了测试管理相关要求，明晰了交通违法责任和事故处理等事项，给出了智能网联汽车自动驾驶功能检测项目。规范的出台，对保障道路交通安全、约束企业任意上路测试行为具有重要的指导意义。

2018年，郑州、温州滴滴顺风车司机杀人案件以及重庆万州“10·28”城市公交车坠江事件受到社会广泛关注，防范出行安全隐患成为政府行业监管的重中之重。9月10日，交通运输部办公厅、公安部办公厅印发《关于进一步加强网络预约出租汽车和私人小客车合乘安全管理的紧急通知》，要求各地对从事或申请从事私人小客车合乘服务的驾驶员一律进行背景核查，对现有网约车和私人小客车合乘服务的驾驶员进行一次全面清理。严格督促企业落实安全生产和维稳主体责任，不得向未经背景核查的驾驶员派单。限制顺风车接单数量，防止以合乘名义从事非法网约车经营服务。严厉打击非法营运行为，加大对平台公司等

① 数据来源：2018年失信黑名单年度分析报告，国家公共信用信息中心。

企业的处罚力度。11 月 9 日，交通运输部办公厅印发《关于进一步加强城市公共汽车和电车运行安全保障工作的通知》，针对各地发生多起乘客侵扰驾驶员驾驶行为，要求加强城市公共汽电车驾驶员安全意识和应急处置能力培训，完善城市公共汽电车驾驶区域安全防护隔离设施，严格防范和正确处置侵扰城市公共汽电车运行安全的违法违规行为。

交通出行安全与人民群众的生命财产安全息息相关，2018 年发生的出行安全事件，给我们敲响了警钟。虽然国家在加强政府监管、规范企业运行、加大违法惩治力度等方面完善了政策、法规和保障措施，但要形成全社会群防群治的良好氛围和防范体系，还任重而道远。

（作者：马林，住房和城乡建设部城市交通工程技术中心副主任，教授级高级工程师）

2018年城市市政基础设施进展

城市市政基础设施是城市的骨架，是新型城镇化的物质基础，也是城市社会经济发展、人居环境改善、公共服务提升和城市安全运转的基本保障。截至2017年年底，全国共有661个城市，其中直辖市4个，地级及以上城市294个，县级城市363个。全国城区人口4.1亿人，城区暂住人口0.85亿人，建成区面积5.6万平方公里，分别比2016年增长1.7%、10.1%、3.4%。2017年，全国城市市政基础设施完成固定资产投资19 328亿元，比2016年增加10.1%。城市市政基础设施固定资产投资占同期全社会固定资产投资比重为3.01%，占同期国内生产总值的比重为2.34%，分别比2016年增加0.13个百分点、减少0.01个百分点。

为促进城市市政基础设施高质量发展，更好地推动《全国城市市政基础设施建设“十三五”规划》的实施，2018年5月，住房城乡建设部、国家发展改革委员会联合开展了《全国城市市政基础设施建设“十三五”规划》实施情况中期评估，重点对规划指标的完成情况、规划任务和重点工程的实施情况、保障措施的落实情况进行评估，采用城市和县城自查、省级评估、综合评估的方式进行。

2018年10月，国务院办公厅发布《关于保持基础设施领域补短板力度的指导意见》（国办发〔2018〕101号），指出要围绕全面建成小康社会目标和高质量发展要求，坚持既不过度依赖投资也不能不要投资、防止大起大落的原则，聚焦关键领域和薄弱环节，保持基础设施领域补短板力度，进一步完善基础设施和公共服务，提升基础设施供给质量。

一、城市供水与节水

2017年年末，城市供水综合生产能力达到3.05亿立方米/日，比上年增长0.5%，供水管道长度79.7万公里，比上年增长5.4%。全年供水总量593.8亿立方米，比上年增加2.3%，其中生产运营用水160.7亿立方米，公共服务用水84.9亿立方米，居民家庭用水229.3亿立方米，其他用水26.7亿立方米。

生活饮用水卫生标准是衡量饮用水质量的主要标尺，是供水设施规划、建设、运营、管理的重要依据。2018年3月21日，国家卫生计生委联合住房城乡建设部、环境保护部等多部门组织实施《生活饮用水卫生标准》修订工作并举行了第一次全体会议，正式启动标准修订工作。

节水已日益成为人们的自觉行动，并带动生产生活方式向节约、绿色方向转变。我国城市节约用水量大幅提升，2017 年，全国城市年度节约用水量约为 65 亿立方米，较 2012 年增加 62%，约占年度城市供水总量的 11%。截至 2018 年，全国已有 78 个城市创建成为国家节水型城市，各地还创建了一批节水型小区、节水型企业和单位。住房和城乡建设部等部门还利用一年一度的全国城市节约用水宣传周，组织开展了不同主题的宣传活动，宣传节水优先理念和意识。2018 年 5 月 13 日至 5 月 19 日是第 27 个全国城市节约用水宣传周，主题是“实施国家节水行动，让节水成为习惯”。13 日上午，全国近 50 座城市同步开启 2018 年城市节约用水宣传周活动。（图 1）

图 1　安徽阜阳开展城市节水宣传

（翰墨　摄）

2018 年 2 月 13，住房城乡建设部、国家发展改革委联合印发新修订的《国家节水型城市申报与考核办法》和《国家节水型城市考核标准》（建城〔2018〕25 号），进一步规范了国家节水型城市申报与考核管理工作。

二、城市燃气与供热

2017 年，人工煤气供气总量 27.1 亿立方米，天然气供气总量 1 263.8 亿立方米，液化石油气供气总量 9 998.8.8 万吨，分别比上年减少 36.7%、增长 7.9%、减少 7.4%。人工煤气供气管道长度 1.2 万公里，天然气供气管道长度 62.3 万公里，液化石油气供气管道长度 0.6 万公里，分别比上年减少 36.7%、增长 13.1%、减少 28.9%。用气人口 4.73 亿人，燃气普及率 96.3%，比上年增加 0.51 个百分点。2017 年年末，城市供热能力（蒸汽）9.8 万吨/小时，比上年增加 26.6%，供热能力（热水）64.7 兆瓦，比上年增长 31.3%，供热管道27.6万公里，比上年增长29.4%，集中供热面积83.1亿平方米，比上年增长12.5%。

2018年6月27日，国务院印发《打赢蓝天保卫战三年行动计划》（国发〔2018〕22号），提出要加大对纯凝机组和热电联产机组技术改造力度，加快供热管网建设，充分释放和提高供热能力，淘汰管网覆盖范围内的燃煤锅炉和散煤。要持续推进供热计量改革，推进既有居住建筑节能改造，重点推动北方采暖地区有改造价值的城镇居住建筑节能改造。在不具备热电联产集中供热条件的地区，现有多台燃煤小锅炉的，可按照等容量替代原则建设大容量燃煤锅炉。2020年年底前，重点区域30万千瓦及以上热电联产电厂供热半径15公里范围内的燃煤锅炉和落后燃煤小热电全部关停整合。

2018年7月23日，财政部、生态环境部、住房城乡建设部、国家能源局联合下发《关于扩大中央财政支持北方地区冬季清洁取暖城市试点的通知》，决定在2017年开展中央财政支持北方地区冬季清洁取暖试点的基础上扩大试点城市范围，试点申报范围扩展至京津冀及周边地区大气污染防治传输通道“2+26”城市、张家口市和汾渭平原城市。文件要求，要认真汲取去冬今春天然气供应紧张、一些地区盲目扩大“煤改气”实施规模、影响部分群众冬季取暖的教训，充分考虑气源保障和工程建设进度等方面因素……宜电则电、宜气则气、宜煤则煤、宜油则油、宜热则热，“以气定改”“先立后破”，多措并举推进北方地区冬季清洁取暖。

2018年10月15日，为指导各地做好城镇供热采暖工作，住房城乡建设部召开北方采暖地区今冬明春城镇供热采暖工作电视电话会议，部署今冬明春城镇供热采暖工作，对北方采暖地区今冬明春城镇供热采暖等有关工作提出具体要求，确保群众温暖过冬。

三、城市交通

2017年年末，全国有32个城市建成轨道交通，线路长度4 594公里，分别比上年增加2个城市，增长28.1%，车站数2 944个，其中换乘站670个，配置车辆数22 663辆。全国50个城市在建轨道交通，线路长度4 913.6公里，分别比上年增加11个城市，车站数3 171个，其中换乘站937个。2018年7月3日，住房城乡建设部发文决定废止《城市轨道交通运营管理办法》（建设部令第140号），自2018年7月1日起施行。2018年5月24日，交通运输部公布《城市轨道交通运营管理规定》（以下简称《规定》），自2018年7月1日起施行。《规定》包括总则、运营基础要求、运营服务、安全支持保障、应急处置、法律责任和附则等内容，明确了城市轨道交通运营管理的各项政策措施。（图2）

2017年年末，城市道路长度39.8万公里，比上年增长4.0%，道路面积78.9亿平方米，比上年增长4.7%，其中人行道面积17.4亿平方米。人均城市道路面积16.05平方米，比上年增加0.25平方米。根据住房和城乡建设部城市交通工程技术中心、中国城市规划设计研究院联合北京四维图新科技股份有限公司于2019年4月联合发布《中国主要城市道路网密度监测报告》，截至2018年年底，全国36个主要城市道路网总体平均密度为5.96千米/平方千米，距离《中共中央国务院关于进一步加强城市规划建设管理工作的若干意见》

图 2　北京地铁尝试“同车不同温”

（赵雅丹　摄）

提出的“到 2020 年，城市建成区平均道路网密度提高到 8 千米/平方千米”仍有较大差距。全国 36 个主要城市中，城市道路网密度处于较高水平的（道路网密度达到 8.0 千米/平方千米以上）仍为深圳、厦门和成都 3 座城市，占比为 8%；城市道路网密度处于中等水平的城市（道路网密度在 5.5～8.0 千米/平方千米之间）共 19 个，包括上海、广州、福州等城市，占比为 53%；城市道路网密度处于较低水平的城市（道路网密度低于 5.5 千米/平方千米）共 14 个，占比为 39%。（图 3）

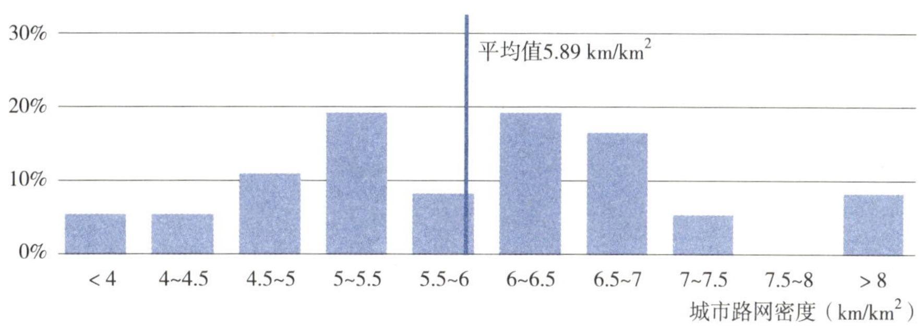

图 3　36 个城市路网密度分布图

资料来源：《中国主要城市道路网密度监测报告》

在“互联网 +”运输服务新业态的推动下，定制客运等新模式不断涌现，汽车租赁规范发展，共享单车日均使用量超过 1 000 万人次。根据交通运输部部长李小鹏的介绍，2018 年以来，建立了交通运输新业态协同监管部际联席会议制度，232 个城市相继出台了网约车配套政策。例如对滴滴公司等网约车平台开展安全专项检查，并督促落实整改要求。39 个城市发布了互联网租赁自行车监管实施细则。

四、城市排水与污水处理

2017年年末，全国城市共有污水处理厂2 209座，比上年增加170座；污水厂日处理能力15 743万立方米，比上年增长5.6%；排水管道长度63.3万公里，比上年增长9.3%，其中污水管道26.6万公里，雨水管道25.4万公里，雨污合流管道11.1万公里。城市年污水处理总量465.5亿立方米，城市污水处理率94.5%。城市再生水日生产能力3 588万立方米，再生水利用量71.3亿立方米，再生水管道1.3万公里。

2018年10月，财政部、住房城乡建设部、生态环境部共同组织实施城市黑臭水体治理示范，中央财政对示范城市给予支持，旨在加强城市环境治理和修复，加快完成黑臭水体治理任务。经综合评审，九江、沈阳、长春、马鞍山、开封、宿州、青岛、长治、漳州、邯郸、信阳、临沂、淮安、福州、广州、重庆、内江、昭通、菏泽、咸宁20个城市确定为2018年城市黑臭水体治理示范城市。(图4)

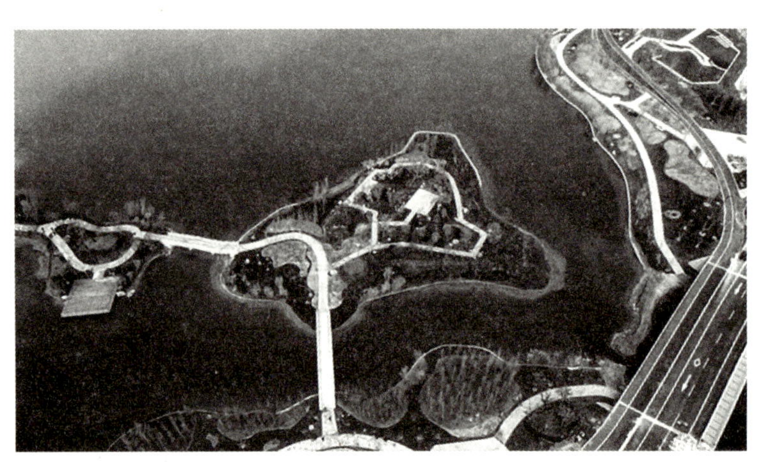

图4　江苏南通紫琅湖

(翟慧勇　摄)

为督促地方加快黑臭水体的治理步伐，2018年5月—6月，住房和城乡建设部联合生态环境部启动黑臭水体整治环境保护专项行动，分三批派出督查组对全国黑臭水体治理情况开展现场督查。本次专项行动将群众是否满意作为首要标准，公众全程参与。10月—11月，两部委开展2018年城市黑臭水体整治专项巡查。

2018年9月30日，住房城乡建设部、生态环境部联合印发《城市黑臭水体治理攻坚战实施方案》(建城〔2018〕104号)，提出到2018年年底，直辖市、省会城市、计划单列市建成区黑臭水体消除比例高于90%，基本实现长制久清。到2019年年底，其他地级城市建成区黑臭水体消除比例显著提高，到2020年年底达到90%以上。鼓励京津冀、长三角、珠三角区域城市建成区尽早全面消除黑臭水体；并就加快实施城市黑臭水体治理工程、建立长效机制、强化监督检查、保障措施等方面提出了具体要求。

为强化排水防涝安全责任制度，切实落实城市人民政府的排水防涝主体责任，确保 2018 年城市安全度汛，2018 年 3 月 14 日，住房城乡建设部公布了 2018 年全国城市排水防涝安全及重要易涝点整治责任人名单（建城函〔2018〕40 号），要求各城市排水防涝安全责任人要依据《城镇排水与污水处理条例》，组织城市排水、交通运输、气象、水利、园林绿化、市容、环境卫生等有关部门做好城市排水防涝工作，加强汛前检查和日常管理，抓紧推进易涝点整治工程并加快实施，组织制定和完善排水防涝应急预案，切实履行排水防涝安全职责。

五、城市园林绿化

2017 年年末，城市建成区绿化覆盖面积 231.4 万公顷，比上年增长 5.0%，建成区绿化覆盖率 40.9%，比上年增加 0.6 个百分点；建成区绿地面积 209.9 万公顷，比上年增长 5.4%，建成区绿地率 37.11%，比上年增加 0.68 个百分点；公园绿地面积 68.8 万公顷，比上年增长 5.3%，人均公园绿地面积 14.0 平方米，比上年增加 0.3 平方米。（图 5）

图 5　北京大兴，市民在林荫道散步

（肖汉男　摄）

为推动各地加强城市园林绿化管理不断提升园林绿化质量，2018 年 8 月，住房城乡建设部开展了对 2015 年及之前的国家生态园林城市、国家园林城市的复查工作，复查的内容包括《国家园林城市系列标准规定指标完成情况》、城市绿线管制情况、国家相关规划中园林绿化重点指标近 3 年发展情况和生态园林城市建设情况、城市园林绿化建设管理情况等。复查采取自查、普查及抽查相结合的方式。对复查合格的城市，保留相关称号。对复查不合格的城市，给予通报并限期整改，整改不合格的，撤销相关称号。

六、城市市容环境卫生

2017年年末，全国城市道路清扫保洁面积84.2亿平方米，其中机械清扫面积54.7亿平方米。全年清运生活垃圾2.15亿吨，比上年增长5.7%。全国城市共有生活垃圾无害化处理场（厂）1 013座，比上年增加73座，日处理能力68.0万吨，全年处理量2.10亿吨，城市生活垃圾无害化处理率97.7%，比上年增加1.1个百分点。市容环卫专用车辆设备总数22万台，比上年增加17.6%。城市公厕总计13.6万座，每万人拥有公厕2.85座。

"无废城市"是以创新、协调、绿色、开放、共享的新发展理念为引领，通过推动形成绿色发展方式和生活方式，持续推进固体废物源头减量和资源化利用，最大限度减少填埋量，将固体废物环境影响降至最低的城市发展模式，也是一种先进的城市管理理念。2018年12月，国务院办公厅印发《"无废城市"建设试点工作方案》，提出在全国范围内选择10个左右有条件、有基础、规模适当的城市，在全市域范围内开展"无废城市"建设试点。到2020年，系统构建"无废城市"建设指标体系，探索建立"无废城市"建设综合管理制度和技术体系，形成一批可复制、可推广的"无废城市"建设示范模式。同时，明确了六项重点任务：一是强化顶层设计引领，发挥政府宏观指导作用；二是实施工业绿色生产，推动大宗工业固体废物贮存处置总量趋零增长；三是推行农业绿色生产，促进主要农业废弃物全量利用；四是践行绿色生活方式，推动生活垃圾源头减量和资源化利用；五是提升风险防控能力，强化危险废物全面安全管控；六是激发市场主体活力，培育产业发展新模式。（图6）

图6 上海虹桥站，孩子在志愿者的引导下扔垃圾

（殷立勤 摄）

七、小结与展望

总体来看，我国城市市政基础设施已经从总量增长转向总量增长与质量提升并举的发展阶段：一方面，市政基础设施要支撑我国新型城镇化的发展需求，不断满足新增人口对市政基本公共服务的刚性需求；另一方面，随着人民群众对美好生活需求的不断提升，要求城市市政基础设施的发展更有品质、更为便捷、更为安全。但同时也应注意到，由于长期历史欠账，市政基础设施发展不充分、不平衡的现象仍非常突出，各类“城市病”在一定时期内还将存在。只有以习近平新时代中国特色社会主义思想为指导，坚持以人民为中心的发展理念，深刻把握城市发展规律，才能促进城市市政基础设施持续高质量发展。

（作者：张志果，中国城市规划设计研究院水务与工程研究分院副院长）

2018年中国城市信息化进展

2018年，我国城市信息化和智慧城市发展既有广度又有深度。党中央、国务院以及有关部委出台一系列政策，引领和规范城市信息化工作，信息化相关法律法规和发展环境进一步完善；多网融合、5G试点建设和云计算环境逐步普及，为城市信息化提供了更为优化的新一代信息基础设施；城市全面深化改革为信息资源的共享提供体制和机制保障，信息化也为全面深化改革攻坚克难和城市转型升级提供技术支撑；以“互联网+”为核心的信息化应用模式在提升公众体验、公众与企业参与度，构建城市信息化生态体系的同时，也在提升城市管理新能级，激发社会经济增长新潜能，引领民生保障新发展，互联网公司加大智慧城市建设的参与度，为城市信息化提供了新动力。面向未来，以新型智慧城市为目标的中国城市信息化呈现出五方面发展趋势：全面深化改革与信息化协同加速新型智慧城市建设，新型数据网络技术进一步推动政务信息共享服务，城市信息化应用建设将更加突出惠民便民服务，互联网公司的深度参与将创新城市信息化模式，网络安全将成为信息化建设的战略重点。

一、国家高度重视信息化工作，引领城市信息化和智慧城市新发展

2018年，党和国家领导人高度重视信息化工作，党中央、国务院及有关部门相继出台了数字中国建设、新一代信息基础设施建设、信息消费升级、共享经济引导等方面多项发展政策和措施，推动了物联网、大数据、人工智能等技术创新和应用发展，为城市信息化和智慧城市建设提供了良好的政策环境支持。

（一）党和国家领导人高度重视信息化和智慧城市工作

2018年4月20日，习近平总书记在全国网络安全和信息化工作会议上讲话时指出，必须敏锐抓住信息化发展的历史机遇，加强网上正面宣传，维护网络安全，推动信息领域核心技术突破，发挥信息化对经济社会发展的引领作用，自主创新推进网络强国建设。11月6日，习近平视察上海浦东新区城市运行综合管理中心，强调指出，城市治理是国家治理体系和治理能力现代化的重要内容，要善于运用现代科技手段实现城市智能化，要通过绣花般的细心、耐心、巧心提高精细化水平，绣出城市的品质品牌。

6月28日，李克强总理在国务院召开全国深化“放管服”改革转变政府职能电视电话会议时，提出要发展“互联网+医疗”“互联网+教育”等，打造全国一体化政务服务平台，三年内实现国务院部门数据共享、满足地方普遍性政务需求，五年内政务服务事项全面实现“一网通办”。10月22日，李克强主持召开国务院常务会议时提出，要依托国家政务服务平台建设“互联网+监管”系统，强化对地方和部门监管工作的监督，通过归集共享各类相关数据，及早发现，防范苗头性和跨行业跨区域风险。

（二）国家多项政策推进“互联网+”和“智慧政务”建设

2018年，中共中央、国务院先后颁布了《关于推进社会公益事业建设领域政府信息公开的意见》《关于促进“互联网+医疗健康”发展的意见》《关于印发进一步深化“互联网+政务服务” 推进政务服务“一网、一门、一次”改革实施方案的通知》《关于加快推进全国一体化在线政务服务平台建设的指导意见》《关于印发政府网站集约化试点工作方案的通知》等政策，明确提出运用大数据、云计算、人工智能等技术，探索构建互联融通的城市信息化平台架构，推动“互联网+医疗健康”的深入发展以及提高政务服务便利化水平。

经中共中央批准，由国家互联网信息办、国家发展改革委、工信部、福建省人民政府主办的首届数字中国建设峰会于2018年4月在福州市举行，习近平总书记专门给峰会发了贺信。来自24个部委，22个省（直辖市、自治区），16家大型央企约1 000余位领导、嘉宾，17位院士，3 000余位专家学者、技术骨干以及一大批国内知名企业负责人参加了峰会的各类活动。峰会成为我国信息化发展政策发布平台、电子政务和数字经济发展成果展示平台、数字中国建设理论经验和实践交流平台，是检阅国家信息化建设丰硕成果和展望未来发展的空前盛会。

（三）相关部委引导信息化规范和城市信息化工作有序开展

2018年5月，国家发展改革委印发《关于做好引导和规范共享经济健康良性发展有关工作的通知》，要求积极利用技术手段创新监管方式，为风险防控、服务评价、网络与信息安全监管等提供有效支撑，鼓励充分利用国家数据共享交换平台和现有平台资源等，依法依规接入相关领域平台企业数据，开展大数据监管①。

7月，工信部、国家发展改革委印发《扩大和升级信息消费三年行动计划（2018—2020年）》，提出多项扩大和升级信息消费的具体措施，包括：利用物联网、大数据、云计算、人工智能等技术推动电子产品智能化升级；在中高端消费领域培育新增长点，进一步扩大在线健康医疗、安防监控、智能家居等领域的应用范围。推进新型智慧城市建设，支持云计算、大数据、物联网综合研发应用，加速提高居民生活信息消费便利化水平；深化制造业和互联网融合，建设一批有较强影响力和带动力的垂直电商平台；加快5G标准研究、技术试

① 关于做好引导和规范共享经济健康良性发展有关工作的通知，http：//www.cac.gov.cn/2018－05/28/c_1122899125.htm.

验，推进5G规模组网建设及应用示范工程等[①]。

8月，工信部印发《推动企业上云实施指南（2018—2020年）》，提出到2020年，力争实现企业上云环境进一步优化，行业企业上云意识和积极性明显提高，上云比例和应用深度显著提升，云计算在企业生产、经营、管理中的应用广泛普及，全国新增上云企业100万家[②]。

9月，国家卫生健康委员会和国家中医药管理局印发《互联网诊疗管理办法（试行）》《互联网医院管理办法（试行）》及《远程医疗服务管理规范（试行）》三个文件，对医疗机构开展互联网诊疗活动的技术要求、人员要求、诊疗要求、电子病历、在线处方、信息安全和患者隐私保护等内容进行了规范。

10月，工信部、国家标准委发布《国家智能制造标准体系建设指南（2018年版）》，该指南着重体现了新技术在智能制造领域的应用，突出强化了标准试验验证、行业应用与实施，为智能制造产业健康有序发展起到指导、规范、引领和保障作用，对于推动我国智能制造标准国际化具有重要意义[③]。

12月，国家发展改革委、工信部颁布《关于组织实施2019年新一代信息基础设施建设工程的通知》，明确将重点面向中西部和东北地区，组织实施中小城市基础网络完善工程，以省为单位开展相关区域内县城和乡镇驻地城域传输网、IP城域网节点设备新建和扩容，开展县城至乡镇、地市至县城之间光缆、通信杆路/管道、光传输设备建设和扩容，为提升农村地区宽带用户接入速率和普及水平提供支撑[④]。

2018年，国家标准委发布了一批智慧城市建设相关国家标准，其中《智慧城市顶层设计指南》规定了智慧城市顶层设计的总体要求、基本过程及需求分析、总体设计、架构设计、实施路径设计等，用于指导智慧城市的顶层设计。这些标准的发布实施，为智慧城市建设提供了标准化支撑，有利于促进城市信息网络宽带化、规划管理信息化、基础设施智能化、公共服务便捷化、产业发展现代化、社会治理精细化发展。

二、信息基础设施创新突破，助力城市信息管理服务新提升

2018年，互联网通信技术提质增速，5G建设进入大提速阶段，提升了城市信息基础设施的整体水平。北斗导航和高分卫星技术取得新突破，为城市精准化治理提供数据信息保

① 两部委关于印发《扩大和升级信息消费三年行动计划（2018—2020年）》的通知，http：//www.cac.gov.cn/2018－08/13/c_ 1123259871.htm.

② 工业和信息化部关于印发《推动企业上云实施指南（2018—2020年）》，http：//news.cnstock.com/news，bwkx－201808－4257402.htm.

③ 两部门关于印发国家智能制造标准体系建设指南（2018年版）的通知，http：//www.gov.cn/xinwen/2018－10/16/content_ 5331149.htm.

④ 两部门关于组织实施2019年新一代信息基础设施建设工程的通知，http：//www.gov.cn/xinwen/2018－12/11/content_ 5347684.htm.

障。大数据平台建设稳步推进，成为智慧城市高质量发展的新引擎，并在政务、通信、金融、工业、旅游、医疗、教育、新零售等领域得到深化应用。各地信息集成共享服务平台加快落地，逐步实现跨城市、跨部门数据资源共享共用格局，推动了城市管理服务的智慧化和精细化。

（一）互联网技术及5G试点步伐加快，提升城市信息基础设施服务能力

《信息基础设施重大工程建设三年行动方案》中明确指出要加快构建高速、移动、安全、泛在的新一代国家信息通信基础设施，力争提前实现“十三五”规划纲要网络建设指标任务，为激活有效投资、拉动信息消费、保障改善民生和培育新动能提供有力支撑。

2018年第四季度《中国宽带速率状况报告》显示，我国固定宽带网络平均下载速率达到28.06Mbps，同比2017年度提升47.6%；移动宽带用户使用4G网络访问互联网时的平均下载速率达到22.05Mbps，同比2017年度提升21.3%；主要城市固定宽带平均可下载速率上海市、北京市、南京市位列前三，平均可用下载速率均超过30Mbps[①]。

中国互联网络信息中心（CNNIC）发布第43次《中国互联网络发展状况统计报告》[②]，据报告统计，截至2018年年底，我国网民规模达8.29亿人，互联网普及率为59.6%；2018年年底我国手机网民规模达8.17亿人，网民通过手机接入互联网的比例高达98.6%。网络购物用户和使用网上支付的用户占总体网民的比例均为73.6%，手机网民中使用移动支付的比例达71.4%。在线政务服务用户规模达3.94亿人，占整体网民的47.5%。

三大通信运营商2018年加快5G试点布局，中国联通将在北京、天津、青岛、杭州、南京、武汉等16个城市开展5G试点，中国移动将在杭州、上海、广州、苏州、武汉5个城市开展5G外场测试，中国电信5G试点城市为“6+6”，包括之前确定的雄安、深圳、上海、苏州、成都、兰州6个地区，还将扩大试点范围再增设6个城市[③]。

2018年2月，江苏省出台“编制发布信息基础设施空间布局规划”“降低信息基础设施进入公共区域成本”“加快推广光纤宽带网络和终端普及应用”等举措，推动加快推进新一代信息基础设施建设，构建宽带、融合、泛在、共享、安全的信息基础设施网络。8月，海南发布《海南省信息基础设施水平巩固提升三年专项行动方案（2018—2020年）》，提出建成高质量高水平的通信网络。8月，浙江出台《关于推进5G网络规模试验和应用示范的指导意见》，提出2018年启动5G试验建设和应用测试，2019年开展部分重点区域试行商用，2020年进入全省5G网络规模部署并实现快速商用。12月，贵阳市发布全国首个5G实验网综合应用示范项目，推动5G与实体经济的深度融合，实现数字化、网络化、智能化高质量发展，智慧医疗、智慧社区、智慧交通等12个5G应用示范初步实现[④]。

---

① 2018年第四季度中国宽带普及状况报告，http://news.chinabaogao.com/dianxin/201902/02163c1642019.html.

② CNNIC发布第43次《中国互联网络发展状况统计报告》，http://www.cnnic.net.cn/hlwfzyj/201902/t20190228_70645.htm.

③ 多地划定发展时间表5G率先落地竞速赛全面打响，http://www.sohu.com/a/247249463_161623.

④ 2018贵阳市大数据发展十大新闻，http://www.cnelc.com/text/1/190122/AD100886056_1.html.

(二) 北斗导航与高分卫星取得新突破，提供精准服务数据信息保障

2018 年，中国北斗高强度组网，形成全球服务能力，一年内完成 10 箭 19 星发射，创下世界卫星导航系统建设和我国同一型号航天发射的新纪录。同时还发射了备份卫星，精化轨控策略，服务性能稳中有升。目前，北斗已在公安、交通、渔业、减灾等行业得到广泛使用，正服务于智慧城市建设和社会治理。

2018 年 3 月，北斗导航服务人群已经超过了 1 亿人，A—北斗加速定位服务覆盖全球 200 多个国家和地区。北斗导航可以在国内提供亚米级精准定位服务，在中国的 21 个省市提供最高厘米级定位服务[①]。9 月，北斗科技发布首款国产双频北斗导航定位芯片，将智能手机带入双频北斗超精准定位时代。12 月 27 日，国新办召开新闻发布会，中国卫星导航系统管理办公室主任冉承其宣布，北斗三号基本系统已经完成建设，于今日开始提供全球服务。这标志着北斗系统服务范围由区域扩展为全球，北斗系统正式迈入全球化应用时代。据报道，北斗系统覆盖了“一带一路”倡议沿线的 30 个国家，初步形成了“太空丝绸之路”。

2018 年我国高分遥感卫星发射取得新成果，并在城市建设、农林水利、地质矿产、环境监测、国防安全和应急减灾等领域得到进一步应用。

2018 年 3 月，高分一号 02、03、04 星成功发射，空间分辨率为全色 2 米、多光谱优于 8 米，3 星组网投入运行后，可实现同一地区 2 天重访，15 天以内对全球覆盖一遍，大幅提高山、水、林、田、湖、草等自然资源全要素、全覆盖调查监测能力。5 月，高分五号卫星成功发射，是世界首颗实现对大气和陆地综合观测的全谱段高光谱卫星，也是我国光谱分辨率最高的卫星，是我国实现高光谱分辨率对地观测能力的重要标志[②]。6 月，高分六号卫星成功发射，是我国首颗设计寿命为 8 年的低轨光学遥感小卫星，也是我国首颗实现精准农业观测的高分卫星[③]，可服务于农业农村、自然资源、应急管理、生态环境等多行业应用。

(三) 时空数据云平台建设稳步推进，助力高质量发展新引擎

2018 年，诸多城市将时空数据云平台建设作为城市信息化发展的核心，统筹规划大数据基础设施。继武汉、重庆时空数据云平台建设取得良好成效后，大连、宝鸡、淄博、佛山、惠州等城市纷纷推进时空数据云平台建设进程。

2018 年 1 月，贵州提出加快大数据与科技创新深度融合，筹建科学数据中心，申建国家超算贵安中心、国家生物医学大数据中心、SKA 亚洲区域中心。作为中国首个大数据综合试验区，贵州搭建了中国首个省级政府主导的基于互联网、电子政务外网的数据管理、交

① 2018 年北斗导航在中国大陆实现厘米级定位服务，http：//www. eeworld. com. cn/qcdz/article_ 2018030721891. html.

② 解密“高分五号”卫星：环境保护再添“天眼”，http：//www. xinhuanet. com/politics/2018 – 05/14/c _ 1122826181. htm.

③ 高分六号：中国首颗设计寿命为 8 年的小卫星，http：//news. sina. com. cn/o/2018 – 06 – 02/doc – ihcikcew8932396. shtml.

换、共享的云服务系统平台[①]。

4 月，上海市大数据中心正式揭牌。该中心承担制定政务数据资源归集、治理、共享、开放、应用、安全等政策法规、技术标准及管理办法的具体工作，推进上海政务信息系统的整合共享，贯通汇聚各部门和各区县的政务数据。

6 月，智慧平顶山时空信息云平台已进入政务版云平台部署上线阶段，阶段性成果已在多项重点工作中示范应用。例如，对老城区 6 个城中村 13 平方公里棚改项目改造进度进行监测，对市不动产登记中心提供时空数据高清影像推送服务、辅助老旧小区的房地统一登记认定等[②]。

8 月，智慧潍坊时空信息云平台圆满完成了各项建设任务，成为全国首个通过验收的地级市试点。云平台汇集了基础地理信息数据、公共专题数据、实时数据和规划数据四大类时空大数据，涵盖 22 个行业部门 2 亿条记录，数据总量超过 100TB，全市（包含各县市区）共推广应用了 260 多个业务系统[③]。

10 月，第五届中国国际大数据大会在京召开，大会以“实体融合新动能　数字经济新发展”为主题，聚焦大数据、互联网、人工智能等数字化产业最新动态，透视发展趋势；深度聚焦观察政务、通信、金融、工业、旅游、医疗、教育、农业、新零售等行业的数字化发展，助力“虚实融合”。

2018 年，阿里的城市大脑升级为 2.0 版本。城市大脑 2.0 除了可以识别和预判道路交通情况之外，还会将自动化的识别结果和管理部门进行联动，城市大脑将向医疗、城管、环境、旅游、平安、民生等七大领域拓展，从智能交通管理全面升级为整个城市的人工智能中枢，并将开放平台的 AI 能力，使城市管理与服务更加高效智能。阿里城市大脑已在杭州、衢州、乌镇、苏州、重庆、澳门、海口等城市先后落地，并取得了很好的效果。

（四）信息共享服务平台纷纷落地，推动服务智慧化和精细化

随着“互联网 +”行动计划的实施和“数字中国”建设的不断发展，以物联网、云计算等技术为核心的智慧城市理念为城市未来发展提供一种全新的模式。但是，长期以来的城市“信息孤岛”问题依然存在，如果不能实现区域大数据的资源共享，将影响新型智慧城市建设的深入推进。

2018 年，信息共享服务平台建设在政策及实践层面都取得显著成效。2 月，科技部、财政部印发《国家科技资源共享服务平台管理办法》，规范管理国家科技资源共享服务平台，推进科技资源向社会开放共享。同时，各个城市纷纷加快构建智慧城市大数据开放共享平台构建，从组织保障、数据采集、数据共享、数据应用等方面入手，形成跨城市、跨部门数据

---

① 中国首个大数据综合试验区将申建“三大中心”，http：//news. sina. com. cn/o/2018 - 01 - 27/doc - ifyqyesy2775665. shtml.

② 智慧平顶山时空信息云平台建设成效初显，http：//www. tjch. com. cn/234/245/8686/content. html.

③ 我市着力推进智慧城市时空信息云平台建设，http：//www. wf. gov. cn/ZF/DT/BMDT/201808/t20180829 _ 5057074. html.

资源共享共用格局。

2018 年 3 月,“深哈合作信息资源共享平台”正式上线,该平台主要包括外部和内部两项功能,其中,外部功能主要面向社会公众,为两市政府、市场主体、社会各界人士提供服务;内部功能主要面向两市有关部门、区县(市)政府,逐步将对口合作有关工作进行平台化、网络化、规范化管理。这种以“互联网 + 深哈对口合作”的模式,为深哈两地市场主体、政府部门和社会各界提供全方位、多视角、宽领域、聚焦精准的信息化服务①。

4 月,内蒙古政务信息资源共享平台完成建设并上线试运行,截至 6 月底,46 个部门网络和平台接入共享平台,589 条目录、6 968 个信息项上线,其中 30 个部门的 239 个目录、2 022个信息项挂接了资源,数据总量达到 1 700 多万条。同时,自治区本级共享平台与国家平台实现了网络、平台、数据互联互通。

9 月,重庆市政务信息资源共享应用推进会上,明确了加快完善五大基础数据库,推进信息系统实时接入和数据共享,抓好政务信息资源的标准化、数字化建设,提升政务信息基础设施承载力和融合度。抓好服务平台、服务资源、服务品牌、咨询问政功能、线上线下服务“五个一体化”,推进政务服务平台建设。

10 月,德州市政务信息资源共享交换平台初步建成人口、法人市级中心共享数据库,分别累积数据 724 万条和 74 万条,已归集市县两级 503 个部门的可共享数据9 216万条,为市县两级共享交换了 300 余类数据共 1. 818 亿条,在便民惠民、加快审批服务效率方面发挥了重要作用②。

2018 年,贵阳市政府数据开放平台累计面向社会免费开放 618 余万条数据,累计访问量 232 余万次,产生了如匯中标、慧停车、贵阳掌上公交等 15 个典型应用,为企业和个人开展政府数据资源社会化开发利用提供了数据支撑。《2018 中国地方政府数据开放报告》显示,贵阳市政府数据开放平台在全国地市级(含副省级)指数排名中名列第一,是中国政府数据开放平台的引领者和探路者。

三、信息化建设助力城市治理,提升智慧城市管理新能级

物联网、大数据、云计算等新型信息技术,不仅是构建新型智慧城市的基础与前提,也可以推动城市治理的现代化,改变城市管理方式,支撑管理服务能力提升,推动管理精细化发展以及保障城市公共安全。

(一)“互联网 +”智慧政务平台建设,支撑管理服务能力提升

在新一代互联网技术快速发展和各地深入推进“互联网 +”行动计划的背景下,不少

① 深哈合作信息资源共享平台上线,http://www.hlj.gov.cn/szf/system/2018/03/29/010867238.shtml.

② 市政务信息资源共享平台交换数据 300 类 1.8 亿条,http://www.wf.gov.cn/ZF/DT/BMDT/201808/t20180829_5057074.html.

城市为了加快现代化转型，更好地引领新形势下的改革创新，纷纷布局智慧政务平台建设，力求先行一步，抢占发展先机。

2018 年 5 月，安阳智慧城市政务服务平台正式上线，实现了自然人、法人、政府机构等不同主体的行政审批电子化、民生支付数字化、行业应用智能化、城市服务综合化、线上线下一体化，单日访问峰值达 2 万余次①。

6 月，深圳市在建立全市统一政务服务标准体系的基础上，充分利用大数据、“互联网 +”、信息共享等新型技术，创新政府管理和服务模式，行政审批事项网上办理率达 88%，社会服务事项网上办理率达 78%。目前，深圳在市场监管、人力资源保障、公安、交通运输、住房建设等领域的 300 个事项实现“审批不见面、办事少跑腿”，简化办事流程，降低企业负担和成本②。

7 月，鄂尔多斯智慧政务（112 + N）平台实现了与自治区政务服务平台的实时对接，成为自治区首个实现政务服务平台五级联动的盟市。为逐步实现全自治区跨层级、跨地区、跨部门政务服务事项全网通办奠定了坚实的基础，实现了数据多跑路、群众少跑腿的工作目标③。

10 月，霍林郭勒市“最多跑一次”智慧政务云平台正式运行，实现网上办事大厅和实体政务大厅无缝对接，形成线上线下功能互补、相辅相成的一体化政务服务新模式，24 家无专网部门单位的 254 项办理事项实现“网上办公”，212 项办理事项实现“网上审批”④。

12 月，安徽省“互联网 + 政务服务”合肥分厅正式上线，推进政务信息系统和资源整合共享，为“互联网 + 政务服务”平台提供数据信息，汇集了 51 家单位、161 个业务系统、81 亿条数据资源，编制资源目录 1 534 项，建成市级政务信息资源交换共享平台，具有数据资源上报、数据治理开发、数据申请审核、数据共享交换、数据在线查询等功能应用⑤。

2018 年，南宁市推出了不动产登记“24 小时不打烊”自助办证模式，实现市、县登记业务同城通办，91% 的登记业务可实现全自助办理且能即时办结，抵押类业务由原来的 7 个工作日压缩至 1 小时。推出了不动产登记电子证照，并实现与住房、税务、公安、民政、教育、金融等多部门互认，实现不动产登记与税务部门“一网通”，实现了不动产登记数据面向司法的在线共享⑥。

---

① 安阳智慧城市政务服务平台正式上线，http：//baijiahao. baidu. com/s? id = 1599801333951718456&wfr = spider&for = pc.

② 深圳智慧政务服务新模式全国领先，http：//sztqb. sznews. com/PC/content/201812/06/content_ 523009. html.

③ 鄂尔多斯智慧政务平台实现五级联动，http：//www. echinagov. com/news/224109. htm.

④ 霍林郭勒市应用智慧政务云平台着力打造“线上线下”政务服务，http：//www. chinasmartcity. org/detail. asp? id = 25350.

⑤ 合肥新型智慧城市呼之欲出搭建政务云平台为“城市超脑”打基础，http：//365jia. cn/news/2018 - 09 - 01/50B21C3B2F50092F. html.

⑥ 南宁市不动产登记“24 小时不打烊”，http：//difang. gmw. cn/gx/2019 - 01/27/content_ 32420612. htm.

（二）互联网+智慧城管深化发展，助推城市管理模式精细化

“智慧城管”作为新一代信息技术支撑环境下的城市管理新模式，是通过物联网技术实现对基础设施的智能感知，变城市被动管理方式为主动管理方式，有利于进一步提升城市精细化管理水平和问题处置效率，让城市管理“聪明”起来。目前，安徽、苏州、贵阳、重庆、海口等多个省市提出了建设智慧城管大数据的要求，大数据对城市发展的推动作用已经成为社会各界的共识，大数据、人工智能、物联感应、人脸识别等技术在城市管理中陆续应用，智慧管理的影响日益突显。同时，一些城市积极开展智慧城管的实践探索，以新信息技术应用为主线的智慧化管理初见成效。

2018 年 6 月，重庆市公布了“大城智管”建设成果，实现了“积水智能监控自动警报远程精准处理”“智能停车管理路边车位信息一目了然”“机器人排查快速定位地下管网隐患”“人脸识别游摊散贩违规将自动记录”。同时，基于 GIS 系统提升万米单元网格管理效益，主城建成区被划分为 21 836 个单元网格，完成基础数据普查面积达 644.54 平方公里，普查准确率达到 99% 以上[①]。上半年主城区累计主动发现城市管理问题 113.58 万件，结案率达 85% 以上。

7 月，上海以建设“智慧城管”为抓手，聚焦市民群众关注的城市管理乱象，着力探索运用信息化、智能化手段，下“绣花”功夫治理城市环境问题，注重严格执法、精细管理、智能管控，共依法拆除违法建筑 2 016.32 万平方米，拆除违法户外广告设施 915 块，查处破坏房屋外貌（破墙开店）案件 403 件、整改恢复 4 499 处，查处违法违规运输处置建筑垃圾案件 3 995 起，有效改善了城市环境秩序，提升了城市环境品质[②]。

8 月，上海发布智慧新城市——智慧城市综合运营管理平台。该平台承载应用展示、接入管理综合能力，具备云化部署、数据安全、快速部署、菜单式选择、灵活开放、大数据分析六大特点，为政府提供高效、科学、全面、便捷的平台，让广大市民享受智慧、快捷、安全的智慧新生活。

8 月初，舟山启动智慧城管系统，该系统采用“智能感知+即时采集+快速处置+市区联动”的运作模式，快速实现城市管理事件、部件的采集（智能感知）、受理、派遣、处置一系列流程，最大限度发挥智慧城管效能，实现了城市管理问题的“第一时间发现、第一时间处置、第一时间解决”。8 月以来，本岛区域共发现城市管理问题 10 000 余起，内容涵盖街面秩序、市容环境、市政公用、园林绿化等城市管理问题[③]。

9 月，浙江省杭州市下城区“云上城管”数字化城市管理服务平台正式上线，这是杭州首个上线的“云上城管”。该平台通过借助路面监控、卫星定位、大数据、云技术等先进技术手段，以“互联网+城管”模式，将城市的精细化治理与技术手段无缝衔接，实现了管

---

① “智慧城管”到来城市管理更“聪明”了，http：//news. ifeng. com/a/20180722/59331244_ 0. shtml.

② 上海：加快建设“智慧城管”提升城市环境品质 https：//baijiahao. baidu. com/s? id = 1604963341713361781.

③ 智慧城管助力舟山创城让城市乱象无处藏身，http：//dy. 163. com/v2/article/detail/DRJQN4P10530VULI. html.

理中的科学调度、云监控、实时发现并处理问题，由传统管理模式向“云上城管”转变[①]。

（三）大数据助推智慧警务，驱动公共安全管理智慧化

城市公共安全是需要重点关注的问题之一，如何防范和化解各类城市风险，为公民提供务实、有效的公共安全，考验现代城市公共安全治理智慧。很多城市勇于创新实践，进行了公共安全智慧管理平台建设，取得了显著的成效，为开展推进智慧安全积累了宝贵的经验。

2018 年 8 月，北京召开“云计算和大数据”重点专项“基于天空地一体化大数据的公共安全事件智能感知与理解”的项目启动会，该项目针对目前公共安全事件预测困难和检测不准的问题，综合利用卫星和航拍影像、地面跨时空视频、网络数据、电磁信息和地理信息等，实现面向公共安全的天空地一体化大数据智能处理，在新疆、上海两地开展三个典型场景应用示范。

10 月，厦门市集美区公共安全管理中心已经建成集 110 联动、网格化中心、数字城管、12345 平台、公安情报等指挥中心于一体的区级公共安全管理大中心，成为多中心合一的区级公共安全管理“最强大脑”，业务范围覆盖集美区公检法、城管、建设、环保、规划、土地、水利、纪检监察、街镇、村居共计 186 个部门。中心平台共受理各类事件 331 277 件，日均 120 件，其中 2018 年受理 4. 8 万件，日均 159 件，1—10 月刑事警情同比下降 33%[②]。

11 月，南京江北新区推出“智慧警务 Mall”，实现了警务服务“O2O”线上线下一体融合新型服务模式。借助智慧警务服务旗舰店的创新运转模式，未来可将智慧警务服务能力逐步扩展到警务服务“便利店”，形成全业务、全渠道、全方式的智能 + 体系[③]。

截至 2018 年 12 月，广西公安“智慧警务”框架的推广应用，使得全区 90% 以上案件通过网上办理，多数刑事案件通过信息化手段侦破，群众安全感达到 96. 1%[④]。

（四）生态环境大数据平台建设，提升生态环境“智理”能力

环境“智理”就是要实现用智慧治理污染，应用大数据、“互联网 +”、云计算、卫星遥感等现代技术，推动工作方式的转变，打造精准治污、科学治污、多方协作的环境治理新模式，包括更加精确地对污染问题进行分析，提升环境问题的综合预警能力，加强动态监管水平，提升治理效果等。不少省市积极构建生态环境大数据平台，探索城市环境污染智理新模式。

2018 年 7 月，全国环境互联网会议在贵阳召开，会议主题为“互联网 + 时代，利用大数据推进生态环境治理”。发布了 2018 智慧环保创新案例，包括北京市环境监察总队应用热点网格技术开展精准大气执法，江苏省卫星遥感强力支撑生态保护红线区环境监管，福建省

---

① “云上城管”推动城市管理智慧升级，http：//www. tjdl. net/2018/typicalcase_ 1127/35846. html.

② 厦门市集美区运用大数据提升公共安全管理质效，http：//www. pafj. net/html/2018/zongzhixinwen _ 1130/103652. html.

③ 南京江北新区推出“智慧警务 Mall”，https：//news. sina. com. cn/o/2018 - 11 - 17/doc - ihnyuqhh5748509. shtml.

④ 广西“智慧警务”惠民生，http：//www. jcrb. com/photo/Lawvisual/201812/t20181224_ 1945963. html.

环境监察执法平台，山东省污染源自动监测动态管控系统，张掖生态环境监测网络管理平台构成“天眼”守护祁连山等[①]。

10月，福建率先建成省级生态环境大数据云平台，通过打造一平台一中心三大体系，让海量数据跑起来、用起来，助力福建环境监管形成一盘棋、一本账，环境决策更高效、更精准、更智慧。平台汇集数据117类80多亿条，包含工商、水利、公安、交通等21个部门41类数据，日容量增长约1TB[②]。

10月，苏州利用环保大数据平台推进污染防治。平台综合运用云计算、大数据、物联网、人工智能等技术，清理、整合了17个部门、135项数据清单，集纳的数据覆盖全市8 657平方公里土地，涵盖10个区（市）、90个乡镇街道、19个工业集中区、159个湖泊、816条河流、3.6万家排污企业、934个入河排污口、121家规模畜禽养殖场、145个污水处理厂，实现环保、水利、农业等各项生态环境数据的互联互通和开放共享，为政府推进环境治理提供“超级大脑”[③]。

10月，重庆建立了服务区、县两级大气环境管理和水环境管理的一体化工作平台，包括“数据舱”和“作战图”，集成仪表盘、热力图、数据表、空间图等可视化形式，实现按全市域、区域、40个区县以及17个国控站和54个市控站不同层级的空气质量、污染因子、首要污染物、超标因子等数据分级、分层应用。重庆市生态环境局通过平台下达任务5 000余项，推送“蓝天行动”6类数据3 000条。共完成各类环境管理遥感监测报告86份，主要助力环保督察取证研判，开展了5个县级自然保护区的疑似人类干扰活动遥感动态变化监测及遥感数据解译，为生态环保集中督查的取证、分析和研判等提供了依据[④]。

四、信息化技术应用不断创新，激发社会经济增长新潜能

国务院2015年发布的《“互联网+”行动指导意见》要求，到2018年基本形成网络经济与实体经济协同互动的发展格局。目前，互联网与各行业各领域不断深度融合、应用持续深化，新经济驱动力持续攀升，推动催生新技术、新产品、新业态、新模式，整体提升实体经济的创新力、生产力、流通力，为各行业各领域的发展带来新机遇、新空间、新活力。

（一）移动互联网不断渗透普及，垂直电商消费规模持续增长

“互联网+”时代为电子商务发展提供了新机遇。电子商务、社交应用、数字内容相互融合，社交电商模式拓展了电子商务业务，第三方电商平台与社交应用融合加深，吸引越来越多的消费者进行网络购物，移动支付使用率保持增长。

---

① 2018全国环境互联网会议凝聚共识大数据提升生态环境治理水平，http://news.ifeng.com/a/20180730/59515202_0.shtml.

② 福建打造全国首个省级生态环境大数据云平台，http://fjnews.fjsen.com/2018-11/05/content_21641058.htm.

③ 苏州首创利用环保大数据平台推进污染防治，http://huanbao.bjx.com.cn/special/?id=715517.

④ 重庆建生态环境大数据平台，http://huanbao.bjx.com.cn/special/?id=715517.

截至2018年12月，我国网络购物用户规模达6.10亿，年增长率14.4%，网民使用率73.6%。同时，手机网络支付用户规模达5.83亿，年增长率10.7%，手机网民使用率达71.4%。网民线下消费时使用手机网络支付比例67.2%。

10月，阿里巴巴集团以20亿元投资新三板公司1919，开始收割垂直电商，在电商和零售领域广撒网，陆续投了京东、唯品会、拼多多、每日优鲜，以及惠下单、多抓鱼、小红书、有赞和好衣库等创业企业[①]。同时，垂直电商平台有效地推动了流通业、制造业、物流快递、宽带、支付等产业发展，并通过提供新的服务、新的市场和新的经济组织方式，推动着传统经济的转型升级，新电商企业趋于聚焦母婴、医疗、家装等垂直电商领域深耕[②]。

11月11日，天猫成交额达到2 135亿元，双十一购物节开创以来首次突破2 000亿元大关，同比增27%。京东11.11全球好物节累计下单金额达1 598亿，再次创造新的纪录，苏宁国际当天成交额同比去年增长428%。

同时，在“一带一路”倡议背景下，跨境出口电商迎来难得的发展机遇。2018年，中国跨境电商规模已稳居世界第一，覆盖绝大部分国家和地区，向全世界提供高质量品牌化的产品，出口交易规模达7.9万亿元中小型卖家占主导[③]，跨境出口电商在广东、浙江、福建等网络、物流比较成熟的沿海区域发展更为活跃，其中广东以56.99%居首，浙江和福建占比均超过10%。

（二）信息化助力智能制造，加速传统制造转型升级

智能制造技术是在现代传感技术、网络技术、自动化技术、拟人化智能技术等先进技术的基础上，通过智能化的感知、人机交互、决策和执行技术，实现设计过程、制造过程和制造装备智能化，是信息技术、智能技术与装备制造技术的深度融合与集成。2018年1月，工信部、国标委印发《国家智能制造标准体系建设指南（2018年版）》。4月，工信部印发《关于开展2018年智能制造试点示范项目推荐的通知》，共有99个项目入围，覆盖家具、材料、医疗、电子、汽车等多个制造业领域。12月，工信部召开全国智能制造试点示范经验交流电视电话会议，明确加强智能制造经验交流与宣传推广，以扎实的成效推动制造业数字化、网络化、智能化发展，为加快制造强国建设做出新的更大贡献。

在上述政策的指导下，各个城市和企业纷纷推进智能制造进程。2018年11月，中南高科·合肥智能制造产业园项目在双凤开发区隆重开工，该项目总投资10亿元，定位于集高端制造、电子信息、生物医疗、集成电路、人工智能、大数据于一体的高端智能生态创新产业园区，建成后可容纳100余家企业，可实现总产值15亿元，解决5 000人就业[④]。12月

① 20亿元投资1919，阿里开始收割垂直电商，http://www.ikanchai.com/article/20181022/243004.shtml.

② 综合电商格局已定垂直领域深耕成新电商的建设趋向，https://www.qianzhan.com/analyst/detail/220/181011-ed0226b5.html.

③ 2018中国跨境出口电商交易规模将达7.9万亿，http://blog.sina.com.cn/s/blog_7962aed80102yf9w.html.

④ 中南高科·合肥智能制造产业园项目在双凤开工，https://www.cnrepark.com/news/2018-11/20181119_182012.shtml.

底，南京已形成了包括江北新区、经开区、雨花台区等在内的“一极三区多点”智能制造发展格局，拥有 11 个国家级智能制造试点示范项目。

2018 年，深圳智能制造、先进制造业蓬勃发展，在不同领域领跑全国甚至全球。华为、中兴等企业领军通信设备产业发展，华星光电、创维等领跑数字视听产业，迈瑞、华大基因等企业领跑生物医药产业，大疆科技、优必选等企业引领无人机、机器人产业。据统计，2018 年深圳先进制造业和高技术制造业增加值分别为 6 564.83 亿元和 6 131.20 亿元，分别增长 12.0% 和 13.3%，占规模以上工业增加值比重分别提升至 72.1% 和 67.3%[①]。

（三）共享经济应用领域拓展，撬动经济社会发展新动能

2018 年，共享经济这一“互联网 +”的时代新业态，由于出现了滴滴顺风车事件等安全事件，引发了诸多关于共享经济的讨论、争议，甚至质疑、抵触。有人呼吁要对共享经济严格监管，还有人喊出了“共享经济已死”的口号。事实上，共享经济发展已进入了一个拐点，这个拐点所昭示的，并非是行业衰退的趋势，而是对整个行业必须回归理性的警醒[②]。目前，农业、教育、医疗领域成为共享经济新“风口”，对于实施创新驱动发展战略、实现高质量发展意义重大，共享经济仍然大有可为。

共享农业方面。2017 年，财政部下发《关于开展田园综合体建设试点工作的通知》，确定要在 18 个省份开展田园综合体建设试点。其中，作为试点省份之一的海南，提出以发展“共享农庄”为抓手，建设田园综合体和美丽乡村。2018 年 2 月，海南选择一批基础条件较好的农业基地，创建各具特色的共享农庄，为消费者提供土地租赁等多种形式的定制服务，培育农旅融合发展新业态[③]。5 月，海南省有关部门公布了第一批 61 个共享农庄。

共享医疗方面。2018 年 6 月，西北首家共享医疗 MALL——月星 · 共享医疗项目落户银川，项目内部整合各类专业医疗机构，让患者可在一地实现多种医疗需求，也为医生患者提供一站式医疗配套输送服务。同时，借助大数据分析，将为患者提供精准的健康管理方案[④]。银川市不仅与丁香园、北大医信、医联等 15 家国内知名互联网医疗企业签约，并陆续与阿里健康、京东医药城、平安健康、360 健康等 60 多家互联网医疗企业对接，成功打造了国内首个互联网医院产业集群，推动优质资源下沉，实现医生与患者跨地域对接。截至 8 月，通过互联网医院在银川备案注册的医生总数已达到 20 583 名，累计服务患者 700 多万人次，节省患者就医时间约 60 万小时[⑤]。9 月，宁夏回族自治区卫计委全民健康平台上的 16 项应用，以及固原市中医院、原州区人民医院全业务系统、区医院的预约挂号系统均实现上

---

① 深圳 2018 年经济数据出炉 GDP 增 7.6%，http：//economy. southcn. com/e/2019 - 02/03/content_ 185051980. htm.

② “跑马圈地”不是共享经济，http：//epaper. southcn. com/nfdaily/html/2018 - 09/18/content_ 7752173. htm.

③ 共享农业：这些案例告诉我们，新商机真的来了！，https：//www. sohu. com/a/221991391_ 99911622.

④ 西北首家共享医疗 MALL 落户银川，http：//nx. cnr. cn/xwdd/20180611/t20180611_ 524265550. shtml.

⑤ 银川打造互联网医院产业集群新高地，http：//www. yinchuan. gov. cn/xwzx/mrdt/201808/t20180809_ 956977. html.

云，打通了各医疗机构之间的信息互联互通①。

共享教育方面。随着互联网、物联网、云计算、VR/MR、智能机器人等技术不断进步，加之消费升级、社会变革等众多因素的影响，教育从“教学空间”到“教育工具”再到“教学内容”均在发展重大变革。以可汗学院、翻转课堂、慕课为代表的互联网教育，掀起教育变革新浪潮，教育资源共享化②。2018年3月，津冀两地共同举办教育论坛，整合津冀优质教育资源，共享优质教育成果，协同解决区域教育发展瓶颈，实现两地教育水平整合提升，形成两地教育领域相互衔接、互为促进、共同支撑、协同发展的新格局③。6月，广东一小学率先引入了全通教育智慧AI共享课堂，通过应用人脸识别、行为识别等AI技术，将帮助学校轻松组建校园班级人脸云考勤网络，实现班级人脸考勤云覆盖④。

五、信息化应用持续升温，推动民生保障新发展

信息化应用打造新生活已渗透居民日常生活的各个层面，利用系统集成、移动互联网、人工智能、大数据挖掘分析等信息技术可创新扶贫模式，释放产业扶贫新动力，可以提供人工智能医疗，开拓医疗服务新模式，推动智慧交通建设，引领民众出行新生态。

（一）“互联网+扶贫”模式创新，释放扶贫澎湃新动力

2018年扶贫工作已经进入攻坚期，互联网助力扶贫脱贫的中国方案随之诞生。工信部发布的《关于推进网络扶贫的实施方案（2018—2020年）》明确提出，要推进贫困村通宽带进程，实施“互联网+健康扶贫”，加强精准扶贫平台开发应用，优先向“三区三州”倾斜等工作措施，安徽、江西、四川、新疆、陕西、湖南等省份，积极探索创新“互联网+扶贫”模式，取得显著成果。

5月，在2018数博会“网络扶贫：大数据助力精准扶贫互联网主力军征战脱贫攻坚主战场”高端对话上，13家全国网信知名企业与贵州省10个深度贫困县达成结对帮扶协议。10月，全国深度贫困地区网络扶贫工作现场推进会暨网络扶贫凉山行活动在凉山州西昌市举行。有40家企业达成签约项目62个，涉及凉山州网络覆盖、农村电商、网络扶智、信息服务、网络公益等网络扶贫多方面。

随着国家加大网络精准扶贫工作力度，“互联网+精准扶贫”成为贫困地区发展赶超的重要抓手。10月，工信部举办“网络扶贫”论坛会议提出切实举措普及重点网络应用，特别是加快推进“互联网+健康扶贫”和远程教育试点，促进公共服务均等化；要加强对

① 宁夏“卫生云”平台助力医疗服务信息互通共享，http：//news.cnr.cn/native/city/20180923/t20180923_524368055.shtml.

② 教育+商业：智慧共享教育综合体产品模式解析，https：//baijiahao.baidu.com/s?id=1605841724694406609&wfr=spider&for=pc.

③ 津冀两地整合优质教育资源共享教育发展成果，http：//news.enorth.com.cn/system/2018/03/11/035170640.shtml.

④ 全通教育共享教育未来，pick智慧AI共享课堂，http：//news.enorth.com.cn/system/2018/03/11/035170640.shtml.

“三区三州”等深度贫困地区的支持，优先安排网络应用试点示范项目。

电子商务已为贫困地区特色产品打通了销售新渠道，撬开了网上大场，成为农民群众增收致富的新利器和脱贫攻坚的新动能，开展电商精准扶贫，大有可为。近年来，张家界市深入开展电商精准扶贫专项行动，充分利用“互联网+”电商平台优势，带动全市经济发展取得显著成效。至2018年年底，张家界市有各类电商企业、网（微）店超过1 800多家，建成农村电子商务站点358多个，电子商务年交易额突破55亿元，并通过创新“互联网+生产基地+合作社+种植户”等电商扶贫模式，使全市16 734贫困农户、58 344名贫困人口受益①。

（二）人工智能医疗领域新发展，提高智慧医疗服务水平

物联网、5G数据、医院信息化建设，使医疗健康领域开始从传统时代的信息不通、资源分配不均中走向医疗智能化、健康模式管理数据化、病历电子化等新的方式。包括AI人工智能和自动诊断、眼科技术、手术机器人、体内植入和血管疗法、康复器械、电子皮肤和柔性电子产品等在内的最新技术得到显著进步。

2018年2月，杭州市发布《建设“智慧健康”打造“智慧医疗升级版”三年行动计划（征求意见稿）》，提出要充分运用新一代信息技术，打造“智慧医疗升级版”，引领全国健康医疗信息化建设和应用，到2020年，形成一朵实用、共享、安全的杭州市“智慧健康云”。截至2018年年底，杭州市全面启动医疗卫生服务领域“最多跑一次”改革，杭州市级医院93%以上的就诊病人在志愿者引导下选择自助服务，市民卡诊间结算率达到88%，医技检查诊间预约率77%，出院病人病区结算率96%，全市智慧医疗活跃用户达834万以上，全市已有6 650万人次以上的门急诊患者享受到了便利②。

8月，清华大学研发出多层石墨烯表皮电子皮肤，该器件具有极高灵敏度，可直接贴覆于皮肤探测呼吸、心率、发声等人体信号，在运动监测、睡眠监测、生物医疗等方面具有重大应用前景。

12月，贵阳市人口健康信息云的手机APP——“健康贵阳”正式上线，可为全市居民提供的“互联网+健康医疗”应用。主要功能包括居民电子病历和电子健康档案、预防接种信息推送、社区随访、家庭医生签约申请等。已对接全市290家市、县、乡三级公立医疗卫生机构，汇聚全市海量的病历、影像、心电、健康档案、社区随访、预防接种等各类健康医疗数据③。

2018年年底，乐山市“移动智慧医院”平台应用成效显著，其中仅金口河区已有14 304名居民成为“智能家庭医生管理信息化平台”电子签约服务对象，慢性病管理对象达到了

① 电商扶贫：让张家界贫困群众“淘”出精准脱贫路，http：//www. 060193. top/zhongwen. html.

② 杭州市全面启动医疗卫生服务领域“最多跑一次”改革，http：//ori. hangzhou. com. cn/ornews/content/2018 - 06/08/content_ 7016715. htm.

③ “健康贵阳”APP发布可掌握自己的健康医疗信息，http：//www. gywb. cn/content/2018 - 12/20/content_ 5959147. htm.

1 615人，远程健康监护提示 543 起，绿色转诊 145 人[①]。

2018 年年底，福州已完成 37 家市、县级医疗机构的互联互通，并开始实现数据实时汇聚数据，目前已汇聚结构化存量数据 8.5TB，影像数据 120TB，数据总量达 165 亿条，取得阶段性成效。如仅在 1.5 秒之内，就能将可疑肺结节的大小、特征等完成筛查，这项名为“智能影像—肺结节筛查”的创新，采用人工智能技术推出的 CT 影像肺结节筛查云服务，目前处于全球领先水平[②]。

（三）信息化引领车联网发展，推动智能出行应用新时代

随着移动 5G、云计算、物联网、中国北斗车载应用、GIS、大数据分析等新一代网络、定位及信息技术的发展，智能车联网系统日渐成熟，以网络信息技术为核心的“智能出行”以其在提高交通资源利用效率和节省出行时间，提供更安全、经济和便利的出行优势成为未来趋势，带动了自动驾驶、人车路融合通信、智能交通设施等新的出行服务与信息消费。

2018 年 2 月，青岛火车站细化服务措施，推出了巡更机器人、旅客评价系统、智能咨询机器人等多种智能化新设备，方便旅客出行，让旅客体验更美好。

3 月，上海发放全国首批智能网联汽车开放道路测试号牌，这标志着无人驾驶汽车正式走出封闭园区，进入上路测试阶段。

9 月，无锡“世界物联网博览会”期间，全球第一个城市级车路协同平台——“车联网（LTE - V2X）城市级示范应用”首次集中展示，该项目完成了现阶段全球最大规模的城市级车联网 LTE - V2X 网络，覆盖无锡主城区、新城主要道路 200 余个信号灯控路口，升级了车路协同路侧管控基础设施及智慧交通信息服务平台，以“人—车—路—云”系统协同为基础，开放 40 余项交通管控信息，提供 26 类应用场景，为无锡市民提供安全便捷的智能网联车生活。

11 月，高德推出“智行战略”，从智能出行、智能驾驶、共享出行三个方面助力合作伙伴智能化升级。智能出行领域，推出了一体化的智能硬件——A + Box，集成了包括导航、语音交互、车载娱乐、无感支付等车内服务能力，可实时在线更新迭代。智能驾驶领域，与千寻位置联合发布了首个高精地图 + 高精定位解决方案，深度融合双方的地图和定位能力，使智能驾驶更加安全高效。

六、信息化深度推进，指导城市信息化未来新发展

随着城市发展转型和互联网、物联网、大数据技术的快速发展，城市信息化内外部环境出现了一系列新变化，未来城市信息化也表现出一些发展趋势。

---

① 互联网 + 医疗：就医体验“高大上”，http://www.leshan.cn/html/list - dtt/view_ 5AB854087D374E91.html.

② 健康医疗大数据，在福州“跑”出新产业，http://fj.people.com.cn/n2/2018/1217/c181466 - 32417425.html.

（一）全面深化改革与信息化协同加速新型智慧城市建设

随着2018年《中共中央关于深化党和国家机构改革的决定》《深化党和国家机构改革方案》的出台，使全面深化改革的措施在组织机构层面上落地。自然资源部、应急管理部、国家市场监督管理总局和生态环境部等部门的组建，优化了组织机构的职能，从机构、业务和流程上为信息化建设提供了体制和机制保障。自然资源部的成立，实现了国土空间规划、自然资源开发利用、自然资源统一登记、自然资源开发利用评价的全过程管理，有助于解决国家管理、城市规划、城乡建设等部门信息共享、业务融合与流程优化等问题，为城市治理提供解决方案，特别是采用信息技术的手段实现信息共享、业务融合与流程优化，呈现全面深化改革与信息化协同的新局面，从智慧政务的层面加速新型智慧城市建设。

（二）新型数据网络技术进一步推动政务信息共享服务

2018年，政府出台了《关于推进社会公益事业建设领域政府信息公开的意见》《关于加快推进全国一体化在线政务服务平台建设的指导意见》等推动政务信息共享的政策。随着计算机和网络技术的不断革新，中国城市进入了时空大数据时代，信息技术已经渗透社会的各行各业，成为推动政府职能部门改革的又一强劲推动力。未来，借助于边缘计算、区块链技术等的支撑，一方面，要加强政府内部规划、经管、园林、环保、公安、税务、工商、交通等部门的数据联通；另一方面，要强化与其他城市之间的数据共享，形成全国范围的巨大城市信息共享网络，实现跨城市、跨领域、跨部门的技术和经验交流，使数据库的应用能效得到充分发挥。

（三）城市信息化应用建设将更加突出惠民便民服务

城市信息化技术的不断提升，城市管理者认识到通过理念和管理手段转变、技术进步和应用深入，可以增强政府的管理效能，更好地实现为居民服务。因而，面对就业、住房、医疗、交通等问题时，更多的城市和行业从信息化建设的角度寻求解决城市问题方法，以推动城市更好的发展。2018年10月，集线上分诊导医、预约挂号、自助缴费、就诊叫号、停诊推送、健康宣教、报告查询等众多便民服务于一体的“无锡智医APP”正式上线公测，该APP目前已接入8家市属医院，自费病人可率先实现支付宝线上支付。12月，西藏推进医疗信息化惠民实现首例远程挂号。未来，信息化技术应用将向居民关心的就业、住房、教育、交通、环境等领域深化和发展，惠民、便民将上新台阶，成效更为显著。

（四）互联网公司的深度参与将创新城市信息化模式

随着人口红利逐步消失、面向消费者（toC）业务增长放缓，互联网公司将业务增长点逐步放在面向政府和企业（toB和toG）的业务上，智慧城市成为互联网公司关注的热点，阿里、腾讯、百度和京东等互联网公司纷纷布局智慧城市建设，利用移动支付、人脸识别和地图服务等一系列支撑技术渗入智慧城市应用，利用云计算、大数据和人工智能技术为政府提供服务，为城市信息化提供一种新模式，这种模式充分利用了互联网公司善于解决痛点和难点问题以及拥有资金、人才、数据和计算资源的优势，从而改变城市信息化格局。阿里城市大脑的发展与应用推广也反映的是这种城市信息化模式。

（五）网络安全将成为城市信息化建设的战略重点

随着物联网、云计算、大数据、区块链、边缘计算等新型信息技术在城市管理中的广泛应用以及信息资源的高度融合，城市信息安全会面临更深层次的风险。国家从制度层面对信息安全更加重视，《中华人民共和国网络安全法》明确提出，坚持网络安全与信息化发展并重，遵循积极利用、科学发展、依法管理、确保安全的方针，推进网络基础设施建设和互联互通，采取措施保护关键信息基础设施免受攻击、侵入、干扰和破坏，依法惩治网络违法犯罪活动，维护网络空间安全和秩序。2018 年，《中共中央关于深化党和国家机构改革的决定》中明确指出，为维护国家网络空间安全和利益，将国家计算机网络与信息安全管理中心调整为由中央网络安全和信息化委员会办公室管理。未来，针对城市信息化安全，必须要构建安全可靠的信息消费环境，深入推进网络综合治理。

（作者：党安荣，清华大学建筑学院教授，博士研究生导师；甄茂成，清华大学建筑学院博士后；王丹，建设综合勘察研究设计院有限公司副院长，研究员；梁军，北京超图软件股份有限公司总工程师，教授级高工）

论坛篇

在国家规划体系改革的过程中
发展人居科学　共筑美好家园

凡事预则立，不预则废。近年来，在中国特色社会主义进入新时代的重要时期，国家对经济社会发展规划工作、生态环境保护规划工作、城乡规划建设管理工作、国土空间规划和区域规划工作等，都做出了顶层设计和战略安排。这些规划都是国家的规划，不是部门的规划，在具体的规划实践中，要有综合的观念，加强统筹协调，体现国家意志和国家规划的战略性，适应高质量发展和人民对美好生活的需求。

第一，国土空间规划重在统筹综合协调。

国家发展的每一项事业几乎都与土地有关，国土空间的保护与利用工作涉及面广，影响大，必须全国一盘棋，进行战略性的大安排，统筹考虑相应的立法与制度安排。国土空间规划是国家空间发展的指南、可持续发展的空间蓝图，是各类开发保护建设活动的基本依据。在建立国土空间规划体系并监督实施的过程中，必然要涉及经济社会发展、生态环境保护、城乡建设管理、地上地下空间利用等具体工作，这些工作需要进行专门的研究与落实，制定规划并监督实施。空间规划要对各相关规划进行统筹、综合与协调，但目的是实现“各美其美、美美与共”，而不是去替代多种部门的不同工作。

第二，落实习近平总书记关于城市规划重要讲话及中央城市工作会议精神。

城市是我国经济、政治、文化、社会等方面活动的中心，在党和国家工作全局中具有举足轻重的地位。习近平总书记在2015年中央城市工作会议上一再强调“城市规划”对城市发展的重要引领作用，强调城市工作中做好规划的价值。对此，我们要尊重城市发展规律，深刻认识城市在经济社会发展、民生改善中的重要作用，科学谋划城市的“成长坐标”。

城市是实现国土空间发展与保护的关键地区。在建立国土空间规划体系并监督实施过程中，我们要认真落实中央要求，抓好城市及其规划工作，处理好城市发展和规划的关系。国土空间规划体系中要对“城市”这个重要的空间层次与地域有所体现，对城市规划在国土空间规划体系中的地位与作用要予以回答，做好国土空间规划管理工作与城市规划建设管理工作的统筹协调。

第三，发展人居科学，共筑美好家园。

改革开放以来，随着我国城镇化快速推进和城乡建设大规模开展，人居环境建设取得实质性改进。党的十九大报告指出，我国社会主要矛盾已经转化为人民日益增长的美好生活需要和不平衡不充分的发展之间的矛盾。这个重大判断为坚持以人民为中心、实现高质量发展和高品质生活、建设美好家园指明了方向。在具体的城乡规划建设工作中，要有人居的观念，聚焦美好人居，共筑美好家园。

1990年以来，针对我国城镇化进程中建设规模大、速度快、涉及面广等特点，我倡议发展人居科学，以人为核心，科学建设有序空间和宜居环境，并以整体论的融贯综合思想，突破原有专业分割和局限，初步建立了一套以人居环境建设为核心的空间规划设计方法和实践模式。当前，在建立国土空间规划体系的过程中，宜乎更为自觉地大力发展人居科学，为建立包括国土空间规划体系在内的国家规划体系提供坚实的科学支撑。建议在我国现有13个学科门类基础上，增设“人居科学”为第14个学科门类。

（作者：吴良镛，中国科学院院士、中国工程院院士、清华大学教授）

中国城镇化下半场的挑战与对策

2018年10月9日，由国务院参事室公共政策研究中心、新华网思客联合主办的2018年第三期《参事讲堂》在新华网举行。我应邀做了“中国城镇化下半场的挑战与对策”主旨演讲，指出中国城镇化前半场有效避免了四类“城市病”，着重探讨了城镇化下半场的六大趋势和来自八方面的主要挑战，并提出了相应的对策建议。下面是根据演讲内容整理的文字材料。

一、有效避免了四类“城市病”

我国的城镇化经历了40年的快速发展，可以说这是人类历史上规模最大的城镇化。在城镇化前半场取得了决定性胜利，差不多把相当于两个美国的人口从农村搬到城市，在这样一个巨大的人口移动过程中，我们避免了先行国家和发展中国家四类严重的城市病：避免了像英国这样的先行工业国家，在城市化初期基础设施严重不足，造成了疾病流行这样悲惨的历史；避免了像阿根廷这样的发展中国家，令大量人口单向度进入到城市，但不能提供相应的就业岗位，经济系统脆弱化从而陷入“中等收入陷阱”；避免了像美国这样的发达国家，在城镇化过程中造成的城市病蔓延，城市能耗比全球平均能耗高出几倍的情况；也避免了非洲等国的城镇化造成了贫民窟遍地，城市60%~70%的人口在贫民窟中居住的现象。

当然，前半场的城镇化是伴随着工业化发展的，这个过程被称为“灰色”城镇化，表现为先污染后治理。展望城镇化的下半场，主要存在六大主要趋势以及八个方面的主要挑战。

二、城镇化下半场的六大趋势

趋势一：城镇化峰值将出现在65%~70%之间

第一个趋势是我国的城镇化峰值将出现在65%~70%之间。城市化发展过程通常呈现出一条“S”形曲线，被称为“诺瑟姆曲线”。世界上存在着两类国家，这两类国家的诺瑟姆曲线第二个拐点是不一样的。第一个拐点在城镇化率达到20%~30%时开始向上走，当城镇化率达到70%以后出现第二个拐点，这时城镇化率慢慢趋向平和。诺瑟姆曲线是在总结北美城市化历程中得出的，对于北美国家来说，人口大部分由新住民组成，原住民大大缩小，这些国家农村人口被压缩到5%甚至更少，这些被称为新大陆国家的城镇化率在诺瑟姆曲线第二拐点后都攀升到85%以上。

作为农耕文明历史最悠久的旧大陆国家，中国的诺瑟姆曲线是不一样的，第二个拐点来得比较早，城镇化峰值将出现在65%~70%之间。我们可以看到，现在外出打工的农民工数量已经基本稳定，每年农村进入城市的人口正在持续减少，55岁以上的农民工返乡的数量正在快速增长，逆城镇化的现象已经普遍存在了。

在这些大趋势之下，提出乡村振兴正当时，我们的乡村将来会成为宜游、宜老、宜业、宜小生产的大舞台。另外可以看到，国家对于大湾区和城市群的规划，通过这类规划来解决传统城市“单打一”的状况，来解决单个城市解决不了而且解决起来又困难的问题，比如说生态共治、环境共保、基础设施共建和资源共享等问题。同时，支柱产业共树、产业链共塑，这些问题都必须在城市群、大湾区这么一个更大尺度的规划中进行城市之间的协调。

当然，我们也应该看到，在这个时候我们城市是追求质量的，现在提出要助推国家中心城市的发展，国家中心城市承担着在全球化进程中提升国际地位的任务，在全球能够参与到高等资源竞争的行列中去，同时带动区域经济持续发展。

趋势二：机动化会加剧郊区化动力

所谓机动化就是小汽车进入家庭，国际上有条规律就是机动化率如果达到30%以上，等于说当每个家庭有一辆车的时候，人们在空间移动的自由度就会上升，这个时候郊区化现象就开始出现。我国高速公路、高铁的里程已经达到了全球第一，再加上城乡人员的流动大大增强，城市之间的人口流动也普遍比以前大大地加速。在这种情况下，高铁、高速公路引导人们跨区域进行流动，这是一个普遍的现象。同时，超大规模城市的高房价、高生活成本也推动了一部分人要移居到小城市和乡村去。

在这种情况下，可以看到：第一，我们着重于特大城市应该进行有机疏散，应该建设卫星城，应该防止扁平化的、美国式的郊区化现象蔓延。第二，农村集体用地应该受到规划和用地性质的双重管制，农村建设用地应该有序地、有数量限制地进入城市的土地市场。第三，城乡紧凑式的改造发展，也就是说城市、乡镇，包括村庄作为一种人类聚居区的模式都应该通过空间紧凑式的改造来节约用地，实现土地减量化发展。只有土地减量化的紧凑式发展，我们才可以避免在机动化过程中出现过度郊区化现象。

趋势三：老龄化快速来临

按照联合国的标准，65岁以上老人占总人口的比重为7%的时候就可以定义为老龄化社会，按照这个指标我国在2000年的时候就已经达到了，而且通过趋势的推演，预计在2027年进入深度老龄化社会，那个时候65岁的老年人口占比会超过15%。这个数据看起来很平常，其实预示着我国老龄化的发展速度是非常快的。法国老龄化的整个进程用了115年，瑞士用了85年，英国用了80年，美国最短用了60年，但是我国只用20多年的时间就完成了这样一个进程。

未来，我们要着重于做以下几件对城市化有重大影响的事情：一要倡导居家养老，对城市社区进行适老化改造，没有电梯的建筑都应该装上电梯；二是城镇和乡村公共品都应该适老化，车站、码头、飞机场都应该迎合高龄老人需求；三是乡村养老将成为普遍现象，医疗服务特别是基于5G的远程医疗服务将会快速普及；四是老龄化社会将带动银发产业或者银发消费的蓬勃发展。

趋势四：城市人口增减分化

我国有三个领头羊式的城市群：长三角、珠三角、京津冀。这三大城市群的人口将会持续增加，但是根据大数据分析，目前已经有近200个城市出现了人口持续减少的情况。根据国际化的规律，东京的人口持续增长已经超过了50年，巴黎人口持续增长超过了120年，纽约人口持续增长超过了200年，所以大都市区人口的持续增长在城市化峰值后仍然会加快、会持续。

在这种情况下，第一，超大城市要规划都市圈，而且要建设周边卫星城，这些卫星城要以宜居城、低碳城的建设为重点；第二，造就一大批三四线城市的再次复兴，使高铁沿线的小城镇成为适宜养老和旅游的聚点；第三，资源枯竭型城市的再改造成为巨大市场，因为任何国民经济的可持续发展都要在城市群拉力与区域均衡发展之间找到一个合适的对策。

趋势五：住房需求逐渐减少

根据国际货币基金组织发布的咨询报告，像法国和日本这样的发达国家，在城镇化率峰值过去之后，人均住房面积为35～40平方米。我国绝大多数省份的抽样调查表明，人均住房面积已经达到这个数值，这就意味着许多三四线城市的住房空置率会逐步上升，许多地方当前已经出现的空城、鬼城现象会加剧。当然，也意味着一线城市随着人口的增长，房价上涨的压力也是非常巨大的。

这个时候，第一，我们的对策应该集中在发展高标准的、节能的绿色建筑，通过绿色建筑来降低建筑的能耗。第二，要对城市的老旧住宅小区进行加固、适老、节水、节能这样的系统改造。我预计我们国家现有的城市建筑面积超过了400亿平方米，其中至少有100亿平方米是需要加固、适老、加电梯、节能、节水改造的。第三，当跃过城镇化率峰值后，我们巨大的建材生产能力，巨大的城市建设能力，巨大的建筑施工能力，将随着“一带一路”倡议而展开，我们可以用积累的丰富经验来改造沿线有些国家的贫民窟。

趋势六：碳排放峰值将会提前

2015年微软创始人比尔·盖茨曾说，中国在2011—2013年期间用掉的水泥，比美国在整个20世纪用掉的还要多。同时中国近几年每年碳排放的总量也很多。对这样的问题应该客观对待，因为中国上半场的城镇化处在高峰期，每年有大量农民移居城市，要满足他们的住房需求，就要建造世界上将近一半的建筑量，而且中国不能像美国那样大量砍伐树木建造木头房子，我们只能用水泥钢筋满足人们对居住的需要。

更重要的是，统计数据显示，从工业革命到1950年，发达国家排放的二氧化碳量占全球累计排放量的95%；从1950年到2000年，发达国家碳排放量占到全球的77%。而中国，包括其他的发展中国家占有的比例较少，所以这是一个客观的现实，谁的积累比例更大谁就应该负有更大的责任。

当然，中国现在决心以绿色建筑和绿色交通应对气候变化，并且有很多有效的对策。第一，以绿色建筑和绿色交通来应对气候变化是最有效的，因为这是我们在工业碳排放减少以后两个最大的单项，而且是持续增长的单项。世界发展的规律表明，城市交通的排放和建筑的排放将会达到总排放的35%和33%，而产业的排放会逐渐缩小到30%之内。第二，建筑能耗可以通过在线监测和显示，在线显示后通过碳税市场进行交换和减排的奖励。第三，在应对气候变化上，应该给所有发展中国家和发达国家建成应对气候变化的共同体，共同为人类未来创造一个更好的地球。第四，城市的生态、绿色的改造将是一个长期的战略，因为根据联合国的统计，75%人为的温室气体排放来自于城市，只有城市绿色了，地球、乡村、自然、环境才会更加绿色。

三、来自八方面的挑战与对策

挑战一：能源和水资源的结构性短缺加剧

我国煤、石油、天然气的人均储量占全球平均比率为58.6%、7.7%、7.1%，实际上是一个缺气、少油、富煤的国家。在城镇化的后半场，需要对环境污染进行治理，需要对能源结构进行调整，这个时候，我国成为世界上最大的天然气进口国和世界上最大的石油进口国。在这种情况下，任何突然增加的用气都会造成气荒。

再从水的方面来看，我国人均水资源量约2 100立方米，仅为世界平均水平的28%，在这样一个水资源缺乏的国家，2016年，我们的农业用水占了62.4%，工业用水占21.6%，城镇用水占13.6%。但是根据国际上城镇化的一个规律，城镇化一旦越过中期进入到后半场，城镇的用水量会恒定，会慢慢减少，不会再增加，这是由用水价格的弹性及节水器具、水循环利用不断发展造成的。

不过，这样的好消息并不能带给我们很大的安慰，为什么？因为我们存在两个巨大的用水方面的挑战。第一，由于极端气候出现，会突发性地造成大面积降雨或者大面积旱涝，极端天气的出现使我们许多旱情超过以往千年的记录。第二，大的化工厂出现事故会造成大面积、突发性的水体污染，这个时候，下游的城市就必须把供水关掉，大面积的缺水就会突然出现。所以，我们应该有以下这些应对措施。

第一，大力发展太阳能、风能、生物质能源等新能源。我国将成为这些新能源比值最高，且数量最大、发展潜力最大的国家。第二，我们的清洁能源技术会大量拓展，煤转油、煤转气，或者煤层气的利用，将是非常重要的方向。第三，国际能源合作共同体的建设，将是我们外贸的一个重要主题。第四，我们要启动西北新能源基地。比如青藏高原、塔里木盆地，这些广袤无边的高原、沙漠，太阳能资源非常丰富。如果能够把这些地方的太阳能开发出三分之一，可以满足两个中国的能源需要。欧洲准备建立一个“撒哈拉沙漠计划”，就是把撒哈拉沙漠的太阳能输送到欧盟去，满足欧盟 30% 的需要。当然，这肯定是一个非常遥远的梦，但是中国在国内可以把更好的太阳能开发出来。我们可以启动深度的海绵城市规划和建设，可以使水在城市里 N 次循环利用，以水定城、以水定人。这个水是可以 N 次使用的，这已经被新加坡等国家证明了。第五，大力发展节水型农业、节水型工业，使水耗大幅度下降，节水本身将成为一个巨大的产业。

挑战二：水体、空气、土壤三大污染治理任务繁重

根据国际规律，每当一个国家的城镇化率达到 50% 以后，三大污染会扑面而来，达到最高峰。发达国家没有一个例外的，像英国在城镇化率超过 50% 的时候，英国主要的河流泰晤士河就成为一条污染非常严重、鱼虾具绝的河。德国、日本都在城镇化峰值左右出现了非常严重的环境污染。

更重要的是，当我们的城镇化和经济发展到了现在这样一种程度，我们的不平衡、不满意最大表现在于解决温饱以后的人民群众对水体污染、空气污染、土壤污染是最不能容忍的，所以党中央明确提出污染防治是三大攻坚战之一，比如说土壤污染的治理、大气污染的治理，再比如对垃圾填埋场进行改造，防止它们继续污染地下水。

挑战三：小城镇人口萎缩和人居环境退化

当前我国城镇化留下来的一个遗憾就是，大城市和中等规模城市不比发达国家逊色，基础设施可能比它们更好，建筑更光鲜，但最大的差距是在小城镇。在发达国家，最宜居的城市是小城镇，而我国的小城镇人居环境退化、环境污染、就业不足、管理粗放四个毛病并存。根据“五五”和“六五”的人口普查，我国在 10 年中，有相当于一个日本的人口从中国的小城镇转移到大城市里来了，所以加剧了大城市的膨胀。

在这种挑战下，首先，我们应该把两万多个小城镇中的一部分进行特色小镇的改造，要在产业特色、形态特色、人文特色和服务特色上加以提升，更大比例地利用最新通讯技术的发展引发“多用信息，少用能源”的竞赛。

其次，大城市应该定向地兼并小城镇的卫生院和小城镇的中小学，把他们改造成为大城市名院的分院和名校的分校，快速地使这些小城镇的公共品质量得到提升。

最后，我们应该把小城镇作为乡村振兴的总基地、总服务器，使得小城镇能够更好地为周边的农村、农民、农业服务。

挑战四：城市交通拥堵加剧

城市的交通拥堵加剧现象，已经从沿海城市扩展到内地城市，从城市早高峰的拥堵变成

了全天候的拥堵，从大城市的交通拥堵向中小城市蔓延。

在这种情况下，我国作为世界汽车制造大国和销售大国的情况还会继续存在。但是这也给我们带来了重大的机遇，第一，旧城区要大力进行增加交通毛细管式的改造，我们许多大院都要多开几个门方便群众出入，减少步行交通和自行交通的阻力。

第二，公共交通设施要进一步发展，因为这些交通工具，特别是地铁的发展不仅有一定的经济效益，它更应该侧重于社会效益、生态效益和城市的防空安全效益。

第三，我们应该利用5G时代，最快地实现共享汽车到无人驾驶的跨越，这样使得城市的实际用车量在未来若干年逐步减少。

第四，可以增加城市的步行道和架空道，使交通更加畅通，我们要大力发展共享单车甚至共享电动单车，使自行车包括电动自行车使用者大幅增加，这将会在5G时代给我们带来便利性。

挑战五：城镇历史文化风貌修复难度增大

许多城市号称自己有2000年历史，但是找不到自己的本地风貌特色。城市化最悲哀的是在完成城市化之后，建筑风格多样，但是缺乏本民族特色的建筑和本地建筑。我们一定要认识到城市的历史风貌是不可再生的、绿色的高等资源，只要保护好，它是不断增值的。

我们已经错过了城市大发展、大改造时期对历史街区、历史建筑保护的最好机会，如果再造历史建筑那就是“假古董”了，所以这方面对我们也有一些机遇。第一，历史文化名城、名镇保护的投资战略将成为主要的、数量极其庞大的新投资领域；第二，修复历史文物、优秀近代建筑、历史名人古居将成为普遍的，而且是从下而上的行为；第三，倡导新地方建筑风格，比如黄山市提出了“新徽派”，泉州提出了“新闽南派”，这都是很好的做法，使当地建筑的风貌，也就是几千年来与气候变化和社会人情能够结合的建筑形式能够延续和传承；第四，历史建筑要进行宜居节能的改造，保留建筑的风貌、符号和重要人文节点，同时应用一些新技术，使它们变得更宜居，使用起来更方便，居住起来更舒心。

挑战六：扼制住房投机泡沫任重道远

在中国民众的资产中，70%以上沉淀在房产里面，而美国不到30%，这是一个客观的现实。由此可以看到，要遏制住房投机泡沫是一个长期艰巨的战役，第一，应该对房地产税进行分类，率先出台能够精准遏制住房投机的消费税、流转税、空置税，然后再从容地考虑物业税如何征收。

第二，把房地产的调控从原来的中央调控为主转变为以地方为主，从行政手段调控为主变成以经济手段为主，从集中的统一调控、突击调控变为分散调控和经常调控，这样我们通过国民经济收入的增长，同时严格控制房价涨幅，逐渐“烫平”房地产泡沫，而不是一脚把它踢破。

第三，土地供应应该和城镇人口变化同步挂钩，现在通过大数据分析可以实时地观察城镇人口的变化。

第四，一线城市，特别是那些超大规模的城市应该推广合作建房和共有产权房，使房地产的波动逐步平缓。

挑战七：城市防灾减灾能力不足

一方面由于我国城市的人口密集度是全世界最高的，人口密度高、城市规模大就成了灾害的放大器；另一方面，城市的主要负责人任期短、交换频繁、外地人为主，会造成城市建设重表面、轻基础，所有这些倾向就导致了城市有内伤。

第一，我们许多城市管网陈旧，桥梁需要进行修复。意大利一个城市的桥梁发生倒塌，这个城市被宣布戒严一年，影响了国民经济的增长以及城市的形象。第二，住宅小区的综合性能提升改造是当务之急，许多建筑已经建成 30 年了，但是这些建筑的抗震性能必须重新进行监测和进行必要的加固。第三，要通过弹性城市来整合现在正在部署的绿色交通城市、智慧城市、新能源城市、园林城市、综合管廊城市和海绵城市，使这些新城市的发展模式整合在防灾减灾绿色发展这样一个总规划中。

挑战八：乡村振兴饱受“城乡一律化”干扰

最后，我们遇到的挑战是乡村振兴将会饱受“城乡一律化”的干扰。因为我们前半场城镇化发展得非常顺利，工业文明也为我们带来了巨大财富，所以在许多决策者的眼里，不由自主地就产生了用城市的发展模式来取代乡村建设，用工业的发展模式来取代农村的乡土建设，这些对乡村振兴的健康发展是不利的。第一，在乡村振兴的过程中，一定要弘扬“一村一品”，要大力发展有机农业、精品农业，一定要把村庄整治、村庄历史文化资产保护放在第一位，使它们成为永远有乡愁的乡村旅游基地。第二，通过乡村旅游再发现乡村传承了 5000 多年的一些独特的农副产品，提质提优多样化地进行发展。第三，传统村落的评比、美丽乡村的奖励应广泛推行，以激励的手段而不是包办的手段，通过农民觉悟的提升和提高，让他们自己动手建立文明的、有历史传承的幸福农村。第四，农村大量的宅基地和空置农房要建立稳定的流转政策，使得城乡能够更好融合。

总的来说，上半场城镇化我们取得了决定性的胜利，但是下半场任务仍然非常艰巨，城市是所有问题包括社会问题、经济问题的本质所在，但是也是解决这些问题的钥匙。

下半场我们要以城市群来引领城镇化的发展，应该启动大湾区战略迎接全球化的挑战；更多地使用 5G、人工智能、智慧城市、物联网、无人驾驶等突破性的新技术来促使城市能够更加绿色、更加宜居；通过城乡的生态修复、人居环境修补、产业的修缮，使我们的经济更加可持续、更平稳发展；通过国家中心城市建设，在全球化的进程中更多地聚集高等资源，发挥我们国家体制和文化的优势；在城镇化下半场这些已经提到的新的投资领域，将会涌现 30 多万亿新的投资机会，这些新的投资机会是传统投资项目本里没有的，这是我国经济持久、快速而且抗波动发展的利器。

（作者：仇保兴，国务院参事、住房和城乡建设部原副部长）

风口浪尖弄潮头

——深圳改革开放四十年回顾

我国改革开放已经走过了四十个春秋，深圳就是在这改革开放过程中，由一个边陲小镇发展成为一座高科技、现代化、国际性特大城市。深圳创造了中国发展史上的深圳速度；创造了由农村快速城市化的典范；创造了在一张白纸上跨越式的发展高科技产业群，并成为以高科技产业为支柱的创新型城市；在高速发展的同时，还加强环境建设，创造了全国环保模范城、全国森林城市等称号；在人口密度全国最高的情况下，创造了最好的人居环境；在经济高速发展的同时，群众生活水平、人均收入水平、社会保障水平、教育水平和医疗水平等都位于全国城市前列。以上这些是怎么做到的呢？为什么深圳能做到呢？

一、方向、路线是根本

党的十一届三中全会，确定了以经济建设为中心，抛弃了以阶级斗争为纲的路线，实现了国家发展方向的大转变，并确定了走社会主义市场经济的道路。没有这一转变，讲经济发展，特别是高速发展是不可能的。接着在邓小平同志的倡导下，把深圳开辟为经济特区，给予税收等优惠政策，让深圳进行社会主义市场经济的探索和试验。深圳市委、市政府带领全市人民，沿着建设社会主义市场经济的方向，在大风大浪中前行，不辱使命，杀出了一条血路，向全国人民交出了满意的答卷。

二、拓荒牛精神万岁

在建市初期，在市委、市政府办公楼前树起了由著名雕塑家潘鹤创作的《孺子牛》雕塑，这尊雕塑就成了深圳的建设者——拓荒牛们的象征，成了深圳精神——“开拓、创新、团结、奉献”的载体。深圳拓荒牛精神鞭策着拓荒者们齐心协力，同心同德，艰苦奋斗，勇敢开拓；激励着拓荒者们冒着酷暑，披着星辰，一往无前，奋不顾身；鼓舞着拓荒者们虚心学习，实践求知，讲求奉献，公而忘私。是这种精神造就了两万工程兵集体转业扎根边陲，克服了难以想象的困难，为深圳的早期发展立下了汗马功劳；是这种精神使中国三建集团等创造了三天一层楼的深圳速度，这是深圳奇迹的开始；是这种精神使任正非等一大批勇士成为名留青史的伟大企业家，正是有了他们创造性的领导才能，才撑起了深圳经济高速增长的大厦；是这种精神造就了新中国第一个拥有百万人的城市义工大军，他们用无私奉献精神谱写了人类的善良、和谐和无私奉献的城市风景线；也是这种精神在深圳这片土地上茁壮生长出近万人的义务抢险救灾大军，他们自买装备、自组训练、自掏腰包、自动上岗，只要哪里有救灾需要，哪里就有他们的身影；也是这种精神，使全市、全民动员开展了轰轰烈烈的特区与老区、山区、少数民族地区心连心、手拉手帮扶活动，仅湖南一省，就帮建了51所学校，解决了浏阳、韶山、宁乡、平江、双慈、张家界等失学儿童（有的到深圳成了流浪卖花女）24 000多人读书问题，在贵州的帮扶投入更多、效果更大。

总之，深圳拓荒牛精神已经成为深圳广大居民的精神财富，已经成为各级党委和政府工作的精神指南，已经成为引领深圳继续开拓前进的鲜艳红旗！

三、改变市场主体，走共同富裕道路

在计划经济时代，除了政府就是国有企业，还有少量集体企业。企业是政府的附属物，企业生产什么，生产多少都由政府用计划决定，可以说政府是生产要素配置的决定者，也是交易、分配的决定者。在这种计划经济体制情况下，中国经济运行了三十年。实践证明，这种以政府为主体、高度集权的计划经济，是短缺经济的根本原因，是不成功的。中央决定经济特区进行社会主义市场经济的探索和试验，当时一切要从头开始。

我们首先从改变市场主体开始。在市场经济条件下，企业不仅有国有、集体经济，又产生了民有、民营经济，还进入了外资所有经济，也产生了混合所有经济，实现了财产占有的多元化。不仅如此，企业由政府的附属物变成了市场的主体。于是，怎么调动市场主体的积极性？怎么提高市场主体的创造能力和提高劳动生产力？就成为我们改革的突破口。

一是推进国有企业改革。我们从两点出发：第一点是一定要扭转国企内部动力不足的问题，通过改革改制增强企业内生动力，增强企业的创新能力；第二点是充分调动企业员工的积极性，使其真正成为财产的主人，不仅要提高劳动报酬，也创造条件使之能分享企业的利润。于是，符合上市条件的企业，都在证券市场上市，成为公众性股份公司，深圳首先创立证券市场，对公众股份公司制度进行试验，接着就通过立法全面实施。

二是对国有中小企业，制订规章，试行企业职工内部持股制的试验，取得可喜成果。

三是在农村全面实行股份合作制，把村民变成股民，把政企不分的体制彻底分开，初见成效后，立法全面实施。

四是在新创建的高新技术企业中，实行劳动、技术、资本都可以拥有股权（产权）的方式。为此我们创立了资产交易所和无形资产交易所，对创造发明进行价值评估，使之更易于与资本的结合。同时，市政府用财政资金创立了高新投资有限公司和创新投资有限公司，在当时没有风险投资机制的情况下，这两个投资公司起到了至关重要的风险投资作用，现在这两个投资公司已经成为风投行业的领军企业。对高科技项目、资金、人才三位一体的高交会在荔枝节的基础上成为国家级高交会，已举办了二十届，对深圳乃至全国高科技产业的发展起到了重要推动作用。

与此同时，大力推动民有（民营）企业发展，给民有（民营）企业提供公平竞争的市场环境和必要的服务。政府的责任就是创造、规范市场环境，依法保护各种产权，建立和完善市场体系和运行机制，给各种组织形态的中、外企业，公、私企业创造公平发展和竞争的市场环境，从而推动生产力的大发展，推动科技进步和城市化及城市现代化进程。

实践证明，作为市场主体——企业财产权的明晰和运行机制的完善，是市场经济繁荣发展的必要条件。

四、着力建立并完善市场经济体制和运行机制

在发展市场经济时，我们始终把握一个有机的链条：政府培育市场、市场解放政府、政府解放企业、企业解放生产力。

一是政府培育市场。因为在计划经济时代没有市场。政府必须首先做培育市场的工作，市场主体需要什么，政府就培育什么。例如：我们在财政局基础上组建了独立的会计师事务所；在审计局基础上组建了独立的审计师事务所；委托司法局、市法院和市检察院组建律师事务所；委托科技局组建无形资产评估事务所；委托国资委组建资产评估事务所；等等。组建后，与政府机关脱钩，进行独立运作，形成为市场主体服务的中介服务体系。

二是市场解放政府。深圳市政府在全国率先减少行政审批，分几次逐步把行政审批减少三分之二以上。政府原有的一些职能在改革后，分别转到企业、市场、社会团体和中介服务机构，政府由全能政府转变为有限责任政府，由审批型政府转变为服务型政府，由全面政府配置资源转变为市场为主体配置资源。把政府从无限的权力中解放出来，使政府集中精力做好该做的事。

三是政府解放企业。政府被解放后，政府也解放了企业，企业（主要是国有企业）由政府附属物地位转变为市场主体地位，政府取消了企业的主管部门、取消了企业行政级别、取消了企业经营范围限制、取消了由政府决定企业待遇，转为由企业经营效益等指标决定企业职工待遇。企业面向市场，独立运作、自负盈亏，激发了企业的积极性和创造精神。

四是企业解放生产力。我们把改革的落脚点放在解放生产力上。国家的富强、人民的幸福，归根结底取决于生产力的提高，取决于科技的进步和劳动生产率的提高。我们千改革、万改革都是为了提高生产力这个目标。深圳的实践结果证明，我们这个目标达到了。我们在社会主义市场经济体制改革过程中，创立了市场经济的十大体系，即：以市场为主形成的价格体系，与国际接轨的经济核算体系，生产要素市场体系，国有资产经营管理体系，社会服务体系，社会保障体系，社会分配体系，精神文明建设体系，法律体系，政府调控体系。早在1996年国家体改委就发布文件，推广深圳的改革做法，并认定深圳已经初步建成社会主义市场经济的基本框架。

与此同时，我们还着力建设了五大运行机制，即：企业发展的内部动力机制，市场竞争的外部压力机制，法律的强制力机制，道德的自制力机制，政府的调控力机制。市场经济在

这五种力的作用下，形成一个合力，保障市场经济的顺利、正常运行。

五、市场经济是法治经济

从一定意义上讲，市场经济就是法治经济，用法律规范市场行为，用法律保护各种产权，用法律制止不正当竞争，用法律打击犯罪。总之，市场经济离不开法律。经济体制改革离不开政治体制改革，经济基础的改革离不开上层建筑改革。

中央要求深圳经济特区先行先试，但建特区初期，深圳经济特区没有立法权，有些市场经济行为又需要法律保护，又没有达到全国立法的程度。为了更好保障深圳对市场经济的探索和试验，深圳应该有立法权。全国人大虽然同意授予深圳经济特区立法权，已经提到全国人大会议上讨论，但是因为深圳没有立法机构而搁置下来。于1990年深圳召开了人代会之后，选举产生了市人大常委会，它的首要的任务就是继续争取立法权，并开展立法工作。

我担任了深圳第一届人大常委会主任，争取立法权的任务就落到了我的头上。这一天终于盼到了，1992年7月1日，七届全国人大常委会第26次会议在北京举行，把授予深圳经济特区立法权列入了议题。我作为深圳市人大常委会主任列席了会议，会上我做了十分钟的大会发言，受到热烈欢迎，最后以没有反对票（有很少几票弃权）的情况下通过。

我们开始立法就对市场主体——企业立法，我们打破以往按不同所有制立法的老框框，按企业组织形态立法，包括股份有限公司条例，有限责任公司条例，股份合作公司条例，合伙公司条例等，给各种不同所有制企业创造一个公平竞争的法律环境，对企业顺利发展起到了保护和推动作用。深圳市拥有一千多万外来务工人员，我们在全国第一个设立了保护外来劳务工条例，使广大劳动者的权益得到法律保护。接着立法工作全面展开，自1992年7月1日深圳获得特区立法权至今，共制定法规228项，其中先行先试类110项、创新变通类58项，先行先试类和创新变通类法规占制定法规的74%，有力保障了市场经济的顺利发展。深圳市已被广东省评为依法治市先进单位。

六、调整产业结构，大力发展高新技术产业

建特区初期，由于没有条件，吸引到深圳投资的“三来一补”企业大多是产业链末端的、附加值低的甚至是污染环境的小印染厂、小电镀厂、小玩具厂等。当时我到蛇口工业区去调研，发现小印染厂就有53家。靠这些企业无法支持深圳的可持续发展，更谈不上高速发展，而且破坏生态环境。于是，市委市政府决定坚决调整产业结构，发展高新技术产业，淘汰落后产业。在城市规划修编中确定了两目标：一是把深圳建设成高新技术产业基地；二是把深圳建设成区域性金融中心。

于是，市委市政府决定对污染环境、破坏生态的“三来一补”企业，要么转型升级，要么退出深圳。实行“腾笼换鸟”。此项工作十分艰难，涉及方方面面的利益，阻力很大，

但我们坚定不移。

一是发展高科技产业没有人才不行，我们实行两手抓，一手是从长远着眼抓教育，招聘教育人才，提高教学质量；提高师资待遇，教师的平均工资比公务员平均工资高10%等；建市初期就创建了深圳大学，接着建立深圳高级职业技术学院，培养实干型高级专才；动员全市建立奖教、奖学的教育基金，奖励优秀教师和优秀学生。我们明确提出：经济要上，教育要热。现在看来，成效卓著：深圳大学培养出以腾讯马化腾、光启刘若鹏为代表的一大批优秀人才，已经在市场经济活动中和高科技创新中崭露头角。深圳高级职业技术学院已经成为全国最好的高职院，人才普遍受到市场的欢迎。另一手是到市外、国外去招聘人才。1992年我率团到美国去招聘留学生回国，那是我国第一次到海外招聘人才，到美国几个著名大学去介绍深圳经济特区，介绍招聘人才的优惠政策，对掌握技术已从事工作的留学生回国优先，科技团队优先，有高科技项目的优先，来去自由，还制订了一系列其他优惠政策。从此以后，形成留学人员归国热潮，现已有近12万留学归国人员在深圳创业。

二是建立科技市场机制（如前所述）。

三是大力推动科技人员和经营者持有股权。在深圳90%以上的高科技企业实行科技人员持股，华为是发展最好的典型实例，在18万职工中有98 000人持股，创始人任正非只占百分之一多一点。

四是奖励创新，推动研发，保护知识产权。深圳的研发机构90%以上设在企业，深圳注册的专利几十年来一直排全国第一。申请专利政府有补助，资识产权严格受到法律保护。

五是进行高科技产业发展空间布局的大调整。我们在南山区建立高科技产业园，园内有吸收国内名校的研发机构和孵化器。南山区2018年GDP为5 018亿元，战略性新兴产业的增加值占GDP的比重达59.1%，国家级高新技术企业3 579家，累计培育上市公司（在南山区成长上市的企业）150家。

我们在偏僻的坪山、坪地两镇设立龙岗大工业区，特区内不再摆大工业项目，特区内只发展高科技产业和研发机构及金融等高端现代服务业，现在按照这个目标完全实现了。

深圳2018年全市高新技术产业增加值8 296.63亿元，占GDP比重34.25%。好多高科技产品填补了国家空白。现在，人们把深圳称为中国的硅谷。深圳已经成为以高新技术产业为支撑的创新型城市。高新技术产业基地和区域性金融中心的规划目标已经实现。

七、风口浪尖弄潮头

风口浪尖弄潮头，改革必伴热血流。
血路杀得伤遍体，夕阳染红孺子牛。

邓小平同志让我们探索出一条新路来，现在回过头来看，才体会到邓小平同志这句话的分量。

建特区之初，有人说特区是租界，坚持反对。有的老干部访问深圳后哭了，说我们白革命了，深圳除了五星红旗还在飘扬以外，都改变颜色了。还有首都学术界人士发文说深圳的资本主义之风向内地猛吹，1989 年之前他们敢讲私有化，1989 年之后他们不敢讲私有化了，他们以股份化代替私有化，股份化是私有化的潜行。特区试验股份制成了某些学术界批判特区搞私有化的一大“罪状”！

特区为试验市场经济争取立法权，在七届全国人大第 26 次常委会即将授予深圳经济特区立法权的时候，有的领导同志甚至提出授予深圳经济特区立法权是“违宪”。多亏万里委员长和曹志秘书长在表决前组织专家研讨的结论：并不违宪，并指定由我取代他在大会发言。否则，授予深圳经济特区立法权可能夭折。

1996 年我在中央党校学习，我借学习机会把深圳关于产权方面的改革总结一下，写成了《关于所有制若干问题的思考》，作为毕业论文交给了党校。文中主张发展股份经济、股份合作经济，主张混合所有制经济，主张发展职工内部持股的新型的公有制经济的实现形式，主张财产占有社会化、分散化、群众化、股份化，形成强大的有产的劳动阶层，避免财产占有向少数人手里集中，产生两极分化。贯彻邓小平同志提出的走共同富裕道路。

我刚离开中央党校回到深圳，就有人领导策划和组织了首都学术界在中央党校召开批判这篇论文的会议，并定性为“反党、反社会主义的政治宣言和经济纲领”，但由于中央主要领导的决断，事情才平息下来。

邓小平同志讲，要在内地再造几个“香港”。我的理解是，通过利用香港式的自由贸易区、自由港机制，进一步扩大对外开放，进一步发展我们自己的生产力，进一步壮大我们的综合国力。我认为深圳最有条件再造一个香港，于是市委决定组织力量设计自由贸易区方案，其主要内容是：双向合作、双线管理、双港起飞、双币流通。

双向合作：一面面向国内，一面面向国际，国内是依托，国际是合作。深圳成为连接国内和国际两个市场的枢纽。双线管理：面临香港这边是一线，一线管出口，不出一线不是出口；面临内地这边是二线，二线管进口，不出二线不是进口。双港起飞：把海港、空港建设成国际自由贸易港，国际物流、人流、资金流、信息流的枢纽港。双币流通：在深圳自由贸易区内，放宽金融管制，人民币和港币都同时流通，自由兑换，等等。

把设计方案向上级领导汇报后，以我挨批和受到口头警告而告终。

在苏联解体之后，中国向何处去？是走邓小平同志倡导的改革开放的路子，还是重回阶级斗争路线？特区是姓资还是姓社？特区向何处去？一时间，风起云涌，有山雨欲来风满楼的架势。有位学者，这时利用各种场合和媒体，剑指邓小平同志的改革开放路线，先从攻击特区开始，给特区罗织了许多罪状，如：特区是剥削内地，特区是国中之国，特区是培养特殊利益集团，特区是寻租，政治寻租是在北京找代理人，经济寻租是向京官行贿，等等，不一而足。在全国造成很大负面影响。尤其是对在特区艰苦奋斗的广大干部群众刺激很大，伤害很深。在无可奈何情况下，我们应战了。我在回答记者提问时，严厉地、正面地回答了记者：建立经济特区是邓小平同志倡导、党中央决策的，根本不存在向中央领导寻租问题。接着《深圳特区报》连续发表了三篇评论文章，正面批驳这位学者对特区的攻击，使特区发展尽可能不受侵扰，保持良好的发展态势。

在深圳第二次党代会上，我们提出了进行产业结构调整，大力发展高端制造业，大力发展高新技术产业和现代服务业，淘汰掉一些污染环境的“三来一补”企业。而这些“三来一补”企业与村民利益结合很紧密，会损害一些村民的眼前利益，工缴费和房租是村民的收入来源。于是村主任联名告我状，罪名是：侵犯村民利益，破坏安定团结。惊动了时任省委书记谢非同志，他找我谈话了解情况，进而他让省委政策研究室主任钟阳胜率团来深圳调研，钟的调查报告是支持深圳产业结构调整。谢非还不放心，又亲自到深圳调研两天，最后他决定，在深圳召开发展高新技术产业现场会，推广深圳的经验。“罪状”变成了经验，谢非同志对深圳发展高科技产业的支持，起到了至关重要的作用。前几年我见到一位村主任，我问他：现在怎么样？他说：“当年我们短视眼，对不起你啦！现在是八个字：坐以待币，度日如年。”他又解释说：“待币是人民币的币，每月我们的账户都会进钱。生活每天都像过年。哈哈！”

我在想：人民群众生活好了！一切挫折都值得。一路走来，风雨交加，雷声大作。但是，深圳拓荒牛们仍然奋不顾身、砥砺前行。

八、几点建议

习近平总书记提出的建设大湾区战略，令人鼓舞。我认为要建成世界级的湾区，在我们的实际情况下，要通过顶层设计解决两大问题：一是香港、澳门与深圳、珠海的人流、物流、资金流、信息流等生产要素要自由流动问题。这是在湾区的核心区内，若生产要素不能自由流动，将无法与世界一流湾区媲美。要做到这样，就应该把深圳和珠海建成自由贸易区和自由港。二是在珠三角九个城市间的经济活动中，实现经济活动同城化。

以上两点做到了，建世界一流湾区的设想就有了实现的体制和机制保障。此其一。

中央早已提出，建立房地产市场的长效机制。我认为深圳可以试验。深圳面临的最大问题是因为房价太高，使打工者租不起房，更买不起房，对在深圳工作生活感到失望。深圳企业生存环境变差，困难重重，并且难度在加大。在此背景下，深圳房地产要采取重大措施：一是工业用地，对符合深圳产业发展的工业项目，政府应采取低价政策；二是由政府组织建设、管理和定价的公租房（廉租房），政府给予补贴。使买不起房的居民、打工者能租得起、住得下，留住人才，对城市发展就没有风险了；三是对房地产商应该主要是靠自有资金开发房地产，银行贷款占比要大幅下降，这样国家银行就没有风险了；四是对符合城市总体规划、建筑质量达标的小产权房，转成大产权房。但有一个限制条件：此房出租时，必须与公租房同价。此其二。

深圳现有户籍人口454.7万人，常住人口1 302.66万人，实际管理的人口超过2 000万人。户籍人口才占总人口的22.7%，占常住人口的37.7%。长期以来户籍人口比例失调，对于较长时间在深圳工作、有正当职业和居所（包括租房）和家庭基础已经在深圳的，都应加快解决他们的深圳户籍问题。这主要是解决存量问题，贯彻共享原则。这是城市化过程中应该解决的问题，可使城市更增加凝聚力。此其三。

最后，祝福深圳在以习近平同志为核心的党中央的正确领导下，深圳在粤港澳大湾区建设中发挥更大作用，取得更大成功。

（作者：厉有为，深圳市原市长、市委书记）

信息技术赋能智慧城市

在介绍全球与中国城镇化发展现状的同时，以数据表现大城市病带来的影响，指出智慧城市建设正当时。从信息技术推动城市数字化、网络化和智能化，论述智慧城市发展的技术基础。从绿色城市、健康城市、平安城市、宜居城市和创新城市等方面说明智慧城市的内涵。最后讨论了智慧城市发展的机遇与挑战。

一、智慧城市建设正当时

联合国经济和社会事务部公布的《2018 年世界城市化趋势》报告显示[1]，今天世界上55%的人口居住在城市中，预计到2050 年，全球城市化率有望达 68%。改革开放以来中国城镇化的发展与经济发展相互促进，2018 年我国城镇化率为 59.58%，超过了全球平均水平，同时全国大多数省会城市城镇化率已经达到 70%。目前，发达国家城市化率大多在75%以上，与此相比，我国的城镇化水平与发达国家还有 15 个百分点的差距。

随着城市越来越大，大城市病越来越突出，表现为人口膨胀、交通拥堵、环境污染、资源环境承载力超限等。根据《2018 年度中国主要城市交通分析报告》[2]，2018 年全国 361 个城市中，有 61%的城市通勤高峰时处于缓行状态，有 13%的城市处于拥堵状态。北京高峰时段出行用时较正常多约一倍，因交通拥堵造成的时间成本占月平均工资的 12.4%。在环保方面，2018 年全国 338 个地级及以上城市中空气质量达到国家标准的为 121 个，比 2017年增加 22 个城市，但仍有 64.2%的城市超标[3]。据世界卫生组织评价，世界上 92%的人口生活在空气质量水平超标的地方[4]。据亚洲开发银行于 2013 年初发布的《迈向环境可持续的未来——中国国家环境分析》一书测算，中国 500 个大型城市中，只有不到 1%的城市达到了世界卫生组织的空气质量标准[5]。世界银行报告对中国空气污染引致的疾病成本估算约为 GDP 的 1.2%[6]。根据 2018 年我国经济—生态生产总值（GEEP）报告，2015 年中国污染损失成本为 2 万亿元[7]。中国拥有的大城市数量全球最多，城市病的问题更为严重和普遍。根据联合国的数据手册《2018 年的世界城市》[8]，人口超过 1 000 万的大城市数量从2014 年的 28 个增长到 2018 年的 33 个，其中我国北京、上海、重庆、天津、广州、深圳共6 个城市上榜，中国百万人口以上的城市有 140 多个，而美国只有 10 个。

城市的问题需要从城市的规划、建设、运营、管理等方面多管齐下来解决，在新一代信息技术快速兴起的时代，将 IT（信息技术）与 OT（城市设施与运营技术）结合应用到城市的建设与管理，将有助于解决城市发展中出现的问题。中国正处在全面建设社会主义现代化国家的新征程，在创新驱动高质量发展的道路上，信息化与城镇化及工业化相伴而行，现在正是将智慧城市为代表的城市信息化理念应用到城市建设与管理中的最好时期。

二、智慧城市的技术基础

城市的信息化从数字城市起步，先进的信息基础设施是数字城市的基础，宽带城市和无线城市是数字城市的必要条件。到 2018 年年底我国固网宽带家庭普及率与移动宽带用户普及率分别达到 86.1% 和 93.6%，均高于对应的全球平均水平（52.3% 和 69.3%），2019 年中国光纤到户占宽带用户之比将超过 90%，在 300 个以上城市部署千兆宽带接入网络[9]。5G 具有用户体验数据率高达 100Mbps 的增强移动宽带能力、99.999% 的高可靠性和空口时延 1ms 的低时延能力、每平方公里百万传感器接入的大连接性能，随着 5G 的商用，将为城市的交通、安防、环保、医疗等智能化管理提供更强有力的手段。

数字城市还需要有较强的计算资源，需要有支撑城市经济和社会发展及民生服务的云计算能力及应用水平。除了集中的云计算外，边缘计算技术的发展将适应车联网和远程医疗及工业互联网等对时延敏感的业务需要，提高城市的机动性和快速响应能力。在数字城市中，以电子政务和线上服务为代表的政府与社会公共服务实现数字化，数字政府、数字企业和数字化生活是数字城市在政治、经济和民生等方面的体现。

感知城市是城市信息化的另一重要特征。运用遥感、全球定位系统、地理信息系统等技术，对城市进行多尺度、多时空、多分辨率和多用途的三维素描，给出城市的虚拟实现。利用物联网实现对城市运行状态的动态监视，对数据进行分析和处理并与城市地理空间信息融合，强化城市空间的实时感知力度。基于许可频段的窄带物联网 NB-IOT 因其广覆盖大连接和低成本低功耗而受到电信运营商的重视，2018 年年底全国已建 NB-IOT 基站覆盖 346 个城市，到 2020 年，我国 NB-IoT 网络将实现全国普遍覆盖，而向室内、交通路网、地下管网等应用场景实现深度覆盖，基站规模达 150 万个[10]。另外，基于非许可频段工作的窄带物联网标准 LoRa 具有低功耗和长距离的特点，现计划升级到 2.0 版本，面向室内应用为主，提供即插即用便捷连接。国际标准化机构还着手在 5G 标准中增加更多种的业务带宽和能力的窄带物联网标准。国内已经开展的窄带物联网应用包括智能抄表、车联网、外勤办公、移动支付、智慧金融、智慧城市和园区、家用电器、安防监控和设备监控 9 大领域。

物联网产生大数据，以城市摄像头为例，根据咨询公司 IHS Markit 2016 年的数据[11]，中国共装有 1.76 亿个监控摄像头。其中属于公安系统天网工程的有 2 000 万个，以北京为例，摄像头数 115 万个，每平方公里 71 个或每千人 59 个，仅为美国平均水平（每千人 96 个）的 60%。1080p 监控摄像头最高码流是 8M，数据量每天 86.4GB，实际上码流与帧率可根据时段和场景预置，如按每天 40GB 存储量计算，具有百万量级摄像头的城市每天将产生 40PB，若需存储一个月则数据量高达 1.2EB。

除了传感器外，网络也产生大数据，每个人都会在网络上留下脚印，网络数据其规模与物理世界产生并收集的数据相当。伴随城市大数据的发展，超算能力每十年提高一千倍，有望在2020年达到百亿亿次每秒，基于深度神经网络技术的算法发展也很快。算力、算法与大数据结合的城市大脑应运而生，利用人工智能技术可从城市大数据中发掘出重要价值，从中可感知社会的脉搏，发现大众关注的热点和捕捉城市的突发事件。人工智能技术与应用的兴起使数字城市、感知城市发展到数据城市和智能城市，切实提升了城市的智能化水平。

三、智慧城市建设的内涵

如果说数字城市、感知城市、数据城市是智慧城市的必要条件，那么绿色城市、健康城市、平安城市、宜居城市、创新城市、人文城市等是智慧城市应有之意。

目前城市人口约占全球人口的50%，但消费全球2/3的能源和产生70%的温室气体排放，绿色城市的意义不言而喻。能源互联网将现代信息技术与可再生能源的应用结合，优化城市的能源供给与消费，为分布式光伏电源并网提供技术支撑。智能电表的普及推动峰谷电价的实施，通过削峰填谷实现负载均衡。利用传感器可以发现建筑物内那些房间没人，可节省照明与空调或暖风供给。1980年到2000年的20年间，欧盟GDP增加56%，而资源消耗量仅增长2%左右[12]，可见依靠科技力量就能减少资源消耗。各类地面和星载或机载环保传感器的应用，可监测城市大气、水体和土壤的污染，通过大数据与人工智能技术的分析，发现污染源和成因。垃圾分类，减少填埋处理，雨污分流，推进海绵城市建设，城市内企业间热能互补，产业上下游物料循环利用，实现资源节约和环境友好，使绿色城市不仅是低碳城市也是生态城市。

世界卫生组织在1994年给健康城市的定义是：“健康城市应该是一个不断开发、发展自然和社会环境，并不断扩大社会资源，使人们在享受生命和充分发挥潜能方面能够互相支持的城市[13]。”信息技术的合理使用将更能体现以人的健康为中心，保障广大市民健康生活和工作。基于人工智能技术的医学影像分析软件对病理图片的癌细胞和CT图片中的肿瘤识别准确率超过90%，还可自动生成具体的放射性照射方案或者手术方案，显著提升医生的工作效率。利用5G+AR辅助解剖试验和手术模拟可缩短培训外科医生的时间。在2019年3月16日，海南总医院医生通过5G网络远程操控电子机械臂，对在北京的帕金森病患者成功完成了“脑起搏器”植入手术，5G的高带宽、高可靠、低时延保证了3小时手术完全成功。数字医疗改进对医务人员的教学、培训、实习，提升医生的诊治水平，提供及时的远程救治指导，降低医疗成本和患者的负担，对实现医疗基本服务均等化有重要意义。

深度学习算法在语音和图像识别领域取得重大突破，基于摄像头的人脸识别准确率已经超过人眼。目前国内企业已开发出城市级别的一万路卡口、一秒查询一年轨迹数据的人像大数据平台。现在国内很多地方80%以上的案件破获都用了“人像大数据”系统，该系统还可用于寻找失踪小孩和老人。深圳的平安城市部署了视频监控工程和移动警务平台，2016年警方破获了1.5万多起案件，抓捕2.45万名嫌犯，报案量从2012年59.4万件降低到

2017年的20.5万件[14]。各地还运用数字地图技术，实现快速查找消防工作薄弱环节，通过“火眼”模型预测建筑火灾风险，通过水电气数据分析预测群租房，通过建设对危化品企业的安全风险数据联网监测系统有效提升危化品事故精细防控水平。现代信息技术还使城市能够快速响应应急事件，保障人民生命财产安全。

便捷的交通出行是宜居城市的重要衡量指标，中国的一二线城市都面临交通拥堵的困惑，智能交通是当务之急。根据地图公司获得的手机定位数据可掌握城市拥堵的路段与时段，可提供实时导航，优化道路与公交路线的设置。杭州在1 300个路口装有4 500路视频接入，将摄像头与红绿灯通过人工智能技术关联，通行效率提升10%。5G将加快车联网的应用，根据IHS预测，2022年全球联网汽车市场占比将达到24%，具有联网功能的新车销量占比达94%[15]。智能交通不仅提升效率且利于节能环保及保障出行安全。美国交通部2015年发布智能交通战略研究计划，预计通过车联网技术可以降低82%潜在的道路安全事故[16]。美国史蒂文斯理工学院在评估智能技术对汽车能源影响的研究中，计算出采用智能汽车技术每年每辆车可减少油耗的6%~23%，即美国每年节约62亿美元的燃料成本[17]。便捷出行、智能家居优化能耗的管理、电子商务等方便市民生活，生态城市和健康城市让市民宜居乐业，人文城市将使生活在城市的人们有归属感。

联合国欧洲经济委员会与国际电信联盟将智慧城市内涵扩展到智慧可持续发展城市，他们联合给出如下定义[18]：“智慧可持续发展城市（SSC）是创新城市，它采用ICT和其他技术来改进生活质量、提高城市运行与服务效率并加强竞争力的同时，确保人们当前和未来的经济、社会、环境和文化等方面的需求得以满足。”国家的创新力体现在城市，一个城市创新水平的高低与当地科技公司、研究机构、风险资本、营商环境以及教育水平等因素息息相关。绿色、平安、健康、宜居的城市为科技创新提供了很好的生态，而智慧城市的可持续发展需要创新能力与数字经济来赋能。新一代信息技术的发展将互联网扩展到工业互联网，为产业转型升级提供新动能。据IHS Markit研究报告[19]，到2035年全球GDP将因5G而增加7%。埃森哲预期[20]，使用人工智能作为全新的生产要素后，2035年有望推动中国劳动生产率提高27%。麦肯锡的调研报告也显示[21]，物联网在2025年可产生高达11.1万亿美元的收入，仅就城市环境改善方面就贡献1.6万亿美元（其中环保贡献约0.7万亿美元、智能交通0.5万亿美元）。

四、智慧城市发展的思考

麦肯锡在2018年关于智慧城市研究报告中提出[22]，联合国可持续发展17项目标中的70%与智慧城市有关，智慧城市的应用能改进人们生活质量的10%~30%，包括降低10%~15%的温室气体排放，减少20%~30%的水消耗，减少10%~20%的固体废弃物；减少生病负担的10%~15%；减少8%~10%的死亡，减少30%~40%的犯罪事件，应急响应时间缩短20%~35%；节约与医院和政府联系的时间45%~65%；正式的工作岗位增加1%~3%；市民生活成本降低1%~3%。

智慧城市的效果会因城市不同而异，上述报告给出了主要城市的比较。在智慧城市的技术（传感器、通信与开放数据门户）方面，满分为37，得分最高的纽约为24.4，斯德哥尔摩为24，中国深圳、北京、香港、上海得分在18.8～20.5，优于东京的14.8分。在智慧城市的应用部署（移动性、安全性、公共事务、医疗保健和经济发展）方面，满分为55，纽约和伦敦得分最高为34.5，中国香港、上海、北京和深圳得分在26.5～31，东京为27分。在本地居民对所在城市智能化应用的感受和满意度方面，满分为30，北京、上海和深圳得分为23.2～24.2，位于全球所调研城市之首。从上述得分看，我国的智慧城市的发展得到市民的认可，但离大众的要求还有很大差距。即便按现有评分标准获得高分，也不意味着智慧城市的发展到头了，智慧城市的建设仅仅是开始，其发展是一个过程而不是结果，智慧城市永远在路上。

信息技术是双刃剑，其应用不当也会适得其反。摄像头已经无处不在，分布广而且24小时在线，全球228个国家和地区，8 063个城市，有2 635万个摄像头暴露在公网，中国占17%[23]。摄像头口令短、认证简单、安全防护能力弱，容易受到DDoS（拒绝服务）攻击、机构安全风险、个人隐私泄露等事件层出不穷。2016年10月，十万多个被木马所控的摄像头组成的僵尸网络发起的DDoS攻击导致美国互联网大面积瘫痪。工业互联网大量使用传感器，即便没有联到外网，也会因管理不善通过U盘在内外网间关联而引入病毒，2010年伊朗部分核设施被“震网”病毒入侵而瘫痪就是一例。自动驾驶用得好会给交通安全加分，但其软件缺陷或其控制被劫持则后果不堪设想。因此，建设和管理智慧城市需要特别重视网络安全，所用的信息技术产品需要成熟稳定和自主可控。

信息技术在智慧城市中将起到很重要的作用，但仅有信息技术是不够的，需要与城市建筑、交通、物流、环保、治安、医疗、产业等技术结合，而且技术离开管理很难发挥作用。城市是一个复杂的大系统，需要多学科结合，多部门合作，技术与管理并重。智慧城市需要城市领导人的大智慧，但市民大众的参与是智慧城市成功的关键，毕竟智慧城市是以人为中心的城市。麦肯锡报告认为，政府是70%的智慧城市应用项目的主体，但智慧城市项目可以采取市场化机制来推进，按照一些城市的经验，私营机构承担了智慧城市建设投资资金的60%。随着智慧城市发展的深入，运行机制和商业模式的探索一定会产生更多可推广的好经验。

（作者：邬贺铨，中国工程院院士，中国互联网协会理事长）

参考文献

[1] UN DESA, World Urbanization Prospects: The 2018 Revision, https://esa.un.org/unpd/wup/Publications/Files/WUP2018-KeyFacts.pdf.

[2] 高德地图，http://www.ha.xinhuanet.com/news/2019-01/17/c_1124000815.htm.

[3] 生态环境部，2018中国生态环境状况公报，http://www.mee.gov.cn/hjzl/zghjzkgb/lnzghjzkgb/201905/

P020190529498836519607. pdf，2019.

[4] WHO，Ambient air pollution：A global assessment of exposure and burden of disease，https：//apps. who. int/iris/bitstream/handle/10665/250141/9789241511353 – eng. pdf? sequence = 1&isAllowed = y，2016.

[5] https：//bbs. pinggu. org/thread – 2739030 – 1 – 1. html.

[6] Worldbank，Cost of Pollution in China，http：//documents. worldbank. org/curated/en/782171468027560055/pdf/392360CHA0Cost1of1Pollution01PUBLIC1. pdf，2007.

[7] 生态环境部环境规划院《中国经济生态生产总值核算发展报告 2018》，http：//finance. sina. com. cn/roll/2019 – 01 – 14/doc-ihqhqcis5926372. shtml，2019.

[8] UN，The World's Cities in 2018，https：//www. un. org/en/development/desa/population/publications/pdf/urbanization/the_ worlds_ cities_ in_ 2018_ data_ booklet. pdf.

[9] http：//www. gov. cn/xinwen/2019 – 05/15/content_ 5391970. htm.

[10] 工业和信息化部办公厅关于全面推进移动物联网（NB – IoT）建设发展的通知，http：//www. miit. gov. cn/n1146290/n4388791/c5692751/content. html. 2017.

[11] https：//technode. com/2017/11/22/china-to-have-626-million-surveillance-cameras-within-3-years/.

[12] 钱易，http：//finance. ifeng. com/c/7nEaNJF8IwA.

[13] https：//baike. baidu. com/item/% E5% 81% A5% E5% BA% B7% E5% 9F% 8E% E5% B8% 82/270149? fr = aladdin.

[14] HIS Markit，2018 平安城市智能视频监控发展趋势和评价体系，https：//wenku. baidu. com/view/d752e5b70875f46527d3240c844769eae109a372. html.

[15] 中国信通院，车联网白皮书 2017，http：//www. caict. ac. cn/kxyj/qwfb/bps/201804/P020170928592209280350. pdf.

[16] U. S. Department of Transportation. Intelligent Transportation Systems（ITS）Strategic Plan Background and Process. http：//www. slideserve. com/larya/intelligent-transportation-systems-its-strategic-plan-background-and-process.

[17] http：//www. chuandong. com/news/news. aspx? id = 224530.

[18] UNECE and ITU，October 2015，https：//www. itu. int/en/ITU-T/ssc/united/Pages/default. aspx.

[19] IHS，5G 经济：5G 技术将如何影响全球经济，https：//www. qualcomm. cn/media/documents/files/ihs-5g-economic-impact-study. pdf，2017.

[20] Accenture，《人工智能：助力中国经济增长》https：//www. accenture. com/cn-zh/insight-artificial-intelligence-china，2017.

[21] Mckinsey，The Internet of Things：Mapping the value beyond the hype，https：//www. mckinsey. com/~/media/McKinsey/Business% 20Functions/McKinsey% 20Digital/Our% 20Insights/The% 20Internet% 20of% 20Things% 20The% 20value% 20of% 20digitizing% 20the% 20physical% 20world/The-Internet-of-things-Mapping-the-value-beyond-the-hype. ashx，2015.

[22] Mckinsey，Smart Cities：Digital solutions for a more livable future，https：//www. mckinsey. com/industries/capital-projects-and-infrastructure/our-insights/smart-cities-digital-solutions-for-a-more-livable-future 2018.

[23] 华顺信安，《网络空间测绘系列—2018 年摄像头安全报告》，https：//www. aqniu. com/industry/42210. html.

5G 助力城市智慧化和高质量发展

2019 年 6 月 6 日，中国发放了四张 5G 牌照，标志着中国正式进入 5G 商用元年。5G 一直是当前全社会关注的热词，尤其是中美经贸摩擦以来，5G 更是成为全球的焦点，那么 5G 究竟是什么？给我们的生活、生产和城市发展能带来什么变化和发展？5G 将在哪些领域应用？5G 的商用进程如何？这些问题是大家普遍关心的问题，本文将从移动通信的发展历程和发展规律，5G 的概念、内涵、能力、产业进展和应用场景等方面进行阐述，希望对认识 5G 和推动 5G 发展，尤其是在城市各领域的应用有参考价值。

一、5G 是什么？

5G 是指第五代移动通信系统（The 5th Generation of Mobile Communication），其在国际电信联盟（ITU）的学名为 IMT－2020。移动通信是 20 世纪 70 年代由美国贝尔实验室发明的技术，80 年代初进入商用，采用模拟技术，用于移动电话业务，被称为第一代移动通信技术（即 1G），1987 年我国引入，手机被称为“大哥大”。移动通信基本上每十年出现一代新技术，当一代技术进入商用时就启动下一代技术的研究，每一代新技术都是追求更高速率、更大容量等，至今经历了 1G、2G、3G、4G 到 5G 的发展，从最初的只有电话业务，发展到今天 4G 的广泛应用，移动互联网的广泛普及，深刻改变了人们的生活方式。

移动通信具有全球漫游的特点，一部手机走天下，无处不在的信号覆盖和无时不能的通信是任何其他手段不可比拟的优势，因而国际标准、全球产业是其突出的特点。但是在移动通信三十几年的发展历程中，从 1G 到 4G 每一代技术都伴随着多个标准之争，5G 是第一个从开始就在全球范围内形成共识，即共同制定全球统一标准的一代技术。5G 也是第一个从开始就要满足移动物联网需求的技术，开启了从人人互联到万物互联，从改变生活到改变社会的新阶段。

5G 定义了三大应用场景和八大能力。三大应用场景（图 1）为增强移动宽带（eMBB）、海量机器类通信（mMTC）和超高可靠低时延通信（uRLLC）。三大应用场景中，一个是面向移动互联网，另外两个都是面向移动物联网应用，其中一个是面向量大面广的全应用场景，可以广泛用于智慧城市，其典型的技术就是现在正在大力推动的 NB－IoT 技术，或称之为窄带物联网技术；另一个是面向自动驾驶、工业控制等的场景。

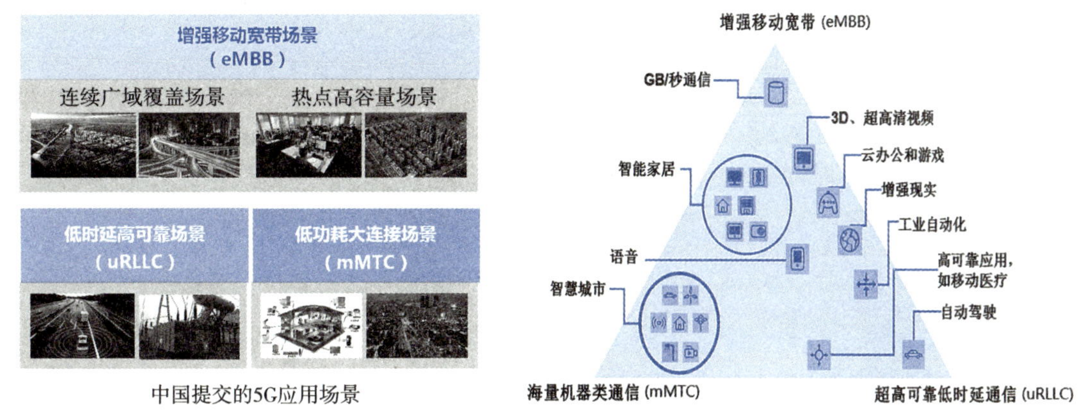

图1　5G三大应用场景

5G的八大能力（图2）包括峰值速率最高20bps、用户体验速率最高达到Gbps、频谱效率比4G提升3倍、时延到毫秒级、单位平方公里百万个连接、移动性500公里/小时、网络能量提升100倍、流量密度每平方米10Mbps八个方面。从中比较可以看出，这些能力与4G相比提高了10倍到100倍。

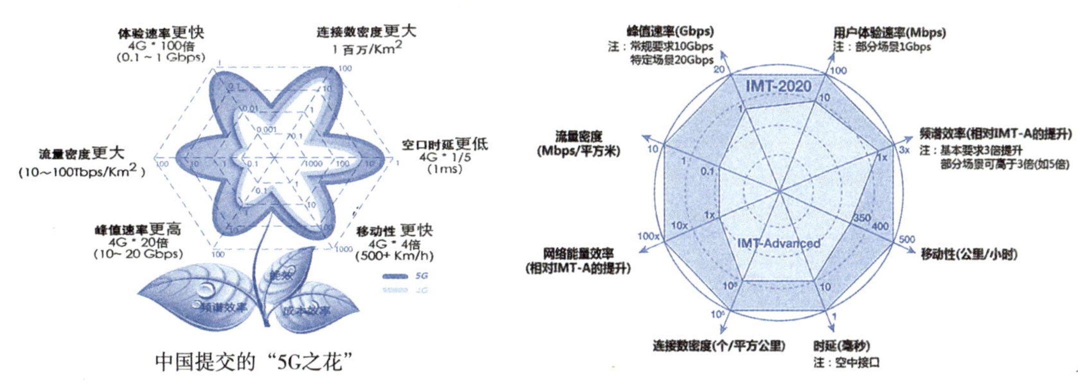

注：IMT－Advanced为4G，IMT－2020为5G

图2　5G的八大能力及较4G的增强

5G主要采用的技术。每一代移动通信发展都是实现能力的数量级的提升，为此在技术和频率等多个层面不断创新。5G综合使用了大规模天线、超密集组网、先进编码、高频段通信等新的无线技术，以及网络虚拟化、网络切片、边缘技术、云化基础设施等网络技术实现定义的八大能力和满足三大场景的需求。

1G到4G都是为面向人的需求而设计的技术，而5G则既满足移动互联网更高速率的要求，也将开启移动物联网时代。也就是说将人与人之间连接，扩展到万物互联。从实现几十亿人的连接，扩展到几百亿、千亿乃至万亿的连接。从面向人需求的消费互联网应用，转向面向行业和企业用户的产业互联网，从消费领域扩展到经济社会的方方面面。5G将成为实现全球数字化、网络化、智能化的重要使能技术。

5G之所以引起全球的高度关注，主要原因是由于5G将用于国民经济各个领域，特别是用于工业、交通、能源、医疗等各个领域，因此5G将成为整个社会的关键基础设施；5G带来的产业规模将超过万亿美元；以5G为代表的移动通信是创新最为集聚的领域；5G对产业上下游的带动巨大，不仅能带动芯片、软件、器件的研发和创新，而且能够带动下游各类应用的无限创新，特别是5G具备了从消费领域走向工业、农业等生产领域的能力和基础，带来产业变革和创新发展，从而促进整个经济的高质量发展，带动国家创新驱动发展的意义重大。

我国移动通信三十年的时间走过了1G空白、2G跟随、3G突破、4G同步，5G引领的创新历程。5G是中国第一个全过程参与的一代移动通信技术，从概念、愿景、需求、关键技术、标准、研发、技术试验到商用，每一个环节都深度参与，积极贡献，成为主导者之一。国际化、市场化和标准化是中国5G研究和推进的显著特点。我国是在一个开放的国际国内市场环境中进行技术研发、标准化、产品研发和试验等工作。一方面积极参与国际标准化活动，与国际同行一道，推动全球统一标准制定和产业的发展；另一方面，中国的5G推进组、中国通信标准化组织，特别是中国的新一代宽带无线移动通信网国家科技重大专项向国外所有的企业开放，爱立信、诺基亚、高通、三星、英特尔等都参与了中国的5G相关组织及项目。

二、5G能带来什么?

5G将带来移动互联网业务全面视频化发展，带来身临其境的立体化体验。与4G相比，5G的大带宽低时延将给普通消费者带来更好的体验和更多新的业务，比如用户可以享受高清视频和3D三维立体视频等；通过使用虚拟现实和增强现实（VR/AR）技术，无论身在何处都可以享受到身临其境的感觉，如虽不在演唱会、体育赛事现场，但却有十足的现场感和实时感，还有浸入式游戏、模拟试穿服饰等新的购物体验。5G将带动移动互联网业务的视频化、直播化快速发展，用户体验更加真实和立体。

5G将迎来移动物联网引领的万物互联时代，加速经济社会网络化、智能化发展。5G的两大物联网应用场景覆盖了从低速到超高速，从低功耗大连接到低时延高可靠，从量大面广的全覆盖到局部高性能高可靠应用等，从而满足不同行业、企业，不同功能性能等的需要。物联网将唤醒万物，如智能水表气表电表、智能烟感、无人驾驶、智慧医疗、智慧工厂等，赋予其“生命”和智慧；物联网将连接动物和植物，如“牛联网”“羊联网”等，赋予其“语言”和智慧，用于畜牧业及农业的智能化。

5G的行业应用将极大地改变以往的产业生态和商业模式，改变目前运营商建设网络、用户购置手机，互联网企业开发应用的面向普通消费者的模式。由于每个行业应用需求不同，功能和性能及可靠性要求不同，采用的终端设备和应用软件也不同。因而，需要5G信息领域与行业领域之间的紧密合作，打破横亘在二者之间的鸿沟，尤其是在5G初期应用时非常重要。

移动物联网（M－IoT）克服了传统物联网技术标准碎片化、应用碎片化和产业碎片化的缺点，由于是国际标准，依托移动网建设，可以很容易实现全覆盖、优质覆盖、规模化，因而可以实现低成本、大规模应用。

5G其中的一个物联网场景是低功耗大连接场景（mMTC），也就是量大面广的低速物联网应用，约占物联网连接数量的三分之二。当前最典型的技术是窄带物联网（NB－IoT），虽然NB－IoT作为4G增强型技术进行标准化和商用化，也被作为5G技术或前5G看待，5G的这一应用场景目前没有定义新的技术，后续也将在NB－IoT的基础上发展演进。其特点是使用低频段（800MHz/900MHz），实现全覆盖，可以覆盖地下2～3米，传输的数据量较小，功耗低，电池寿命达几年，模组成本已经低于20元人民币，明年可望达到10元以内，目前已经广泛用于水电气表、烟感、路灯、停车、共享单车、电动车防盗等领域，在河湖水质监测、气象监测、桥梁、交通、防汛等各个领域都有着巨大的潜力。2017年商用一年多来，全球已经有78个商用网络，连接数量已达5 000万。

三、物联鹰潭的实践

信息技术作为使能技术正在带来城市全方位的提升，特别是5G应用将带来的巨大机遇，重塑城市经济发展、城市管理和百姓生活等方方面面。鹰潭市被中国电信、中国联通、中国移动先后列为全国首批5G试点城市，2017年1月启动窄带物联网NB－IoT的发展，并将之作为核心技术推动智慧新城的建设实践。市委提出用“新理念引领、新技术支撑，带来产业发展新业态、政府管理新手段、百姓生活新体验”的发展思路，并采取了“网络先行、平台支撑、应用牵引、产业为本”的原则，将物联网的发展与城市的产业、生活和管理紧密结合，为各行各业插上智慧的翅膀，加上新动能的引擎。

经过两年多的努力，目前在鹰潭市已经形成了智慧水务、智慧交通、智慧党建、智慧路灯、智慧停车等一批具备向全省全国推广的城市级示范应用平台。智慧党建平台实现服务全市3 240个基层组织、服务50 184名全体党员、服务广大人民群众。在智慧水务方面，市中心城区水表用户约13万户，智能水表改造12.4万户，智能水表应用率约为95.4%。在智慧路灯方面，市中心城区7 000多盏路灯完成智能化改造，相同条件下节约30%电量，全域一体智慧路灯项目（28 000余盏路灯）已正式施工建设。在智慧光伏扶贫方面，推动智慧光伏扶贫智能监管平台上线，通过物联网技术，将全市所有扶贫电站纳入监管平台，实现设备运行精准高效、故障处理精准定位、扶贫效益精准透明。在智慧城市方面，在智慧停车、智慧烟感、智慧垃圾桶、智慧充电桩、智慧井盖等方面均开展了综合试点运用，积累了成功经验。2018年全市物联网终端产品出货量增加至546.9万件；纳入省政府协议供货目录产品21款；物联网企业206家，其中制造类企业90家；物联网核心及关联产业产值211亿元。而且，物联网产品逐步从鹰潭拓展到国内，辐射到国际。“物联鹰潭”品牌初现端倪。

鹰潭制造企业转型升级的典型是三川智慧，这是一家传统的水表企业，他们抓住移动物联网发展的机遇于2016年开始与华为合作研发基于NB－IoT的智能水表，2018年销售100万台，2019年1—5月同比增长100%，预计2019年将销售200万台，三川智慧成为全球最大的 NB－IoT 水表生产商，超声波远传水表系列正式获得澳大利亚国家计量院认证，电子远传水表在北京、深圳、上海等一线城市取得突破应用，并已出口到安哥拉、澳大利亚等国家，预计全年 NB－IoT 水表订单近百万台。

江西省是“新一代宽带无线移动通信网国家科技重大专项成果转移转化试点示范”（简称 03 专项试点示范），目前也是全国唯一一个试点示范，鹰潭则是试点示范基地。03 专项就是负责 4G、5G 研发和产业化的国家科技重大专项，在江西进行试点示范的目的就是促进专项成果在地方快速应用推广，又带动地方经济社会的发展。

当前，鹰潭也已经开始了 5G 的应用，包括龙虎山的视频直播推介、鹰潭火车站的 5G 高速互联网接入等。鹰潭移动物联网实践为采用新技术建设智慧城市和带动高质量发展进行了有益的探索。

四、5G 的商用进程

2019 年工信部为四家运营商发放了 5G 牌照，标志着 5G 进入网络加速建设和商用加速推进的新阶段。由于网络建设和网络优化至少需要 1～2 年时间，芯片和终端需要不断成熟，应用需要开发和培育，因此 5G 的应用将陆续逐步开展。2019 年是 5G 商用元年，但从网络建设、设备成熟度和应用探索等多个层面来讲，5G 的规模商用将需要 2～3 年的努力。5G 的三大应用场景中，增强移动宽带和低功耗大连接将率先应用，而超高可靠低时延场景则需要逐步在一些领域或企业开始应用，再逐渐扩大到更大范围和更广应用。

面向普通消费者的基于智能手机的业务将率先商用，用户将享受到更高的速率，更多的高质量视频业务、直播业务、高清视频以及虚拟现实 VR、增强现实 AR 等新业务和新体验。

NB－IoT 窄带物联网低功耗大连接场景已经具备良好的基础，三个运营商均实现了全国范围的覆盖，已经在智能水表、电表、气表、共享单车、电动车防盗等领域广泛应用。预计将可能在 2019 年年底或明年上半年进入快速增长期，总连接数突破亿级，更多的行业、更多的物体将接入网络，应用的深度和广度都会快速扩展，物联网带来的“智慧＋”将愈加显现。

5G 高可靠低时延的物联网应用需要一个培育和发展的过程，由于这类应用对性能要求很高，而且需要不同类型的终端设备，需要实现网络切片技术等，所以从网络到设备到应用都需进一步研发，如工业互联网、车联网应用等，可以在一些重点地区、重点行业和重点企业率先创新突破，再逐步扩大范围和规模。

5G 的应用是 5G 成功发展的关键，5G 具备了赋能各个行业的能力，即“5G＋”。同时，各个行业也要主动拥抱 5G，即“＋5G”。这无论是对通信产业还是对其他各行业都是新的机遇，也必须跨越彼此之间的鸿沟。

当前很多地方政府发展 5G 的积极性很高，以 5G 为代表的信息技术将极大地改变城市管理、产业的发展，带动城市智慧化、高质量全面发展。虽然 5G 潜力巨大、应用前景广阔，但是由于 5G 的发展是跨行业、跨产业的交叉和融合，应用初期需要城市强有力地牵引和带动。政府能将跨行业的资源有效组织，极大地缩短行业间融合的周期，以智慧城市的建设带动 5G 的应用，以 5G 的应用带动 5G 产业，以及 5G 与各行各业的快速融合，从而带动经济高质量发展，快速培育新动能。

5G 已经正式起航，让 5G 为成为发展，为各行各业插上高质量发展的翅膀。

（作者：曹淑敏，北京航空航天大学党委书记、新一代宽带无线移动通信网国家重大科技专项副总师）

充分发挥人工智能在城市建设中的“头雁”作用

人工智能是引领这一轮科技革命和产业变革的战略性技术，具有溢出带动性很强的“头雁”效应。

——习近平总书记2018年10月31日在中共中央政治局第九次集体学习时的讲话

一、理性认识人工智能

近几年来，人工智能发展势头很猛。在轰轰烈烈的造势活动中，我们能观察到一种“围城”现象：真正做人工智能研究的专家说话都比较谨慎，而吹嘘人工智能万能或散布人工智能威胁论的大多不是真正研究智能技术的专家。一般而言，媒体和投资者较多宣传人工智能技术的颠覆性作用，对智能技术的应用前景偏于乐观；而学术界较多看到目前人工智能的局限性，担心人工智能再次进入“寒冬”时期。我们究竟要如何认识人工智能的威力，如何理性地判断人工智能的应用前景，特别是如何发挥人工智能在城市建设中的“头雁”作用，本文谈一点个人看法，供大家参考。

总的来讲，发展人工智能要排除“左”“右”两方面的干扰。“右”的干扰是对人工智能等新一代信息技术麻木不仁，墨守成规，导致错失发展机遇；极“左”的干扰是盲目冒进，对人工智能抱不切实际的幻想，或者过分夸大人工智能的威胁，使人工智能再次进入寒冬，可能断送发展新经济的大好机遇。

（一）人工智能究竟发展到什么程度？

人工智能的火爆不是吹出来的，从应用效果来看，确实有一些过去机器做不到的事现在能做到了。语音识别在安静环境下准确率超过98%，人脸识别准确率已高达99.7%，比人眼还准确。“11：11”当天，如果完全采用人工客服，蚂蚁金服需要3.3万服务人员才能较好承接。2016年94%的客服已由计算机自动解决，近两年蚂蚁金服全面开放AI客服能力，比人工客服效率高出30～60倍。这样的人工智能应用案例比比皆是。人工智能系统在一些特定任务方面已胜过人类，例如国际象棋（1997年）、图像识别（2015年）、语音识别

(2015年)、围棋(2016年)以及德州扑克(2017)等。

人工智能的复兴很大程度上是由于风险资本的介入和大企业的投入。目前，中国私募股权投资市场中，人工智能领域相关投资额已达3 658.6亿元。最受资本欢迎的人工智能领域包括：智能金融(智能风控等)、智能安防(身份认证系统等)、智能健康(智能影像诊疗等)、智能驾驶(高级驾驶辅助系统等)、智能企业服务(智能营销等)、智能机器人(仓储/物流机器人、工业机器人等)、AI + 互联网服务(智能推荐等)、AI + 家居建筑(智能家电等)、AI基础元件(智能应用加速芯片)等。人工智能领域国内估值超过10亿美元的独角兽公司已有十几家。投资者的狂热往往形成短期泡沫，理性地判断技术商业化的临界点，更可信的依据是专利和专利诉讼。2008年语音识别的授权专利数达到最高峰，近几年开始下降，说明此项技术已基本成熟。同时相关的专利诉讼激增，这说明人工智能技术已经有钱可赚。

但是，我们也要看到人工智能应用目前还有较多限制。人工智能还不是像交流电一样接上插头就能用的通用技术。一般而言，人工智能技术在完成任务中能发挥较好作用，需要有较丰富的数据或者较丰富的知识，需要有较完全和较确定的信息，规则比较明确，任务较为单一。目前多数智能程序还需要采用借助样本的有监督学习，计算机通过自我博弈做到无师自通需具备集合封闭、规则完备、约束有限等苛刻条件。人工智能下棋可以超过人类，但打麻将、玩桥牌目前难以胜过人类。不限领域的开放性的人机对话还难以实现，目前科大讯飞的机器翻译还取代不了同声翻译专业人员，在复杂路况条件下无人驾驶还要走很长的探索之路，短期内不可能实现。人工智能产业还处于起步阶段。据统计，目前90%以上的人工智能企业还处于亏损状态。人工智能产品开发和服务依赖于数据和平台，用户数量是成败的关键。与互联网企业类似，初期的关注点不是盈利而是尽快扩大用户规模，目前还处在烧钱锁定用户阶段。我们对人工智能技术的大规模普及应用要有足够的耐心。

对人工智能持悲观态度的学者认为，目前深度学习的火热与20世纪80年代的专家系统盛行十分类似，人工标注与人工输入专家的规则知识一样困难，深度学习也有通用性、鲁棒性(robutness)不强的局限性，走出特定的应用领域，人工智能往往变成人工智障，因此人工智能必然会第三次进入“严冬”。这种看法有点偏颇。经过第二次寒冬以后，一批不被人工智能主流学派看好的从事“计算智能”研究的学者，在逆境中坚持对人工神经网络的研究，确实将人工智能推进了一大步，在视觉听觉等感知领域达到的水平远远超出当年的专家系统，在机器翻译等理解和决策领域也提高了机器的智能水平，许多智能技术已达到实用程度，今天的人工智能技术与20世纪80年代不可同日而语。2018年图灵奖得主、“深度学习之父”Geoffrey Hinton教授明确表示：“不会有‘人工智能寒冬’，因为AI已经渗透到你的生活中了，在之前的寒冬中，AI还不是你生活的一部分，但现在，它是了。”

(二)现在是否已从信息时代跨入“智能时代”

由于人工智能火爆，许多人认为信息时代已经过去了，大数据的热潮也已经过去了，现在已进入人工智能新时代。究竟现在处在什么时代，需要有历史的眼光。作为一种基础的科学范式，数据科技的影响可能要比人工智能更持久，但人工智能技术更具有颠覆性。

信息时代与工业时代一样，应该延续较长的时间。信息时代将走过数字化、网络化、智能化等几个阶段。人工智能的复兴标志着信息时代已进入智能化新阶段。以下赢一盘围棋分界，现在就将信息时代和智能时代划分成两个时代有点牵强。

由于深度学习在语音和图像识别等领域的成功，许多人把基于人工神经网络的深度学习技术作为进入智能时代的标志。导致深度学习流行的基础技术是反向传播（Back Propagation），此技术的发明者、2018 年图灵奖得主 Hinton 教授最近指出："我的观点是把反向传播全部丢下，重起炉灶。"今年诺贝尔经济学奖得主威廉·诺德豪斯 2015 年曾发表了一篇名为《我们正在接近经济奇点吗?》的论文，分析指出：大部分的经济指标都不支持"奇点即将来临"的判断。工业时代的划时代发明是蒸汽机和电动机，信息时代的标志性发明是计算机和互联网，进入智能时代需要有比深度学习更基础的划时代发明。

我们绝不能低估大数据和人工智能的战略作用，但也不能对人工智能抱有不切实际的过高期望。我国各地的人工智能造势活动已经起到很好的启蒙作用，现在是技术落地生根的时候了，要务实务实再务实。

（三）理性看待人工智能的基础研究与技术应用

对人工智能技术的判断出现比别的学科更明显的分歧，其原因可能在于对"智能"的看法很不一致。从基础研究和实际应用两个不同角度，看到的人工智能判若云泥。从基础理论的角度来看，人工智能必须以认知科学为基础，而认知科学还不是一门成熟的学科。认知和计算的关系不能单靠推理或计算分析来解决，只能通过实验来回答，认知科学本质上是实验科学。尽管脑科学有许多进展，但至今对人脑的认识还很肤浅，现在还没有步入可以利用对脑的认识来指导搭建智能系统的时代。要基于对人脑的了解来模拟人的智能，还要走很长的路。对上百亿年宇宙演化形成的极为精巧的人脑应有足够的敬畏，破解人脑的奥秘可能需要几百年甚至更长的时间。

从实际应用的角度来看，所谓人工智能就是计算机的非平凡应用。人工智能的权威学者 M. 明斯基定义："人工智能的任务是研究还没有解决的计算机问题。"人工智能应用问题，如图像识别、语音识别、计算机下棋、机器翻译等，多数是具有指数复杂性的问题，用常规的方法对付不了。所谓人工智能算法研究就是要找到在多项式时间内求解这些问题的方法，不断扩展计算机可求解问题的范围。所谓"问题求解"不是要求在最坏情况下找到最优解，也不是非要找到模仿人脑思考解决问题的方法，而用计算机的"思维"方式是在可容忍的时间内找到满意的解。因此，现在讲的"智能化"本质上就是"计算机化"。

计算技术发展走的是一条"非脑"道路。从第一台电子计算机开始，计算机的发展就与模拟神经网络分道扬镳。集成电路的发明和后来几十年在摩尔定律引导下的狂奔，使得用计算机实现人工智能的方式与人脑的思维机制几乎不沾边。近年来人工智能的复兴有深度学习算法的贡献，但主要是得益于数据资源的极大丰富和计算能力的飞速提高，人工智能技术本身还没有本质性的突破。因此可以说，人工智能的复兴主要是计算技术的胜利，摩尔定律的胜利！

在人类历史上，技术走在科学前面的例子比比皆是。对第一次工业革命起关键作用的蒸汽机的发明和改进，主要来自工程师和能工巧匠之手，热力学的科学研究完成在热机大量普及之后。人工智能走的道路可能与热机发展之路类似，在破解人脑之谜之前，借助计算的力量、数据的力量、知识的力量，人工智能可能会引领一次新的工业革命，计算机的智能应用会广泛普及。等到认知科学取得根本性突破后，新一波的人工智能还会形成更大的浪潮。

二、发挥人工智能的头雁作用

（一）人工智能为什么是数字经济的“领头雁”？

2018 年 10 月 31 日，习近平总书记在政治局第九次集体学习的讲话中特别指出，人工智能具有溢出带动性很强的“头雁”效应，这一判断也就是说智能化是发展数字经济的主攻方向。

理解人工智能的引领作用要从智能学科的本质特点找原因。人工智能与其他学科不一样，它不是静止的有限范围的技术，其研究内容不断向未知领域延伸，永远处在计算机科学研究的最前沿。人工智能总是探索像“下围棋胜过人类”那样的令人惊喜的“禁区”，将“不可能”变成“可能”，将尖端技术变成老百姓司空见惯的常用技术，这就是“领头雁”的作用。

人工智能也是我国经济转型的新动力。2017 年，我国电子信息产业收入总规模 18 万亿元，人工智能产品的直接市场 200 亿元左右。人工智能核心产业收入只占电子信息产业总收入的千分之一左右，如此弱小的 AI 核心产业如何能成为推动经济转型发展的新动力？理解人工智能等引领技术的贡献，可用“蜜蜂模型”来解释。我国蜂蜜市场每年不到 100 亿元，但蜜蜂的价值主要不是蜂蜜而是传粉，蜜蜂对农业有不可替代的重大贡献。人工智能对其他产业的作用如同蜜蜂对各种农作物的作用一样。人工智能不是单项技术，实际上是计算机和其他信息技术的集成应用，在实际应用中很难分清楚哪些是人工智能应用，哪些是一般的计算机技术应用。人工智能技术渗透各行各业，将促进全社会方方面面的变革和技术升级换代，从数字化、网络化走向智能化。

（二）理解人工智能的作用不能只看 GDP 统计

人们习惯于从 GDP 的统计中看一个产业的贡献，但 GDP 的统计不能全面反映人工智能的贡献。人工智能和大数据的作用不仅仅体现在经济增长上，更多的体现在生产方式、生活方式、科研模式、政府管理模式的改变和福利改进，特别是思想观念和认知方式的改变。智能技术的许多免费应用没有计入 GDP，老百姓的获得感和幸福感也很难统计到 GDP 中。我们需要关注的不是在原来的经济大饼中划出多大一块饼算成人工智能的 GDP，而是要关注人工智能究竟提供了多少原来没有的新产品和新服务，给民众带来了多大实惠。

人工智能主要体现为无形资产。1975 年标普 500 公司无形资产只有几千亿美元，占总资产的 17%；到 2018 年无形资产达到 2 万亿美元，占总资产的 83%。目前全球市值 Top 6 公司都是人工智能公司。按 2018 年 7 月的统计：苹果公司 9 360 亿美元，亚马逊 8 800 亿美元，Alphabet（谷歌的母公司）8 250 亿美元，微软 8 077 亿美元，Facebook 6 033 亿美元，阿里巴巴 4 872 亿美元。这些公司的市值主要来自投资者对他们掌握的人工智能技术的估值。

三、在智慧城市建设中让人工智能落地

（一）我国智慧城市建设现状

据国家发展和改革委员会提供的数据显示：截至 2018 年 8 月，全国 100% 的副省级以上城市，包括 76% 以上的地级城市和 32% 的县级市，总计大约 500 座城市已经明确提出正在建设新型智慧城市。到 2018 年年底，国家发布的智慧城市领域相关政策性文件共计 17 项，地方性的政策法规性文件 16 项。我国智慧城市建设经历了三个阶段：第一阶段是数字化，2010 年以前是我国智慧城市的萌芽期，主要强调数字化建设，利用 3S 技术（遥感技术 RS、地理信息技术 GIS、全球定位系统 GPS）对城市及相关信息进行采集监测。第二阶段是网络化。2010—2015 年是国内智慧城市建设的探索发展期，主要搞网络化建设。从国家层次到各省市地方制定了多项发展规划，在（移动）互联网、物联网等技术的支撑下，掀起了国内智慧城市建设的潮流，出现了一批试点城市。第三阶段从 2016 年至今，重点是大数据化和智能化，进入新型智慧城市建设阶段。习近平总书记 2016 年提出要推进新型智慧城市建设，2016 年 12 月，国务《“十三五”国家信息化规划》，明确了新型智慧城市建设的行动目标：“到 2018 年，分级分类建设 100 个新型示范性智慧城市；到 2020 年，新型智慧城市建设取得卓著成效。”

中国的“智慧城市”的内涵比国外的“Smart city”广阔，发展途径也与国外不同。因为中国的城市管理者不但要进行城市管理，还要推进城市的工业化、城镇化、信息化、农业现代化与绿色化，中国的智慧城市需要同时推进这“五化”，智能化是“五化”的重要抓手。仅仅在技术和设备层面推进智慧城市建设，难以解决中国城市发展中的问题。

目前各地的智慧城市建设红红火火，但建设的效果还没有达到预期的目标，城市大数据的作用还没有充分发挥，人工智能技术的应用不够广泛深入。目前，相同属性的数据分散在各个孤立的系统之中，真正做到数据共享和充分公开的城市还不多。收集到的数据也缺少常态化的更新机制，往往只有一个时态。智慧城市建设缺乏统一的整体规划和集中设计，容易导致部门之间、省市之间、市区之间重复建设。标准化的滞后也是当前制约智慧城市建设的“瓶颈”之一。数据格式各异，分类、编码不统一，给数据获取、更新和维护带来很多困难，也给信息资源共享、交换带来许多不便，严重制约了信息资源的开发利用。

以物流行业为例，多种运输方式之间缺乏有效衔接，短驳、搬倒、装卸、配送成本较高。我国的多式联运方式尚未普及，地域经济结构导致运输的来回满载率不平衡，空车率达

40%，平均运距只有182千米，一次卸货到下次装货平均要等待72小时，导致我国的物流成本居高不下。这些现象背后是信息化、网络化、智能化水平的问题，通过大力推广智慧物流，物流成本肯定可以明显降低。必须指出，物流成本占GDP比重与经济结构密切相关，中国是制造业大国，美国现在制造业空心化，不能用这一指标简单地比较中美两国的物流成本。有企业家说要通过新技术将中国物流成本占GDP比例从现在的14.6%降到5%以下，这个指标定得不科学，一味降低物流业占比也不符合中国国情。其实，通过智慧物流能将物流成本占比降低3到4个百分点，就会产生巨大的经济效益。

（二）建设智慧城市要构建“城市大脑”

智慧城市是多个垂直行业的数字化系统智能联动形成的大系统，衡量智慧城市的一个基础指标是建成承载大数据的大平台。智慧城市建设的主力是各大互联网科技公司，阿里、腾讯、百度、京东、华为等龙头公司的“平台化”趋势最为明显。阿里打造的平台是“ET城市大脑”，包括一体化计算平台、数据资源平台、智能平台和应用支撑平台。腾讯曾推出“城市超级大脑”，最新战略是“WeCity未来城市解决方案”，用微信、小程序等应用实现数字政务、城市治理等方案的落地。百度倡导“AI City”智能城市概念，车路协同+自动驾驶是百度的主攻方向。华为提出“数字平台”方案，对云平台、大数据、GIS、视频云等实现统筹。这些公司从不同角度发力，目标都是构建“城市大脑”。

城市是一个动态变化的复杂巨系统，充满不确定性和不一致性，必须从整个系统着眼才能把握城市的脉搏，头痛医头、脚痛医脚的办法治不好“大城市病”。以城市交通为例，路况瞬息万变、交通关系错综复杂，计算模型必须在很短时间内做出反应。中国千万人口以上的大城市，都有数百万辆汽车，究竟一个城市每天有多少量汽车在路上，过去的估计都是拍脑袋拍出来。比如，杭州市估计每天有200万辆汽车在路上，但通过阿里公司“ET城市大脑”的复杂计算，发现平时杭州市的路上平均只有20万汽车，高峰时刻也只有30万辆车。解决杭州市的交通堵塞问题，实际上就是这多出来的10万辆汽车的实时调度问题。现在ET城市大脑已接管杭州128个信号灯路口，试点区域通行时间减少15.3%，高架道路出行时间节省4.6分钟，120救护车到达现场时间缩短一半。阿里城市大脑已在杭州、苏州、上海等城市相继落地。取得这些成绩的背后是靠巨大的计算平台和管理调度复杂资源的飞天操作系统的支持。

（三）智慧城市的落地要靠建设各个行业的智能应用系统

人工智能技术的落地不外乎两种途径：一种是先掌握单点技术，如人脸识别、语音识别等，再去找单项技术的应用机会，试图把单项技术应用到不同行业；另一条途径是从市场需求出发，提供行业垂直解决方案，综合利用各种人工智能技术。前一种途径有点像手里有一把锤子，就到处找钉子，容易把看上去像钉子的东西都当成钉子。过去多年的实践表明，这种所谓“成果转化”的做法往往难以成功。比较见效的做法还是构建行业应用平台和系统。各行业的智能应用系统不是孤立的“烟囱”，相互之间一定要数据共享，通过城市大脑形成协作的大平台。

构建行业智能应用平台的关键是领域知识的计算机化。20 世纪红火一阵的专家系统虽然不十分成功，但重视领域知识的传统不能丢。有些人认为，有了大数据和深度学习技术，领域知识就无关紧要了，这是一种偏见。今后的努力方向应该是知识推理与数据学习相结合。没有知识推理，人工智能系统就缺乏可解释性，而不能解释因果性的机器学习结果，很多行业都不敢作为正式产品或服务项目。比如医学图像识别，如果只给出机器统计学习的结论是什么病而不说明为什么，医生就很难确信。领域知识的积累是一个行业的宝贵财富，这笔知识财富主要体现在行业软件上。我国的工业软件比集成电路更落后，是我国产业高质量发展最大的软肋，在推进智慧城市的过程中要集中力量研究开发行业软件，特别是制造业的 CAD、CAE、CAM 软件。

四、推动人工智能技术加速落地的几点建议

（一）坚持问题导向和效果导向，不做表面文章

人工智能的应用落地要听到响声。人工智能技术落地有三个层次：第一层次是有真实可见的实际应用案例，第二层次是有规模化应用的产品，第三层次是有可统计的应用成效。人工智能技术往往和常用的计算机技术交织在一起，要关注解决了什么问题，不必纠缠“智能在哪里”。不仅要关心高消费人群的“锦上添花”需求，更要关注用智能技术满足老百姓的“刚需”。比如，把图像识别和 OCR 技术嵌入到盲人买得起的智能眼镜中，让盲人带上眼镜就能走路、能看书，对数千万盲人来讲就是一种刚需。

（二）重视开辟新市场的智能产品

宏观上看，经济发展过程中交织着三类创新：新市场创新、渐进型创新和效率型创新。人工智能的作用主要是优化，因此主要表现为效率型创新。效率型创新的特色是会消灭工作，因为效率提升了，多余的人力就会释出。同样地，资金也会因为效率的提升而释出到市场上。渐进创新是产品的不断升级，它可以为企业带来更多利润，但市场总量没有改变，不会创造新的就业机会。只有新市场创新能够创造就业，吸收效率创新释出的人力和资金，PC 机和智能手机是创造新市场的典型案例。因此，只有新市场创新才是经济由衰转盛的关键。推广人工智能应用不能只考虑机器换人，用机器取代重复性强、照本宣科的白领职工，还要多关注开辟新市场，创造新就业机会甚至新的行业。

（三）改变人工智能领域“头重脚轻”的局面

目前，我国的人工智能基础层、技术层、应用层的人才比例是 3.3%、34.9%、61.8%。人才多集中在应用层，基础层人才比例严重偏低，头重脚轻，根基不牢。发展人工智能和大数据不能只停留在算法上，需要关注计算机系统架构和基础软件。由于摩尔定律遇到了天花

板，器件升级速度变慢，未来 10 年可能出现新计算机系统结构的“寒武纪大爆发”。要高度重视高能效结构、领域专用结构、可重塑结构、事件驱动计算等新结构。

（四）充分发挥企业在技术攻关中的骨干作用

我国科研队伍的精兵强将集中在国家重点实验室，一半以上的中国科学院院士、40% 以上的杰青工作都集中在国家重点实验室。国家把突破人工智能关键技术的希望也寄托在大学和国家科研机构。但是，我国关键技术难以突破的根本原因在于企业的技术创新能力薄弱。我们必须从思想上认识到这一问题严重性和紧迫性，从国家经济转型的高度重视这一涉及高质量发展全局的战略问题，制定有力度的政策切实提高企业的创新能力。最关键的措施是激励了解世界科技前沿的青年才俊进入企业，减轻企业税负促使企业增加研发投入。

（作者：李国杰，中国科学院计算技术研究所研究员，中国工程院院士，发展中国家科学院院士）

观察篇

2018年中国市长协会舆情观察

一、舆情综述

2018年，谷尼舆情大数据平台共监测到约44万条相关信息，主要分布在教育、环保、反腐、改革、安全维稳、招商旅游等领域。(图1)

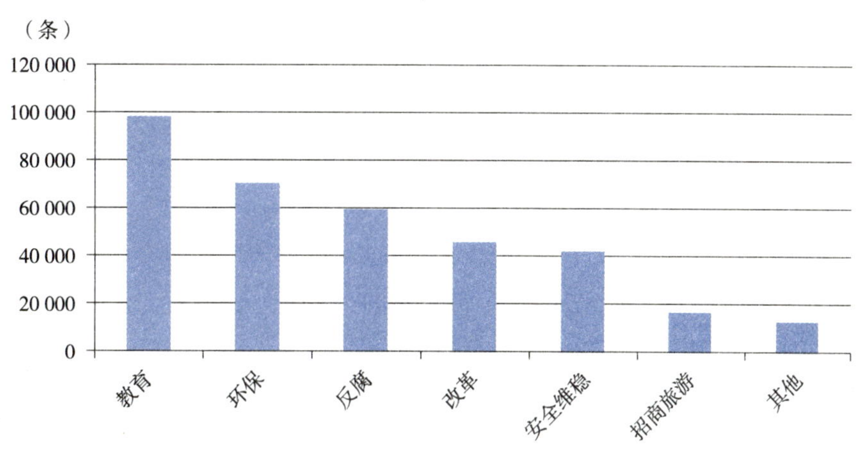

图1　2018年谷尼舆情大数据平台监测信息统计图

“教育”“环保”“反腐”等得到最高关注度。其中，今年教育话题较多“北交大实验室爆炸事件、学生‘减负’、学前教育、校园欺凌等”话题持续走热，总体占28%，居第一位；因环保政策的颁布一浪高过一浪，各个细分市场的崛起一波接着一波，环保产业“备受追捧”，占比为21%，跃居第二位；反腐话题占比17%，占第三位；改革类话题占13%，因今年相关改革话题较多，关注度也一直较高。(图2)

2018年，关于市长的新闻稿件有31 299篇，从媒体关注度舆情趋势图中11月和12月关注度最高。发布新闻量占比较高的是人民网（27.95%）、新浪新闻（28.89%）、中国经济网（11.32%）等媒体。值得关注的事件有：网络媒体“搜狐网”发布的《海南三亚市长阿东首度回应春节后现“天价机票”：机场要扩容》（转载179）；新浪微博“人民日报”发布的《江西副市长王成兵暗访发现窗口人员戴耳机听歌：当天辞退》（转载量7 026，评论

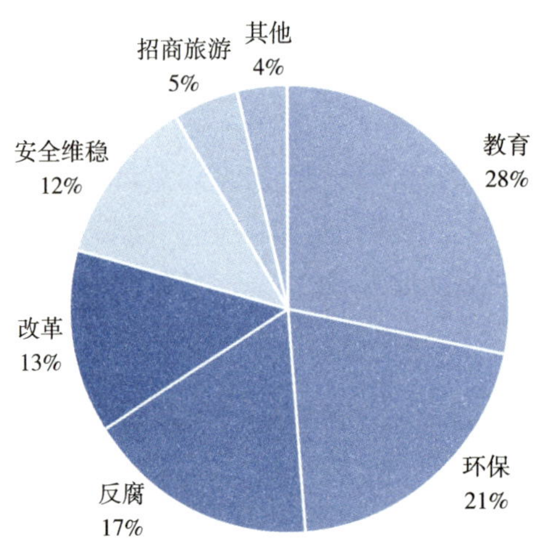

图 2　各类信息战比图

5 415）；微信公号“佛山发布”发布的《2 月 7 日佛山地铁 2 号线坍塌事故通报》（阅读数 10 万 +，点赞数 773）。（图 3 ~ 图 6）

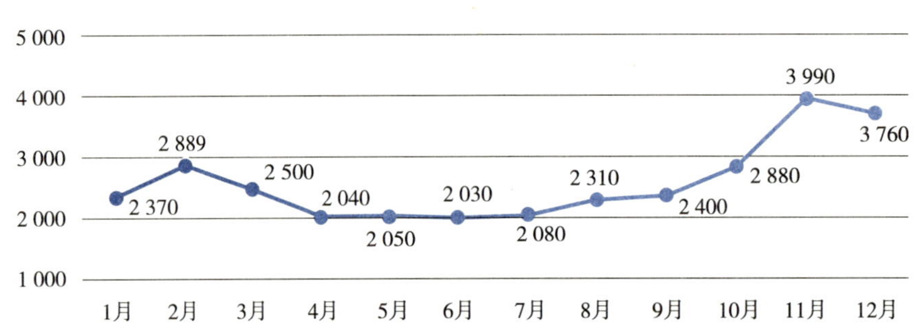

图 3　媒体涉“市长”每月数据图（1 月 1 日至 12 月 31 日）

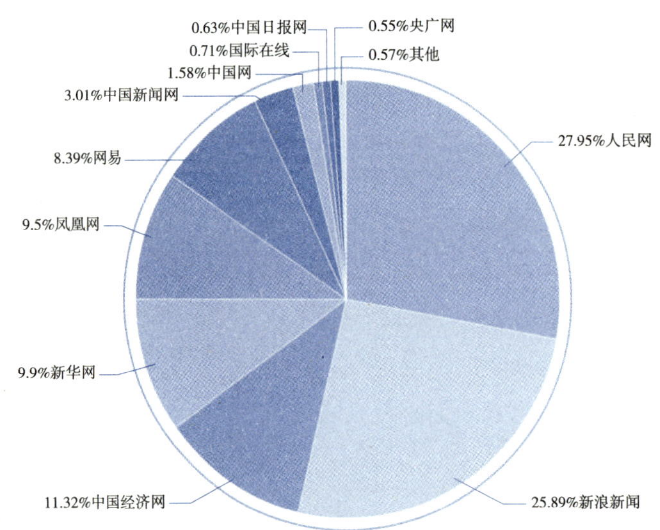

图 4　主流媒体关注比例

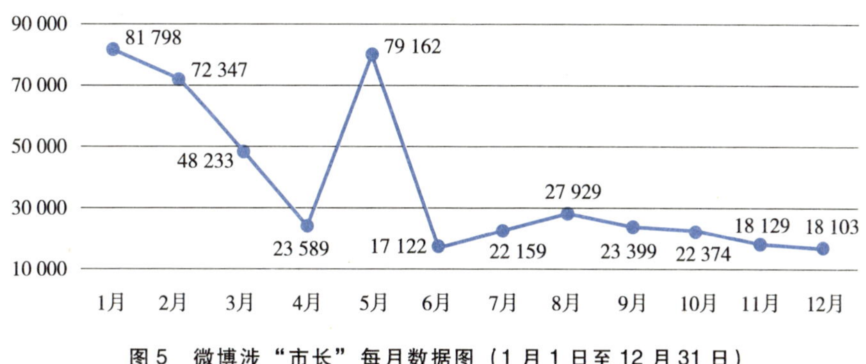

图5　微博涉“市长”每月数据图（1月1日至12月31日）

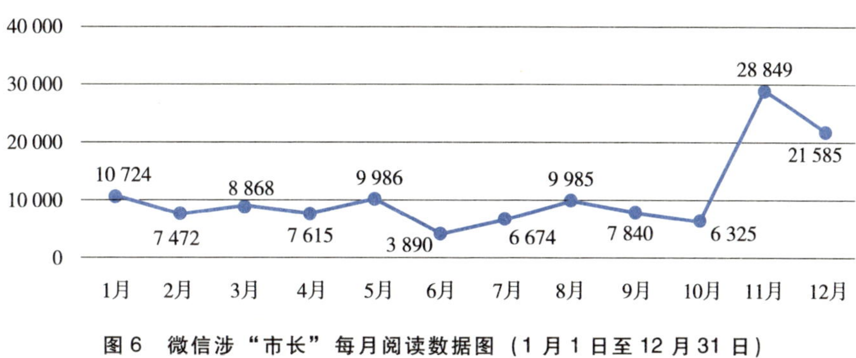

图6　微信涉“市长”每月阅读数据图（1月1日至12月31日）

新闻

序号	事　件	来源	转载量
1	海南三亚市长阿东首度回应春节后现“天价机票”：机场要扩容	搜狐网	179
2	安徽池州市市长雍成瀚：扎实推进长江生态环境保护	中国新闻网	154
3	上海常务副市长周波：100条开放举措中90%以上可在年内实施	人民网	149
4	丽江市长郑艺：丽江古城、泸沽湖每天游客将限流	中国经济网	138
5	北京副市长杨斌：采暖季重污染易发多发　要强化有效应对	新浪新闻	112
6	天津市常务副市长马顺清：支持引导高技术民营企业来天津投资兴业	网易网	109
7	贵阳市长陈晏：助力网络强国建设　打造“中国数谷”	新浪新闻	94
8	绍兴市长盛阅春：古城绽放“高端制造”新花骨朵儿	搜狐网	82
9	湖南邵阳市长回信志愿者：环境保护是人民战争，需要人人参与	网易网网	79
10	佛山市委书记鲁毅透露以铁的手腕坚决打好污染防治攻坚战	凤凰网	71

微博

序号	事　件	来源	转载量	评论
1	江西副市长王成兵暗访发现窗口人员戴耳机听歌：当天辞退！	人民日报	7 026	15 593
2	乌鲁木齐市长：维吾尔族不是突厥人后裔	环球时报	3 502	1 594
3	长江协调会第十八届市长联席会举行　沿岸27城市开启区域合作新篇章	国网重庆电力	2 632	2 605

续表

序号	事　件	来源	转载量	评论
4	纪录片《中国市长》,现实版李达康让办事不力的下属当场辞职	这个我服	1 650	1 176
5	北京副市长殷勇:应避免为了稳定而频繁干预市场	案多多平台	731	124
6	9.19日安徽芜湖两家幼儿园涉嫌“给孩子吃霉变食品”事件	连鹏	482	417
7	西安市上官吉庆在“12345”市民服务热线中心调研时强调“提高站位　夯实责任　加快推进　确保各类民生项目早建设早见效早惠民”	西安发布	398	107
8	重庆市原市长黄奇帆:资本市场上这六种功能已经在国民经济中逐步体现出来,今后二三十年必将更深刻的显现出来	全景网	358	79
9	昌都市副市长赵明用骑行的方式,向媒体介绍这座神奇的城市	周群	305	51
10	北京市副市长殷勇:建议金融机构准入和监管适度分开	财新网	182	30

微信

序号	事　件	公众号	阅读数	点赞数
1	2月7日佛山地铁2号线坍塌事故通报	佛山发布	10万+	773
2	黄奇帆一走　重庆房价和火锅一样火爆	叶檀财经	10万+	576
3	国家税务总局党组书记、局长王军与北京市委副书记、市长陈吉宁共同为国家税务总局北京市税务局揭牌	央视财经	10万+	456
4	深圳市长陈如桂、华为公司董事长梁华代表双方签署协议	买房之前	8万+	43
5	武汉市市长万勇做客央视财经《对话》演播室,谈突飞猛进的人才引进速度是怎么来的	杭州交通918	7万+	45
6	朔州要建机场了! 市委副书记、代市长高键与朔州机场专家评审组熊朝一行座谈	朔州那些事儿	6万+	13
7	日前,(江西)抚州人的朋友圈被这样一段视频刷屏了,副市长、金溪县委书记王成兵突击暗访,因为这事一名单位工作人员当天被辞退	凤凰网	5万+	326
8	两会期间,秦皇岛市市长张瑞书做客央广《谁不说咱家乡好》栏目	爆料秦皇岛	5万+	26
9	晋州市长袁永福到晋州市第三中学检查指导春季绿化工作	晋州贴吧	4万+	13
10	5月16日,天津副市长孙文魁在会上介绍“海河英才”行动计划,放宽对学历型人才、资格型人才、技能型人才、创业型人才和急需型人才的落户条件	澎湃新闻	3万+	31

二、反腐倡廉舆情分析

(一) 舆情走势

由图7可以看出，2018年反腐舆情信息量走势较有起伏。1月，中纪委发布《关于做好2018年元旦春节期间有关工作的通知》，引发全网互动热潮。3月，舆论对全国两会的关注热度不减，聚焦反腐议题。8月，随着中央军委党的建设会议的召开，主流媒体纷纷在显著位置转载，致使8月后相关信息量持续增加。

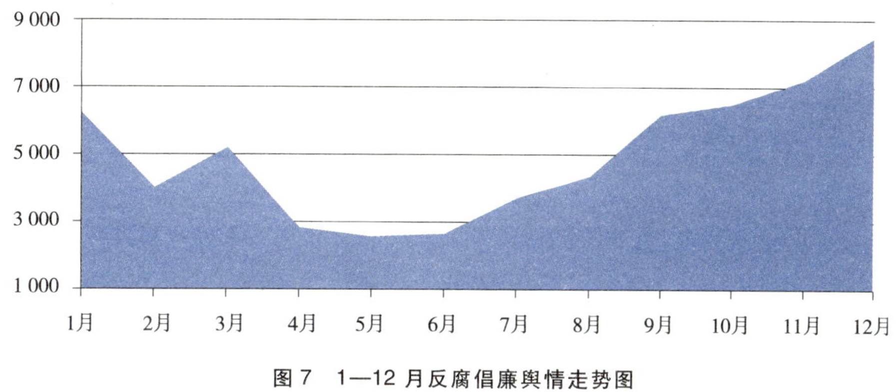

图 7　1—12 月反腐倡廉舆情走势图

（二）2018 年重点话题事件

1. 习近平：反腐败斗争不会变风转向

监测数据：共检测到 776 000 条相关数据

事件背景：中央军委党的建设会议 2018 年 8 月 17 日至 19 日在北京召开。中共中央总书记、国家主席、中央军委主席习近平出席会议并发表重要讲话。他强调，全面加强新时代我军党的领导和党的建设工作，是推进党的建设新的伟大工程的必然要求，是推进强国强军的必然要求。全军要全面贯彻新时代中国特色社会主义思想和党的十九大精神，深入贯彻新时代党的强军思想，落实新时代党的建设总要求，落实新时代党的组织路线，坚持党对军队绝对领导，坚持全面从严治党，坚持聚焦备战打仗，全面提高我军加强党的领导和党的建设工作质量，为实现党在新时代的强军目标、完成好新时代军队使命任务提供坚强政治保证。他还指出，反腐败斗争必须坚定不移抓下去，不会变风转向。要坚持无禁区、全覆盖、零容忍，坚持重遏制、强高压、长震慑，坚持受贿行贿一起查，健全完善权力运行制约和监督体系，扎紧制度笼子，不给权力脱轨、越轨留空子。

2. 中纪委国家监委发规定规范立案相关工作程序

监测数据：共检测到 360 000 条相关数据

事件背景：近日，《中央纪委国家监委立案相关工作程序规定（试行）》（以下简称《规定》）印发实施。作为中央纪委国家监委推进国家监察体制改革的一项重要制度，《规定》对于确保依规依纪依法、一体两面履行党的纪律检查和国家监察两项职责具有重要的推动作用。《规定》共四章 33 条，对中央纪委国家监委监督检查和审查调查工作中立案、交办案件和指定管辖以及结案等相关程序进行规范，特别是明确了以事立案、对涉案人员立案、对单位立案等程序，并设计了 5 种相关文书格式。

3. 哈尔滨交通执法“塌方式”腐败事件

监测数据：共检测到 337 000 条相关数据

事件背景：在黑龙江省哈尔滨市，大货车给人的印象是肆无忌惮地疯狂违章，超载、超速、超限、闯红灯。恶性竞争之下这些大货车经常发生重大交通事故致行人死亡。而负有主要监管责任的公安交通管理部门却对此视而不见，原因就是他们已经沦为这些“疯狂大货车”的“保护伞”了。

2018年6月25日，哈尔滨纪委、监委发布通报，向社会公布了对122名为疯狂大货车充当“保护伞”的领导干部以及公职人员的查处情况。在这122名被查处的领导干部及公职人员中，既有哈尔滨市交警支队副支队长，也有多个区交警大队的大队长、中队的中队长以及普通民警。

三、安全维稳舆情分析

(一)舆情走势

由图8可以看出，安全维稳舆情在2018年信息量起伏较大。4月，因每逢假期，各类安全事故频繁发生，成为网络媒体和网民的关注焦点；8月，因温州一名女乘客搭乘滴滴顺风车遇害，滴滴顺风车下线等信息再次引发社会强烈关注，致使8月的信息量又达到一个小高峰。

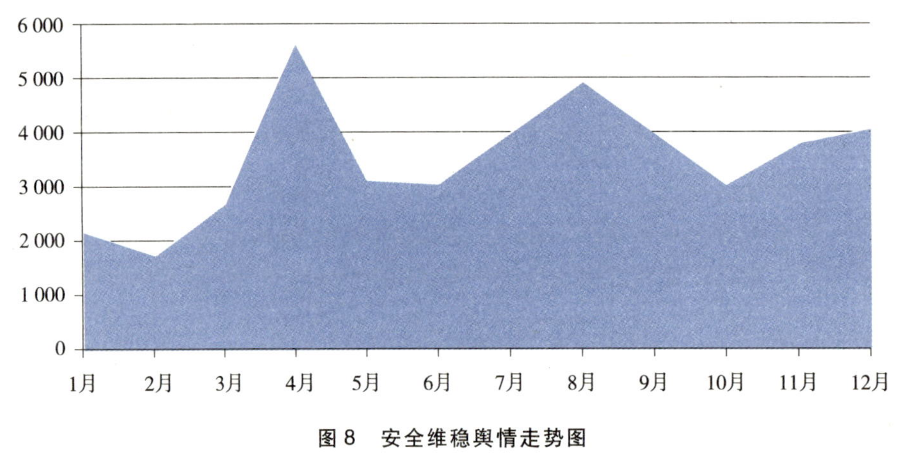

图8　安全维稳舆情走势图

(二)2018年重点话题事件

1. 朝鲜发生涉中国游客的重大交通事故

监测数据：共检测到359 000条相关数据

事件背景：2018年4月22日18时许，在朝鲜黄海北道发生一起重大交通事故，一辆载有34名中国游客的旅游大巴从当地一处大桥坠落。截至4月23日，已造成中国游客32人死亡、2人重伤。

事故发生后，党中央、国务院高度重视。中共中央总书记、国家主席、中央军委主席习近平立即作出重要指示，要求外交部及我国驻朝使馆要立即采取一切必要措施，协调朝鲜有关方面全力做好事故处理工作。要全力抢救受伤人员，做好遇难者善后工作。相关地方要主动开展伤亡人员家属安抚工作。习近平总书记强调，近期，各类安全事故频繁发生，必须引起高度重视。

2. 国务院食品安全办召开 2018 年食品行业组织座谈会

监测数据：共检测到 394 000 条相关数据

事件背景：按照食品相关部门与行业协会协作工作机制，2018 年 11 月 21 日，国务院食品安全办联合相关部门在京召开 2018 年食品行业组织座谈会。会议围绕行业组织推进“放管服”改革，发挥食品安全社会共治作用进行了充分讨论，就推动食品产业高质量发展，保障食品质量安全提出意见建议。

会议指出，一年来食品行业组织积极参与食品安全法律法规和标准制修订，协助解决食品安全监管重点难点问题，共同推动食品安全风险预警交流，在促进食品安全社会共治、推动食品产业持续健康发展中发挥了不可或缺的重要作用。

会议强调，要完善食品安全相关部门与行业组织联络协作机制，更好地发挥行业组织在政府、企业、消费者之间的桥梁纽带作用。一是深化“放管服”改革，更好地服务民营企业发展；二是发挥行业组织自律作用，引导企业诚信经营；三是积极开展双向沟通，传递企业需求和监管要求，共同提升食品安全保障水平；四是加强食品安全风险预警交流，更好地维护消费者和各类市场主体的合法权益，科学释疑解惑，营造公平竞争的市场秩序。

3. 交通运输部联合公安部等单位约谈滴滴公司

监测数据：共检测到 88 400 条相关数据

事件背景：2018 年 8 月 26 日，交通运输部联合公安部以及北京市、天津市交通运输、公安部门，对滴滴公司开展联合约谈，责令其立即对顺风车业务进行全面整改，加快推进合规化进程，严守安全底线，切实落实承运人安全稳定管理主体责任，保障乘客出行安全和合法权益，及时向社会公布有关整改情况。交通运输部运输服务司司长徐亚华在约谈中指出，今年 5 月初，空姐李某在郑州搭乘滴滴顺风车，途中遭司机残忍杀害，短短三个月时间，又再次发生“8・24”温州恶性事件，引起社会各界广泛关注。

四、改革舆情分析

（一）舆情走势

由图 9 看出，改革舆情在 2018 年信息量起伏较平缓，每次习近平主席主持召开中央深改会议都引起媒体和网民的大量关注。其中 3 月，经济体制改革措施逐步落实，舆情迅速上升并达到全年最高值。

（二）2018 年重点话题事件

1. 习近平庆在庆祝改革开放 40 周年大会上的讲话

监测数据：共检测到854 000条相关数据

事件背景：庆祝改革开放 40 周年大会 2018 年 12 月 18 日上午在北京人民大会堂隆重举

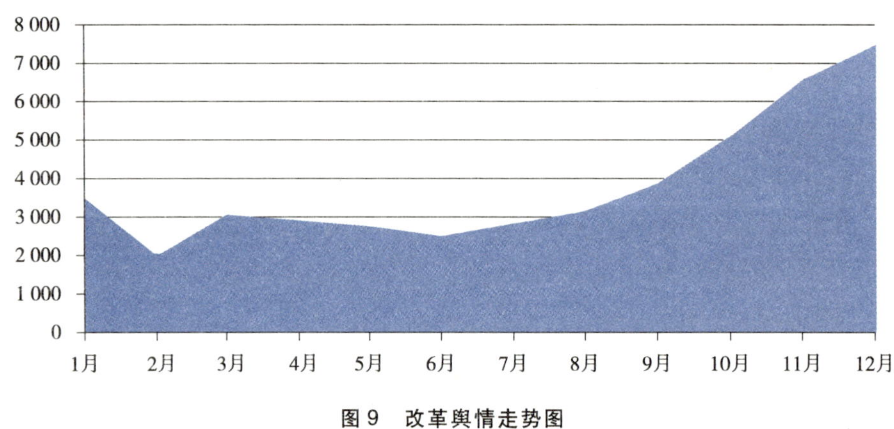

图9　改革舆情走势图

行。中共中央总书记、国家主席、中央军委主席习近平在大会上发表重要讲话。习近平强调，40 年的实践充分证明，党的十一届三中全会以来我们党团结带领全国各族人民开辟的中国特色社会主义道路、理论、制度、文化是完全正确的，形成的党的基本理论、基本路线、基本方略是完全正确的。

习近平强调，40 年的实践充分证明，中国发展为广大发展中国家走向现代化提供了成功经验、展现了光明前景，是促进世界和平与发展的强大力量，是中华民族对人类文明进步作出的重大贡献。

习近平强调，40 年的实践充分证明，改革开放是党和人民大踏步赶上时代的重要法宝，是坚持和发展中国特色社会主义的必由之路，是决定当代中国命运的关键一招，也是决定实现“两个一百年”奋斗目标、实现中华民族伟大复兴的关键一招。

2. 习近平主持召开中央全面深化改革委员会第二次会议

监测数据：共检测到 75 300 条相关数据

事件背景：中共中央总书记、国家主席、中央军委主席、中央全面深化改革委员会主任习近平 2018 年 5 月 11 日下午主持召开中央全面深化改革委员会第二次会议并发表重要讲话。他强调，党的十九届三中全会以来，中央和国家机关机构改革取得重大进展，要注意边实践、边总结，把好经验运用好，周密组织地方机构改革，使中央和地方机构改革在工作部署、组织实施上有机衔接、有序推进，确保深化党和国家机构改革取得全面胜利。

3. 医疗卫生领域央地权责划分改革方案发布

监测数据：共检测到 3 800 条相关数据

事件背景：2018 年 8 月 14 日，国务院办公厅印发《医疗卫生领域中央与地方财政事权和支出责任划分改革方案》（以下简称《方案》），将于 2019 年 1 月 1 日起实施。《方案》明确，我国将通过财政事权和支出责任划分改革，形成中央领导、权责清晰、依法规范、运转高效的医疗卫生领域中央与地方财政事权和支出责任划分模式，提高基本医疗卫生服务的供给效率和水平。

具体而言，在公共卫生方面，基本公共卫生服务明确为中央与地方共同财政事权，由中央财政和地方财政共同承担支出责任。全国性或跨区域的重大传染病防控等重大公共卫生服务，上划为中央财政事权，由中央财政承担支出责任。此外，医疗保障方面（主要包括城乡居民基本医疗保险补助和医疗救助），以及计划生育方面，明确为中央与地方共同财政事权，由中央财政和地方财政共同承担支出责任。

《方案》指出，以全国性或跨区域的公共卫生服务为重点，适度强化中央财政事权和支出责任。属于中央与地方共同财政事权的，由中央统一制定国家基础标准或提出原则要求。

五、招商旅游舆情分析

（一）舆情走势

由图 10 可以看出，2018 年招商旅游舆情信息波动较大。因春节来临及国庆节日放长假，人们出游较多，使 3 月、10 月招商旅游舆情信息量达到最高。其他时间段相关舆情信息较为稳定。

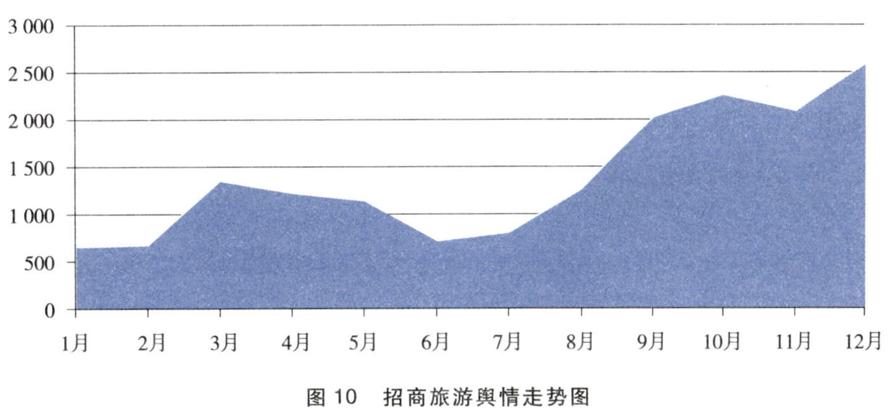

图 10　招商旅游舆情走势图

（二）2018 年重点话题事件

1. 文化和旅游部出台《国家级文化生态保护区管理办法》

监测数据：共检测到201 000条相关数据

事件背景：24 日获悉，文化和旅游部近日出台《国家级文化生态保护区管理办法》（以下简称《管理办法》），将于 2019 年 3 月 1 日起正式施行。

《管理办法》规定，申报国家级文化生态保护区要具备良好的文化生态区域性整体保护工作基础，应当在本省（区、市）内已实行文化生态区域性整体保护两年以上，成效明显；国家级文化生态保护区设立后，总体规划不再由文化和旅游部批复实施，改为由省级文化主管部门审核，报省级人民政府审议通过后发布实施，并报文化和旅游部备案；总体规划实施三年后，省级文化主管部门可向文化和旅游部申请组织验收，验收合格的，正式公布为国家级文化生态保护区并授牌。

《管理办法》明确，要对国家级文化生态保护区总体规划实施和建设情况进行检查评估。建设成绩突出的，予以通报表扬，并给予重点支持。因保护不力使文化生态遭到破坏的，将严肃处理，并予以摘牌。

2. 雪乡旅游事件：国家旅游局责成黑龙江立案调查

监测数据：共检测到 24 600 条相关数据

事件背景：2018 年 1 月 15 日，针对网络曝光的“雪乡导游车上强售套票”事件，国家旅游局高度重视，责成黑龙江省旅游委迅速调查核实，对涉事导游和旅行社要依法严肃查处，绝不姑息。目前已初步查明，涉事导游为商某某，涉事旅行社为哈尔滨康华国际旅行社有限公司龙腾四海分公司。黑龙江省旅游委正按照法律程序，进一步调查取证，一经核实，将依法依规严肃处罚。

国家旅游局已发出通知，要求各地旅游主管部门进一步重视旅游市场监管工作，举一反三，加大旅游市场整治力度，尤其要加强对冰雪旅游、森林旅游等旅游新业态的监管，督促景区主管部门加强日常管理，严厉打击“不合理低价游”、强迫消费和欺客宰客等各类侵害游客合法权益的违法行为，切实履行起行业监管职责。

3. 中秋期间　国内旅游收入 435 亿元

监测数据：共检测到 11 100 条相关数据

事件背景：2018 年 9 月 25 日，从文化和旅游部获悉，中秋假日期间，全国旅游市场供需稳定。经中国旅游研究院（文化和旅游部数据中心）综合通讯运营商、线上旅行服务商和各地旅游部门数据，中秋假日期间全国接待国内游客 9 790 万人次，实现国内旅游收入 435 亿元。

六、教育舆情分析

（一）舆情走势

从图 11 看出，教育舆情在 2018 年信息量起伏较平缓。9 月，习近平出席全国教育大会并发表重要讲话在全国速成为网络热门话题，引起了人们的广泛关注。

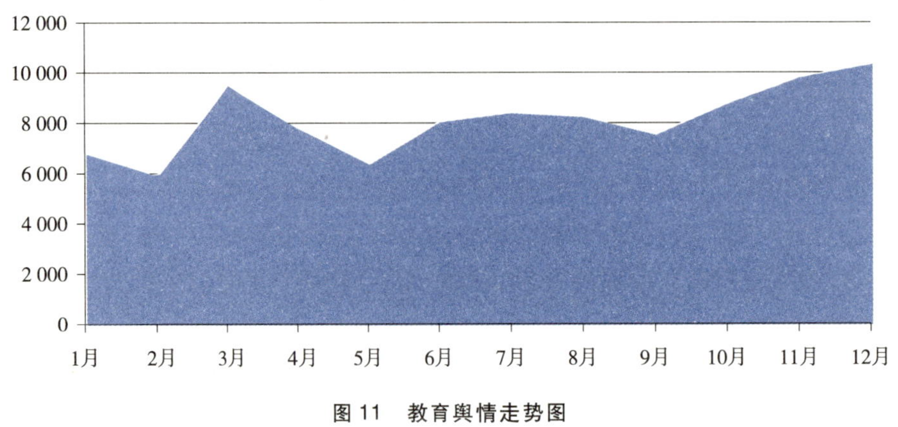

图 11　教育舆情走势图

（二）2018 年重点话题事件

1. 教育部公布：高考改革试点方案将出台

监测数据：共检测到740 000条相关数据

事件背景：教育部官网公布了 2018 年工作要点，包括北京在内的第二批试点省份要制订出台高考综合改革试点方案。同时，推动《学前教育法》起草，完成《学校未成年学生保护规定》起草等被列入重点工作。

2020 年，北京市实施新高考，目前的高一学生是新高考首批考生。新高考不分文理，除语文、数学、外语必考外，考生还要依据向往的高校和专业的要求，在思想政治、历史、地理、物理、化学、生物 6 门科目中自选 3 门参加考试。

工作要点中明确提出，要指导北京、天津、山东、海南等第二批试点省份制订出台高考综合改革试点方案，并发布《普通高校本科招生专业选考科目要求指引（试行）》，指导高校在高考综合改革试点省份优化选考科目要求。此外，今年还将深入推进中考改革，建立地方中考改革动态跟踪机制，以及推进外语能力测评体系建设。

2. 习近平出席全国教育大会并发表重要讲话

监测数据：共检测到 105 000 条相关数据

事件背景：9 月 10 日上午，全国教育大会在北京召开。中共中央总书记、国家主席、中央军委主席习近平出席会议并发表重要讲话。他强调，长期以来，广大教师贯彻党的教育方针，教书育人，呕心沥血，默默奉献，为国家发展和民族振兴作出了重大贡献。教师是人类灵魂的工程师，是人类文明的传承者，承载着传播知识、传播思想、传播真理，塑造灵魂、塑造生命、塑造新人的时代重任。全党全社会要弘扬尊师重教的社会风尚，努力提高教师政治地位、社会地位、职业地位，让广大教师享有应有的社会声望，在教书育人岗位上为党和人民事业作出新的更大的贡献。

3. 教育部：校外培训机构有望实现全国联网查询

监测数据：共检测到 42 700 条相关数据

事件背景：11 月 25 日，教育部开发的全国中小学生校外培训机构管理服务平台即将上线，各地审批的全国中小学生校外培训机构有望通过平台实现联网查询。

教育部要求，各地要用好平台，通过系统完成校外培训机构的摸排、整改、审批、学科类培训备案、社会监督等工作，面向社会公布校外培训机构的有关政策、白名单、黑名单、学科类培训班等信息，依托平台受理群众投诉，接受社会各界监督，切实通过信息化手段实现校外培训全过程精细化管理，方便群众了解相关信息。此外，截至 11 月 15 日，全国2 963 个县（市、区）已启动专项治理整改工作，其中 1 247 个县（市、区）已基本完成专项治理整改任务。全国共摸排校外培训机构 401 050 所，存在问题机构 272 842 所，现已完成整改 163 203所，整改完成率近 60%。

七、环保舆情分析

(一) 舆情走势

由图12可见，环保舆情在2018年信息量浮动较小。因十三届全国人大一次会议开幕会上李克强强调雾霾治理，使3月的信息量达到最高。由此看出影响我们健康的环境问题，媒体和网民的关注度一直较高。

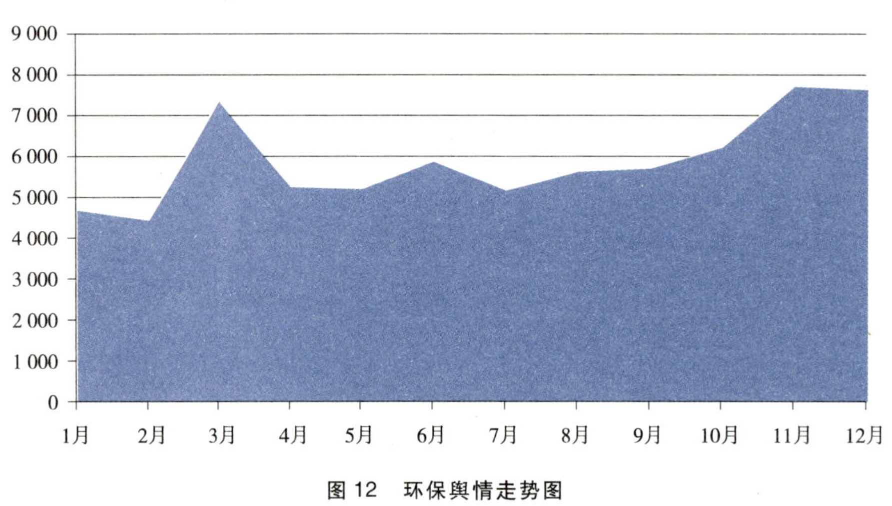

图12 环保舆情走势图

(二) 2018年重点话题事件

1. 生态环境部发布:《环境空气质量标准》修改单

监测数据：共检测到512 000条相关数据

事件背景：2018年7月31日，生态环境部部长李干杰主持召开的生态环境部常务会议审议并原则通过《环境空气质量标准》修改单和《非道路移动柴油机械排气烟度限值及测量方法》。

会议强调，尽快发布《环境空气质量标准》修改单，抓紧配套监测方法标准制修订，按照新的监测状态建立全面、系统的环境空气污染物监测标准规范体系，建立必要的气象参数监测、记录、报告工作制度，确保监测数据准确。充分做好监测状态转换，抓紧完成国控监测点仪器设备更新调试，指导各地做好地方监测点位的监测状态转换，做好大气颗粒物及其组分监测数据的历史回溯。组织专家做好宣传解读，及时回应社会关切。

2. 五部门喊你一起保护生态环境

监测数据：共检测到83 700条相关数据

事件背景：2018年6月5日是新《环境保护法》规定的第4个环境日。生态环境部、中央文明办、教育部、共青团中央、全国妇联五部门联合发布《公民生态环境行为规范

（试行）》（以下简称《规范》），倡导简约适度、绿色低碳的生活方式，引领公民践行生态环境责任，携手共建天蓝、地绿、水清的美丽中国。

据了解，这十条行为规范主要包括关注生态环境、节约能源资源、践行绿色消费、选择低碳出行、分类投放垃圾、减少污染产生、呵护自然生态、参加环保实践、参与监督举报、共建美丽中国内容。《规范》的编制和发布旨在牢固树立社会主义生态文明观，推动形成人与自然和谐发展现代化建设新格局，强化公民生态环境意识，引导公民成为生态文明的践行者和美丽中国的建设者，共包括“十条”行为规范。

3. 生态环境部：加快推动碳排放权交易管理暂行条例出台

监测数据：共检测到67 400条相关数据

事件背景：国新办11月26日就《中国应对气候变化的政策与行动2018年度报告》有关情况举行发布会。生态环境部气候司司长李高在发布会上表示，下一步，要进一步加快碳市场建设的相关工作。具体而言，包括以下几个方面：一是相关法规制度的建设，要和有关部门一道，加快推动碳排放权交易管理暂行条例的出台。该条例非常重要，是建立碳市场运行的法律基础。这一条例出台后，还要进一步陆续推动相关配套制度出台，这些相关的配套制度都在起草过程中。

二是推动相关基础设施建设。碳排放权交易市场有几大基础设施，包括注册登记系统、交易系统、企业直报系统等。企业碳排放数据的直报系统已经初步建成，还要进一步完善优化。注册登记系统和交易系统有了初步的方案，接下来要抓紧对这些方案进行论证，进一步完善方案，在完善方案的基础上抓紧推进基础设施建设。

三是进一步做好重点排放单位碳排放报告、核查和配额管理工作。在碳市场建设中，数据基础非常关键。

四是进一步强化能力建设。整个碳市场的建设涉及很多方面，包括生态环境系统，也包括相关部门、机构，都需要具有相关的能力，开展相关的能力建设。

（作者：中国市长协会；技术支持：谷尼舆情库）

香港的现状与未来

我想要说明的是，在撰写这篇文章之前和期间，笔者没有进行任何独立的数据统计和田野调查，故而这篇文章谈不上有什么学术价值。文中所述所议，均为个人的体验和感受。尽管体验和感受是真实的，但相对于科学研究而言，无疑也是主观的。

而主观的感受，正是我想要强调的。坦白地说，如果这篇文章有可读的价值，那么，其价值正在于其主观性。这是因为，自从人类出现城市之后，其演变和发展都从来没有离开过人们的主观感受。一个城市好不好，人们很少根据科学的标准去衡量，绝大多数人都是根据个人的体验和感受去判断。虽然科学方法和统计数据能够解释一些问题，但却不能领会人们的主观感受。既然城市是为人而建、为人而存在，那么，城市的研究者和规划者，就必须把公众的主观感受作为科学研究和科学行为的第一考虑因素。

一、香港人的出行模式

在城市规划和管理中，最大的难处就是如何照顾好、管理好居民的感受。其中最大的挑战之一，就是确保大量人口在拥挤的空间里，能够有秩序、有效率地流动。在世界范围内，这是所有城市每天都要面对的难题，它让很多城市的管理者和规划者困扰不已。

在过去几十年里，我先后在海内外几个城市长期生活过，包括在布鲁塞尔4年，在新加坡15年，在香港已近10年。在这三个城市里，我感觉香港人口的日常流动最为高效，也最有秩序。香港有700多万人口，土地面积原本就不大，而用于居住和工作的空间就更狭窄。就在这么狭小的空间里，其日复一日的人口流动却做到了顺畅而有效，着实不易。这首先要归功于发达的公共交通网络以及各种交通设施的合理配置与布局。

国际上有一个机构名为Arcadis，每隔几年就对世界主要城市的公共交通状况发布研究报告。2017年，香港被列为世界上公共交通网络最好的城市，位于100个城市之首，名列其后的是苏黎世和巴黎。还有其他几个亚洲城市也见于榜首，例如排名第四的首尔和排名第八的新加坡。该机构在研究报告中认为，香港的地铁网络具有创新性，衔接良好、使用率高、管理优良、资金配置高效，达到了现代城市交通的很多目标，包括带动了经济发展，丰富了市民的生活，促进了商业和旅游业等。

然而，这种学术性的评价还是过于抽象，我还是要回到个人的体验和感受上。我在香港经常搭乘有轨交通，大多时候是从新界的大埔墟站乘坐火车，前往九龙塘转乘地铁，由海底穿过，目的地是港岛的湾仔、铜锣湾或者中环。这条交通线很长，中途换乘三次地铁列车，听上去很折腾，其实非常便捷。因为每次换乘不同方向的地铁，都无需在车站里、在人群中穿来绕去，只需朝对面的月台走几步，稍等片刻，下一趟地铁就会抵达。上文所说的“创新性”“衔接良好”，指的就是这一点。虽然是频繁地换乘，但感觉不到任何不便与烦躁，这样的感受在很多城市里都不能获得。以习以为常的思维来看，香港人口如此的密集，其公共交通难免是混乱和拥挤不堪的，但事实却相反，这里的交通井然有序。

我和一些内地来的朋友聊天时，只要谈到香港的公共交通，就禁不住地感慨。可以这么说，越是在人流高峰时段，香港火车和地铁就越能展现出其管理和运行的高效本色。比如早晨上班时间，差不多大半个香港的人口同时出动，先是从四面八方聚集到地铁站，然后朝着同一个方向，也就是向九龙和港岛地区排山倒海般地移动，最后在不同的地点下车，快速地分散。这个过程在很多大城市都是稀疏平常的景象，但效率和秩序却是差别很大。若要探究为何有这种差别，答案都藏在细节之中。

这些年里，前来香港考察的内地官员络绎不绝，我好几次亲耳听到几位市长感叹说，香港道路上的车辆也很多，为什么见不到严重堵塞的情况？这是怎么做到的？其实，要了解一座城市的公共交通，最好的办法就是花几天时间亲自坐公交，亲眼观察，亲身感受。

凡是在香港坐过公交的人都知道，无论是地铁还是公交车，“准点抵达”是构成其可靠服务的最核心要素。举个例子，我的儿子过去每天早晨从新界去港岛上学，只要他自己准时出门，那就一定能够赶上按照时刻表准时抵达的那趟地铁。从小学四年级直到高中毕业，在长达 9 年的时间里，除了个别的日子，他没有遇到过地铁不准点的情况。因为准点，因为靠谱，所以香港市民对公交网络的服务有着不假思索的信赖。所谓现代化城市，这一点应该是必须有的基本素质之一。

在人潮蜂拥而至的高峰时段，香港地铁的效率之高，也是很多外地人所不可想象的。列车班次的频率极高，间隔时间只有一分钟，有时候甚至更短。很多香港人即使有私家车，也不愿意驾车出门，其中的主要原因就在于公共交通更便捷、更靠谱，当然成本也低。

城市人口的日常流动，是一个非常复杂而细致的庞大工程，公交网络只是其中的一环。若只是依赖公交系统，那还是无法保证日常出行的顺畅和高效。因此，在公交网络之外，其他交通工具的合理布局和配置同样十分重要。

很多内地人都知道香港有著名的小巴服务，但对它的认识只限于画面层次的观感，并没有深究小巴服务为何有其长期存在的价值。香港小巴一般穿梭于地铁站与住宅区的沿线，承担着人潮聚集和分散的功能，虽然车费高于公交车，但由于比公交车灵活快捷，所以是一个不可缺少的选择。我记得 90 年代的时候，北京也有类似的小巴服务，但因为管理不当，运行中不讲规矩，反而给城市交通增加了混乱，结果自然是很快消失。这一点也告诉我们，不规范的管理和不规范的运行，是制造无序状态的因素之一。

与此同时，香港大多数屋苑（住宅小区）都为住户提供出行交通服务。凡是距离地铁站和巴士站有较长路程的屋苑都有自己的穿梭巴士，内地叫摆渡车。从早到晚，这些穿梭巴士在公交车站和住宅之间循环运行，弥补了公交网络不能覆盖每个角落的缺陷。

我想特别提一下人的因素，因为一座城市的有序与无序，决定性因素是人本身。若人群本身不守秩序，再怎么发达的交通网络，其效率也会被大打折扣，甚至会变得一团糟。我曾经不厌其烦地跟一些朋友谈过一件事，这里再啰嗦一次，目的是要强调人的因素对一个城市的秩序是多么重要。

九龙塘地铁站是人潮非常集中的一个交通枢纽，前面我已经提到自己常在这里转乘地铁。每天早晨上班时段，这里的人潮和拥挤程度若用“人山人海”“汹涌澎湃”来形容都嫌不够。大量的人群从不同的方向不断地聚集于此，接着又朝着不同的方向逐渐分散。在某些城市，这种大规模聚集和分散的过程，人们可以凭经验去想象，有多么混乱就多么混乱。而在香港，人们也可以反过来尽情地想象，庞大的人潮聚集在一个狭小的空间里，并且在不断地移动，那该如何维持有序和高效?

凡是上班族都有这样的体验，那就是在赶着去上班时，难免都有争先恐后的心理，香港人当然也是如此。但在九龙塘车站，却看不到你争我抢的混乱场面，虽然所有的个体都急急忙忙，但把人群当一个整体来看，却是忙而不乱。外人所想象不到的是，在不算宽阔的通道里，两股声势浩大的人流各占一半空间，彼此朝着相反的方向快速移动，各行其道，互不逾矩，既没有熙熙攘攘，更没有大呼小叫。置身于数以万计的人群中，唯一能够听到的声响，就是鞋底与地面摩擦的声音。这是一个令人十分震撼的场面，甚至会令人为之感动。秩序是一种内在的力量，安静是一种含蓄的力量。相比于混乱和嘈杂，前者会让人肃然起敬。

由于土地稀缺，香港的街道和马路都比较窄，但路上的交通大多时候都很通畅，既保证了出行的效率，同时又让出行的人们有一个好心情。听起来，这好像是小事，其实这攸关城市人的生活质量。我有时候会在高峰时段驾车去港岛，路上要穿越好几个隧道。进入隧道之前，四五条车道合并成两条，车辆拥挤是肯定的，但每个人都很规矩，不会因为争抢车道、互不相让而导致大堵塞。在内地很多城市，塞车是常态，但很多时候，只要礼让三分，塞车是可以避免的。香港人守规矩，守秩序，重自律，确实是内地人应该学习的。

几年前，香港部分民众产生了排斥内地游客的激烈情绪和行动。从内地人的角度看，香港人很不友善。其实不友善的人毕竟是少数，而这少数人往往怀有政治目的，他们在利用某些现象鼓动其他人的情绪。我的感觉是，绝大多数香港人对无关自己利益的事情都是选择避让，不会无缘无故地卷入是非。内地人在看待这个问题时，需要设身处地地站在对方的角度思考，更需要好好反省自己的行为举止是否符合香港社会所普遍遵循的规矩和秩序。乘坐地铁时一哄而上，抢占座位，在车厢里旁若无人的喧哗或者大声地打电话，类似的行为举止基本上都发生在内地人身上。虽然不是所有内地人都是如此，但地铁车厢里有那么几个不文明的人，就足以让所有的内地人为他们背上黑锅。毫不夸张地说，我每次乘坐地铁都能遇到这类事情。若要说香港人歧视内地人，那就很难解释我的反应。我也是内地人，同样看不惯这种情况。我每天生活在香港人中间，但从来就没有被歧视的感觉。这是为什么？因为我不给他们任何歧视的理由。

二、香港人的生活空间

以住房面积来衡量，香港人的生活空间小得可怜。除了非富即贵者之外，绝大部分香港家庭的住处都令人感到很憋屈。很多年前，一位香港朋友的孩子对我说，她从小到大都在沙发上睡觉，从来没有睡过床。我那时对香港不怎么了解，所以很是惊讶。直到后来，我从新加坡移居到香港，因为要租房子住，终于有机会参观了很多香港人的居住环境，真真切切地体会到了什么叫“蜗居”。70 平方米的私人屋宇算是豪宅，价格惊人，且年年大幅上涨，低收入家庭只能望而兴叹。至于一家几口挤在三四十平米的房子里，那是非常普遍的。

为了解决低收入家庭的住房问题，香港实行一套政府补贴的租住公屋制度，通称“公屋”，面积很小，租金便宜。但是，由于低收入人口的数量很庞大，加上土地开发受到各种因素的掣肘，这些家庭要申请公屋，至少需要等待 4 年时间。在漫长的等待时间里，一些无房户别无选择，只好租住“劏房”。所谓“劏房”，是香港的一个非常悲惨的特色。几十平方米的房子被分隔成好几个空间，分租给多户人家，有的甚至被分成十几个床位租给不同的住户。粗略估算，租住这种房子的家庭大约 9 万户，人口几十万。

香港已经连续八年被评为世界上房价最贵的城市，但问题不只在于贵，而且还在于供不应求，当中存在的结构性问题十分突出。这种困局与土地稀缺有关，但与土地分配的不合理性同样有关。论土地，香港新界地区其实有很多闲置的地方，按道理应该予以征用，但英国统治时期留下来的土地政策限制了土地的开发和利用，这是香港特区政府解不开的绳索。

与此同时，各种既得利益者，包括拥有土地的村民、从高房价中牟利的地产商，都不支持这些土地的开发。除此之外，还有形形色色的社会团体，例如环保组织、自然保护组织、打着本土主义旗号的政客，都一直在阻挠乡郊地区的土地征用。这是一个非常矛盾、非常奇特的现象：很多香港人一边抱怨买不起住房，批评政府不想办法提供足够的房源，一边却以各种理由反对政府开发闲置的土地。至于中产阶级家庭，他们一方面抱怨房价太高，房贷支出不堪重负，一方面却又反对政府建设更多的廉租房，因为这样会导致房价下降，使他们的财产缩水。

由于现有的土地难以顺利开发，行政长官林郑月娥在 2018 年度施政报告中正式提出“明日大屿愿景”的填海计划，以此扩大香港的发展和生活空间。这个计划的基本内容是，用二三十年时间，在大屿山附近的海域填海造地、建设人工岛，总面积为 1700 公顷。大屿山是香港机场的所在地，也是港珠澳大桥的起始端，特区政府希望把大屿山及其填海新增土地，变成港珠澳大桥和香港机场的“双门户”，将这一片土地建成香港的另一个核心商业中心和住宅区，这样就可以分散香港的人口，也可为现有的老旧公屋腾出重建的空间。2019

年3月，香港立法会通过了这一发展规划，首期财政拨款已经到位，但这是个需要耗时几十年的建设工程，暂时无法缓解目前所存在的困难。

居住空间的狭小，并不等同于香港人整体的生活空间同样小。我定居香港之后就惊讶地发现，香港的运动和休闲空间竟然比我熟悉的其他几个城市要大得多。无论在哪一个区，无论道路和高楼大厦多么拥挤，大大小小的体育场和面积很大的公园都随处可见。这个寸土寸金的城市，舍得为普通市民腾出宽敞的公共活动空间，这就体现出城市管理者和规划者的远见与情怀。无论是港岛、九龙，还是新界，凡是河边和滨海的土地，必定都建有绿树成荫的公园、运动场地、步行道、自行车道等。我所居住的大埔区，面积不是很大，但这里分布着几个足球场，室内室外的运动场多达六七个，而且所占空间都很大。这些运动休闲场所不只为居民们扩展了生活的空间，而且也有效地降低了青少年的犯罪率。有一个理论是这么说的，青少年精力充沛，当他们无所事事的时候，也就是容易滋事和犯罪的危险时候。因此，为他们提供充足的运动空间，可以规范他们的行为方式，可以有效地引导他们朝着健康的方向成长。

尽管如此，香港人的生活空间在根本上还是狭小的。它毕竟只是一个城市，即使不断地填海造地，香港依然摆脱不了天生的局限。因此，香港人，尤其是年轻一代，不能画地自限，而应该认识到视野就是空间。他们应该把整个中国作为寻求自我发展、满足生活目标的大舞台。而粤港澳大湾区的建设宏图，正是香港人可以充分利用的大舞台，是他们人生中不可错过的宝贵机遇。

三、香港人的守成与自满

无论从哪个角度看，香港早就是一个成熟的大都市。凡是从其他国际城市移居到这里的人，方方面面都很容易适应。虽然香港的生活方式有其自身的特色，但整个城市的运行规则与其他现代化城市没有太大差别。

可是，正因为一切都有既定的规矩，社会各阶层的利益关系也已固定经年，所以香港社会也就缺乏自我调适、自我改变的想象力和进取意识。香港固然需要坚持自己的成功模式，但若不能虚怀若谷地吸收新时代带来的新机会和新事物，那就等于是自我封闭和不思进取。

香港和新加坡过去一直被视为具有竞争的关系，所谓的“双城记”曾经是两地官员和媒体津津乐道的话题。但是，最近这些年，新加坡似乎已经不再把香港作为竞争对手。我每次从香港到新加坡旧地重游，都明显感觉到新加坡的变化完全说得上是“日新月异”。新加坡政府和民众始终有一种强烈的危机意识，他们永远不甘落后，永远努力地与时代的节奏保持一致。新加坡其实一直很羡慕香港，认为香港背后依托广袤的中国内地，而新加坡却没有。李光耀先生曾经感慨地说，中国内地是香港继续发展和繁荣的腹地，为香港提供了无限的发展空间和机遇。只可惜，香港所具备的这个巨大的潜在优势，并没有被香港人好好地利用。

从香港去深圳，现在变得越来越方便了。除了罗湖、落马洲、文锦渡、沙头角、皇岗和深圳湾这几个通关口岸之外，今年又增加了莲塘口岸，从莲塘口岸通往九龙的公路已经建成通车。从九龙西车站乘坐高铁，12 分钟就可到达深圳的福田。而港珠澳大桥的落成，更是大大缩短了香港至珠海和澳门的行车时间。所有这些基础设施的建成，都为香港与内地的深度融合提供了便利，香港和珠三角地区实现“一小时生活圈”的硬件设施已经完全具备。但是，在具备了基础设施之后，香港人的心态和视野也需要跟着改变。

多少年之前，从香港进入深圳的那一刻，我们都会感觉到强烈的反差，这主要是因为两地发展阶段的不同，导致人们对深圳的所有方面都感觉到有落差。但最近这些年，这种差异性已变得越来越不明显。当然，差异还是有的，比如香港显得很安逸平和，一切按部就班、有条不紊；深圳则依然显得比较凌乱，触目所及之景象似乎都比较躁动。但是，除此之外，我们再也不能用“落后”二字来形容。在躁动的表象之下，深圳每时每刻都释放着强大的能量和爆发力，街道上的每个人似乎都在不知疲倦地奔向美好的人生目标。很坦白地说，在很多方面，深圳已经把香港抛在了后头。

比如住房，虽然深圳这些年的房价如同内地其他城市一样一路猛涨，但人均居住面积远远大于香港，性价比当然已远远优于香港。我所在的公司位于香港大埔，距离深圳只有四个地铁站的距离，半个小时即可抵达，所以很多同事都愿意住在深圳，因为房子大，租金低于香港，消费又方便又便宜。

深圳的科技创新能力已经成为世界关注的焦点，华为、中兴、腾讯、大疆等都是最近这些年兴起的。反观香港，很多年轻人都感到迷茫，有些年轻人更因某些政客的唆使而误入歧途。而经济结构的转型，在香港始终没有发生。几大地产业巨头依然居于龙头地位，至今没有出现凭借科技创新而崛起的新兴产业。

在深圳消费，不需要怀揣现金和钱包，一部手机就可以解决几乎所有问题。但在香港，现金依然是王。要坐出租车，还是要通过原始的电话预约，或者必须站在路边耐心地碰运气。曾经有人提出香港应该学习内地，用手机二维码给出租车司机付费，但香港的出租车司机们群起反对。不久之前，一位香港朋友才发现，在深圳消费原来都不用现金了，深圳人身上都没有钱包，他为此感到十分的新鲜和诧异，并且感慨地说，他这些年好像都在睡大觉，对内地的迅速发展竟然没有感觉，实在是井底之蛙。

其实，相比于内地，香港的传统优势依然存在，金融、航运、自由港、与外部世界的密切联系等，都领先于内地。但是，若香港继续躺在过去的成功之上吃老本，那将来就是龟兔赛跑的新版故事。我个人认为，香港必须正视和克服两大问题，才能使其传统优势获得新的生命力。第一，香港必须在自己的命运和前途问题上形成更广泛的共识，减少内部纷争，尤其是要减少反对派政客的分裂性和破坏性的作用；第二，全体香港人必须认清世界大势，不能迷失自我、迷失方向。香港人必须清醒地认识到，国家的未来就是香港的未来，国家的繁荣就是香港的繁荣，国家的命运就是香港的命运。

四、香港，我最喜欢的城市

我从新加坡迁到香港之初，好几位香港同事都这么问我：新加坡那么好，你为何非要来香港？每次遇到这样的问题，我都没有办法用一两句话说清楚。当初在决定是否要来香港时，我在内心挣扎了很长时间，凡是能够想到的问题，我都反反复复地考虑了很多遍。

我还征求了三个好朋友的意见，第一个说："你不会讲粤语，去香港干什么？"第二位说："你要去香港，还不如回大陆。"第三位说："我在香港生活了好几年，房子小得要死，坐在客厅沙发上看电视，膝盖都能碰到电视机。"但是，我终究还是顺从了自己的意愿，作出了自己的决定。几年之后，这三位朋友先后来香港看望我，每个人跟我说的话几乎一模一样："你来香港是对的！"

我当初决定迁居香港，首要原因并非香港本身，而是因为聘用我的公司在香港，我对这家公司一直充满向往之情，觉得自己可以在这个舞台上更好地体现自身价值。我始终认为，喜不喜欢一个城市，这个城市是否适合自己长期居住，在很大程度上并非取决于城市本身，而是取决于这个城市能否为自己提供更好的机会。我们常常说"安居乐业"，其实这四个字的顺序应该调换过来，改为"乐业安居"才显得顺理成章。

在全球范围内，除了经济移民和难民之外，人口流动的方向主要是由"机会"所主导的。哪个城市可供选择的机会多，人口就自然地流向哪里。中国从改革开放直到今天，其他地区的人口一直向北上广深四大城市流动；日本其他地区的人口向东京地区流动，美国各领域专才向纽约湾区和旧金山湾区流动，都足以说明这个道理。

至于香港，它的主要吸引力也在于此。虽然香港的住房条件是个很大的劣势，但很多人来到香港之后都不愿意离开，就是因为香港给他们提供的机会，在其他城市不易获得。比如，在香港读书的中国内地学生，明明知道香港的房价和物价要远远高于内地城市，但大多数都还是愿意留在香港。所以，一个城市到底好不好，评判的标准千差万别。每个人的机会不同，每个人的际遇不同，所以对同一个城市的感受也很不相同。但最根本的标准是相同的，那就是，凡是能够为各类人才创造更多机会的城市，就必定是一座好城市。

至于我自己，在几个不同的城市长期生活之后，我还是觉得香港是我心目中最好的城市。除了它能够满足我安居乐业的基本需求之外，我觉得香港具备了现代都市所应该具备的所有元素。政府服务部门的高效，公共设施的完善和简便，私营部门的规范化，城市文化的多元性，高度国际化的都市生活，文明、守纪和自律的社会环境，还有畅通无阻的信息流通，所有这些都是香港的魅力所在，也是中国内地城市所努力的方向。

我始终认为，城市的发展不只是高楼大厦，不只是经济指标，也不只是各种冷冰冰的统计数据，而更应该有鲜活的人以及他们的所思所想与行为方式。这是因为，一座城市应该呈现出什么样的灵性、什么样的性格、什么样的气质，这些都需要居住在这座城市的人来塑造。而在塑造所有这些内涵的时候，人的自我塑造应置于最优先的位置。

致谢：

这篇文章是应朋友亲自邀约而写。自领命之日，我一直怀着敬畏之心，诚惶诚恐，其原因是，对于城市发展这个大课题，我既没有任何学术训练的背景，也没有任何实践的经验。朋友们很坚持，鼓励我以媒体人的视角来分享一下自己的观察。我将此番鼓励视为莫大的光荣。

（作者：杜平，凤凰卫视评论员、香港三策智库理事长、四川大学特聘教授）

澳门回归和澳门大学的改革发展

1999 年 12 月 20 日，中华人民共和国国旗在澳门上空冉冉升起，澳门长达 400 多年被殖民统治的历史宣告结束，回归后的澳门经历了历史的变革，旅游、经济、治安、教育等各方面的飞速发展让澳门生机勃勃，澳门人民寻找到了未来广阔的发展空间。

澳门回归祖国 20 年来，"一国两制""澳人治澳"、高度自治的方针在澳门得到了全面的贯彻和落实，在中央政府的大力支持和特区政府、社会各界的共同努力下，澳门取得了令人瞩目的发展成就，社会安定、经济发展、居民安居乐业，多元文化得到了很好的发展。澳门在国家"十二五"规划期间被赋予建设一个中心——"世界旅游休闲中心"和一个平台——"中国与葡语国家商贸合作服务平台"的战略定位。现在澳门人均生产总值超 8 万美元，居全国之首，世界领先。澳门旅游业近 20 年获得腾飞。1999 年澳门回归祖国前，每年旅客为 700 万到 800 万人次。而 2018 年，拥有 30 余万居民的澳门竟然全年接待 3 580 万人次外地游客。2019 年第一季度访澳旅客已达 1 035 万人次。回归后的澳门积极拓展对外交往，着力打造中葡商贸合作服务平台。近年来，在参与和助力"一带一路"的建设过程中，澳门不仅成为中葡友好的一个合作桥梁，也为中国和葡语国家开展合作搭建了重要平台。

在澳门经济和社会快速发展，朝着多元化和可持续的方向迈进的过程中，挑战与机遇并存，尤其需要有高水平的大学教育。为此，澳门特区政府在中央的支持下，采取一系列战略举措，发展提升澳门大学，力图将其打造成高水平的旗舰型大学。在重重挑战与机遇之下，澳门大学在这一历史时刻的发展提升具有多重意义。

第一，澳门的需要。虽然澳门经济已有较快的发展，但要达到"世界旅游休闲中心"的目标，社会要可持续发展，经济要多元化，还需要更多优秀人才的支持。澳门不但要有一流的旅游休闲设施，更需要有高水平的大学教育。澳门大学作为本地高等教育的旗舰，承担着为澳门培养更多更好的人才的使命。正如我们常说的："澳大要为澳门培养特首"。为达此目的，澳门大学必须积极改革发展，提升竞争力，把自身打造成具有区域特色、高水平的大学。

第二，国家的期待。中国处在改革发展的关键阶段，经济社会发展方式加快转变。因此，中国急需提高高等教育的质量以适应国家的发展。最近国家一系列政策都凸显了高等教育改革和发展的重要性和紧迫性。澳门作为国家战略的组成部分，也应利用"一国两制"的特点，积极打造本地高水平的世界级大学，为国家未来之发展，探索提升高等教育质量的成功之道。

第三，世界的趋势。高等教育改革发展是当今世界的趋势。提升高等教育质量已不仅是学生的愿望和家长的期盼，也是澳门特区的共识及政府的策略。近年来，许多国家和地区都对高等教育加大投放资源，改革教育模式，更新管治系统，提升师资质量，致力发展高水平大学。事实上，澳门邻近的地区在提升高等教育质量的进程中都有显著的进展，北京大学、新加坡国立大学、台湾大学、香港大学等都已名列世界前百名。澳门不应该也不能在这一进程中被边缘化，澳门大学作为澳门的旗舰型大学必须与世界发展趋势同步，迎头赶上。

一、管治模式改革

澳门大学的发展改革是一个长期的过程，面临着许多困难和挑战。就澳门而言，什么样的管治模式才最有利于大学的提升？澳门大学如何按照其发展趋势制定合适的管治模式？这是要突破的第一个问题。澳门特别行政区政府在2002年启动澳门大学管治模式的改革。澳门地域虽小，但澳门特区政府和澳门社会对大学所担当的重要角色的认同，是与国际社会一致的，并将顺应世界大学的发展趋势，作出有助于增强澳门大学竞争力、深化大学管治水平的决定。这个改革只涉及澳门大学，但足见澳门特区政府、澳门社会的视野与世界趋势发展同步。在2002年，澳门特区政府委任了一个修章工作小组，分析检讨澳门大学的章程和人事规章等，研究如何修改才能让澳门大学配合特区在“一国两制”下可以预见的整体发展。澳门特区立法会在2006年制定了一项管治澳门大学的专用法律，而《澳门大学章程》也按该法律进行了修改。这个初步的改革，从澳门大学角度来看，极为重要，它使得澳门大学能够在此后几年内晋身成为今天的现代化大学。澳门大学横琴新校区开始建设以后，澳门特区政府于2011年6月再次委任修章工作小组，启动第二次大学管治改革，研究修改澳门大学的法律、章程及规章等，务求有关法律条规能满足澳门大学迁入横琴新校园后的发展需要。由此可见，澳门地域虽小，但是回归以后，澳门特区政府和澳门社会高度认同教育所担当的重要角色，作出有助于增强澳门大学发展改革、深化大学管治水平的决定。足见澳门特区政府、澳门社会的视野与世界趋势发展同步。

二、横琴校区建设

澳门地域狭小，土地严重短缺，只有29.2平方公里。澳门大学原来在凼仔的老校区，只有0.2平方公里，设施拥挤，学生基本上是走读，无法进一步发展。为了帮助突破澳门大学“有校无园”的困境，2009年，澳门特别行政区政府和广东省商议，向中央政府提出，希望在广东省珠海市横琴岛为澳门大学提供新校址，并依照澳门特区法律实施管辖。2009年6月27日，全国人大常委会授权澳门特别行政区政府管辖横琴岛东部一幅约一平方公里土地，专门用于澳门大学新校园。2009年12月20日，中共中央总书记、国家主席胡锦涛和澳门特区行政长官崔世安一起为澳门大学横琴校区奠基，并为大学题词。

澳门大学横琴校区由澳门特区政府出资，华南理工大学何镜堂院士设计，广东南粤公司施工，占地109公顷，有60多栋楼宇，总建筑面积90多万平方米。经过三年半的紧张设计施工，2013年7月20日，澳门大学横琴校区宣布竣工，移交澳门特区政府，开始依照澳门特区法律管辖。2013年11月5日，中共中央政治局委员、国务院副总理汪洋为澳门大学横琴校区主持启用仪式。2014年8月24日，澳门大学完成了从凼仔老校区的整体搬迁，正式启用横琴校区。

“一国两制”是史无前例的崭新事物。中央政府支持澳门特别行政区政府，同意澳门大学在横琴建立校区，并授权澳门特区依照澳门特区法律对其实施管辖，是我国在“一国两制”实践过程中的一项创新举措，有着极为深刻的历史和现实意义。

三、教育体制创新

新校园的建设给澳门大学提供了极佳的物质环境。澳门大学与此同时抓住发展机遇，在教育体制方面开展了全面而系统的改革创新，努力提升自身的办学水平和学术声望。澳门大学的发展改革因而也日益为世界高等教育界所关注。

（一）目标

进入21世纪以来，国际形势的变化为学生带来更多的不稳定感和焦虑感，而高等教育的改革方向并未在此着力。追本溯源，从组成社会的基本单元——个体及教育过程的主体——学生的角度出发，我们提出以“自知”为教育改革的出发点和目标。“自知”，即认识自我。提倡自知即鼓励青年学生在不稳定的形势下更多地反观自身，鼓励高等教育的改革重新探索人的发展的内涵，回归教育育人的本真意涵，从源头处解决国际形势变化与高等教育改革动向不相匹配的问题，从而更好地发挥高等教育培养人才、服务社会、推动社会变革的职能。

我们认为，在以学生为本的价值理念之下，教育目标是自知，即培养学生认识自我。只有在自知的基础上，个体才能获得完整和充分的发展，也才能更好地将个体优势与社会需求相结合，发挥最大效用。在这里，通过自我与外部之间的良性互动，让学生发现认识自己，明白“我想做什么”和“我能做什么”。

第一，引导学生思考和探索“我想做什么”，是从个体兴趣和个人抱负的角度出发对自我的认识，将个人抱负和外部激励相结合。调动学生在个体发展和选择中的内部积极性和内生动力，充分重视学生作为教育对象的主体性，鼓励学生自愿、主动确定志向及发展目标。

第二，“我能做什么”则是从现实条件的角度考虑个体发展的可能性，将个人才干与外部资源相结合。个体的发展既具备极强的可塑性，同时也具有一定的局限性。不同的个体在不同领域所拥有的天赋和优势、局限各有不同，这是一切教育活动开展的前提和基础。除去个体内部自身的条件和发展基础之外，个体作为社会成员，其发展必然受到包括经济社会发展水平、价值观念、教育制度等社会结构因素和外部资源的支持和制约。

换言之，通过自知，一人方可自信，自立，从而自强，最终获得自由，在社会中充分发挥个人才能，积极为社会做贡献。

（二）模式

根据“自知”的教育目标，我们对学生培养模式进行创新性变革，提出“四位一体”的新模式，即以专业教育、通识教育、研习教育、社群教育四种要素为主，培养学生。

专业教育和通识教育是通过课堂进行的，而研习教育和社群教育则将视角延伸到课堂外，将学生在课堂内的学习与课堂外的学习联系在一起，努力创建一种整体的、全方位的教育教学活动，打通教育与生活之间的联系，让学生在“做中学”，在“学中做”，“知行合一”，达到“教育即生活”“生活即教育”的教育效果，促进学生发展，以达到“自知”的教育目标。

专业教育是大学的基本元素，奠定了大学在知识创新和学术发展方面的重要地位。我们在专业教育中注重语言、历史、数学、科学等基础学科的建设与发展。同时，为了适应全球化与现代化的社会变革，在学科结构上进行创新性变革，打破传统的学院学科布局，鼓励跨学科教育。

通识教育（General education）与专才或分科教育，共同构成了大学教人、育人的完整轮廓。通识教育有利于打破不同学科的界限，让学生在具备扎实的专业基础和知识结构的同时，能够融会贯通，兼有多种不同视角。澳门大学通识教育课程于2010年5月经教务委员会批准，于2011—2012学年全面推行。澳门大学通识课程中的必修科注重中国文化与语言，强调澳门与中华文明之间的血脉联系，体现澳门大学作为澳门地区的一所旗舰型高等院校所承担的社会责任，以及对于“一国两制”基本国策在高等教育中的创新性实践。

研习教育将教育延伸到传统的课堂教学之外，是一种以学科知识为基础、以学术研究和社会实践为主要形式的教育实践活动。我们常说“大学不是买卖学分的超级市场”，研习教育是澳门大学实现以“自知”为目标的教育的重要一环。学生通过研习教育可以将所学的专业知识与学术研究、社会实践联系在一起，分析、研究和探讨社会现象与理论问题，提升自己的反思能力、实践能力与理论素养。学生在“做”和“用”知识的同时，认识自我，明白自己“想做什么”和“能做什么”。

社群教育是“四位一体”教育模式的重要组成部分，主要通过住宿式书院这种特殊的大学内部组织实现其教育功能，为学生营造了特殊的文化环境、学习环境与生活环境。在自由、自然的氛围中促进学生之间的相互学习以及自我教育。

住宿式书院不是单纯的学生宿舍，而是具有独特的文化教育功能。住宿式书院通过在住宿区的公共区域植入大量的文化元素，举办丰富多样的师生交往活动和文娱活动，营造特殊的文化氛围，培育学生的文化精神。例如，在高桌晚宴中，学生与书院院长共进晚餐，亲密交流，形成独特的师生共同体，让学生在这种文化氛围中成长。

目前澳门大学共有十所书院，每所书院可容纳约500名本科生，学生不分专业、年级、背景，打乱分配到书院生活和学习。书院的学生来自不同专业，打破了传统的学科专业局限，拓宽了学生的社会交往范围。不同专业的学生住在一起实际上可以使每个学生在多个方面受益。一方面，可以促进学生进行学科的交流，拓展知识与视野，有利于培养全面发展的创新性人才；另一方面，也可以增进学生对于自己所学专业的认识以及对自我的认知，同时学会包容不同的思想与见解。

澳门大学十所书院的院长，都是来自不同学术领域的知名教授，院长、驻院导师与学生一起住在书院内，一方面便于对学生进行监管与指导，另一方面这种住宿式的方式使得学生有更多的时间和机会与老师相处，形成亲近密切的师生关系，有利于老师的言传身教，同时学生在日常生活的耳濡目染中也可自然而然地受教。学生与教师在住宿式书院中交往频繁、相处融洽，就像一个大家庭，对学生各方面的成长都是有益的。为了评估学生是否达到了“社群教育”的满意程度，书院制定了三类评价方法：自我评价、同伴评价及教师评价。所有评价都会在学生进入书院学习的四年内持续进行。

四、结语

澳门回归后，澳门特区政府和社会高度认同教育所担当的重要角色。在中央的支持下，采取一系列战略举措，发展提升澳门大学，力图将其打造成高水平的旗舰型大学。澳门大学管治模式的改革和横琴校区的建立为澳门大学的发展提供了管理制度和物质环境保障。在此基础上，澳门大学积极创新，改革教育体制，以自知为教育目标，鼓励学生在不稳定的形势下更多地反观自身，克服焦虑，培养学生认识自我，将个体优势与社会需求相结合，发挥最大效用。

澳门回归后，澳门大学的改革成效已经初现。有数据显示，学生整体素质提高。学科建设方面，澳门大学中文、数学、历史等基础学科得到广泛认可，微电子、中医药、生命健康、材料、计算机等学科发展迅速，经科技部批准成立了 3 所国家重点实验室。澳门大学的发展展示了“一国两制”这一史无前例的崭新事物的优越性，日益为世界高等教育界所关注。

（作者：赵伟，澳门大学原校长。现任沙迦美国大学科研总监（副校长），国际欧亚科学院院士）

风雨兼程七十载　砥砺前行城市化

——新中国城市化建设述评

2019 年 3 月 6 日，全国政协副主席、国家发展改革委员会主任何立峰向采访十三届全国人大二次会议的中外记者宣布：中国新型城市化正在加速，2018 年常住人口城市化率达到 59.58%。按照国家的统一部署，城市化率将继续保持每年提高一个百分点的速度，这就意味着每年 1 400 万农民成为市民。这不仅激活巨大的消费需求，更是让越来越多的中国人过上美好的新生活。

60% 的城市化率，对于数千年以农立国的中国，含义实在太多，它标志着传统生产方式的根本变革，标志着人们生活方式的彻底转变，标志着社会主义是那么具体、那么细致、那么有温度。

一、中国城市化之梦

早在新中国成立之前，毛泽东同志在西柏坡党的七届二中全会上讲，我们党的工作重点要从农村转向城市。过去人们对这句话的理解主要是从政治上，就是说中国共产党执掌全国政权，其实，这何尝不是中国城市化的起步。

城市是文明的标志，是先进生产方式的象征。世界最早的原始城市，大约出现于新石器时代。目前考古挖掘的古城市文明遗迹主要分布在美索不达米亚、埃及、印度河峡谷和中国黄河流域。

从公元前 3500 年到 18 世纪期间，地球上的城市数量增加，城市规模扩大，城市人口比例上升，城市功能和形态逐渐演化，但这种传统的城市化进程相当缓慢。18 世纪的工业革命，既开启了人类的现代化进程，又使作为工业化载体的城市装上了强大的引擎。就全球来说，2007 年世界城市人口首次超过农村人口，人类社会迈入城市社会成为社会主体的发展阶段。

对于中国人来说，什么是城市化呢？大家都是一个感觉，越是熟之极详的概念却往往玄而又玄。什么是城市？目前汉语中最少有三十多种定义，用比较学术化的语言，城市是非农业人口为主的人类聚居地，它具备一定的人口规模、人口密度，具有相应的法律地位、基础设施、公共服务、公共管理和社会功能。如果用普通人的亲身体验来说，那就是工业化生产、由广泛的社会分工协作联系在一起的宜居、宜业、宜教、宜医、宜养、宜游、宜乐的生活状态，它包括硬环境与软环境。与新中国同龄的那一代人特别是农村人，当时所向往的城市无非“楼上楼下、电灯电话”。改革开放之初，一位南方作家高晓声发表了一部小说《陈奂生进城》，写一位农民进城后的种种窘态，形象地刻画出当时的农民对城市生活羡慕嫉妒怕的复杂心态。小说从一个侧面反映出了城市化的迟滞与当时城乡分割的无奈。

中国是城市文明的发源地之一，中国原始城市大约出现于4000年前。古代的城市更多的是行政权力的聚集地和名门望族的享乐场。杜甫的“朱门酒肉臭，路有冻死骨”，写尽了城市里的生与死。

中国的现代城市可以追溯到19世纪中叶。列强用坚船利炮轰开中国的大门，开始赤裸裸的殖民侵略与剥削。一代又一代志士仁人哪里甘心遭受如此屈辱，“师夷长技以制夷”，城市化由此发轫。可是中国幅员实在太大，她的人口实在太多，她的城市化任务远远超过发达国家的总和。经过60年几代人的奋斗，进入20世纪的时候，中国的城市化率只有4%，真是汪洋大海中的几个似隐似现的小岛。又过了50年，当五星红旗在天安门升起的时候，中国城市化率只有11.2%，新中国城市化的家底太薄弱了。

为什么从1900年到1950年，我们的城市化率仅仅增长7.2%？是懒惰、荒唐，还是无能？作为晚辈，我们必须对前辈予以充分的尊重，他们以血肉之躯承担起的是救亡之责。国家将亡，种犹不存，惶论其他！如果一定要追责，那责在帝国主义列强，中国人民奋起反抗侵略，无量英雄无量血，平救战乱图生存。正如曹操所叹：“铠甲生虮虱，万姓以死亡。白骨露於野，千里无鸡鸣。生民百遗一，念之断人肠。”行文至此，对20世纪前半叶顽强坚守的前辈充满敬意，正是前辈的流血牺牲才有新中国的独立自主，才为中国城市化建立了基本前提。即使是筚路蓝缕，也要有一个稳定和平的环境啊！

从1950年到1980年，这30年时间里，我们走过的城市化道路曾经出现波折。主要是由于严峻的国际环境导致我们长期处于战时和准战时状态，虽然没有在中国大陆发生大的战争，但是由于“冷战”局面，由于朝鲜战争和越南战争，中国要声张国际正义，要保卫边境安全，要反对当时肆虐的超级大国霸权主义，特别是“大跃进”的失败和“文革”动乱严重破坏了国内的建设进程，城市化虽然也有一定程度的进步，但城市化率仅仅提高了8.2%。其中的经验可贵，其中的教训可叹。对于善于学习的中国共产党来说，我们对历史进行了充分的反思，一场人类历史上从来没有过的惠及中国和整个人类的城市化风生水起了。

从毛泽东同志晚年改善中美关系起，特别是党的十一届三中全会确定的改革开放，中国共产党痛定思痛，真诚地果断地严肃地总结经验教训，做出一系列重大的战略决策。在邓小平同志的主持下，从以阶级斗争为纲转向经济建设为中心，从闭关锁国转向全方位对外开放，拨乱反正，全面转向经济、政治、社会改革，城市化建设迈出雄伟的步伐，曾经压抑的城市化需求如同火山喷发，蔚为大观。1980年到2010年，又是一个30年，中国的城市化率提高到49.7%，提高了30.3%，平均每年一个百分点。从2011年到2018年的八年时间，正如本文开头所引用的数据，又增长约10%。14亿中国人中的60%生活在城市，这不正是圆了中华民族的城市梦么！

特别需要指出的是，城市化使几亿农民先是变成农民工，再变成城市居民。我们可以想一想，这是多么伟大的人口迁徙。20世纪末与21世纪初，每到春节，中国的列车挤满回乡过年的农民工，压得铁路钢轨呀呀作响，长途汽车超载几乎是常态，任何一个有同情心的人都会为此感到难过。党和国家领导人更是将春节农民工返乡过年作为头等大事。近年来这种山呼海啸的回乡潮越来越弱，道理很简单，农民既然已经进城，既然已经成为城市居民，将父母妻儿接来团聚，这种守夜对于城里人司空见惯，对于农民则是命运的重大转折。

人人都是追梦人，每一个追梦人都是有血有肉有爱有忧有追求的张三李四，而一个农民，他（她）的梦首先就是城市梦。中国的城市化为几亿中国人造梦，功莫大焉！中国的农民圆了自己的城市梦，福莫大焉！

二、中国城市化之路

任何一个社会管理的概念都需要结合当时当地的实际情况。同样讲城市化，现在所讲的城市化与70年前的城市化相比已经具备许多不同的内涵，它是过去的升级版、转型版、N次版。过去所说的“楼上楼下、电灯电话”早就是一种新的戏谑了。

目前所说的中国城市化是一个向着社会主义现代化强国急行军的大国的城市化，是一个正在复兴其光荣并日益接近其复兴的伟大民族的城市化。它包括城市经济、城市社会、城市政治、城市文化、城市居民，需要从功能形态、建筑住房、基础设施、公共服务、公共管理、国际联系等方面设计、规划、运行、组织与改善。

中国科学院中国现代化研究中心经过长期潜心研究，精准地分析判断了中国城市化的基本状况：

第一是城市经济。中国目前的城市经济是一种混合经济，包括都市农业、工业经济、服务经济和知识经济等。中国共产党第十八次全国代表大会提出新型工业化和创新驱动战略，中国城市的经济发展模式，正在向市场化、全球化和绿色化转变。

深圳是中国改革开放以来的一座新兴移民城市，建市之前只是一个渔村。1979年设市，2018年辖区面积2 000平方千米，常住人口1 300万人，是中国第一个没有农村人口的城市，是国务院批准的以创新引领超大型城市可持续发展为主题，建设国家可持续发展议程创新示范区。其经济总量长期位列中国大陆城市第四位，是中国大陆经济效益最好的城市，2018年深圳经济总量2.4万亿元，创造了世界城市化的奇迹。

第二是城市社会。中国城市化率低于发达国家但高于发展中国家，城市社会部分指标则远远高于世界平均水平，这体现了中国共产党和中国政府以人民为中心的执政理念。如2014年中国儿童DPT免疫接种率、儿童麻疹免疫接种率都高于世界平均值，结核病患病率约为世界平均水平的一半，2013年中国结核病治愈率高于世界平均值。长期困扰我们的人均住房面积的难题迎刃而解，目前中国人均住房面积已经超过德国与日本。

第三是城市政治。中国城市政治具有中国特色，与发达国家和发展中国家有所不同。统计数据显示，中国政府收入占 GDP 的比例低于世界平均值。西方某些集团或者由于无知或者由于偏见往往对中国城市政治的实情予以扭曲。中国的城市积累了非常丰富的政治协商经验，许多决策都是通过反复协商形成的。比如，2019 年 6 月，青岛市政协组织部分政协委员，围绕青岛市如何“做好双拥工作，共创模范城市”进行专题考察。青岛市政协负责人、市政府负责人、当地驻军首长一起参与。大家考察该市退役军人事务局，召开相关方面出席座谈会，广泛征求意见。强调牢固树立爱军就是爱国、拥军就是政治的理念，要求各方办实事、解难题，大力支持驻军的战斗力建设，帮助部队解决实际问题。建立定向招聘、职业培训、自主创业扶持机制和社会化就业助推机制，促进随军随调家属安置就业，积极协调各方推动军地基础设施建设和国防教育等方面实现融合发展。这对于军队是安心，对于军人和复（员）转（业）军人是暖心，对于社会是同理心。

第四是城市文化。中国地大物博，大（超过百万人口城市）中（50 万至百万人口城市）小（50 万人口以下城市）城市齐头并进，东（部）中（部）西（部）城市异彩纷呈，南（方）北（方）城市各有千秋。我们随便走进某一座城市，往往都有千年以上的历史传承与不绝如缕的文化血脉，让其他国家的城市叹为观止，心悦诚服。联合国教科文组织和世界遗产委员会近年来加强对世界文化遗产的确认与保护，这里试举经其确认拥有文化遗产的几座城市。北京是元明清三代帝都，周口店北京猿人遗址、故宫、长城、颐和园、天坛、明十三陵，哪位中国人不知？哪位外国人不想知？洛阳的龙门石窟、大运河、白马寺，历千年风雨而依然精彩。苏州的古典园林独步天下，拙政园、留园、狮子林、网师园、沧浪亭、退思园等闻名遐迩。杭州西湖美不胜收，吴越的秀气与灵气随波荡漾，中外游人赞不绝口。西安的秦始皇陵及兵马俑坑、汉代未央宫遗址、唐大明宫遗址、大雁塔诉说着先秦汉唐的雄浑与壮阔。郑州的历史建筑群居“天地之中”，少林寺、东汉三阙、中岳庙、嵩岳寺塔、嵩阳书院、观星台让郑州再放光辉。

第五是城市环境。世界各国工业化现代化的过程都难以避开一个工业污染与治理的悖论，这是 20 世纪第二次世界大战结束以来让各国政府和学者头疼的大问题。究竟我们人类应该要一个什么样的工业化现代化？应该说，中国城市化过程中的环境问题解决得比较妥当。就一时来说，大家往往批评较多，但就相对长的过程来看，我们的城市化较早地警惕环境污染，加大治理与惩处，特别是党的十八大以来，各种各样的蓝天、碧水、净土保卫战打响，城市居民对干净空气、洁净饮水和食物安全的愿望得到积极的回应。

第六是城市居民。人是一切的尺度，城市居民既是城市的主人，又是城市的服务对象。前 30 年是打基础的城市化，后 40 年是大发展的城市化，中国由一个农民为主体的国家转变为城市人口为主体的国家，人的现代化素养得到了逐步的提升。知恩、知责、知止的社会公德、职业道德和家庭美德步步推进，人爱人、人助人、人成全人、人宽恕人正在取代人斗人、人害人、人提防人、人算计人。古话讲，“十年树木，百年树人”，所谓树人就是树一代新风，让我们所有当代人和我们的后代得到文明的滋养，同时又让每一个人的善心滋养文明。

就一般意义而言，中国城市化具有世界各国的普遍共性，也有自己的个性。如中国城市

（其实也包括发达地区的农村）居民普遍地享用着电气化、信息化和国际化。早在2010年中国城市的电视、空调、移动电话、洗衣机、电冰箱、热水器、电脑已经普及，家用汽车拥有率约为13%。城市家庭的恩格尔系数仅为三分之一。中国人2018年的平均预期寿命为76岁，仅仅比美国低两岁（美国78岁）。尤其让我们兴奋的是，中国的城市观念开放多元，文明城市、宜居城市、卫星城市、创新城市、绿色城市、生态城市、低碳城市、花园城市、山水城市、世界城市、国际城市、数字城市、智慧城市、城市群、城市带、城市圈等。

中国共产党第十九次全国代表大会提出新的“两步走”战略和“两个一百年”的奋斗目标，中国原定的基本实现现代化的目标提前15年，到2035年就要基本实现社会主义现代化；再奋斗15年，到新中国成立一百周年的时候，把我国建成富强民主文明和谐美丽的社会主义现代化强国。城市化是未来30年的重要主题，未来30年，我们要保证城市化率每年增长一个百分点。

今天是明天的起点。正如前述，中国的城市化比发达国家晚了一百年。清朝末年的城市化是小打小闹，中华民国时期的城市化是局部起步，新中国的城市化则以全面、大规模、高速度令世界瞠目。目前我们的城市化相当于世界初等发达水平，处于发展中国家前列。一代人跑好自己的那一棒，新中国七十年的城市化使中国的现代化建设满纸云霞。

如果从学理层面总结中国城市化的特点，可以概括为如下几点：

一是因为中国的特殊，世界上没有任何一个国家能够与她相比，国际经验不足以解决中国的问题，所以中国的城市化很难简单地学习别国，必须走自己的路。有人也许会说，世界上没有两片相同的树叶，似乎这样讲是废话。曾经有人总结美国的特点，提出“美国例外论”，美国的地理环境、历史传承、文化汇聚等，使她与欧洲母国大相径庭。此处不说中国例外，但中国确实与众不同。作为某一个城市，可以借鉴某一个发达国家的某个城市，但是总体上，中国的城市化只能独辟蹊径。

二是中国城市化毕竟是一种后发追赶型，且是一种工业化优先的城市化。中央和各级地方政府的作用格外重要与明显。这种情况，可以说是一柄双刃剑。可能事半功倍，也可能灾祸连连。怎样处理好“有效的市场”与“有为的政府”之间的关系，确实积累了大量的正反两方面的经验教训。

三是中国城市化面临双重压力，许多时候决策者面对的都是两难选择。城市化需要大量的基础设施建设，可是土地越来越珍贵；需要大量的能源供给，可是能源越来越枯竭；需要大量的人口转移，可是户籍管理却往往造成“农民进城还是农民”；需要环境生态改善与美化，可是这大大提高了城市化的成本。

就中国的城市化前景看，每一位客观冷静的分析者都应该充满信心。中国人身处其中，有时往往感受到的只是某些城市化的不便或不妥。根据联合国发布的《世界城市化展望2011》和相关估算，2050年中国城市总数可能达到1 632个，其中大城市338个，中等城市358个，小城市936个；大城市人口比例占到所有城市人口的60%，中等城市人口比例占到所有城市人口的19%，小城市人口比例占到所有城市人口的21%。

理想丰满，现实途径同样充实。我们未来30年的城市化，要走质量与规模并重、经济与环境双赢、城市化与城市现代化协调的新路，真正实现城市化模式的六个转变：从简单城市化向城市化与城市现代化协同转变，从城市优先向城市现代化与农村现代化协同转变，从城区优先向城区现代化与郊区现代化协调发展转变，从工业化优先向新型工业化与新型城市化协调发展转变，从工业和经济优先向工业与服务业协调发展、经济与环境双赢转变，从重视地面基础设施向地面基础设施与地下基础设施并重转变。

一座现代化的城市，一般都会具有一些基本特点，例如建筑优质美观，服务公平高效，生活舒适便捷，环境世界一流，收入全球或区域最高，福利全球或区域最佳，等等。而且这些特点也是与时俱进、不断被自己或其他城市刷新的。

三、中国城市化之鉴

如此大的国家，如此大规模的城市化，人类历史上亘古未有，这何尝不是百年未有之大变局！一座座工厂开工造物，一幢幢高楼拔地凌空，一所所学校书声琅琅，一条条高速路车流如织，一道道大桥天堑通途，一个个公园花香鸟语……与新中国同龄的当代人，都会感受到这种巨大变迁所包含的历史底蕴：中国的城市化生逢其时、势之必至，城市化的中国理所当然、水到渠成！

面对2008年美国金融危机引发的全球经济疲弱，十年过去仍然难见真正的起色。令人不解的是美国不但不反思自己的失误给本国和世界造成的损失，反而嫁祸他国，放弃大国应当承担的国际责任，生生地搞出一起起国际闹剧。如今的国际经济、国际政治、国际文化，相互之间紧密相连，修墙断路的孤立主义行不通，蛮横固执的“浑不吝”徒增笑料。

中国显示出沉着淡定的强大素养，一方面作为新兴大国，勇于担当，倡议“一带一路”，联合沿线国家和参与此倡议的国家抱团取暖，欢迎大家搭乘中国发展的顺风车；另一方面大力振兴国内需求，习近平同志在2018年中央经济工作会议上提出要促进形成强大国内市场。中国拥有1.1亿户市场主体，其中企业3 470多万户，14亿消费人口（无论是市场主体、企业还是消费者都主要集中在城市），这就说明中国庞大的生产资料消费市场和生活资料消费市场是一片广阔的“蓝海”。

城市化最重要的是规划。城市领导者必须有一张蓝图绘到底、功成不必在我的气魄与胸襟。城市规划不是简单地盖房子、修街道，更不是制作不伦不类的假古伪洋，而是必须从全球产业链创新链为自己定位，这就需要组织各方面专家学者，知本来，学外来，创未来。比如，现在就要特别重视新产业、新业态、新商业模式这“三新”对于城市化的作用。2015—2017年统计数据表明，“三新”对经济发展新动能指数的年均增幅达到28%，“三新”经济增加值占GDP的比重已经达到了15.7%。

“中国创造”与“中国制造”并不矛盾，而是相辅相成、互为表里。传统产业特别是传统制造业改造升级潜力天量。现在规模以上工业企业总资产超过110万亿元，按照正常的设备更新改造升级，本身就是巨大的需求，再叠加不断快速发展的科技包括互联网等影响，设备更新改造升级的速度还会进一步加快。这对于城市居民就业或再就业，对于年轻人特别是每年毕业的800万大学生创业创新，提供了广阔的平台。就业稳才能城市安，能够比较容易的就业与再就业才表明一座城市的包容与博大。

城市化必然带来居民对于自身生活品质的更高要求。如各个大城市日益突出的“（养）老（托）小”问题，既表明了居民的消费能力，又暴露出我们的供给短板。“老吾老以及人之老，幼吾幼以及人之幼”是中国文化早熟的政治智慧，“养老”“托幼”是下一步大力推动的服务性产业。至于家用电器、汽车乃至住房的更新，也应列入各级政府与各类企业的总体考虑。2018年中央经济工作会议确定了“巩固、增强、提升、畅通”的八字方针，要求深入推进供给侧结构性改革，不断提供更多高品质高质量的产品与高品质高质量的服务，这同样要作为我们城市化的题中之意。

大规模的城市化难免会出现始料不及的弊端。比如某些城市由于战略思维弱与文化修养差，对于历史文化缺乏敬畏之心，破坏历史文化的现象屡有发生。2014年2月25日，习近平同志视察北京市时有一番语重心长的讲话。习近平同志说：“历史文化是城市的灵魂，要像爱惜自己的生命一样保护好城市历史文化遗产。北京是世界著名古都，丰富的历史文化遗产是一张金名片，传承保护好这份宝贵的历史文化遗产是首都的职责，要本着对历史负责、对人民负责的精神，传承历史文脉，处理好城市改造开发和历史文化遗产保护利用的关系，切实做到在保护中发展、在发展中保护。搞历史博物展览，为的是见证历史、以史鉴今、启迪后人。要在展览的同时高度重视修史修志，让文物说话、把历史智慧告诉人们，激发我们的民族自豪感和自信心，坚定全体人民振兴中华、实现中国梦的信心和决心。”这是对全党全国的要求。城市建设要保护好“灵魂”，一个人没有“灵魂”即行尸走肉，一座城市没有“灵魂”则只剩钢筋水泥。

七十年往矣，未来已来。当下一个七十年结束的时候，那就是2089年了。回望2089年的二百年前，中国诞生了一批革命先驱和科学先驱。他们成为五四运动的领导者，由他们和他们培育的一代代圣贤君子推动的制度革命与科技革命，使中国已经和正在天地翻覆，农业中国已经成为工业中国、信息中国、知识中国，农村中国同样成为城市中国，我们可以告慰列祖列宗了。

（作者：刘洪海，高级编辑，中国科学报社原社长兼总编辑、国家纳米科学中心原党委书记）

中国主要城市道路网密度监测与分析

一、引言

（一）背景

2016 年 2 月，中共中央、国务院发布《中共中央国务院关于进一步加强城市规划建设管理工作的若干意见》（中发〔2016〕6 号）（以下简称《意见》），对今后城市的发展提出了具体的要求，其中提出明确而具体的时间目标和工作要求共 9 项，城市交通占 2 项。文件第十六条提出了对城市道路网密度的定量要求。

《意见》中指出：优化街区路网结构。加强街区的规划和建设，分梯级明确新建街区面积，推动发展开放便捷、尺度适宜、配套完善、邻里和谐的生活街区。新建住宅要推广街区制，原则上不再建设封闭住宅小区。已建成的住宅小区和单位大院要逐步打开，实现内部道路公共化，解决交通路网布局问题，促进土地节约利用。树立“窄马路、密路网”的城市道路布局理念，建设快速路、主次干路和支路级配合理的道路网系统。

《意见》中强调指出：打通各类“断头路”，形成完整路网，提高道路通达性。科学、规范设置道路交通安全设施和交通管理设施，提高道路安全性。到 2020 年，城市建成区平均路网密度提高到 8 公里/平方公里，道路面积率达到 15%。积极采用单行道路方式组织交通。加强自行车道和步行道系统建设，倡导绿色出行。合理配置停车设施，鼓励社会参与，放宽市场准入，逐步缓解停车难问题。

（二）密度要求解读

以平均街区宽度作为指标，对《意见》中的路网密度要求进行直观解释（图 1）：

$4km/km^2$ 的道路网密度，折算为平均街区的尺度相当于街区宽度为 500m；

$6km/km^2$ 的道路网密度，折算为平均街区的尺度相当于街区宽度为 330m；

$8km/km^2$ 的道路网密度，折算为平均街区的尺度相当于街区宽度为 250m。

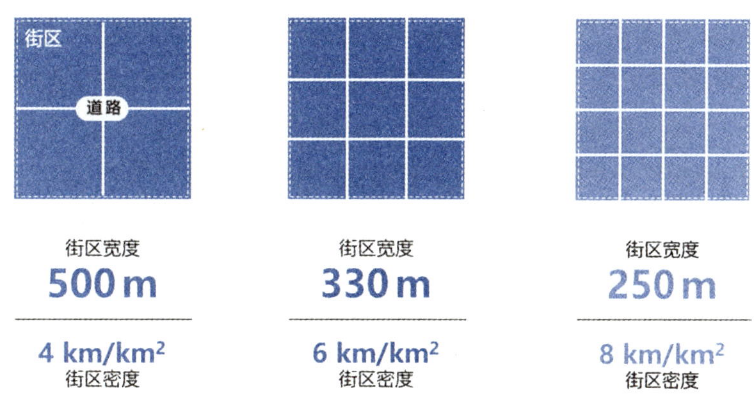

图 1　不同路网密度要求的街区宽度示意

（三）城市选取

本报告共选取 36 个全国重点城市作为研究对象。其中直辖市 4 个（北京、上海、天津、重庆）、计划单列市 5 个（大连、青岛、宁波、厦门、深圳）、省会城市 27 个（广州、成都等）。

（四）名词解释及计算方法

路网密度：一定范围内的道路总里程与该范围面积的比值。为了保证各城市路网密度的可比性、统计口径的一致性，本报告明确了城市路网密度的计算方法。本报告以中心城区建成区为指标计算范围，以中心城区建成区内道路总里程与面积的比值作为城市路网密度。

中心城区建成区：中心城区内的建设用地范围。中心城区范围为全国 36 个重点城市现行城市总体规划中明确提出的中心城区范围（北京、上海等城市涉及新版总规编制，在本报告中以上版城市总规为参考标准）；建设用地为根据地表覆被的遥感影像（地理国情普查 2015 年数据）解译识别范围；本次统计的中心城区建成区为中心城区和建设用地重叠的区域。

除了关注城市整体的路网密度外，本报告也对城市下辖的各行政区路网密度进行了计算和比较。以行政区纳入城市建成区的部分作为指标计算范围，以该范围内的道路总里程与该范围面积比值作为行政区的路网密度。对于仅有较小的局部范围被纳入建成区内的行政区而言，本报告所计算的路网密度仅使用该行政区名称表征路网密度的空间分布特征，而不用以表征该行政区的整体路网密度情况。

二、总体情况

（一）中国主要城市路网总体密度

1. 城市路网总体密度与国家目标要求仍有较大差距

本报告选取的 36 个全国主要城市中，路网总体平均密度为 5.89km/km^2，总体平均密度与国家目标要求之间仍有较大的差距（表1）。密度处于较高水平的城市有深圳、厦门、成都、上海、广州5座城市，路网总体密度达到7.0km/km^{2}以上，占全部研究城市的13.9%。其中深圳、厦门、成都三市达到国家提出的8km/km^{2}的目标要求。路网总体密度水平低于4.5km/km^{2}的城市有4个，占全部研究城市的11.1%，分别为乌鲁木齐、拉萨、兰州、呼和浩特。路网密度介于5.5~7.0km/km^{2}的城市有16个，占全部研究城市的44.4%。在北京、上海、广州、深圳四个一线城市中，路网密度水平依次为深圳（9.50 km/km^2）>上海（7.10 km/km^2）>广州（7.02 km/km^2）>北京（5.59 km/km^2）。

表1 中国主要城市路网密度一览表

排名	城市	密度	排名	城市	密度
1	深圳	9.50	19	武汉	5.77
2	厦门	8.45	20	北京	5.59
3	成都	8.02	21	南京	5.55
4	上海	7.10	22	西安	5.49
5	广州	7.02	23	海口	5.41
6	杭州	6.90	24	青岛	5.35
7	福州	6.81	25	长春	5.33
8	昆明	6.72	26	太原	5.17
9	宁波	6.67	27	石家庄	5.15
10	合肥	6.61	28	西宁	5.04
11	南宁	6.57	29	哈尔滨	4.94
12	重庆	6.49	30	银川	4.76
13	长沙	6.27	31	沈阳	4.74
14	郑州	6.22	32	济南	4.68
15	南昌	6.12	33	呼和浩特	4.24
16	贵阳	6.07	34	兰州	4.04
17	天津	6.04	35	拉萨	3.78
18	大连	6.03	36	乌鲁木齐	3.41

2. 城市路网密度总体呈现“南方城市高于北方城市”统计规律

从城市区位角度来看，以秦岭—淮河地理分界线为城市分类标准统计，南方城市路网密度普遍高于北方城市。北方城市路网密度总体平均值为5.07km/km^2，北方城市中路网密度水平较高的为郑州和天津，路网密度分别为6.22km/km^{2}和6.04km/km^2，路网密度水平较低的为乌鲁木齐和兰州，路网密度分别为3.41km/km^2、4.04km/km^2。南方城市路网密度总体平均值为6.62km/km^2，南方城市路网密度水平较高城市为深圳、厦门、成都，分别为9.50km/km^2、8.45km/km^2、8.02km/km^2，路网密度水平较低的城市为海口，路网密度为5.41km/km^2。

（二）主要城市行政区路网密度

本报告在统计分析城市整体路网密度的基础上进一步统计了组成各城市主要行政区的路网密度，共涉及214个行政区（县）。

全国行政区路网密度差异性较大，与《意见》目标标准相差较远。介于5~6km/km^{2}的行政区最多，所有涉及行政区的路网密度平均值仅为6.24km/km^2，可见从行政区层面分析，我国城市路网密度距离8km/km^{2}理想目标还有较大差距。

214个行政区中路网密度达标的仅有34个，占比仅15.8%，这些行政区普遍分布于西南、华南、华东地区。路网密度达标的行政区主要为城市中心城区的老城区，如上海黄浦区、深圳福田区、杭州上城区、天津和平区、广州越秀区等，老城区由于建设历史久远，人口聚集度较高，在老城区的历史成型时期就已形成了“窄而密”的路网肌理，较少受到近年来大地块开发模式的影响，因而整体路网密度处于较高水平。其中路网密度超过10km/km^{2}的行政区共7个，占比3%，路网密度最高的行政区是上海黄浦区（14.06km/km^2）。主要城市行政区路网密度指标见表2。

表2　主要城市行政区路网密度指标（前44名）

排名	区（县）	城市	路网密度	排名	区（县）	城市	路网密度
1	黄浦区	上海	14.06	23	集美区	厦门	8.41
2	福田区	深圳	11.67	24	静安区	上海	8.39
3	上城区	杭州	10.88	25	云岩区	贵阳	8.39
4	和平区	天津	10.85	26	青羊区	成都	8.33
5	虹口区	上海	10.52	27	南山区	深圳	8.27
6	罗湖区	深圳	10.52	28	下城区	杭州	8.22
7	越秀区	广州	10.07	29	荔湾区	广州	8.21
8	渝中区	重庆	9.52	30	江汉区	武汉	8.19
9	思明区	厦门	9.47	31	中山区	大连	8.07
10	市南区	青岛	9.42	32	西湖区	南昌	8.07
11	东湖区	南昌	9.30	33	台江区	福州	8.06
12	锦江区	成都	9.10	34	西城区	北京	8.06
13	海曙区	宁波	9.06	35	雨花台区	南京	7.96
14	长宁区	上海	9.04	36	沈河区	沈阳	7.92
15	同安区	厦门	8.93	37	建邺区	南京	7.90
16	良庆区	南宁	8.68	38	江东区	宁波	7.65
17	西岗区	大连	8.61	39	碑林区	西安	7.59
18	翔安区	厦门	8.55	40	沙河口区	大连	7.59
19	成华区	成都	8.54	41	金牛区	成都	7.54
20	湖里区	厦门	8.50	42	鄞州区	宁波	7.51
21	和平区	沈阳	8.48	43	海珠区	广州	7.43
22	武侯区	成都	8.46	44	江北区	重庆	7.43

本报告从行政区层面分析了各城市路网密度的匀质性，也即城市多个行政区间路网密度的差异性。本报告采用各行政区的路网密度标准差作为衡量行政区间路网密度的差异性的指标，指标越高则各行政区间路网密度差异越大、城市路网密度匀质性越差，反之则反。各城市所属行政区的路网密度和差异性指标见汇总图（图2）。

（三）城市形态与路网密度关系分析

1. 组团型城市 > 团块型城市 > 带型城市

按照城市建成区形态分类，可将全国主要城市分为团块形态、组团形态和带状形态三类。在全国36个主要城市中，团块形态城市共计15个，例如北京、石家庄、西安等；组团形态城市共计17个，例如重庆、深圳、武汉等；带状形态城市共计4个，例如兰州、济南等。

根据全国主要城市道路网密度计算结果，团块型城市平均路网密度为5.79km/km^2，组团型城市平均路网密度为6.33km/km^2，带型城市平均路网密度为4.38km/km^2。从平均路网密度指标来看，城市形态对路网密度有影响作用，呈现组团形态 > 团块形态 > 带状形态的现象规律，组团型城市平均路网密度相对较高，带型城市路网密度普遍较低。

2. 组团城市：地形分隔，组团内部建设集中

由于山地河流等自然屏障的分隔作用，城市空间难以平面化的自由拓展。一般情况下，城市组团内部空间受到地形制约，建设用地十分有限，在人口聚集度较高的情况下，组团内用地布局较为紧凑，形成高密度的集中建设开发，路网密度相对较高。

3. 团块城市：连片开发，路网密度内高外低

平坦的地形有利于城市空间的扩展和连片开发，由于受到地形制约较少，在城市建设发展过程中，团块型城市中普遍老城中心区密度高，外围新城区及开发区密度低的圈层结构，平均路网密度相对较低。

4. 带型城市：轴向发展，道路级配不尽合理

带型城市受到地形制约形成沿轴向发展的城市布局，狭长的带状城市空间对轴向方向骨干道路设施需求较大，而集散性道路以及非轴向方向道路设施建设相对不足，道路级配比例不合理，导致路网密度普遍偏低。

（四）城市规模与路网密度关系分析

1. 城市规模划分“新标准”

2014年11月，国务院印发《关于调整城市规模划分标准的通知》，对原有城市规模划分标准进行了调整，明确了新的城市规模划分标准。标准以城区常住人口为统计口径，将城市划分为五类七档。

其中，城区是指在市辖区和不设区的市，区、市政府驻地的实际建设连接到的居民委员会所辖区域和其他区域。常住人口包括：居住在本乡镇街道，且户口在本乡镇街道或户口待定的人；居住在本乡镇街道，且离开户口登记地所在的乡镇街道半年以上的人；户口在本乡

排名	城市	总密度	行政区路网密度标准差	主要行政区路网密度									
1	深圳	9.50	1.41	福田区 11.67	罗湖区 10.44	南山区 8.27							
2	厦门	8.45	0.86	思明区 9.47	同安区 8.93	翔安区 8.55	湖里区 8.50	集美区 8.41	海沧区 6.68				
3	成都	8.02	0.50	锦江区 9.10	成华区 8.54	武侯区 8.46	青羊区 8.34	金牛区 7.54					
4	上海	7.10	2.48	黄浦区 14.06	虹口区 10.52	长宁区 9.04	静安区 8.39	徐汇区 7.00	普陀区 6.99	闵行区 6.97	浦东新区 6.76	杨浦区 6.32	宝山区 4.84
5	广州	7.02	1.38	越秀区 10.07	荔湾区 8.21	海珠区 7.43	白云区 6.97	天河区 6.96	黄埔区 5.55				
6	杭州	6.90	1.52	上城区 10.88	下城区 8.22	江干区 7.30	滨江区 7.12	西湖区 6.87	拱墅区 6.28	余杭区 6.26	萧山区 5.73		
7	福州	6.81	0.77	台江区 8.06	连江县 7.47	仓山区 7.41	鼓楼区 7.40	晋安区 7.12	马尾区 6.57	闽侯县 5.47			
8	昆明	6.72	0.18	西山区 6.98	呈贡区 6.79	官渡区 6.70	五华区 6.60	盘龙区 6.45					
9	宁波	6.67	1.27	海曙区 9.06	江东区 7.65	鄞州区 7.51	江北区 7.28	北仑区 5.48	镇海区 5.47				
10	合肥	6.61	0.35	包河区 7.02	蜀山区 6.52	瑶海区 6.27	庐阳区 6.08						
11	南宁	6.57	1.18	良庆区 8.68	青秀区 7.39	邕宁区 7.00	江南区 6.01	西乡塘区 5.44	兴宁区 5.38				
12	重庆	6.49	1.17	渝中区 9.52	江北区 7.43	南岸区 6.79	渝北区 6.56	九龙坡区 6.30	北碚区 5.82	沙坪坝区 5.78	大渡口区 5.68	巴南区 5.66	
13	长沙	6.27	0.56	开福区 7.23	芙蓉区 6.64	岳麓区 6.60	雨花区 6.37	望城区 5.78	天心区 5.57				
14	郑州	6.22	0.82	二七区 7.42	金水区 6.70	管城区 6.17	惠济区 6.09	中原区 4.93					
15	南昌	6.12	1.56	东湖区 9.30	西湖区 8.07	新建区 7.41	青山湖区 5.47	青云谱区 5.20					
16	贵阳	6.07	1.41	云岩区 8.39	乌当区 7.04	南明区 6.86	花溪区 5.13	白云区 4.77	观山湖区 4.48				
17	天津	6.04	1.71	和平区 10.85	河东区 7.04	红桥区 6.89	河北区 6.85	河西区 6.54	南开区 6.40	西青区 5.25	东丽区 5.04	津南区 4.88	北辰区 4.64
18	大连	6.03	1.36	西岗区 8.61	中山区 8.07	沙河口区 7.59	金州区 5.57	甘井子区 5.49	旅顺口区 5.28				
19	武汉	5.77	1.08	江汉区 8.19	汉阳区 6.84	武昌区 6.72	东西湖区 6.44	江岸区 6.17	硚口区 5.74	蔡甸区 5.72	江夏区 4.68	洪山区 4.42	
20	北京	5.59	1.26	东城区 7.31	西城区 8.06	海淀区 5.54	朝阳区 5.39	丰台区 5.33	石景山区 4.42				
21	南京	5.55	1.32	雨花台区 7.96	建邺区 7.90	秦淮区 7.18	鼓楼区 6.84	浦口区 5.42	六合区 5.23	玄武区 5.01	江宁区 4.97	栖霞区 4.23	
22	西安	5.49	0.90	碑林区 7.59	莲湖区 6.14	灞桥区 6.05	新城区 5.84	雁塔区 5.27	未央区 5.01	长安区 4.64			
23	海口	5.41	0.66	龙华区 6.55	琼山区 5.79	秀英区 5.02	美兰区 4.92						
24	青岛	5.35	1.78	市南区 9.42	市北区 6.97	城阳区 5.41	崂山区 5.28	李沧区 5.14	黄岛区 3.80				
25	长春	5.33	0.39	宽城区 6.06	朝阳区 5.55	二道区 5.48	南关区 5.14	绿园区 4.90					
26	太原	5.17	0.61	迎泽区 6.35	小店区 5.61	杏花岭区 5.26	晋源区 5.16	万柏林区 4.75	尖草坪区 4.45				
27	石家庄	5.15	0.38	新华区 5.62	桥西区 5.46	裕华区 5.02	长安区 4.64						
28	西宁	5.04	0.41	城西区 5.92	城中区 5.38	城东区 5.34	城北区 4.77						
29	哈尔滨	4.94	0.84	道里区 6.04	南岗区 5.74	松北区 4.89	香坊区 4.71	道外区 4.54	呼兰区 3.88	阿城区 3.79	平房区 3.59		
30	银川	4.76	0.67	兴庆区 5.45	金凤区 5.05	西夏区 3.87							
31	沈阳	4.74	1.84	和平区 8.48	沈河区 7.92	铁西区 6.86	浑南区 4.78	皇姑区 4.19	苏家屯区 4.18	于洪区 3.74	沈北新区 3.68		
32	济南	4.68	0.68	槐荫区 5.74	历下区 5.25	天桥区 4.95	市中区 4.45	长清区 4.04	历城区 3.80				
33	呼和浩特	4.24	0.67	赛罕区 4.77	新城区 4.68	回民区 4.27	玉泉区 3.09						
34	兰州	4.04	0.74	城关区 4.71	安宁区 4.10	七里河区 4.09	西固区 2.69						
35	拉萨	3.78	0.63	堆龙德庆[4.75	城关区 3.48								
36	乌鲁木齐	3.41	0.60	新市区 4.40	沙依巴克[4.01	头屯河区 3.37	水磨沟区 3.20	天山区 2.95	米东区 2.65				

图 2　主要城市路网密度与差异性汇总图

镇街道，且外出不满半年或在境外工作学习的人。

> 划分标准：城区常住人口50万以下的城市为小城市，其中20万以上50万以下的城市为Ⅰ型小城市，20万以下的城市为Ⅱ型小城市；城区常住人口50万以上100万以下的城市为中等城市；城区常住人口100万以上500万以下的城市为大城市，其中300万以上500万以下的城市为Ⅰ型大城市，100万以上300万以下的城市为Ⅱ型大城市；城区常住人口500万以上1 000万以下的城市为特大城市；城区常住人口1 000万以上的城市为超大城市。

2. 城市规模越大，路网密度越高

根据全国主要城市的路网密度结果来看，超大型城市平均路网密度为7.30km/km^2，特大型城市平均路网密度为6.06km/km^2，Ⅰ型和Ⅱ型大城市分别为5.76km/km^{2}和5.39km/km^2（图3）。

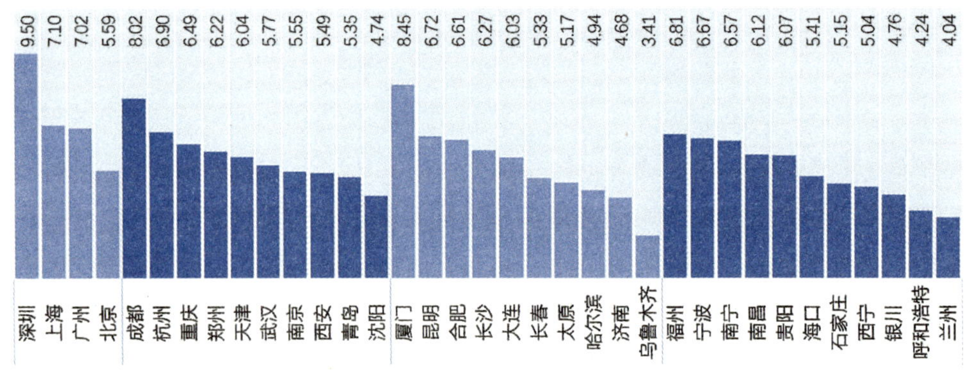

图3　城市规模与路网密度关系

依据城市规模分类，城市道路网密度呈现出“城市规模越大，路网密度水平越高”的统计规律。一方面，由于城市规模越大，建成区人口聚集度相对越高，城市市政基础设施的建设相对完善，城市规模效应促进了城市经济的发展，进一步为城市道路设施建设提供保障；另一方面，城市人口集聚程度越高，交通基础设施的利用率相对越高，道路交通环境也倾向于越拥堵，城市则增加建设相应的道路设施以缓解交通拥堵，道路设施建设水平也相对较高。

三、主要城市路网密度详情

本报告对全国4个直辖市、5个计划单列市、27个省会城市等共计36个城市的路网密度指标进行了系统性分析和梳理，实现了城市级、行政区级、网格级路网密度指标的动态监测。下面主要介绍路网密度指标前三位城市、直辖市及计划单列市等部分城市的路网密度详情。

（一）深圳市

深圳市是我国计划单列市之一，位于珠江三角洲城市群，其中心城区建成区城市形态为组团型。根据《深圳市城市总体规划（2009—2020年）》中心城区的明确定义，2018年深圳中心城区建成区面积为181平方公里，建成区道路里程为1 718.7公里。

根据深圳市城市总体规划定义，中心城区仅包括福田区、罗湖区、南山区三个行政区。深圳中心城区建成区总体路网密度为9.50km/km^2，在36个城市中排名第1位。在建成区各行政区中，3个行政区的路网密度全部已达标，其中福田区（11.67km/km^2）和罗湖区（10.44km/km^2）的路网密度超过了10km/km^2。（表3）

表3　深圳主要行政区路网密度指标

行政区	路网密度
福田区	11.67
罗湖区	10.44
南山区	8.27

自深圳特区建立以来，深圳经历了从无到有、日新月异的发展过程，这种平地而起的发展机遇在科学规划和有序建设的加持下确保了深圳城市道路网结构的合理性。深圳市起步于罗湖区和福田区，此后向西延展至南山区形成初期的带状形态。而后，围绕西、中、东三条放射发展轴梯度向北推进，进一步形成组团结构。虽然30余年来深圳保持高速发展，但由于其遵循有序扩展的发展理念，宏观上保证了骨干路网结构的合理性，微观上维护了道路等级级配的合理性和较高的路网密度。未来，在进一步采用“窄马路、密路网”的发展理念后，中心城区外围组团路网密度还有很大提升空间。

（二）厦门市

厦门市是我国计划单列市之一，位于海峡西岸城市群，其中心城区建成区城市形态为组团型。根据《厦门市城市总体规划（2011—2020年）》中心城区的定义，2018年厦门中心城区建成区面积为244.5平方公里，建成区道路里程为2065.1公里。

厦门中心城区建成区路网密度为8.45km/km^2，在36个城市中排名第2，是36个城市中全市建成区路网密度达标（8km/km^2）的城市之一。在建成区的各行政区中，共有5个行政区的路网密度已达标，位于厦门本岛、发展最早的思明区（9.47km/km^2）路网密度最高，以临港产业、航运物流为主导产业的海沧区路网密度（6.68km/km^2）相对较低。（表4）

自开埠以来，厦门由思明区核心区逐渐向外扩张，在跨过鹰厦铁路后逐渐覆盖厦门本岛，由于岛内地理空间有限，2003年后厦门开始向岛外扩展，由海岛城市转变为海湾城市。厦门市的城市路网特征与其发展历程密不可分，在岛屿城市阶段充分利用了岛内的有限空间，形成了“一环四横七纵”的岛内骨干道路结构和高密度的方格路网；随着城市发展向岛外扩张，厦门进一步形成了由高等级道路构成环形放射状骨架路网，实现了海湾、海岛各组团间的联络，有效支撑了城市转型和发展。

表 4 厦门主要行政区路网密度指标

行政区	路网密度
思明区	9.47
同安区	8.93
翔安区	8.55
湖里区	8.50
集美区	8.41
海沧区	6.68

（三）成都市

成都市是我国四川省省会，位于成渝城市群，是西南地区核心城市，其中心城区建成区城市形态为团块型。根据《成都市城市总体规划（2011—2020 年）》中心城区的定义，2018 年成都中心城区建成区面积为 326.1 平方公里，建成区道路里程为 2614 公里。

成都中心城区建成区路网密度为 8.02km/km^2，在 36 个城市中排名第 3 位，总体建成区路网密度已经达标。在纳入建成区的各行政区中，共有 4 个行政区的路网密度已达标，锦江区（9.10km/km^2）路网密度最高，金牛区路网密度（7.54km/km^2）相对最低。（表 5）

表 5 成都主要行政区路网密度指标

行政区	路网密度
锦江区	9.10
武侯区	8.46
成华区	8.54
青羊区	8.34
金牛区	7.54

成都市路网呈典型的环形放射结构，现已基本形成了五条环线和高达二十余条的射线高快速路网，高快速路网规模大、密度高。成都的路网形态体现了其扩张发展模式，由新中国成立初期的一环内扩张至 80 年代的二环内，在 21 世纪初扩张至三环内，再逐步扩张至今天的四环乃至部分五环圈层，扩展方向也由 80 年代的东、北方向转变为全方向扩展。虽然成都市核心区域街区尺度较小，路网密度较高，但仍难以承载其不断扩张的城市形态带来的向心交通压力。随着“天府新区”的建设推进，成都将由单核城市转变为多核城市，以期缓解老城压力，但其本质上是再一次的城市扩张。

（四）北京市

北京市是我国首都，位于京津冀城市群，其中心城区建成区城市形态为团块状。根据《北京市城市总体规划（2004—2020年）》中心城区的明确定义，2018年北京中心城区建成区面积为912.3平方公里，建成区道路里程为5 112公里。

北京市中心城区建成区路网密度为5.59km/km²，整体偏低，在36个城市中排名第20。在中心城区建成区的各行政区中，位于北京市核心位置的西城区（8.06km/km²）、东城区（7.31km/km²）因次支路较多因而路网密度较高，基本达标，其他区路网密度相对较低，朝阳区、丰台区、海淀区路网密度均处于5～6km/km²，石景山区路网密度最低，仅为4.42km/km²。（表6）

表6　北京主要行政区路网密度指标

行政区	路网密度
西城区	8.06
东城区	7.31
朝阳区	5.39
海淀区	5.54
丰台区	5.34
石景山区	4.42

北京市近年来在城市交通建设方面投入巨大，如“十二五”期间交通领域固定资产投资达3300亿元。近年来北京在城市道路建设方面更倾向于骨干道路的建设，形成了典型的环形放射式结构，而低等级道路建设较为迟缓，使得北京市路网级配不尽合理。目前北京市快、主、次、支路级配结构为1:2.5:1.7:11.5，致使路网密度整体较低。另外，由于北京市街区尺度与《意见》中250米的理想街区尺度差距较大，进一步造成了路网密度较低的现象。

（五）上海市

上海市是我国直辖市之一，位于长江三角洲城市群，其中心城区建成区城市形态为团块状。根据《上海市城市总体规划（2004—2020年）》中心城区的明确定义，2018年上海中心城区建成区面积为564.9平方公里，建成区道路里程为4012公里。

上海总体规划定义中心城区范围为外环线以内区域，其中心城区建成区路网密度为7.10km/km²，在36个城市中排名第4，城市总体路网密度较高。在中心城区建成区的各行政区中，黄埔区、虹口区、长宁区、静安区4个行政区的路网密度已达标，且黄浦区（14.06km/km²）、虹口区（10.52km/km²）的路网密度超过了10km/km²，而各个行政区中，宝山区（4.84km/km²）路网密度相对最低。（表7）

表7　上海主要行政区路网密度指标

行政区	路网密度
黄浦区	14.06
虹口区	10.52
长宁区	9.04
静安区	8.39
徐汇区	7.00
浦东新区	6.76
普陀区	6.99
杨浦区	6.32
闵行区	6.97
宝山区	4.84

上海早在1927年即成为“上海市特别市”，最早发展建设的老城区为外滩以西、以北区域，也即今黄浦区、虹口区、静安区，由于发展较早、建设较为完善，故路网密度较高。此后上海在浦西纵向发展，直至20世纪80年代末才跨过黄浦江全面开发浦东，由于发展相对较晚，故浦东新区路网密度相对浦西较低。宝山区、闵行区在20世纪90年代设立，发展建设较晚，且主要以工业、物流等产业为支柱产业，故基础设施建设不尽完善，故路网密度相对较低。

（六）天津市

天津市是我国直辖市之一，位于京津冀城市群，其中心城区建成区城市形态为团块状。根据《天津市城市总体规划（2005—2020年）》中心城区的明确定义，2018年天津中心城区建成区面积为339平方公里，建成区道路里程为2 012.5公里。

天津城市总体规划定义中心城区为外环线、外环绿化带所围合的范围，其中心城区建成区路网密度为6.04km/km^2，在36个城市中排名第17位，路网密度处于中等水平。在中心城区建成区各行政区中，和平区路网密度最高，达到10.85km/km^2，远高于国家目标标准；河东区（7.04km/km^2）、河西区（6.54km/km^2）、河北区（6.85km/km^2）、红桥区（6.89km/km^2）、南开区（6.40km/km^2）比较接近，路网密度处于中高水平；东丽区、西青区、津南区、北辰区路网密度相对较低。（表8）

天津城市建成区呈典型的圈层结构，路网密度由内向外递减。位于老城中心的和平区路网密度最高，远高于目标标准（8km/km^2）；外围河东、河西、河北、南开、红桥五区处于中高水平（约6.5～7.0km/km^2）；随着城市建设发展，城市空间尺度拉大，外围行政区东丽区、西青区、津南区、北辰区建设用地较为分散，道路设施以骨架路网为主，集散性道路相对不足，路网密度仍处于较低水平。

表 8　天津主要行政区路网密度指标

行政区	路网密度
和平区	10. 85
河东区	7. 04
河西区	6. 54
南开区	6. 40
河北区	6. 85
红桥区	6. 89
东丽区	5. 04
西青区	5. 25
津南区	4. 88
北辰区	4. 64

（七）重庆市

重庆市是我国直辖市之一，位于成渝城市群，其中心城区建成区城市形态为组团型。根据《重庆市城市总体规划（2007—2020 年）》中心城区的明确定义，2018 年重庆中心城区建成区面积为 439 平方公里，建成区道路里程为 2 849 公里。

重庆市中心城区建成区路网总体密度为 6. 49km/km^2，处于中游水平，在 36 个城市中排名第 12 位。在中心城区建成区各行政区中，仅渝中区（9. 52km/km^2）路网密度达标，路网密度最低的行政区是巴南区（5. 66km/km^2）。（表 9）

表 9　重庆主要行政区路网密度指标

行政区	路网密度
渝中区	9. 52
江北区	7. 43
南岸区	6. 79
渝北区	6. 56
九龙坡区	6. 30
北碚区	5. 82
大渡口区	5. 68
沙坪坝区	5. 78
巴南区	5. 66

重庆是我国典型的山城，受地形和历史原因影响，城市发展为多中心组团结构。重庆路网整体上结合地形特点呈自由式发展。渝中区作为重庆老城区，起步早，建设密度大，故其路网密度相对较高。重庆作为我国工业重镇，初期的城市化进程主要由工业引领，如江北

区、南岸区等辖区，使得这些辖区的路网密度较高。与平原城市路网密度主要受发展历史的影响不同，重庆市路网密度在很大程度上还受到地形影响，如沙坪坝区虽然建设较早，但由于地形复杂使得其路网密度仍然相对较低。

（八）大连市

大连市是我国计划单列市之一，位于辽中南城市群，其中心城区建成区城市形态为组团型。根据《大连市城市总体规划（2001—2020年）》中心城区的明确定义，2018年大连中心城区建成区面积为368平方公里，建成区道路里程为2 219.4公里。

大连市中心城区建成区路网密度为6.03km/km^2，在36个城市中排名第18位，处中游水平。在中心城区建成区各行政区中，仅路网密度最高的西岗区（8.61km/km^2）密度达标，旅顺口区（5.28km/km^2）路网密度相对最低。（表10）

表10　大连主要行政区路网密度指标

行政区	路网密度
西岗区	8.61
中山区	8.07
沙河口区	7.59
金州区	5.57
甘井子区	5.49
旅顺口区	5.28

西岗区、中山区是大连市的老城区，发展较早，开发强度较大，故其路网密度相对较高。随着城市化进程推进，与老城区隔海相望的金州区以及位于半岛西端的旅顺口区成为了新兴发展区域，逐步使得大连由单中心演变为多中心组团城市，但由于这些组团建设相对较晚，其路网密度相对较低。

（九）青岛市

青岛市是我国计划单列市之一，位于山东半岛城市群，其中心城区建成区城市形态为组团型。根据《青岛市城市总体规划（2011—2020年）》中心城区的明确定义，2018年青岛中心城区建成区面积为514平方公里，建成区道路里程为2 751公里。

青岛市中心城区建成区路网密度为5.35km/km^2，在36个城市中排名第24位。在各行政区中，市南区（9.42km/km^2）路网密度最高，已超过8km/km^{2}的目标标准；其次为市北区，路网密度6.97km/km^2，基本达标；崂山区、李沧区、城阳区等保持在5km/km^{2}左右；黄岛区路网密度较低仅为3.80km/km^2。（表11）

表 11　青岛主要行政区路网密度指标

行政区	路网密度
市南区	9.42
市北区	6.97
城阳区	5.41
崂山区	5.28
李沧区	5.14
黄岛区	3.80

市南区、市北区为青岛传统老城区，建设发展历史悠久，具备良好的城市道路设施基础，路网密度较高；随着城市发展和空间扩展，逐渐形成多组团发展格局，外围李沧区、城阳区、崂山区作为功能性组团发展起步较晚，道路建设相对不完善；黄岛区作为国家级新区、西岸经济技术开发区，近年开始发展建设，以高新技术产业和大学城为主，道路建设仍处于不断规划建设时期，城市路网密度相对较低。

（十）宁波市

宁波市是我国计划单列市之一，位于长江三角洲城市群，其中心城区建成区城市形态为组团型。根据《宁波市城市总体规划（2006—2020 年）》中心城区的明确定义，2018 年宁波中心城区建成区面积为 341.6 平方公里，建成区道路里程为 2 276.7 公里。

宁波市中心城区建成区路网密度为 6.67km/km^2，在 36 个城市中排名第 9 位，处于中上游水平。在建成区各行政区中，仅路网密度最高的海曙区路密度达标（9.06km/km^2），路网密度最低的行政区是镇海区（5.47km/km^2）。（表 12）

表 12　宁波主要行政区路网密度指标

行政区	路网密度
海曙区	9.06
江东区	7.65
鄞州区	7.51
江北区	7.28
北仑区	5.48
镇海区	5.47

宁波市依江而建，三江穿城而过，宁波市老城区海曙区即位于奉化江和姚江汇流的合流处，宁波的城市发展也受水系影响主要呈沿江发展的态势。相对于老城区而言，沿江逐渐拓展的市辖区如江东区、鄞州区等路网密度相对较低。镇海区和北仑区是宁波市的工业和港口聚集区，由于主要以制造、物流为主要功能，同时起步相对较晚，故其路网密度相对更低。

四、结语

我国主要城市道路网密度监测工作，克服了传统城市工作中道路网密度统计标准不统一、数据更新时效性差等问题，以科学的城市建成区边界、规范化的道路分级标准、标准化的指标计算方法和技术规程，结合信息化技术，实现了对全国36个重点城市的路网密度动态监测。为合理控制城市道路网密度，落实“窄马路、密路网”的城市布局理念、促进城市交通规划的建设实施提供了有效支撑。

（作者：赵一新，中国城市规划设计研究院交通分院院长，教授级城市规划师）

中国城市服务业发展特点及提升路径

2018 年，中国服务业增加值达 469 575 亿元，比上年同期增长 7.6%，增速比第一产业和第二产业分别高出 4.1 和 1.8 个百分点，持续领跑国民经济增长；服务业占全国 GDP 比重 52.2%，比第二产业高出 11.5 个百分点；服务业对经济增长贡献率接近 60%，为中国经济平稳运行持续发挥关键作用。服务业特别是生产性服务业中的信息传输、软件和信息技术服务业、金融业、租赁和商务服务业以及生活性服务业中的批发零售、文化旅游、健康养老业的快速发展，对稳增长、促政策、调结构、保就业、惠民生的功能与作用不断增强。随着创新要素的不断积聚，中国服务业新动能快速发展，新产业、新业态和新模式不断涌现，不仅促进了服务业内部结构优化和质量提升，更有力地推动了产业结构调整和转型升级。

对中国城市而言，服务业同样具有重要的战略意义。它是推动城市其他产业现代化的催化剂、促进经济保持中高速增长的活性剂。同时，服务业也是中国城市加强对外开放的重点领域和激发经济发展活力的重要源泉，通过建立统一开放、竞争有序的现代服务业市场体系，放宽市场准入，加强公正监管，营造出国际化、法治化、便利化的营商环境，激发了市场主体活力和社会创造力，城市经济内生发展动力、防范和应对风险的能力显著提升。当前，在以供给侧改革为主线、创新驱动为引擎的发展背景下，加快发展城市现代服务业是优化城市产业结构、推动新旧动能转换和促进城市高质量发展的必然要求。

一、中国城市服务业发展特点

（一）城市服务业带动经济增长的作用日益凸显，发展活力不断增强

城市服务业的经济规模逐步扩大，发展速度快速提升。一方面，服务业在城市经济中所占份额持续上升，2017 年，中国城市服务业增加值达 37.3 万亿元，占全国服务业增加值的 87.35%，较上年增长 11.4%，其中，北京、上海、广州、深圳、天津的服务业增加值已突破 1 万亿元大关，北京和上海更是超过了 2 万亿元；城市服务业增加值占到地区生产总值的 48.5%，较上年增长 39.0%，其中，北京、海口、广州的占比均在 70% 以上，服务业已成为拉动城市经济增长的“稳定器”和“助推器”。另一方面，城市服务业稳定就业的能力突出，2016 年的服务业从业人员总数达到 9 019.7 万人，占城市就业总人数的 44.2%，其中生

产性服务业占服务业从业人数的52.5%。服务业充分发挥了“蓄水池”的作用，成为吸纳就业的主要渠道。此外，城市服务业的经济效益显著，人均服务业增加值为5.5万元，服务业劳动生产率为43.1万元/人，对城市经济增长的贡献率达50.9%，其中，北京、天津、海口的服务业贡献率均超过了85%；同时，服务业投资领域发展活跃，以北京为例，其第三产业投资额高达7 639亿元，较上年增长6.1%，占固定资产投资总额的90.3%，以房地产业、交通运输、仓储和通讯业为主，城市服务业的经济活力正在不断增强。(图1)

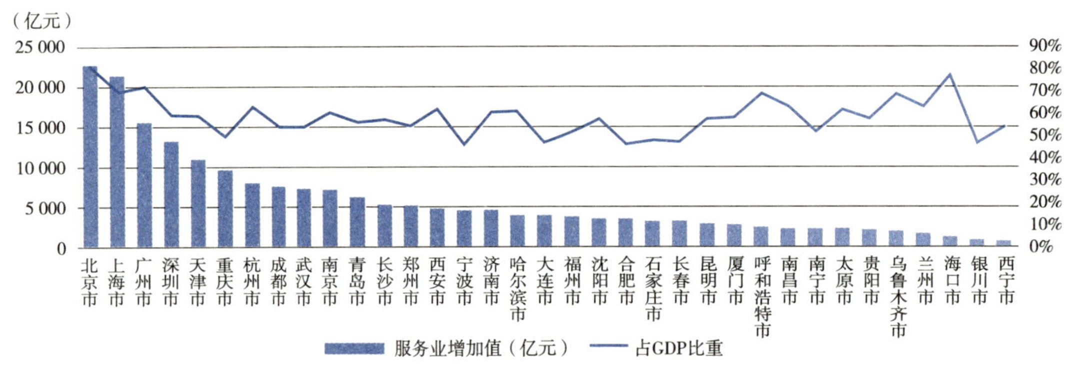

图1　中国各主要城市服务业增加值及其在国民经济中的比重(2017年)

(二)城市服务业新兴业态不断涌现，信息技术助推服务业融合发展

随着全球产业价值链分工的不断深化，基于移动互联网、物联网、大数据、云计算等的新一代信息技术，特别是以电子商务第三方支付和众创空间为核心的平台型企业的大量涌现，直接推动了服务业内部金融、商贸、物流、交通运输、文化、旅游、高技术服务等重点行业门类及其相关领域，以及服务业与第一、二产业间的跨界融合发展，催生出分享经济、数字经济、创意经济、智能经济、生物经济等新领域、新业态、新模式，服务业的发展活力、竞争力与运行效率得到迅速提升，成为服务业创新的新引擎和产业融合的新增长点。

服务业跨界融合往往导致产业边界的模糊化、技术的复杂化和运行组织方式的深刻变化。生产性服务业与先进制造业的关系越来越密切，有利于推动制造业由生产型向生产服务型转变，构建以现代服务业为主体、战略新兴产业为引领、先进制造业为支撑的新型产业体系，不断提升服务经济特别是实体经济的发展质量与水平。例如，杭州充分运用“互联网+”、人工智能等技术手段，打造以智慧物流“公路港”和“信息港”为重点的全国智慧物流中心，同时加快发展信息经济核心产业，聚焦信息与软件服务、电子信息产品制造、集成电路、机器人、信息安全等特色领域，推动云操作系统、智能终端操作系统、人机交互系统等的研发和应用。

消费结构的转型升级、人口老龄化等发展趋势，为文化旅游、商贸会展、健康养老、体育休闲等需求潜力大、带动作用强、贴近人民生活的生活性服务业类型带来了新的发展机遇，推动生活性服务业由生存型、传统型、物质型向发展型、现代型、服务型转变，有利于扩大消费市场，培育新的消费热点，深入挖掘生活性服务业的发展潜力。呼和浩特立足于本地独特的草原文化，通过文化公园、影视基地、古城遗址公园等项目，和极具少数民族风情的文化节与艺术节活动，提升城市旅游品牌影响力，进而增强城市的整体吸引力与竞争力。厦门则依托其国际知名旅游城市建设，加速旅游业与会展业的深度融合，吸引高端客源，提升旅游消费层次。

（三）城市服务业集聚区的功能特色日益突出，中心城市的集聚效益相对较高

服务业集聚发展的态势日益增强，诸多城市相继建设了一批主体功能突出、辐射范围广泛、带动作用显著的服务业集聚发展示范区，成为带动城市整体服务业高质量发展的先导区。目前，城市服务业集聚区的主导产业和发展特色日以鲜明，各地认定的服务业集聚区大体包括中央商务区、现代物流园、信息软件园、金融商务与后台服务集聚区、服务外包产业园、科技创业园、文化创意产业园、旅游休闲度假区、空港服务产业园等，几乎涵盖了大多数的服务业领域，但总体上以高端生产性服务业为主。例如上海的虹桥商务区依托虹桥综合交通枢纽、国家大型会展项目等重大功能性项目，以现代服务业集聚区、国际贸易中心新平台、企业总部基地汇集区、世界级高端商务中心为功能定位，促进城市产业空间格局调整，带动城市经济发展方式转型，从而更好地服务于长三角一体化发展战略。

然而，主导行业不同的服务业集聚区的空间分化态势逐渐显著，不同城市的服务业集聚效益差异也十分明显。对于大部分城市而言，中央商务区、现代物流园、信息软件园、金融服务业集聚区、文化创意园的集聚效益相对较高，对城市经济社会发展的带动能力较强，有少数服务业集聚区已经形成了规模化、专业化、高端化的发展格局，并在区域经济发展中发挥了重要的引导作用。例如杭州、宁波、大连等城市面向跨境电商而配套发展的现代物流园，重点发展嵌入式操作系统和应用软件研发的西安软件新城软件研发基地，以动漫制作、时装和珠宝设计为特色的武汉光谷文化创意产业园，有些甚至发展成为具有国际影响力的服务业集聚区，如北京金融街、上海陆家嘴等。从区域尺度来看，服务业主要分布在35个中心城市①，其发展规模、结构和效益水平普遍较高，而其他城市服务业发展规模、集聚水平与效益则相对偏低。这与服务业集聚区是城市经济发展和产业结构演变达到一定阶段的产物，需要较高的产业基础、人力储备、消费水平与需求等的支撑密切相关。

（四）城市服务业发展水平的空间差异明显，规模、结构、效益水平发展不均衡

在上述35个中心城市中，遵循科学性、系统性与数据可获得性原则，从服务业规模（服务业增加值、服务业从业人员数）、服务业结构（服务业增加值占GDP比重、服务业从

① 包括北京、上海、天津、重庆4个直辖市，石家庄、太原、沈阳、长春、哈尔滨、南京、杭州、合肥、福州、南昌、济南、郑州、广州、长沙、武汉、海口、成都、贵阳、昆明、西安、兰州、西宁、呼和浩特、南宁、银川、乌鲁木齐26个省会城市（由于数据不全，未包括拉萨），以及深圳、厦门、宁波、青岛、大连5个计划单列市。

业人员比重、生产性服务业从业人员比重)、服务业效益(人均服务业增加值、服务业劳动生产率、服务业对城市经济增长贡献率)三方面构建服务业发展水平综合评价指标体系，所需数据主要源自《中国城市统计年鉴》(2017)以及上述各市2018年的统计年鉴与统计公报。

采用客观赋值的熵值法求得各级指标的权重值，同时参考已有研究并结合各中心城市的发展实际对权重值进行修正，最后通过SPSS软件中的K-means聚类分析模块将全国35个中心城市的服务业发展水平综合得分依次划分为高水平、较高水平和中等水平3类，其中，高水平城市有北京、上海、广州3个；较高水平城市有深圳、天津、杭州、南京、呼和浩特、成都、乌鲁木齐、海口、西安、武汉、哈尔滨、济南、长沙、青岛14个；中等水平城市有太原、兰州、重庆、沈阳、郑州、昆明、厦门、石家庄、贵阳、大连、福州、西宁、宁波、长春、南昌、南宁、银川、合肥18个。

城市服务业发展呈现以北京、上海、广州三足鼎立的态势，但三者间亦存在水平差异，北京服务业发展水平的综合得分位居全国首位，较第二位的上海高出近30%。在服务业规模方面，2017年北京、上海、广州的服务业增加值分别为22 567.8亿元、21 191.5亿元、15 271.7亿元；三市服务业从业人员数分别为641.4万人、406.9万人和217.6万人。在服务业结构方面，北京稳居首位，其服务业增加值占GDP比重、服务业从业人员比重、生产性服务业从业人员比重分别为80.6%、80.6%、51.1%；而上海和广州服务业增加值占GDP比重大体为70%，服务业从业人员占比不到70%，生产性服务业从业人员在服务业中占比也未超过50%。在服务业效益方面，广州的表现最为优异，人均服务业增加值达10.5万元，服务业劳动生产率为70.2万元/人，服务业对城市经济增长的贡献率超过80%，均位居全国前列；北京市紧随其后，其服务业劳动生产率约为广州的一半，而服务业对城市经济增长的贡献率则高于广州，达到87.4%；上海的服务业效益水平表现欠佳，其服务业对城市经济增长的贡献仅为75.8%，服务业劳动生产率仅为广州的52.1%。中国35个中心城市服务业的规模、结构和效益水平见图2。

(五) 城市服务业地域分工明显，科技服务业的专业化程度最高

本文采用区位熵来表征城市服务业的专业化发展水平。将服务业分生产性服务业(包括交通运输业、仓储和邮政业、信息传输和计算机服务与软件业、金融业、租赁和商务服务业、科学研究和技术服务业)和生活性服务业(包括批发和零售业、住宿和餐饮业、房地产业、文化和体育及娱乐业、居民服务与修理和其他服务业)进行分析，由于公共服务业的专业化水平普遍不高，因此不包括在内。研究结果表明，城市服务业的专业化发展进程也表现出显著的空间分异特征，东部地区城市的专业化水平普遍较高，北京、上海、广州生产性服务业及其分行业专业化水平突出，这既符合城市在经济社会发展过程中的实际需求，也与三市多元化、综合化、高端化的发展方向相吻合；在生活性服务业方面，成都、北京、上海、海口则名列前4位，其区位熵分别为2.44、2.24、2.22和2.21，与其在批发零售、住宿餐饮、房地产等行业的优势和竞争力密切相关(表1)。

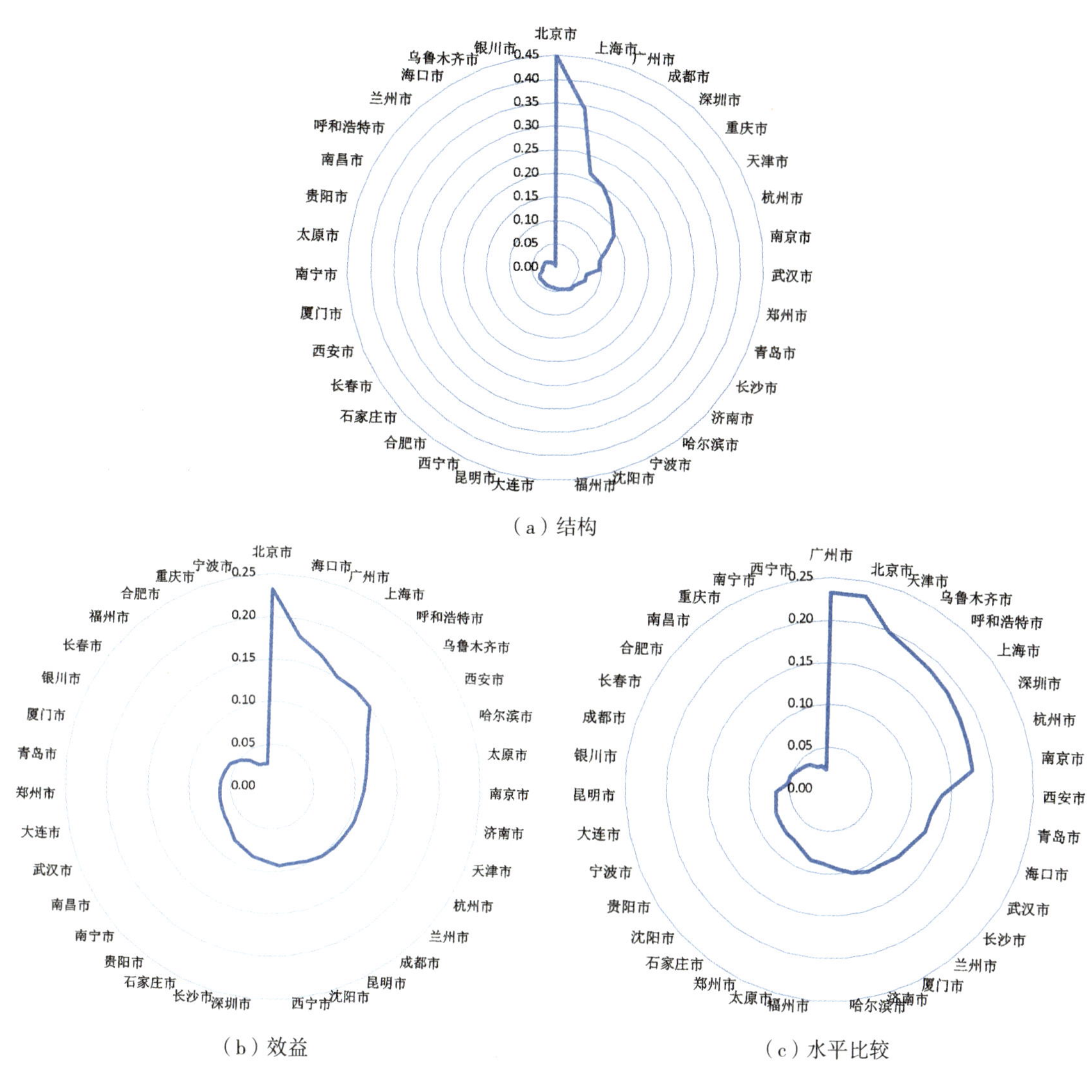

图2　2017年中国35个中心城市的服务业规模

表1　中国35个中心城市按生产性与生活性服务业及其内部各行业专业化水平分类（2017年）

行　业	按区位熵划分的城市服务业专业化水平					平均值
生产性服务业	北京 2.66	上海 1.93	广州 1.82	西安 1.79	乌鲁木齐 1.60	1.32
	成都 1.57	太原 1.55	南京 1.53	海口 1.52	西宁 1.52	
	哈尔滨 1.47	大连 1.47	石家庄 1.46	呼和浩特 1.45	济南 1.42	
①交通运输、仓储和邮政业	兰州 5.05	太原 2.62	海口 2.15	银川 2.09	广州 1.93	1.43
	昆明 1.76	西安 1.74	成都 1.72	上海 1.71	哈尔滨 1.60	
	呼和浩特 1.58	沈阳 1.57	石家庄 1.56	贵阳 1.56	北京 1.55	
	西宁 1.52	南京 1.47				
②信息传输、计算机服务和软件业	北京 4.30	南京 3.39	大连 2.91	济南 2.88	成都 2.78	1.42
	杭州 2.18	上海 2.10	西安 2.08	深圳 1.99	广州 1.96	

续表

行　业	按区位熵划分的城市服务业专业化水平					平均值
③金融业	银川 2.11	济南 1.89	北京 1.75	大连 1.74	哈尔滨 1.54	1.15
	上海 1.52	天津 1.50	海口 1.49	石家庄 1.48	呼和浩特 1.48	
	长沙 1.47	宁波 1.43	南宁 1.35	沈阳 1.26	西安 1.21	
	郑州 1.21	西宁 1.21				
④租赁和商务服务业	北京 3.71	上海 3.05	广州 2.68	深圳 2.31	成都 1.93	1.27
	西安 1.51	杭州 1.45	南宁 1.42	昆明 1.37	石家庄 1.35	
	福州 1.32	兰州 1.29	哈尔滨 1.28			
⑤科学研究和技术服务业	北京 3.72	西安 2.85	兰州 2.36	呼和浩特 2.21	西宁 1.95	1.50
	广州 1.80	天津 1.71	南京 1.70	沈阳 1.69	杭州 1.69	
	昆明 1.68	长沙 1.68	石家庄 1.67	太原 1.63	武汉 1.61	
	上海 1.57	乌鲁木齐 1.55	南宁 1.52	长春 1.52		
生活性服务业	成都 2.44	北京 2.24	上海 2.22	海口 2.21	广州 1.98	1.36
	昆明 1.60	南京 1.54	武汉 1.54	天津 1.48	济南 1.46	
	哈尔滨 1.43	西安 1.42	长沙 1.41	深圳 1.41	呼和浩特 1.39	
①批发和零售业	兰州 3.67	成都 2.59	上海 2.55	北京 2.02	南京 1.81	1.40
	广州 1.78	武汉 1.74	西宁 1.74	昆明 1.64	济南 1.62	
	哈尔滨 1.57					
②住宿和餐饮业	成都 4.42	上海 2.57	北京 2.46	海口 2.23	广州 2.15	1.42
	昆明 1.93	西安 1.87	厦门 1.72	武汉 1.54	长沙 1.54	
	深圳 1.52	杭州 1.52	南京 1.52	呼和浩特 1.48	哈尔滨 1.43	
③房地产业	海口 3.81	广州 2.46	北京 2.30	贵阳 1.87	深圳 1.85	1.39
	兰州 1.73	上海 1.68	厦门 1.58	杭州 1.57	大连 1.52	
	西安 1.52	长沙 1.49	昆明 1.41	济南 1.40		
④居民服务、修理和其他服务业	天津 7.77	厦门 2.75	北京 2.57	长春 2.50	上海 2.38	1.29
	广州 2.04	贵阳 1.73	哈尔滨 1.58	昆明 1.56	青岛 1.43	
⑤文化、体育和娱乐业	呼和浩特 3.03	北京 2.80	长沙 2.14	银川 2.12	南昌 1.94	1.47
	乌鲁木齐 1.94	石家庄 1.86	成都 1.84	太原 1.78	海口 1.77	
	兰州 1.67	南宁 1.59	西宁 1.56	南京 1.55	武汉 1.51	
	哈尔滨 1.50					

（六）城市服务业营商环境持续优化，服务业对外开放领域和规模不断扩大

城市服务业的高质量发展离不开良好营商环境的塑造，而首先需要改善的就是服务业发展的制度环境。服务业具有制度密集型的特征，对制度具有高度的敏感性和依赖性，同时也是制度的载体，主要体现在城市现代企业的产权体系和治理结构、现代市场体系的秩序和运作规则、政府公共服务职能的法制化和现代化等方面，因而营造公平竞争的市场环境、便捷高效的政务服务环境，以及强化事中事后监管成为城市服务业营商环境改造的重中之重。杭州在优化服务业制度环境的过程中，十分注重服务业政策体系的完善，积极开展服务业企业认定高新技术企业等探索，同时不断创新监管方式，探索建立跨行业、跨领域的服务业准入

和监管机制。同时，服务业因其分工的复杂化和行业的专业化，对监管机构的能力和监管人员的素质都提出了较高的要求。长春和贵阳在服务业融合发展的过程中十分注重专业人才队伍建设，鼓励市场主体加大对从业人员的培训力度和专项考核，提升从业人员的服务意识、业务水平和专业技能。

在城市服务业营商环境不断改善的同时，城市服务业对外开放水平也稳步提升，通过服务业综合改革试点与自贸试验区的建设，加大了在对外投资管理体制、金融管理制度、外籍高层次人才激励保障机制、监管体系和监管模式等方面的改革力度，进一步放开服务业领域的市场准入，同时鼓励引导各类社会资本投向高端服务业和新兴服务业领域，优化服务业对外开放的空间格局，使城市在更大范围、更广领域、更高层次上参与服务业的国际合作与竞争。在这一方面，北京率先打造服务业扩大开放综合试点，对标国际先进理念、领先标准和最佳实践，加快实施“负面清单 + 正向激励”“产业开放 + 园区开放”的新模式，扩大金融、科技、信息、文化创意、商务等领域的服务出口，在不断扩大服务业对外开放的同时，着力提升服务行业的国际竞争力。

二、影响中国城市服务业发展的主要因素

（一）城市规模与经济发展水平是城市服务业的发展基础

城市规模对城市服务业发展水平的影响程度最大，且显著性也最强，即随着城市规模的扩大，城市服务业发展水平将进一步提高。通常认为，城市规模与服务业发展水平之间呈现一种非线性关系，城市规模的逐步扩大，其对服务业发展水平的正向效应也会不断增强。这是因为城市规模水平越高，其市场规模相应越大，劳动分工也更为专业化，这使得城市的服务业发展趋于多样化，从而有利于吸引人力资源和企业进入城市。同时，随着市场规模的逐步扩大，产业间的分工进一步深化，劳动生产效率显著提升，这意味着城市能够提供更多的工作岗位和更完备的基础设施与公共服务体系，由此更多的人口向城市集聚，为城市服务业创造了更为广阔的发展空间，这一点在批发零售、住宿餐饮、交通运输、仓储和邮政业表现得尤为明显。

服务业特别是现代服务业呈现出较高的复杂性和较强的产业关联性，但经济发展水平仍然是制约城市服务业发展水平的基本因素，较高的经济发展水平会为城市服务业提供持续稳定的发展动能，很大程度上决定了服务业的质量水平、行业选择和未来发展路径，是城市服务业发展活力的根本来源。

（二）信息网络技术是推动传统服务业转型升级和提质增效的主要支撑

传统服务业作为劳动密集型行业，具有无形性、非标准化、同步性和不可贸易性等特点，由此导致服务业布局分散、缺乏规模效应、劳动生产率低、难以管理等问题。随着信息网络技术的快速发展及其在城市服务业中的广泛应用，加快了传统服务业的转型升级步伐。

如“互联网＋”等现代信息技术，不仅大大拓展了服务业的维度，精细服务环节、延伸服务链条、发展智慧服务，并通过线上线下融合，培育新型服务业，促进服务业新业态、新模式的发展壮大；而且有利于加强服务业的规范管理，提升服务质量水平，健全消费者的权益保护。同时，还可消除上下游企业间或企业与消费者之间交易过程中的信息不对称，降低企业和消费者的交易成本。此外，信息技术在服务业内部管理上的应用，也有助于服务企业实现管理程序的简化与科学化，提升管理水平。

（三）工业化水平是城市生产性服务业迅速崛起和第二、三产业融合发展前提条件

城市服务业特别是生产性服务业的持续稳定繁荣离不开坚实的工业发展基础，二者之间呈现相互作用、相互依赖、共同发展的互补性关系。工业是生产性服务业发展的前提和基础，工业扩张所引致的服务需求是生产性服务业发展动力的重要来源。具体来看，城市工业化水平的提升为生产性服务业的发展创造了广阔的市场需求空间，技术变化所引发的“垂直分离”。

（四）对外开放程度与人才科技水平是城市服务业发展的内生动力

扩大对外开放水平是提升城市服务业发展质量和国际竞争力的重要举措，将加大服务市场的竞争强度，经营状况欠佳、竞争力较差的一些服务业企业的经营效益会出现大幅下滑甚至会因此被市场淘汰，但就整体而言，扩大服务业开放对中国城市服务业发展的积极影响要远大于负面影响。首先，国外服务机构在知识、技术、管理能力、服务理念、风险防范等方面的示范作用，催生知识溢出和学习效应，带动城市内的服务开放部门提高劳动生产率；其次，通过引入竞争，加大城市服务市场的竞争强度，推动市场结构向较为充分的完全竞争结构转变，促进服务业企业改善经营并提高服务质量，从而实现优胜劣汰，提高资源配置效率；再次，为吸引高质量外资营造良好的投资环境，包括培育高水平的法律、金融、保险、会计、审计等专业服务市场；最后，通过扩大服务业的对外开放水平，引进新业态、新服务、新商业模式和高端服务业人才，支撑和带动制造业转型升级。此外，科技人力资源对城市服务业的贡献也愈发显著，通过提升科技人力资源的利用程度，进一步释放人才活力，能够为城市服务业的持续高速发展注入新的活力。

（五）政策扶持是城市服务业发展的重要保障

政府的政策扶持是确保城市服务业持续快速发展的重要保障。如国家“十三五”经济和社会发展规划纲要在“加快推动服务业优质高效发展”部分明确提出，要促进生产性服务业专业化，提高生活性服务业品质，完善服务业发展体制和政策。2015 年 11 月，国务院办公厅发布的《关于加快发展生活性服务业促进消费结构升级的指导意见》，要求以增进人民福祉、满足人民群众日益增长的生活服务需要为主线，大力崇尚绿色环保，讲求质量品质，注重文化内涵的生活消费理念，创新政策支持，积极培育生活性服务业新业态新模式，全面提升生活性服务业质量和效益。以上文件不仅为城市服务业的发展指明了方向，而且还

提出要加大财税、金融、土地政策引导支持，如适时推进“营改增”方案，大力推广政府和社会资本合作（PPP）模式，逐步推进政府购买养老、健康、体育、文化、社区等服务。

三、提升中国城市服务业发展的主要路径

（一）整合优势资源，将北京、上海、广州打造成具有国际竞争力的现代服务业中心

作为国家首批服务业综合改革试点区，北京、上海、广州应以全球化的视野、充分发挥自身先发优势，加快打造以科技创新、现代金融、国际商贸、综合交通、文化旅游为主并具有全球影响力的现代服务业中心，成为推进全国现代服务业发展的重要引导力量。北京市应根据政治中心、文化中心、国际交往中心和科技创新中心的战略发展定位，大力推进科技创新和服务于国际交往的软硬件环境建设。以建设国际一流的科技创新中心为目标，依托国家科研院所和重点高校，建设创新网络服务平台，提高对全球创新资源的吸引集聚能力，不断提升自主创新能力；同时要以发展总部经济和现代金融为切入点，扩大金融对外开放，加强国际文化合作交流，服务于“一带一路”建设和国际经贸合作。上海市应依托雄厚的产业基础、通达的立体交通及信息网络等基础设施、良好的营商环境、高素质的人力资本等优势，大力推进国际金融、航运及贸易中心建设。广州市基于国家中心城市和综合性门户城市的发展背景，着力打造成粤港澳大湾区区域发展的核心引擎、国际商贸中心、综合交通枢纽和科技教育文化中心。同时，积极运用各种新技术改造提升零售、餐饮等传统服务业，提高服务业的技术含量和专业化程度，引导服务业企业充分运用“互联网+”技术，积极创新服务模式，通过跨界联动、业务流程再造等实现业态创新、商业模式创新，着力培育产业新增长点。

（二）培育高端现代服务业，推动东部沿海城市生产性服务业与制造业的融合发展

培育法律、会计、咨询等高端现代服务业，推动东部沿海城市服务业向价值链高端延伸，提升现代服务业的能级水平。一方面，充分利用得天独厚的区位优势、发达的港口经济和总部经济优势，加快构建高端、高效的生产性服务业体系，打造电子商务、会展商务、国际金融等生产性服务业集聚区，推动城市向具有竞争力的区域性生产性服务业中心发展；另一方面，加快现代服务业与先进制造业的联动发展，充分利用“互联网+”、人工智能等技术手段，在生物医药、集成电路、装备制造等领域实现与现代制造业的跨界融合；推进基于大数据、云计算、物联网、移动互联网的公共服务平台建设，促进服务业向专业化、精细化、高端化的方向转变。有条件的城市可考虑将软件和信息服务作为重点扶持产业，顺应信息时代发展潮流，推动与其他生产性服务业的融合发展，如互联网与金融服务业的有机结合，有利于培育科技金融、文化金融、互联网金融等特色金融服务业；物流业信息化水平的提高，有利于港口城市发展电商物流、智能仓储、供应链物流等新业态，扩大港口、机场、高铁等交通设施的服务效应，引导传统外贸企业、专业市场向跨境电商转型，强化现代国家

物流枢纽功能。

（三）发展高品质生活性服务业，减少城市经济增长对房地产业的过度依赖

生活性服务业的发展应突出便利性、精细化、个性化、定制化的特点，顺应消费结构升级、人口老龄化等趋势，逐步向发展型、现代型、服务型转变。首先，着力发展需求潜力大、带动作用强、贴近人们生活的文化旅游、商贸会展、健康养老、体育休闲等朝阳产业，同时加快批发零售、住宿餐饮等传统生活性服务业的转型升级，鼓励发展夜间经济，逐渐形成专业化的生活性服务体系。以文化旅游业为例，可立足于本地都市文化资源和风景名胜资源，发展如滨海旅游、商展旅游、休闲旅游等特色旅游产品，服务产品应紧密贴合现代人的生活习惯与需求，避免因流于形式以及行业内部的同质或恶性竞争而造成的资源浪费；同时，加速旅游会展深度融合，吸引高端客源，提升旅游消费层次。如厦门等旅游业基础雄厚的城市，可全面推进全域旅游创建工作，完善旅游发展政策，拓展旅游发展空间，优化旅游发展环境，建设高品位、主题型、体验式的精品文化旅游景区。其次，推动生活性服务业的创新转型，以集约化组织形式、信息化管理手段、标准化运营体系提升服务质量，可考虑发展高端医疗健检、医养结合、体育健身等健康养老产业，更好地发挥生活性服务业保障和改善民生的作用。最后，要促进房地产业的健康有序发展，合理调控商品房市场，通过公租房、廉租房、棚改安置房等手段有效化解房地产供需问题，推动养老地产、旅游地产等多元化地产均衡发展，减少经济增长对房地产业的过度依赖。

（四）推动形成优势互补的竞合关系，完善合理有序的城市服务业梯度发展格局

中国城市服务业发展水平的空间差异十分显著，东部城市的经济总量与质量仍然处于领先地位，也是服务业发展水平最高的地区。随着近年来西部城市的加速赶超，东西发展差距逐渐缩小，西部城市服务业的发展环境逐步得到改善，而部分东部城市则出现了服务业增速放缓甚至发展水平下降的情况；与此同时，南北方城市发展差距日益扩大，北方城市经济增长疲软，服务业发展活力普遍不强，其中，东北城市的衰落迹象十分明显，各类经济社会发展问题尤为突出。在东部城市服务业转型升级与中西部城市服务业提速增效的背景下，应充分结合城市自身功能定位与特点错位发展，形成优势互补、分工明确、健康有序的竞合关系。以城市群为基础，以城市群的中心城市为龙头，带动周边城市和地区实现差异化发展，通过发挥自身产业能级优势，对周边地区进行产业辐射，促其产业结构的优化升级、服务业的高质量发展并向价值链高端延伸，要重视维护健康和谐的发展环境，避免同质化甚至恶性竞争，建成产业互补的关系网络，最终形成以城市等级为依托的服务业梯度发展格局。

（五）扩大城市服务业对外开放格局，提升服务业国际竞争力

加大城市服务业各领域的对外开放力度，首先需要构建统一、创新、竞争、有序的开放型服务业市场，以服务业综合改革试点为契机，探索新型服务业态发展的市场准入和管理标准，减少重点领域的前置审批和资质认定，制定落实支持服务业“走出去”的优惠政策，

推进服务业在体制机制、技术和内容等领域的创新。其次，引导社会资本成为服务业发展的主体力量，推动教育、医疗、健康、养老等非基本公共服务的市场化、产业化、国际化；同时，充分发挥服务业 FDI 的溢出效应，延伸外资企业服务链，促进研发、物流、销售、信息等高端和新兴服务业领域发展。再次，重视城市服务业品牌建设，加强与国际知名企业的交流合作，制定并实施本地服务业宣传计划，利用主流媒体、知名网站、社交软件等平台，实施全方位、多角度、精准化、互动式的品牌营销，打造“中国服务”品牌。最后，着力提升城市服务业国际竞争力，与发达国家相比，中国生产性服务业发展相对滞后，多数行业的研发设计、检验检测水平有待提高，物流、金融等产业虽发展速度较快，但依然存在成本过高、结构不完善等问题，与传统产业的融合程度有待提升，制造业降本增效亟待增强。未来城市服务业应在对外开放中逐步强化质量基础支撑，提升产品和服务品质，加快推进与国际先进水平和评价标准的有效对接，拓展应用“智能 +”等创新手段，为制造业的转型升级赋能，努力提升中国城市服务业的国际竞争力与影响力。

（作者：申玉铭，首都师范大学资源环境与旅游学院副院长、教授、博士生导师；李哲，首都师范大学资源环境与旅游学院，博士）

参考文献

[1] 任旺兵．论中国产业服务化的战略问题［J］．宏观经济管理，2018，（10）：29 - 35.

[2] 王佳元，李子文，洪群联．推动服务业向高质量发展［J］．宏观经济管理，2018，（5）：24 - 29，63.

[3] 来有为．推动服务业高质量发展对策［J］．新经济导刊，2018，（11）：83 - 85.

[4] 肖高．大力推进生产性服务业高质量发展［N］．浙江日报，2018 - 8 - 28（005）.

[5] 潘峰华，杨博飞．国家中心城市竞争力及其职能演变——基于上市企业总部的研究［J］．地理研究，2018，37（7）：1364 - 1376.

[6] 邱灵，申玉铭，任旺兵．国内外生产性服务业与制造业互动发展的研究进展．世界地理研究，2007，16（3）：71 - 77.

1.5℃温控目标下中国城市近零碳排放工作进展及展望

一、1.5℃温控目标与中国城市近零碳排放工作

（一）背景介绍

2015年12月12日，在巴黎举行的联合国气候变化大会第21次缔约方大会会上通过了一份具有里程碑意义的协定，由此确立了2020年后全球气候治理的新秩序，即为《巴黎协定》。该协定以“在本世纪内，将全球平均气温较工业化前水平升幅控制在2℃之内，并为把温升控制在1.5℃内而努力。全球将尽快实现温室气体排放达峰，本世纪下半叶（2080年前后）实现温室气体净零排放”为目标，明确各方以“自主贡献”为基础的减排机制，以期在全球应对气候变化方面起到切实效果，并承担“共同而有区别”的责任。

近年来，随着相关科技的发展进步，科学家们对于碳排放的具体影响的认识越来越深入。研究报告显示，人类以二氧化碳的形式排放一万亿吨碳，将会导致全球地表平均温度升高1.7℃（正负波动0.4℃），但不同区域的具体升温情况会有所差别，其中高纬度大陆地区、沿海地区与岛屿所受影响最大。

为进一步应对人类活动导致地球升温的影响，2018年10月，联合国政府间气候变化专门委员会（IPCC）发布了《全球升温1.5℃特别报告》（以下称《特别报告》）和《1.5℃城市决策者摘要》（以下称《摘要》）。《特别报告》重点强调，若不将全球温升控制在1.5℃，任由其突破2℃的红线或更高，不仅自然生态会遭受明显的系统性破坏，全球秩序、社会公平与可持续发展也都会因气候变化导致的过度能源消耗而受到影响；明确指出，为了达成1.5℃温控目标，人类需要在2030年之前将全球温室气体排放量较2010年降低40%~60%，并在本世纪中叶达到（近）零排放。

《摘要》指出，要将全球温控限制在1.5℃，城市的政策制定者必须了解气候科学，并做出迅速深远且前所未有的变革。至2050年，将全球建筑物的碳排放量较2010年减少80%~90%；至2050年，可再生能源替代化石染料，能源供应以可再生能源为主导，利用可再生能源实现70%~85%电力供应。

由此，近零碳排放被正式提上日程。

（二）现状及展望

目前，中国乃至全世界正在经历高速的城镇化进程。据统计，目前全球超过50%的人口生活在城市中，而这一数字还在逐年增长。到2050年，城市人口预计将从目前的35亿增加到67亿。而与此相对应，城市对全球化石能源碳排放的贡献率已经超过了70%。城市居民对交通运输、食物、商品和能源等资源的需求越来越大，给土地、水资源和气候带来了更大的压力。在中国，城市更是贡献了超过90%的二氧化碳排放量。因此，为实现1.5℃温控目标，城市的近零碳排放工作是重中之重。

首先，1.5℃温控目标的达成需要有效的治理框架。该治理框架应该是需要分工明确、权责匹配，有城市和城市地区、区域、工业、民间社会以及科学机构参与的多层次治理框架。有效的多层次治理能够提升地区的气候适应能力和减缓气候变暖能力，强化部门间政策的协调，更好达成各利益相关方合作伙伴关系。与此同时，还可以更快提升公众可持续发展的意识，改善与气候相关的环境教育，从而推动实现公众行为的转变。将温控目标与可持续发展紧密结合。

其次，于中国而言，1.5℃温控目标的实际推动将会助力社会发展，引导经济产业转型。其中，能源、陆地和生态系统、城镇化和城镇基础设施建设以及工业四个方面的建设工作将会得到快速推进。其中，城镇系统和城镇化是贯穿其他重要体系转型的关键因素，完成上述四个体系的转型工作，需要具备城市规划的专业知识、多层治理经验以完善的低碳、零碳技术。这也是未来中国低碳城市建设的工作重点。

最后，从能源角度切入，1.5℃温控的目标的达成，需要能源系统的去碳化速度的大幅提高。能源相关的二氧化碳排放需在2010年的水平上以每年2.0%~2.8%的速度下降，这比2℃温控的相关要求（1.0%~1.8%）提高了整整一个百分点。具体来说，电力行业、工业、建筑和交通领域都是减排工作的重点。[1]

二、近零碳排放的概念、分类及意义

（一）低碳、零碳与近零碳排放的概念与区别

目前，国内城市建设近零碳排放示范区的工作还处于经验积累的探索阶段，而近零碳排放的概念也会随实际工作的展开不断增加新的内涵，为此，笔者将其与低碳排放、零碳排放等相关概念进行了对比分析。

1. 低碳排放

“低碳排放”是相对于当前的高碳排放而提出的概念，英国率先提出低碳经济概念时，强调的是碳排放与经济增长的绝对脱钩，即在经济增长的同时，碳排放总量要不断降低。而对于发展中国家而言，考虑到发展阶段和碳排放的规律性特征，碳排放与经济增长相对脱钩，即单

位GDP碳排放的下降，就被看作低碳排放。总之，低碳排放是低碳经济建设的初步阶段，通过碳排放总量、人均排放量以及碳排放强度的降低，实现低碳发展过程的不断演进。

2. 零碳排放

“零碳排放”指的是在一定区域、一定时间内的生产活动和消费活动净碳排放量为零。零碳排放是建设低碳经济、应对气候变化所要达到的最终目标，可从以下途径探索实现：①在减少甚至杜绝使用煤炭、石油、天然气等高碳排放的化石能源基础上，完全使用零碳能源，包括风能、核能、可再生能源等，降低碳排放；②通过增加森林碳汇、草地碳汇等抵消碳排放；③通过碳捕获与封存技术（CCS）实现减碳和零碳。

3. 近零碳排放

“近零碳排放”是处于低碳排放和零碳排放之间的低碳发展阶段，是接近零碳排放的一种状态，表明低碳发展的进程已接近零碳排放的终点。

若将三者进行对比，则近零碳排放比低碳的要求更高。一方面，低碳通常指相对碳排放量的下降，即碳排放强度的下降，而近零碳排放则是指绝对碳排放总量接近于零；另一方面，近零碳排放又与零碳排放存在一定区别。近零碳排放考虑碳排放源汇平衡，允许采用碳汇等抵消机制，只要总的“净排放”（即碳源减去碳汇）接近于零即可。而零碳排放要求的条件更为苛刻，必须要从源头实现零碳排放（如全部使用零碳能源），不采用碳汇等抵消机制。

实现近零碳排放应以先进的生产力为支撑，通过合理有效的途径，在不限制经济发展的前提下，实现经济与生态环境的协同可持续发展，建设成为生态文明社会。[2]

（二）近零碳排放的意义

推广近零碳排放是维持1.5℃升温目标的重要手段，在全球生态层面上，它将有助于抑制全球升温，维持生态环境稳定，保护全人类共同的家园。而具体到我国，施行近零碳排放也有着深远、广泛的意义：

1. 近零碳排放是我国生态文明建设工作的具体落实

生态文明建设是我国目前“五位一体”总体战略布局中重要的一环，而应对气候变化则是生态文明建设的主要工作之一。实施近零碳排放将有助于增强我国对于碳排放经济领域的把控，必然成为我国在应对气候变化领域以及整个生态文明建设体系中一项重要的具体工作。

2. 推动产业转型、技术进步

目前，从中央到地方各个层面均已在低碳领域开展了系统性工作，包括低碳城镇、低碳园区、企业碳排放权交易、低碳产品认证等，形成了全面化、系统化的低碳工作局面。

施行近零碳排放势必将进一步推动节能减排，促进我国的传统产业转型，推动创新科技发展。

3. 增强中国在气候变化领域的国际话语权，提高国际地位

在美国退出《巴黎协定》的大背景下，中国全方位实施近零碳排放，建设近零碳排放

区示范工程。此举将会有力推动中国与其他国家在应对气候变化领域的合作，有助于推动和提升中国国际形象以及在该领域的话语权。[3]

三、国内外城市的近零碳排放区实践

示范区一般是指先行发展或建设的典型区域，在发展模式上具有示范作用，具有可复制、可推广的发展经验。在推广近零碳排放概念、发展近零碳排放经济的工作中，近零碳排放区将会起到重要作用。近零碳排放示范区的内涵定义如下，即在指定评价范围内，通过优化空间布局、发展低碳产业、使用清洁能源、运用低碳技术、加强低碳管理、倡导低碳生活、增加森林碳汇、购买自愿减排量等综合性措施，实现该区域的净碳排放量逐步趋近于零并最终实现绿色低碳发展的典型区域。

（一）国外城市的实践

城市总体建设层面。2009 年 3 月，丹麦哥本哈根提出到 2025 年将建成世界首个零碳排放城市，并提出了分阶段的发展目标：2015 年二氧化碳排放在 2005 年的基础上减少 20%；2025 年全市二氧化碳排放量降低到零。哥本哈根市政府成立了专门的行动小组，提出具体的降碳行动计划，主要措施包括大力发展绿色可再生资源、鼓励更多市民选择绿色出行、推广绿色环保建筑、对城市进行绿化改造等。2012 年，第一阶段的目标已提前实现，目前正在向零碳目标努力迈进。

社区建设层面。英国贝丁顿零碳社区位于英国伦敦西南部的萨顿镇，占地 1.65 公顷，包括 82 套公寓和 2 500 平方米的办公和商住面积，于 2002 年完工。该社区设计遵循绿色低碳理念，建设采用可循环利用的建筑材料，采取各种措施减少社区建筑热损失并充分利用太阳热能，采用热电联产系统为社区居民提供生活用电和热水，建立了循环利用的节水系统，社区全部实现绿色出行模式。

新城建设层面。阿联酋马斯达尔（Masdar）位于阿拉伯联合酋长国首都阿布扎比郊区，规划面积 6 平方公里，其规划建设完全融入绿色低碳理念，规划设计充分利用环境条件实现降温节能；能源供应全部采用可再生能源；全城禁止燃油车通行，交通依靠慢行交通和电动车；水资源利用方面，大量建设雨水回收设施、中水系统及污水的回收再利用，推动水资源的高效利用；通过回收再利用，减少废弃物产生及其排放，推动 2020 年实现零废物、零填埋目标。

（二）国内近零碳排放示范区概念的提出

在 2015 年 11 月的《联合国气候变化框架公约》会议上，中国在“国家自主贡献”中提出了“将于 2030 年左右使二氧化碳排放达到峰值并争取尽早实现，2030 年单位国内生产总值二氧化碳排放比 2005 年下降 60%~65%，非化石能源占一次能源消费比重达到 20% 左右”等多个目标。2017 年联合国气候变化会议期间，全球 25 个城市市长（伦敦、里约热内卢等）在波恩先行承诺，2050 年之前将使各自城市碳排放量净值降为“零”。

在全球气候变化与各类环境问题等多重压力下，深入开展低碳建设，尽早达到碳排放峰值，实现零碳排放目标，成为当下我国生态文明建设的重要任务。《中华人民共和国国民经济和社会发展第十三个五年规划纲要》提出深化各类低碳试点，实施近零碳排放区示范工程。《“十三五”控制温室气体排放工作方案》明确提出，选择条件成熟的限制开发区域和禁止开发区域、生态功能区、工矿区、城镇等开展近零碳排放区示范工程建设，到 2020 年建设 50 个示范项目。

（三）国内城市的近零碳实践

在全球气候变化与各类环境问题等多重压力下，深入开展低碳建设，尽早达到碳排放峰值，实现零碳排放目标，成为当下中国生态文明建设的重要任务。《中华人民共和国国民经济和社会发展第十三个五年规划纲要》提出深化各类低碳试点，实施近零碳排放区示范工程。《“十三五”控制温室气体排放工作方案》明确提出，选择条件成熟的限制开发区域和禁止开发区域、生态功能区、工矿区、城镇等开展近零碳排放区示范工程建设，到 2020 年建设 50 个示范项目。

依据国家相关部署，各省市积极响应近零排放示范区建设工作，广东省、江苏省、浙江省、陕西省、北京市等成为率先提出建设实施近零碳排放区示范工程的省市。

1. 广东省

广东省“十三五”规划建议明确提出“珠三角地区实施近零碳排放区示范工程”，并将其列为 2016 年广东省政府工作报告中的重点项目之一。2017 年，广东省发布了《广东省近零碳排放区示范工程实施方案》（粤发改气候函〔2017〕50 号）和《关于征集近零碳排放区示范工程试点项目的通知》（粤发改气候函〔2017〕1530 号），在全省范围内征集一批近零碳排放示范工程试点项目，创建类型包括城镇、建筑、交通、社区、园区和企事业单位 6 类。同年，广东省相关部门组织了近零碳排放区示范工程试点项目遴选工作安排，选定了 4 个省级近零碳排放区示范工程试点项目，包括汕头市南澳县近零碳排放区城镇试点、珠海市万山镇近零碳排放区城镇试点、广东状元谷近零碳排放区园区试点、中山市小榄镇北区近零碳排放区社区试点。

2. 陕西省

2016 年，陕西省发布了《关于组织开展近零碳排放区示范工程试点的通知》，重点在工矿区、农业园区和民用建筑三个领域进行试点示范，其中：①工矿区：包括煤矿、油气田、大型化工企业及火电厂等，示范工程可再生能源消费及余热余气余压等能源循环利用占到能源消费总量的 60% 以上；能耗强度和碳排放强度均为全省同行业平均水平的 30% 以下；②农业园区：以设施农业集中区和特色农庄为主；③民用建筑：包括居民小区建筑和公共机构建筑，试点民用建筑节能设计目标为供暖、制冷、照明三项消耗小于 25 千瓦时/平方米·年，达到绿色建筑三星级标准。

3. 浙江省

2017 年，浙江省发布了《关于开展第二批省级低碳试点工作的通知》（浙发改资环〔2017〕939 号），提出在城镇、社区、园区和企业领域“四位一体”打造近零碳排放区试点示范，选定了凤林镇等 6 个近零示范城镇、余村等 4 个近零示范社区、长兴画溪等 2 个近零示范园区、传化智联股份有限公司等 4 个近零示范企业。

4. 其他

上海市：在 2010 年和 2015 年分别启动了第一批、第二批低碳发展实践区创建工作，力求突破低碳发展遇到的瓶颈，进一步创新机制体制，为推进全市试点积累经验，其中第二批试点区域以更新建筑碳排放为主。

截至目前，低碳发展各项基础工作逐步夯实，目标及责任考核工作不断加强，各项创新政策和机制体制陆续出台，节能低碳技术被广泛运用，重点建设项目的示范效应得到充分显现。

其中，部分实践区建立了较为完善的能耗统计监测体系和相关服务平台；部分实践区明确了低碳发展推进机构及职责，并将低碳发展目标任务纳入区域有关责任评价考核体系。与此同时，政策机制持续创新以及低碳技术和举措全面推广，使得全社会节能低碳氛围得到显著增强。

江苏省：常州市和扬中县分别推动发展绿色建筑与绿色能源。常州市绿色建筑博览园，通过打造绿色建筑主题公园，运用海绵城市体系、太阳能与建筑一体化技术，打造接近零碳排放示范区。镇江市扬中县提出打造“绿色能源岛”，通过规划建设屋顶分布式光伏发电、风电、新能源微电网、生物质能等清洁能源项目，打造清洁、低碳、安全、高效的高比例可再生能源生产和消费模式。

河北承德：建立可再生能源供应体系。河北承德建设零碳城市包括实施清洁电力、替煤供热、绿色交通、绿色建筑、森林碳汇五大工程。到 2020 年，承德市 100% 的电力消费来自可再生能源，基本形成以可再生能源为主的能源保障和供应体系。

北京市：提出重点区域打造零碳排放示范区。城市副中心、冬奥会场馆、新机场及临空经济区等将重点打造新能源高端应用示范区。到 2020 年，城市副中心行政办公区率先建成“近零碳排放示范区”，新能源和可再生能源利用比重力争达到 40% 以上。城市副中心整体区域新能源和可再生能源利用比重力争达到 15% 以上。冬奥会场馆将大力发展地热、热泵、太阳能等新能源和可再生能源应用。延庆区新建冬奥会场馆将推广地热及热泵系统供暖、分布式光伏发电，基本实现赛区电力消费全部使用绿色电力，打造国际一流的绿色低碳冬奥会。到 2020 年，新机场及临空经济区可再生能源比重，预期将达到 15% 以上。

此外，很多城市在申报国家发展改革委第三批低碳试点城市方案中，也把实施近零碳排放示范区作为创新性的举措。

四、中国实现近零排放的技术路径

在近零碳排放区示范工程的具体建设方面，中国的近零碳排放建设按技术类型可分为如下四类：

1. 100%可再生能源示范型近零碳排放示范区

对于可再生能源富集地区，如内蒙古拥有丰富的风能资源，西藏拥有丰富的水能和太阳能资源，同时内蒙古和西藏边远地区经济欠发达，能源需求量小，可以实现清洁能源自给自足。具备零碳发展的能源资源基础与条件，开展近零碳排放示范还可以有效解决局部地区严重的弃风、弃光问题，对优化能源消费结构、促进绿色低碳发展具有重要意义。

2. 碳中和型近零碳排放示范区

探索在碳汇资源丰富的部分林牧区和建成景区开展近零碳排放示范工程建设。中国边远地区的林区和牧区，主要产业是牧业和林下产业，能源消费主要为生活能源消费，完全可以通过开发利用太阳能、风能及水能等可再生能源得以满足，通过建设再生能源微电网或局域电网模式，促进分布式能源开发与利用，有条件开展近零碳排放示范区建设。一些已开发建成的旅游景区、风景名胜区、国家公园等，主要功能为发展旅游业或开展生态保护，其能源消费主要用于景区建筑运行、设施维护和区内交通工具，能源消费量十分有限，在不破坏自然景观的前提下，通过合理开发可再生能源，推动所在区域实现近零碳排放。

3. 局部行业性近零碳排放示范区

以国外成功的零碳建筑与零碳汽车标准为参考依据，推动建设行业性近零碳排放示范区，推动近零碳排放企事业单位建设。以广东省低碳公共交通试点运行为例，学校、机关事业单位、部分服务业的能源消费主要用于维持建筑运行，大力推动零碳校园、零碳企业和零碳事业单位等示范工程建设。局部行业性近零碳排放示范区的建设将有力促进中国交通部门的零碳技术研发与应用，最终以近零碳产业带动近零碳社会的发展。

4. “升级版”低碳排放示范区

在现有低碳城市、低碳城（镇）、低碳园区、低碳社区等低碳试点基础上，进一步强化区域经济发展的“去碳化”，制定更加严格的低碳目标（更加趋近于零碳排放），通过零碳技术和产品的普及使用，推动建设零碳生产和生活体系，最终推动形成零碳社会。[4]

与此同时，推动近零碳排放区示范工程建设主要有减源、增汇和替代三条路径，总目标是实现区域内净碳排放接近于零。以上三方面互为补充，各区域根据产业和能源结构、资源禀赋等实际情况，合理选择适宜路径，推进近零碳排放区示范工程建设。

（1）“减源”要求强化现有节能降碳工作，继续优化产业结构，淘汰落后产能，实现能源资源的梯级利用，采用节能低碳技术，在低碳转型的基础上实现近零碳排放。

（2）“增汇”指加强生态系统管理，提高现有森林、草地、农田等生态系统固碳能力，通过增加人工林和绿地面增加碳汇能力，或购买少量 CCER 自愿减排量，抵消区域内碳排放。

（3）“替代”指充分利用区域内水电、风能、太阳能、生物质能及地热能等可再生能源，替代化石能源，实现零碳排放。

五、中国城市近零排放工作的主要问题及展望

1. 近零碳排放区示范建设存在概念不清、配套措施不足的问题

近零碳排放示范工程建设作为新生事物，尽管各地推动相关工作的积极性较高，但是在遴选和建设近零碳排放区示范工程方面仍存在概念不清、遴选评价指标体系缺失、激励政策和保障措施不到位等问题。近零碳排放并不仅仅是“低碳发展”，作为低碳发展的“升级版”，需要在当前低碳发展的基础上付出更大努力才能实现。

2. 支撑近零碳排放区目标评价的区域碳排放核算体系不完善

从目前上海市区域碳排放统计和核算情况来看，大部分低碳实践区和低碳社区的碳核算体系还未建立，部分低碳实践区实施了区域内部分建筑统计、报告制度，搭建区域建筑能耗在线监测平台，但在交通、市政、碳汇等领域的碳排放统计和核算还应强化，另外也有必要按相关规范进一步厘清区域碳排放测算边界。考虑到近零碳排放示范区碳排放目标的科学性和可考核性，应设置合理的区域碳排放核算边界和方法。

3. 近零碳排放区示范工程建设的政策、制度有待完善

近零碳排放示范区建设与经济社会发展、产业发展、基础设施建设等规划之间的协调和统筹机制缺失，后续的监管和评价机制有待完善，如低碳发展氛围亟须强化，能源与碳排放监测、计量管理体系有待完善，低碳技术和产品的使用比例有待提高。另外，由于缺乏有效的配套支持政策，一定程度上限制了近零碳排放区示范工程建设相关工作的开展。

目前中国城市近零排放工作尚处于初期阶段，但是各地区业已开展积极有效的尝试，笔者希望通过本文对于现今已有的近零排放工作的介绍，各城市决策者得以将应对全球气候变化的1.5℃温控目标与城市近零排放建设工作实现有机结合，从而最终有效贡献在本世纪中叶实现（近）零碳排放的工作。

（注：上海市节能减排中心对本文亦有重大贡献）

（作者：王伟康，世界自然基金会（瑞士）北京代表处气候与能源、绿色金融项目总监；李瑛，世界自然基金会（瑞士）北京代表处气候与能源项目高级项目专员；单诗尧，世界自然基金会（瑞士）北京代表处项目协调办助理专员）

参考文献

[1] 张永香，等．全球温控目标浅析［J］．气候变化研究进展，2017，13（04）．

[2] 李艳梅，等．近零碳排放示范区的内涵及建设路径分析［J］．企业经济，2017（10）．

[3] 史志呈，许文强．从低碳到近零碳排放——我国实施近零碳排放区示范工程的思考与建议［J］．广东科技，2018（11）．

[4] 刘长松．我国近零碳排放区示范工程建设路径与配套措施［J］．中国经贸导刊，2017（36）．

专题篇

空间规划体系改革

一、编者按

1949 年 1 月 31 日北平和平解放后，成立中华人民共和国、规划建设新首都即刻被提到议事日程。同年 5 月 22 日，北平市都市计划委员会举行成立大会并决议，“正式授权梁思成先生及清华建筑系师生起草新市区设计”。新中国的城市规划事业由此拉开序幕，迄今已走过 70 年辉煌历程。

改革开放以来，我国城市规划的制度建设，经历了 1984 年的《城市规划条例》、1989 年的《中华人民共和国城市规划法》、2007 年的《中华人民共和国城乡规划法》三个阶段。在城市规划走向逐步成熟的过程中，城市规划工作中存在的种种问题，包括空间约束性规划无力，各类规划自成体系、互不衔接，规划的科学性和严肃性不够等日趋凸显。习近平总书记在 2013 年 12 月 12 日的中央城镇化工作会议上指出：“要建立空间规划体系，推进规划体制改革，加快推进规划立法工作，形成统一衔接、功能互补、相互协调的规划体系。城市规划要由扩张性规划逐步转向限定城市边界、优化空间结构的规划。城市规划要保持连续性，不能政府一换届、规划就换届。”①

在中央的直接指导下，空间规划体系的改革工作开始起步。2015 年 4 月 25 日，《中共中央国务院关于加快推进生态文明建设的意见》指出：“国土是生态文明建设的空间载体。要坚定不移地实施主体功能区战略，健全空间规划体系，科学合理布局和整治生产空间、生活空间、生态空间。……构建平衡适宜的城乡建设空间体系，适当增加生活空间、生态用地，保护和扩大绿地、水域、湿地等生态空间。”

中共中央国务院随后印发《生态文明体制改革总体方案》，对“建立空间规划体系”提出三项要求：

（1）编制空间规划。整合目前各部门分头编制的各类空间性规划，编制统一的空间规划，实现规划全覆盖。空间规划是国家空间发展的指南、可持续发展的空间蓝图，是各类开发建设活动的基本依据。空间规划分为国家、省、市县（设区的市空间规划范围为市辖区）

---

① 见《十八大以来重要文献选编（上）》，中央文献出版社 2014 年版。

三级。研究建立统一规范的空间规划编制机制。鼓励开展省级空间规划试点。编制京津冀空间规划。

（2）推进市县“多规合一”。支持市县推进“多规合一”，统一编制市县空间规划，逐步形成一个市县一个规划、一张蓝图。市县空间规划要统一土地分类标准，根据主体功能定位和省级空间规划要求，划定生产空间、生活空间、生态空间，明确城镇建设区、工业区、农村居民点等的开发边界，以及耕地、林地、草原、河流、湖泊、湿地等的保护边界，加强对城市地下空间的统筹规划。加强对市县“多规合一”试点的指导，研究制定市县空间规划编制指引和技术规范，形成可复制、能推广的经验。

（3）创新市县空间规划编制方法。探索规范化的市县空间规划编制程序，扩大社会参与，增强规划的科学性和透明度。鼓励试点地区进行规划编制部门整合，由一个部门负责市县空间规划的编制，可成立由专业人员和有关方面代表组成的规划评议委员会。规划编制前应当进行资源环境承载能力评价，以评价结果作为规划的基本依据。规划编制过程中应当广泛征求各方面意见，全文公布规划草案，充分听取当地居民意见。规划经评议委员会论证通过后，由当地人民代表大会审议通过，并报上级政府部门备案。规划成果应当包括规划文本和较高精度的规划图，并在网络和其他本地媒体公布。鼓励当地居民对规划执行进行监督，对违反规划的开发建设行为进行举报。当地人民代表大会及其常务委员会定期听取空间规划执行情况报告，对当地政府违反规划行为进行问责。

经过三年的酝酿筹备，根据中共十九届三中全会通过的《深化党和国家机构改革方案》，2018 年 3 月 17 日，第十三届全国人民代表大会第一次会议批准了《国务院机构改革方案》，将国土资源部的职责，国家发展和改革委员会的组织编制主体功能区规划职责，住房和城乡建设部的城乡规划管理职责，水利部的水资源调查和确权登记管理职责，农业部的草原资源调查和确权登记管理职责，国家林业局的森林、湿地等资源调查和确权登记管理职责，国家海洋局的职责，国家测绘地理信息局的职责整合，组建自然资源部，作为国务院组成部门。

2018 年 8 月 1 日，中共中央办公厅、国务院办公厅印发《自然资源部职能配置、内设机构和人员编制规定》。其中，新组建的国土空间规划局的职责是：拟订国土空间规划相关政策，承担建立空间规划体系工作并监督实施。组织编制全国国土空间规划和相关专项规划并监督实施。承担报国务院审批的地方国土空间规划的审核、报批工作，指导和审核涉及国土空间开发利用的国家重大专项规划。开展国土空间开发适宜性评价，建立国土空间规划实施监测、评估和预警体系。

2018 年 11 月 18 日，中共中央、国务院发布《关于统一规划体系更好发挥国家发展规划战略导向作用的意见》（以下简称《意见》）。

《意见》指出：“以规划引领经济社会发展，是党治国理政的重要方式，是中国特色社会主义发展模式的重要体现。科学编制并有效实施国家发展规划，阐明建设社会主义现代化强国奋斗目标在规划期内的战略部署和具体安排，引导公共资源配置方向，规范市场主体行为，有利于保持国家战略连续性稳定性，集中力量办大事，确保一张蓝图绘到底。”《意见》

要求："坚持下位规划服从上位规划、下级规划服务上级规划、等位规划相互协调，建立以国家发展规划为统领，以空间规划为基础，以专项规划、区域规划为支撑，由国家、省、市县各级规划共同组成，定位准确、边界清晰、功能互补、统一衔接的国家规划体系。"

《意见》明确了国家级空间规划的功能定位是：以空间治理和空间结构优化为主要内容，是实施国土空间用途管制和生态保护修复的重要依据。

《意见》同时指出，国家发展规划根据党中央关于制定国民经济和社会发展五年规划的建议，由国务院组织编制，经全国人民代表大会审查批准，居于规划体系最上位，是其他各级各类规划的总遵循。国家级专项规划、区域规划、空间规划，均须依据国家发展规划编制。国家级专项规划要细化落实国家发展规划对特定领域提出的战略任务，由国务院有关部门编制，其中国家级重点专项规划报国务院审批，党中央有明确要求的除外。国家级区域规划要细化落实国家发展规划对特定区域提出的战略任务，由国务院有关部门编制，报国务院审批。国家级空间规划要细化落实国家发展规划提出的国土空间开发保护要求，由国务院有关部门编制，报国务院审批。国家级专项规划、区域规划、空间规划，规划期与国家发展规划不一致的，应根据同期国家发展规划的战略安排对规划目标任务适时进行调整或修编。国家级空间规划对国家级专项规划具有空间性指导和约束作用。

2019 年 1 月 23 日，习近平主持召开中央全面深化改革委员会第六次会议，审议通过了《关于建立国土空间规划体系并监督实施的若干意见》。会议指出，将主体功能区规划、土地利用规划、城乡规划等空间规划融合为统一的国土空间规划，实现"多规合一"，是党中央作出的重大决策部署。要科学布局生产空间、生活空间、生态空间，体现战略性、提高科学性、加强协调性，强化规划权威，改进规划审批，健全用途管制，监督规划实施，强化国土空间规划对各专项规划的指导约束作用。

会议强调，改革工作重点要更多放到解决实际问题上，发现问题要准，解决问题要实。要抓好任务统筹，精准推进落实，加强调查研究，坚持问题导向，画好工笔画，提出的改革举措要直击问题要害，实现精确改革。改革方案落地过程中要因地制宜，逐层细化，精准有效，改什么、怎么改都要根据实际来，不能一刀切。特别是直接面向基层群众的改革，要把抓改革落实同做群众工作结合起来，讲究方式方法，确保群众得实惠。要防止空喊改革口号，防止简单转发照搬中央文件，防止机械式督察检查考核。要处理好政策顶层设计和分层对接、政策统一性和差异性的关系，加强政策解读和指导把关。要强化责任担当，对推出的各项改革方案要进行实效评估，及时发现和解决问题。

2019 年 5 月，《中共中央、国务院关于建立国土空间规划体系并监督实施的若干意见》正式发布。在此，我们将有关文件以及选编的几篇已在媒体/网络上发表的文章一并刊出，以飨读者。

——毛其智

二、专栏一：《中共中央　国务院关于建立国土空间规划体系并监督实施的若干意见》

国土空间规划是国家空间发展的指南、可持续发展的空间蓝图，是各类开发保护建设活动的基本依据。建立国土空间规划体系并监督实施，将主体功能区规划、土地利用规划、城乡规划等空间规划融合为统一的国土空间规划，实现“多规合一”，强化国土空间规划对各专项规划的指导约束作用，是党中央、国务院作出的重大部署。为建立国土空间规划体系并监督实施，现提出如下意见。

一、重大意义

各级各类空间规划在支撑城镇化快速发展、促进国土空间合理利用和有效保护方面发挥了积极作用，但也存在规划类型过多、内容重叠冲突，审批流程复杂、周期过长，地方规划朝令夕改等问题。建立全国统一、责权清晰、科学高效的国土空间规划体系，整体谋划新时代国土空间开发保护格局，综合考虑人口分布、经济布局、国土利用、生态环境保护等因素，科学布局生产空间、生活空间、生态空间，是加快形成绿色生产方式和生活方式、推进生态文明建设、建设美丽中国的关键举措，是坚持以人民为中心、实现高质量发展和高品质生活、建设美好家园的重要手段，是保障国家战略有效实施、促进国家治理体系和治理能力现代化、实现“两个一百年”奋斗目标和中华民族伟大复兴中国梦的必然要求。

二、总体要求

（一）指导思想。以习近平新时代中国特色社会主义思想为指导，全面贯彻党的十九大和十九届二中、三中全会精神，紧紧围绕统筹推进“五位一体”总体布局和协调推进“四个全面”战略布局，坚持新发展理念，坚持以人民为中心，坚持一切从实际出发，按照高质量发展要求，做好国土空间规划顶层设计，发挥国土空间规划在国家规划体系中的基础性作用，为国家发展规划落地实施提供空间保障。健全国土空间开发保护制度，体现战略性、提高科学性、强化权威性、加强协调性、注重操作性，实现国土空间开发保护更高质量、更有效率、更加公平、更可持续。

（二）主要目标。到2020年，基本建立国土空间规划体系，逐步建立“多规合一”的规划编制审批体系、实施监督体系、法规政策体系和技术标准体系；基本完成市县以上各级国土空间总体规划编制，初步形成全国国土空间开发保护“一张图”。到2025年，健全国土空间规划法规政策和技术标准体系；全面实施国土空间监测预警和绩效考核机制；形成以国土空间规划为基础，以统一用途管制为手段的国土空间开发保护制度。到2035年，全面提升国土空间治理体系和治理能力现代化水平，基本形成生产空间集约高效、生活空间宜居适度、生态空间山清水秀，安全和谐、富有竞争力和可持续发展的国土空间格局。

三、总体框架

（三）分级分类建立国土空间规划。国土空间规划是对一定区域国土空间开发保护在空间和时间上作出的安排，包括总体规划、详细规划和相关专项规划。国家、省、市县编制国土空间总体规划，各地结合实际编制乡镇国土空间规划。相关专项规划是指在特定区域（流域）、特定领域，为体现特定功能，对空间开发保护利用作出的专门安排，是涉及空间利用的专项规划。国土空间总体规划是详细规划的依据、相关专项规划的基础；相关专项规划要相互协同，并与详细规划做好衔接。

（四）明确各级国土空间总体规划编制重点。全国国土空间规划是对全国国土空间作出的全局安排，是全国国土空间保护、开发、利用、修复的政策和总纲，侧重战略性，由自然资源部会同相关部门组织编制，由党中央、国务院审定后印发。省级国土空间规划是对全国国土空间规划的落实，指导市县国土空间规划编制，侧重协调性，由省级政府组织编制，经同级人大常委会审议后报国务院审批。市县和乡镇国土空间规划是本级政府对上级国土空间规划要求的细化落实，是对本行政区域开发保护作出的具体安排，侧重实施性。需报国务院审批的城市国土空间总体规划，由市政府组织编制，经同级人大常委会审议后，由省级政府报国务院审批；其他市县及乡镇国土空间规划由省级政府根据当地实际，明确规划编制审批内容和程序要求。各地可因地制宜，将市县与乡镇国土空间规划合并编制，也可以几个乡镇为单元编制乡镇级国土空间规划。

（五）强化对专项规划的指导约束作用。海岸带、自然保护地等专项规划及跨行政区域或流域的国土空间规划，由所在区域或上一级自然资源主管部门牵头组织编制，报同级政府审批；涉及空间利用的某一领域专项规划，如交通、能源、水利、农业、信息、市政等基础设施，公共服务设施，军事设施，以及生态环境保护、文物保护、林业草原等专项规划，由相关主管部门组织编制。相关专项规划可在国家、省和市县层级编制，不同层级、不同地区的专项规划可结合实际选择编制的类型和精度。

（六）在市县及以下编制详细规划。详细规划是对具体地块用途和开发建设强度等作出的实施性安排，是开展国土空间开发保护活动、实施国土空间用途管制、核发城乡建设项目规划许可、进行各项建设等的法定依据。在城镇开发边界内的详细规划，由市县自然资源主管部门组织编制，报同级政府审批；在城镇开发边界外的乡村地区，以一个或几个行政村为单元，由乡镇政府组织编制“多规合一”的实用性村庄规划，作为详细规划，报上一级政府审批。

四、编制要求

（七）体现战略性。全面落实党中央、国务院重大决策部署，体现国家意志和国家发展规划的战略性，自上而下编制各级国土空间规划，对空间发展作出战略性系统性安排。落实国家安全战略、区域协调发展战略和主体功能区战略，明确空间发展目标，优化城镇化格局、农业生产格局、生态保护格局，确定空间发展策略，转变国土空间开发保护方式，提升国土空间开发保护质量和效率。

（八）提高科学性。坚持生态优先、绿色发展，尊重自然规律、经济规律、社会规律和城乡发展规律，因地制宜开展规划编制工作；坚持节约优先、保护优先、自然恢复为主的方针，在资源环境承载能力和国土空间开发适宜性评价的基础上，科学有序统筹布局生态、农业、城镇等功能空间，划定生态保护红线、永久基本农田、城镇开发边界等空间管控边界以及各类海域保护线，强化底线约束，为可持续发展预留空间。坚持山水林田湖草生命共同体理念，加强生态环境分区管治，量水而行，保护生态屏障，构建生态廊道和生态网络，推进生态系统保护和修复，依法开展环境影响评价。坚持陆海统筹、区域协调、城乡融合，优化国土空间结构和布局，统筹地上地下空间综合利用，着力完善交通、水利等基础设施和公共服务设施，延续历史文脉，加强风貌管控，突出地域特色。坚持上下结合、社会协同，完善公众参与制度，发挥不同领域专家的作用。运用城市设计、乡村营造、大数据等手段，改进规划方法，提高规划编制水平。

（九）加强协调性。强化国家发展规划的统领作用，强化国土空间规划的基础作用。国土空间总体规划要统筹和综合平衡各相关专项领域的空间需求。详细规划要依据批准的国土空间总体规划进行编制和修改。相关专项规划要遵循国土空间总体规划，不得违背总体规划强制性内容，其主要内容要纳入详细规划。

（十）注重操作性。按照谁组织编制、谁负责实施的原则，明确各级各类国土空间规划编制和管理的要点。明确规划约束性指标和刚性管控要求，同时提出指导性要求。制定实施规划的政策措施，提出下级国土空间总体规划和相关专项规划、详细规划的分解落实要求，健全规划实施传导机制，确保规划能用、管用、好用。

五、实施与监管

（十一）强化规划权威。规划一经批复，任何部门和个人不得随意修改、违规变更，防止出现换一届党委和政府改一次规划。下级国土空间规划要服从上级国土空间规划，相关专项规划、详细规划要服从总体规划；坚持先规划、后实施，不得违反国土空间规划进行各类开发建设活动；坚持"多规合一"，不在国土空间规划体系之外另设其他空间规划。相关专项规划的有关技术标准应与国土空间规划衔接。因国家重大战略调整、重大项目建设或行政区划调整等确需修改规划的，须先经规划审批机关同意后，方可按法定程序进行修改。对国土空间规划编制和实施过程中的违规违纪违法行为，要严肃追究责任。

（十二）改进规划审批。按照谁审批、谁监管的原则，分级建立国土空间规划审查备案制度。精简规划审批内容，管什么就批什么，大幅缩减审批时间。减少需报国务院审批的城市数量，直辖市、计划单列市、省会城市及国务院指定城市的国土空间总体规划由国务院审批。相关专项规划在编制和审查过程中应加强与有关国土空间规划的衔接及"一张图"的核对，批复后纳入同级国土空间基础信息平台，叠加到国土空间规划"一张图"上。

（十三）健全用途管制制度。以国土空间规划为依据，对所有国土空间分区分类实施用途管制。在城镇开发边界内的建设，实行"详细规划+规划许可"的管制方式；在城镇开发边界外的建设，按照主导用途分区，实行"详细规划+规划许可"和"约束指标+分区准入"的管制方式。对以国家公园为主体的自然保护地、重要海域和海岛、重要水源地、文物等实行特殊保护制度。因地制宜制定用途管制制度，为地方管理和创新活动留有空间。

（十四）监督规划实施。依托国土空间基础信息平台，建立健全国土空间规划动态监测评估预警和实施监管机制。上级自然资源主管部门要会同有关部门组织对下级国土空间规划中各类管控边界、约束性指标等管控要求的落实情况进行监督检查，将国土空间规划执行情况纳入自然资源执法督察内容。健全资源环境承载能力监测预警长效机制，建立国土空间规划定期评估制度，结合国民经济社会发展实际和规划定期评估结果，对国土空间规划进行动态调整完善。

（十五）推进"放管服"改革。以"多规合一"为基础，统筹规划、建设、管理三大环节，推动"多审合一""多证合一"。优化现行建设项目用地（海）预审、规划选址以及建设用地规划许可、建设工程规划许可等审批流程，提高审批效能和监管服务水平。

六、法规政策与技术保障

（十六）完善法规政策体系。研究制定国土空间开发保护法，加快国土空间规划相关法律法规建设。梳理与国土空间规划相关的现行法律法规和部门规章，对“多规合一”改革涉及突破现行法律法规规定的内容和条款，按程序报批，取得授权后施行，并做好过渡时期的法律法规衔接。完善适应主体功能区要求的配套政策，保障国土空间规划有效实施。

（十七）完善技术标准体系。按照“多规合一”要求，由自然资源部会同相关部门负责构建统一的国土空间规划技术标准体系，修订完善国土资源现状调查和国土空间规划用地分类标准，制定各级各类国土空间规划编制办法和技术规程。

（十八）完善国土空间基础信息平台。以自然资源调查监测数据为基础，采用国家统一的测绘基准和测绘系统，整合各类空间关联数据，建立全国统一的国土空间基础信息平台。以国土空间基础信息平台为底板，结合各级各类国土空间规划编制，同步完成县级以上国土空间基础信息平台建设，实现主体功能区战略和各类空间管控要素精准落地，逐步形成全国国土空间规划“一张图”，推进政府部门之间的数据共享以及政府与社会之间的信息交互。

七、工作要求

（十九）加强组织领导。各地区各部门要落实国家发展规划提出的国土空间开发保护要求，发挥国土空间规划体系在国土空间开发保护中的战略引领和刚性管控作用，统领各类空间利用，把每一寸土地都规划得清清楚楚。坚持底线思维，立足资源禀赋和环境承载能力，加快构建生态功能保障基线、环境质量安全底线、自然资源利用上线。严格执行规划，以钉钉子精神抓好贯彻落实，久久为功，做到一张蓝图干到底。地方各级党委和政府要充分认识建立国土空间规划体系的重大意义，主要负责人亲自抓，落实政府组织编制和实施国土空间规划的主体责任，明确责任分工，落实工作经费，加强队伍建设，加强监督考核，做好宣传教育。

（二十）落实工作责任。各地区各部门要加大对本行业本领域涉及空间布局相关规划的指导、协调和管理，制定有利于国土空间规划编制实施的政策，明确时间表和路线图，形成合力。组织、人事、审计等部门要研究将国土空间规划执行情况纳入领导干部自然资源资产离任审计，作为党政领导干部综合考核评价的重要参考。纪检监察机关要加强监督。发展改革、财政、金融、税务、自然资源、生态环境、住房城乡建设、农业农村等部门要研究制定完善主体功能区的配套政策。自然资源主管部门要会同相关部门加快推进国土空间规划立法工作。组织部门在对地方党委和政府主要负责人的教育培训中要注重提高其规划意识。教育部门要研究加强国土空间规划相关学科建设。自然资源部要强化统筹协调工作，切实负起责任，会同有关部门按照国土空间规划体系总体框架，不断完善制度设计，抓紧建立规划编制审批体系、实施监督体系、法规政策体系和技术标准体系，加强专业队伍建设和行业管理。自然资源部要定期对本意见贯彻落实情况进行监督检查，重大事项及时向党中央、国务院报告。

来源：中国政府网 http：//www.gov.cn/xinwen/2019－05/23/content_ 5394187.htm

三、专栏二:《中共中央　国务院关于建立国土空间规划体系并监督实施的若干意见》新闻发布会（实录）

国新办新闻局局长、新闻发言人胡凯红:

女士们、先生们，大家上午好。欢迎出席国务院新闻办今天举办的新闻发布会。最近，中央印发了《中共中央　国务院关于建立国土空间规划体系并监督实施的若干意见》，大家都很关注，今天我们很高兴请来了自然资源部副部长赵龙先生，请他向大家介绍有关情况，并回答大家的提问。出席今天发布会的还有：自然资源部总规划师庄少勤先生，国土空间规划局副局长张兵先生。首先有请赵部长做介绍。

自然资源部副部长赵龙:

谢谢主持人。女士们、先生们，媒体朋友们，大家上午好!

国土空间规划是国家空间发展的指南、可持续发展的空间蓝图，是各类开发保护建设活动的基本依据，党中央、国务院高度重视。习近平总书记对国土空间规划工作多次作出重要论述，今年3月在参加十三届全国人民代表大会内蒙古代表团审议时再次强调，“要坚持底线思维，以国土空间规划为依据，把城镇、农业、生态空间和生态保护红线、永久基本农田保护红线、城镇开发边界作为调整经济结构、规划产业发展、推进城镇化不可逾越的红线，立足本地资源禀赋特点、体现本地优势和特色。”

今年1月23日，中央全面深化改革委员会第六次会议审议通过《关于建立国土空间规划体系并监督实施的若干意见》(以下简称《若干意见》)，已正式印发，新华社也已全文发布，我不再赘述，这里强调说明四个方面内容。

一、贯彻党中央重大决策部署，坚定不移推进“多规合一”

新中国成立特别是改革开放以来，各级各类空间规划在支撑城镇化快速发展、促进国土空间合理利用和有效保护方面发挥了积极作用，但也存在规划类型过多、内容重叠冲突，审批流程复杂、周期过长，地方规划朝令夕改等问题。为从体制机制上解决这些问题，按照党中央部署，国家发展改革委、原国土资源部、原环境保护部、住房和城乡建设部联合开展了省级和市县“多规合一”试点工作，积累了宝贵经验。在此基础上，党中央作出组建自然资源部、实现《多规合一》、建立国土空间规划体系并监督实施的重大决策。《若干意见》开篇强调：“建立国土空间规划体系并监督实施，将主体功能区规划、土地利用规划、城乡规划等空间规划融合为统一的国土空间规划，实现“多规合一”，强化国土空间规划对各专项规划的指导约束作用，是党中央、国务院作出的重大部署。”可以说，从空间规划改革试点、决策到顶层设计，都是在党中央坚强领导下进行的。下一步，我们将继续坚持党对规划工作的领导，按照确定目标，坚定不移推进和实施“多规合一”，形成“一本规划、一张蓝图”，建立统一的编制审批体系、实施监督体系、法规政策体系和技术标准体系，构建统一的基础信息平台，形成全国国土空间开发保护“一张图”，落实好《若干意见》各项部署，实现国土空间开发保护更高质量、更有效率、更加公平、更可持续。

二、坚持科学编制，严格实施监督

习近平总书记指出，“规划科学是最大的效益，规划失误是最大的浪费，规划折腾是最大的忌讳”。要提高规划编制科学性。落实新发展理念，坚持以人民为中心，促进高质量发展，在资源环境承载能力和国土空间开发适宜性评价的基础上，科学有序统筹布局生态、农业、城镇空间，划定生态保护红线、永久基本农田、城镇开发边界等管控边界，优化国土空间结构布局，保护生态屏障，开展生态保护和修复，完善基础设施和公共服务设施，延续历史文脉，突出地域特色。要强化规划实施监管权威性。规划一经批复，就具有法律效力，任何部门和个人不得随意修改、违规变更，坚决防止出现换一届党委政府改一次规划的现象。坚持先规划、后实施，严禁违规建设；坚持按法定程序修改规划，严格审批。对国土空间规划编制实施过程中的违规违纪违法行为，要严肃追究责任。

三、坚持“放管服”改革，着力提高行政效率

积极落实党中央、国务院推进政府职能转变、深化“放管服”改革要求。在规划审批中，要减少报国务院审批的城市数量，同时按照“管什么就批什么”原则，精简规划审批内容，重点从目标定位、底线约束、控制性指标、相邻关系等方面进行控制性审查，大幅压缩审批时间，提高行政效率；要结合“多规合一”，推进用地审批和规划许可“多审合一”“多证合一”，切实优化营商环境，体现“多规合一”改革效果。

四、坚持上下联动、多方合作、久久为功，一张蓝图干到底

《若干意见》的发布，标志着国土空间规划体系顶层设计和“四梁八柱”基本形成。建立一个全国统一、责权清晰、科学高效的国土空间规划体系是一项系统性工程，不可能一蹴而就。需要各地区各部门按照党中央、国务院部署，明确目标要求，落实主体责任，上下联动，形成合力，以钉钉子精神久久为功，一张蓝图干到底。

自然资源部将强化统筹协调，切实负起责任，会同有关部门按照国土空间规划体系总体框架，整体谋划布局，不断完善制度设计，抓紧建立国土空间规划体系并监督实施，把每一寸土地规划得清清楚楚、明明白白，形成生产空间集约高效、生活空间宜居适度、生态空间山清水秀，安全和谐、富有竞争力和可持续发展的国土空间格局，把党中央、国务院的重大决策部署落实、落地。

我简单介绍这么多。下面，我和我的同事愿意回答媒体朋友提出的问题。谢谢大家！

胡凯红：谢谢赵部长。下面开始提问，提问之前请通报所代表的新闻机构。

中央广播电视总台央视记者提问：

我的问题是新的国土空间规划与原来的，也就是我们现在现有的主体功能区规划和土地利用规划以及城乡规划等这些空间规划，它们之间有什么区别和新的特点是什么？谢谢。

赵龙：谢谢你的提问。这一次国土空间规划体系是按照国家的总体改革要求进行的，与原有的主体功能区规划、土地利用规划和城乡规划还有其他的空间类规划相比，新的空间规划体系首先是更加注重落实新发展理念，促进高质量发展，更加注重坚持以人民为中心，满足人民对高质量美好生活的愿望，更加致力于提高空间治理体系和治理能力现代化。这是总的指导思想，以及与原有空间规划最主要的区别。具体有几个方面：

第一，新的规划体系有利于实现“多规合一”。大家知道，我刚才也提到，我们过去的空间规划类型很多，同时各个规划之间相互协调不够，交叉重叠比较多。这次党中央、国务院明确将主体功能区规划、土地利用规划和城乡规划等空间规划相融合，今后就是一个名称，叫作国土空间规划。同时形成一个平台，即国土空间基础信息平台，形成全国的国土空间规划“一张图”，

从而实现规划编制更加科学，实施监管更加严格，这是一个新的特点。

第二，这是体现国家意志的约束性规划。这次文件里明确规定，国土空间规划是自上而下编制，同时还规定下级规划要服从上级规划，专项规划和详细规划要落实总体规划。目的是要把党中央、国务院的重大决策部署，把国家安全战略、区域发展战略、主体功能区战略等国家战略，通过约束性指标和管控边界逐级落实到最终的详细规划等实施性规划上，保障国家重大战略落实和落地。因为我们过去的规划有不同的管制方式，比如土地利用总体规划是自上而下组织编制，但是城乡规划可能更加注重的是本地区的发展，是一个缺乏上下联通的管理模式。

第三，这是一个强化规划权威的规划体系。这次《若干意见》非常明确，第一是明确国土空间规划的法定性，提到国土空间规划一经批准，任何单位和个人不得随意修改和违规变更，改变了过去规划调整比较随意、朝令夕改等问题。第二是明确规定要先规划、后实施，各项开发建设活动要符合规划，不能违规进行建设。第三是规划也不是一成不变的，但对规划的调整和修改要有严格的限制。限制大致包括以下几个方面：一是国家新的重大战略变化和调整；二是国家重大建设项目的调整；三是行政区划的调整；四是在定期评估中，如果发现规划与当地的经济社会发展出现了一些不相适应的内容，也可以进行调整。但是这些调整规定了明确的前置条件，就是必须先征得规划原审批机关的同意，才能相应地按程序进行调整。第四明确严格规划的实施监管，要求管控边界和约束性指标要落地。第五是对违反规划的行为进行严格查处。这些规定使规划在权威性方面更加严格，实施监管更加严格。

第四，这是一个用先进技术支撑的规划体系。为什么这么说呢？这次《若干意见》明确提出，要建立全国统一的国土空间规划的基础信息平台，并形成全国国土规划的“一张图”。信息平台建设也有明确的要求，就是要利用最新的自然资源调查数据，应用全国统一的测绘基准和测绘系统，整合各类空间数据，利用先进的信息化手段来构建全国统一的空间基础信息平台。同时结合各地编制的规划，形成全国统一的“一张图”。就保证了下一步在规划实施监管方面更加科学，更加有效，手段也更加先进。

第五，这是落实“放管服”改革的规划体系。刚才跟大家介绍了，这次对规划审批怎么提高行政审批效率提了很多要求。比如说，一是减少报国务院审查总体规划的城市数量，二是按照管什么就批什么的原则，重点实行控制性审查，减少过去审查内容承载过多的问题。同时把县以下的规划审批权力交给省级政府，这样更能提高效率。同时，实现“多规合一”以后，使我们有机会按照“放管服”改革的要求，改进用地审批和其他行政许可，切实改善营商环境，提高行政审批效率，促进营商环境更加优化、更加有利。大概是这几个方面。谢谢。

光明日报记者提问：

赵部长您刚才在发言中提出“四梁八柱”基本形成，我的问题是国土空间规划体系的“四梁八柱”具体是指的哪些内容？谢谢。

赵龙：下面请庄少勤总规划师来回答这个问题。

庄少勤：刚才赵龙副部长介绍了文件发布以后“四梁八柱”已基本形成，我们知道，这次国土空间规划体系的改革是国家系统性、整体性、重构性改革的重要组成部分，国土空间规划“四梁八柱”的构建，也是按照国家空间治理现代化的要求来进行的系统性、整体性、重构性构建。我们可以把它简单归纳为“五级三类四体系”。

具体可以这样分，从规划运行方面来看，我们可以把规划体系分为四个子体系：按照规划流程可以分成规划编制审批体系、规划实施监督体系，从支撑规划运行角度有两个技术性体系，一是法规政策体系，二是技术标准体系。这四个子体系共同构成国土空间规划体系。跟以往的规划体系相比，我认为一方面是着力改善了大家比较关注的规划编制审批的环节，同时特别加强了规划的实施监督。对两个基础体系也是按照新时代的新要求进行了重构。

《若干意见》指出，2020年要基本建立国土空间规划体系。去年自然资源部组建以来，我们就着手来推动这四个子体系重构的前期工作，目前已经形成了一些阶段性成果。随着《若干意见》印发以后，相关的一些成果也会陆续发布。这是从规划运行体系的角度来看。

另一方面，从规划层级和内容类型来看，我们可以把国土空间规划分为"五级三类"。"五级"是从纵向看，对应我国的行政管理体系，分五个层级，就是国家级、省级、市级、县级、乡镇级。当然不同层级规划的侧重点和编制深度是不一样的，其中国家级规划侧重战略性，省级规划侧重协调性，市县级和乡镇级规划侧重实施性。这里需要说明的是，并不是每个地方都要按照五级规划一层一层编，有的地方区域比较小，可以将市县级规划与乡镇规划合并编制，有的乡镇也可以以几个乡镇为单元进行编制。

"三类"是指规划的类型，分为总体规划、详细规划、相关的专项规划。总体规划强调的是规划的综合性，是对一定区域，如行政区全域范围涉及的国土空间保护、开发、利用、修复做全局性的安排。详细规划强调实施性，一般是在市县以下组织编制，是对具体地块用途和开发强度等作出的实施性安排。详细规划是开展国土空间开发保护活动，包括实施国土空间用途管制、核发城乡建设项目规划许可，进行各项建设的法定依据。这次我们特别明确，在城镇开发边界外，将村庄规划作为详细规划，进一步规范了村庄规划。相关的专项规划强调的是专门性，一般是由自然资源部门或者相关部门来组织编制，可在国家级、省级和市县级层面进行编制，特别是对特定的区域或者流域，比如我们正在开展的长江经济带流域，或者城市群、都市圈这种特定区域，或者特定领域，比如说交通、水利等等，为体现特定功能对空间开发保护利用作出的专门性安排。这是三类相关专项规划的类型。

刚才您问到具体内容有哪些？我这里需要再补充强调一下，这次新的国土空间规划体系"四梁八柱"，不是简单换一个名称，比如说我们把它统称为国土空间规划，也不是形式上的拼凑，我认为体现的是生态文明新时代空间供给侧结构性改革的要求。《若干意见》里面特别强调，新的规划要体现战略性，提高科学性，强化权威性，加强协调性，注重操作性，要实现国土空间开发保护更高质量、更有效率、更加公平、更可持续。因此，"多规合一"以后的国土空间规划要在原来的主体功能区规划、土地利用规划、城乡规划等空间规划的基础上，融合它们的优势，既注重宏观也注重微观，既注重自然也注重人文，既有管控也有发展，既注重技术性能也注重政策性，既要研究实体空间也关注经济社会问题，既要强调全国的统一性也考虑到地方因地制宜的差异性。所以新的国土空间规划要按照文件里指出的，要成为能用、好用、管用的规划。所谓"能用"，我理解为要适应新时代要求，适合于国情。所谓"管用"，就是要能够解决空间治理和空间发展的问题。所谓"好用"就是运行成本要低、效率要高，切实提高空间治理体系和治理能力的现代化水平，为实现两个一百年的目标和中华民族永续发展提供支撑，也为全球生态文明建设作出我们应有的贡献。谢谢。

经济日报记者提问：

我的问题是《若干意见》已经对国土空间规划提出了路线图和时间表，应该说这个蓝图我们已经绘出来了，但是如果它真正要落实的话，应该是一个系统的工程，地方政府这一块接下来应该怎么样做好进一步的工作？谢谢。

赵龙：谢谢你的提问。刚才说到了国土空间规划路线图和“四梁八柱”已经确定，现在当务之急是加快建立各项制度，同时着手开展规划的编制工作。从地方政府的角度，《若干意见》也明确规定，要求加强组织领导，要求加快编制进度。在国家的统一部署下，当前地方政府可能要重点做好以下工作：

第一，加强组织领导。《若干意见》要求把每一寸土地规划得清清楚楚，形成有利于空间开发保护的格局。要求落实国土空间开发保护的主体责任，主要负责同志要亲自抓，组建规划的编制专班，明确责任分工，同时提出要加强经费保障，加强宣传，加强实施监管等一系列要求。大家知道，组织上的保障是一个非常重要的保障，这是当前地方党委和政府首先要做的一项工作。

第二，做好前期准备工作。刚才说了，因为我们这个规划是自上而下编制，在编制的过程中，要自上而下、上下结合、压茬推进，现在全国的国土空间规划已经开始着手编制，国家级规划制定的各项指标和管控边界要逐步落实到省和市县一级的规划中。在约束性指标下达之前，各级地方党委政府要做好前期工作，主要有几个方面：第一要做好双评价，我们所说的双评价，一是资源环境承载能力评价，二是国土空间开发适宜性评价。说白了，就是有多少资源干多少事，用资源的约束来实现科学发展，落实新发展理念。第二做好基础性工作，要收集最新规划编制的基础数据，包括调查的数据、相关空间规划的基础数据，还有各地国民经济社会发展规划的一些数据，来作为编制国土空间规划的前提和基础。这些前期工作各地方现在也正在做。第三要坚持“开门编规划”。为了保证规划的科学性，要坚持上下结合、社会协同、公众参与的组织方式。特别是在社会协同和公众参与方面，因为这个规划最后给大家用的，要体现生活空间、生产空间和生态空间的统筹布局，所以发挥公众参与的作用非常重要。同时，我们还提出要发挥不同领域专家的作用。这句话的意思是要专业的人做专业的事，因为国土空间规划不仅仅是一个方面的事情，它涉及自然的、经济的、文化的、历史的等各个方面，所以需要各方面的专家来参与。在各方面专家不同意见的共同指导和相互融合中，形成空间规划布局结构达到最优和最科学。第四现在要抓紧同步建立基础信息平台。刚才讲了基础信息平台要抓紧构建，原来各地可能有一些相关的信息系统，下一步要按照全国统一的标准，按照统一的基础数据的技术规则，包括测绘基准、测绘体系和先进的信息化技术，开始着手搭建基础信息平台，尽快建成，待规划编制完以后，能够马上利用基础信息平台实施监管。第五统筹规划管理的各个环节。这里最重要的还是要树立规划的权威意识。在规划编制、规划实施和规划体系建立过程中，希望各级党委政府一定要树立规划的权威意识，要保证规划一旦批准，就要认真执行。这个权威性要体现在从规划编制到规划管理的各个环节，而不是说最后到实施的时候才要想起这件事。科学规划是一个基础，需要强调的是要心无旁骛，在思想上就要强化规划要贯彻执行的意识，要久久为功，要一张蓝图干到底，而不是说在规划编制过程中总想下一步可能要修改。文件中对规划修改有严格的程序要求，各级地方党委和政府一定要强化这种意识，这样才能保证规划的权威和管用。谢谢。

中国日报记者提问：

我想问一下过去我们在民间有很多关于政府规划的看法，有的人说“规划规划，墙上挂挂”，还有人说“政府一换届，规划也就跟着换届了”。我想问一下我们新的国土空间规划体系怎么样解决规划落地困难和朝令夕改这两个问题。谢谢。

赵龙：谢谢你的提问。你提到的这个问题在过去的一段时间确实存在，因为我也在地方做过副市长，也确实看到，在规划的调整过程中不能说随意，程序上是比较简单的，确实造成你说的经常出现换一届党委政府可能就修改一次规划的现象，甚至也出现过这一届政府提出要往东边发展，下一届政府可能要提出往西边发展，把规划的落实搞得七零八落、支离破碎。

刚才你提到的规划的权威性涉及两个方面的问题，第一是如何保证规划编制的科学性，第二是如何保证规划实施监管的严肃性。因为规划科学是基础，如果这个规划不科学，很难达到实施的权威性。严格监管是保障，只有严格监管才能保证规划的落地。对于规划的科学性，规划本身关注的是空间格局和功能布局，是空间布局和结构的整体优化，是需要统筹谋划的。我们中华文化一直叫谋定而后动，如果不谋定好，可能你造成的失误和损失是无法挽回的。所以习近平总书记强调，规划的科学是最大的效益，规划的失误是最大的浪费。在科学性方面重点要把握几个方面：

一是基础工作要扎实，要做好资源的“双评价”，要用最新的基础数据和最先进的技术手段来编制规划。

二是要体现国家意志，要把党中央、国务院的决策部署，把国家发展战略通过自上而下规划编制层层落实，特别是一些约束性指标的传导和落实。比如生态文明建设，比如新发展理念，国家都有一些重要的管控指标，要把它们通过国家、省、市、县一直落实到详细规划上。同时，中央要求划定好“三条线”，即生态保护红线、永久基本农田保护红线、城镇开发边界。这三条管控边界也要通过规划层级层层落实，体现战略性。

三是要明确生态文明建设的要求。这次规划，刚才庄总规划师也介绍到，一个很大的特点是强调生态优先、绿色发展，强调节约优先、保护优先、自然恢复为主，强化山水林田湖草是一个生命共同体的理念。这里对生态文明建设有很多的要求。举几个具体的例子，比如要实施生态环境的分区管控，要保护好生态屏障，要构建好生态网络和生态廊道，要做好生态保护的修复，等等，这些问题都要在规划的过程中体现出来。

四是要优化用地结构和布局。这个规划，刚才也介绍到还有一个很大的特点，就是要以人民为中心，我们国家现在主要矛盾发生了变化，变成了人民群众对美好生活的向往和不平衡不充分发展之间的矛盾，这种不平衡不充分的矛盾也要在空间规划上得以一定程度的解决。比如如何统筹布局的问题，如何做好基础设施规划的问题，如何满足基本公共服务的问题，如何做好住房、医疗、文化、体育、养老、教育等各方面的用地保障，还有如何把社区构建得更加舒适宜居，有更多的公共开放空间。同时要保证城市的安全，包括公共安全、防灾减灾安全，这些方面都是规划里要充分考虑的。还要传承历史文脉，体现风貌特色和地域特征。

五是开门编规划，特别强调要公众参与，公众参与是一个民主的过程，同时也是落实规划宣传规划的过程，只有在规划编制过程中，把大家的一些疑虑、大家的一些矛盾、大家的一些问题充分协商和解决后，才能使这个规划更加科学、更加有利于实施。

六是发挥专家的作用。专业的人干专业的事。过去遇到过，也听说过，很多的规划调整是由行政来主导的，当然行政主导也没有错，但是一定要有专家意见的充分表达，这样才能保证规划的科学性。

七是一些手段的应用，比如城市设计、乡村营造、大数据等等，这些理念和方法要应用进去。第一是保证规划的科学性，第二是在实施监管方面树立一个理念，就是再好的规划如果你不认真执行，不落实到底，最后也不是一个好规划，或者是一个差规划。为什么这样说？规划实际上就是画出一张蓝图，本来我们想画一个风景优美山水画，最后你今天改一下，明天改一下，今天涂一下，明天涂一下，最后可能就像大家讲的笑话一样，画张飞最后变成画石头，最后没办法只能搞成一个黑色的扇面。所以说规划的实施也是非常重要的。习近平总书记提出，规划折腾是最大的忌讳。如何避免折腾？刚才也介绍了，《若干意见》里已经有了明确规定，第一是强调规划的权威性，规划一经确定就具有法律效力。第二是坚持先规划后实施。第三是对于规划的调整有严格的限制条件和程序要求。第四是上级部门要加强对规划执行的监管。第五是对违法违规行为要严肃查处。这样才能保证规划的权威性。当然科学性也好、权威性也好，制度规定是一个重要的方面，更重要的是大家从落实新发展理念上来重视、来认识，来执行。制度和理念共同结合，才能够切实解决刚才您提到的“规划规划，墙上挂挂”这样的问题，从而实现空间治理体系和治理能力的现代化，保证“一张蓝图绘到底”。谢谢。

中央广播电视总台国广记者提问：

想问一下国土空间规划体系建立有没有具体的时间表？在新规划编制审批完成前，如何与现有的规划做好衔接？谢谢。

赵龙：这个问题请张兵副局长来回答。

张兵：谢谢你的提问。按照您提的问题，我先讲讲目标。在《若干意见》的文件里已经非常明确了我们建立国土空间规划体系并监督实施的时间表，我们有三个重要的时间节点，第一是到2020年基本建立国土空间规划体系，逐步建立起“多规合一”的规划编制审批体系，实施监管体系，法规政策体系和技术标准体系。刚才庄总规划师也讲到了“四梁八柱”的规划体系。2020年底要基本完成市县以上国土空间总体规划的编制，在先进的数字技术和统一的技术标准基础上，逐步形成全国统一的国土空间基础信息平台，建立形成全国国土空间开发保护的“一张图”。第二是到2025年要健全国土空间规划的法规政策和技术标准体系。这是一个非常重要的基础性工作，同时全面实施国土空间的监测预警和绩效考核机制，形成以国土空间规划为基础，以统一的用途管制为手段的国土空间开发保护制度。第三是到2035年，和十九大报告给我们设定2035年大的目标是一致的，要全面提升国土空间治理体系和治理能力现代化水平。基本形成生产空间集约高效、生活空间宜居适度、生态空间山清水秀的国土空间开发保护格局，让我们国土空间开发保护能够达到一个安全和谐、富有竞争力和可持续发展的状态。这是我们在三个时点上的安排。

刚才提到的第二个问题，是关于和现有规划的衔接。这部分工作我从三个方面展开：第一，要加快开展全国的国土空间规划编制工作。这是非常重要的一项工作，这个工作是我们整个国土空间开发保护利用修复的一个总纲，体现的是战略性、系统性的安排，是非常重要的内容。这个规划由自然资源部和相关部门一起来组织编制，最后要由党中央、国务院审定后向全国公布，这就是全国需要共同遵循的“一张图”。目前各省已经在开展省级国土空间规划的编制，在一些特定的区域或流域也已经开展相关规划的编制工作。比如自然资源部正在组织编制长江经济带覆盖11个省市的国土空间规划，同时在市县这个层面，国土空间总体规划也在逐步展开。刚才赵部长也讲到如何让地方政府发挥主体责任，抓紧把这项工作尽快启动，形成规划成果，目的是要明确国土空间开发保护利用在各个空间尺度上的规划依据，让整个开发保护修复的行动有规可依。这是我们要做的第一项工作。

第二，目前，我们还有一部分法定规划在有效期内运行，在新的规划没有完成前的过渡时期内，我们要做的很重要的一项工作，是对现行的城市或者镇的总体规划和土地利用总体规划，在实施中存在矛盾的差异图斑进行协调性、一致性处理，保证营商环境有一个非常顺畅的衔接。但是在做好协调性和一致性处理的过程中，有四个“不得突破”：第一是不得突破我们土地利用总体规划确定的耕地保有量等约束性指标；第二是不得突破已经确定的生态保护红线和永久基本农田控制线；第三是不得突破城市、镇的总体规划所确定的禁止建设区等规划强制性内容；第四是不得突破新的国土空间规划提出的一些新的管理要求。这四个“不得突破”是在协调性和一致性中间的工作底线，是非常重要的。

第三，在规划立法方面的工作。目前，《土地管理法》《城乡规划法》都是有效法律，我们要继续落实好这些法律，同时要加快国土空间规划相关法律法规的建设工作。自然资源部也将牵头抓紧梳理和国土空间规划相关的现行法律法规和部门规章，对“多规合一”改革涉及要突破现行法律法规的有关内容要进行梳理，按程序报批，取得授权以后进行实施，做好过渡期内法律法规的衔接工作。谢谢。

中国新闻社记者提问：

我们了解到之前有不少人反映包括城市总体规划、土地利用总体规划审批过程十分漫长，请问在这次国土空间规划当中，在提高审批效率方面有哪些考虑？谢谢。

赵龙：谢谢。原来的土地利用总体规划、城市规划，重点是这两个规划，确实存在着审批比较慢的问题，甚至出现过规划的审批之日就是规划的期限到期之时，这也对规划的权威性造成了很大的影响。这一次实现“多规合一”，对进行规划审批制度改革、投资审批制度改革都提供了一个很好的条件。文件明确要求，要解决规划审批周期过长的问题，大幅压缩规划的审批时间。主要有几个方面，我们现在也是在研究，马上要制定审批的办法。

第一，减少报国务院审批总体规划的城市数量。过去土地利用总体规划和城市规划报国务院审批的城市，土地利用总体规划是106个，城市总体规划报国务院审批的是108个，这里面是31个省会城市和直辖市，还有5个计划单列市，是36个，剩下的主要是按城市规模来确定的。这个量非常大。所以这一次我们下决心要体现地方对规划的自主权，主要是落实国家的控制性指标和管控边界。我们考虑国务院审批城市重点是计划单列市、省会城市、直辖市这三类，一共是36个城市，其他指定城市要大大减少。我们有一个初步设想的名单，大概在50个以下，起码在审批数量上要减少一半。

第二，改变审查的内容。过去的审查承载了太多的东西，偏重于技术性审查，特别是对于规划内容好不好、合理不合理等都进行审查。这一次《若干意见》里面非常明确，就是叫管什么就批什么，上一级政府审查下一级政府的规划，要明确上一级政府对下一级政府规划有什么要求，从技术性审查转换到控制性审查。重点审查发展目标、约束性指标、管控边界、相邻关系这四个方面，审查内容会大大减少。我们有一个初步的设想，就是把报国务院审批总体规划的审查时间尽量控制在90天之内。

第三，取消了编制大纲或叫规划纲要的审查环节，就是在规划成果正式上报前的一个中间审查环节，减少重复性的审查，取消这个环节也可以压缩时间。

第四，对于市县一级不是报国务院批准的城市审查的内容和程序，由省一级人民政府根据自身的实际情况来确定。把这个权力交给了地方，地方根据自身的实际确定审批的内容和程序，这样也会进一步提高审批的效率。

总体上说，我们希望结合新的规划体系的建立，把规划审查的行政效率大幅度提高。

之前我也做过了介绍，这次“多规合一”为我们优化营商环境，促进投资体制改革提供了一个非常好的机会和条件。大家知道，原来土地的审批是遵循土地利用规划，规划许可的审批主要遵循的是城市规划，这两个规划因为之间不融合，甚至是不协调，各有各的审批体系，各有各的审批内容，但是在实践中我们也发现这两个审批有很多内容相近、相互重复，甚至是相互制约的情况，这次机构改革，第一个是把两个规划整合到一起，形成一个“多规合一”的体系。第二个是职能统一转到自然资源部，一个部门来管理，这样对于我们同类项合并，简化投资审批手续，实行“放管服”，改善营商环境提供了非常好的条件。

自然资源部也已经起草了一个通知，这个通知名字最后还要进一步确定，基本上叫以“多规合一”为基础，推进用地和规划许可的“多审合一”“多证合一”。具体是同一个事项由一个部门来管理，同一个阶段的审查，同一类事项要进行整合。具体地讲，大家对投资审批比较熟悉的可能知道，在项目立项阶段，原来项目立项在用地规划上有两个前置条件，一是用地的预审，二是用地的规划选址意见书。这两个审查内容有很多相近的地方，这次我们决定将两个审查合并，变成一项审查内容，叫一个窗口接件，一个事项办理，最后一个窗口发放。

另外，正式的用地审批阶段，原来规划上有建设用地规划许可证，土地上有建设用地批准书和划拨决定书，同时出让的地还要签订合同，这也是功能非常相近的，我们也准备把这三个事项合并，建设用地规划许可、用地批准书和划拨决定书合并，变成一个事项。同时，对于项目位置相对比较固定，也可以把建设工程规划许可把它适当进行合并，我们也做了一个基本的测算，这样通过这种方式可以大大减少用地和规划的审批时间，为我们的投资领域的工程建设领域的审批制度改革提供一个很好的样板。这也是党中央进行空间规划体制的改革，实行“多规合一”的一个非常重要的内容。

需要说明的是，因为这两项改革都涉及现有的法律的修改，在法律修改之前，我们采用一些技术性的方法，我刚才说的一个窗口受理，同时审查，最后一个窗口发放。下一步，随着空间规划的法规政策体系的完善，我们要对现有的法规体系进行重新构建，对现有的规划进行修改。我预测或者是我们觉得将来在投资特别是用地和规划的审批上面，最终要走向规划许可的路子上去，大幅减少用地规划的审批事项，当然这是要结合我们的法律修改和结合规划的科学性得到进一步增强以后，下一步继续往前推进，这一步在不久的将来也会实现。谢谢。

胡凯红：今天的发布会到此结束。谢谢三位发布人，谢谢各位。

发布时间：2019年5月27日　来源：国新网

四、专栏三：《中共中央国　务院关于建立国土空间规划体系并监督实施的若干意见》解读

上篇：构建“多规合一”的国土空间规划体系

《中共中央　国务院关于建立国土空间规划体系并监督实施的若干意见》（以下简称《若干意见》）正式印发，标志着国土空间规划体系构建工作正式全面展开。建立国土空间规划体系并监督实施，将主体功能区规划、土地利用规划、城乡规划等空间规划融合为统一的国土空间规划，实现“多规合一”，强化国土空间规划对各专项规划的指导约束作用，是党中央、国务院作出的重大决策部署。

新时代，新规划。在时间与空间标注的方位中，国土空间规划体系将如何布局？如何落子？记者就此采访了自然资源部国土空间规划局有关负责人。

一、破解规划“打架”，实现“多规合一”

问：长期以来，“规划打架”“马拉松式审批”“政府一换届、规划就换届”等问题制约着我国空间利用质量和效率，新的国土空间规划体系的建立是基于怎样的考量，建立的背景又是什么？

答：新中国成立以来，各级各类空间规划在支撑城镇化快速发展、促进国土空间合理利用和有效保护方面发挥了积极作用，但也存在一些突出问题：一是规划类型过多、内容重叠冲突，“规划打架”容易导致空间资源配置无序、低效，也割裂了“山水林田湖草”生命共同体的有机联系，不利于科学布局生产、生活、生态空间。二是审批流程复杂周期过长，“马拉松式审批”时有发生。三是地方规划朝令夕改，甚至“政府一换届、规划就换届”，规划权威性、稳定性不够。

习近平总书记高度重视国土空间规划工作，多次提出明确和具体的要求。2013 年 5 月习近平总书记在十八届中央政治局第六次集体学习时指出，“国土是生态文明建设的空间载体。从大的方面统筹谋划、搞好顶层设计，首先要把国土空间开发格局设计好。要按照人口资源环境相均衡、经济社会生态效益相统一的原则，整体谋划国土空间开发”。2014 年 2 月习近平总书记在北京考察时强调，“考察一个城市首先看规划，规划科学是最大的效益，规划失误是最大的浪费，规划折腾是最大的忌讳”。2018 年 4 月习近平总书记在深入推动长江经济带发展座谈会上指出，“要按照‘多规合一’的要求，在开展资源环境承载能力和国土空间开发适宜性评价的基础上，抓紧完成长江经济带生态保护红线、永久基本农田、城镇开发边界三条控制线划定工作，科学谋划国土空间开发保护格局，建立健全国土空间管控机制，以空间规划统领水资源利用、水污染防治、岸线使用、航运发展等方面空间利用任务，促进经济社会发展格局、城镇空间布局、产业结构调整与资源环境承载能力相适应”。今年 3 月全国人民代表大会期间，习近平总书记再次强调，“要坚持底线思维，以国土空间规划为依据，把城镇、农业、生态空间和生态保护红线、永久基本农田保护红线、城镇开发边界作为调整经济结构、规划产业发展、推进城镇化不可逾越的红

线，立足本地资源禀赋特点、体现本地优势和特色”。

国土空间规划在国土空间治理和可持续发展中起着基础性、战略性的引领作用。党的十八大以来，在生态文明建设新时代的新理念新要求下，党中央和国务院对空间规划提出了一系列改革要求。党的十九届三中全会以来，中央加快了生态文明体制改革的步伐，深入推进了党和国家机构改革，从体制上对过去存在的各类规划“打架”的问题提出了解决方案。《中共中央关于深化党和国家机构改革的决定》要求“强化国土空间规划对各专项规划的指导约束作用，推进‘多规合一’，实现土地利用规划、城乡规划等有机融合”；《深化党和国家机构改革方案》明确了组建自然资源部，并提出了建立国土空间规划体系并监督实施的任务。

自然资源部从去年3月成立以来，将建立国土空间规划体系并监督实施作为战略性、基础性和综合性工作来抓。组建了专项工作组，开展了深入调查研究，系统总结和继承发展了原土地利用规划和城乡规划等空间规划体系，借鉴了国外空间规划经验，总结了相关部委和地方的空间规划试点经验，提出了《关于建立国土空间规划体系并监督实施初步方案》，并代拟形成了《若干意见》。今年1月23日，中央全面深化改革委员会第六次会议审议通过了《若干意见》；5月9日，中共中央、国务院正式印发了《若干意见》。

二、引领绿色发展和高质量发展，能用、管用、好用

问：作为新时代的新规划，新的国土空间规划体系与之前相比，有哪些突出的特点？

答：新的国土空间规划体系是“多规合一”的规划体系，有利于解决原有空间规划存在的冲突问题。新的国土空间规划体系对主体功能区规划、土地利用规划、城乡规划等空间规划进行了优势互补和继承发展，从规划编审内容、管理机构、体制机制、技术规范、人员队伍等各方面在原有基础上进行了整合和优化，强调“一级政府一级事权”，强调总体规划和详细规划、专项规划之间的指导约束和衔接协调，强调部门之间形成合力，着力解决过去规划“打架”、约束和引领作用不突出、行政效能不高等问题。

新的国土空间规划体系是体现国家意志的规划体系，保障国家发展战略有效实施。国土空间规划自上而下编制，对空间发展作出战略性系统性安排，全面落实党中央、国务院重大决策部署，落实国家乡村振兴、区域协调发展、可持续发展等战略。作为国家规划体系中的基础性规划，国土空间规划从空间角度对社会经济发展、城镇空间布局、产业结构调整等进行指导和约束，从而促进转变发展方式，提升国土空间开发保护质量和效率，为实现“两个一百年”奋斗目标提供空间保障。

新的国土空间规划体系是促进生态文明建设的规划体系，体现了生态优先、绿色发展的导向。新的国土空间规划体系以促进绿色发展、安全发展、可持续发展为目标；坚持保护优先、节约集约，严控增量、盘活存量，加快形成绿色生产方式和生活方式；强化底线约束，划定生态保护红线、永久基本农田、城镇开发边界等空间管控边界以及各类海域保护线；注重风险防范，积极应对未来发展不确定性，提高规划韧性。

新的国土空间规划体系是引领高质量发展的规划体系，体现了以人民为中心的发展思想。针对我国社会主要矛盾，从空间开发保护方面提出解决方案，满足人民群众对美好生活的向往。优化生态保护格局、历史文化保护格局、城乡开发利用格局等，合理配置住房、就业、休闲、游憩等空间功能布局，推动形成生产空间集约高效、生活空间宜居适度、生态空间山清水秀的空间格

局；着力完善交通基础设施和公共服务设施，促进基本公共服务均等化，打造宜居、宜业、宜游、宜学、宜养的社区生活圈，实现高品质生活、建设美好家园。

新的国土空间规划体系是国家治理体系现代化的重要组成部分，注重能用管用好用。能用，是指要适应我国国情和新时代发展要求；管用，是指能够有效解决问题，强调因地制宜，适用各地具体情况；好用，是指新的体系要能够有效运行，降低成本，方便实操。具体地，将按照明晰事权、权责对等原则，结合“放管服”改革要求，理顺各层级政府及其自然资源主管部门职责划分，明确各级各类国土空间规划编制和管理的要点；规划编制要充分考虑地方特色，实事求是，避免工业化思维下编制“标准化”但不好用的规划；编制规划的同时，要搭建国土空间基础信息平台，逐步实现全国国土空间规划“一张图”，推进数据共享和信息交互；同时，统筹规划、建设、管理三大环节，优化行政审批许可管理流程，提高空间治理体系和能力的现代化水平。

三、四大体系构建国土空间规划蓝图

问：作为一整套运行系统，国土空间规划体系的架构是怎样的，包括哪些组成部分？

答：建立“多规合一”的国土空间规划体系是系统性、整体性、重构性的改革，是一整套运行体系制度设计，而不只是规划成果本身。新的国土空间规划体系包括运行体系四个子体系，即规划编制审批体系、实施监督体系、法规政策体系、技术标准体系。其中，规划编制审批体系和实施监督体系包括从编制、审批、实施、监测、评估、预警、考核、完善等完整闭环的规划及实施管理流程；法规政策体系和技术标准体系是两个基础支撑。

具体而言，规划编制审批体系即各级各类国土空间规划编制和审批以及规划之间的协调配合。融合了主体功能区规划、土地利用规划、城乡规划等空间规划的新的国土空间规划，包括“五级三类”：五级规划体现一级政府一级事权，全域全要素规划管控，强调各级侧重点不同；三类包括总体规划、相关专项规划和详细规划，总体规划是战略性总纲，相关专项规划是对特定区域或特定领域空间开发保护的安排，详细规划作出具体细化的实施性规定，是规划许可的依据。

实施监督体系即国土空间规划的实施和监督管理。包括以国土空间规划为依据，对所有国土空间实施用途管制；依据详细规划实施城乡建设项目相关规划许可；建立规划动态监测、评估、预警以及维护更新等机制；优化现行审批流程，提高审批效能和监管服务水平；制定城镇开发边界内外差异化的管制措施；建立国土空间规划“一张图”实施监督信息系统，并利用大数据、智慧化等技术手段加强规划实施监督等。

法规政策体系是对国土空间规划体系的法规政策支撑。一方面，要在充分梳理研究已有相关法律法规的基础上，加快国土空间规划立法，做好过渡时期的法律衔接；另一方面，国土空间规划的编制和实施需要全社会的共同参与和各部门的协同配合，需要有关部门配合建立健全人口、资源、生态环境、财政、金融等配套政策，保障规划有效实施。

技术标准体系是对国土空间规划体系的技术支撑。“多规合一”对原有城乡规划和土地利用规划的技术标准体系提出了重构性改革要求，要按照生态文明建设的要求，改变原来以服务开发建设为主的工程思维方式，注重生态优先绿色发展，强调生产、生活、生态空间有机融合。按照本次改革要求，自然资源部将牵头建构统一的国土空间技术标准体系，并加快制定各类各级国土空间规划编制技术规程。

四、“五级三类”编制实施国土空间规划

问：国土空间规划包括哪些层次、类型，彼此之间的相互关系是什么？

答：国土空间规划的编制审批和监督实施要分级分类进行，即包括“五级三类”。五级指与我国行政管理层级相对应的国家、省、市、县、乡镇，不同层级的规划体现不同空间尺度和管理深度要求。其中，国家和省级规划侧重战略性，对全国和省域国土空间格局作出全局安排，提出对下层级规划约束性要求和引导性内容；市县级规划承上启下，侧重传导性；乡镇级规划侧重实施性，实现各类管控要素精准落地。五级规划自上而下编制，落实国家战略，体现国家意志，下层级规划要符合上层级规划要求，不得违反上层级规划确定的约束性内容。

三类指总体规划、详细规划和相关专项规划。在国家、省、市、县编制国土空间总体规划，各地结合实际编制乡镇国土空间规划。各层级的国土空间总体规划是对行政辖区范围内国土空间保护、开发、利用、修复的全局性安排，强调综合性。

相关专项规划可在国家、省、市、县层级编制，强调专业性，是对特定区域（流域）、特定领域空间保护利用的安排。其中，海岸带、自然保护地等专项规划及跨行政区域或流域的国土空间规划（如长江经济带国土空间规划等），由所在区域或上一级自然资源主管部门牵头组织编制；以空间利用为主的某一领域的专项规划，由相关部门组织编制。

详细规划在市县及以下编制，强调可操作性，是对具体地块用途和强度等作出的实施性安排，是开展国土空间开发保护活动、实施国土空间用途管制、核发城乡建设项目规划许可、进行各项建设等的法定依据。城镇开发边界内的详细规划由市县自然资源主管部门编制，报同级政府审批；城镇开发边界外的乡村地区，由乡镇人民政府编制村庄规划作为详细规划，报上一级政府审批。

总体规划与详细规划、相关专项规划之间体现“总—分关系”。国土空间总体规划是详细规划的依据、相关专项规划的基础；详细规划要依据批准的国土空间总体规划进行编制和修改；相关专项规划要遵循国土空间总体规划，不得违背总体规划强制性内容，其主要内容要纳入详细规划。

需要说明的是，并不是所有地方都要求编制“五级三类”的国土空间规划。例如，各地可以因地制宜，将市县域乡镇国土空间规划合并编制，也可以几个乡镇为单元编制乡镇级国土空间规划；村庄规划编制也应该按照“应编尽编”的原则编制“多规合一”的实用性村庄规划。

下篇：将国土空间规划一张蓝图绘到底

《中共中央　国务院关于建立国土空间规划体系并监督实施的若干意见》（简称《若干意见》）明确了构建什么样的国土空间规划体系，但如何让统领全局的国土空间规划落实为全国一盘棋的行动，将规划蓝图转化为全方位治理的实践，考验着执政水平，更锤炼着治理能力。

一分部署，九分落实。本轮国土空间规划编制工作有哪些新要求？如何处理与原有规划的关系？规划编制的时间表和路线图又是什么？近日，自然资源部空间规划局相关负责人对此进行了解读。

五、强化国土空间规划的战略引领地位

问：本轮国土空间规划编制工作有哪些新要求？

答：首先，要贯彻生态文明思想和新发展理念，突出体现国土空间规划的战略性、科学性、协调性、操作性、权威性。要体现国土空间规划在空间开发保护方面的战略引领地位，各级国土空间总体规划编制要按照生态文明建设和中华民族永续发展的要求，对空间开发保护作出战略性系统性长远安排，强调底线约束，探索以生态优先、绿色发展为导向的高质量发展新路子。要采用科学的理念、方法、工作方式编制和实施规划，运用城市设计、乡村营造、大数据等手段，提高规划编制水平。要协调好国土空间规划和相关规划的关系。一方面，国土空间规划要结合主体功能定位，为国家发展规划确定的重大战略任务落地实施提供空间保障；另一方面，要坚持底线思维，充分发挥国土空间规划在国家规划体系中的基础作用，发挥好对各专项规划的指导约束作用，促进经济社会发展格局、城镇空间布局、产业结构调整与资源环境承载力相适应，约束不合理的发展诉求。要注重操作性，在规划编制的过程中要考虑规划如何实施，综合运用各种政策工具，保障规划实施。要强化规划权威，规划一经批复，不得随意修改、违规变更，对规划编制和实施中的违规行为，要严肃追责。

其次，统一规划数据基础和规划期限，谋划全域全要素、陆海统筹、区域协调发展的国土空间开发保护格局。基础数据要以三调数据作为规划现状底数和底图基础，统筹考虑全国水资源、森林资源、草原资源、湿地资源、矿产资源等调查监测评价成果。规划成果数据库按照统一的国土空间规划数据库标准与规划编制工作同步建设。实现城乡国土空间规划管理全域覆盖、全要素管控。

将各类相关专项规划叠加到统一的国土空间基础信息平台上，形成全域“一张图”。做好陆海统筹，编制陆海统筹规划的“一张图”，确定陆海统一分区，明确管制要求，做好海域、海岛和海岸带保护利用，推进陆海空间整体优化。实施好区域协调发展战略，优化生产力的空间布局，促进协调发展、开放发展。

第三，夯实基础研究，在全面摸清家底、深入分析评价的基础上开展规划编制工作。开展原有空间规划实施评估，对国土空间开发保护现状和未来风险点的评估，以及自然资源承载能力和国土空间开发适宜性评价，在评估评价的基础上制定国土空间规划。根据中央要求，要在科学评估既有生态保护红线等重要控制线划定情况基础上，结合国土空间规划编制提出优化调整意见，在2020年前完成“三线”划定工作。划定城镇开发边界要尽可能避让永久基本农田红线和生态保护红线，科学优化城镇布局形态和功能结构，提升城镇人居环境品质，促进城镇发展由外延扩张向内涵提升转变。

再次，坚持问题导向和目标导向相结合，因地制宜编制规划。国土空间规划的编制必须做到立足实际、实事求是、因地制宜、分类指导。根据当地自然条件、人文特色、发展阶段等特点，找准实际问题，有针对性地开展规划编制。比如，大城市、特大城市、超大城市要提出都市圈、城镇圈以及跨行政区域规划协调要求；沿海市县要统筹陆海分区做好海域、海岛和海岸带保护利用；地级市要加强对所辖县（市、区）的统筹，合理分配建设用地规模指标，统筹安排市域交通基础设施网络，均衡配置各类空间资源；自然保护地、海岸带、生态敏感脆弱区等特殊区域，要在规划中明确特殊保护要求和实施措施；村庄规划要结合县和乡级国土空间规划编制，优化村庄布局，通盘考虑土地利用、产业发展、居民点布局、人居环境整治、生态保护和历史文化传承等，按照“应编尽编”的原则编制“多规合一”的实用性规划。

最后，同步搭建信息系统。以国土空间基础信息平台为基础，同步搭建国土空间规划“一张图”实施监督信息平台，统筹建设国家、省、市、县各级系统，实现上下贯通，做到自上而下一个标准、一个体系、一个接口，形成国土空间规划“一张图”。

六、“管什么就批什么”，大幅缩减审批时间

问：国土空间规划的审批制度和原来相比有哪些不同？

答：国土空间规划体系构建中将更加注重处理好政府和市场的关系，中央政府和地方政府的关系，以及国土空间总体规划和详细规划、相关专项规划的关系。与原来的城市总体规划、土地利用总体规划审批制度相比，主要有以下五方面不同：

一是减少国务院审批的城市数量，提高行政效能。原来的城市总体规划和土地利用总体规划由国务院审批的城市数量分别有108个和106个，国土空间规划体系改革后，由国务院审批国土空间总体规划的城市数量将减少到一半左右。

二是精简规划审批内容，压缩审查时间。按照“管什么就批什么”的原则，对省级和市县国土空间规划从目标定位、空间格局、底线约束、要素配置、实施传导机制、技术标准、信息平台等方面进行实质性审查，从程序及成果的合法合规性等方面进行程序性审查。简化报批流程，取消大纲编制报批环节，严格控制征求部门意见时间，自审批机关交办之日起，在限定时间内完成审查工作，提出审查意见，上报国务院审批。

三是简政放权，对地方的国土空间规划审批留了弹性空间。一方面，事权下沉，对于国务院审批以外城市和县、乡镇国土空间规划，由省级人民政府根据当地实际明确编制审批内容和程序要求；另一方面，考虑到我国各地差异大，对乡镇国土空间规划编制审批作了灵活规定，各地可以因地制宜，将市县与乡镇国土空间规划合并编制，也可以几个乡镇为单元编制乡镇级国土空间规划。

四是强调了省级和国务院审批城市的国土空间规划报批前需经同级人大常委会审议的要求。原来的城市总体规划有这个要求，但土地利用总体规划没有要求。国土空间规划体系构建中，为了更好发挥人大参与监督、规划编制和实施的作用，继续保留和强化人大常委会审议这一环节。

五是增加了相关专项规划与国土空间规划的衔接及“一张图”核对的要求。为避免规划打架的老问题，切实发挥国土空间规划对各专项规划的指导约束作用，要求相关专项规划在编制和审查过程中应加强与有关国土空间规划的衔接及“一张图”的核对，批复后纳入同级国土空间规划“一张图”实施监督信息系统上。国土空间规划成果及有关数据与专项规划编制部门共享。

七、将原有规划融合为统一的国土空间规划

问：此前，我国已有主体功能区规划、土地利用规划、城乡规划、海洋功能区划等，国土空间规划体系构建中，与原有城乡规划、土地利用规划的关系如何处理？

答：按照“多规合一”要求，各地不再新编和报批主体功能区规划、土地利用总体规划、城市（镇）总体规划、海洋功能区划等，今后行政工作中，上述规划统称为“国土空间规划”。

在总体层面，国土空间总体规划将作为行政辖区内国土空间保护、开发、利用、修复的政策和总纲。针对存在差异的现行城市（镇）总体规划、市（县）土地利用总体规划，在不突破土地利用总体规划确定的2020年建设用地和耕地保有量等指标、不突破生态保护红线和永久基本农田保护红线的前提下，以国土空间基础信息平台为基础，按照规划“一张图”要求，对存在矛盾的

差异图斑进行协调性、一致性处理，作为国土空间用途管制的基础。已开展规划编制工作和原“多规合一”试点工作的地方，要按照新的规划编制要求，将既有规划成果融入同级国土空间总体规划中。在详细规划层面，城镇开发边界内，以原有法定的详细规划为基础，丰富完善有关内容，用于指导和约束各项建设活动，作为核发建设项目相关规划许可的依据；在城镇开发边界外，整合原有法定的村庄规划，以及村级土地利用规划、整治规划、保护规划等，形成村域层面“多规合一”的实用性村庄规划，作为详细规划。在海域海岛，可以根据具体情况编制海域海岛规划作为详细规划。

八、2020年基本建立国土空间规划体系

问：国土空间规划体系的时间表是什么，下一步将围绕哪些重点开展工作？

答：按照《若干意见》，到2020年国土空间规划体系将基本建立，并初步形成全国国土空间开发保护“一张图”。到2025年，将进一步健全国土空间规划法规政策和技术标准体系，全面实施监测预警和绩效考核；到2035年，将全面提升国土空间治理体系和治理能力现代化水平。

2019年是国土空间规划体系建设的关键年度，今年我们将围绕落实《若干意见》，加快推进国土空间规划体系建设，力争到今年年底，国土空间规划体系的四个体系建设能初见成效，取得阶段性成果。

一是积极推动国土空间规划立法。十三届全国人大常委会已将国土空间规划有关法律的制定工作列入了立法规划，我们将加快推进立法工作。《中华人民共和国土地管理法》修正案（草案）已经于1月4日在中国人大网上全文公布，其中将落实国土空间开发保护要求作为土地利用总体规划的编制原则，规定经依法批准的国土空间规划是各类开发活动的基本依据，已经编制国土空间规划的，不再编制土地利用总体规划和城市总体规划（第四条）。同时，自然资源部将梳理与国土空间规划相关的现行法律法规和部门规章，对“多规合一”改革涉及突破现行法律法规规定的内容和条款，按程序报批，取得授权后施行，并做好过渡时期的法律法规衔接。

二是全面推进各级国土空间规划编制。按《若干意见》要求，自然资源部将抓紧启动全国、省级、市县和乡镇国土空间规划编制工作（规划期至2035年，展望期至2050年）；今年将编制完成《长江经济带国土空间规划》，按程序呈报国务院审定；同时，研究提出国土空间规划标准体系框架，发布规划编制相关标准和技术规程，并研究制定规划审查机制。

三是在规划编制过程中落实主体功能区战略和制度、统筹三线划定。将完成全国、长江经济带“双评价”，部署省以下“双评价”工作，健全资源环境承载能力监测预警长效机制，研究提出新时期主体功能区战略布局方案，深化主体功能区配套政策研究；指导地方结合国土空间规划编制，统筹协调生态保护红线、永久基本农田、城镇开发边界，实事求是、因地制宜地处理好有关矛盾，切实发挥空间管控边界的底线约束作用。

四是扎实推进国土空间规划监督实施。将在全国范围内部署国土空间规划监测评估预警管理系统建设工作，年底前实现市县、省级与国家级系统的初步对接；同时，建立国土空间规划监测评估预警指标体系，并应用在国土空间规划监测、评估、预警工作中。

五是加强行业队伍建设。一方面，积极广泛开展培训工作，分批次举办面向市县镇村国土空间规划主管部门领导和业务人员、参与国土空间规划编制实施监督的有关技术人员等的培训班和培训会，做好任务部署和《若干意见》及相关文件解读，明确工作重点，提升国土空间规划编制、审查、实施、监督等业务能力。另一方面，完善行业有关资质、资格管理制度，会有关部门加强国土空间规划相关学科建设，积极整合行业、学界，以及社会各界的优势资源，汇聚各领域人才，形成更有创造力、凝聚力、影响力的规划“生态”。

来源：中国自然资源报 作者：焦思颖 时间：2019 年 5 月 29—30 日

五、专栏四：自然资源部关于全面开展国土空间规划工作的通知

各省、自治区、直辖市自然资源主管部门，新疆生产建设兵团自然资源主管部门：

为贯彻落实《中共中央 国务院关于建立国土空间规划体系并监督实施的若干意见》（以下简称《若干意见》），全面启动国土空间规划编制审批和实施管理工作，现将有关事项通知如下：

一、全面启动国土空间规划编制，实现“多规合一”

各级自然资源主管部门要将思想和行动统一到党中央的决策部署上来，按照《若干意见》要求，主动履职尽责，建立“多规合一”的国土空间规划体系并监督实施。按照自上而下、上下联动、压茬推进的原则，抓紧启动编制全国、省级、市县和乡镇国土空间规划（规划期至 2035 年，展望至 2050 年），尽快形成规划成果。部将印发国土空间规划编制规程、相关技术标准，明确规划编制的工作要求、主要内容和完成时限。

各地不再新编和报批主体功能区规划、土地利用总体规划、城镇体系规划、城市（镇）总体规划、海洋功能区划等。已批准的规划期至 2020 年后的省级国土规划、城镇体系规划、主体功能区规划，城市（镇）总体规划，以及原省级空间规划试点和市县“多规合一”试点等，要按照新的规划编制要求，将既有规划成果融入新编制的同级国土空间规划中。

二、做好过渡期内现有空间规划的衔接协同

对现行土地利用总体规划、城市（镇）总体规划实施中存在矛盾的图斑，要结合国土空间基础信息平台的建设，按照国土空间规划“一张图”要求，作一致性处理，作为国土空间用途管制的基础。一致性处理不得突破土地利用总体规划确定的 2020 年建设用地和耕地保有量等约束性指标，不得突破生态保护红线和永久基本农田保护红线，不得突破土地利用总体规划和城市（镇）总体规划确定的禁止建设区和强制性内容，不得与新的国土空间规划管理要求矛盾冲突。今后工作中，主体功能区规划、土地利用总体规划、城乡规划、海洋功能区划等统称为“国土空间规划”。

三、明确国土空间规划报批审查的要点

按照“管什么就批什么”的原则，对省级和市县国土空间规划，侧重控制性审查，重点审查目标定位、底线约束、控制性指标、相邻关系等，并对规划程序和报批成果形式做合规性审查。其中：

省级国土空间规划审查要点包括：①国土空间开发保护目标；②国土空间开发强度、建设用地规模，生态保护红线控制面积、自然岸线保有率，耕地保有量及永久基本农田保护面积，用水总量和强度控制等指标的分解下达；③主体功能区划分，城镇开发边界、生态保护红线、永久基本农田的协调落实情况；④城镇体系布局，城市群、都市圈等区域协调重点地区的空间结构；⑤生态屏障、生态廊道和生态系统保护格局，重大基础设施网络布局，城乡公共服务设施配置要求；⑥体现地方特色的自然保护地体系和历史文化保护体系；⑦乡村空间布局，促进乡村振兴的

原则和要求；⑧保障规划实施的政策措施；⑨对市县级规划的指导和约束要求等。

国务院审批的市级国土空间总体规划审查要点，除对省级国土空间规划审查要点的深化细化外，还包括：①市域国土空间规划分区和用途管制规则；②重大交通枢纽、重要线性工程网络、城市安全与综合防灾体系、地下空间、邻避设施等设施布局，城镇政策性住房和教育、卫生、养老、文化体育等城乡公共服务设施布局原则和标准；③城镇开发边界内，城市结构性绿地、水体等开敞空间的控制范围和均衡分布要求，各类历史文化遗存的保护范围和要求，通风廊道的格局和控制要求；城镇开发强度分区及容积率、密度等控制指标，高度、风貌等空间形态控制要求；④中心城区城市功能布局和用地结构等。

其他市、县、乡镇级国土空间规划的审查要点，由各省（自治区、直辖市）根据本地实际，参照上述审查要点制定。

四、改进规划报批审查方式

简化报批流程，取消规划大纲报批环节。压缩审查时间，省级国土空间规划和国务院审批的市级国土空间总体规划，自审批机关交办之日起，一般应在90天内完成审查工作，上报国务院审批。各省（自治区、直辖市）也要简化审批流程和时限。

五、做好近期相关工作

做好规划编制基础工作。本次规划编制统一采用第三次全国国土调查数据作为规划现状底数和底图基础，统一采用2000国家大地坐标系和1985国家高程基准作为空间定位基础，各地要按此要求尽快形成现状底数和底图基础。

开展双评价工作。各地要尽快完成资源环境承载能力和国土空间开发适宜性评价工作，在此基础上，确定生态、农业、城镇等不同开发保护利用方式的适宜程度。

开展重大问题研究。要在对国土空间开发保护现状评估和未来风险评估的基础上，专题分析对本地区未来可持续发展具有重大影响的问题，积极开展国土空间规划前期研究。

科学评估三条控制线。结合主体功能区划分，科学评估既有生态保护红线、永久基本农田、城镇开发边界等重要控制线划定情况，进行必要调整完善，并纳入规划成果。

各地要加强与正在编制的国民经济和社会发展五年规划的衔接，落实经济、社会、产业等发展目标和指标，为国家发展规划落地实施提供空间保障，促进经济社会发展格局、城镇空间布局、产业结构调整与资源环境承载能力相适应。

集中力量编制好“多规合一”的实用性村庄规划。结合县和乡镇级国土空间规划编制，通盘考虑农村土地利用、产业发展、居民点布局、人居环境整治、生态保护和历史文化传承等，落实乡村振兴战略，优化村庄布局，编制“多规合一”的实用性村庄规划，有条件、有需求的村庄应编尽编。

同步构建国土空间规划“一张图”实施监督信息系统。基于国土空间基础信息平台，整合各类空间关联数据，着手搭建从国家到市县级的国土空间规划“一张图”实施监督信息系统，形成覆盖全国、动态更新、权威统一的国土空间规划“一张图”。

各级自然资源部门要按照《若干意见》和本通知精神，结合本地区实际制定落实方案，把建立国土空间规划体系并监督实施作为当前工作的重中之重，抓紧、抓实、抓好。

自然资源部

2019年5月28日

六、专栏五：专家视点（选登）

2019年5月，《中共中央　国务院关于建立国土空间规划体系并监督实施的若干意见》（以下简称《若干意见》）发表，受到各界关注。我们节略选编了几篇已在相关媒体/网络上刊出的文章观点，以飨读者。

1. 重视国土空间规划战略思路的科学性完整性

（陈为邦，中国城市科学研究会原副理事长，教授级高级规划师）

这次中央提出的“开发保护”大战略思路，是对于国土空间规划体系建设总体战略思路和基本政策的一种调整和完善。空间规划体系的提出是由于国家生态文明制度建设的需要，它也正成为国家生态文明制度的一部分。国家强调生态文明建设，是对于长期出现的自然资源浪费、生态环境破坏问题的战略性大政策，是关系国家可持续发展的大事，是关系子孙后代的千秋大业，全党全国必须非常重视。强调国土空间规划对于自然资源的保护和生态环境的保护，是非常必要，完全正确的。

开发建设与保护约束是国土空间规划的两大根本要素，如果没有开发建设，国家和城市就不能发展；如果没有保护约束，国家和城市发展就不可持续。权衡处理开发建设与保护约束的关系，就成为国土空间规划的根本战略和基本任务。因此，在大战略和大政策中，在国土空间规划体系建设过程中，在规划编制以及实施过程中，甚至在管理机构改革中，两者必须兼顾，综合平衡，缺一不可。

一个时期以来，对于国土空间规划肩负的“开发建设”任务出现了某种忽视，并开始体现到规划思想和规划制定工作中。在一些城市，在新规划编制的过程中，城市方面对于开发建设和发展的强烈需求和新规划对于保护约束的一再强调的矛盾已经不同程度显现出来。在机构改革中，对于城市规划管理力量与土地管理力量的安排权衡过程中，也发生了某些倾向，等等。中央《若干意见》大战略思想的提出，对于发现和克服某些偏向，应当说，还是比较及时的。规划的权威性来自科学性。我们需要权威性，但首先更需要科学性。对于城市规划，对于土地利用规划，对于新的国土空间规划都是相同的。难道不是吗？

2. 深刻理解、抓住机遇、主动参与

（吕斌，中国城市规划学会副理事长，北京大学城市与环境学院教授）

“建立空间规划体系推进规划体制改革，加快规划立法工作”是习近平总书记在2013年12月召开的中央城镇化工作会议上首次提出的，我国空间规划管理体制的改革顺应了生态文明时代的价值导向和发展理念，体现了一个负责任大国的使命与担当。国土空间规划是国土空间用途管制和综合治理的顶层设计，是经济、社会、文化和生态政策与措施的空间表达，其核心是保障和促进空间资源的合理、效率、公平的可持续利用。国土空间规划是多尺度、多维度的，《若干意见》要求分级分类建立国土空间规划，明确各级国土空间总体规划编制重点，强化对专项规划的指导约束作用，在市县及以下编制详细规划。关于健全用途管制制度，《若干意见》指出，要依据国土空间规划，对所有国土空间分区分类实施用途管制，不仅在城镇开发边界内的建设要实行

“规划＋许可”的管制方式，就是在城镇开发边界外的建设也要按照用途分区，实行“详细规划＋规划许可”和“约束指标＋分区准入”的管制方式，充分体现了对所有国土空间实行统一用途管控的原则，这也正是我本人多年来一直期待的空间用途管制模式。

《若干意见》彰显了国土空间用途管制目标导向和价值理念，即实现以人民为中心的社会经济高质量发展为目标的绿色发展理念，也给出了构建符合中国国情的国土空间规划体系的清晰路线图，这无疑对我们从事城乡规划教育和实践的规划师而言是一次难得的参与机会。

3. 以国土空间规划体系助力生态文明之路

（杨保军，中国城市规划学会常务理事，中国城市规划设计研究院院长；董珂，中国城市规划设计研究院绿色城市研究所所长）

我国的城镇化已进入快速发展的中后期，但区域差距、城乡差距并未明显缩小，部分领域甚至逐步扩大。经济增速和结构发生深刻变化，经济质量、效率、动力亟待变革；以“工业园区、房地产”为代表的空间产品跟不上人民日益增长的美好生活需要，呈现普遍性的空间供给“过剩”和资本循环“断路”，而在“良好生态环境”这种最普惠民生福祉上，空间供给能力却是逐渐下降的。

综合发展的“目标”是由国土空间规划的基本属性决定的。与以往各类空间性规划相对单一或片面的发展目标不同，国土空间规划是全要素、全空间、全过程的规划，应当“紧紧围绕统筹推进‘五位一体’总体布局和协调推进‘四个全面’战略布局”。兼顾保护与发展，兼顾各类空间要素的统筹协同。国土空间蓝图是“多要素紧约束条件”下的综合效益最优解，其基本原则是有限国土空间上“物尽其用”，即让每个空间单元承担最适宜的功能，目的是实现综合、整体效益的最优。

国土空间规划最艰巨的任务不是“识问题”，也不是“定目标”，而是“寻路径”。即在有限时间、有限资源的紧约束条件下，如何从“问题复杂”的现状到达“美好图景”的未来。这归根结底是一个道路问题，即如何“贯彻新发展理念，统筹好经济发展和生态环境保护建设的关系，努力探索以生态优先、绿色发展为导向的高质量发展新路子”。

国土空间规划把“三类空间”“三条红线”作为调整经济结构、规划产业发展、推进城镇化不可逾越的红线，做好“双评价”“双评估”“双评判”的基础性工作，以此作为合理规划的前提。国土空间规划应“保持加强生态文明建设的战略定力”，采取从紧的土地供给政策，严控增量、盘活存量、释放流量、提高质量，提高各类资源能源的利用效率。国土空间规划应抛弃机械、无机、线性的解析思维，将“山水林田湖草”当作相生相息、复杂有机、内生关联的生态系统来看待，遵循生态系统的整体性、多样性、复杂性规律，对山上山下、地上地下、陆地海洋以及流域上下游，进行整体保护、系统修复、综合治理，增强生态系统自我调节、自我修补、自我平衡、自我循环能力，维护生态平衡。

国土空间规划是人民的规划，它需要全社会的共同参与，以人民的满意度为衡量，解决好人民群众反映强烈的突出问题；国土空间规划是层级传导、事权对应的规划，需要上下级政府间的刚性传递与动态反馈；国土空间规划是各类利益主体充分博弈、沟通协调的平台，需要建立协调的程序、规则和标准；新时代下，城市设计、乡村、营造、大数据等手段大大提升了规划的数据支撑、技术支撑和决策支撑。上述机制创新，是提升国土空间规划科学性的重要手段。

4. 开启多规合一新时代，迈向空间规划新征程

（方创琳，国际欧亚科学院院士，中国科学院地理科学与资源研究所研究员）

日前，中共中央国务院下发了《关于建立国土空间规划体系并监督实施的若干意见》（以下简称《若干意见》），标志着我国自此终结了长达40多年之久的“多规演义”和各类空间规划“分治”冲突的局面，从此进入国土空间规划实现“多规合一”的新时代。这是我国空间规划编制与实施从“多规分治”的浅水区进入“多规合一”的深水区的重要里程碑，必将为优化我国国土空间格局、提高国土空间利用质量、为推动生态文明和美丽中国建设发挥重要作用，做出重要贡献。科学解读《若干意见》可知，新时代国土空间规划编制与实施的基本思路可归结为：整合形成“唯一”的国土空间基础信息平台，明确“两大规划”的上下位关系，贯穿“三合一”的主线思维，突出“四条红线”的刚性管控，强化“五大特性”的高度衔接，突出“六统一”的技术路径。

一是整合成“唯一”的国土空间基础信息平台。《若干意见》将建立健全和完善统一的国土空间基础信息平台作为实现“多规合一”的底板，明确规定以自然资源调查监测数据为基础，并将其作为“多规合一”的战略资源，整合各类空间关联数据，建议自下而上、全国统一的国土空间基础信息平台，推进政府部门之间的数据共享以及政府和社会之间的信息交互，确保了主体功能区战略和各类空间管控精准落地，对推动国土空间规划“一张图纸绘制到底”“一张图纸实施到底”发挥了重要的基础支撑作用。这将从根本上解决长期以来存在的各部门基础数据不统一、平台自成体系，相互封闭、互不认可、互相推诿导致国土空间管控无序、利用效率低下等顽疾。

二是明确了两大规划的上下位关系。《若干意见》明确提出国家发展规划是国土空间规划的上位规划，是一切规划的总遵循，国土空间规划是对国家发展规划的空间落地和落实，要体现国家发展规划的战略性，自上而下编制各类国土空间规划，为国家发展规划落地实施提供空间保障。强调国土空间规划重在落实国家安全战略、区域协调发展战略和主体功能区战略，体现国家意志。

三是贯穿了“三合一”的主线思维。《若干意见》自始至终将“多规合一”作为国土空间规划编制的总目标和总遵循，将不同空间尺度的主体功能区规划、土地利用规划、城乡规划等空间规划统一为国土空间规划，同时首次推动“多审合一”和“多证合一”，提出了优化现行建设项目用地用海预审、规划选址以及建设用地规划许可、建设工程规划许可等“多证多审合一”的审批流程，将大大提高国土空间规划的审批效能及监管水平。

四是突出了“四条红线”的刚性管控。《若干意见》从“把每一寸土地都规划得清清楚楚”的管控目标出发，提出了坚持底线思维，立足资源禀赋和环境承载能力，加快构建生态功能保障基线、环境质量安全底线、自然资源利用上线、生态保护红线等“四线”管控的要求，体现了国土空间规划在国土空间开发保护中的战略引领和刚性管控作用。

五是强化了“五大特性”的高度衔接。在《若干意见》中突出强调了国土空间规划编制要体现战略性，提高科学性，强化权威性，加强协调性，注重可操作性。通过这“五性”的衔接和落实，将实现国土空间开发保护更高质量、更有效率、更加公平、更可持续的“四更”目标。

六是突出了“六统一”的技术路径。《若干意见》在不同部分先后提出了统一的测绘基准和测绘系统、统一的规划用地分类体系、统一的规划技术标准体系、统一的规划编制审批体系、统

一的规划监督实施体系、统一的规划法规政策体系。这六大“统一”为编制、审批、实施国土空间规划提供了全过程控制的技术路径和制度保障。解决了以往各类空间规划中存在的规划主体、技术标准和编制办法不统一、技术标准不统一、坐标系不统一、用地指标不统一、用地分类不统一、表述方式不统一、规划周期不统一等一系列不统一的现实问题。

5. 规划的三个维度

（张泉，中国城市规划学会副理事长，江苏省住房和城乡建设厅原巡视员）

从规划工作全局的维度，把原来互不统属的各种规划整合纳入一个体系，以“整合”为基础，分级分类解决实用、适用问题。构建统一的国土空间规划体系，包括总体规划、详细规划和相关专项规划；分级编制国家、省、市县国土空间总体规划，并结合各地实际编制乡镇国土空间规划；分类（分级）编制专项规划，以满足特定区域（流域）、特定领域、特定功能的需要。并明确了这三类规划之间的基础、依据和协同、衔接关系。

从规划统筹协调的维度，关注差异、强调传导，指出国土空间规划体系中各类规划和而不同，即总体目标和方向一致，但各有任务、各有侧重、各有特点。国土空间规划要统筹综合平衡各专项领域的空间需求；详细规划要依据批准的国土空间总体规划进行编制和修改；相关专项规划不得违背总体规划强制性内容，其主要内容要纳入详细规划。健全规划实施传导机制，明确规划约束性指标、刚性管控要求和指导性要求，提出下级国土空间总体规划和相关专项规划、详细规划的分解落实要求，确保规划能用、好用、管用。

从规划实施管理的维度，立足于用、立足于法，提出加快建立规划的编制审批、实施监督、法规政策、技术标准四个体系，以强化规划的权威性、严肃性和稳定性，杜绝“一届政府一个规划”，杜绝“多个规划打架”。按照谁组织编制、谁负责实施的原则，明确各级各类国土空间规划编制和管理的要点；按照谁审批、谁监管的原则，分级建立国土空间规划审查备案制度。推进“放管服”改革，统筹规划、建设、管理三大环节，推动“多审合一”“多证合一”，提高审批效能和监管服务水平。

6. 国土空间规划——重塑规划操作体系的新契机

（赵燕菁，中国城市规划学会副理事长，厦门大学教授）

改革开放四十年，中国城市规划取得了巨大的成就。进步之巨大当初谁也没有料到。但经过四十年的运行，现有各类空间规划体系之间的不兼容所带来的制度性摩擦也变得越来越大。中共中央、国务院《关于建立国家空间规划体系并监督实施的若干意见》提供了一个重塑规划体系的机会。让规划有机会在操作系统层次重新理解、设计、安装并重启。这个文件并没规定这个体系是什么，而是给这个体系的形成提出了一个方向性的“意见”，以及2020年、2025年和2035年三个时间节点。这就为未来的规划体系设计留下了巨大的空间。这和40年前城市规划初创非常类似——真正的规划体系不是预先给定，而是在不断回答现实问题的过程中逐步形成的。

现有的城市规划，脱胎于计划经济。那时候还并没有土地招牌挂制度，以及与之相关联的“两证一书”，在这样的语境下，规划编制从诞生之日，就更加注重自上而下、面面俱到的科学性，而不太注意不同层级管理事权划分对规划实施的实际影响。可以说，规划体系从一开始就是围绕着“编制”而不是“审批”和“监管”而设计的，以至于在今天，还把《城乡规划法》称为《规划编制法》。重“编制”、轻“管理”成为规划体系的先天缺陷。针对这一问题，《若干意见》在标题中特地把"监督实施"提升到和规划体系同等重要的位置。这就要求新的"国土空间规划体系"要从传统的编制为核心，转向审批为核心。

同四十年前相比，今天的规划在国家治理中的作用要大得多，如果说四十年前我们还可以通过摸索慢慢构筑规划体系，今天我们则必须在两个体系间快速切换。一个好的构架可以节省大量的摸索，这就要求国土空间规划主管部门对这一体系未来的运行方式，具有非凡的想象力和高超的设计技巧。出现在这个位置的人，必定会在规划历史上留下一笔——可能是功臣，也可能是罪人。

7. 学科发展的改革机遇：从单一到综合

（段进，中国城市规划学会常务理事，东南大学建筑学院教授）

需要从单一学科拓展走向多学科综合。规划内容的单一性，是以往规划不能够很好的实施以及造成很多城市问题的主要原因之一。无论是国土规划还是城乡规划都有类似的问题，尽管各自也都在发生改变和改进，例如城乡规划早期单一以物质规划为目标的方式受到了批判，随后在规划过程中，重视了空间规划与社会经济发展的关系，强调维护公共利益，支持社会安定，合理利用资源，延续历史文化，并且建立了公众参与的机制，以及应用了大量的社会经济管理的其他学科优秀方法，但是仍然缺乏整体的、综合的资源评估与利用等内容。未来的规划要求加强规划学科中对空间资源环境与区域经济社会发展重要基础要素的全系统的分析，因此与自然环境学科，地理资源学科的研究内容和研究方法需融会贯通，要梳理影响城乡发展的全要素体系，建立资源与自然环境的约束概念。新的规划范式不是在原有单一学科上的拓展而是各学科的综合。

综合发展中的改革初心不能变。建立一套空间规划体系，完成一次机构改革，实现规划合一只是手段，我们需要解决的是问题。这次改革解决了政府体制机制的自身结构性问题，解决了规划作为一种行政职能存在多年的交叉重复和矛盾冲突问题，是政府行政管理的理念与方式变化而做出的调整，是行政权力和责任的配置调整，以及行政程序的梳理和行为模式的方式调整，不是部门之间话语权的争夺，更不能各编各的规划，随着国土空间规划的实施以及当代新技术的发展和生态时代发展的需求，城乡规划学科一定需要新的整合和统一，需要有新的发展，只有面对不断的变化，与时俱进才有生存和发展的空间。但我们回到改革的初心和目标，我们也应该认识到一些基本的原理和方法，学理并没有发生变化。

综合发展中的学科挑战思考。目前虽然国土空间规划作为一个整体体系，更加集中在国土资源、空间资源环境的分析和利用，重点集中在国土空间资源，但是对于整个的规划来说仍然是更加综合和复杂，不仅涉及从国家全域到乡村各种层次和尺度，也增加了国土、农林、资源地理等各种学科的综合，所以对于规划来说已经向更加综合的规划体系发展，对于未来规划的教学和学习，应该仍然是分层次和分专业的，除了基本原理学习之外，应该形成有特色的专业学习，要一个个人能够全面掌握所有知识十分困难。原有的城乡规划学科，作为一级学科下设6个二级学科，5个领域和10门核心课，对学生来说已经量大面广，从这些核心课的内容来看，与国土空间规划体系所要求的规划内容，尤其是关于生态资源分析、评价等等方面还是有很大的缺项，还需要进一步优化资源管理、社会生态等方面的内容，学科之间的交叉，互相借鉴也将会催生出新的知识和内容，所有这些内容都作为教学和学习的基本内容难度很大，尤其是要做精难度更大。所以进一步完善学科的基本要求和推进特色发展十分重要。

8. 优化国土空间开发格局的基本遵循

（史育龙，国家发展改革委中国城市和小城镇改革发展中心主任、研究员）

新的国土空间规划体系致力于解决各级各类空间规划存在的规划类型过多、内容重叠冲突，审批流程复杂、周期过长，地方规划朝令夕改等问题，定位于建立全国统一、责权清晰、科学高效的国土空间规划体系，体现了鲜明的问题导向、目标导向和应用导向的结合。一是层级类型兼顾的规划体系结构具有充分的指向性和兼容性。包括国家、省、市县三个层级，总体规划、详细规划和其他相关专项规划三级三类的国土空间规划体系基本框架。此外，还特别允许因地制宜，将市县与乡镇国土空间规划合并编制，或以几个乡镇为单元编制乡镇级的国土空间规划的安排，既有鲜明的功能指向性，体系内也有充分的兼容性和灵活性。二是各层级规划不同的目标取向能够有效防止规划"空转"。从国家级、省级到市县和乡镇级，分别确定战略性、协调性和实施性的侧重要求，有助于更好实现空间发展指南、可持续发展空间蓝图和各类开发建设保护活动依据三大目标。三是市县以下与空间用途管制、项目规划许可以及开工建设等密切关联的详细规划，根据与城镇开发边界的相对关系，提出了更加务实的解决方案。四是注重监督实施。对不同层级和类型规划间的服从关系、规划建设时序做出明确规定，明确体系外不得另设其他空间规划，同时对规划审批、修改都作出了明确规定。五是强化用途管制，建立了"详细规划＋规划许可"和"约束指标＋分区准入"等不同管制方式，确保实现管制目标。

2018 年 11 月，党中央、国务院发布了《关于统一规划体系更好发挥国家发展规划战略导向作用的意见》，要求在明确规划功能定位、理顺规划关系基础上，统一规划体系，形成规划合力，尤其是特别强调国民经济和社会发展五年规划纲要作为国家发展规划，居于规划体系最上位、是其他各级各类规划总遵循的地位，并要求空间规划与国家级专项规划、区域规划均须依据国家发展规划编制。通过上述安排，基本厘清了国家发展规划与国土空间规划之间的关系，即国家发展规划突出战略指导性，国土空间规划体现发展规划的意图并在空间上做出安排。尽管如此，有些问题还没有完全清晰。如两个文件都提到关于跨行政区域或流域的规划，在统一规划体系的文件中将其确定为跨行政区的国家级区域规划，在健全国土空间规划体系的文件中则表述为专项规划。对于一个经济联系紧密、跨行政区的连片区域，以空间治理和空间结构优化为主要内容的国土空间专项规划，与以贯彻实施重大区域战略、协调解决跨行政区重大问题为重点的区域规划，其重点内容、规划目标和实现方式都是相互交织、密不可分的，分别冠名的规划在编制和实施过程中如何衔接，还需要通过实践进一步明确。此外，关于统一规划体系的文件明确要求："国家级专项规划、区域规划、空间规划，规划期与国家发展规划不一致的，应根据同期国家发展规划的战略安排对规划目标任务适时进行调整修改。"这意味着大量规划的目标任务应调整到 5 年。对于国土空间规划关注的一些慢变量而言，如何与 5 年左右的时间尺度确定的经济社会发展等快变量衔接，需要进一步研究。

9. 因势利导地推进国土空间规划时期城乡规划学科的新发展

（武廷海，中国城市规划学会学术工作委员会副主任委员，清华大学建筑学院教授）

建立国土空间规划体系并监督实施，将主体功能区规划、土地利用规划、城乡规划等空间规划融合为统一的国土空间规划，实现"多规合一"，强化国土空间规划对各专项规划的指导约束作用，是党中央、国务院作出的重大部署。

国土空间规划是对一定区域国土空间开发保护在空间和时间上作出的安排。按照《若干意见》提出的国土空间规划分级分类构架，城市作为一种国土空间形态，其规划可以分为总体规划、详细规划和相关专项规划三大类，这是城市规划的新形式。习近平总书记多次强调，“城市规划在城市发展中起着重要引领作用，考察一个城市首先看规划，规划科学是最大的效益，规划失误是最大的浪费，规划折腾是最大的忌讳。”70年来中国社会主义建设已经积累了丰富的城市规划实践经验。在开展城市国土空间规划的过程中，要自觉地发挥城市规划专业知识与技术基础优势，并针对生态文明建设与美丽中国建设的新要求对城市规划重点和内容作出相应的调整，切实保障城市规划对城市发展发挥重要引领作用。

《若干意见》要求市县及以下空间编制覆盖城乡全域的详细规划，为城乡规划学强化完善乡村规划提供了条件。长期以来，城市规划关注城市地区的发展，相比之下对于城市周边广大农村地区的规划只能局限在“城市规划区”的有限范围内。按照《中华人民共和国城乡规划法》规定，城市规划区是指城市、镇和村庄的建成区以及因城乡建设和发展需要，必须实行规划控制的区域。显然，在乡村振兴的战略要求下，必须将规划的范围覆盖到城乡空间全域作统一的安排。《若干意见》关于市县及以下空间编制覆盖城乡全域的详细规划的要求，为城乡规划学强化完善乡村规划提供了条件。即使未来中国实现了较高程度的城镇化，仍然将有大约四分之一的人口要居住在广大乡村，乡村规划是建立新型城乡关系、实现城乡融合发展的重要工具，做优做美乡村规划是国土空间规划时期城乡规划发展大有可为且大有作为的广阔空间。

《若干意见》提出加强国土空间规划相关学科建设，城乡规划学要创造性地发展人居科学指导下的规划理论、技术方法与实践应用，为国土空间规划提供坚实的学科支撑。中央城市工作会议要求，城市工作要把创造优良人居环境作为中心目标，努力把城市建设成为人与人、人与自然和谐共处的美丽家园。学科建设上，吴良镛先生建议，在我国现有的13个学科门类基础上，增设“人居科学”为第14个学科门类；“以城乡规划学、建筑学、风景园林学三个一级学科为核心，融贯综合工学、地理学、社会学、管理学、人类学、环境学等与人居环境相关的其他学科内容，形成人居科学学科门类。”城乡规划学是“人居科学”的三个核心组成学科之一。

2019年5月22日，清华大学城市规划系与同济大学城市规划系共同开展城乡规划学科发展教学交流研讨，一致认为国土空间规划是城乡规划实践的重要领域，城乡规划学科发展要放眼美丽国土，规划美丽城乡，聚焦美好人居，共筑美好家园。具体说来，第一，要适应国家不同部门对国土空间规划编制、实施、监督和城乡人居环境建设、管理等多类型高层次人才需求，因势利导地推进城乡规划学科发展，培养新时代卓越规划人才。第二，要以人居科学理论为指导，创造性地发展城乡规划科学理论与技术方法，加强城乡规划学在国土空间规划领域的实践应用，为国土空间规划提供坚实的学科支撑。第三，要积极开展国土空间规划知识体系建设，促进相应的城乡规划课程教学改革，鼓励教学过程中的交流与合作，加强学科之间的交叉融合，广泛吸纳学术同道探讨教学中的迫切和重大问题，促进城乡规划学更好地满足新时代国土空间规划的知识与技能需求。

基于边界生产的《粤港澳大湾区发展规划纲要》解读

粤港澳大湾区包括香港特别行政区、澳门特别行政区和广东省广州市、深圳市、珠海市、佛山市、惠州市、东莞市、中山市、江门市、肇庆市，总面积5.6万平方公里，2017年年末总人口约7000万人，GDP总量超过约1.34万亿美元，约占中国经济总量的12.17%，其港口集装箱吞吐量、机场旅客量、进出口贸易总额等指标在全球主要湾区中均名列前茅。当前，粤港澳大湾区已成为当之无愧的中国开放程度最高、经济活力最强的区域之一，在国家发展大局中具有重要战略地位。

粤港澳大湾区战略是在过去良好合作基础上逐渐升级的过程。香港、澳门与珠三角九市文化同源、人缘相亲、民俗相近、优势互补，具有良好的合作基础。自1994年香港科技大学创校校长吴家玮首次提出"香港湾区"始，湾区的名称和内涵不断演化，有学者后续提出了"港深湾区""环珠江口湾区""伶仃洋湾区""港珠澳湾区"等概念[1]。2015年开始，类似的讨论及各种方案开始逐步由地方向中央层面升级，并频繁出现在国家部委所发布的各类文件中——2015年4月，国家发展改革委、外交部和商务部共同发布《推动共建丝绸之路经济带和21世纪海上丝绸之路的愿景与行动》，首次提出深化与港澳台合作，明确了粤港澳大湾区概念。及至2017年3月，政府工作报告中提出"研究制定粤港澳大湾区城市群发展规划"，首次将粤港澳大湾区提升为国家战略。2017年10月，十九大报告提出"支持香港、澳门融入国家发展大局，以粤港澳大湾区建设、粤港澳合作等为重点"，将支撑港澳发展作为湾区建设的基准点。2018年3月的政府工作报告明确提出"出台实施粤港澳大湾区发展规划"。至2019年2月18日，筹备多时的《粤港澳大湾区发展规划纲要》（以下简称《规划纲要》）终于公布于世，一个国际一流的湾区和世界级城市群愿景逐渐显现。

一、规划概况

《规划纲要》是指导粤港澳大湾区当前和今后一个时期合作发展的纲领性文件，确立了建设粤港澳大湾区的基本原则、主要内容，体现高层次战略，涉及的内容广泛而又具体。总体来说，《规划纲要》的主要内容为"一个中心，一个愿景，两大目标、五大定位、八大重点，四项措施"。

“一个中心”是指《规划纲要》以支持港澳融入国家发展大局为中心。“一个愿景”是指建设富有活力和国际竞争力的一流湾区，成为扎实推进高质量发展的示范。“两大目标”是指确定了2022年的近期目标和2035年的远期目标。“五大定位”是指明确了充满活力的世界级城市群、具有全球影响力的国际科技创新中心、“一带一路”建设的重要支撑、内地与港澳深度合作示范区、宜居宜业宜游的优质生活圈五大战略定位。“八大重点”是指明确了空间布局、建设国际科技创新中心、加快基础设施互联互通、构建具有国际竞争力的现代产业体系、推进生态文明建设、建设宜居宜业宜游的优质生活圈、紧密合作共同参与“一带一路”建设、共建粤港澳合作发展平台八个重点领域的工作。“四项措施”，包括加强组织领导、推动重点工作、防范化解风险、扩大社会参与。(图1)

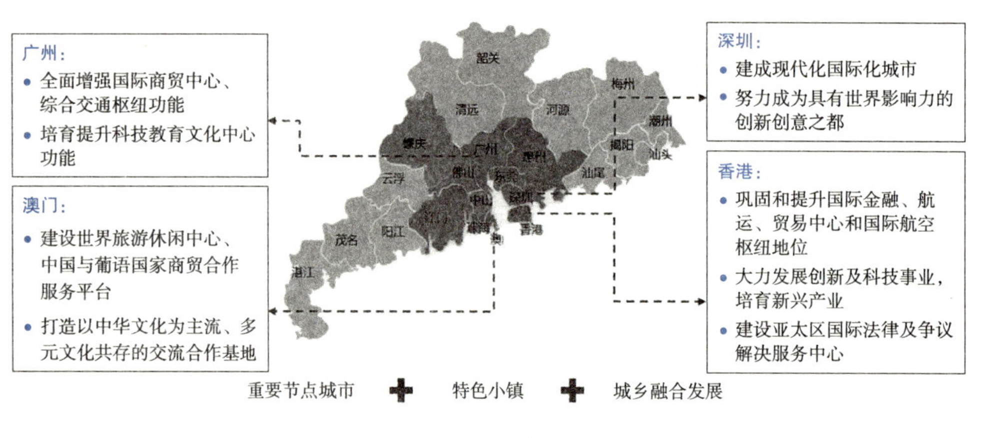

图1　粤港澳大湾区空间布局

资料来源：德勤中国

当前官方抑或民间对《规划纲要》内容的解读已然繁多，但是对其更深层次的规划动力的解读较少，更缺乏立足于一个统一的框架去整体解释宏观的背景和战略、微观的变革和行动、政府的策略和措施。而边界和边界生产作为一个泛空间概念和逻辑，对从宏观到微观、从物质空间到制度文化的多个层次的机制，对牵涉其中的多个主体的行动逻辑都具有较强的解释力。故本文以边界及其生产为整体的逻辑，解读《规划纲要》背后的边界尺度调整、边界生产的转型、边界再生产的空间生产等核心机制，揭示其规划逻辑。

二、边界生产的逻辑

(一) 边界的复合化概念

“边界”是各种社会系统、要素的存在范围和活动领域[2]，亦是事物间本质或现象发生变化的标志线[3]，既涉及真实存在的物质空间，又涉及意识和文化、规则和制度、社会关系等虚拟的空间，代表了这些要素的空间秩序和空间关系[4]。真实的抑或虚拟的空间边界是复杂社会中不断生产与再生产的产物，反映的是边界生产和再生产的结果。边界再生产反馈到空间上，表现为空间的再生产。

（二）边界再生产的逻辑

边界天然地具有尺度的特征，这种尺度特征来源于物质空间、意识和文化、规则和制度、社会关系本身具有的尺度。不同尺度的清晰抑或模糊的边界是垂直且相互嵌套的[5]，在空间上就形成了边界和尺度体系，每一个边界都有一个耦合的尺度及其适应的边界效应。边界会因为权力的再分配、区域管治而在尺度上产生变革。通过“尺度重组”，不同尺度的边界主体能够进入更高层次区域治理网络，从而获得边界拓展的更多机会。

边界并不是一成不变的，其范围的大小、尺度特征等边界要素会因为主体的作用而变化，即边界的再生产。各方主体基于利益的考量，通过动用资源和使用策略，扩大行动的空间，并扩展边界或者调整边界的尺度。边界生产就是多主体边界拓展范围和领域、调整尺度的相互作用过程。空间、法律、制度、文化等边界与实践需求的空隙和差距是产生边界生产的前提，治理主体通过边界生产过程，增加法律与制度与实践的契合度。

在实践过程中，边界表现为各种系统和要素的互动关系，这决定了主体的行动空间和界限。不同主体因为差异化的政治经济社会资源具有不同的调整边界的行动能力和行动策略，改变边界的作用范围和相对界限的能力亦相应不同。即主体在利益、权力和权利的互动、对抗中持有差异化的行动界限和机会空间。双方的互动和博弈，不仅使双方行动维持在一定界限之内，强化着某种可能的对抗边界，而且还会生产出新的边界、开辟出新的空间，实现对抗边界的再生产和转化。

边界的再生产会空间化，表现为空间的再生产。边界的屏蔽效应和中介效应依附于有形或无形的边界，会再地化为响应的空间，表现为空间的生产。边界地区“接触带”特征使其更容易接触边界两侧的差异要素，因为具有政策、制度等的选择空间而发展起来，并成为基础设施等物理去边界化的首要地区。同时，边界地区在区域一体化的进程中能够改变原有区位特征，一体化使得边缘区转化为核心区，成为“中心边界区”[6]。区位的改变使得原边界地区获得更进一步发展。

边界具有不同程度的屏蔽效应和中介效应。屏蔽效应是指边界阻碍边界空间两侧的相互作用及跨界交流直至一体的效应，如行政区经济就因为行政边界产生的明显阻碍效应而产生，阻碍了要素跨区域的高效流动，导致了要素结构或者特质上的差别，边界也成为区域发展摩擦的集中地区。中介效应是指边界“交流”“融合”的潜质为两侧的文化、物质、信息等各种要素的交流起到中介和桥梁作用的现象，是指边界的“接触带”的特征。如因为区域一体化的拓展，部分边界及其周边地域成为区域合作的主要载体，边界进而由原来的空间网络的边缘位置向空间的中心位置转移。

三、《规划纲要》的边界再生产解构

从边界生产的逻辑解构《规划纲要》，一方面需要紧扣《规划纲要》文本解读边界再生产的最新动向，另一方面更需要跳出《规划纲要》文本本身解读其出台的背景和所处的区域发展现实，从文本里和文本外相结合的角度揭示边界再生产的复杂动因和过程。

(一) 粤港澳大湾区边界再生产的背景

从成熟的“前店后厂”区域发展模式到现今三个核心城市共同发展，港澳和珠三角地区在新的发展阶段具有一些优势，也面临一些结构性问题。“香港经济增长缺乏持续稳固支撑，澳门经济结构相对单一、发展资源有限，珠三角九市市场经济体制有待完善，区域发展空间面临瓶颈制约”。这些结构性问题很大程度上来源于政治和经济制度、治理结构在区域内的差异。不同于京津冀和长三角一体化在单一的行政体内的区域一体化，粤港澳大湾区面临着一个国家基础上的两种制度、三种关税区的这一最大差异，这种差异也是大湾区边界的最核心特征。

在粤港澳大湾区的空间地域上，港澳和大陆地区发展阶段的代差和“一国两制”的制度框架分别为区域的发展提供了经济和政治上的动因。这个制度框架一方面保障了香港和澳门的繁荣稳定，使之成为国际一流的自由贸易港和博彩中心；另一方面随着区域经济一体化的发展，“一国两制”可能成为大湾区规划和建设的最终制度底线。

在这个框架下的可调制度边界成为区域发展的主要障碍。正如《规划纲要》在规划背景中所说，粤港澳大湾区的区域一体化受到边界显著的边界屏蔽效应——“在‘一国两制’下，粤港澳社会制度不同，法律制度不同，分属于不同关税区域，市场互联互通水平有待进一步提升，生产要素高效便捷流动的良好局面尚未形成。”在大湾区内部，还存在明显的行政壁垒和制度障碍。

在制度边界普遍存在的条件下，边界主体的价值观也影响着边界效应的增减。在合作的背景下，边界主体的行动并不总是秉持导向积极一体化的价值观。在对话层面，以前香港在建设紧密型经济体的设想上并不像内地那么积极，甚至在特定领域存在排斥与内地合作的现象，少数群体的理念甚至背道而驰；香港有时候不愿意跟珠三角的省、市对话，而是想跟中央政府直接对话。在行动层面，地方保护主义的举措也很常见：边界的权力主体仍然局限于当前的边界空间利益，实施市场分割策略是省一级政府的普遍偏好[7]，也是城市政府的普遍偏好。如湾区跨江通道的曲折决策建设过程无不体现了这种地方保护主义。

同时，社会文化边界的融合潜力也受到制度边界的不断挤压。当前，香港经济增长动力不足，收入差距拉大，青年失业率高企，社会撕裂现象严重，出现了部分民众与香港政府、与内地的对抗，经济社会文化矛盾凸显。制度边界是这些矛盾的根源，其存在严重限制了香港经济腹地和人口的流动。

(二) 边界尺度的调整：为了港澳与内地的融合发展

《规划纲要》的提出是从地区议程逐步上升为国家战略的边界尺度调整的结果。2009年，香港、澳门及广东省三方政府提出《大珠三角城镇群协调发展规划研究》，并提出了跨界交通合作、跨界地区合作、生态环境保护合作和协调机制建设四项跟进工作。2010年，三地政府制定了《环珠三角宜居湾区建设重点行动计划》，以落实上述跨界地区合作。2014年，深圳出台《关于大力发展湾区经济建设21世纪海上丝绸之路桥头堡的若干意见》，明确指出"通过湾区经济并主动融入'一带一路'战略"。2015年，广东省政协委员谭刚提出《构建粤港澳大湾区，推动广东经济发展新常态》，明确提出"粤港澳大湾区"的名称。2017年7月，国家发展改革委与广东省、香港及澳门政府签署《深化粤港澳合作推进大湾区建设框架协议》，确立大湾区建设的合作目标和重点领域；2018年8月，粤港澳大湾区建设领导小组成立，旨在提供顶层设计，并加强对大湾区发展的统筹协调。

《规划纲要》成为国家对边界尺度进行调整的工具。区域规划目前普遍成为边界尺度调整的工具，《规划纲要》的发布代表着国家力量对这个"一个国家、两种体制、三个关税区"特色区域的尺度调整，以实现制度边界的调整，人、资本、信息等要素的互通和区域的全方位一体化管治。区域一体化构筑了新的边界，新的边界在空间、领域上和尺度上同步实现拓展和提升。新的边界既是物理边界的锁定，也是制度、经济、社会、文化等各种关系/边界的再生产。依托于尺度上升了的主体力量对边界内联系的发生进行干预，空间干预的能力上升，包括对边界内部分要素的支配权力的强化和部分支配权力的下放。中央利用调控职能，通过制定区域规划，推进基础设施一体化、社会公共服务一体化、劳动力就业一体化、产业布局一体化、生态环境整治一体化等[3]，促使边界效应由屏蔽效应向中介效应转化。

《规划纲要》提出核心导向是要确保港澳的繁荣稳定，促进港澳与内地的融合发展。对《规划纲要》各城市词频统计的分析表明，香港（100次）、澳门（90次）的词频远远高于大湾区的另外两个核心城市（广州41次、深圳39次），香港和澳门是《规划纲要》最为关注的城市。也正是因为中央一级《规划纲要》对于香港和澳门的偏重，获得了香港和澳门政府的积极响应。一方面香港和澳门特首频繁考察大湾区的各个城市，积极和省、市一级政府展开对话；另一方面在特区内部成立高规格组织和机构推动《规划纲要》落实。如香港为更全面统筹及推动香港参与大湾区建设，其已成立由特首亲自主持、成员包括特区政府所有司局长的"粤港澳大湾区建设督导委员会"；在特区政府政制及内地事务局亦将成立粤港澳大湾区发展办公室，并委任大湾区发展专员。

（三）边界生产的转型：从物理边界的再生产转向制度、社会关系边界的再生产

近年来，粤港澳合作不断深化，基础设施、投资贸易、金融服务、科技教育、休闲旅游、生态环保、社会服务领域合作有了较为明显的进展，特别是在经济产业合作和以交通为主的基础设施去边界化尤为显著。前期的去边界化以物理边界的再生产为主。然而经济以及其他要素的扩散性和制度边界的矛盾凸显。要解决资本、人员、货物、劳务、信息、技术等各种要素自由流动，必须解决原有市场的深度制度分割问题，改革需要突破重点领域和关键环节的制度障碍。同时，现存复杂的社会和价值观矛盾又要求消解制度、各种发展机遇和公共服务边界，以推动湾区人口能够充分享受均衡化的公共服务和发展机会。

基于这样的背景，在保障政治边界稳定的前提下，《规划纲要》在强调物理边界再生产

的基础上更强调制度和社会关系边界的再生产，推动大湾区边界生产的转型。交通、信息基础设施、能源设施、水资源设施的互联互通以及生态防护和环境保护的共同合作仍然是大湾区边界生产的重点。针对制度去边界，《规划纲要》更深入制度边界障碍的核心环节和关键领域。如在优化区域创新环境方面，《规划纲要》提出中出入境、工作、居住、物流等更加便利化的政策措施，在创业孵化、科技金融、成果转化、国际技术转让、技服务业等领域开展深度合作，深度推进知识产权保护和利用；在产业体系方面，《规划纲要》提出推进金融市场的互联互通、放宽投资的资质要求、推动金融产品的跨境交易和跨境集资、再保险等制度。《规划纲要》的深度制度边界再生产不仅仅停留在文本上，已经反馈到政府部门的管理工作中：2019 年的广东省政府工作报告称，广东将以“规则相互衔接”为重点，加快编制大湾区建设专项规划。

《规划纲要》进一步突破社会、文化的边界障碍，形成以人为本的社会、文化边界再生产。更细微的、以人为本的边界再生产成为《规划纲要》的工作重点，由经济、物理要素的再生产转向社会文化边界的再生产，由生产要素的再配置转向人本要素的再配置。据此提出了建设宜居宜业宜游的优质生活圈的战略任务，推动在就业创业、教育、医疗、养老、休闲度假、文化交流、社会治理等方面的边界再生产。

正如深圳创新发展研究院的研究所揭示的，除了政治制度和政治体制外，经济、社会、保障居民基本权利和自由的体制和特定的生活方式成为大湾区一体的主要方向，形成“政治上两制，经济社会一体”的基本格局[8]。

（四）聚焦于边界再生产的空间生产

粤港澳大湾区一直朝着降低屏蔽边界效应的方向发展，以交通基础设施去边界化为先导，逐步迈向产业、制度、人口、服务的边界再生产过程，这种边界再生产集聚在特定的空间。

1. 边界地区的崛起

边界再生产的作用和政府部门的主动作为推动边界地区的崛起。因为边界的屏蔽效应和中介效应，边界地区会因为截留某些要素、临近边界两侧的市场和空间而具有的突出的桥梁作用、边界的尺度调整获得更大的发展制度空间而发展起来。同时，边界地区的现有制度红利成为推动边界区域发展以及边界尺度调整的激励因素。政府主导的边界地区成为边界的尺度调整的实施平台，为各种流要素的再地域化提供了空间基础。即边界的存在创造了新阶段发展的红利，有序的去边界化成为释放制度红利的重要调整的手段。

边界地区因为多领域的去边界化和交流合作，边界地区从“边缘区”转变成为“核心区”而中心化为“中心边界区”。边界地区产业的核心竞争力和集聚效应不断增强，由边界屏蔽效应的“再领域化”转向中介效应的“再领域化”，实现了边界再生产的空间化。另外，地方政府也普遍将边界地区作为区域合作的重点：2009 年广州和佛山签署同城化建设协议后强化了同城化的管治，特别是边界地区成为同城化的重点地区，边界地区成为迎来人口增长的主要地区；2010 年，深莞惠针对边界区召开联席会，探讨了边界地区的属地规划管理和整体协调发展。在发展实践上，研究表明，深莞、深惠、莞惠、广莞、广佛、佛中等边界地区也呈现去边界化趋势，城市之间边界逐步模糊，边界地区成为机会空间得到增长[9]。(图2)

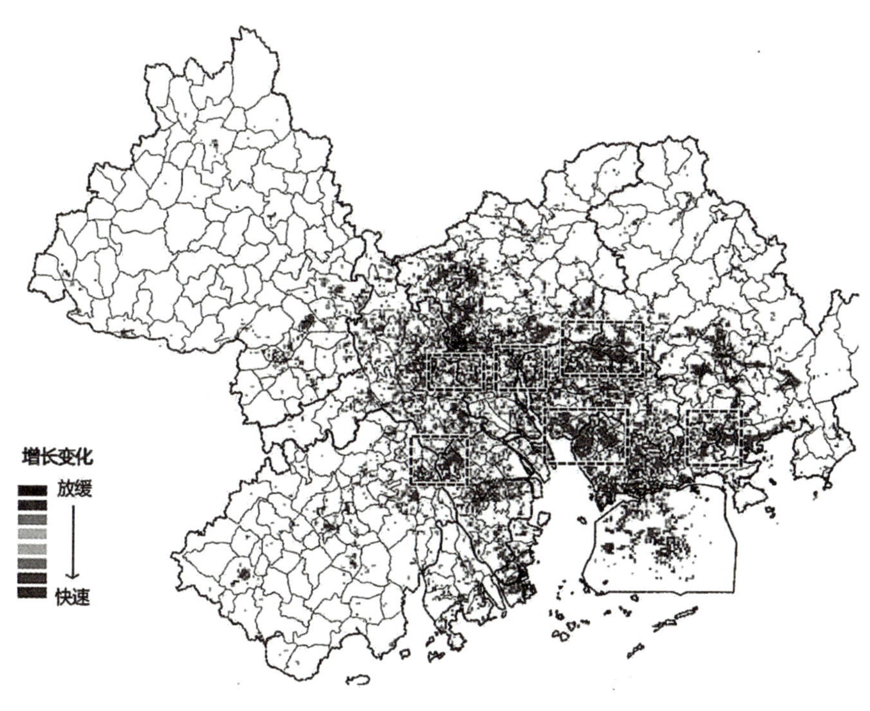

图2 2013—2017年粤港澳灯光增长变化图

资料来源：李郇，周金苗，黄耀福等，从巨型城市区域视角审视粤港澳大湾区空间结构，地理科学进展，2018.12

2. 制度社会关系边界的再生产赋能重点平台

从国家角度出发，在普遍性的边界再生产的基础上，更深层次的、改革式的边界再生产需要一些空间平台去承载、集聚其可控的、显性化的效应；从地区政府出发，不同尺度的边界再生产需要紧密地和城市发展战略相协调，城市试图利用好边界再生产的显著效益带来的战略机遇。因此，一种聚合边界再生产的各种效应和城市发展战略意图的重点平台成为边界再生产的重点。

交通、信息基础设施、能源、水资源、生态等基础设施的边界再生产是一种普遍的去边界化，金融、贸易、关税、社会保障等制度障碍的突破等交织着普遍化的边界再生产和“飞地型”的边界再生产。普遍化的边界再生产有序、可期地普惠作用于边界效应全域。“飞地型”边界再生产是在原边界以外拓展的、制度要素突出边界的再生产，其推动了以重点平台为核心的改革先锋探索。而重点平台在普遍化边界再生产和“飞地型”边界再生产的共同作用下崛起。

《规划纲要》谋划了多种类型的重点平台，包括粤港澳合作重要平台、发展特色合作平台、科技创新载体和平台、临空经济区、港澳青年创业就业基地等，通过边界再生产对这些重点平台赋能。这些平台分别承担了不同要素边界再生产的探索，如广州南沙作为粤港澳合作发展平台，被赋予了营造高标准的国际化市场化法治化营商环境、提供与港澳相衔接的公共服务和社会管理环境、探索建设国际航运保险等创新型保险要素交易平台、在跨境资金管理、人民币跨境使用、资本项目可兑换等方面先行先试的“飞地型”边界再生产。

四、结论

目前《粤港澳大湾区发展规划纲要》的各种官方解读并没有明确提出边界生产和再生产的概念，但是通过边界生产的逻辑解构《粤港澳大湾区发展规划纲要》，可以发现《规划纲要》贯穿着边界生产和再生产的整体框架，揭示了国家虽没有将边界生产作为有意识的追求，但是在实际的规划中无意架构其边界生产的框架逻辑，以“边界思维”推动粤港澳大湾区开放发展。

进一步解读《规划纲要》中边界尺度调整、边界生产的转型、边界再生产的空间生产逻辑，发现《规划纲要》的出台是为了促进港澳和内地的融合发展、支持香港、澳门融入国家发展大局而对边界尺度进行的调整。物理边界的再生产已经成为区域规划的标准动作，而《规划纲要》意推的边界生产因为“一个国家、两种体制、三个关税区”的特殊区域特征，和港澳凸显的经济社会文化矛盾，而重点转向制度和社会关系边界的再生产。同时，边界地区因为边界制度红利、中介效应的彰显和区域去边界化使得边界地区成为“中心边界区”而崛起；重点平台因为普遍化的边界再生产和“飞地型”的边界再生产赋予了更多的制度、社会关系边界再生产的职责，成为区域发展的重点地区。

（作者：贺辉文，广州市城市规划勘测设计研究院；廖远涛，广州市城市规划勘测设计研究院政府规划编制部副主任、教授级高级工程师）

参考文献

[1] 闵杰．粤港澳大湾区：探索香港“再融入”[J]．中国新闻周刊，2017，(24)：8 - 10.

[2] 刘威．制造边界：业主行动与秩序缤纷的社区［M］．北京：社会科学文献出版社，2018：230 - 231.

[3] 任以胜，陆林，朱道才．区域协调发展战略下的行政边界研究框架［J］．经济地理，2019，39（03）：29 - 36.

[4] 唐雪琼，杨茜好，钱俊希．社会建构主义视角下的边界——研究综述与启示［J］．地理科学进展，2014，33（07）：969 - 978.

[5] 陈航航，贺灿飞，毛熙彦．区域一体化研究综述：尺度、联系与边界［J］．热带地理，2018，38（1）：1 - 12.

[6] 王亮，刘卫东．西方经济地理学对国家边界及其效应的研究进展［J］．地理科学进展，2010，29（5）：601 - 608.

[7] 陆铭，陈钊．分割市场的经济增长——为什么经济开放可能加剧地方保护？[J]．经济研究，2009，44

(03)：42 - 52.
[8] 张思平．“一国两制”与大湾区——粤港澳大湾区建设中的制度创新［R］．深圳创新发展研究院，2017.
[9] 李郇，周金苗，黄耀福，等．从巨型城市区域视角审视粤港澳大湾区空间结构［J］．地理科学进展，2018，37（12）：1609 - 1622.

从“深圳特区”到“大湾区”的跨越

粤港澳大湾区，是中国继“一带一路”倡议、京津冀协同发展、长江经济带发展之后提出的第四个国家战略。2019 年 2 月 18 日，中共中央国务院正式印发《粤港澳大湾区发展规划纲要》，标志着以深圳特区为突破口的 40 年改革开放之后，大湾区将成为代表中国下一个现代化的崭新模板。

如何理解大湾区未来的价值和方向？回溯历史，“特区现象”也许有所启示。

一、从“经济特区”到“大湾区”

改革开放的 40 年在珠三角创造了以经济特区为引领的发展奇迹。作为经济特区的深圳从 1980 年一个城区面积 3 平方公里、县域人口 30 余万的边陲“渔村”，发展成为建成区约 900 平方公里、1 800 万人口的现代化都市。深圳的基因或者初心就是“敢为天下先”的特区精神。深圳的发展激发了“特区速度，升级速度，转型速度，创新速度”的一系列引领全国的城市—产业—经济迭代升级。

（一）特区速度

1980 年 8 月，五届全国人大常委会第十五次会议批复深圳经济特区成立，正式拉开了深圳特区作为全国经济体制改革先锋的序幕。特区建立之初，在经济发展模式方面提出了“四个为主”的理论，即：特区的建设资金以引进外资为主、企业结构以发展外资企业为主、产品销售以外销为主、经济活动以市场调节为主。由于享有特区立法权和单行经济法规制定权的优势，深圳以接受香港制造业转移为契机，通过市场经济体制改革，发展“三来一补”为主的劳动密集型的加工制造业。深圳的产业结构发生了巨大变化，初步实现了从传统农业到工业化的产业转变。与此同时，在“小政府，大社会”的政府体制下，深圳通过推行针对境外人士的灵活入境政策、便利劳动力自由流动的合同工制度、双轨制的住房供应模式等，成为国内最早聚集打工者的城市之一，形成“百万劳工下深圳”的现象。华为、平安、金蝶等企业均创立于这一时期。

“时间就是金钱，效率就是生命”折射出特区速度背后务实创新的精神内涵。特区速度展示了深圳从计划经济体制中杀出了一条血路，全面地建立起开放的市场经济的艰辛历程。

（二）升级速度

20 世纪 90 年代初期，全球信息通讯领域迅速发展，移动通信和互联网技术不断进步，同时大规模的制造业开始向发展中国家进行转移。在国际大分工背景下，深圳出台了一系列推进高新技术产业发展的政策，使深圳的产业发展从原来的“三来一补”为主的劳动密集型产业结构得到迅速提升，被高新技术产业为主的技术密集、资本密集、知识密集的产业结构所取代。

1995 年，深圳的“科教兴市”战略明确提出“把深圳建设成为高新技术产业基地和区域性金融中心、信息中心、商贸中心、运输中心和旅游胜地”。随后的五年里，在市政府的推动下，深圳成立高新区，批复《深圳市高新技术产业园区发展规划》，举办首届“中国国际高新科技成果交易会（高交会）”，其后发展成为“中国科技第一展”。出台《深圳经济特区创业投资条例》，并提出构建市域高新技术产业带。同时，与北京大学、香港科技大学联合，在深圳建设深港产学研基地。成立深圳虚拟大学园，实行“一园多校、市校共建”的独特建设模式，吸引全国 22 所高校进入，成为国家科教改革的重要载体和先行示范。民营企业在此阶段迅速发展，占据深圳企业的半壁江山。

升级速度展示了深圳抓住世界科技革命的历史性机遇，跨越产业阶梯，直接迈入信息互联网时代。

（三）转型速度

进入 21 世纪初，深圳经济增长速度开始放缓，在经济话语权和高级人才竞争中的劣势逐渐显现。2002 年年底，《深圳，你被谁抛弃?》在人民网强国论坛首发，引出了一场关于深圳命运的大讨论。一方面，深圳的发展也正面临土地空间有限、能源水资源短缺、人口不堪重负、环境承载力严重透支“四个难以为继”的困境；另一方面，中国正式加入世界贸易组织（WTO），参与全球竞争，激发深圳企业的竞争意识倒逼转型。

在空间资源紧约束的背景下，深圳加快发展高新技术产业、现代金融业和现代物流业三大战略性支柱产业，2003 年在全国率先提出“文化立市”战略。至此，深圳逐渐趋向于形成以高新技术产业、金融业、现代物流业、文化创意产业四大支柱产业为主的产业体系，产业发展进入到优化产业结构、参与全球竞争的新的发展阶段。

深圳的对外政策也从“引进来”过渡到“走出去”。2006 年，《深圳市实施“走出去”战略规划纲要》出台，首次把“走出去”列入城市重点发展战略。以华为、中兴、万科、腾讯、比亚迪等为代表的民营企业，拓展跨国投资和全球运营业务，逐步形成“政府引导与企业自主扩张并行，龙头企业领跑与广大中小企业跟随”的海外发展格局。

城市规划也明确深圳作为“全国性经济中心城市和国际化城市”的地位，“严控新增，盘活存量”。在空间拓展上建设重心向原特区外转移，原特区内以城市更新为主。探索深圳城市社会经济转型路径，城市发展从速度规模型向效益质量型转变，从单纯地注重城市功能和空间布局向全面统筹和协调城市管理转变。

转型速度在“四个难以为继”的紧约束条件下，率先走出了一条内涵发展的转型之路。

（四）创新速度

2010年以后，深圳发展进入“无人区”，从0到1的源头创新短板显现。习近平总书记的一系列重要批示和国家创新型城市试点、国家综合配套改革试验区、国家自主创新示范区、自贸试验区、粤港澳大湾区等多个国家政策的叠加，为深圳“争创特区新优势”指明了方向。

深圳推动经济发展方式加快转变，实现从“深圳速度”向“深圳质量”跨越。增强源头创新能力，打造创新型产业集群，战略性新兴产业成为经济增长主导力量。新一代信息技术领域的华为、中兴通讯，生物领域的华大基因、迈瑞、海普瑞，互联网领域的腾讯、迅雷、宜搜，新能源领域的中广核、比亚迪，新材料领域的通产丽星、星源材质，文化创意领域的华强文化、雅昌集团等都已成为国内行业龙头企业，部分企业已跻身国际前列。下一步，深圳将向创新引领型全球城市、具有国际影响力的创新创意之都迈进。

创新速度展示了深圳面向未来，从追赶到引领，逐渐进入科创“无人区”，勇于探索一条创新驱动的高质量的发展道路。

深圳特区作为先行先试的实验平台，经历了四次迭代，展示了“深圳速度”，创造了人类发展史上的城市奇迹。深圳特区完成了历史赋予的使命，为大湾区乃至全国的各个城市提供了一个现代化的城市发展模板，掀起了一个风起云涌的城市英雄时代!

但是，近年的粤港澳地区，成长的烦恼日显：香港产业空心化、澳门的过度单一化、深圳空间成本的难以为继和创新成本持续高涨、广州的新动能转换瓶颈、东莞的街镇碎片化、珠海与核心城市渐行渐远、中山日益成为中间城市……一个个城市之殇，预示着“经济特区模式”下的城市英雄主义时代的终结，全力追赶与速度增长时代的终结。而“一带一路”倡议下的粤港澳大湾区最独特的制度特色与多年厚积的发展优势，将支持共建共享、彼此融通的“大湾区模式”，有望在下个30年引领粤港澳进入繁荣、公平、美丽、高质量发展的世界级城市群。

从“经济特区”到“大湾区”的理念跨越、价值认知跨越、模式跨越、行动路线的跨越，将成为区域发展的重点。

二、发展理念的跨越

全球化2.0时代，中国的开放格局需要经济转型、空间转型和外交转型。过去，通过WTO引入资本，把中国廉价的劳动力和园区、特区的政策结合起来，形成了一个庞大的世界工厂，下一步要真正成为全球有影响力的国家，就要“走出去”在全球尺度组织和推进产业、经济、文化、治理等各项事务。其中，粤港澳作为创新发展的核心地区，将在国家转型进程中发挥重要作用。

（一）国际视角：在全球化下半场竞争中，中国需要新的对外开放平台

当前，在全球贸易保护和国际政治围堵的现状下，中国“走出去”面临极大的障碍，港澳地区仍是我国实施“走出去”战略的最佳平台。粤港澳大湾区因为有多种制度、多元文化、多种的资本形式以及最丰富的创新形态等，在人民币国际化、企业走出去中扮演着“超级联系人”的角色。（表 1）

表 1　营商效率全球排名（2018）

排名	经济体	DTF 评分	DTF 变化
01	新西兰	86.55	－0.18
02	新加坡	84.57	＋0.04
03	丹麦	84.06	－0.01
04	韩国	83.92	0.00
05	中国香港	83.44	＋0.29
06	美国	82.54	－0.01
07	英国	82.22	－0.12
08	挪威	82.16	－0.25
09	格鲁吉亚	82.04	＋2.12
10	瑞典	81.27	＋0.03

数据来源：世界银行《2018 年营商环境报告》

（二）转型视角：中国经济需要转型模式的引领，从世界工厂转变为全球经济引领者

中国已成为世界第一制造业大国。制造业产出占世界比重达到 20%，在 500 余种主要工业产品中一半产量位居世界第一，是唯一拥有全部工业门类的国家，产业链完备。随着技术模仿空间缩小和改革红利逐渐减弱，近年来中国全要素生产率增速持续下降，亟须探索通过科技创新、产业升级向国际价值链高端攀升，培育新经济动能。

湾区是当今全球经济的增长极与技术变革领头羊，也是区域经济形态转型的重要趋势。在国家转型发展背景下，粤港澳作为创新发展的核心地区，是新常态下国家创新发展引擎，将在国家转型进程中发挥重要作用。（表 2）

表 2　2016 年四大湾区指标表

指标（2016）	纽约湾区	旧金山湾区	东京湾区	粤港澳大湾区
陆地面积（万平方公里）	2.15	1.79	3.68	5.65
常住人口（万人）	2 340	760	4 383	6 494
GDP（万亿美元）	1.6	0.8	1.8	1.35

续表

指标(2016)	纽约湾区	旧金山湾区	东京湾区	粤港澳大湾区
土地产值(亿美元/平方公里)	0.74	0.45	0.49	0.24
人口密度(人/平方公里)	1 088	425	1 191	1 212
人均 GDP(万美元)	6.8	10.5	4.1	2
GDP 增长率(%)	3.51	2.7	3.61	7.35
地区 GDP 集中度(%)	8.87	4.31	38.43	12.5
第三产业比重(%)	89.35	82.76	82.27	77.57
全球金融中心指数	780	724	740	755
100 强大学数量(所)	2	3	2	4
世界 500 强企业(家)	28	22	60	16
最具创新力企业(家)	3	8	20	4
港口集装箱吞吐量(万标箱/年)	465	227	766	7 118
机场旅客吞吐量(亿人次/年)	1.3	0.71	1.12	1.86
海外游客人数(万人)	5 200	1 651	556	169

数据来源：根据世界银行、日本国土交通省、美国统计局、WIND 数据、英国 Z/Yen 公司《全球金融中心指数》、美国《财富》杂志、《QS 世界 100 强大学排名》整理

（三）“一国两制”视角：将香港自由经济和制度优势转化为竞争优势，促进港澳繁荣稳定

近年，香港受全球经济冲击明显，转口贸易、服务贸易及酒店等相关产业竞争力降低，四大支柱产业（贸易及物流业、金融服务业、专业及工商业支援服务业、旅游业）的增长持续减弱；高端服务业竞争力下降。（图 1）

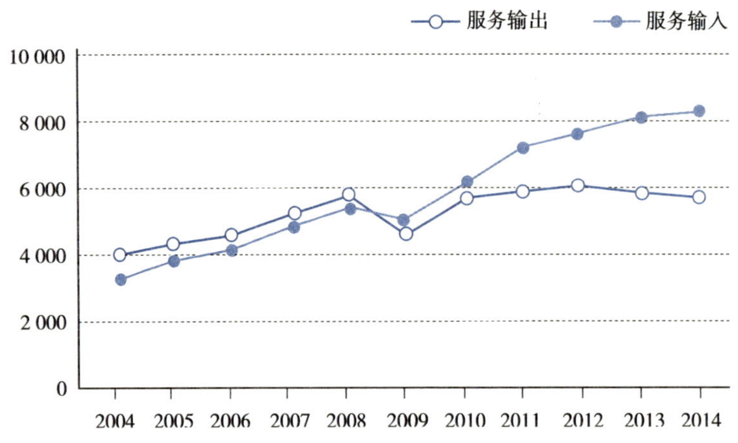

图 1　2004—2014 年香港服务贸易标化（亿港元）走势图

数据来源：香港特别行政区政府统计处

香港连续 5 年被评为全球房价收入比负担最重的地区，生活成本过高，贫富差距过大，青年人就业成为难题。(图 2)

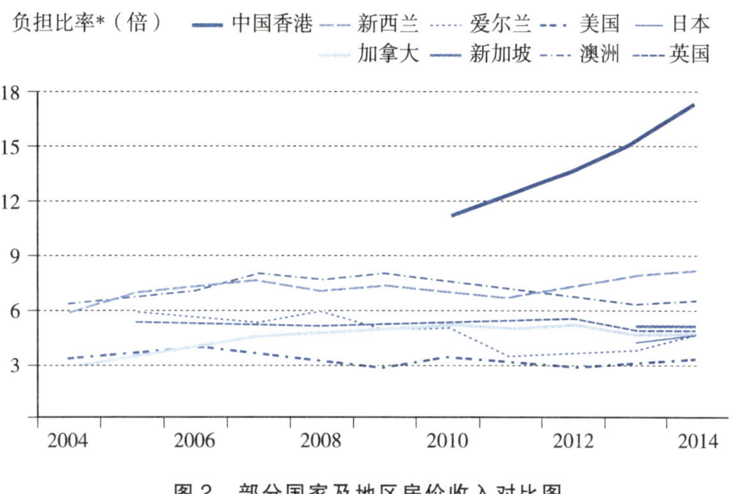

图 2　部分国家及地区房价收入对比图

数据来源：香港特别行政区政府统计处

习近平总书记在庆祝香港回归祖国二十周年大会的讲话中明确提到：“支持香港在推进‘一带一路’建设、粤港澳大湾区建设、人民币国际化等重大发展战略中发挥优势和作用。”——通过粤港澳大湾区建设为香港提供机会，实现长期繁荣稳定，缓解香港资源环境压力及社会问题，使香港从粤港澳合作中受益。(图 3)

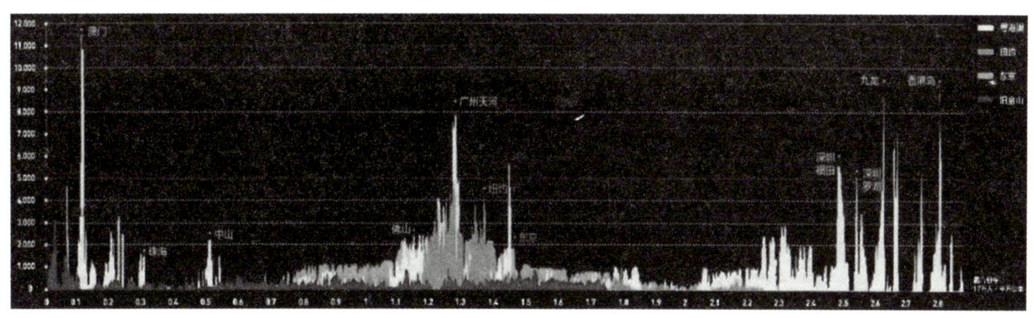

图 3　粤港澳大湾区是世界“最高密度”的湾区城市群

三、全球价值的认知跨越

从地理大发现以来，世界贸易格局逐步经历环大西洋时代—环太平洋时代—环印度洋时代的更迭。环印度洋地区的中国、印度等新兴市场国家的城镇人口、进出口贸易、外商直接投资规模的全球占比不断上升，成为全球投资的热点地区，世界贸易迎来新格局。

（一）价值一：粤港澳大湾区是国内市场和东南亚新兴市场的枢纽

“一带一路”倡议下，我们走出去的方式是海路并举。丝绸之路有两个方向，一是从上海这个方向远洋，到达太平洋地区；二是中亚地区。这两个地区在近域都没有足够的人口和经济市场，恰恰在大湾区周边有庞大的东盟国家，人口加起来将近6亿左右。所以，我们看到港口航运网络与铁路体系都在推进，以实现经济共同体的建设。

（二）价值二：与海上丝绸之路国家海港互联、航线最短

以广州港为例，广州港与世界100多个国家和地区的400多个港口有海运贸易往来，开辟外贸直航航线46条，世界前十大集装箱班轮公司均在广州港开辟班轮航线；从珠三角各港口至海上丝绸之路沿线国家的航线里程，比国内其他港口距离均较短；以珠三角港口群为核心，形成向海洋开放的海运扇面，以及向内陆开放的腹地扇面，珠三角毋庸置疑将成为我国内陆连接21世纪海上丝绸之路的重要枢纽。

（三）3.3 价值三：对外联系网络——港口通航和运营网络遍布全球

大湾区主要港口的运营商遍及全球。在整个东南亚地区，就有很多中国对外承建或者运营的港口。其中，深圳港主要运营商和记黄埔、招商局国际、中远太平洋参与运营的港口遍布全球，还有吉布提、科伦坡等与沿线国家共建的港口航线。广州和深圳也积极开展友好港口建设，遍布“一带一路”的沿线国家。

（四）价值四：拥有世界级海港群、空港群及高效物流体系

大湾区各机场航空客货运总量超过其他三大湾区，港口货运量居全球第一。（图4）

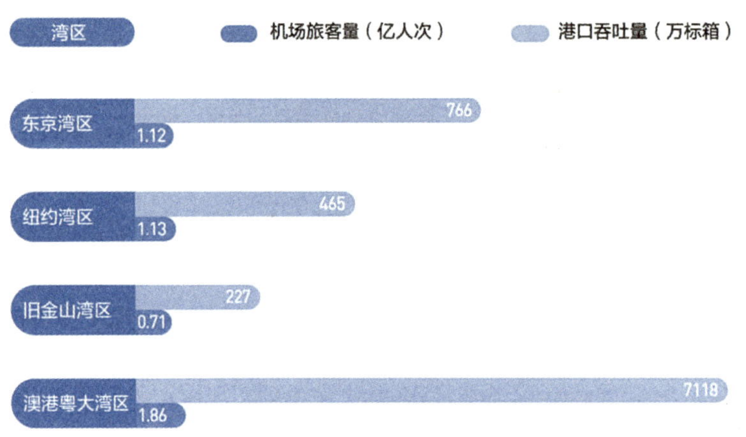

图4　四大湾区机场旅客量及港口吞吐量对比（2016）

随着未来高铁和城际轨道与机场的结合，在粤港澳大湾区将形成高等级交通网络密切联系的快速交通网。例如，珠三角的旅客可以乘坐广深港高铁抵达西九龙，再换乘机场快线抵

达香港国际机场，包括港珠澳大桥的开通，香港机场将更好地服务整个大湾区。穗莞深城际也将区域两大机场白云机场和宝安机场联系起来，未来机场的合作，大有文章可做。

（五）价值五：企业国际化和"走出去"优势明显

大湾区企业的优势也很明显。深圳新兴产业走出去比较早的、以华为和中兴为代表的珠三角企业凭借创新优势已广泛走向世界市场，并逐步占领产业高端环节，基本上实现了全球运营的模式。深圳的企业带领着全国的企业走向国际，可以看到两个资本：一是国家资本，包括港口、"一带一路"的建设、基础设施；二是市场的资本，包括大湾区在新的产业、战略性的技术方面，都在走出去。

四、行动路线的跨越

《粤港澳大湾区发展规划纲要》对粤港澳大湾区的定位为充满活力的世界级城市群、具有全球影响力的国际科技创新中心、"一带一路"建设的重要支撑、内地与港澳深度合作示范区、宜居宜业宜游的优质生活圈。这些定位涉及创新、协同、生态、宜居、文化等诸多领域。

（一）创新湾区——创新是动力

中央城市工作会议提出未来的新动力不是资本、不是技术，而是改革、文化和创新。创新就是培育未来的新动力。

基于全球资本服务体系的 GAWC 排名，大湾区已有港、广、深三个城市进入 α 层级，但核心城市地位仍有待提升（广、深地位弱于北、上）；基于全球资本控制体系的排名，大湾区只有港、深控制力较强，但地位相比北京、上海仍有不足。趋势上，全球顶尖总部的集聚度呈现多极化趋势，发展中国家的核心城市有较好上升趋势。（表 3）

表 3　基于全球资本服务体系的 GAWC 排名

层级		2010 年中国	2012 年中国	2016 年中国	2018 年中国
Alpha	Alpha + +				
	Alpha +	香港、上海	香港、上海、北京	香港、上海、北京	香港、北京、上海
	Alpha	北京			台北、广州
	Alpha -	台北	台北	台北、广州	深圳
Bata	Bata +		广州		成都、杭州
	Bata	广州	澳门	深圳	天津、南京、武汉
	Bata -	深圳	深圳	成都、天津	重庆、苏州、大连、厦门、长沙、沈阳、青岛、济南

续表

层级		2010 年中国	2012 年中国	2016 年中国	2018 年中国
Gamma	Gamma +		天津	南京、杭州、青岛	西安、郑州
	Gamma			大连、重庆、厦门	昆明、太原
	Gamma -			台中、武汉、苏州、长沙、西安、沈阳	福州
High Sufficiency		天津	成都、青岛、杭州、南京、重庆	济南、高雄	宁波
Sufficiency		南京、成都、杭州、青岛、大连、澳门	大连、高雄、厦门、武汉、西安	昆明、福州、澳门、太原、长春、合肥、宁波、郑州、南宁、哈尔滨、乌鲁木齐	乌鲁木齐、哈尔滨、澳门、贵阳、石家庄、长春、南昌、兰州、海口、无锡、珠海、南宁、澳门、呼和浩特、西宁、潍坊

Alpha + +：全球经济的最高整合能力，伦敦、纽约；

Alpha +：在全球经济中具有高度的服务能级，香港、北京、新加坡、上海、悉尼、巴黎、迪拜、东京；

Alpha 和 Alpha -：链接全球大多数地区的高端服务进入全球经济网络，圣保罗、米兰、多伦多、首尔、台北、广州、旧金山、深圳等；

Beta：链接部分地区的高端服务进入全球经济网络，波士顿、成都等；

资料参考：http：//www. lboro. ac. uk/

大湾区已经从城市竞争走向区域合作，从城市群时代走向湾区时代，从城市创新走向湾区创新。大湾区发展需要破除壁垒，补齐短板，降低成本，促进要素自由流动，发挥集成优势。(图 5)

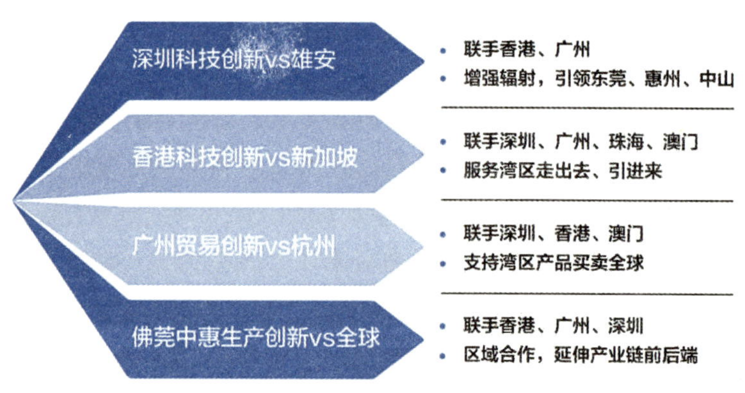

图 5　粤港澳大湾区城市竞争与区域合作图

（二）协同湾区——制度是特色

创新，特别是颠覆性的创新，一定是在边缘的地方生长出来的。大湾区拥有全世界独一无二的“1 个国家、2 种制度、3 个关税区”的制度特色，治理结构包含多种制度，存在很多边界，可以为创新孕育氛围。“一国两制”下的互利合作，与京津冀的协同发展、长三角一体化发展完全不同；同时，与欧盟“一制多国”合作不同，当前制度门槛高于国家门槛，粤港澳三地的流通便利性远不及欧盟。随着“一带一路”倡议的实施，人类共同命运体的理念践行，粤港澳多样的制度、融通的合作模式、包容的文化恰恰是“一带一路”倡议的全球样板。香港的欧美体制与金融专业服务、澳门与葡语系国家的天然链接、深圳的全球科创中心、广州中国商贸门户……还有前海、南沙、横琴三个自贸区作为深度合作的承载平台，推动自由贸易发展，探索两种制度下如何破解就业、医保、税收以及教育之间的壁垒。

从城市到区域，大湾区不是减少差异，而是求同存异、异中求和，将各自优势转换为粤港澳共同的国际竞争力。在宏观层面，顶层设计指导的跨境协商管治机制；在中观层面，沟通机制与合作平台；在微观层面，促成多种形式的合作。通过更深入的合作，实现更广度的开放。

（三）生态湾区——海湾是核心

国外知名湾区，生态环境品质都非常好。比如，纽约湾地区纽华克湾下游部分区域水质为“鱼类存活”标准，其他区域水质均达到“渔业标准”及以上，为全美最洁净海港之一。而珠江口湾区已经是华南第一大、国内第二大污染型海口，水污染形势严峻，海洋环境质量现状堪忧，环珠江口湾区水环境质量与国际三大湾区差距有 20～30 年；在岸线方面，大湾区填海造陆面积居世界前列，海湾面积快速萎缩，1973—2017 年，珠江口海域面积缩减了 15%。大湾区海岸带开发强度不断提高，可开发岸线余量小。生态是大湾区最大的短板。

大湾区因海而生，从地区到湾区，从流域到海湾，背后是生态逻辑之变、是发展理念之变，大湾区需要一个美好的环境来容纳城市未来的转型迭代。生态是大湾区的核心价值，各城市相拥一湾，构成了难以割裂的生态共同体。

（四）宜居湾区——民生是根本

大湾区人的流动是最关键的。粤港澳三地市民来往活动频繁，据 2015 年数据，每天有 40 万的深港市民在深港之间奔波，占香港与内地每日跨境人次总量的 60%。来往内地的居港人士中有 7 成的目的地是深圳，大约是 23 万人次/日。内地赴港旅客中有 6 成来自深圳，大约 7.5 万人次/日。从经济联系度来看，更像是一个双核的城市。但目前仍存在阻碍人员等自由流通的各类障碍，这种障碍已不再是简单的交通问题，而是社保、教育、医疗制度体系等，恰恰是这些看不到的问题才是大湾区下一轮发展最重要的东西。下一步真正关键的就在于各种制度和政策的创新整合。

近期，应开展公共服务跨境衔接试点，建设粤港澳优质生活圈：比如研究养老、医疗等福利的跨境可携带性；引进香港教育模式，实现前海教育与香港标准的统一和相互认证；远期，可以通过制度创新，在大湾区与港澳之间真正实现要素自由流动，包括人才通、信息通、规则通。

（五）人文湾区——文化是灵魂

一流的产业和竞争力需要一流的人才，一流的人才需要一流的栖息环境，而文化是滋润人才最主要的载体。洛杉矶、旧金山有着众多不同的族裔、信仰、文化和建成环境，都是吸引大量人才的因素。大湾区应该思考如何用文化竞争力源源不断地吸引人才，以提升文化国际性为核心目标建设国际文化交往中心，加强文化的跨区域协作平台与体系建设，强化多元文化繁荣发展，才真正具备造血能力。

未来，在“一带一路”倡议下的粤港澳大湾区有着全球最独特的制度特色与优势，共建共享、彼此融通的“大湾区模板”，将在下个30年引领粤港澳进入繁荣、公平、美丽、高质量发展的世界级城市群。

五、结语

从特区到湾区，从追赶融入到引领担当，从高速增长到高质量发展，从全球化到“一带一路”倡议，大湾区是一次从工业文明到生态文明跨越的地理新发现，是一种不同制度共同合作发展的新范式，是一个自主创新与全球生态共同驱动的新平台，是一部面向未来不同文化彼此包容而大气磅礴的新史诗！

（作者：方煜，中规院深圳分院院长）

案例篇

海绵城市建设

——以常德为例

一、背景

为缓解城市水危机，修复城市水生态，涵养水资源，增强城市防涝能力，扩大公共产品有效投资，提高新型城镇化质量，促进人与自然和谐发展，2015 年年初，由住房城乡建设部、财政部和水利部三部委组织海绵城市建设试点，100 多个城市参与申报，首批 16 个城市脱颖而出，2016 年第二批 14 个城市成为海绵城市建设试点城市。根据试点要求，国家海绵城市建设试点期为 3 年，2019 年 3 月份，国家三部委组织专家对第一批海绵城市建设进行验收，第一批海绵城市建设试点阶段性结束。

常德为我国首批海绵城市建设试点城市之一，常德地处湘西北，是长江经济带的重要节点城市、洞庭湖生态经济区的重要组成部分，头枕长江、腰缠二水（沅水、澧水），东靠洞庭湖，西连张家界。全市总面积 1.82 万平方公里，辖 9 个区县（市）和 6 个管理区，总人口 620 万。常德年降水高达 1 365mm，水面率高达 17.6%，是我国中部典型的丰水型城市。

常德海绵城市建设的目的在于探索我国中南部丰水型城市海绵城市建设的技术途径，建管模式，为我国海绵城市进一步推广出经验、出模式。

二、系统谋划，统筹推进

（一）主要问题

1. 水体黑臭

常德市确定护城河、穿紫河、夏家垱水系、屈原公园水面、白马湖公园水面等 7 处水体为常德市海绵城市建设试点区内的黑臭水体。

根据计算，污水直排口为城市河道的主要污染源；护城河流域为合流制，污水直排污染物占护城河入河污染物的 90% 以上；穿紫河流域为分流制，由于混接错接导致的污水直排污染物占入河污染物的 79% 以上。（图 1）

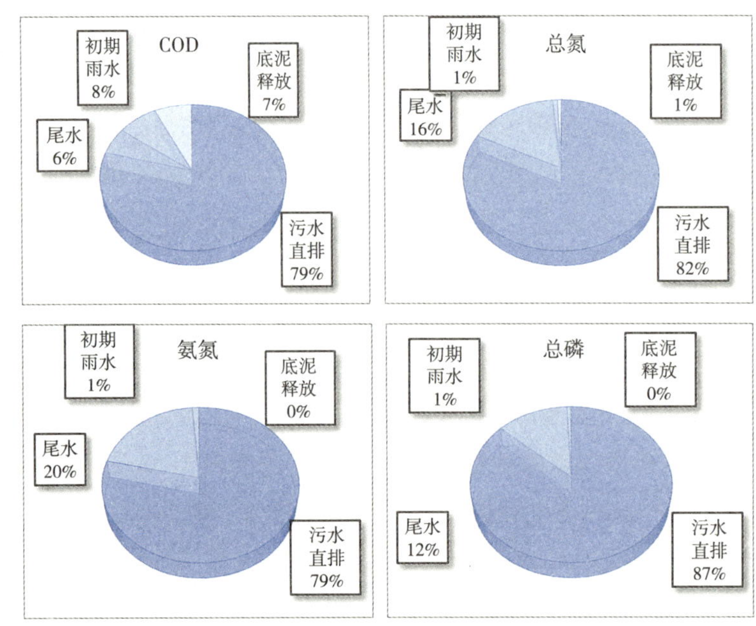

图1 穿紫河污染物来源解析图

2. 内涝易发

由于地势平坦，管网坡度小，管网内水流不畅，壅水溢流情况严重，常德时常发生内涝，试点范围内有16处内涝积水点。

导致城市内涝的成因较多，如设施能力不足、雨水排水分区改变、调蓄空间减少，但常德内涝积水最主要的成因有两个：

一是管网及附属设施运维缺失，导致过水能力大幅下降。根据调查，管网缺陷等级较高的3级与4级占总数的64%，已经严重影响了排水管网的正常安全运行。(图2)

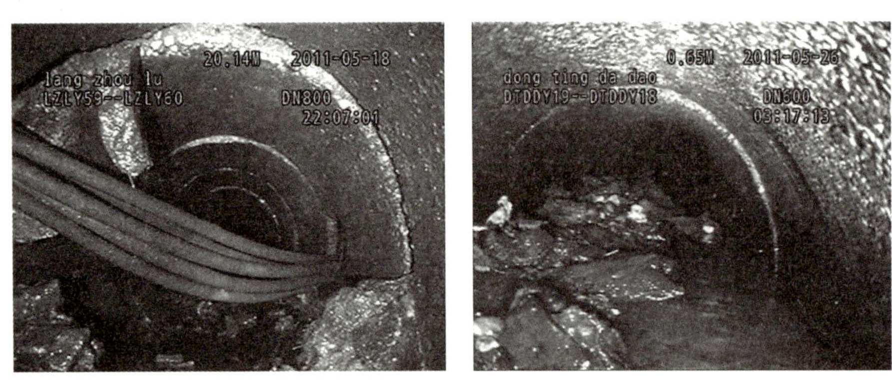

管道材料破碎，异物侵入管道底部有石头等障碍物，断面损失约为管径的50%

图2 管网破损

二是管网不按规划实施，导致管网服务范围过大，排水能力不足。常德大道沿线的内涝积水点主要是由该原因导致的。根据《常德市江北城区排水专项规划（2011)》，常德大道以北、铁路线以南、火车站以西的区域应该排往前进泵站，但由于往前进泵站的道路还没有修通，该区域的雨水管网接到夏家垱排水分区的雨水管网，增大了夏家垱雨水分区的面积，导致该区域成为常德市主要的内涝区域之一。

3. 文化断代

公元前 277 年，秦蜀守张若在常德筑城，修建了护城河，拱卫城池。在随后发展中，常德又因为沅江常德段水势平缓，常德成为水上交通枢纽城市，在常德沅江边上形成了河街。(图 3)

图 3　常德老河街

凭借沅水天然的运输优势，常德成为沅水上的咽喉，西南各地的土特产要顺沅水而下，从常德装上大船转运武昌下江入海，下游的物质又要从常德装船，上溯五岭，近代以前常德是水和船的世界。

抗战胜利后，因无暇顾及护城河的环境保护和综合治理，以至于护城河许多地段藏污纳垢，居民形成随意往河里乱扔垃圾和在河中砌石筑屋的陋习。1986 年对护城河进行为期 3 年的治理，将护城河改为明渠，1988 年又将明渠改为暗渠，成为地下洞河。将祝家堰、龙坑建成屈原公园，将濠坪湖建成滨湖公园。随着城市的发展，护城河变成了黑臭河流，屈原公园、滨湖公园也都变成了臭气难闻的地方。

由于水运的没落，河街日渐萧条，20 世纪 90 年代，为修建沅江防洪堤，彻底取消了河街；由于护城河被盖板，传承 2000 多年的护城河空间消亡，护城河文化、漕运文化逐渐消亡。(图 4)

4. 空间缺失

地处城郊的穿紫河见证了农耕文明向城市文明的发展。穿紫河本是一条连通上游水系的河流，20 世纪 70 年代，为了泄洪，修建了渐河、新河，穿紫河成了无源之河；随着城市发展，穿紫河由远郊变为近郊，成了藏污纳垢之地，垃圾随意丢，污水直接排，穿紫河成为一条黑臭河流，市民活动的高品质空间严重缺乏。(图 5)

(a) 护城河所在城市区间

(b) 护城河上的高密度棚户区

图4 护城河被侵占

(a) 船码头泵站调蓄池原貌

(b) 船码头泵站周边河道原貌

图5 穿紫河黑臭现象

(二) 系统方案

1. 建设目标

以海绵城市建设为抓手，解决城市水体黑臭和内涝问题，恢复和传承城市水文化，统筹促进城市转型发展。

水环境：消除试点范围内的黑臭水体，城市河道水环境质量达到《湖南省主要地表水系水环境功能区划（DB43/023—2005)》的要求，即城区内部重点河道穿紫河水质目标为地表水环境质量IV类。

水安全：消除试点范围内内涝积水点，即30年一遇24小时降水189.83mm不发生内涝灾害。当发生30年一遇暴雨时，一般道路积水深度超过15cm的时间不超过30分钟且最大积水深度不超过40cm。

水文化：

(1) 沅江作为常德的母亲河，养育着城头山古文化，善卷文化，为常德水文化之源。

（2）护城河两千多年保护着常德城市的发展，与常德共生共长，为常德水文化之根。

（3）穿紫河近50年发展为城市河流，为常德水文化集中展示区，是常德休闲旅游之河。

2. 建设方案

以流域为基本单元，构建海绵城市建设方案。常德市海绵城市建设试点范围分为3个流域，分别为护城河流域、穿紫河流域和新河流域。因护城河和穿紫河流域分别代表老城区合流制和新城区分流制，本次仅简要说明护城河和穿紫河系统方案。

为治理护城河黑臭水体，首先沿护城河建设截污干管，将直排护城河的污水接入市政污水管网；在此基础上，重点考虑对溢流污染的治理。

建设截污干管后，护城河水系及排水系统运行如下：

（1）晴天时，合流制排水管网收集的污水通过污水管送到污水厂。

（2）小雨时，收集的污水加初期雨水，通过污水管送到污水厂；超过污水泵输送能力的合流污水临时存储在雨水调蓄池中，降雨结束后，再送到污水处理厂。

（3）大雨时，收集的污水加初期雨水，通过污水管送到污水厂；超过污水泵输送能力的合流污水临时存储在雨水调蓄池中，降雨结束后，再送到污水处理厂；超过调蓄池容积的合流污水量，经调蓄池沉淀处理后溢流到护城河。

护城河海绵城市建设的核心在于构建合理的截污干管、溢流池、生态滤池，控制排入护城河河道污染物的浓度。在此基础上进行源头减排、河道清淤，减少入溢流频次、底泥释放量等。

结合水文化建设，护城河流域以屈原公园和滨湖公园为界，将护城河流域分为四段（图6）：

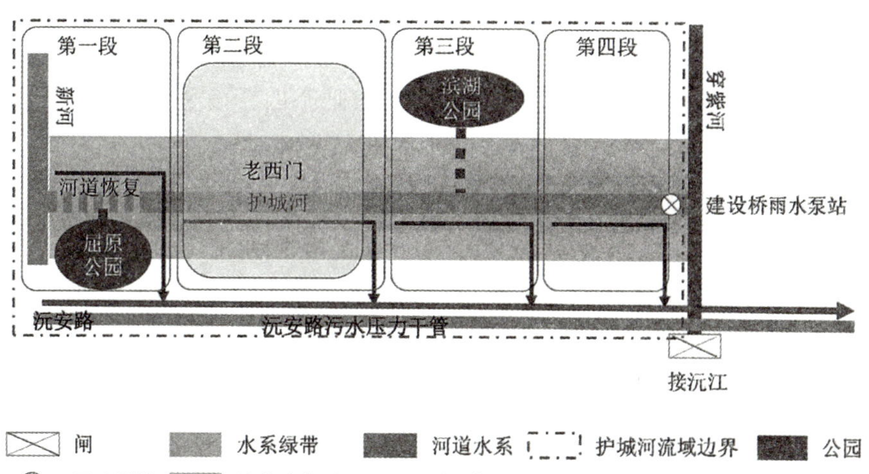

图6 护城河流域海绵城市建设概念图

第一段：以屈原公园提质改造为核心的海绵城市建设。

第二段：老西门为代表的老城区有机更新。

第三段：以滨湖公园为代表的水生态修复。

第四段：建设桥雨水溢流池汇水区综合改造。

穿紫河流域排水系统为分流制，穿紫河的治理采用源头减排 + 清污分流 + 末端初期雨水调蓄池及生态滤池的技术方案，主要采取以下措施：

（1）初期雨水污染削减 45%，即源头低影响开发设施处理能力大于 7mm。

（2）末端集中式生态滤池初期雨水削减率达到 60%，即生态滤池处理能力应大于 7mm。

（3）污水管或者合流制小区管错接入市政雨水管道小于 5%；市政雨污混接比例大幅降低，小于 10%；通过两者综合措施，削减 50% 以上混接入雨水管网的污水量。

（4）雨水口旱流污水消除。

（5）消除江北污水处理厂尾水直排污染，建设湿地，净化尾水水质，主要水质指标达到补水水质要求。

（6）污水处理厂提标扩容，江北城区污水处理能力达到满足污水处理能力要求。

（7）通过灰色基础设施 + 源头减排，共同达到 78% 的年径流总量控制率。

（8）河道整治，消除河道内源污染，河道清淤深度介于 40 ~ 60cm 之间。

（9）滨河打造常德水文化，包括复建常德河街，恢复非物质文化遗产。

通过以上措施形成穿紫河流域性海绵城市建设工程。其中包括：船码头等八个雨水泵站和其周边区域改造；以德国风情街为代表的海绵滨水小区建设；以白马湖和丁玲公园为代表的海绵公园改造；以管网修改、运行维护为主体的灰色基础设施建设；以河街为主的水文化工程。(图 7)

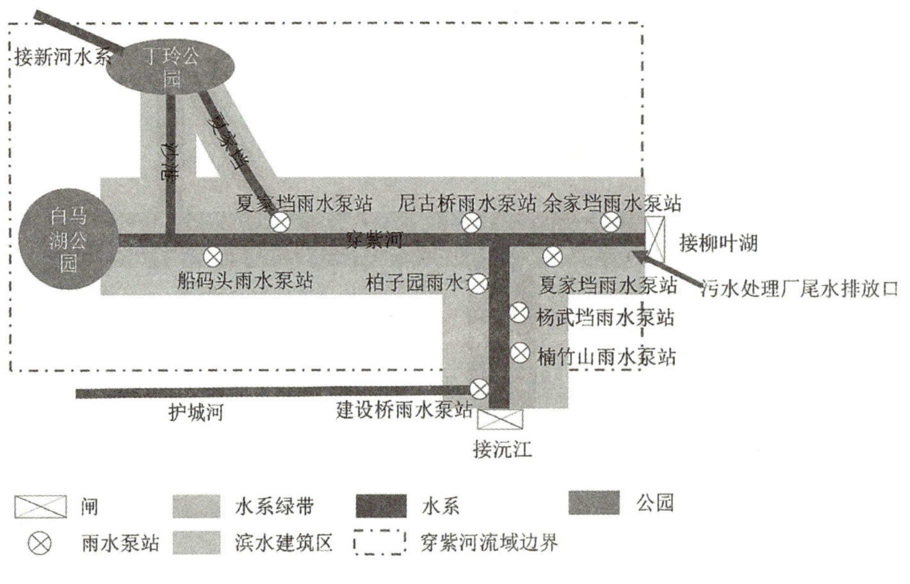

图 7　穿紫河流域海绵城市建设分区图

（三）实施保障

1. 效果导向

在实施时序上，为保障海绵城市建设效果，常德市首先从雨污水排口开始治理，消除水体主要污染源；在此基础上，建设河道水系，将水文化内容植入，传承和发扬水文化；开展源头小区及管网建设，进一步提高城市品质，还给市民高品质空间，水环境、水安全达到海绵城市建设要求。

以穿紫河为例，建设时序上，结合常德市黑臭水体治理的经验，先对泵站、调蓄池、生态滤池及泵站周边的水系、绿地进行改造，消除城市河道点源污染，削减泵站周边面源污染；以水文化定位为要求，对滨水建筑区进行改造，统筹落实海绵城市及水文化战略要求；在此基础上，海绵城市建设目标和指标为要求，落实源头小区改造、管网改造与建设。

2. 建章立制

2015 年 4 月，常德市正式入选第一批海绵城市建设试点，当时正有 79 个项目处于在建阶段，为不耽误工期、同时发挥各部门、专家的能动性，弥补海绵城市建设技术标准规范的不足，采用联审制。所谓联审制是指规划局、住建局、专家等联合审查海绵城市建设方案。当然，该规划建设管控体系也存在一定的局限性，其中之一就是打破了常规的建设规划管控程序。

2016 年 8 月，常德市海绵办明确指出今后所有海绵城市建设项目，必须严格遵守执行《常德市规划局关于印发〈常德市海绵城市建设项目规划管理规定〉》和《常德市住房和城乡建设局关于印发〈常德市海绵城市建设管理规定的通知〉》。

为将海绵城市纳入“两证一书”。常德市政府出台了《常德市海绵城市项目建设暂行管理实施细则》，明确：①在土地出让环节，应纳入海绵城市规划设计要求；②“两证一书”为标准格式，在“两证一书”标准格式变更之前难以将相关指标纳入，但是在相关附件或者审批单中应纳入海绵城市条件。

3. 民生导向

城市居民，特别是老城区居民最头疼的停车位缺乏、没有邻里休闲空间、运动器材老旧、道路年久失修等问题，都在海绵城市建设中得到一定改善。地下停车场不再怕被淹，即使暴雨时，道路上也不会出现污水横流的情况。

海绵城市建设过程中，常德对老旧小区进行了改造，小区环境有了翻天覆地的变化，5 万余居民直接受益。同时彻底解决了老城区内涝积水问题。改造公园及广场 5 个，城市居民休闲游憩空间大幅增加，城市变得更加宜居。市海绵办收到了近百份试点区外小区进行海绵改造的申请。

4. 贴身服务

常德治水启动较早，引入了欧洲治水的理念，但由于降水条件、发展阶段、建设理念不一样、面临的主要问题不一样，欧洲的技术需要和中国的海绵城市有机融合。常德市政府聘请中国城市规划设计研究院作为技术咨询组，一是统筹协调整体海绵城市建设技术路线，为此，中国城市规划设计研究院编制了《常德市海绵城市建设专项规划》《常德市海绵城市建设系统方案》《常德市海绵城市监测方案》等整体性、系统性的文件，将欧洲的治水技术和中国的海绵城市理念融合；二是对海绵城市建设项目方案等设计文件进行技术审核及现场巡视，保障项目落实海绵城市建设要求；三是针对常德市海绵城市建设的共性的技术和程序问题，建议管理部门组织编制相关标准规范，规范海绵城市实施；四是总结海绵城市经验，推广常德海绵城市试点经验，形成常德经验、常德模式。通过以上措施，保障常德市海绵城市建设目标可达，出经验、出模式，达到国家海绵城市建设试点的初心。

三、成效斐然，绿色发展

（一）绿水青山

2019 年市城区主要黑臭水体消除，城内各水体水质达到地表水标准 IV 类以上。城市的 16 个内涝积水点也已经消除。穿紫河从过去市民避而远之的臭水沟，变成了如今市民休闲娱乐的风光带。（图 8、图 9）

（a）改造前的水系和土堤

（b）改造后的水系和生态驳岸

图 8　穿紫河船码头段水系和驳岸改造前后对比

（a）运行前拍摄，2014 年 7 月 17 日

（b）运行两年后，2016 年 10 月 14 日

图 9　穿紫河船码头段咖啡馆处水质对比图

水系生态环境也因生态治理措施与水质的提升，发生巨大的变化。曾经发黑、发臭、沿岸鱼鸟绝迹的水体，随着生态环境的改善，河湖中动植物数量有了显著增长，重现了昔日水鸟成群的景象。水中的生态浮岛，长满挺水、沉水植物的水系驳岸，它们都是鸟类、鱼类、

两栖类的家园，穿紫河生态多样性得到恢复和保护。（图 10）

图 10　水系生态环境得到改善的穿紫河

（二）文脉传承

常德市先后修复并建成了老常德时期码头文化代表的麻阳街、河街、老西门等一批展现常德历史文化、风格多样、内涵丰富的水文化载体群落。在老西门建造了常德丝弦剧场，挖掘整合常德丝弦、花鼓戏两项非物质文化遗产，传统艺术历久弥新。新建德国风情街，让德国风格的建筑落户在穿紫河畔，形成一个外国人的家园，常德的对外之窗。婚庆产业园、金银街等特色商业街，使老常德的内河码头文化、商业文明得到传承。（图 11 ~ 图 13）

图 11　常德河街

（三）市民点赞

常德市海绵城市建设最直观、最重要的效果是城市主要河流水质和生态环境得到改善，为居民提供了休闲空间，增强了幸福感。由此，也改变了老百姓的生活方式。下班后不再打

图 12　常德老西门商业街

图 13　德国风情街

麻将，而是去穿紫河散步，还能沿河骑车上班。大小河街上逢年过节人潮涌动，还举办穿紫河龙舟赛、环柳叶湖马拉松。

针对主要黑臭水体，每处发放 100 份调查问卷，随机了解常驻人员或游人回馈意见。根据问卷调查，各个水体的满意度都能达到 90% 以上，特别是水域面积最大的穿紫河、白马湖、屈原公园均达到了 92%~98%，说明市民认可改造效果。

针对内涝感受情况，进行了民意调查，调查地点集中在内涝点所在地街道，如芷兰、芙蓉等 11 个街道。发放并填写调查问卷 151 份，其中填写非常满意 105 份，占 69.5%，满意 35 份，占 23.2%，一般 11 份，占 7.3%，不满意 0 份，占 0%。通过本次调查问卷反映，16 处内涝点所在居民对防洪排涝工作是相当满意的，整治效果也是卓有成效的。

（四）旅游带动

常德市在海绵城市建设中注重融入大量旅游元素，赋予其城市景观、生态廊道、旅游休闲等新功能，先后打造形成了柳叶湖环湖景观带、穿紫河水上风光带、德国风情街、大小河街、老西门历史文化街等一批海绵亮点项目，目前已成了炙手可热的旅游目的地。老西门文化与商业双赢；大小河街、穿紫河水上观光巴士游客如织；万达金银街、武陵阁步行街流金淌银。（图 14）

图 14　停靠在大小河街码头的水上巴士

数据显示：穿紫河水上巴士运营以来，短短 7 个多月累计接待游客超 5 万人次，实现门票收入约 1 000 万元；“常德欢乐水世界”开园 2 年累计接待游客近 122.1 万人次，门票收入 1.53 亿元。2016 年，常德市海绵城市建设助推旅游效果显著，全市接待国内外游客 4048 万人次，同比增长 25.7%，实现旅游综合收入 318 亿元，同比增长 25.7%。2017 年农历正月初二，中央电视台在黄金时段向全国特别推介了穿紫河 · 河街夜景风光。

穿紫河特色商业街于 2016 年 10 月 18 号开街（常德河街及德国风情街、婚庆产业园目前在建），项目在运营初期主要取得商铺租金收入及住房销售收入。待所持有商业资产运营逐渐成熟，资产升值后再进行销售。目前周边房均价 7 000 元/平方米左右，根据测算商业租金及销售收入预计 2018 年还可实现收入 2 亿元。该项目经过 2 年商业运营资产总值预估为 1.8 亿元。预计上缴税金约 2.4 亿元。

（五）筑巢引凤

随着环境提质进行的城市开发，带来土地大幅升值，拉活地方经济，提升城市品质。以生态水城为定位，经过多年的经营，常德悄然绽放、让人惊艳，多次国际会议在这里召开，如 2017 年 5 月的中德法治国家对话研讨会，2017 年 8 月的气候适应型城市试点建设国际研讨会等，城市影响力逐渐加强。

2018 年 3 月，常德市 708、709 地块拍卖地价创历史新高，分别达到 704 万元/亩、781 万元/亩，楼面地价达 3 756 元/平方米、4 188 元/平方米。现在环柳叶湖、穿紫河沿岸土地出让市场炙手可热，全国著名房产开发商来常德市洽谈络绎不绝。随着保利、恒大、万达、碧桂园、华侨城、绿地、同元、景域、禾田居等实力企业进驻常德，常德正在成为真正意义上的湘西北现代化区域中心城市。

常德成为海绵城市试点城市后，试点区内地价、房价上升幅度要高于一般城区；而穿紫河沿岸，随着水质和环境提升，地价、房价上涨比例更是达到一般城区的2倍。

以船码头周边房地产开发为例，以前由于船码头泵站黑臭现象严重，周边区块一直是常德市城区典型的脏乱差区域。2010年机埠启动改造后，实现了水体由差变好，吸引了众多开发商。2013年建成了当时市城区占地面积最大，品质最高的公园世家小区，开创了全国在雨污泵站旁建设高档房产小区的先例。(图15)

图15　船码头生态滤池对面的公园世家小区

2015—2017年，海绵城市建设试点范围内土地出让2 773亩，因海绵城市建设引起的土地出让溢价收入达到6.65亿元；商品房销售面积达到496万平方米，因海绵城市建设引起的房屋销售溢价收入达到15.14亿元，相应增加政府税费收入3.78亿元。截至2017年年末，海绵城市建设试点范围内剩余可商业出让土地预计有2 527亩，因海绵城市建设引起的土地出让溢价收入预计可达28.82亿元，房屋销售溢价收入预计可达41.41亿元，相应增加政府税费收入预计可达10.35亿元。

四、启示

(一) 水城共生

一方面，治水营城的理念始终贯穿于常德海绵城市建设试点，给内涝洪水预留空间，建设分散式和集中式的绿色基础设施净化雨水；另一方面，城市充分利用预留的蓝色空间，把水当成城市高品质发展的核心资源，充分挖掘城市水文化，打造城市水景观。

穿紫河、护城河河面的恢复及拓宽则是给洪水以出路，协调城市与水的关系，打造水安常德。以护城河老西门为核心的城市水文化复兴、老城复兴项目，以穿紫河河街为代表的千年沅江文化的传承，以常德丝弦为代表的非物质文化遗产重现等，充分挖掘了常德的水文化。

（二）群众路线

群众路线表现为解决市民关注的问题，如高品质公共空间的打造以及市民关注小区环境的改造。通过整治穿紫河、大型公园（滨湖公园、屈原公园、白马湖公园等），为市民提供了高品质的公共空间。

通过老旧小区的改造，解决市民房前屋后积水和黑臭水体问题，以及小区居住中实际的需求，如停车等问题。老旧小区在改造之前，海绵办先对小区情况进行摸底，包括小区建设年代、小区面临的主要问题。对于问题较突出的老旧小区，进一步与业主座谈，确定业主需求等。

（三）综合统筹

行政统筹。海绵城市建设是一项系统的工作，政府部门涉及规划、建设、财政、水利、国土、发改、园林、市政、房管等部门，常德市海绵城市建设领导小组的由市主要领导挂帅，综合协调各部门。在具体的运作模式上，主要通过海绵办的周例会、主管领导的月例会、主要领导的季度调度来实现。在 2019 年的机构改革中，常德市以海绵办为基础，成立常德市海绵城市建设服务中心，协调海绵城市建设各行政层面的关系，统筹推进。

技术统筹。常德海绵城市建设参与项目设计的技术单位有 8 家，这 8 家设计单位中有欧洲背景的设计单位，有美国背景的设计单位，也有国内一线城市的设计单位，也有常德本地的设计单位，各家对海绵城市建设的理解并不一致，技术途径也不一致。常德市聘请中国城市规划设计研究院作为技术支撑单位的目的之一就在于融合各家技术，综合达到海绵城市建设效果。中国城市规划设计研究院在常德通过总体把控，充分发挥各家技术优势，形成常德海绵城市建设技术途径，达到了海绵城市建设的目标。

（作者：陈利群，中国城市规划设计研究院教授级高级工程师）

以共同缔造助力乡村精准扶贫

——以红安县柏林寺村为例

一、背景

新中国成立70年来，我国经济社会得到巨大发展，但是，农业、农民和农村问题一直是制约我国经济社会发展的短板，“三农”问题是关系国计民生的根本性问题，破解“三农”问题一直寄托着中华民族的强国之梦。然而，当前我国城市与农村发展失衡已严重阻碍了经济社会的可持续发展，城乡发展不平衡是我国最大的发展不平衡，农村发展不充分是最大的发展不充分[1]，2013年，习近平总书记在湘西十八洞村考察时首次作出了“精准扶贫”的重要指示。深入推进精准扶贫，其薄弱环节在乡村，主战场也在乡村，因此要打赢这场攻坚的“硬战”，实现全面小康的百年奋斗目标，基层治理是一个重要课题。[2]党的十九大报告提出乡村振兴战略的总要求，即产业兴旺、生态宜居、乡风文明、治理有效、生活富裕，并要求健全乡村治理体系，打造共建、共治、共享的社会治理格局，为打赢脱贫攻坚战提供了思路。

在打赢脱贫攻坚战与实施乡村振兴战略的历史交汇期和任务叠加期，为切实贯彻落实十九大重要精神和习近平总书记重要指示，把人民对美好生活的向往作为奋斗目标，完成2020年全面脱贫任务，住房城乡建设部在四个对口扶贫县各选了一个村进行共同缔造乡村治理试点。共同缔造以吴良镛先生的人居环境科学为基础；[3]以群众为主体，从空间的使用者的需求出发，建设民生工程；核心是参与，通过参与来动员群众、组织群众，对承载社会各群体利益的空间资源进行合理的分配与协调；基础在社区，即以社区为平台，发动群众共同参与社区公共事务，增强认同感、归属感，实现美好环境与和谐社会共同缔造。[4]实际上，从十九大习总书记提出“共建共治共享”的治理体系，到2017年8月《农村人居环境整治三年行动方案》中提出的“共谋、共建、共管、共评、共享”机制，这是社会治理的具体化。

本文以在红安县柏林寺村试点的实践为基础，探索通过共同缔造的方法调动农民的积极性、主动性，建立乡村治理的新模式，激发乡村内生发展动力，进一步改善乡村人居环境，巩固脱贫成果，落实乡村振兴战略。

二、案例村庄概况及代表性

柏林寺村位于黄冈市红安县七里坪镇东南部的浅丘陵山区，距镇区约17公里，距红安县城约25公里，到武汉市约1个半小时车程，属于典型的“远郊型村庄”（图1）。全村辖9个村民小组、15个自然湾，共416户、1 607人，首批试点的自然村大塘黄格湾户籍120户、530人，均为汉族，常住人口为121人，以中老人为主，平均年龄在62岁左右。村民主要经济收入来自务工，农业收益主要来自于水稻、花生种植和少量猪、牛、鱼等养殖。自然村原有贫困人口42户、131人，2017年年底贫困户全部脱贫，进入巩固提升脱贫成果阶段。大塘黄格湾背山面水，自然环境优美，人居环境整治处于起步阶段，呈现出以下特点及问题：

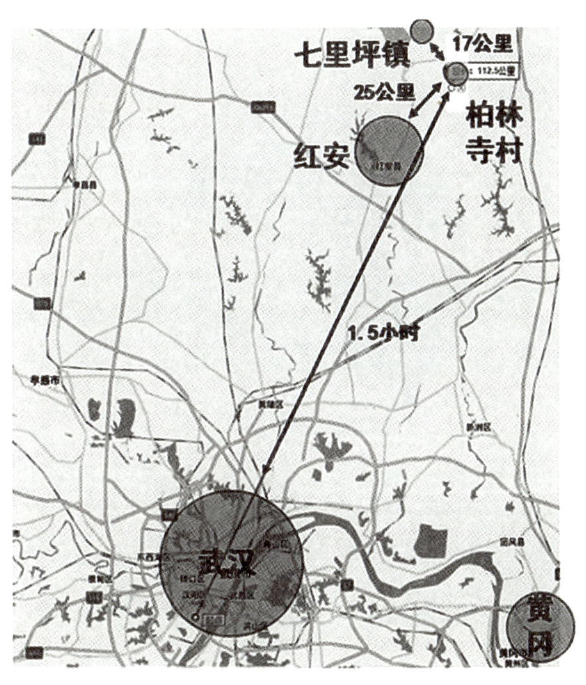

图1　柏林寺村区位图

（1）人口“老龄化”“空心化”现象明显。柏林寺村属于典型的“空心化老龄村”，村庄60%以上的村民选择村外工作居住（图2），村内60岁以上老人占人口比重达到19%，40～60岁以上人口占比达到41%（图3）。

（2）村民建设主动性不强，思想容易反复。村庄规划建设中，村民的主体意识不强，“等、靠、要”的思想比较严重，普遍存在等待观望情绪。在共同缔造过程中，由于区别于以往政府大包大揽，建设快、效果明显的“输血”式的乡村建设，以村民为主体的“造血”式乡村建设周期较长，村民参与共同缔造的热情和思想多次出现反复。

（3）村落凝聚力不强，沟通机制不畅。共同缔造开展之前，村委书记刘有福常常感叹

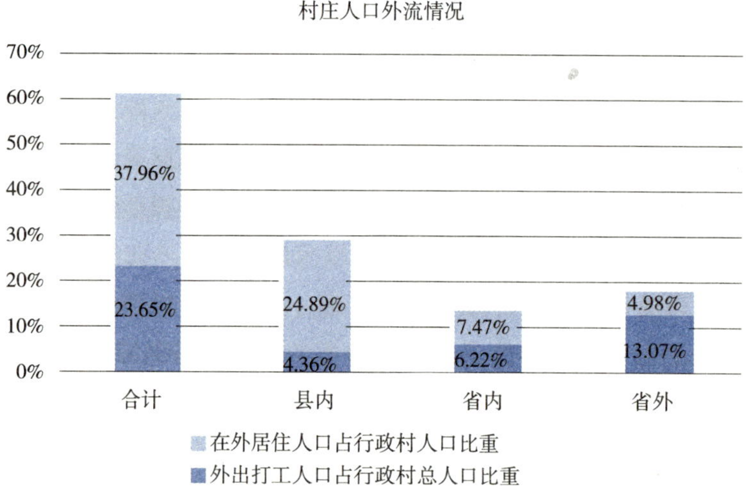

图 2　柏林寺村人口外流统计

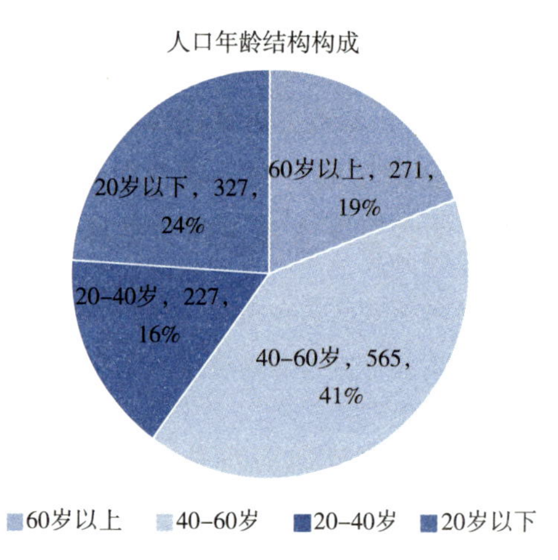

图 3　柏林寺村人口年龄结构

“村里办事形不成合力”，无论是环境维护还是产业发展，村民各自为政，不愿协作办事。同时，缺乏有效反映问题的途径，村民经常抱怨村庄问题不能及时解决。

（4）政策机制壁垒，资金缺乏统筹。以前村庄建设靠政府自上而下走招投标流程，村庄只需被动接受改造即可，村内缺乏相应的支持、监督和管理制度，村民很难参与村庄建设，在一定程度上也影响了工程的后期维护。同时，支持村庄建设的涉农资金缺乏有效统筹，不从实际问题和需求出发，容易造成建设上的浪费。

（5）基础设施存在短板，乡村风貌有待提升。村庄经过美丽乡村建设，基础设施逐渐完善，但在污水排放及处理、化粪池建设、垃圾收集处理和池塘水质净化等方面仍存在短板，村内局部存在过度硬化、景观园林化等问题，破坏了村庄乡土风貌，影响村庄的居住环境和村庄品质（图 4）。

红安县柏林寺村作为以农业为主，又没有明显区位优势的普通村庄，所面临的空心化、老龄化、村庄治理结构松散、人居环境有待改善提升等问题，具有较强的普遍性和代表性，

图4 柏林寺村村容村貌问题

因此以柏林寺村为代表进行共同缔造的实践，对于量大面广的普通村庄具有借鉴意义。

三、共同缔造的方法与过程

（一）共同缔造的基础：转变思想，发动群众

思想转变既是前提，也是共同缔造工作的难点，政府、规划团队和村民都需要转变思想观念，改变自上而下的工作方式，政府部门从由原来的“决策者”变为“辅导员”，规划师从“专家”变为“参谋”，村民由“旁观者”变为“参与者”，形成政府、社会、村民协商共治的局面（图5）。

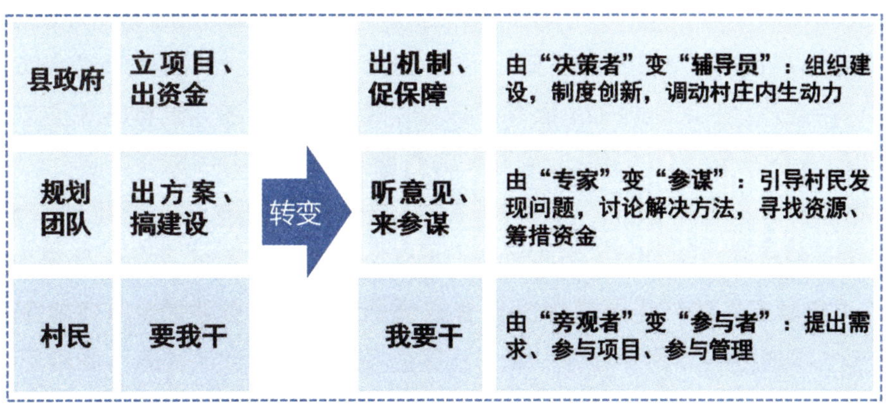

图5 思想转变及角色转变

（1）改变政府的工作方式。地方政府是村庄规划建设的责任主体，过去习惯通过“立项目、出资金”家长式管理主导村庄建设，共同缔造则是转变政府主导模式，结合社区自治模式，通过“出机制、促保障”，促进政府服务重心下沉，指导支持农村基础组织建设，调动村庄内生动力，从“大包大揽建设”变为“支持引导激励”。

（2）转变规划团队的理念。在传统规划模式中，规划师以专家身份成为制定规划方案的主体，其所拟定的规划方案受到委托方影响较大，无法完成以村民为主体的共同缔造工作。规划师主动通过理论学习、定期交流讨论以及成功案例考察等方式，实现了由最初的“专家主导”向现在的“协同参谋”的思想转变，从过去的“出方案、搞建设”变为“听意见、来参谋”，让村民成为主人，引导村民主动查找村庄问题，自行商议解决方法，寻找资源筹措资金，规划团队提供相应的技术咨询。

（3）激发村民的主体意识。村民的思想转变最难，也是共同缔造工作瞄准的“靶心”。规划团队进村后，常常入户访谈找不到人，开会见不到人，村民对新事务、新观念的接受速度也较慢。为了使村民从被动冷淡、消极观望到主动谋划、捐工捐力，规划团队改变工作方法，并总结了四点经验：

第一，口说千遍，不如眼见为实。除了反复给村民宣讲共同缔造理念，规划团队还邀请村两委、村内乡贤、村民代表赴罗平县苍葭冲村、信阳郝堂村等美丽乡村考察参观，对村民思想触动明显（图6）。

图6 美丽乡村考察参观

第二，采取群众喜闻乐见的沟通方式。比如用地图扎大头针的“游戏”方式采集群众意见，效果立竿见影（图7）。

第三，将共同缔造“软性植入”到村民活动中。为了吸引更多村民关注，规划团队联合村委举办百家宴活动，趁机向村民宣传共同缔造的理念（图8）；组织小学生开展“我心中美丽的柏林寺村”演讲赛吸引家长参与，演讲稿还发布在公众号平台上（图9）。

第四，关注一老一小，建立情感传输纽带。老年食堂和亲人见面角维系了老年人和外出务工子女之间的情感联系，间接传递共同缔造理念；暑期为村内留守孩子举办的“四点半”课堂，成为持续宣传共同缔造理念的媒介（图10），带动更多村民从关注共同缔造到理解共

图 7　村民在航拍图上扎针表示“满意”“不满意”的地方

图 8　百家宴活动

图 9　“我心中美丽的柏林寺村”演讲赛

图 10　“四点半”课堂

同缔造，最后参与共同缔造。

经过这一系列耐心细致的工作，村民逐渐明白共同缔造是为自己和后辈谋福利，从原来的“要我干”变为“我要干”。

(二)共同缔造的保障:组织建设,机制创新

组织机制建设是共同缔造工作的重中之重。当工作重点从物质环境建设转变为组织发动村民,从政府主导项目实施转变为村民主导项目实施,制度创新的作用远比规划方案更为重要。规划团队在柏林寺村建立了“纵向到底,横向到边,多方力量共治共管”的乡村治理体系。

(1)以县为面,纵向到底,政府工作下沉。将党的领导从县委、镇党委、村党支部到村庄每位党员贯彻到底,更好地发挥党的领导作用及党员的带头作用。同时,将政府的管理服务和技术服务从县政府到镇政府到村委会,最终惠及到每一位村民。

(2)以村为点,横向到边,发挥村民自治。为凝聚村民,激发村民内生动力,柏林寺村建立了“1+4N”的组织机制,“1”是村两委班子,“4N”包括村组理事会、村经济合作社、专项责任组和村落事务监事会,四个组织以理事会为核心,各司其职,推动村落共同缔造(图11)。

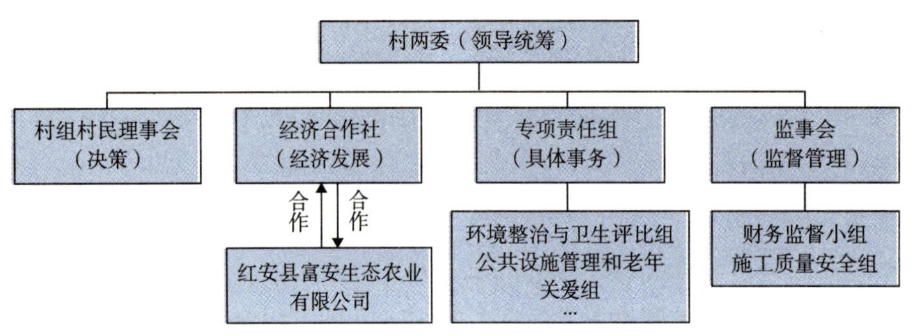

图11 “1+4N”的组织机制架构

为确保乡村共同缔造的各项建设公开透明,机制设计进行灵活创新,在监事会的财务监管组和施工质量安全小组中引入县、镇技术人员,协助对村内重大事项把关。同时,在共同缔造工作推动过程中,还需要及时将运行效果好的工作流程、方式确定下来,出台村规民约,形成长效机制,也是防止村民思想反复的一个“紧箍咒”。红安县政府层面也由政研室牵头,联合县、镇各部门出台了《柏林寺村“美丽乡村、共同缔造”示范点项目建设与奖补办法(试行)》的通知,制定详细的针对村落农房改造和村落环境整治以奖代补政策,细化资金支出和监管流程,通过“以奖代补,同工同劳”等方式,鼓励村民自发参与共同缔造过程(图12)。

(三)共同缔造的过程:村民参与,协商推动

“五共”是共同缔造的灵魂,强调以村民参与为核心,充分发挥村民在村庄规划与建设方面的潜能与作用,规划团队在柏林寺村共同缔造实践中,探索出“共谋、共建、共管、共评、共享”的工作路径。

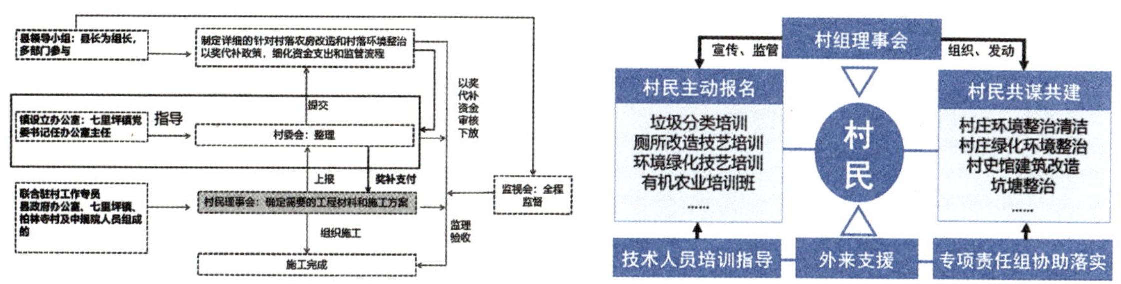

图 12 “纵向到底，横向到边，多方力量共治共管”的工作机制

1. 决策共谋，坚持问题导向

决策共谋是共同缔造的核心，直接决定了工作的内容及方式。决策共谋的目的是动员村民群策群力，共同谋划村庄各项事务，形成村民和理事会、乡贤、规划师、村民之间协商共谋的局面。规划团队驻村后，首先，以问题为导向，引导村民共谋。规划团队通过逐户走访与问卷调查，了解群众需求，并贴近村民，用群众语言说活，比如在村落航拍图上扎红蓝双色大头针的方式了解村民对村庄建设的满意度（图 13），用简易模型和村民推演方案等直观简洁的方式，发动村民一起思考（图 14）。其次，搭建信息平台，支持村民共谋。针对村民大多外出打工，召开村民代表大会颇为不易的现实情况，规划团队帮助设立了“柏林寺之声”微信公众号和微信群，发布村内信息，讨论发展意愿，协商解决问题（图 15）；再次，“慢一点”表态，推动村民共谋。为了让村民具有主人翁意识，规划团队内部强调要“采取慢一点表达意见”的工作方法。村民要求建筑风格不能太“土气”，规划团队不急于否定，而是在组织参观优秀示范村落时再次抛出这个问题，村民们立刻意识到房屋建筑还是要保留乡村特色更好，凝聚了群众经验共识。最后，确立乡贤引领，带领村民共谋。乡贤是村庄的意见领袖，其言论和行动对村民有极强的导向性，规划团队和村两委积极联络关心乡村发展的在外乡贤，通过邀请他们加入微信群、回村开座谈会等方式，为村庄发展出谋划策（图 16），成为村民共谋的“领头羊”。

图 13 村民反映的村庄问题

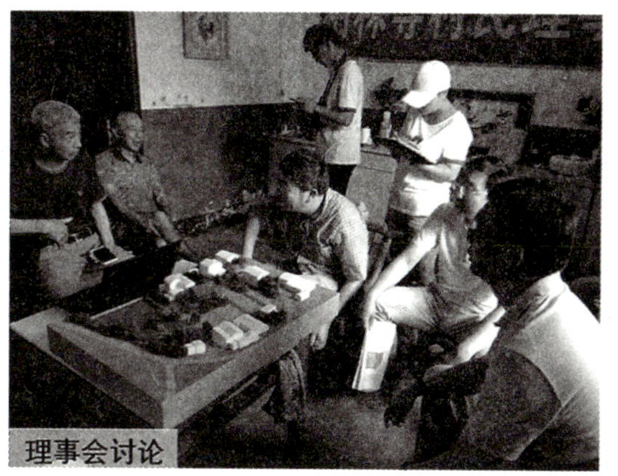

图 14 以简易模型为载体讨论

图 15　信息平台共谋议事

图 16　“七一”组织乡贤党员座谈

2. 发展共建，注重因村施策

村庄的建设项目可分为三种类型：一是简易项目，村民可自行投工投劳完成；二是技术含量低的项目，可由村民组织施工队，聘请技术指导；三是技术含量较高的项目，由村民代表大会遴选专业施工队，村民按工计酬参与共建。针对村庄不同的建设改造需求，规划团队探索了三种共建模式：

一是家庭自建。对于农房院落绿化美化等简易项目，设计师给予引导和技术培训，依据相关的“以奖代补”政策，鼓励村民自建。

二是“能人”组织共建。应对村内用地紧张，简单基础设施项目如化粪池建设可采取加强邻里合作，共同分摊成本的方式连户合建，由村内施工经验丰富的村民领头，完成技术难度不大的工程。

三是集体共建。难度较大的工程由村委会作为甲方，经议事程序选择合适的施工队伍进行建设，同时可邀请村民投工投劳。

同时，针对柏林寺村人口严重老龄化情况，尊老助老，探索村庄适老化设计也是工作重点之一（图 17）。在村委、理事会商议下，村内成立了公共设施管理与关爱老人小组，规划团队协助村民改造了村史馆并在功能上向老年人倾斜，村史馆增加专人管理的老年活动室和亲人见面角。村内老年人多使用老年手机，亲人见面角则提供免费视频服务，便于老人和子女在网上联系。此外，村内还建设了老年共享食堂，计划面向全村所有 65 岁以上的空巢老人提供敬老餐。

3. 建设共管，解决长效机制

建设共管是共同缔造有效的支撑与保障，是村民参与长效机制的重要内容。村两委领导，协同村民、县镇相关部门、专业技术团队等多方成员形成合力，在“村民主体、多方参与、责任明确、分工协作”共同管理机制下，齐抓共管村里的环境卫生、财务收支、项目质量。

一是建制村规民约，共管环境卫生。村委和理事会组织村民讨论，划定了村落公共环境责任分区，每位理事会成员负责一个环境责任区的“四清”工作，并明确村民自觉管理房

● 柏林寺村老人的"四个烦恼"

一是村里没有老人乘凉喝茶闲聊的去处；二是大部分老人持老年手机，子女常年在外不能见面，也不舍得多打电话；三是部分老人行动不便，日常做饭不便；四是村落距离县城较远，老人担心出现紧急健康情况无法及时就医。

● 改造村史馆，突出老人服务功能

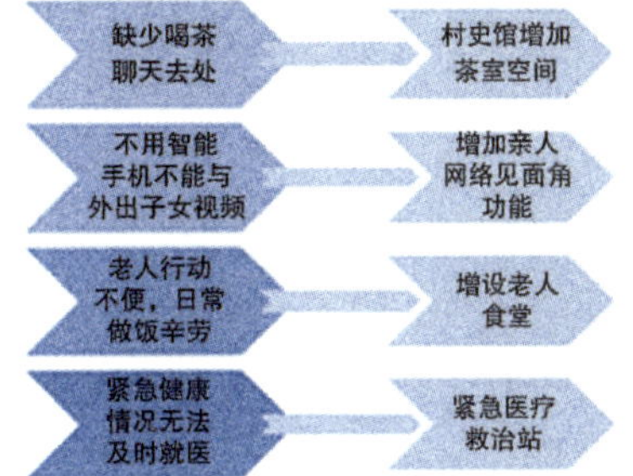

● 相关设备筹集

桌椅——村民自备；亲人网络见面角电脑——中规院捐赠；紧急治疗器材——县医院捐赠

图 17　村史馆适老化改造及功能调整

前屋后的卫生环境。（图 18）

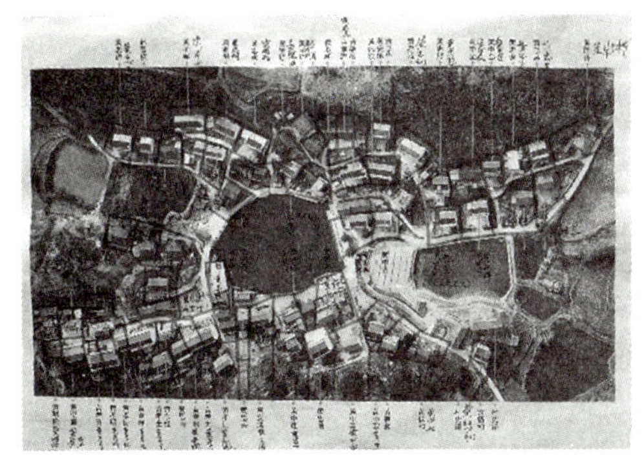

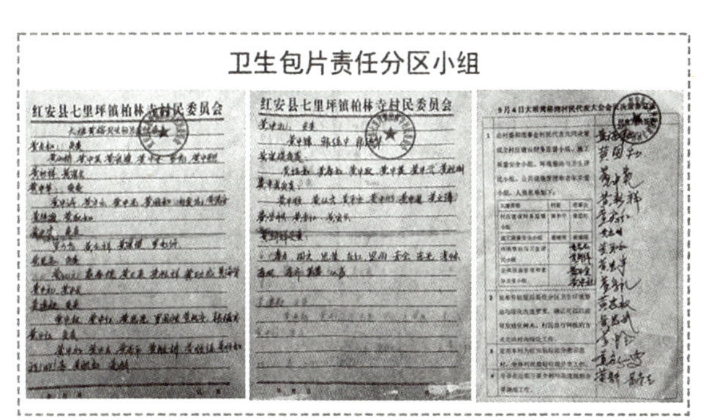

图 18　责任分区共管环境卫生

二是监督财务收支，共管资金安全。村内成立了财务监督小组，负责管理和监督村内公共资金使用，所有资金拨付的关键环节，以及项目工程开工前的资金估算和施工完成后的资金结算，均需财务监督小组四位成员签字许可，并将相关财务情况在村内予以公示。

三是严格监管流程，共管施工质量。村内成立了施工质量安全监督小组，兼有施工技术员和工程监理的双重责任，村内工程的每一个关键环节，均需由施工质量小组人员到场监督确认并集体签字，方能进入下一施工环节，施工开工前的技术评估和施工完成后的工程验收均由施工质量安全小组成员组织完成，并将相关情况于村内公示，接受村民监督检查。

4. 效果共评，形成奖惩激励

效果共评是共同缔造必不可少的重要环节，既能总结阶段性工作，及时调整行动计划，又能激发村民的参与热情。村落美不美，村民说了算，柏林寺村建立了事先明确评比内容与细则，事中组织中小学生和理事会成员为主的评定团认真评比，事后张榜公布成绩并给予物质奖励的共评机制方法。共同缔造开展后，村两委和理事会发布了村内卫生环境评比标准，建立了每月一次的评比制度，组织了“大手拉小手”环境卫生打分评比活动（图19），最后总结出村庄十大环境卫生问题，并作为下次评比整改的核心内容，同时，还评选出十户卫生文明家庭在村内张榜公示，并发放奖励。

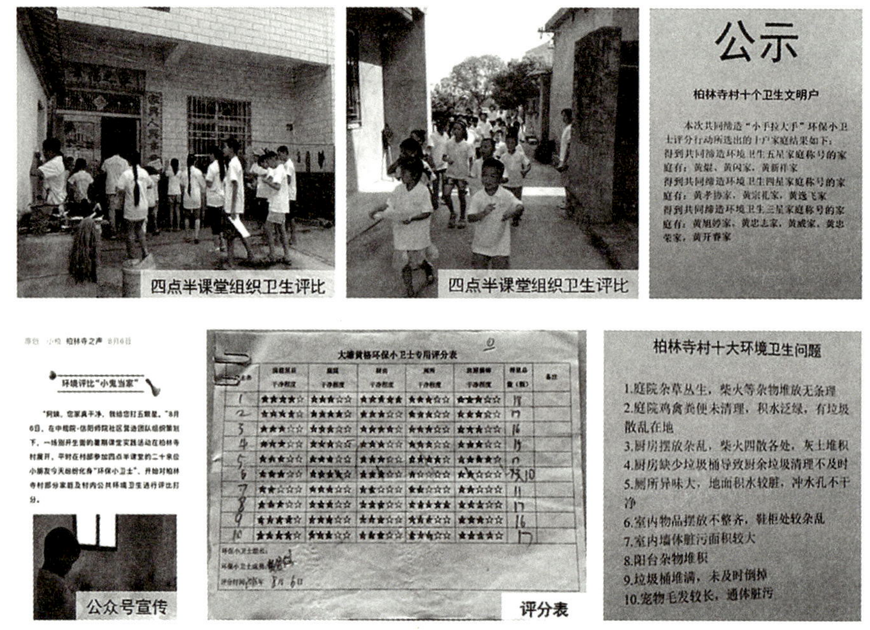

图19 “大手拉小手”环境卫生评比活动

5. 成果共享，实现多方共赢

通过“共谋、共建、共管、共评”，村民切实参与到共同缔造过程中，推动了项目，建立了组织，开展了活动，村庄面貌焕然一新，村民感受着村容整洁、乡风文明、管理民主、生产发展的美丽乡村新气象，享受着共同缔造结出的硕果。

一是乡风文明共同享受。老年人食堂已建成运营，并形成较为完善的管理机制（图20），村内65～70岁年龄段的老人，一日三餐只需要付5元；71～80岁年龄段的老人，一日三餐只需要付3元；80岁及以上高龄的老人免费就餐。村内全体党员及部分在外打工的年轻人、村理事会捐款，作为老年食堂运营的资金，充分体现了村落内部凝聚力，让老人真正老有所养、老有所依。紧急医疗救治站已投入使用（图21），镇医院的医生对村里比较年轻的村民进行了医疗急救培训，还和村民互加微信，解决了村内留守老人较多，看病不方便的问题。亲人网络见面室已布置启用，并组织培训老年人微信视频，加强与在外打工孩子的情感交流。

图 20　老年人食堂建成运营

图 21　医疗公益健康检查

二是美好环境共同享受。从开展村落四清四化环境提升，到村民划定责任自觉维护村内环境卫生，村里的房前屋后垃圾得到及时清理，村内绿化得到极大改善，村内还建立了垃圾分类制度，每户分两个垃圾桶，一个放会腐烂的垃圾，一个放不会腐烂的垃圾，腐烂垃圾由村民自己送到垃圾站去，不腐烂的垃圾定期送到废品回收站。

三是产业发展共同享受。产业兴旺是乡村振兴的基础，发展产业是脱贫攻坚的根本决策。乡贤刘灵敬教授回乡创业，创办的生态农业基地一共带动 121 户贫困户，600 余人增收，为村民就业和脱贫攻坚贡献了极大的力量（图 22），共同缔造工作开展后，村理事会牵头组织村民学习培训、参观考察，并以生态农业基地为依托，组建经济合作社，规划团队利用技术优势，为村民们开发了一套用于生态蔬菜销售和劳动用工组织的微信小程序（图 23），打开线上销售的广度和深度，并配套设计了生态蔬菜销售的外包装，树立品牌观念，促进村庄有机农业良性、更好、更快的发展。

红安县富安生态农业有限公司合作养羊分红领款单

图 22　产业带领村民脱贫致富

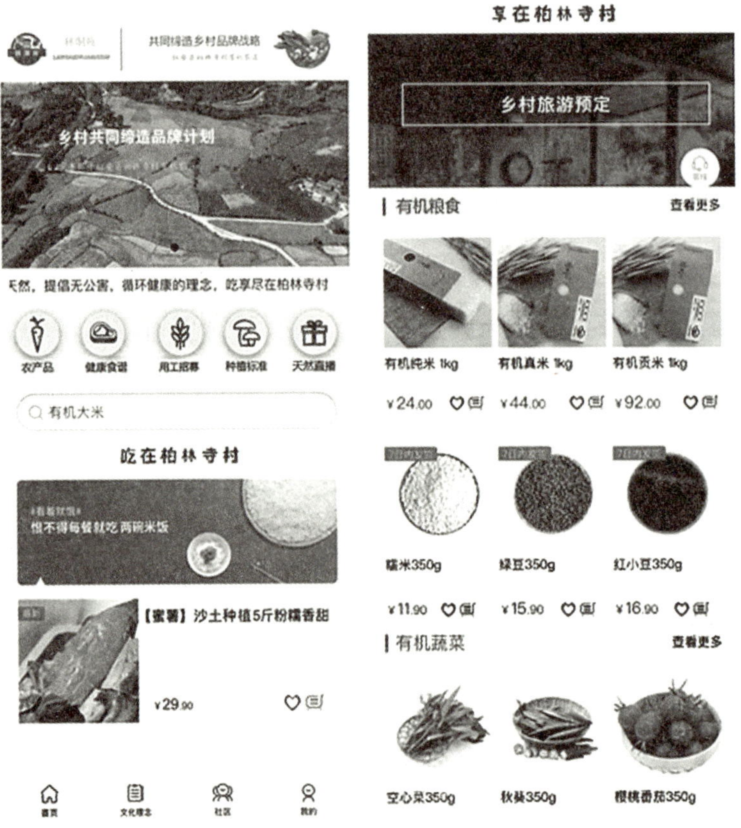

图23　生态蔬菜销售和劳动用工组织的微信小程序

四、结语

精准扶贫的实施离不开有效的乡村治理，乡村治理的高效也必然会加速精准扶贫的推进。我国现阶段乡村治理仍然十分薄弱，尤其是城镇化快速发展导致长时期形成的乡村社会结构发生了巨大变化，大批农村青壮年劳动力涌向城市，能人乡贤流失，动摇了村民自治的根基。本次红安柏林寺村共同缔造实践的探索区别于只强调物质空间形态和功能布局的传统村庄规划编制，而是从思想到行动，紧紧围绕共同缔造为核心，从小事到大事，贯彻共同缔造的理念和方法，充分激活村庄的内生动力，以村民参与为核心，以问题为导向，以美好环境与幸福生活为目标，构筑政府、村民与社会力量多方良性互动平台，实现精准扶贫、乡村治理和乡村振兴的有效实践，提高村民的满意度、幸福感、获得感。“共谋、共建、共管、共评、共享”作为共同缔造的重要内容，清晰地展现了共同缔造过程中村民参与的路径和方法，实现村庄的自我“造血”，为脱贫攻坚和乡村振兴建立长效机制，是可复制、可推广的乡村治理模式的探索。

（作者：彭小雷，中国城市规划设计研究院科技处处长，教授级高级规划师；邓鹏，中国城市规划设计研究院村镇所高级规划师）

参考文献

[1] 孙景淼. 乡村振兴战略 [M]. 杭州: 浙江人民出版社, 2018.

[2] 秦良芳, 陈卓, 游昭妮. 精准扶贫背景下的乡村治理研究综述 [J]. 社会科学动态 2019, (2): 40-47.

[3] 王蒙徽, 李郇. 城乡规划变革: 美好环境与和谐社会共同缔造 [M]. 北京: 中国建筑工业出版社, 2016.

[4] 李郇, 彭惠雯, 黄耀福. 参与式规划: 美好与和谐社会共同缔造 [J]. 城市规划学刊 2018, (1): 24-30.

规划引领：横道河子镇高质量建设发展历程

一、前言

横道河子镇位于黑龙江省海林市市域西部，地理坐标为北纬 44°48'，东经 129°04'，处于黑龙江省“哈牡绥东对俄经济带”上。2007 年，由于其身处独特的自然环境之中并拥有特色的中东铁路历史建筑群落，横道河子镇获批为第三批“中国历史文化名镇”的称号，是黑龙江省获得该项殊荣的首个乡镇。其镇区因山势河道呈带状分布，铁路线南北贯穿，周边翠岭青山环抱，横道河自西北向东南从镇中流过，以河水为界，镇区可分为“北部老区”“南部新区”两部分。“北部老区”是山脉、水系等自然景观遗存和 107 栋俄式历史建筑遗存的核心分布区域，包括全国重点文物保护单位 8 栋（5 处），省级文物保护单位 27 栋，市县级文物保护单位 17 栋，第三次全国文物普查登记的不可移动文物 55 栋。(图 1)

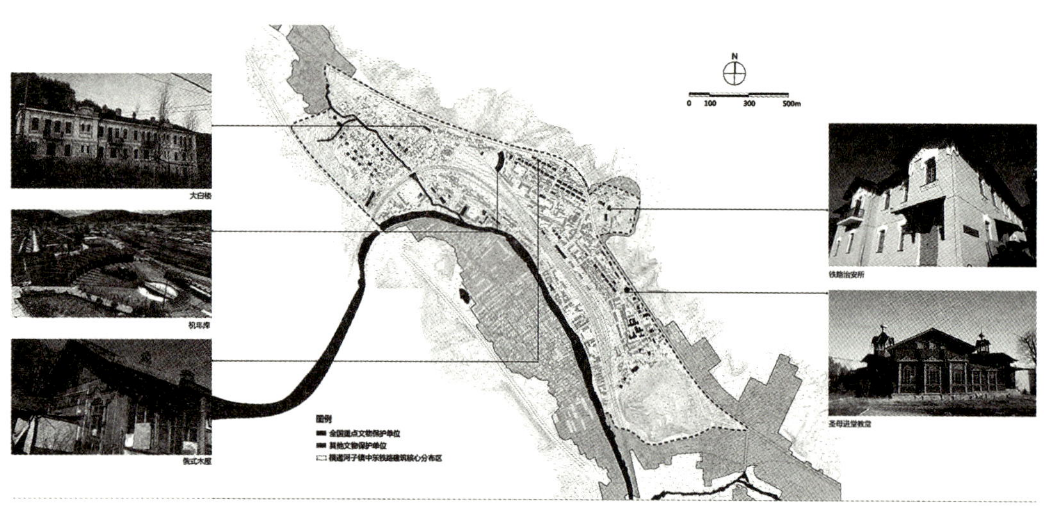

图 1　横道河子镇中东铁路建筑核心分布区

自 2010 年至今，为保持历史城镇风貌特征、传承历史文脉、提升人居环境、复兴地方活力及维持横道河子镇作为中东铁路线性文化遗产重要构成部分的完整性，在当地政府、民众、各建设单位和哈工大规划团队的密切合作下，横道河子镇历经多轮有序的规划设计及建设，包括总体规划、保护规划、城镇风貌规划、建筑本体修缮、环境整治、基础设施提升、旅游规划、使用后评估及后期宣传策划等。在国家新型城镇化政策指导下，规划严守“保护与生态”底线，坚持“低影响低开发”的建设理念和发展原则，将其定位为“以文化保护和生态优先带动利用发展的自然历史文化风貌复兴型的特色小镇”。

在各项规划的编制、实施到建设的8年过程中，横道河子镇逐渐彰显出自然与历史风貌特色及新时代魅力（图2）。相关规划共获得华夏建设科学技术二等奖1项，全国十佳文物保护工程1项，全国优秀城乡规划设计一、三等奖各一项。尤其是2018年，小镇得到了来自联合国等多个国际组织和专家的高度评价。5月，《横道河子机车库修缮设计工程》在迪拜荣获“世界不动产联盟国际卓越建设奖文化遗产保护类金奖”，是该奖项自2009年开设文化遗产保护类别项目评选以来，首个获得该项金奖的中国大陆地区参赛作品；11月，《横道河子镇历史区域》获得“联合国教科文组织文化遗产保护荣誉奖”，成为中国东北地区首个获得联合国教科文组织认可的近现代历史城镇文化遗产保护案例，为向世界推介横道河子镇以及黑龙江省独特的旅游文化魅力做出了卓越贡献，为在世界范围内搭建更广阔的文旅合作与交流平台提供了新契机。

图2　横道河子镇区局部风貌（2018年4月航摄）

省领导们专为此文化遗产保护工作及对当地旅游的带动作用作出重要批示，指示地方加强文旅资源协调和建设工作。联合国教科文组织、住房和城乡建设部、国家文物局、中国城市规划学会、中国建筑学会、黑龙江省人民政府及各大新闻机构等官方媒体平台皆对此作出详细的报道和宣传。规划团队在腾讯视频中发布的奖项申报视频，已达到12.5万的点击率，来自海内外的旅游者、摄影师络绎不绝、慕名前往，热切地一睹小镇风采。

而8年前的小镇，在“中国历史文化名镇”的桂冠下却面临着“保护”与“发展”的两难选择，历史建筑及其周边环境遭到严重建设性破坏，部分珍贵的百年建筑岌岌可危，市政基础设施落后，环境卫生条件恶劣，镇区人口结构呈老龄化特点，居民生活满意度极低，并且民众急于脱离原有生活环境，住进楼房的强烈意愿恰恰处于历史城镇保护工作中维护居民生活延续性的对立面，加之财政资金的严重不足与相关产业支持的匮乏，加剧了小镇保护形势的严峻性。（图 3、图 4）

图 3　七号木屋周边环境旧貌（摄于 2010 年 7 月）

图 4　俄式木屋周边环境旧貌（摄于 2011 年 4 月）

二、夯实前期基础工作，评估文化遗产价值

在昔日魅力无限，到如今境遇却如此窘迫的横道河子小镇面前，规划团队师生明确以改善民生和保护文化遗产相融合为规划理念，迅速开展现状调研与实地走访工作，并在与当地老百姓访谈交流过程中巧妙地将文物保护理念、历史资料研读中发掘的小镇历史文化价值、小镇的发展前景向居民宣传讲述。在前期内、外工作的同期稳步开展中，小镇丰富的文化遗产价值得以逐步彰显。

（一）解读人文历史资料，挖掘社会文化价值

相关的历史照片、画册、明信片、影像、史志及中俄文献是能真实反映小镇在中东铁路建设时期空间面貌及民俗民风的宝贵资料。横道河子镇是伴随着中东铁路的建设而逐渐兴起的“花园城镇”。1898 年 6 月，中东铁路正式动工，并在此处设二等站；1901 年 3 月，中东铁路东部线在此处接轨；1903 年 7 月，中东铁路全线竣工通车。为了配合铁路铺设工程管理并解决张广才岭段的施工难题，大批的俄国工程技术人员和中国工人涌至此地工作生活、交流往来，城镇的规划及建设也随之展开，并在后来铁路的运营中逐步发展兴旺起来，由此俄罗斯文化与东北特有的淳朴热情民风结合为独特的人文景观。

对照历史图纸及照片可见（图 5），与建镇初始之风貌相比，现在的小镇自然景观风貌格局依然保持如初，在群山环绕和水系穿流之中，呈现出典型的东北山地风光，植被及气象变化等因素使小镇的季相变幻颇具美感。百余栋历史建筑群落皆原址保存，但花园式的独户庭院设计已被后期使用者的改造和搭建所破坏。建筑群落就地势呈组团式分布，错落有致，

公共建筑与铁路建构设施分布其间，道路骨架结构未有改变，景观、建筑与道路形成的轴线关系明显，镇区功能分区清晰，是中东铁路站区的典型城镇代表。整体规划兼具现代城镇建设意识和铁路工业城镇的布局特点，堪为研究中东铁路城镇史和建筑史的重要实物史料，其场所空间是特殊历史时期俄罗斯移民生存环境的历史见证。

图 5　横道河子镇历史照片

（二）全面评测历史建筑，详录艺术技术价值

对建筑群落艺术和技术价值的细致发掘，虽然历经百年的风雨沧桑和居住者人为造成的私搭乱建，群落整体显露出破败沧桑之感，但通过测绘勘察统计和对文物建筑进行价值评估，横道河子镇从建筑群体看，是现为中东铁路东部线上设站城镇中风貌特色最鲜明、建筑保有数量最多、功能类型最齐备的小镇，统一采用黄色调墙面、深色屋面、精致的门斗和阳光间、转角隅石、砖砌落影的山墙等俄罗斯传统建筑语汇设计；从建筑单体看，是存世个体建筑最珍贵的小镇，在建筑材料、建筑结构、施工工艺等建筑艺术及技术上具有独创性、先进性，一些建筑的特征甚至具备唯一性，如：圣母进堂教堂是中国现存唯一的一座具有百年历史的木结构教堂；15 门的扇形机车库是中东铁路线上尚存机车库中艺术价值最高的一座，空间处理手段和结构设计巧妙，建筑细节考究，在铁路工业遗产中是具有较高的艺术欣赏价值、审美价值与技术价值的典型代表。

此外，对历史建筑群形成风貌协调性干扰及艺术价值破坏的周边非文物建筑也进行了一系列全面评估，如非文物建筑层数、屋顶形式、立面材质、保存现状评估等，力求剥丝抽茧地将遗产的真实性、完整性完美呈现出来。

（三）确定规划建设重点，引领工作有序深化

史料研究及调研勘察工作使规划师对小镇的建筑、环境与人文关系有了从宏观至细微的把控，规划确定了保护小镇包含自然景观、建筑本体（色彩、材质、高度、风格、装饰）、宅院格局、路网结构的框架性风貌控制原则，并明确了单体建筑分级分期的修缮计划，非文物建筑风貌协调规划及横道河污水治理、镇区垃圾清运管理等环境整治要点和重要节点空间的景观设计、展示利用等初步意向。

三、多专业多层级协同规划，保障小镇风貌延续

城镇风貌应源自物质文化和非物质文化的丰富展现。物质文化之于城镇风貌大到空间格局、建筑群落、道路肌理，小到街道立面、建筑质量、牌匾家具，非物质文化还包括传统工艺、民间艺术、生活习俗、饮食文化等，均为城镇风貌延续与发展的重点。其涉及的空间载体既有镇域的宏观范围、镇区的中观范围，同时也包含历史街区和以全国重点文物保护单位（以下简称国保单位）为核心的建筑本体及周边环境区域。因此，考虑到城镇风貌的层次性特征，在规划制定上采用“层层递进，重点有序”逻辑方式，分别从《海林市横道河子镇总体规划（2010—2030年）》《黑龙江省海林市横道河子镇保护规划（2010—2030年）》和《全国重点文物保护单位——中东铁路建筑群（横道河子镇）保护规划（2014—2030年）》进行从宏观、中观到微观三个层次的规划编制，从整体定位到重点把控再到细节修正，着力于解决镇区空间布局、保护区划及保护措施、国保单体展示利用方向等核心问题，层层递进助力历史文化名镇横道河子的活化再生。

（一）镇域发展定位下的宏观统筹

《海林市横道河子镇总体规划（2010—2030年）》从城镇全域发展的战略高度出发，明确城镇性质职能，结合镇区与周边村屯的现状特点部署城镇体系规划，阐明城镇空间的供给与布局关系，就镇区历史文化遗产的资源优势，制定了相对应的保护专题。

城镇定位兼顾小镇特色和国家、省政策等外部环境因素，如《国务院关于加快发展旅游业的意见》《中东铁路沿线保护规划》和《黑龙江省十二五规划》等一系列政策，明确了横道河子镇作为牡丹江市及海林市旅游产业重点发展的地区，性质确定为以旅游服务、生态疗养为主的国家级历史文化名镇。同时按照社会主义新农村建设和发展旅游经济的宏观要求，依托丰富的旅游资源、优越的区位条件、良好的生态基础以及深厚的文化底蕴，规划从全局的高度确定了横道河子镇“中国东北虎之乡”“中东铁路建筑群文化创意产业发展新镇”和“森林中的山水小镇”三大战略定位。

规划整合分析了历版规划中的实施问题，结合小镇自身资源发展条件和生态空间承载力，同时借鉴了德国埃斯林根、山西平遥古城、安徽宏村和西递等国内外优秀实践案例，理

清了一条发展的新思路。即从城镇性质角度出发，以保护城镇自然山水和历史格局等因素为要，分别对镇村统筹发展、村镇体系构建和中心镇区发展三方面进行规划。具体涵盖了产业经济发展、人口与城镇化发展、村镇体系空间布局（空间结构、等级规模和职能结构）、城镇性质与规模、建设用地发展方向、绿地与景观建设、建设用地布局等内容（图6）。

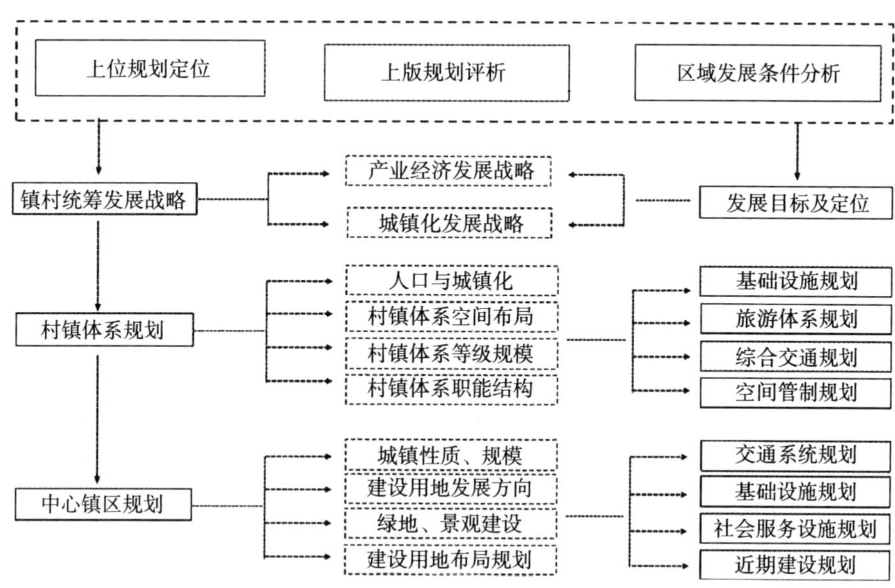

图6 《海林市横道河子镇总体规划（2010—2030年）》技术路线图

规划在工作开展和保护对象分析方面均具有创新性。在工作方法上采取政府组织、专家领衔、部门合作、公众参与、科学决策的工作方法，建立政府重要会议和规划专业会议相结合的会议制度，形成“产、学、研”一体化工作模式，联合中国文化遗产研究院、中国文化大学等科研机构，广泛吸取各部门及专家的意见和建议，增强总体规划的科学性。此外，规划对象解析重视资源条件及生态本底分析，运用生态评价技术对城乡用地条件进行生态适宜性评价、用地布局方案进行环境质量评价，对城镇现状闲置土地进行盘整，从生态容量角度分析城镇人口及用地合理发展规模，建立用地对人口的弹性容量引导。规划重视全面性、实施性和指导性，使小镇重新焕发新时代的活力与光彩。

（二）镇区保护推动下的中观优化

《黑龙江省海林市横道河子镇保护规划（2010—2030年）》在满足上位总体规划要求基础上，接续并深化了其中对于城镇历史风貌保护的内容，规划采用“分级分类”的保护策略：一方面将保护对象确定为镇区范围内的物质文化遗产和非物质文化遗产，另一方面在物质文化遗产的具体保护过程中将其分为小镇整体格局、重点历史街区和各级文物保护单位及登记不可移动文物建筑保护范围三个层次进行分级保护。同时在“保护、完善、发展”规划思想和目标的指引下，提出了“全面保护”“保护与整治相结合”“保护与开发利用相结合”三大保护方法与措施（图7）。

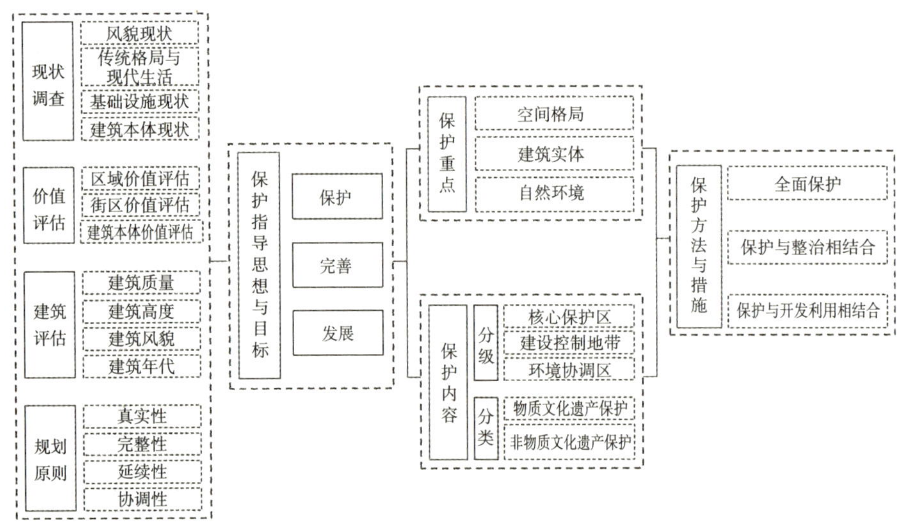

图7 《黑龙江省海林市横道河子镇保护规划（2010—2030年）》技术路线图

小镇整体格局涉及山体、河流、街区、历史街巷、古树名木等主要要素，保持其历史延续性进而保持天际线和轮廓线是首要一步。历史街区的保护以老街历史街区、顺桥历史地段、佛手历史地段和工业遗址地段四处为重点，针对每处历史街区分别划定核心保护范围、建设控制地带和环境协调区，控制要求如下：对核心保护范围的街巷空间和文物保护单位进行保护和维修，不可随意新建、拆建，对确需新建、拆建的建筑，必须符合保护规划的原则和审批程序，同时保证建筑风格一致；建设控制地带内经批准可新建、改建、扩建建筑，在高度、体量、色彩等方面与传统风貌相协调，不得破坏古镇传统风貌；环境协调区要求不得随意建设项目，最大程度上保护历史地段与周围环境的关系。各级文物保护单位及登记不可移动文物建筑根据《黑龙江省文物管理条例》逐一划定特别保护区、重点保护区和一般保护区，并依据实际价值和现状情况对特色突出者划出建设控制地带，以此达到分级保护的要求。

非物质文化遗产的保护首先通过建立文化遗产档案和资料库的方式，运用文字、录音、录像、数字化多媒体、网络等手段对其进行真实、系统全面的记录。其次，建立切实可行的非物质文化遗产传承机制，对列入非遗的代表性事物采取授予称号、表彰鼓励、资助扶持等方式，鼓励和支持其开展带徒授艺等传习活动，确保优秀非物质文化遗产的传承，努力改变目前非物质文化遗产后继乏人的状态。

（三）单体展示利用措施的微观深入

《全国重点文物保护单位——中东铁路建筑群（横道河子镇）保护规划（2014—2030年）》在镇保护规划的基础上，更加细致地挖掘每一栋历史建筑的价值所在，进而进行详细的展示利用和游览线路的设计。

保护对象包括建筑本体——5处全国重点文物保护单位、16处市级文物保护单位、41处登记不可移动文物及其相关历史环境——4座山体、横道河、构筑物机车库大转盘、25条道路、3 座桥梁、植被及非文物建筑 2 327 栋（图 8），其中以 5 处国保单位为重点保护对象。保护原则为在历史建筑的修缮过程中秉承保持其原有属性和特色，妥善处理保护与开发的矛盾，兼顾与城镇建设的协调发展，促进其功能延续与合理利用，增强其展示与宣传。

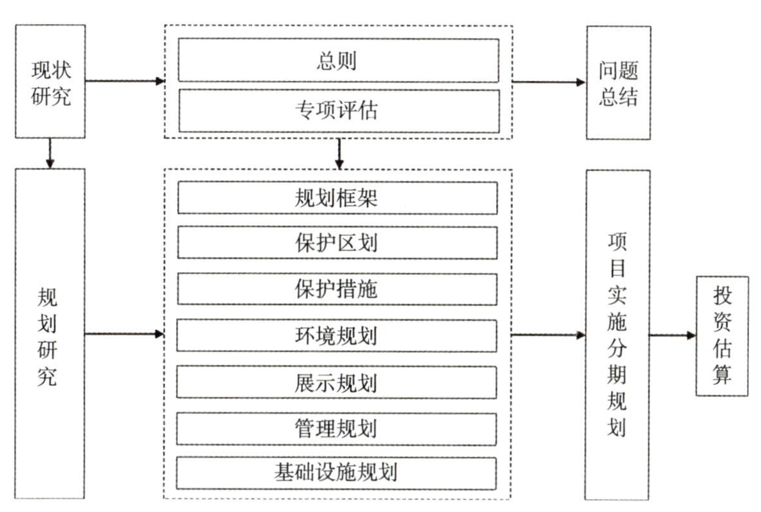

图 8 《全国重点文物保护单位——中东铁路建筑群（横道河子镇）保护规划（2014—2030 年）》技术路线图

整体上构建“一条线路、五个分区”的展示框架：“一条线路”指毛子坟—七号木屋—圣母进堂教堂—铁路治安所驻地—俄式木屋—横道河子机车库—铁路大白楼这一游览参观路线，“五个分区”是指 5 处国保单位的展示片区。展示内容上不仅包括建筑本体的展示，同时包含周边环境的展示，从而给游客呈现出完整的历史文化景象。并以建筑文化特色为出发点，分别确立保护性展示、利用性展示、环境性展示、游览性展示和传播性展示五大展示向。其中：保护性展示是针对 5 处国保单位的不同单体建筑特色确定不同展示要素，例如铁路大白楼保护性展示要素有四坡屋顶、清水砖墙、贯通式扶壁柱、凹凸花饰、露天阳台、窗楣、水磨石地面、白色装饰，而圣母进堂教堂保护性展示要素有条石基础、十字平面、两坡房顶、帐蓬顶塔楼、圆葱头、山花墙面、窗型、门楣、窗楣，要素间有交叉也有侧重；利用性展示将每一栋建筑赋予适于城镇发展的具体功能以体现其新时代意义，例如圣母进堂教堂主要通过恢复教堂功能、恢复钟楼原貌进行展示，利用方向为宗教文化艺术展览馆；环境性展示以其历史环境特征为本底，通过铁轨、院落格局、地势台阶、地下空间等外部环境特征体现其历史文化内涵；游览性展示以观赏、体验参与为主，包括面包制作、啤酒畅饮、民俗歌舞，观赏横道河子镇山水景色、现场作画、画廊展示等；传播性展示通过清晰的文字说明、教育展板、导游手册、纪念品、不同语言的参考书、音像制品、实景模型呈现，并聘请训练有素的导游或教师展开相关宣传。

展示利用的规划思路实现了文物保护、历史文化知识普及、生态环境优化、塑造民众文化休闲场所、促进地方社会经济发展的初衷，使单体建筑、历史环境、城镇发展有机结合起来，赋予老建筑新功能的做法不仅有效利用了原有闲置空间，更成为宣传展示小镇文化的良好平台。

(四)信息采集分析手段的大数据全过程应用

三轮规划制定过程中综合运用计算机技术、空间信息技术和数据库技术，分别建立了“无人机遥测技术平台”“GIS 空间信息分析平台”和“B/S 结构数字化空间信息展示平台”，辅助并优化了历史城镇保护规划的编制技术。

技术的创新首先体现在调研方法的升级：依托无人机正射影像、倾斜摄影和 360 度全景空中信息采集技术替代了原有现场调研拍照、测绘等方法，提升了调研的真实性和全面性。

其次体现在基于信息数据提取与处理的三维模型构建过程：将已采集的具有矢量信息的影像数据，利用倾斜摄影计算软件进行空三运算后，生出三维模型（图 9）。该三维模型可根据空间分析需要，转译成多种数据格式，如倾斜三维模型数据（如 OSGB、OBJ）、数字表面模型（DSM）以及数字正射影像（DOM）（图 10）。

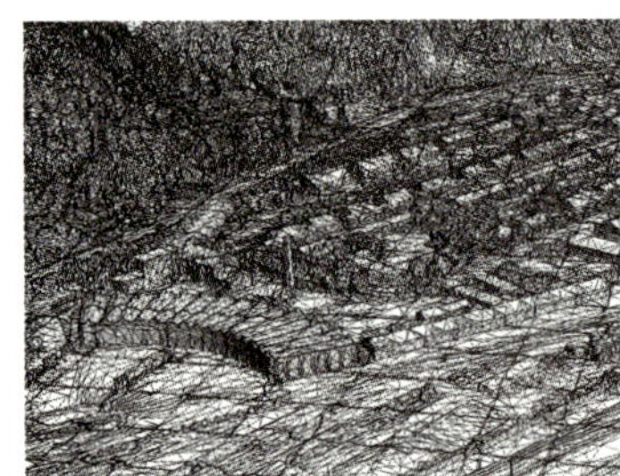

图 9 机车库周边环境数字模型

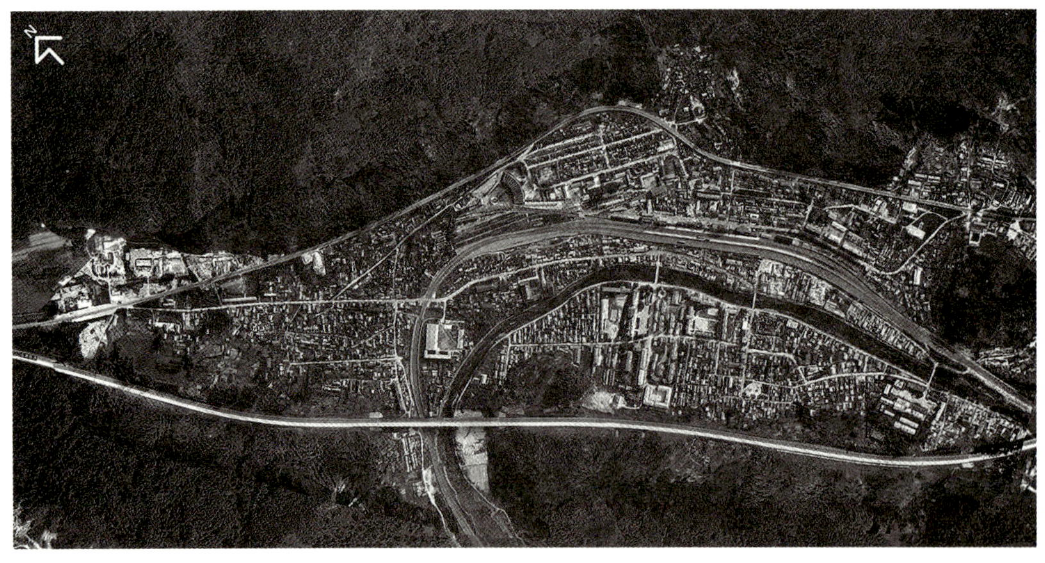

图 10 横道河子镇区正射影像

另外，利用 GIS 通过对地形、缓冲区、视线等方面进行综合叠加分析，阐释用地现状及存在的问题，科学划定保护区划，因地制宜地对土地利用性质进行适度调整。

最后在信息展示方面实现了技术突破，为配合保护规划编制、利于规划实施以及高效进行后期保护规划管理及展示利用的实践工作，构建了“智慧横道河子镇”（图 11）这一数字化空间信息平台。该平台以镇区内 6.15 平方公里的“360 度全景影像”和“倾斜影像”为数据载体，载入丰富的地理信息数据，包括横道河子镇建筑和历史信息的属性数据、图片、保护规划相关成果等，实现三维地理信息数据的创建、浏览、分析和发布，并能将信息进行动态更新维护。

图 11　智慧横道河子镇数字化空间信息平台

（五）规划的稳定落实促动重点项目渐次实施

通过村镇发展总体规划、历史文化名镇与全国重点文物保护单位的保护规划这三种不同层级规划的协调一致、层级深化完善这一工作思路的空间落实，间接地达成了不同时序规划的“多规合一”，令横道河子镇的原始风貌在快速城市化的建设时局下得以完整保留，并去伪存真，场景再现，这既是永久性地保护了小镇历史文化价值的核心所在，并为下一步控制性详细规划的一系列开展奠定了稳定的框架基础，又为未来的规划管理和实施建设制定了清晰目标。

四、重点项目推动小镇功能转型与民生持续改善

在三轮规划的基础上，重点项目（图 12）的推动工作也渐次展开。环境整治类项目注重面域及条带状大环境基底的视觉形象及功能品质提升，如亮化规划、交通道路景观设计与工程施工、滨河景观设计、桥梁改造等；俄风恢复类项目旨在通过复原单体建筑、街道、广

场等老旧空间载体来营造浓郁的历史氛围，以最少干预、工程设计与未来展示利用相结合、解决文物建筑的结构安全隐患、保留历史信息和整洁沧桑美为设计理念，项目包括单体历史建筑抢救性保护工程、历史街道及广场的景观设计等；展示利用类项目主要借助在体量和形态布局上具有优势的单体和组团融入文化活动属性加以开放利用，如机车库、圣母进堂教堂、治安所的修缮和展示利用及油画村的塑造，使其成为建筑文化形象和小镇活力的双重地标；环境协调类项目则是以小镇历史建筑的风格、色彩、构件为参照系对周边非文物建筑及环境进行协调性规划，如非文物建筑立面改造、毗邻村落形象整合规划及概念规划、色彩规划、栅栏改造设计等；空间信息管理类是将小镇置于黑龙江省段中东铁路建筑群总体保护规划的框架下，为其建筑及周边环境建立信息化的档案数据。

这些重点项目通过规划手段为使用者提供了富于历史气息并拓展有时代功用的优质空间，承载各种公共文化功能和艺术活动，切实发挥了传承历史文化特色、改善民众生活环境、联动周边旅游资源的支撑性作用，将产业和经济力量注入小镇的职能角色中，令其从原始凋落的守望型居住城镇逐渐丰富为多元化可吸引旅游者、学者等大众的开放型特色旅游小镇。

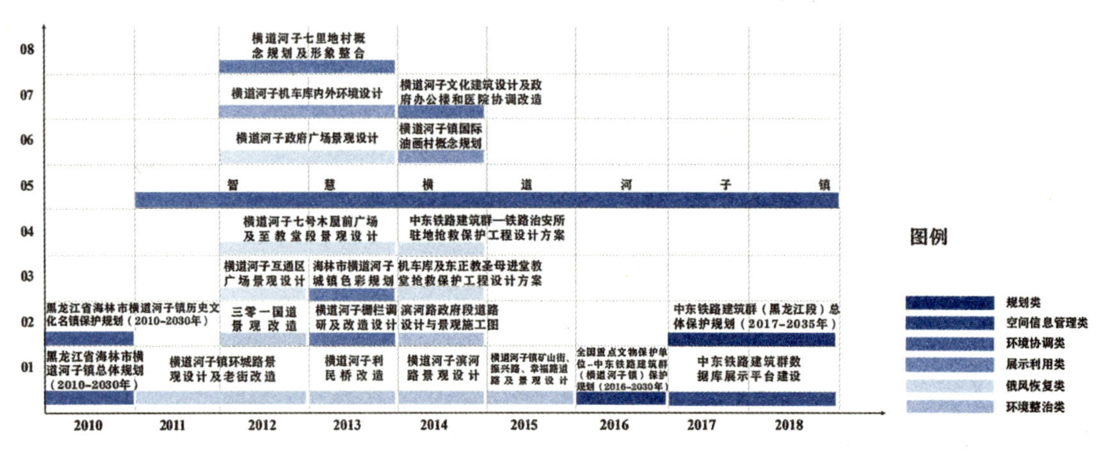

图 12　重点项目时序表

五、学术研究理性引导小镇空间规划和社会治理

随着规划工作的全面落实，更多的研究方法被运用到小镇空间规划的解析和对社会治理的理解中来。如调研前期采用“AHP 层次分析法”建立遗产价值和保存状态的评价体系，并以评价结果来辅助保护力度的分级和修缮方法的判定；中期应用“空间句法”研究小镇改造后的空间布局序列特征，并重点研究历史建筑核心分布区段内各要素间的整体关联性，以辅助制定保护小镇空间形态（地块利用方式、开放空间、非历史建筑等）的规划措施。在保护工作取得初步成效的中后期，则面向居民、经营者和游客三大使用群体，对历史空间保护、历史文脉延续、社区环境改善和街区活力复兴这四个方面进行基于“IPA 分析法”的

实施后评价。这些研究方法始终助力规划者在不同阶段对历史文化名镇的规划实践进行客观修正和进一步的理性引导。

六、结语

自2010年横道河子镇全面推动中国历史文化名镇建设工作至今，在镇域经济中充分担负起文化遗产旅游的经济价值职能，吸引年游客数达20万～30万人次，就此，进一步的规划工作中已启动了遗产安全监测、游客满意度和居民需求调查，并计划于2020年（纳入海林市“十四五”规划）启动横道河子镇空间容量、设施容量和生态资源容量这三大旅游活动管理规划工作，为横道河子小镇旅游发展的持续、健康地运行提供保障。

联合国教科文组织亚太地区文化遗产保护奖专家评委会对横道河子镇所开展规划工作的评语为：“位于中国北部的19世纪铁路城镇横道河子镇的成功保护得益于其统观全局的保护方法，涵盖了历史建筑、基础设施以及相关的公共空间。项目彰显了对地域和功能性的深刻理解，重塑并延续了这一历史工业城镇的精神。保护工作以克制的方法开展，充分尊重了当地建筑及其环境的历史韵味和功能特性。”

小镇的保护严守“克制”之道，秉承踏实的工作态度，不忘初心，通过规划有序引领小镇的高质量建设发展，在8年的建设过程中，始终以文脉延续为本，人居环境渐进式改善为阶段任务，学术研究为治理辅助，多元参与为共建方式，真正将这一系统性工程放置于严谨开放的工作架构中，其每一步的筹划、规划与实施皆得到公众的监督与参与其中。未来，小镇将敞开怀抱，以国际化的视野与智慧，共同助力特色小镇的建设蓝图。

备注：①图5提供者为横道河子镇宣传部；②文中实景、数字影像、框架图等其他图片，皆出自哈尔滨工业大学城市规划设计研究院所编制的横道河子镇相关项目。

（作者：赵志庆，哈尔滨工业大学建筑学院教授、博士生导师，哈尔滨工业大学城市规划设计研究院院长；张璐，哈尔滨工业大学建筑学院博士研究生；张欢，哈尔滨工业大学建筑学院博士研究生）

亳州市建设“世界中医药之都”的规划与实践

亳州市位于安徽省西北部，地处苏鲁豫皖四省交界区域中心，是老子、庄子、曹操、华佗等世界级历史文化名人的故里，是道家文化、中医药文化、酒文化的重要发祥地，是国家历史文化名城、首批中国优秀旅游城市、中国长寿之乡，素有“天下道源、曹操故里、中华药都、华夏酒城”美誉。2015 年 10 月，党的十八届五中全会明确提出了推进“健康中国”建设任务。2017 年 1 月，安徽省委、省政府提出要“把亳州打造成国内外知名的中医药之都”。近年来，亳州市坚决贯彻党中央、国务院关于“健康中国”和中医药发展的系列重大战略，落实省委、省政府的部署要求，大力推动以人为核心的新型城镇化建设，举全市之力建设“世界中医药之都”，积极探索构建现代经济体系、实现高质量发展的新路径。

一、亳州市中医药产业发展优势

亳州市于 2000 年 5 月经国务院批准设立，是安徽省最年轻的地级市。近年来，亳州市坚持以习近平新时代中国特色社会主义思想为指导，深入贯彻落实党的十八大和十九大精神，坚持稳中求进工作总基调，坚持“三严三实”“马上就办、真抓实干”，深入实施五大发展行动计划，突出抓好防范化解重大风险、精准脱贫、污染防治“三大攻坚战”，主动融入中原城市群、长江三角洲区域一体化、淮河生态经济带等发展战略，加快建设新兴工业强市、现代农业强市、文化旅游强市、新型智慧城市和健康养生城市“五大城市”，经济社会始终保持高质量发展的良好态势。2018 年，在安徽省统计局公布的 23 项主要经济指标中，亳州市有 21 项增速居全省 16 个地级市前八位，13 项居前三位，7 项居第一位，主要经济指标增速继续保持在全省先进行列。特别是，GDP 完成 1 277. 2 亿元，增长 10. 1% 、连续两年居全省第一位，是全省唯一增速超过两位数的市；财政收入突破 200 亿元，增长 17. 1% ，提前两年完成“十三五”规划目标任务。(图 1)

中医药产业是亳州市的首位产业。自神医华佗开辟中华大地第一块“药圃”起，亳州中药材种植、经营、炮制、诊疗的历史已达 1800 多年。到了明代，亳州就已成为闻名全国的“中华药都”。改革开放后，亳州中医药产业得到飞速发展，目前已初步形成种植、加工、贸易、科研、医疗、保健、教育、文化等整体发展格局，产业发展优势明显。

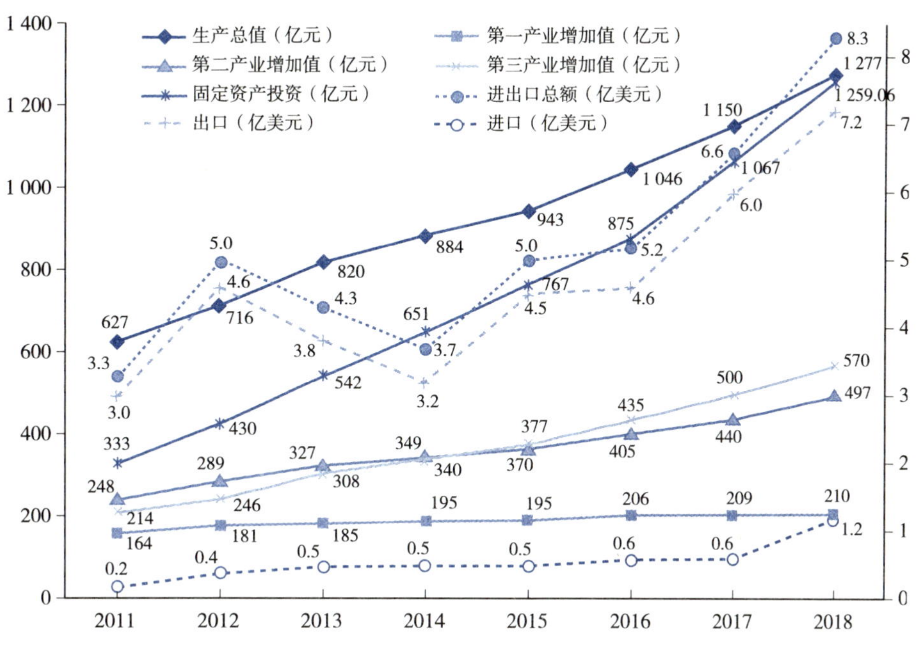

图 1　亳州市近 8 年主要经济指标走势图

（一）区位优势愈发显著

亳州位于中原战略要地，素有“南北通衢，中州锁钥”之称。公路交通四通八达，境内拥有 2 条国道和 6 条省道，济广、南洛、泗许、济祁高速公路形成“井字形”高速路网，亳涡蒙高速立项获批。铁路交通日益便捷，京九、徐阜铁路直通“京津冀”“长三角”“珠三角”三大经济圈，商杭高铁即将通车。航空、水路交通加快升级，亳州机场获批建设，涡河四级航道改造全面展开，承南启北、东进西出的区位优势进一步凸显。（图 2）

（二）中药资源得天独厚

亳州现有中药材资源 171 科、410 种，其中植物类有 107 科、295 种，其中亳芍、亳菊、亳花粉、亳桑皮等“亳”字冠名药材列入《中国药典》，是全国重要的中药材种植加工基地。中医药文化资源丰富，华佗麻沸散是世界麻醉药物的先例，五禽戏是导引练形以养生的最早记载，该市先后荣获首批国家中医药健康旅游示范区创建单位、国际健身气功五禽戏之都等国家级称号。（图 3）

（三）产业链条比较完整

亳州现代中药产业被安徽省列入首批省级战略性新兴产业集聚发展基地，2018 年产业规模突破 1 000 亿元、达 1 096.8 亿元。现有规模以上中药工业企业 178 家，其中通过 GMP 认证 175 家，全国中医药百强企业已有 57 家落户亳州，3 家本土企业入选中华民族医药百强。拥有全国最大的中药饮片加工产业集群，年生产能力超 100 万吨、约占全国的 30%。中药材种植面积超 8 万公顷。亳州中药材特色产业发展服务基地被人力资源与社会保障部批

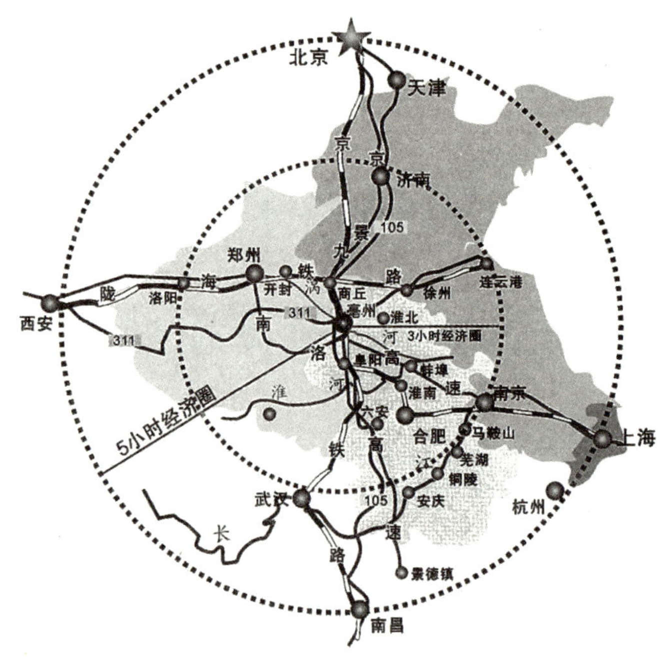

图 2　亳州市承南启北、东进西出的区位优势明显

图 3　亳药花海休闲观光大世界 57.9 万平方米芍药花田创吉尼斯世界纪录

准为全国首批国家级专家服务基地。

（四）贸易流通全国领先

亳州是全国最大的中药材集散地，被列为全国首批中药材流通追溯体系建设试点城市、全国供应链创新与应用试点城市，2018 年中医药流通贸易额 743.2 亿元，其中中国·亳州中药材专业交易市场交易额 400 亿元；中药材及饮片出口 2.8 亿美元，4 家企业进入全国中

药材及饮片出口前10强；中药材电子商务快速发展，各类电商平台从业人员22万人。中国·亳州中药材专业市场占地1 000亩，建筑面积120万平方米，入驻药企700多家，摊位总量超6 000个，日上市中药材2 600余种，日人流量4万~5万人，是全国面积最大、上市品种最多、交易最为活跃的中药材专业交易市场。（图4）

图4　中国·亳州中药材专业市场年交易额400亿元

（五）科创能力显著提升

亳州拥有药业国家级农业产业化龙头企业2家，国家级中药类工程研究中心2个，涉药类高新技术企业44家，建成运行地方首家国家中药材产品质量监督检验中心（安徽）。现有中药类院士工作站、博士后工作站11家，获批国家级众创空间2家、星创天地3家。设立7支、总额超过100亿元的中医药大健康产业基金，中医药领域有效发明专利拥有量约300件，济人药业有限公司疏风解毒胶囊荣获国家发明专利金奖，九方制药公司牡荆素填补了安徽省中药一类新药的空白。坚持传承和发展两手抓，大力引进“老字号”、经典名方、古法炮制技艺，加快推进中成药提取、中药配方颗粒、中药破壁饮片等，先后出台17项激励政策，获批省中药配方颗粒生产基地，5家企业获批配方颗粒生产试点，4家企业获批破壁饮片生产试点；目前，已从全国转入药品技术品种6个、待转入394个，报批中药配方颗粒品种1 294个，引进兽药品种2个。（图5）

（六）健康服务蓬勃发展

现有中医医院10家，其中“三甲”中医医院、三级中医医院各1家，省级中医重点专科（专病）11个，国医大师、全国名中医工作室4个，全国综合医院中医药工作示范单位3个，89个乡镇卫生院、13个社区卫生服务中心全部建成中医馆，92个社区卫生服务站和

图5 国家中药材产品质量监督检验中心落户亳州

85%的村卫生室具有中医药服务能力。拥有中医药健康饮食产品2 000余种，中医药健康养生旅游产品30余种，2018年实现中医药健康服务收入220亿元。先后被授予全国基层中医药工作先进单位（地级市）、全国中医药文化建设先进单位、全国药膳之都等称号。

（七）品牌影响逐步扩大

亳州连续举办了13届国际（亳州）中医药博览会、34届全国（亳州）中药材交易会，已成为国内规模最大、参与人数最多、交易额最大的中医药文化经贸活动。中国传统道家文化与中医药文化相互浸润、契合，形成源远流长、内涵丰富、独具特色的中医药健康养生文化及思想体系，“华佗故里、药材之乡”“中华药都、养生亳州”等品牌享誉海内外。

二、亳州市建设“世界中医药之都”的制约因素分析

“世界中医药之都”是指在中医药产业领域具备雄厚的产业发展基础、全球领先的产业发展水平、持续旺盛的产业发展潜力的城市。具体而言，就是该城市中医药产业规模、创新能力、品牌塑造、文化建设等方面处于世界领先水平，能实现中医药产业和地区经济社会整体性、引领性和辐射性发展。亳州市现代中医药产业发展虽然基础良好，有些方面达到了世界领先水平，但要建设“世界中医药之都”，仍有不少制约因素。

（一）产业发展结构不优

产业整体处于中医药产业链的中低端，主要产品为中药材及饮片等原材料或初加工产品，正处在资源优势转化为产业优势的转型期。药材种植规范化、规模化水平偏低。工业产品以饮片加工为主，中成药占比仅10%，主流产品科技含量偏低、知名品牌偏少、利润空间偏小。传统的中药材集约交易功能占主流，线上交易量占比小，中药材期货交易所的审批

难度大。

（二）科技研发人才短缺

缺乏高水平的研发创新平台和国家级创新平台，科技研发力量薄弱，原创性研究较少。药品技术转让时间过长、成本过高，获批难度较大，严重制约了该市药品技术转让市场化进程。中医药人才短缺，普遍缺乏企业管理、科技研发、专业技术和中医医疗等高端人才、专业人才。

（三）中医服务相对滞后

中医药服务的质量和水平与“世界中医药之都”的要求差距较大。中医医疗体系需要进一步完善，中医名院、名科、名医、名药建设滞后，在国内知名的中医特色专科较少，中医药优势未充分发挥，缺少学科带头人和拔尖人才。

（四）文化交流载体缺乏

中医药文化缺乏重量级、代表性、标志化的载体。药博会市场化改革刚刚起步，缺乏高水平、标志性的学术论坛和经贸项目。中医药品牌策划宣传推广不够，品牌国际化运作水平亟待提升。

（五）城市基础设施欠账较多

由于建市迟、底子薄，城市道路、商业服务、医疗卫生、文化教育等基础设施存在不少历史欠账。综合立体交通网尚未形成，城市内外交通一体化衔接不够，不能充分满足对出行效率、服务质量的要求和中远距离交通运输需求。

（六）宏观环境复杂多变

从全国大的宏观环境看，实体经济困难仍然较多，企业生产经营成本较高，民间投资积极性不高。从行业看，药理基础研究薄弱，中成药技术标准不够统一，质量控制标准体系尚未建立，行业健康发展困难较多。

三、亳州市建设“世界中医药之都”的实践路径

习近平总书记指出，中医药学是中华民族的瑰宝，是打开中华文明宝库的钥匙。亳州市贯彻落实党和国家决策部署，抢抓中医药发展的重大历史机遇，立足亳州、辐射全国、面向全球，精心编制了《世界中医药之都（安徽亳州）建设发展规划（2019—2030年）》，重点建设“一核一带三中心”，着力构建中药与中医并重、一二三产有机融合、经济效益与社会效益共赢的现代中医药产业发展体系，到2030年产业规模突破3 500亿元，努力建设成为具有重要国际影响力的“世界中医药之都”。（图6、图7）

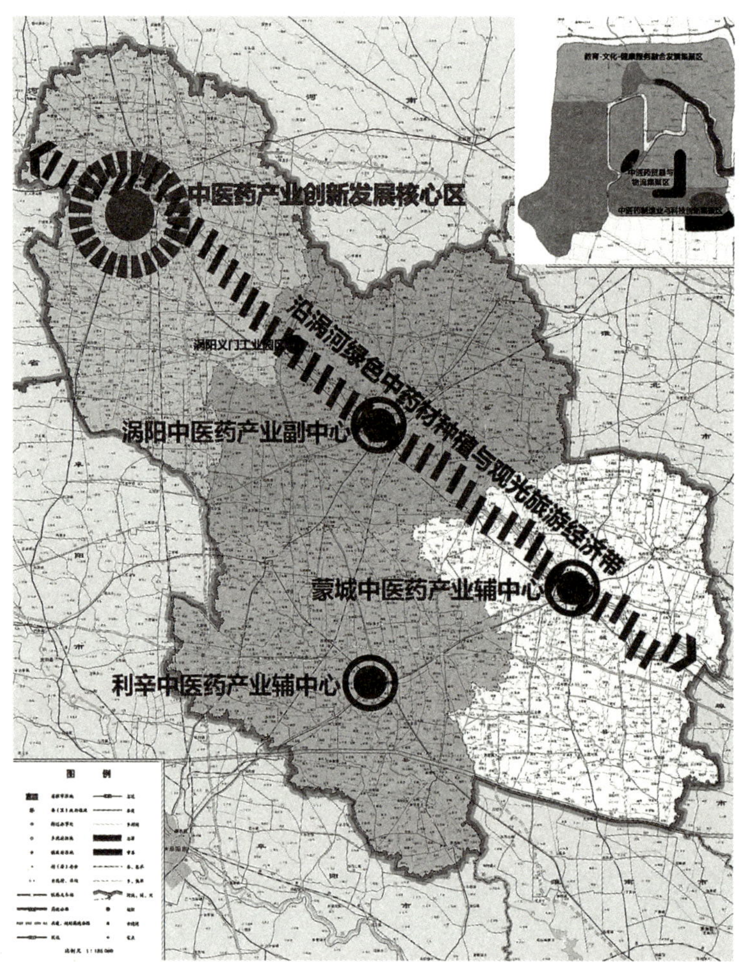

图6 “一核一带三中心”功能布局示意图

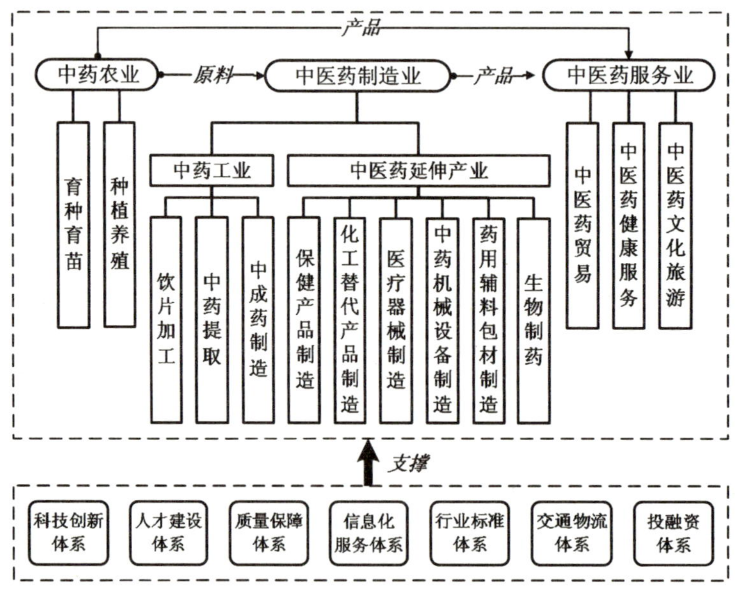

图7 亳州市中医药产业高质量发展示意图

（一）立足资源禀赋，建设中药材规范种植中心

（1）加强中药资源保护利用。建立中药材种质资源库和种子、种苗组培研发中心，发挥中药材种植研究所作用，逐步提升优质种子、种苗供应能力。推广种子种苗标准繁育技术及种植技术，持续加大“亳”字道地药材保护力度。

（2）推动中药材规范化种植。以14个中药材种植重点乡镇为核心区域，指导粮农向药农转变，推广GAP种植，发展中药材订单农业，建设面向全国的中药材现代化初加工（趁鲜加工）基地，推动中药材标准化、规范化、规模化种植。

（3）壮大中药农业新兴业态。发展现代中药农业新产业、新业态，促进中药材种植养殖、初加工、文化旅游等融合发展，提升传统中药农业的整体附加值。引入发展药用动物养殖，建设规范性药用动物繁育基地。发展生态循环中药农业，开发具有一定养生祛病功能的特色循环经济产品。

（二）瞄准发展方向，建设中医药高端制造中心

（1）做精做优饮片加工。引导鼓励饮片产业向差异化、精深化、品牌化、标准化方向发展，开发单味小包装、口服饮片、破壁饮片等新型产品，叫响“亳州饮片”品牌。推进中药饮片标准化，加强饮片加工炮制、贮存运输、生产器械、包装材料等技术及设施设备研究，积极参与全国中药饮片标准研究制定，增强话语权。加快推进破壁饮片生产企业试点工作。

（2）做大做强成药制造。发挥龙头带动效应，鼓励优势企业开展新药创制，支持基于经典名方、民间验方、特色制剂等，推动技术、方药等研究成果的知识产权化、商品化和产业化。推动企业兼并重组和上市融资，提升产业竞争实力。加强自主创新产品的品种规划、市场培育和品牌建设，形成一批市场占有率高、社会影响大的知名品牌。推进药品品种技术转移，推动拟转入品种早日落地投产。

（3）做专做实中药提取。围绕全省唯一配方颗粒生产基地建设，扎实开展中药配方颗粒生产工艺和标准试点研究，支持有条件的企业发展配方颗粒，扩大中药配方颗粒生产能力和市场范围。鼓励有条件的饮片企业拓展提取物生产能力，培育高质量的大品种和特色品种，重点发展出口型高端提取物创新产品，迅速提升提取物产业规模。

（三）巩固龙头地位，建设中医药流通贸易中心

（1）推动传统交易市场转型升级。着力推进实体交易市场设施升级、特色培育、专业化经营、错位发展，加强12个地产药材集中交易区和仓储区建设，鼓励有条件的企业建设产地加工、仓储物流、药材追溯等形式的现代化中药材流通体系，巩固“买全国、卖全国”的道地药材交易集散地优势地位。加快建设全国领先的中医药大数据研发中心和全国性中药材信息中心。

（2）培育电子商务市场特色品牌。建设一批具有交易、物流、支付、信息、信用等综

合服务功能的大型电商平台，完善中药材电子商务服务功能。积极开展中药材商品等级分类标准研究，推进中药材大数据云智慧管理与应用系统建设，积极争取建设中药材期货交易中心。

（3）增强货运物流市场服务能力。加快物流基础设施建设和统筹整合，推动大型物流企业基础配套设施建设和资源整合，形成覆盖全国的物流体系。完善中药材专业市场的配套物流服务功能，推动电子商务和物流服务融合发展，提高中药材物流的信息化、智能化、专业化水平。

（4）拓展服务贸易市场产品范围。整合医、教、研、产、服资源，建立科研成果向服务贸易产品的转化机制，重点推出华佗五禽戏传习体验、华佗夹脊穴理疗等一批具有亳州特色的中医药服务贸易产品，培育国际知名品牌，扩大中医药服务贸易范围。

（四）强化科技支撑，建设中医药创新研发中心

（1）完善中医药技术创新体系。鼓励和引导科研人员针对中药选育栽培、加工提取、成药生产等共性关键技术问题进行科技攻关，解决发展瓶颈。鼓励中医药企业加强与中科院、大专院校、科研机构合作，建立产学研战略联盟关系，培育和提高企业自主创新能力。围绕生物医药、生物技术等产业，强化中医药协同创新和成果转化，形成一批重大技术成果和产品。

（2）促进中医药科技成果转化。建设中国（亳州）中医药创新研究院，推进公共研发和科技服务平台建设，形成集研发、转化、孵化、成长于一体的公共科研平台和高新企业孵化平台。推进亳州高新区创建国家级高新技术产业开发区。

（3）创新中医药人才培养模式。以科技合作项目为纽带，积极培养本地人才，柔性引进领军人才、高端人才，建立院士工作站和博士后工作站，构筑高层次创新人才高地。与北京中医药大学、上海中医药大学、安徽中医药大学等高等院校，探索开展联合办学，建设亳州（华佗）中医药大学。发展职业教育，加强中医药技能型人才基地和教育科研基地建设。

（五）紧盯消费需求，建设中医药健康服务中心

（1）提高中医医疗服务能力。深入开展名院、名科、名医、名药建设，创新中医医院发展模式，与国内知名中医院建立合作关系，带动提升中医诊疗水平。着力培养名中医，加强名老中医传承工作室建设，提高中医诊疗的便捷度。

（2）提高中医养生保健能力。实施中医治未病健康工程，建设全国性治未病研究中心，加强中医治未病技术、方法、药品、用品开发研究和推广应用。开展慢性病管理、残疾人康复、工伤康复等中医特色康复服务，推动中医院与大型康复机构开展中西医结合康复技术合作。

（3）发展中医药健康养老服务。推动中医药与养老融合发展，鼓励中医院积极开办有中医药特色的医养结合机构，鼓励社会资本新建护理院、老年病医院，促进中医医疗资源进入养老机构、社区和居民家庭。支持养老机构设立中医医疗机构。

（4）发展中医药健康旅游服务。以创建国家中医药健康旅游示范区为抓手，推动中医药健康服务与旅游产业、体育健身产业深度融合。发展以中医药养生和老庄清修养生为核心的健康养生休闲旅游，形成一批特色的中医药健康旅游品牌，打造具有地域特色的健康旅游线路。

（六）厚植文化底蕴，建设中医药文化传承中心

（1）继承中医药理论方法。深入挖掘华佗流派历代传人传记及代表性著作、流派典籍、医话医论、方志记载、历史实物等文史资料，进一步发展、完善华佗学术思想，开发华佗养生文化产品，面向全世界推广华佗“五禽戏”。

（2）推动中医药文化传播。探索设立国家级中医药文化研究院，谋划建设国家级中医药博物馆，传承、传播、普及中医药知识。广泛开展中医药文化教育，推动中医药文化进校园、进社区、进乡村、进家庭。

（3）发展中医药文化产业。将中医药文化纳入文化产业发展规划，创作一批承载中医药文化的创意产品和文化精品，发展新型文化产品和服务。充分挖掘整理道家养生、中医药养生、健身功法养生以及民间秘方养生等资源，策划神医华佗、道源问道、长寿之乡等系列文化产品，加大“亳”字号品牌对外宣传、展示和推介力度。

（七）深化开放合作，建设中医药国际交流中心

（1）加强中医药对外合作。依托亳州药博会，与中医药行业国际组织合作，高规格谋划举办世界（亳州）中医药大会。推进药博会市场化运营，与世界中医药学会联合会等机构交流合作，聚力打造国际中医药会展中心。

（2）扩大国际化人文交流。加强与国际组织和海外知名文化传播机构交流与合作，提升亳州中医药文化外向度。开展亳州市中医药国外行活动，支持中医传统养生健身运动国际推广，开拓入境中医健康旅游市场。

（3）畅通中医药国际贸易。紧抓“一带一路”建设机遇，发挥饮片市场优势，加强与韩国、日本、东南亚、欧美等标准对接，突破准入限制，提升海外认可度，扩大中药材海外市场，推动国际贸易发展。

（作者：中国市长协会城市咨询委员会，安徽省亳州市政府发展研究中心）

附录篇

附录 1

2018 年中国城市规划发展大事记

1 月 2 日　中共中央国务院发布关于实施乡村振兴战略的意见：实施乡村振兴战略，是党的十九大作出的重大决策部署，是决胜全面建成小康社会、全面建设社会主义现代化国家的重大历史任务，是新时代“三农”工作的总抓手。

1 月 3 日　国务院办公厅印发《省级政府耕地保护责任目标考核办法》，自印发之日起施行。

1 月 3 日　为指导城市绿地防灾避险设计，提升城市防灾减灾能力，住房城乡建设部印发《城市绿地防灾避险设计导则》。

1 月 4 日　河北省住房城乡建设厅印发《河北省小城镇污水处理设施建设行动方案》。提出 2018 年不具备污水处理能力的小城镇，力争全部启动污水处理项目建设；到 2019 年，小城镇实现污水处理设施全覆盖，污水处理率达到 70%；到 2020 年，重点镇污泥无害化处置率提高 5 个百分点，初步实现小城镇污泥统筹集中处置。

1 月 5 日　广西壮族自治区人民政府正式印发《北部湾城市群发展规划广西实施方案》（以下简称《方案》），《方案》从城市发展、城市产业、交通设施、生态环境、开放合作、发展机制六大方面提出要求，加快推进北部湾城市群发展，全力打造国际一流品质的蓝色宜居海湾城市群。

1 月 6 日　为促进深圳经济特区一体化发展，结合特区建设发展面临的新形势新使命新任务，国务院同意撤销深圳经济特区管理线。

1 月 7 日　中共中央办公厅、国务院办公厅印发《关于推进城市安全发展的意见》，以强化城市运行安全保障，有效防范事故发生，推进城市安全发展。

1 月 9 日　国务院同意《关中平原城市群发展规划》（以下简称《规划》）。《规划》实施要全面贯彻党的十九大精神，以习近平新时代中国特色社会主义思想为指导，统筹推进“五位一体”总体布局和协调推进“四个全面”战略布局，坚持以人民为中心的发展思想，牢固树立和贯彻落实新发展理念，以供给侧结构性改革为主线，加快培育发展新动能，拓展发展新空间，以建设具有国际影响力的国家级城市群为目标，以深度融入“一带一路”建设为统领，以创新驱动发展、军民融合发展为动力，以延续中华文脉、体现中国元素的风貌塑造为特色，加快高端要素和现代产业集聚发展，提升人口和经济集聚水平，打造内陆改革开放新高地，充分发挥关中平原城市群对西北地区发展的核心引领作用和我国向西开放的战略支撑作用。

1月10日 张高丽主持召开推动长江经济带发展工作会议，深入学习贯彻党的十九大、中央经济工作会议、中央农村工作会议精神，总结近年来推动长江经济带发展工作，审议有关文件，研究部署下一步重点工作。

1月10日 国土资源部办公厅下发《关于开展新一轮土地利用总体规划编制试点工作的通知》（以下简称《通知》)，《通知》称，为推动形成绿色发展方式和生活方式，经国务院同意，国土资源部拟在部分省（自治区、直辖市）部署开展新一轮土地利用总体规划编制试点工作，以点带面探索土地利用总体规划编制方法及管理方式，为全面开展新一轮土地利用总体规划编制工作积累实践经验。

1月11日 《湖北长江经济带绿色宜居城镇建设专项规划（2016—2020年)》（以下简称《规划》）出台。《规划》提出，要实现湖北长江经济带的城乡统筹发展，成为长江经济带新型城镇化与绿色宜居城镇发展及“两型”社会建设的先行区。

1月12日 国务院批复《山东新旧动能转换综合试验区建设总体方案》（以下简称《方案》)。批复指出，《方案》实施要全面贯彻落实党的十九大精神，以习近平新时代中国特色社会主义思想为指导，贯彻新发展理念，坚持质量第一、效益优先，以供给侧结构性改革为主线，以实体经济为发展经济的着力点，以新技术、新产业、新业态、新模式为核心，以知识、技术、信息、数据等新生产要素为支撑，积极探索新旧动能转换模式，推动经济发展质量变革、效率变革、动力变革，提高全要素生产率，着力加快建设实体经济、科技创新、现代金融、人力资源协同发展的产业体系，推动经济实现更高质量、更有效率、更加公平、更可持续的发展，为促进全国新旧动能转换、建设现代化经济体系作出积极贡献。

1月16日 国土资源部办公厅、住房城乡建设部办公厅原则同意沈阳、南京、杭州、合肥、厦门、郑州、武汉、广州、佛山、肇庆、成都11个城市利用集体建设用地建设租赁住房试点实施方案。

1月16日 国务院办公厅印发《关于推进农业高新技术产业示范区建设发展的指导意见》，对促进农业科技园区提质升级、推进农业高新技术产业示范区建设发展进行部署。

1月17日 推进“一带一路”建设工作会议在北京召开。国务院副总理张高丽主持会议并讲话。会议深入学习贯彻党的十九大和中央经济工作会议精神，贯彻落实习近平总书记重要讲话和指示精神，总结推进“一带一路”建设工作进展情况，讨论有关文件，研究部署下一步重点工作。中共中央政治局常委、中央书记处书记王沪宁出席会议。

1月22日 国土资源部印发《关于做好2018年度报国务院批准城市建设用地申报工作的通知》（以下简称《通知》)，部署启动2018年报国务院批准城市建设用地申报工作。《通知》明确要求各地继续严控城市新增建设用地规模，组织做好城市用地申报，确保在今年3月底前完成年度报国务院批准城市建设用地申报工作；今年申报工作将全部实行远程电子申报。

1月29日 从青海省十三届人大一次会议上获悉，青海大力实施高原美丽乡村建设、城镇棚户区改造和农牧民危旧房改造项目。2017年，全省300个高原美丽乡村建设与脱贫攻坚结合，惠及6.8万户、约28万农牧民。

1月31日　浙江省在全国率先上线覆盖省、市、县、乡、村五级的河长制信息化平台，率先实现河长制信息化全覆盖。

2月1日　国务院同意兰州、白银2个高新技术产业开发区建设国家自主创新示范区，区域范围为国务院有关部门公布的开发区审核公告确定的四至范围。

2月2日　中国工业遗产保护名录（第一批）名单正式公布。这批名录包含了创建于洋务运动时期的官办企业，也含有新中国成立后的“156项”重点建设项目，覆盖了造船、军工、铁路等门类，是具有代表性、突出价值的工业遗产。

2月5日　国务院原则同意《呼包鄂榆城市群发展规划》（以下简称《规划》）。《规划》实施要全面贯彻党的十九大精神，以习近平新时代中国特色社会主义思想为指导，统筹推进“五位一体”总体布局和协调推进“四个全面”战略布局，坚持以人民为中心的发展思想，牢固树立和贯彻落实新发展理念，坚持质量第一、效益优先，以供给侧结构性改革为主线，推动经济发展质量变革、效率变革、动力变革，着力推进生态环境共建共保，着力构建开放合作新格局，着力创新协同发展体制机制，着力引导产业协同发展，着力加快基础设施互联互通，努力提升人口和经济集聚水平，将呼包鄂榆城市群培育发展成为中西部地区具有重要影响力的城市群。

2月6日　海南省政府出台《关于支持美丽乡村建设的若干意见》（以下简称《意见》）。《意见》指出，社会投资建设经营美丽乡村项目，涉及房屋建设的应在村庄公示7天征求村民意见，经项目所在地村民小组或行政村2/3以上村民签名同意，与村民小组、村委会签订项目建设经营合作协议后，由投资方会同村委会将《农村房屋建设规划报建申请表》、村民同意项目建设签名书、项目设计方案与建设经营（合作）协议报乡镇规划建设管理所，由乡镇规划建设管理所在7个工作日内（不含方案设计及公示时间），对村庄建设规划进行审核和反馈，符合村庄建设规划和相关政策的项目，作出意见报乡镇政府；乡镇政府在7个工作日内作出审查意见，报市县规划主管部门审批，给予建设单位核发《乡村建设规划许可证》。

2月8日　国务院办公厅公布辽宁五花顶等6处新建国家级自然保护区名单。

2月8日　国务院同意宁波、温州2个高新技术产业开发区建设国家自主创新示范区，区域范围为国务院有关部门公布的开发区审核公告确定的四至范围。

2月13日　为推动长江流域生态保护和治理，财政部发布《关于建立健全长江经济带生态补偿与保护长效机制的指导意见》（以下简称《指导意见》）。《指导意见》提出，通过统筹一般性转移支付和相关专项转移支付资金，建立激励引导机制，明显加大对长江经济带生态补偿和保护的财政资金投入力度。《指导意见》明确，到2020年，长江流域保护和治理多元化投入机制更加完善，上下联动协同治理的工作格局更加健全，中央对地方、流域上下游间生态补偿效益更加凸显，为长江经济带生态文明建设和区域协调发展提供重要的财力支撑和制度保障。

2月13日　国务院同意深圳市建设国家可持续发展议程创新示范区，深圳市将以创新引领超大型城市可持续发展为主题，建设国家可持续发展议程创新示范区。

2 月 13 日　国务院同意太原市建设国家可持续发展议程创新示范区，太原市将以资源型城市转型升级为主题，建设国家可持续发展议程创新示范区。

2 月 13 日　国务院同意桂林市建设国家可持续发展议程创新示范区，桂林市将以景观资源可持续利用为主题，建设国家可持续发展议程创新示范区。

2 月 13 日　国务院批准了京津冀 3 省（市）、长江经济带 11 省（市）和宁夏回族自治区共 15 省份生态保护红线划定方案。生态保护红线将形成全国“一张图”。

2 月 22 日　中共中央政治局常务委员会 2 月 22 日召开会议，听取河北雄安新区规划编制情况的汇报。中共中央总书记习近平主持会议并发表重要讲话。

2 月 22 日　国务院批复《兰州—西宁城市群发展规划》（以下简称《规划》），强调《规划》实施要全面贯彻党的十九大精神，以习近平新时代中国特色社会主义思想为指导，统筹推进“五位一体”总体布局和协调推进“四个全面”战略布局，坚持以人民为中心的发展思想，牢固树立和贯彻落实新发展理念，坚持稳中求进工作总基调，以供给侧结构性改革为主线，解放思想、实事求是，尽力而为、量力而行，着力优化城镇空间布局，着力加强生态建设和环境保护，着力补齐基础设施和公共服务短板，着力推进产业优化升级和功能配套，着力融入“一带一路”建设，积极推动高质量、特色化发展，把兰州—西宁城市群培育发展成为支撑国土安全和生态安全格局、维护西北地区繁荣稳定的重要城市群。

2 月 23 日　北京市召开推进疏解整治促提升、促进首都生态文明与城乡环境建设动员大会，明确今年疏解整治促提升重点任务，将拆除违法建设 4 000 万平方米，城市副中心 155 平方公里范围内基本无违法建设，疏解退出 500 家一般制造业企业，整治提升核心区 615 条背街小巷，完成 PM2.5 精细化来源解析等。

2 月 24 日　环境保护部发布《关于加强“未批先建”建设项目环境影响评价管理工作的通知》（以下简称《通知》），《通知》要求，各级环境保护部门要按照“属地管理”原则，对“未批先建”建设项目进行拉网式排查并依法予以处罚。

2 月 25 日　京津冀协同发展工作推进会议在北京召开，国务院副总理张高丽主持会议并讲话。

2 月 27 日　国土资源部印发《关于全面实行永久基本农田特殊保护的通知》，以守住永久基本农田控制线为目标，以建立健全“划、建、管、补、护”长效机制为重点，巩固永久基本农田划定成果，完善保护措施，提高监管水平，确保到 2020 年，全国永久基本农田保护面积不少于 15.46 亿亩，基本形成保护有力、建设有效、管理有序的永久基本农田特殊保护格局。

2 月 27 日　湖南省易地扶贫搬迁工作会议在长沙召开，今年是全面完成“十三五”易地扶贫搬迁任务的攻关年。到今年年底，湖南省将全面完成“十三五”期间易地扶贫搬迁 72 万人的总任务。

2 月 28 日　从黑龙江省水利厅获悉，截至目前黑龙江省河长制组织体系和制度体系基本建立，河湖保护专项行动陆续开展，全省提前半年全面建立河长制。

2月28日　河北省住房城乡建设厅印发《2018年全省城乡规划工作要点》，全面贯彻落实党的十九大精神，以习近平新时代中国特色社会主义思想为指导，按照省委九届五次、六次全会决策部署，坚持以科学规划为引领，以城镇高质量发展为根本，深入推进新型城镇化与城乡统筹示范区建设，全面推动“五级两规一导则”体系建设，创新规划理念，改进规划编制方式，提高规划设计水平，严格规划执行，加强规划实施考核评估，强化规划管控作用，促进城乡健康有序发展，为新时代全面建设经济强省、美丽河北提供规划保障。

3月1日　国土资源部、财政部发出通知，要求进一步做好中央支持土地整治重大工程的有关工作。

3月2日　交通运输部发出通知，决定在北京、河北、吉林、江苏、浙江、福建、江西、河南、广东九省（市）加快推进新一代国家交通控制网和智慧公路试点。通知将基础设施数字化、路运一体化车路协同、北斗高精度定位综合应用、基于大数据的路网综合管理、“互联网+”路网综合服务、新一代国家交通控制网6个方向作为重点。

3月7日　国务院同意12个高新区升级为国家级开发区，严禁房地产开发。此次升级的高新区中，湖北省有3个：荆州高新技术产业园区、黄石大冶湖高新技术产业园区、潜江高新技术产业园区。江西省有2个：九江共青城高新技术产业园、宜春丰城高新技术产业园。广东省有2个：湛江高新技术产业开发区、茂名高新技术产业开发区。云南省有1个：楚雄高新技术产业开发区。安徽省有1个：淮南新技术产业开发区。重庆2个：荣昌高新技术产业开发区、永川高新技术产业开发区。湖南省有1个：怀化高新技术产业开发区。

3月9日　国务院办公厅印发《关于促进全域旅游发展的指导意见》，就加快推动旅游业转型升级、提质增效，全面优化旅游发展环境，走全域旅游发展的新路子作出部署。

3月9日　国家发展改革委印发《关于实施2018年推进新型城镇化建设重点任务的通知》，要求做好2018年新型城镇化工作，推动新型城镇化高质量发展，努力实现在新起点上取得新突破。

3月10日　为规范有序实施跨省域补充耕地国家统筹，严守耕地红线，根据《中华人民共和国土地管理法》和《中共中央国务院关于加强耕地保护和改进占补平衡的意见》《中共中央国务院关于实施乡村振兴战略的意见》有关规定，国务院制定并发布《我国跨省域补充耕地国家统筹管理办法》和《城乡建设用地增减挂钩节余指标跨省域调剂管理办法》。

3月10日　辽宁省住房城乡建设厅发布《关于加快推进海绵城市建设工作的通知》。要求2018年每个市至少要确定一个海绵城市建设示范区，并组织项目实施。2018年10月底前，各市要完成海绵城市建设专项规划编制并批复。各市要结合实际，制定2018、2019、2020年海绵城市建设三年项目计划，建立项目库。

3月12日　西藏自治区住房城乡建设厅积极推进边境地区小康村建设，编制全区边境地区小康村规划。全区628个边境地区小康村的规划正在加紧编制和开展专家技术审查。截至目前，4个边境地区共上报455个村庄规划，通过专家技术审查的共358个。

3月14日　住房城乡建设部发布《关于加强2018年城市排水防涝工作　确保安全度汛的通知》，并公布2018年全国城市排水防涝安全及重要易涝点整治责任人名单。住房城乡建设部强调，对于因排水防涝设施建设、汛前安全检查、汛期应急保障等方面工作不力，汛期城市发生内涝灾害导致人员伤亡和重大财产损失的，要依法追究相关责任。

3月21日 北京市政府出台《北京市人民政府办公厅关于加强传统村落保护发展的指导意见》(以下简称《指导意见》)，公布北京首批44个市级传统村落名录。《指导意见》称，传统村落中严禁各类不符合保护发展规划的建设行为，严禁以保护利用为由将村民全部迁出、实施房地产开发。

3月23日 国务院办公厅印发《关于保障城市轨道交通安全运行的意见》(以下简称《意见》)。《意见》强调，要全面贯彻党的十九大精神，坚持以习近平新时代中国特色社会主义思想为指导，以切实保障城市轨道交通安全运行为目标，遵循“以人为本、安全第一，统筹协调、改革创新，预防为先、防处并举，属地管理、综合治理”的基本原则，完善体制机制，健全法规标准，创新管理制度，强化技术支撑，夯实安全基础，提升服务品质，增强城市轨道交通安全防范治理能力。

3月24日 北京发布《建设项目规划使用性质正面负面清单》。这份清单主要为落实《北京城市总体规划(2016年—2035年)》，加强“四个中心”功能建设，发挥市场配置资源决定性作用，按照鼓励疏解非首都功能，鼓励补齐地区配套短板，鼓励完善地区公共服务设施，鼓励加强职住平衡的原则编制而成。

3月28日 浙江省《浙江省农村住房建设管理办法》，将于5月1日实施，标志着浙江省农房建设管理有法可依，填补长期以来农村住房质量安全管理的空白，实现对城镇建设活动和农村建设活动的闭合管理。

4月2日 国务院同意调整湖南东洞庭湖、重庆金佛山、云南白马雪山和西藏珠穆朗玛峰国家级自然保护区的范围。调整后保护区的面积、范围和功能分区等由生态环境部予以公布。

4月8日和9日 中共中央政治局常委、国务院副总理韩正分别到生态环境部、住房城乡建设部调研。他强调，要以习近平新时代中国特色社会主义思想为指导，全面贯彻落实党的十九大和十九届二中、三中全会精神，按照党中央、国务院决策部署，加快转变政府职能，全面提高政府效能，坚持问题导向，回应群众关切，密切结合实际，以更加务实的态度解决问题，把为人民群众造福的事办实办好。

4月9日 住房城乡建设部办公厅发布《农村危房改造基本安全技术导则》，为农村危房改造基本安全划出底线，并要求各地在参照执行的同时，结合实际细化，针对不同结构类型农房，制定既能保证安全又不盲目提高建设标准的地方标准，切实让农村困难群众住得安全又不增加负担。

4月11日 中共中央国务院出台《关于支持海南全面深化改革开放的指导意见》。

4月13日 国家发展改革委、自然资源部、环境保护部、住房城乡建设部、文化和旅游部5部委日前联合印发《关于规范主题公园建设发展的指导意见》，提出，要防止一哄而起、盲目发展、重复模仿、同质化竞争，防范地方债务、社会、金融等风险；要严控房地产倾向，对拟新增立项的主题公园项目要科学论证评估，严格把关审查，防范“假公园真地产”项目。

4月13日 湖北省住房城乡建设厅印发《湖北省美丽宜居乡村示范项目建设方案》，2018年至2020年，全省每个县市区都将打造精品型、提升型美丽宜居乡村示范项目。

4月17日 在法国巴黎召开的联合国教科文组织执行局第204次会议通过决议，正式批准了新一批世界地质公园。其中，中国提交申报的四川光雾山—诺水河、湖北黄冈大别山地质公园入选。

4月20日 中共中央国务院批复《河北雄安新区规划纲要》。《河北雄安新区规划纲要》深入贯彻习近平新时代中国特色社会主义思想，深入贯彻党的十九大和十九届二中、三中全会精神，坚决落实党中央、国务院决策部署，牢固树立和贯彻落实新发展理念，紧扣新时代我国社会主要矛盾变化，按照高质量发展要求，紧紧围绕统筹推进“五位一体”总体布局和协调推进“四个全面”战略布局，着眼建设北京非首都功能疏解集中承载地，创造“雄安质量”和成为推动高质量发展的全国样板，建设现代化经济体系的新引擎，坚持世界眼光、国际标准、中国特色、高点定位，坚持生态优先、绿色发展，坚持以人民为中心、注重保障和改善民生，坚持保护弘扬中华优秀传统文化、延续历史文脉，符合党中央、国务院对雄安新区的战略定位和发展要求，对于高起点规划、高标准建设雄安新区具有重要意义。

4月24日 国家发展改革委、自然资源部、住房城乡建设部、中国铁路总公司日前联合发布《关于推进高铁站周边区域合理开发建设的指导意见》，指导意见提到，新建铁路选线尽量减少对城市的分割，新建车站选址尽可能在中心城区或靠近城市建成区，确保人民群众乘坐高铁出行便利。

4月25日 工业信息化部、住房城乡建设部、国家能源局等6部门联合发布《智能光伏产业业发展行动计划（2018—2020年）》。计划分为5个方面、17项工作，其中住房城乡建设部牵头开展智能光伏建筑及城镇应用示范。

4月25日 中国证监会、住房城乡建设部联合发布了《关于推进住房租赁资产证券化相关工作的通知》。

4月26日 中共中央总书记、国家主席、中央军委主席习近平在武汉主持召开深入推动长江经济带发展座谈会并发表了重要讲话。

4月26日 全国改善农村人居环境工作会议在浙江省安吉县召开。会议全面贯彻落实党的十九大精神，深入学习贯彻习近平总书记关于乡村振兴和改善农村人居环境的重要指示精神，认真落实李克强总理批示要求，进一步推广浙江“千村示范、万村整治”工程经验做法，全面部署改善农村人居环境各项任务。

5月1日 为有效保护和合理利用风景名胜资源、加强和规范风景名胜区管理，《湖北省风景名胜区条例》自2018年5月1日正式施行。

5月2日 国务院批复同意将河北省蔚县列为国家历史文化名城。河北省、张家口市及蔚县人民政府按照《历史文化名城名镇名村保护条例》的要求，加强文物保护利用和文化遗产保护传承，正确处理城市建设与保护历史文化遗产的关系，深入研究挖掘历史文化遗产的内涵与价值，明确保护的原则和重点。

5月9日 浙江省颁布国内首部城市景观风貌条例，这是国内首部城市景观风貌专项立法，是浙江“走在前列谋新篇”的又一次成功实践。

5月9日 《2018中国海绵城市建设白皮书》在福州发布，全面解析中国海绵城市的最新进展，分析目前典型城市的成功案例，为其他地区建设海绵城市提供更多参与和借鉴，并指出海绵城市建设可以更好地通过创新性、适应性、包容性的思路从而达到发展的新高度。

5月11日 住房和城乡建设部、文化和旅游部、国家文物局、财政部、自然资源部、农业农村部联合下发通知，要求各省（区、市）有关部门要严格按照建村〔2014〕61号文件和《住房城乡建设部 文化部 国家文物局 财政部关于做好中国传统村落保护项目实施工作的意见》（建村〔2014〕135号）要求，认真做好中央财政支持的中国传统村落各类保护项目组织实施工作，加强监督检查，督促相关传统村落在使用中央财政资金前将项目实施信息录入中国传统村落保护项目管理信息系统，并于每年2月底前，将本省（区、市）上年度传统村落保护项目实施情况报告送住房城乡建设部和财政部。公布2018年第二批列入中央财政支持范围的中国传统村落名单。

5月12日 《粤港澳大湾区建设报告（2018）》发布。报告指出，在“一带一路”背景下，粤港澳大湾区在国家战略布局中具有独特地位和优势。“一国两制”和三个独立关税区为对接国际、推动“一带一路”建设提供了更加灵活的制度安排。自由港、特别行政区、经济特区、自由贸易试验区等在大湾区的制度叠加效应扩大了贸易和产业合作的选择面。

5月14日 中共中央政治局常委、国务院副总理韩正在河北雄安新区调研时强调，规划建设雄安新区是以习近平同志为核心的党中央作出的重大决策，是疏解北京非首都功能、推动京津冀协同发展的历史性工程，是千年大计、国家大事。要以习近平新时代中国特色社会主义思想为指引，深入贯彻落实党的十九大精神，坚持世界眼光、国际标准、中国特色、高点定位，着眼打造北京非首都功能疏解集中承载地，创造“雄安质量”，高标准高质量规划建设雄安新区。

5月14日 国务院办公厅印发《关于开展工程建设项目审批制度改革试点的通知》，决定在北京市、天津市、上海市、重庆市、沈阳市、大连市、南京市、厦门市、武汉市、广州市、深圳市、成都市、贵阳市、渭南市、延安市和浙江省开展试点。

5月18日—19日 全国生态环境保护大会在京召开。中共中央总书记、国家主席、中央军委主席习近平出席会议并发表重要讲话。习近平强调，要自觉把经济社会发展同生态文明建设统筹起来，充分发挥党的领导和我国社会主义制度能够集中力量办大事的政治优势，充分利用改革开放40年来积累的坚实物质基础，加大力度推进生态文明建设、解决生态环境问题，坚决打好环境污染防治攻坚战，推动我国生态文明建设迈上新台阶。中共中央政治局常委、国务院总理李克强在会上讲话。中共中央政治局常委、全国政协主席汪洋，中共中央政治局常委、中央书记处书记王沪宁，中共中央政治局常委、中央纪委书记赵乐际出席会议。中共中央政治局常委、国务院副总理韩正作总结讲话。

5月24日 甘肃省发展改革委、省自然资源厅、省生态环境厅、省住房城乡建设厅研究制定了《关于规范推进特色小镇和特色小城镇建设的实施意见》。

5月25日 全国政协在京召开双周协商座谈会聚焦历史文化名城名镇保护。中共中央政治局常委、全国政协主席汪洋主持会议并讲话。汪洋强调，历史文化名城名镇是培育文化自信和文化认同的重要物质基础。双周协商座谈会以“历史文化名城名镇保护”为议题，发挥政协委员的智力优势，为历史文化名城名镇保护资政建言，具有重要意义。

5月28日 中共中央政治局常委、国务院副总理韩正在北京市通州区调研北京城市副中心规划建设工作时表示，建设北京城市副中心是以习近平同志为核心的党中央作出的重要决策，是疏解北京非首都功能、推动京津冀协同发展的重大战略举措，是千年大计、国家大事。要以习近平新时代中国特色社会主义思想为指导，全面贯彻党的十九大精神，按照世界眼光、国际标准、中国特色、高点定位的要求，高起点、高标准、高水平规划建设管理北京城市副中心，着力打造国际一流的和谐宜居之都示范区、新型城镇化示范区和京津冀区域协同发展示范区，促进北京优化提升首都功能、有序疏解非首都功能。

5月28日 辽宁省住房和城乡建设厅发布《关于加强无障碍设施建设管理的通知》，要求新建、改建、扩建各类居住建筑和公共建筑以及城市道路等公共设施，要严格执行《无障碍设计规范（GB 50763—2012）》等相关标准和规定，设计坡道、盲道等相关无障碍设施。无障碍设施要与主体工程同步设计、同步施工、同步验收投入使用，并与周边无障碍设施相衔接。

5月28日 根据《国务院办公厅关于印发〈省级政府耕地保护责任目标考核办法〉的通知》要求，自然资源部会同农业农村部、国家统计局联合印发《关于开展2016—2020年省级政府耕地保护责任目标期中检查工作的通知》，对省级政府“十三五”前两年（2016—2017年）耕地保护责任目标履行情况进行期中检查。

5月30日 交通运输部印发《交通运输脱贫攻坚三年行动计划（2018—2020年）》（以下简称《计划》）。《计划》明确到2020年，贫困地区基本建成“外通内联、通村畅乡、客车到村、安全便捷”的交通运输网络，贫困地区具备条件的乡镇和建制村通硬化路，具备条件的县城通二级及以上公路，具备条件的建制村通客车，基本完成乡道及以上行政等级公路安全隐患治理，建立健全农村公路建设管理养护和运行体制机制。督导帮助定点扶贫县、对口支援县、六盘山片区如期完成脱贫任务。

5月31日 中共中央政治局召开会议审议《乡村振兴战略规划（2018—2022年）》和《关于打赢脱贫攻坚战三年行动的指导意见》。

6月1日 住房城乡建设部、生态环境部、水利部、农业农村部印发《关于做好非正规垃圾堆放点排查和政治工作的通知》，要求各地重点整治垃圾山、垃圾围村、垃圾围坝、工业污染“上山下乡”，积极消化存量，严格控制增量，到2020年年底基本遏制城镇垃圾、工业固体废物违法违规向农村地区转移问题，基本完成农村地区非正规垃圾堆放点整治。

6月3—4日 中共中央政治局常委、国务院副总理韩正在工程建设项目审批制度改革试点工作座谈会上强调，以市场主体和群众感受为标准构建科学便捷高效的工程建设项目审批制度。

6月5日　生态环境部、中央文明办、教育部、共青团中央、全国妇联五部门在长沙联合发布《公民生态环境行为规范（试行）》，旨在牢固树立社会主义生态文明观，推动形成人与自然和谐发展现代化建设新格局，引导公民成为生态文明的践行者和美丽中国的建设者。

6月11日　国务院办公厅公布山西太宽河、吉林头道松花江上游、吉林甑峰岭、黑龙江细鳞河、贵州大沙河5处新建国家级自然保护区名单。新建国家级自然保护区的面积、范围和功能分区等由生态环境部另行公布。有关地区要按照批准的面积和范围组织勘界，落实自然保护区土地权属，并在规定的时限内标明界区，予以公布。

6月13日　国务院总理李克强主持召开国务院常务会议，部署实施蓝天保卫战三年行动计划，持续改善空气质量；确定进一步扩大进口的措施，促进调结构、惠民生和外贸平衡发展。

6月14日　按照国务院关于推广使用2000国家大地坐标系的有关要求，之前国土资源部（现自然资源部）确定，2018年6月底前完成全系统各类国土资源空间数据向2000国家大地坐标系转换，2018年7月1日起全面使用2000国家大地坐标系。

6月21日　北京市规划国土委、通州区政府共同发布通知，《北京城市副中心控制性详细规划（街区层面）》草案已经编制完成，按照《中华人民共和国城乡规划法》《北京市城乡规划条例》，规划草案于6月21日至7月20日向社会公告，听取公众意见建议。

7月2日　司法部下发《关于全面推动长江经济带司法鉴定协同发展的实施意见》，提出7个方面措施，为全面推动长江经济带11省（市）司法鉴定协同发展，更好地服务长江经济带经济社会发展作出部署。

7月3日　江苏、上海两地陆续划定生态红线，切实保护生态环境，维护生态安全。

7月3日　国务院印发《打赢蓝天保卫战三年行动计划》，明确了大气污染防治工作的总体思路、基本目标、主要任务和保障措施，提出了打赢蓝天保卫战的时间表和路线图。

7月3日　山东省青岛市十六届人大常委会第十次会议表决通过了关于修改《青岛市崂山风景区条例》的决定。新条例规定，未经批准，不得在风景区内进行各类建设活动；风景区内禁止修坟立碑、禁止建设经营性墓地。

7月5日　中共中央总书记、国家主席、中央军委主席习近平对实施乡村振兴战略作出重要指示，强调实施乡村振兴战略，是党的十九大作出的重大决策部署，是新时代做好"三农"工作的总抓手。各地区各部门要充分认识实施乡村振兴战略的重大意义，把实施乡村振兴战略摆在优先位置，坚持五级书记抓乡村振兴，让乡村振兴成为全党全社会的共同行动。

7月6日　中共中央总书记、国家主席、中央军委主席、中央全面深化改革委员会主任习近平主持召开中央全面深化改革委员会第三次会议并发表重要讲话。习近平强调，党的十九大以来，党中央在深化党的十八大以来改革成果的基础上，不失时机推进重大全局性改革，全面深化改革取得新的重大进展。继续推进改革，要把更多精力聚焦到重点难点问题上来，集中力量打攻坚战，激发制度活力，激活基层经验，激励干部作为，扎扎实实把全面深化改革推向深入。

7 月 6 日　自然资源部批复同意《浙江省实施全域土地综合整治助推乡村振兴战略行动计划工作方案》。

7 月 6 日　司法部、生态环境部联合发布《环境损害司法鉴定机构登记评审细则》。细则针对污染物性质鉴定、地表水和沉积物、空气污染、土壤与地下水、近海海洋与海岸带、生态系统和其他环境损害 7 个鉴定类别，分别提出鉴定机构和人员登记准入的具体要求和条件，确保环境损害司法鉴定高资质、高水平。

7 月 7 日　国务院同意调整内蒙古大黑山、河南丹江湿地、广西九万山、四川花萼山、西藏芒康滇金丝猴和西藏羌塘国家级自然保护区的范围。调整后保护区的面积、范围和功能分区等由生态环境部予以公布。

7 月 12 日　为推动完善京津冀及周边地区大气污染联防联控协作机制，经党中央、国务院同意，将京津冀及周边地区大气污染防治协作小组调整为京津冀及周边地区大气污染防治领导小组。

7 月 12 日　北京市正式印发生态保护红线。根据划定范围，北京市生态保护红线面积 4290 平方公里，占市域总面积的 26.1%，包含水源涵养、水土保持、生物多样性维护和重要河流湿地 4 种类型。北京市生态保护红线严禁不符合主体功能定位的各类开发活动。

7 月 13 日　中共中央总书记、国家主席、中央军委主席、中央财经委员会主任习近平主持召开中央财经委员会第二次会议并发表重要讲话。习近平强调，关键核心技术是国之重器，对推动我国经济高质量发展、保障国家安全都具有十分重要的意义，必须切实提高我国关键核心技术创新能力，把科技发展主动权牢牢掌握在自己手里，为我国发展提供有力的科技保障。

7 月 13 日　国务院办公厅发布《关于进一步加强城市轨道交通规划建设管理的意见》。

7 月 18 日　国家发展改革委、住房城乡建设部发布通知，决定对《“十三五”全国城镇污水处理及再生利用设施建设规划》和《“十三五”全国城镇生活垃圾无害化处理设施建设规划》开展中期评估。

7 月 19 日　河北省政府出台《河北省生态保护红线》，划定全省生态保护红线总面积 4.05 万平方公里，主要分布于承德市、张家口市、唐山市北部山区、秦皇岛市中北部以及保定市、石家庄市、邢台市、邯郸市西部山区。通过评估，河北省划定了生态保护红线 4 个重点区域，基本形成护佑京津、雄安新区和华北平原，优化京津冀区域生态空间安全格局。

7 月 25 日　国务院印发《关于加强滨海湿地保护　严格管控围填海的通知》（以下简称《通知》）。《通知》指出，进一步加强滨海湿地保护，严格管控围填海活动，有利于严守海洋生态保护红线，改善海洋生态环境；有利于构建国土空间开发保护新格局，推动实施海洋强国战略；有利于构建海洋生态环境治理体系，推进生态文明建设。

7 月 25 日　央行营业管理部联合四部门出台支持北京市共有产权住房专项信贷政策。其中规定，适用首套房贷政策的共有产权住房贷款最低首付比例按照政策性住房执行，不低于30%；不适用首套房贷政策的共有产权住房贷款最低首付比例参照普通住房执行，不低于60%。

7月30日 北京市发布《推进京津冀协同发展2018—2020年行动计划》，提出到2020年，要高质量完成京津冀协同发展中期目标任务，初步形成协同发展、互利共赢的新局面。

7月31日 中共中央办公厅、国务院办公厅印发《关于实施革命文物保护利用工程(2018—2022年)的意见》的通知，要求各地区各部门结合实际认真贯彻落实。

7月31日 自然资源部原规划司、原城乡规划司、国家林业和草原局保护司和江西省上饶市人民政府在北京共同召开“多规合一”背景下的世界自然遗产保护与发展研讨会，交流、讨论世界自然遗产规划建设管理的实践与经验，探讨适应“多规合一”和机构改革要求的世界自然遗产规划建设管理模式和体制机制建议。

7月31日 经江苏省委、省政府同意，省委办公厅、省政府办公厅正式印发《关于在全省湖泊实施湖长制的意见》。

8月10日 按照国务院要求，根据国家发展改革委、科技部、原国土资源部、住房城乡建设部、商务部、海关总署发布的《中国开发区审核公告目录（2018年版)》，自然资源部、住房城乡建设部对各省、自治区、直辖市上报的开发区四至范围文字表述和边界拐点坐标进行核对，形成了《国家级开发区四至范围公告目录》(2018年版)。同时，在自然资源部网站（www. mlr. gov. cn）公布国家级开发区四至范围、界桩坐标号及开发区边界形状图。省级开发区的四至范围由各省、自治区、直辖市人民政府自行公告，并报自然资源部备案。

8月14日 经国务院同意，天津市将开展天津市城市总体规划（2017—2035年）编制工作，并下发了《关于印发天津市城市总体规划（2017—2035年）编制工作方案的通知》。

8月15日 中共中央政治局常委、国务院副总理、粤港澳大湾区建设领导小组组长韩正在北京人民大会堂主持召开粤港澳大湾区建设领导小组全体会议，深入学习贯彻习近平总书记关于粤港澳大湾区建设的重要讲话精神，讨论审议有关文件，研究部署下一阶段工作。

8月16日 交通运输部办公厅发出《关于加快推进建制村通客车有关工作的通知》(以下简称《通知》)，《通知》指出，建制村通客车是保障广大农民群众“行有所乘”的民生服务，对改善农民群众生活条件、提升人民群众获得感、促进农业农村现代化建设具有重要意义。《中共中央国务院关于打赢脱贫攻坚战三年行动的指导意见》和《国务院关于印发“十三五”现代综合交通运输体系发展规划的通知》(国发〔2017〕11号）均提出了到2020年“具备条件的建制村全部通客车”的明确要求。

8月20日 根据机构设置、人员变动情况和工作需要，国务院决定，第三次全国土地调查调整为第三次全国国土调查，国务院第三次全国土地调查领导小组调整为国务院第三次全国国土调查领导小组，对领导小组组成单位和人员进行相应调整。

8月20日 农业农村部和中共浙江省委、浙江省人民政府在北京签署合作框架协议，共同推动浙江乡村振兴示范省建设。根据合作框架协议，双方将以省部共建、以省为主、试点先行、示范推广、整体推进为工作路径，在多规融合引领发展、高质量发展乡村产业、建设新时代美丽乡村、繁荣发展乡村文化、健全现代乡村治理体系、促进城乡融合发展、全面深化农村改革7个方面深度合作，全面实施乡村产业振兴行动、新时代美丽乡村建设行动、乡村文化兴盛行动、自治法治德治“三治结合”提升行动、富民惠民行动“五大行动”，高水平打造农业农村现代化浙江样板。

8月21日　中共中央政治局常委、国务院总理、国务院西部地区开发领导小组组长李克强主持召开国务院西部地区开发领导小组会议，部署深入推进西部开发工作。

8月23日　山西省政府正式印发《关于2018年实施乡村振兴若干政策措施的通知》，决定投入90.23亿元实施乡村振兴战略，并将2018年强农惠农富农政策纳入其中统筹实施。

8月28日　重庆市第五届人大常委会第四次会议日前表决通过了《重庆市历史文化名城名镇名村保护条例》，这是重庆市对名城、名镇、名村以及历史文化街区、传统风貌区、历史建筑和传统风貌建筑七类历史文化资源进行保护的首部地方性法规，并于9月1日起施行。

8月29日　收录了我国333万余条自然和人工河流、湖泊、水库、水渠等水系实体数据的全国水网数据库正式建成。自此，每条长度500米以上的河流和每个面积大于5000平方米的湖泊、水库、坑塘等都有了自己唯一的“身份证号”，这将极大地方便今后开展水资源管理、国土空间规划、灾害应急和政府决策等工作，为自然资源调查监测管理提供基础数据服务。

8月29日　全国首个地市级绿色矿山建设规划——《包头市绿色矿山建设规划》通过了由自然资源部、内蒙古自治区国土资源厅以及包头市相关专家组成的专家组的评审。

8月29日　中共中央政治局常委、国务院副总理韩正主持召开大气污染防治专题工作会议，贯彻落实党中央、国务院关于打赢蓝天保卫战的决策部署，审议《京津冀及周边地区2018—2019年秋冬季大气污染综合治理攻坚行动方案》等文件，对京津冀及周边地区、汾渭平原大气污染防治重点工作作出安排。

9月13日　根据党的十九届三中全会审议通过的《深化党和国家机构改革方案》和第十三届全国人民代表大会第一次会议批准的《国务院机构改革方案》，中共中央办公厅、国务院办公厅发布关于调整住房和城乡建设部职责机构编制的通知。

9月13日　《重庆市海绵城市建设管理办法（试行）》（以下简称《办法》）正式发布，《办法》对重庆市海绵城市建设的规划和用地管理、建设管理、运行维护以及监督管理提出了要求。到2020年，重庆城市建成区20%以上面积将达到海绵城市指标要求，到2030年，这一数字将达到80%以上。

9月14日　为贯彻党中央、国务院关于引导设计下乡提升乡村规划建设水平的工作部署，落实《中共中央国务院关于实施乡村振兴战略的意见》和《农村人居环境整治三年行动方案》有关要求，住房城乡建设部发布《关于开展引导和支持设计下乡工作的通知》。

9月18日　为贯彻党中央、国务院关于提升乡村规划建设水平的部署，落实《农村人居环境整治三年行动方案》关于村庄规划管理基本覆盖的要求，满足农民群众对美好生活的期待，住房城乡建设部发布《关于进一步加强村庄建设规划工作的通知》。

9月20日　中共中央总书记、国家主席、中央军委主席、中央全面深化改革委员会主任习近平主持召开中央全面深化改革委员会第四次会议并发表重要讲话。习近平强调，改革重在落实，也难在落实。改革进行到今天，抓改革、抓落实的有利条件越来越多，改革的思想基础、实践基础、制度基础、民心基础更加坚实，要投入更多精力、下更大气力抓落实，加强领导，科学统筹，狠抓落实，把改革重点放到解决实际问题上来。

9 月 26 日　中共中央国务院印发《乡村振兴战略规划（2018—2022 年）》，并发出通知，要求各地区各部门结合实际认真贯彻落实。

10 月 6 日　国务院批复《淮河生态经济带发展规划》。

10 月 8 日　国务院总理李克强主持召开国务院常务会议，部署推进棚户区改造工作，进一步改善住房困难群众的居住条件。

10 月 8 日　为深入贯彻落实党的十九大精神，进一步做好文物保护利用和文化遗产保护传承工作，中共中央办公厅、国务院办公厅印发《关于加强文物保护利用改革的若干意见》。

10 月 8 日　国务院批复《汉江生态经济带发展规划》。

10 月 9 日　福建省国土资源厅发出通知，决定在福清市开展陆海统筹自然生态空间用途管制试点，推进陆海统筹发展，探索解决用地用海矛盾，建立健全陆海自然生态空间用途管制制度体系，实现陆海资源严格保护、有效修复、集约利用，为构建蓝色生态屏障和蓝色经济试验区、建设生态文明提供试点经验。

10 月 10 日　为进一步促进乡村旅游发展提质扩容，发挥乡村旅游对促进消费、改善民生、推动高质量发展的重要带动作用，国家发展改革委会同有关部门共同研究制定了《促进乡村旅游发展提质升级行动方案（2018 年—2020 年）》。

10 月 13 日　辽宁省委、省政府印发《辽宁“一带一路”综合试验区建设总体方案》，标志辽宁省在全域范围内，开启了以“一带一路”建设引领全面开放、推动全面振兴的高质量发展新时期。

10 月 15 日　北京市平谷区、河北省秦皇岛市等 27 个城市被国家林业和草原局授予“国家森林城市”称号。截至目前，全国国家森林城市已达 165 个。

10 月 15 日　住房和城乡建设部、生态环境部发布《城市黑臭水体治理攻坚战实施方案》，进一步扎实推进城市黑臭水体治理工作。

10 月 16 日　国务院批复同意设立中国（海南）自由贸易试验区并印发《中国（海南）自由贸易试验区总体方案》。

10 月 19 日　根据《国务院办公厅关于政府向社会力量购买服务的指导意见》《政府购买服务管理办法（暂行）》有关要求，为进一步完善公租房运营管理机制、更好地吸引企业和其他机构参与公租房运营管理，近日，住房城乡建设部、财政部下发通知，确定在浙江、安徽、山东、湖北、广西、四川、云南、陕西 8 个省（自治区）开展政府购买公租房运营管理服务试点工作，在试点地区建立健全公租房运营管理机制，完善政府购买公租房运营管理服务的管理制度与流程，形成一批可复制、可推广的试点成果，为提升公租房运营管理能力提供支撑。

10月24日　习近平总书记对自由贸易试验区建设作出重要指示，强调继续解放思想，积极探索，加强统筹谋划，改革创新，把自由贸易试验区建设成为新时代改革开放新高地。

10月24日　习近平总书记视察广州市恩宁路历史文化街区永庆坊片区，在听取广州市城市规划建设管理工作汇报时指出：城市规划和建设要高度重视历史文化保护，不急功近利，不大拆大建；要突出地方特色，注重人居环境改善，更多采用微改造这种“绣花”功夫，注重文明传承、文化延续，让城市留下记忆，让人们记住乡愁。

10月31日　住房城乡建设部、江苏省人民政府、联合国人居署共同在徐州举办2018年世界城市日中国主场活动。

10月31日　为贯彻落实党中央、国务院决策部署，深化供给侧结构性改革，进一步增强基础设施对促进城乡和区域协调发展、改善民生等方面的支撑作用，国务院办公厅印发《关于保持基础设施领域补短板力度的指导意见》。

11月5日　为贯彻落实《国务院关于印发“十三五”加快残疾人小康进程规划纲要的通知》和《国务院关于印发“十三五”国家老龄事业发展和养老体系建设规划的通知》要求，进一步做好无障碍环境建设工作，力争到2020年实现无障碍环境建设工作机制、地方性法规、规章、标准体系进一步健全，无障碍设施覆盖面进一步扩大，无障碍环境建设水平明显提升，全社会关心、支持、参与无障碍环境建设与维护的社会氛围不断增强，农村无障碍环境得到较大改善的目标，住房城乡建设部、工业和信息化部、民政部、中国残联、全国老龄办决定组织开展无障碍环境市县村镇创建工作，联合发出《关于开展无障碍环境市县村镇创建工作的通知》。

11月15日　文化和旅游部等17部门印发《关于促进乡村旅游可持续发展的指导意见》的通知，乡村旅游是旅游业的重要组成部分，是实施乡村振兴战略的重要力量，在加快推进农业农村现代化、城乡融合发展、贫困地区脱贫攻坚等方面发挥着重要作用。

11月19日　国务院第三次全国国土调查领导小组办公室印发《第三次全国国土调查实施方案》（以下简称《方案》）的通知。《方案》提出三调的主要目标是：在第二次全国土地调查成果基础上，全面细化和完善全国土地利用基础数据，掌握翔实准确的全国国土利用现状和自然资源变化情况，进一步完善国土调查、监测和统计制度，实现成果信息化管理与共享，满足生态文明建设、空间规划编制、供给侧结构性改革、宏观调控、自然资源管理体制改革和统一确权登记、国土空间用途管制、国土空间生态修复、空间治理能力现代化和国土空间规划体系建设等各项工作的需要。

11月23日　为贯彻落实《中共中央办公厅、国务院办公厅印发〈关于推进城市安全发展的意见〉的通知》，做好住房城乡建设系统推进城市安全发展工作，住房城乡建设部办公厅印发《贯彻落实城市安全发展意见实施方案》的通知。

11月23日　国务院批复同意关于乌区的鲁木齐、昌吉、石河子高新技术产业开发区建设国家自主创新示范区。

11月30日　中共中央、国务院发出《关于建立更加有效的区域协调发展新机制的意见》（以下简称《意见》）。《意见》指出，实施区域协调发展战略是新时代国家重大战略之一，是贯彻新发展理念、建设现代化经济体系的重要组成部分。党的十八大以来，各地区各部门围绕促进区域协调发展与正确处理政府和市场关系，在建立健全区域合作机制、区域互助机制、区际利益补偿机制等方面进行积极探索并取得一定成效。同时要看到，我国区域发展差距依然较大，区域分化现象逐渐显现，无序开发与恶性竞争仍然存在，区域发展不平衡不充分问题依然比较突出，区域发展机制还不完善，难以适应新时代实施区域协调发展战略的需要。

11 月 30 日　为遏制工程建设领域专业技术人员职业资格“挂证”的现象，维护建筑市场秩序，促进建筑业持续健康发展，住房城乡建设部、人力资源社会保障部、工业和信息化部、交通运输部、水利部办公厅以及铁路局、民航局综合司联合下发通知，决定开展工程建设领域专业技术人员职业资格“挂证”等违法违规行为专项整治，坚持“全覆盖、零容忍、严执法、重实效”，依法从严查处工程建设领域职业资格“挂证”等违法违规行为。

12 月 6 日　住房城乡建设部在广西首府南宁举办了“推动城市高质量发展系列标准发布”活动，发布包括《海绵城市建设评价标准》《绿色建筑评价标准》在内的 10 项标准，旨在适应中国经济高速增长阶段转向高质量发展阶段的新要求，以高标准支撑和引导我国城市建设、工程建设高质量发展。

12 月 12 日　2018 年 7 月 6 日，中共中央总书记、国家主席、中央军委主席习近平主持召开中央全面深化改革委员会第三次会议，审议通过了《关于建立健全基本公共服务标准体系的指导意见》（以下简称《指导意见》），近日中共中央办公厅国务院办公厅印发《关于建立健全基本公共服务标准体系的指导意见》，《指导意见》指出建立健全基本公共服务标准体系，明确中央与地方提供基本公共服务的质量水平和支出责任，以标准化促进基本公共服务均等化、普惠化、便捷化，是新时代提高保障和改善民生水平、推进国家治理体系和治理能力现代化的必然要求，对于不断满足人民日益增长的美好生活需要、不断促进社会公平正义、不断增进全体人民在共建共享发展中的获得感，具有重要意义。

12 月 20 日　为全面贯彻党的十九大精神，落实党中央、国务院关于打赢脱贫攻坚战三年行动的决策部署，完成建档立卡贫困户等重点对象农村危房改造任务，实现中央确定的脱贫攻坚“两不愁、三保障”总体目标中住房安全有保障的目标，住房城乡建设部联合财政部印发《农村危房改造脱贫攻坚三年行动方案》，把建档立卡贫困户放在突出位置，全力推进建档立卡贫困户、低保户、农村分散供养特困人员和贫困残疾人家庭 4 类重点对象的危房改造，并探索支持农村贫困群体危房改造的长效机制。

（作者：徐辉，中国城市规划设计研究院学术信息中心副主任；胡文娜，中国城市规划设计研究院学术信息中心高级规划师）

附录 2

2018 年城市政策法规文件索引

名称	批号（文号）	发布机构	发布日期
国家发展改革委办公厅关于总结推广第二批国家新型城镇化综合试点阶段性成果的通知	发改办规划〔2018〕1453 号	国家发展改革委	2018－11－15
生态环境部 农业农村部关于印发农业农村污染治理攻坚战行动计划的通知	环土壤〔2018〕143 号	生态环境部、农业农村部	2018－11－7
关于印发《汉江生态经济带发展规划》的通知	发改地区〔2018〕1605 号	国家发展改革委	2018－11－5
关于印发《淮河生态经济带发展规划》的通知	发改地区〔2018〕1588 号	国家发展改革委	2018－11－2
自然资源部办公厅关于印发《围填海项目生态评估技术指南（试行）》等技术指南的通知	自然资办发〔2018〕36 号	自然资源部办公厅	2018－11－1
关于城镇低效用地再开发工作推进情况的通报	自然资源部通报第 28 期	自然资源部	2018－10－20
国务院关于汉江生态经济带发展规划的批复	国函〔2018〕127 号	国务院	2018－10－18
国务院关于淮河生态经济带发展规划的批复	国函〔2018〕126 号	国务院	2018－10－18
关于印发自然资源科技创新发展规划纲要的通知	自然资发〔2018〕117 号	自然资源部	2018－10－16
国家发展改革委办公厅 文化和旅游部办公厅关于印发《“三区三州”等深度贫困地区旅游基础设施提升工程建设方案》的通知	发改办社会〔2018〕1223 号	国家发展改革委办公厅、文化和旅游部办公厅	2018－10－10
住房城乡建设部 生态环境部关于印发城市黑臭水体治理攻坚战实施方案的通知	建城〔2018〕104 号	住房和城乡建设部、生态环境部	2018－9－30
农业农村部办公厅关于印发《乡村振兴科技支撑行动实施方案》的通知	农办科〔2018〕22 号	农业农村部办公厅	2018－9－30
关于加快推进长江两岸造林绿化的指导意见	发改农经〔2018〕1391 号	国家发展改革委、水利部、自然资源部、林草局	2018－9－25
农业农村部关于支持长江经济带农业农村绿色发展的实施意见	农计发〔2018〕23 号	农业农村部	2018－9－21
住房城乡建设部关于进一步加强村庄建设规划工作的通知	建村〔2018〕89 号	住房和城乡建设部	2018－9－18
关于进一步做好全国环保设施和城市污水垃圾处理设施向公众开放工作的通知	环办宣教〔2018〕29 号	生态环境部办公厅、住房和城乡建设部办公厅	2018－9－18
国务院办公厅关于开展生态环境保护法规、规章、规范性文件清理工作的通知	国办发〔2018〕87 号	国务院	2018－9－18
农业农村部 自然资源部印发《关于开展“大棚房”问题专项清理整治行动坚决遏制农地非农化的方案》的通知	农农发〔2018〕3 号	农业农村部、自然资源部	2018－9－15

续表

名　称	批号（文号）	发布机构	发布日期
关于发布《环境影响评价技术导则 土壤环境（试行）》国家环境保护标准的公告	公告 2018 年 第 38 号	生态环境部	2018－9－14
国家发展改革委办公厅关于建立特色小镇和特色小城镇高质量发展机制的通知	发改办规划〔2018〕1041 号	国家发展改革委办公厅	2018－8－30
农业农村部办公厅关于开展第五批中国重要农业文化遗产发掘工作的通知	农办加〔2018〕10 号	农业农村部办公厅	2018－8－2
自然资源部关于印发《城乡建设用地增减挂钩节余指标跨省域调剂实施办法》的通知	自然资规〔2018〕4 号	自然资源部	2018－7－30
国务院关于加强滨海湿地保护严格管控围填海的通知	国发〔2018〕24 号	国务院	2018－7－25
国务院办公厅关于调整内蒙古大黑山等 6 处国家级自然保护区的通知	国办函〔2018〕42 号	国务院	2018－7－16
住房城乡建设部关于发布国家标准《城市居住区规划设计标准》的公告	公告 2018 第 142 号	住房和城乡建设部	2018－7－10
农业农村部关于印发《农业绿色发展技术导则（2018—2030 年）》的通知	农科教发〔2018〕3 号	农业农村部	2018－7－6
自然资源部关于健全建设用地“增存挂钩”机制的通知	自然资规〔2018〕1 号	自然资源部	2018－6－25
国家发展改革委办公厅 住房城乡建设部办公厅关于开展“十三五”城镇污水垃圾处理设施建设规划中期评估的通知	发改办环资〔2018〕724 号	国家发展改革委办公厅、住房城乡建设部办公厅	2018－6－14
国务院办公厅关于公布山西太宽河等 5 处新建国家级自然保护区名单的通知	国办发〔2018〕41 号	国务院	2018－6－7
关于公布《公民生态环境行为规范（试行）》的公告	公告 2018 年 第 12 号	生态环境部、中央精神文明建设指导委员会办公室、教育部、中国共产主义青年团中央委员会、中华全国妇女联合会	2018－6－4
住房城乡建设部关于发布国家标准《城市轨道交通线网规划标准》的公告	公告 2018 第 78 号	住房和城乡建设部	2018－4－25
关于印发全国沿海渔港建设规划（2018—2025 年）的通知	发改农经〔2018〕597 号	国家发展改革委、农业农村部	2018－4－19
国务院办公厅关于调整湖南东洞庭湖等 4 处国家级自然保护区的通知	国办函〔2018〕19 号	国务院	2018－4－2
关于印发兰州—西宁城市群发展规划的通知	发改规划〔2018〕423 号	国家发展改革委、住房城乡建设部	2018－3－13
关于在第三次全国土地调查中先行开展城镇内部土地利用现状调查工作的通知	国土调查办发〔2018〕7 号	国务院第三次全国土地调查领导小组办公室	2018－3－5
关于印发呼包鄂榆城市群发展规划的通知	发改地区〔2018〕358 号	国家发展改革委	2018－2－27
国家发展改革委关于扎实推进农村人居环境整治行动的通知	发改农经〔2018〕343 号	国家发展改革委	2018－2－26
国土资源部关于全面实行永久基本农田特殊保护的通知	国土资规〔2018〕1 号	国土资源部	2018－2－13
关于印发关中平原城市群发展规划的通知	发改规划〔2018〕220 号	国家发展改革委、住房城乡建设部	2018－2－2

续表

名 称	批号(文号)	发布机构	发布日期
关于印发《第三次全国土地调查实施方案》的通知	国土调查办发〔2018〕3号	国土资源部	2018-2-2
国土资源部办公厅 住房城乡建设部办公厅关于沈阳等11个城市利用集体建设用地建设租赁住房试点实施方案意见的函	国土资厅函〔2018〕63号	国土资源部办公厅	2018-1-16
国务院办公厅关于公布辽宁五花顶等6处新建国家级自然保护区名单的通知	国办发〔2018〕9号	国务院	2018-2-13
关于印发山东新旧动能转换综合试验区建设总体方案的通知	发改地区〔2018〕67号	国家发展改革委	2018-1-12
关于印发三江源国家公园总体规划的通知	发改社会〔2018〕64号	国家发展改革委	2018-1-12
国土资源部 财政部 中国人民银行 中国银行业监督管理委员会关于印发《土地储备管理办法》的通知	国土资规〔2017〕17号	国土资源部、财政部、中国人民银行、中国银行业监督管理委员会	2018-1-3

（作者：徐辉，中国城市规划设计研究院学术信息中心副主任；沈喜明，中国城市规划设计研究院学术信息中心工程师）

附录3

2018年中国历史文化名镇名村
（2019年1月21日公布）

根据《住房城乡建设部、国家文物局关于组织申报第七批中国历史文化名镇名村的通知》（建规函〔2016〕177号）和《中国历史文化名镇（村）评选办法》等规定，住房和城乡建设部、国家文物局决定公布山西省长治市上党区荫城镇等60个镇为中国历史文化名镇、河北省井陉县南障城镇吕家村等211个村为中国历史文化名村。

第七批中国历史文化名镇名单

1. 山西省长治市上党区荫城镇
2. 山西省阳城县横河镇
3. 山西省泽州县高都镇
4. 山西省寿阳县宗艾镇
5. 山西省曲沃县曲村镇
6. 山西省翼城县西阎镇
7. 山西省汾阳市杏花村镇
8. 内蒙古自治区牙克石市博克图镇
9. 上海市宝山区罗店镇
10. 江苏省苏州市吴中区光福镇
11. 江苏省昆山市巴城镇
12. 江苏省高邮市界首镇
13. 江苏省高邮市临泽镇
14. 浙江省慈溪市观海卫镇（鸣鹤）
15. 浙江省平阳县顺溪镇
16. 浙江省湖州市南浔区双林镇
17. 浙江省湖州市南浔区菱湖镇
18. 浙江省诸暨市枫桥镇
19. 浙江省临海市桃渚镇

20. 浙江省龙泉市住龙镇
21. 安徽省六安市裕安区苏埠镇
22. 安徽省东至县东流镇
23. 安徽省青阳县陵阳镇
24. 福建省永安市贡川镇
25. 福建省晋江市安海镇
26. 福建省永春县岵山镇
27. 福建省南靖县梅林镇
28. 福建省宁德市蕉城区洋中镇
29. 福建省宁德市蕉城区三都镇
30. 江西省修水县山口镇
31. 江西省贵溪市塘湾镇
32. 江西省樟树市临江镇
33. 山东省淄博市周村区王村镇
34. 山东省泰安市岱岳区大汶口镇
35. 湖北省当阳市淯溪镇
36. 湖南省浏阳市文家市镇
37. 湖南省临湘市聂市镇
38. 湖南省东安县芦洪市镇
39. 广西壮族自治区阳朔县福利镇
40. 广西壮族自治区防城港市防城区那良镇
41. 重庆市万州区罗田镇
42. 重庆市涪陵区青羊镇
43. 重庆市江津区吴滩镇
44. 重庆市江津区石蟆镇
45. 重庆市酉阳土家族苗族自治县龚滩镇
46. 四川省崇州市元通镇
47. 四川省自贡市大安区三多寨镇
48. 四川省三台县郪江镇
49. 四川省洪雅县柳江镇
50. 四川省达州市达川区石桥镇
51. 四川省雅安市雨城区上里镇
52. 四川省通江县毛浴镇
53. 云南省通海县河西镇
54. 云南省凤庆县鲁史镇
55. 云南省姚安县光禄镇

56. 云南省文山市平坝镇
57. 西藏自治区定结县陈塘镇
58. 西藏自治区贡嘎县杰德秀镇
59. 西藏自治区札达县托林镇
60. 甘肃省永登县红城镇

第七批中国历史文化名村名单

1. 河北省井陉县南障城镇吕家村
2. 河北省蔚县南留庄镇南留庄村
3. 河北省蔚县南留庄镇水西堡村
4. 河北省蔚县宋家庄镇宋家庄村
5. 河北省蔚县宋家庄镇大固城村
6. 河北省蔚县涌泉庄乡任家涧村
7. 河北省蔚县涌泉庄乡卜北堡村
8. 河北省怀来县瑞云观乡镇边城村
9. 河北省沙河市册井乡北盆水村
10. 河北省沙河市柴关乡西沟村
11. 河北省沙河市柴关乡绿水池村
12. 河北省邢台县南石门镇崔路村
13. 河北省邢台县路罗镇鱼林沟村
14. 河北省邢台县将军墓镇内阳村
15. 河北省邢台县太子井乡龙化村
16. 河北省武安市午汲镇大贺庄村
17. 河北省武安市石洞乡什里店村
18. 河北省涉县固新镇原曲村
19. 河北省磁县陶泉乡南王庄村
20. 河北省磁县陶泉乡北岔口村
21. 山西省大同市新荣区堡子湾乡得胜堡村
22. 山西省天镇县马家皂乡安家皂村
23. 山西省阳泉市郊区荫营镇辛庄村
24. 山西省平定县冠山镇宋家庄村
25. 山西省平定县张庄镇桃叶坡村
26. 山西省平定县东回镇瓦岭村
27. 山西省平定县娘子关镇上董寨村
28. 山西省平定县娘子关镇下董寨村

29. 山西省平定县巨城镇南庄村
30. 山西省平定县巨城镇上盘石村
31. 山西省平定县石门口乡乱流村
32. 山西省盂县孙家庄镇乌玉村
33. 山西省盂县梁家寨乡大宋村
34. 山西省长治市上党区荫城镇琚寨村
35. 山西省平顺县石城镇东庄村
36. 山西省平顺县石城镇岳家寨村
37. 山西省平顺县虹梯关乡虹霓村
38. 山西省黎城县停河铺乡霞庄村
39. 山西省沁源县王和镇古寨村
40. 山西省高平市河西镇牛村
41. 山西省阳城县凤城镇南安阳村
42. 山西省阳城县北留镇尧沟村
43. 山西省阳城县润城镇上伏村
44. 山西省阳城县固隆乡府底村
45. 山西省阳城县固隆乡泽城村
46. 山西省阳城县固隆乡固隆村
47. 山西省泽州县大东沟镇东沟村
48. 山西省泽州县大东沟镇贾泉村
49. 山西省泽州县周村镇石淙头村
50. 山西省泽州县晋庙铺镇天井关村
51. 山西省泽州县巴公镇渠头村
52. 山西省泽州县山河镇洞八岭村
53. 山西省泽州县李寨乡陟椒村
54. 山西省泽州县南岭乡段河村
55. 山西省陵川县西河底镇积善村
56. 山西省沁水县中村镇上阁村
57. 山西省沁水县嘉峰镇尉迟村
58. 山西省沁水县嘉峰镇武安村
59. 山西省沁水县嘉峰镇嘉峰村
60. 山西省山阴县张家庄乡旧广武村
61. 山西省晋中市榆次区东赵乡后沟村
62. 山西省太谷县范村镇上安村
63. 山西省平遥县段村镇段村
64. 山西省介休市洪山镇洪山村

65. 山西省介休市龙凤镇南庄村
66. 山西省介休市绵山镇大靳村
67. 山西省灵石县南关镇董家岭村
68. 山西省寿阳县宗艾镇下洲村
69. 山西省寿阳县西洛镇南东村
70. 山西省寿阳县西洛镇南河村
71. 山西省寿阳县平舒乡龙门河村
72. 山西省稷山县西社镇马跑泉村
73. 山西省翼城县隆化镇史伯村
74. 山西省翼城县西阎镇曹公村
75. 山西省翼城县西阎镇古桃园村
76. 山西省霍州市退沙街道许村
77. 山西省吕梁市离石区枣林乡彩家庄村
78. 山西省交口县双池镇西庄村
79. 山西省临县三交镇孙家沟村
80. 山西省临县安业乡前青塘村
81. 山西省柳林县三交镇三交村
82. 山西省柳林县陈家湾乡高家垣村
83. 山西省柳林县王家沟乡南洼村
84. 山西省交城县夏家营镇段村
85. 辽宁省沈阳市沈北新区石佛寺街道石佛一村
86. 江苏省常州市武进区前黄镇杨桥村
87. 江苏省溧阳市昆仑街道沙涨村
88. 浙江省建德市大慈岩镇上吴方村
89. 浙江省建德市大慈岩镇李村村
90. 浙江省桐庐县富春江镇茆坪村
91. 浙江省宁波市海曙区章水镇李家坑村
92. 浙江省宁波市鄞州区姜山镇走马塘村
93. 浙江省慈溪市龙山镇方家河头村
94. 浙江省余姚市大岚镇柿林村
95. 浙江省义乌市佛堂镇倍磊村
96. 浙江省磐安县尖山镇管头村
97. 浙江省磐安县双溪乡梓誉村
98. 浙江省江山市凤林镇南坞村
99. 浙江省江山市石门镇清漾村
100. 浙江省龙游县溪口镇灵山村

101. 浙江省龙游县塔石镇泽随村
102. 浙江省临海市东塍镇岭根村
103. 浙江省天台县平桥镇张思村
104. 安徽省歙县北岸镇瞻淇村
105. 安徽省歙县昌溪乡昌溪村
106. 安徽省池州市贵池区棠溪镇石门高村
107. 安徽省绩溪县上庄镇石家村
108. 安徽省绩溪县家朋乡磡头村
109. 福建省福州市仓山区城门镇林浦村
110. 福建省永泰县洑口乡紫山村
111. 福建省永泰县洑口乡山寨村
112. 福建省大田县桃源镇东坂村
113. 福建省宁化县曹坊镇下曹村
114. 福建省泉州市泉港区涂岭镇樟脚村
115. 福建省永春县五里街镇西安村
116. 福建省晋江市龙湖镇福林村
117. 福建省南靖县书洋镇石桥村
118. 福建省南靖县书洋镇塔下村
119. 福建省南靖县书洋镇河坑村
120. 福建省邵武市金坑乡金坑村
121. 福建省政和县岭腰乡锦屏村
122. 福建省龙岩市永定区下洋镇初溪村
123. 福建省长汀县古城镇丁黄村
124. 福建省长汀县濯田镇水头村
125. 福建省长汀县四都镇汤屋村
126. 福建省龙岩市永定区抚市镇社前村
127. 福建省龙岩市永定区洪山乡上山村
128. 福建省连城县莒溪镇壁洲村
129. 福建省福安市社口镇坦洋村
130. 福建省福安市晓阳镇晓阳村
131. 福建省福安市溪柄镇楼下村
132. 福建省福鼎市管阳镇西昆村
133. 福建省古田县城东街道桃溪村
134. 福建省古田县吉巷乡长洋村
135. 福建省古田县卓洋乡前洋村
136. 福建省寿宁县下党乡下党村

137. 江西省浮梁县蛟潭镇礼芳村
138. 江西省浮梁县峙滩镇英溪村
139. 江西省贵溪市耳口乡曾家村
140. 江西省龙南县里仁镇新园村
141. 江西省寻乌县澄江镇周田村
142. 江西省安福县金田乡柘溪村
143. 江西省泰和县螺溪镇爵誉村
144. 江西省金溪县合市镇游垫村
145. 江西省金溪县合市镇全坊村
146. 江西省金溪县琅琚镇疏口村
147. 江西省金溪县陈坊积乡岐山村
148. 江西省乐安县湖坪乡湖坪村
149. 江西省婺源县江湾镇篁岭村
150. 江西省婺源县思口镇西冲村
151. 山东省济南市章丘区相公庄街道梭庄村
152. 山东省淄博市淄川区洪山镇蒲家庄村
153. 山东省招远市张星镇徐家村
154. 山东省昌邑市龙池镇齐西村
155. 山东省邹城市石墙镇上九山村
156. 山东省巨野县核桃园镇前王庄村
157. 河南省宝丰县李庄乡翟集村
158. 河南省郏县薛店镇冢王村
159. 河南省郏县薛店镇下宫村
160. 河南省郏县茨芭镇山头赵村
161. 河南省修武县云台山镇一斗水村
162. 河南省修武县西村乡双庙村
163. 河南省三门峡市陕州区西张村镇庙上村
164. 湖北省大冶市金湖街道上冯村
165. 湖北省阳新县排市镇下容村
166. 湖北省大冶市大箕铺镇柯大兴村
167. 湖北省阳新县大王镇金寨村
168. 湖北省枣阳市新市镇前湾村
169. 湖北省南漳县巡检镇漫云村
170. 湖北省红安县华家河镇祝家楼村
171. 湖北省通山县闯王镇宝石村
172. 湖南省醴陵市沩山镇沩山村

173. 湖南省汝城县文明瑶族乡沙洲瑶族村
174. 湖南省汝城县土桥镇永丰村
175. 湖南省汝城县马桥镇石泉村
176. 湖南省新田县枧头镇龙家大院村
177. 湖南省道县清塘镇楼田村
178. 湖南省蓝山县祠堂圩镇虎溪村
179. 湖南省沅陵县荔溪乡明中村
180. 湖南省中方县中方镇荆坪村
181. 湖南省永顺县灵溪镇双凤村
182. 广东省汕头市澄海区莲下镇程洋冈村
183. 广东省云浮市云城区腰古镇水东村
184. 广东省郁南县大湾镇五星村
185. 广西壮族自治区南宁市江南区江西镇同江村三江坡
186. 广西壮族自治区宾阳县古辣镇蔡村
187. 广西壮族自治区阳朔县高田镇朗梓村
188. 广西壮族自治区岑溪市筋竹镇云龙村
189. 广西壮族自治区灵山县新圩镇萍塘村
190. 广西壮族自治区玉林市福绵区新桥镇大楼村
191. 广西壮族自治区玉林市玉州区南江街道岭塘村（硃砂垌）
192. 广西壮族自治区陆川县平乐镇长旺村
193. 广西壮族自治区兴业县石南镇庞村
194. 广西壮族自治区兴业县石南镇谭良村
195. 广西壮族自治区兴业县葵阳镇榜山村
196. 广西壮族自治区兴业县龙安镇龙安村
197. 广西壮族自治区贺州市平桂区沙田镇龙井村
198. 广西壮族自治区富川瑶族自治县古城镇秀山村
199. 广西壮族自治区钟山县回龙镇龙道村
200. 广西壮族自治区钟山县公安镇荷塘村
201. 广西壮族自治区钟山县公安镇大田村
202. 广西壮族自治区钟山县清塘镇英家村
203. 广西壮族自治区钟山县燕塘镇玉坡村
204. 广西壮族自治区天峨县三堡乡三堡村
205. 贵州省贵阳市花溪区石板镇镇山村
206. 云南省沧源县勐角乡翁丁村
207. 云南省泸西县永宁乡城子村
208. 西藏自治区普兰县普兰镇科迦村

209. 甘肃省兰州市西固区河口镇河口村

210. 甘肃省静宁县界石铺镇继红村

211. 甘肃省正宁县永和镇罗川村

（资料整理：廖远涛，广州市城市规划勘测设计院政府规划编制部副主任，高级工程师）

附录4

中国人口方面的基本数据（2017年及历年）

一、本篇资料的主要内容

本篇资料反映我国2017年及历年人口方面的基本情况，包括全国及31个省、自治区、直辖市的主要人口统计数据，如：全国历年人口数、城镇人口、乡村人口；2017年各地区人口数、出生率、死亡率、自然增长率、人口负担系数、家庭户规模、人口受教育程度等。

二、本篇的资料来源

本篇资料由国家统计局人口和就业统计司整理。其中表1～表7中，1981年及以前数据为户籍统计数；1982年、1990年、2000年、2010年数据为当年普查数据推算数；其余年份数据为年度人口抽样调查推算数据，部分年份数据根据人口普查数据进行了修订。表8为2017年全国人口变动情况抽样调查推算数据，表9～16为2017年全国人口变动情况抽样调查样本数据。

本篇各表如不做特殊说明，均未包括香港特别行政区、澳门特别行政区和台湾地区的人口数据。

三、本篇的统计调查方法

目前由国家统计局人口和就业统计司实施的人口统计调查有：

在逢“0”的年份进行全国人口普查；在逢“5”的年份进行全国1%人口抽样调查；其余年份进行全国人口变动情况抽样调查，其样本量约占全国总人口的1‰。人口抽样调查是以全国为总体，省级单位为次总体，采用分层、多阶段、整群概率比例抽样方法抽取样本。

表1　人口数及构成

单位:万人

年份	总人口(年末)	按性别分				按城乡分			
		男		女		城镇		乡村	
		人口数	比重(%)	人口数	比重(%)	人口数	比重(%)	人口数	比重(%)
1949	54 167	28 145	51. 96	26 022	48. 04	5 765	10. 64	48 402	89. 36
1950	55 196	28 669	51. 94	26 527	48. 06	6 169	11. 18	49 027	88. 82
1951	56 300	29 231	51. 92	27 069	48. 08	6 632	11. 78	49 668	88. 22
1955	61 465	31 809	51. 75	29 656	48. 25	8 285	13. 48	53 180	86. 52
1960	66 207	34 283	51. 78	31 924	48. 22	13 073	19. 75	53 134	80. 25
1965	72 538	37 128	51. 18	35 410	48. 82	13 045	17. 98	59 493	82. 02
1970	82 992	42 686	51. 43	40 306	48. 57	14 424	17. 38	68 568	82. 62
1971	85 229	43 819	51. 41	41 410	48. 59	14 711	17. 26	70 518	82. 74
1972	87 177	44 813	51. 40	42 364	48. 60	14 935	17. 13	72 242	82. 87
1973	89 211	45 876	51. 42	43 335	48. 58	15 345	17. 20	73 866	82. 80
1974	90 859	46 727	51. 43	44 132	48. 57	15 595	17. 16	75 264	82. 84
1975	92 420	47 564	51. 47	44 856	48. 53	16 030	17. 34	76 390	82. 66
1976	93 717	48 257	51. 49	45 460	48. 51	16 341	17. 44	77 376	82. 56
1977	94 974	48 908	51. 50	46 066	48. 50	16 669	17. 55	78 305	82. 45
1978	96 259	49 567	51. 49	46 692	48. 51	17 245	17. 92	79 014	82. 08
1979	97 542	50 192	51. 46	47 350	48. 54	18 495	18. 96	79 047	81. 04
1980	98 705	50 785	51. 45	47 920	48. 55	19 140	19. 39	79 565	80. 61
1981	100 072	51 519	51. 48	48 553	48. 52	20 171	20. 16	79 901	79. 84
1982	101 654	52 352	51. 50	49 302	48. 50	21 480	21. 13	80 174	78. 87
1983	103 008	53 152	51. 60	49 856	48. 40	22 274	21. 62	80 734	78. 38
1984	104 357	53 848	51. 60	50 509	48. 40	24 017	23. 01	80 340	76. 99
1985	105 851	54 725	51. 70	51 126	48. 30	25 094	23. 71	80 757	76. 29
1986	107 507	55 581	51. 70	51 926	48. 30	26 366	24. 52	81 141	75. 48
1987	109 300	56 290	51. 50	53 010	48. 50	27 674	25. 32	81 626	74. 68
1988	111 026	57 201	51. 52	53 825	48. 48	28 661	25. 81	82 365	74. 19
1989	112 704	58 099	51. 55	54 605	48. 45	29 540	26. 21	83 164	73. 79
1990	114 333	58 904	51. 52	55 429	48. 48	30 195	26. 41	84 138	73. 59
1991	115 823	59 466	51. 34	56 357	48. 66	31 203	26. 94	84 620	73. 06
1992	117 171	59 811	51. 05	57 360	48. 95	32 175	27. 46	84 996	72. 54
1993	118 517	60 472	51. 02	58 045	48. 98	33 173	27. 99	85 344	72. 01
1994	119 850	61 246	51. 10	58 604	48. 90	34 169	28. 51	85 681	71. 49
1995	121 121	61 808	51. 03	59 313	48. 97	35 174	29. 04	85 947	70. 96
1996	122 389	62 200	50. 82	60 189	49. 18	37 304	30. 48	85 085	69. 52

续表

年份	总人口（年末）	按性别分				按城乡分			
		男		女		城镇		乡村	
		人口数	比重(%)	人口数	比重(%)	人口数	比重(%)	人口数	比重(%)
1997	123 626	63 131	51.07	60 495	48.93	39 449	31.91	84 177	68.09
1998	124 761	63 940	51.25	60 821	48.75	41 608	33.35	83 153	66.65
1999	125 786	64 692	51.43	61 094	48.57	43 748	34.78	82 038	65.22
2000	126 743	65 437	51.63	61 306	48.37	45 906	36.22	80 837	63.78
2001	127 627	65 672	51.46	61 955	48.54	48 064	37.66	79 563	62.34
2002	128 453	66 115	51.47	62 338	48.53	50 212	39.09	78 241	60.91
2003	129 227	66 556	51.50	62 671	48.50	52 376	40.53	76 851	59.47
2004	129 988	66 976	51.52	63 012	48.48	54 283	41.76	75 705	58.24
2005	130 756	67 375	51.53	63 381	48.47	56 212	42.99	74 544	57.01
2006	131 448	67 728	51.52	63 720	48.48	58 288	44.34	73 160	55.66
2007	132 129	68 048	51.50	64 081	48.50	60 633	45.89	71 496	54.11
2008	132 802	68 357	51.47	64 445	48.53	62 403	46.99	70 399	53.01
2009	133 450	68 647	51.44	64 803	48.56	64 512	48.34	68 938	51.66
2010	134 091	68 748	51.27	65 343	48.73	66 978	49.95	67 113	50.05
2011	134 735	69 068	51.26	65 667	48.74	69 079	51.27	65 656	48.73
2012	135 404	69 395	51.25	66 009	48.75	71 182	52.57	64 222	47.43
2013	136 072	69 728	51.24	66 344	48.76	73 111	53.73	62 961	46.27
2014	136 782	70 079	51.23	66 703	48.77	74 916	54.77	61 866	45.23
2015	137 462	70 414	51.22	67 048	48.78	77 116	56.10	60 346	43.90
2016	138 271	70 815	51.21	67 456	48.79	79 298	57.35	58 973	42.65
2017	139 008	71 137	51.17	67 871	48.83	81 347	58.52	57 661	41.48

注：1. 1981年及以前数据为户籍统计数；1982年、1990年、2000年、2010年数据为当年人口普查数据推算数；其余年份数据为年度人口抽样调查推算数据（下相关表同）。

2. 总人口和按性别分人口中包括现役军人，按城乡分人口中现役军人计入城镇人口。

表2　人口出生率、死亡率和自然增长率

单位：‰

年份	出生率	死亡率	自然增长率
1978	18.25	6.25	12.00
1980	18.21	6.34	11.87
1981	20.91	6.36	14.55
1982	22.28	6.60	15.68
1983	20.19	6.90	13.29

续表

年份	出生率	死亡率	自然增长率
1984	19. 90	6. 82	13. 08
1985	21. 04	6. 78	14. 26
1986	22. 43	6. 86	15. 57
1987	23. 33	6. 72	16. 61
1988	22. 37	6. 64	15. 73
1989	21. 58	6. 54	15. 04
1990	21. 06	6. 67	14. 39
1991	19. 68	6. 70	12. 98
1992	18. 24	6. 64	11. 60
1993	18. 09	6. 64	11. 45
1994	17. 70	6. 49	11. 21
1995	17. 12	6. 57	10. 55
1996	16. 98	6. 56	10. 42
1997	16. 57	6. 51	10. 06
1998	15. 64	6. 50	9. 14
1999	14. 64	6. 46	8. 18
2000	14. 03	6. 45	7. 58
2001	13. 38	6. 43	6. 95
2002	12. 86	6. 41	6. 45
2003	12. 41	6. 40	6. 01
2004	12. 29	6. 42	5. 87
2005	12. 40	6. 51	5. 89
2006	12. 09	6. 81	5. 28
2007	12. 10	6. 93	5. 17
2008	12. 14	7. 06	5. 08
2009	11. 95	7. 08	4. 87
2010	11. 90	7. 11	4. 79
2011	11. 93	7. 14	4. 79
2012	12. 10	7. 15	4. 95
2013	12. 08	7. 16	4. 92
2014	12. 37	7. 16	5. 21
2015	12. 07	7. 11	4. 96
2016	12. 95	7. 09	5. 86
2017	12. 43	7. 11	5. 32

表 3　流动人口数

单位：亿人

年份	人户分离人口	流动人口
2000	1.44	1.21
2005		1.47
2010	2.61	2.21
2011	2.71	2.30
2012	2.79	2.36
2013	2.89	2.45
2014	2.98	2.53
2015	2.94	2.47
2016	2.92	2.45
2017	2.91	2.44

注：2000 年、2010 年分别为当年人口普查时点数据，其余年份数据根据年度人口抽样调查推算。

表 4　平均预期寿命

单位：岁

年份	合计	男	女
1981	67.77	66.28	69.27
1990	68.55	66.84	70.47
1996	70.80		
2000	71.40	69.63	73.33
2005	72.95	70.83	75.25
2010	74.83	72.38	77.37
2015	76.34	73.64	79.43

表 5　人口年龄结构和抚养比

单位：万人

年份	总人口（年末）	按年龄组分						总抚养比（%）	少儿抚养比（%）	老年抚养比（%）
		0～14 岁		15～64 岁		65 岁及以上				
		人口数	比重（%）	人口数	比重（%）	人口数	比重（%）			
1982	101 654	34 146	33.6	62 517	61.5	4 991	4.9	62.6	54.6	8.0
1987	109 300	31 347	28.7	71 985	65.9	5 968	5.4	51.8	43.5	8.3
1990	114 333	31 659	27.7	76 306	66.7	6 368	5.6	49.8	41.5	8.3
1991	115 823	32 095	27.7	76 791	66.3	6 938	6.0	50.8	41.8	9.0
1992	117 171	32 339	27.6	77 614	66.2	7 218	6.2	51.0	41.7	9.3

续表

年份	总人口(年末)	按年龄组分						总抚养比(%)	少儿抚养比(%)	老年抚养比(%)
		0~14岁		15~64岁		65岁及以上				
		人口数	比重(%)	人口数	比重(%)	人口数	比重(%)			
1993	118 517	32 177	27.2	79 051	66.7	7 289	6.2	49.9	40.7	9.2
1994	119 850	32 360	27.0	79 868	66.6	7 622	6.4	50.1	40.5	9.5
1995	121 121	32 218	26.6	81 393	67.2	7 510	6.2	48.8	39.6	9.2
1996	122 389	32 311	26.4	82 245	67.2	7 833	6.4	48.8	39.3	9.5
1997	123 626	32 093	26.0	83 448	67.5	8 085	6.5	48.1	38.5	9.7
1998	124 761	32 064	25.7	84 338	67.6	8 359	6.7	47.9	38.0	9.9
1999	125 786	31 950	25.4	85 157	67.7	8 679	6.9	47.7	37.5	10.2
2000	126 743	29 012	22.9	88 910	70.1	8 821	7.0	42.6	32.6	9.9
2001	127 627	28 716	22.5	89 849	70.4	9 062	7.1	42.0	32.0	10.1
2002	128 453	28 774	22.4	90 302	70.3	9 377	7.3	42.2	31.9	10.4
2003	129 227	28 559	22.1	90 976	70.4	9 692	7.5	42.0	31.4	10.7
2004	129 988	27 947	21.5	92 184	70.9	9 857	7.6	41.0	30.3	10.7
2005	130 756	26 504	20.3	94 197	72.0	10 055	7.7	38.8	28.1	10.7
2006	131 448	25 961	19.8	95 068	72.3	10 419	7.9	38.3	27.3	11.0
2007	132 129	25 660	19.4	95 833	72.5	10 636	8.1	37.9	26.8	11.1
2008	132 802	25 166	19.0	96 680	72.7	10 956	8.3	37.4	26.0	11.3
2009	133 450	24 659	18.5	97 484	73.0	11 307	8.5	36.9	25.3	11.6
2010	134 091	22 259	16.6	99 938	74.5	11 894	8.9	34.2	22.3	11.9
2011	134 735	22 164	16.5	100 283	74.4	12 288	9.1	34.4	22.1	12.3
2012	135 404	22 287	16.5	100 403	74.1	12 714	9.4	34.9	22.2	12.7
2013	136 072	22 329	16.4	100 582	73.9	13 161	9.7	35.3	22.2	13.1
2014	136 782	22 558	16.5	100 469	73.4	13 755	10.1	36.2	22.5	13.7
2015	137 462	22 715	16.5	100 361	73.0	14 386	10.5	37.0	22.6	14.3
2016	138 271	23 008	16.7	100 260	72.5	15 003	10.8	37.9	22.9	15.0
2017	139 008	23 348	16.8	99 829	71.8	15 831	11.4	39.2	23.4	15.9

表6 分地区年末人口数

单位：万人

地区	2006	2007	2008	2009	2010	2011	2012	2013	2014	2015	2016	2017
全国	131 448	132 129	132 802	133 450	134 091	134 735	135 404	136 072	136 782	137 462	138 271	139 008
北京	1 601	1 676	1 771	1 860	1 962	2 019	2 069	2 115	2 152	2 171	2 173	2 171
天津	1 075	1 115	1 176	1 228	1 299	1 355	1 413	1 472	1 517	1 547	1 562	1 557
河北	6 898	6 943	6 989	7 034	7 194	7 241	7 288	7 333	7 384	7 425	7 470	7 520

续表

地区	2006	2007	2008	2009	2010	2011	2012	2013	2014	2015	2016	2017
山西	3 375	3 393	3 411	3 427	3 574	3 593	3 611	3 630	3 648	3 664	3 682	3 702
内蒙古	2 415	2 429	2 444	2 458	2 472	2 482	2 490	2 498	2 505	2 511	2 520	2 529
辽宁	4 271	4 298	4 315	4 341	4 375	4 383	4 389	4 390	4 391	4 382	4 378	4 369
吉林	2 723	2 730	2 734	2 740	2 747	2 749	2 750	2 751	2 752	2 753	2 733	2 717
黑龙江	3 823	3 824	3 825	3 826	3 833	3 834	3 834	3 835	3 833	3 812	3 799	3 789
上海	1 964	2 064	2 141	2 210	2 303	2 347	2 380	2 415	2 426	2 415	2 420	2 418
江苏	7 656	7 723	7 762	7 810	7 869	7 899	7 920	7 939	7 960	7 976	7 999	8 029
浙江	5 072	5 155	5 212	5 276	5 447	5 463	5 477	5 498	5 508	5 539	5 590	5 657
安徽	6 110	6 118	6 135	6 131	5 957	5 968	5 988	6 030	6 083	6 144	6 196	6 255
福建	3 585	3 612	3 639	3 666	3 693	3 720	3 748	3 774	3 806	3 839	3 874	3 911
江西	4 339	4 368	4 400	4 432	4 462	4 488	4 504	4 522	4 542	4 566	4 592	4 622
山东	9 309	9 367	9 417	9 470	9 588	9 637	9 685	9 733	9 789	9 847	9 947	10 006
河南	9 392	9 360	9 429	9 487	9 405	9 388	9 406	9 413	9 436	9 480	9 532	9 559
湖北	5 693	5 699	5 711	5 720	5 728	5 758	5 779	5 799	5 816	5 852	5 885	5 902
湖南	6 342	6 355	6 380	6 406	6 570	6 596	6 639	6 691	6 737	6 783	6 822	6 860
广东	9 442	9 660	9 893	10 130	10 441	10 505	10 594	10 644	10 724	10 849	10 999	11 169
广西	4 719	4 768	4 816	4 856	4 610	4 645	4 682	4 719	4 754	4 796	4 838	4 885
海南	836	845	854	864	869	877	887	895	903	911	917	926
重庆	2 808	2 816	2 839	2 859	2 885	2 919	2 945	2 970	2 991	3 017	3 048	3 075
四川	8 169	8 127	8 138	8 185	8 045	8 050	8 076	8 107	8 140	8 204	8 262	8 302
贵州	3 690	3 632	3 596	3 537	3 479	3 469	3 484	3 502	3 508	3 530	3 555	3 580
云南	4 483	4 514	4 543	4 571	4 602	4 631	4 659	4 687	4 714	4 742	4 771	4 801
西藏	285	289	292	296	300	303	308	312	318	324	331	337
陕西	3 699	3 708	3 718	3 727	3 735	3 743	3 753	3 764	3 775	3 793	3 813	3 835
甘肃	2 547	2 548	2 551	2 555	2 560	2 564	2 578	2 582	2 591	2 600	2 610	2 626
青海	548	552	554	557	563	568	573	578	583	588	593	598
宁夏	604	610	618	625	633	639	647	654	662	668	675	682
新疆	2 050	2 095	2 131	2 159	2 185	2 209	2 233	2 264	2 298	2 360	2 398	2 445

注：2010年数据为当年人口普查数据推算数；其余年份数据为年度人口抽样调查推算数据。各地区数据为常住人口口径。

表7　分地区年末城镇人口比重

单位:%

地区	2009	2010	2011	2012	2013	2014	2015	2016	2017
全国	48.34	49.95	51.27	52.57	53.73	54.77	56.10	57.35	58.52
北京	85.00	85.96	86.20	86.20	86.30	86.35	86.50	86.50	86.50
天津	78.01	79.55	80.50	81.55	82.01	82.27	82.64	82.93	82.93
河北	43.74	44.50	45.60	46.80	48.12	49.33	51.33	53.32	55.01
山西	45.99	48.05	49.68	51.26	52.56	53.79	55.03	56.21	57.34
内蒙古	53.40	55.50	56.62	57.74	58.71	59.51	60.30	61.19	62.02
辽宁	60.35	62.10	64.05	65.65	66.45	67.05	67.35	67.37	67.49
吉林	53.32	53.35	53.40	53.70	54.20	54.81	55.31	55.97	56.65
黑龙江	55.50	55.66	56.50	56.90	57.40	58.01	58.80	59.20	59.40
上海	88.60	89.30	89.30	89.30	89.60	89.60	87.60	87.90	87.70
江苏	55.60	60.58	61.90	63.00	64.11	65.21	66.52	67.72	68.76
浙江	57.90	61.62	62.30	63.20	64.00	64.87	65.80	67.00	68.00
安徽	42.10	43.01	44.80	46.50	47.86	49.15	50.50	51.99	53.49
福建	55.10	57.10	58.10	59.60	60.77	61.80	62.60	63.60	64.80
江西	43.18	44.06	45.70	47.51	48.87	50.22	51.62	53.10	54.60
山东	48.32	49.70	50.95	52.43	53.75	55.01	57.01	59.02	60.58
河南	37.70	38.50	40.57	42.43	43.80	45.20	46.85	48.50	50.16
湖北	46.00	49.70	51.83	53.50	54.51	55.67	56.85	58.10	59.30
湖南	43.20	43.30	45.10	46.65	47.96	49.28	50.89	52.75	54.62
广东	63.40	66.18	66.50	67.40	67.76	68.00	68.71	69.20	69.85
广西	39.20	40.00	41.80	43.53	44.81	46.01	47.06	48.08	49.21
海南	49.13	49.80	50.50	51.60	52.74	53.76	55.12	56.78	58.04
重庆	51.59	53.02	55.02	56.98	58.34	59.60	60.94	62.60	64.08
四川	38.70	40.18	41.83	43.53	44.90	46.30	47.69	49.21	50.79
贵州	29.89	33.81	34.96	36.41	37.83	40.01	42.01	44.15	46.02
云南	34.00	34.70	36.80	39.31	40.48	41.73	43.33	45.03	46.69
西藏	22.30	22.67	22.71	22.75	23.71	25.75	27.74	29.56	30.89
陕西	43.50	45.76	47.30	50.02	51.31	52.57	53.92	55.34	56.79
甘肃	34.89	36.12	37.15	38.75	40.13	41.68	43.19	44.69	46.39
青海	41.90	44.72	46.22	47.44	48.51	49.78	50.30	51.63	53.07
宁夏	46.10	47.90	49.82	50.67	52.01	53.61	55.23	56.29	57.98
新疆	39.85	43.01	43.54	43.98	44.47	46.07	47.23	48.35	49.38

注：2010年数据为当年人口普查数据推算数；其余年份数据为年度人口抽样调查推算数据，部分省份2008－2009年数据根据2010年普查数据进行了修订。

表8 分地区人口的城乡构成和出生率、死亡率、自然增长率（2017）

地区	总人口(年末)(万人)	城镇人口		乡村人口		出生率(‰)	死亡率(‰)	自然增长率(‰)
		人口数	比重(%)	人口数	比重(%)			
全国	139 008	81 347	58.52	57 661	41.48	12.43	7.11	5.32
北京	2 171	1 878	86.50	293	13.50	9.06	5.30	3.76
天津	1 557	1 291	82.93	266	17.07	7.65	5.05	2.60
河北	7 520	4 136	55.01	3 383	44.99	13.20	6.60	6.60
山西	3 702	2 123	57.34	1 579	42.66	11.06	5.45	5.61
内蒙古	2 529	1 568	62.02	961	37.98	9.47	5.74	3.73
辽宁	4 369	2 949	67.49	1 420	32.51	6.49	6.93	-0.44
吉林	2 717	1 539	56.65	1 178	43.35	6.76	6.50	0.26
黑龙江	3 789	2 250	59.40	1 538	40.60	6.22	6.63	-0.41
上海	2 418	2 121	87.70	297	12.30	8.10	5.30	2.80
江苏	8 029	5 521	68.76	2 508	31.24	9.71	7.03	2.68
浙江	5 657	3 847	68.00	1 810	32.00	11.92	5.56	6.36
安徽	6 255	3 346	53.49	2 909	46.51	14.07	5.90	8.17
福建	3 911	2 534	64.80	1 377	35.20	15.00	6.20	8.80
江西	4 622	2 524	54.60	2 098	45.40	13.79	6.08	7.71
山东	10 006	6 062	60.58	3 944	39.42	17.54	7.40	10.14
河南	9 559	4 795	50.16	4 764	49.84	12.95	6.97	5.98
湖北	5 902	3 500	59.30	2 402	40.70	12.60	7.01	5.59
湖南	6 860	3 747	54.62	3 113	45.38	13.27	7.08	6.19
广东	11 169	7 802	69.85	3 367	30.15	13.68	4.52	9.16
广西	4 885	2 404	49.21	2 481	50.79	15.14	6.22	8.92
海南	926	537	58.04	389	41.96	14.73	6.01	8.72
重庆	3 075	1 971	64.08	1 105	35.92	11.18	7.27	3.91
四川	8 302	4 217	50.79	4 085	49.21	11.26	7.03	4.23
贵州	3 580	1 648	46.02	1 932	53.98	13.98	6.88	7.10
云南	4 801	2241	46.69	2 559	53.31	13.53	6.68	6.85
西藏	337	104	30.89	233	69.11	16.00	4.95	11.05
陕西	3 835	2 178	56.79	1 657	43.21	11.11	6.24	4.87
甘肃	2 626	1 218	46.39	1 408	53.61	12.54	6.52	6.02
青海	598	317	53.07	281	46.93	14.42	6.17	8.25
宁夏	682	395	57.98	287	42.02	13.44	4.75	8.69
新疆	2 445	1 207	49.38	1 238	50.62	15.88	4.48	11.40

注：1. 本表数据根据2017年全国人口变动情况抽样调查数据推算。全国总人口根据抽样误差和调查误差进行了修正，分地区人口未作修正。
2. 全国总人口包括现役军人数，分地区数字中未包括。

表 9 按年龄和性别分人口数（2017）

本表是 2017 年全国人口变动情况抽样调查样本数据，抽样比为 0.824‰。

年龄	人口数（人）			占总人口比重(%)			性别比（女=100）
		男	女		男	女	
总计	1 145 246	586 072	559 174	100.00	51.17	48.83	104.81
0～4	68 313	36 468	31 845	5.96	3.18	2.78	114.52
5～9	63 314	34 344	28 969	5.53	3.00	2.53	118.55
10～14	60 727	32 929	27 798	5.30	2.88	2.43	118.46
15～19	59 251	32 034	27 217	5.17	2.80	2.38	117.70
20～24	73 185	38 496	34 689	6.39	3.36	3.03	110.98
25～29	100 701	51 451	49 251	8.79	4.49	4.30	104.47
30～34	88 959	44 709	44 249	7.77	3.90	3.86	101.04
35～39	82 553	41 944	40 609	7.21	3.66	3.55	103.29
40～44	87 713	44 730	42 983	7.66	3.91	3.75	104.06
45～49	105 476	53 661	51 815	9.21	4.69	4.52	103.56
50～54	96 760	48 982	47 778	8.45	4.28	4.17	102.52
55～59	59 823	30 244	29 579	5.22	2.64	2.58	102.25
60～64	68 044	34 027	34 017	5.94	2.97	2.97	100.03
65～69	51 552	25 281	26 271	4.50	2.21	2.29	96.23
70～74	32 590	15 790	16 799	2.85	1.38	1.47	93.99
75～79	22 553	10 774	11 779	1.97	0.94	1.03	91.46
80～84	14 708	6 660	8 048	1.28	0.58	0.70	82.76
85～89	6 606	2 758	3 849	0.58	0.24	0.34	71.66
90～94	1 964	660	1 304	0.17	0.06	0.11	50.61
95+	455	131	324	0.04	0.01	0.03	40.36

注：由于各地区数据采用加权汇总的方法，全国（部分省区）人口变动情况抽样调查样本数据合计与各分项或分组相加略有误差（以下表同）。

表 10 分地区户数、人口数、性别比和户规模（2017 年）

本表是 2017 年全国人口变动情况抽样调查样本数据，抽样比为 0.824‰。

地区	户数（户）			人口数（人）			性别比（女 = 100）	家庭户人口数（人）			集体户人口数（人）			平均家庭户规模（人/户）
		家庭户	集体户		男	女			男	女		男	女	
全国	375 187	367 273	7 915	1 145 246	586 072	559 174	104. 81	1 114 610	570 037	544 573	30 636	16 035	14 600	3. 03
北京	6 631	6 151	480	17 801	9 017	8 784	102. 65	16 134	8 042	8 092	1 667	975	692	2. 62
天津	4 479	4 162	317	12 778	6 725	6 053	111. 10	11 423	5 790	5 632	1 355	934	421	2. 74
河北	19 221	19 092	129	62 086	31 523	30 563	103. 14	61 239	31 373	29 867	847	150	697	3. 21
山西	10 210	10 104	106	30 550	15 887	14 664	108. 34	29 971	15 415	14 556	579	472	108	2. 97
内蒙古	7 775	7 644	131	20 849	10 465	10 384	100. 79	20 430	10 366	10 064	419	100	319	2. 67
辽宁	13 483	13 382	101	35 969	17 996	17 973	100. 12	35 451	17 906	17 545	518	90	428	2. 65
吉林	8 444	8 426	18	22 424	11 346	11 078	102. 42	22 374	11 317	11 056	50	29	22	2. 66
黑龙江	11 924	11 872	52	31 251	15 919	15 332	103. 83	31 020	15 878	15 142	232	42	190	2. 61
上海	7 906	7 729	177	19 826	10 085	9 740	103. 54	19 269	9 718	9 551	557	367	189	2. 49
江苏	21 275	20 575	699	66 100	33 542	32 558	103. 02	63 536	32 217	31 319	2 564	1 325	1 239	3. 09
浙江	17 686	17 238	448	46 573	24 550	22 023	111. 48	45 157	23 464	21 693	1 416	1 086	330	2. 62
安徽	16 213	16 110	103	51 658	26 449	25 209	104. 92	51 204	26 087	25 118	454	363	91	3. 18
福建	10 625	10 142	482	32 221	16 435	15 786	104. 12	30 746	15 617	15 129	1 475	819	656	3. 03
江西	10 689	10 658	32	38 163	19 840	18 323	108. 28	37 992	19 740	18 252	171	100	71	3. 56
山东	29 103	28 862	241	82 502	41 595	40 907	101. 68	81 408	41 387	40 021	1 094	208	886	2. 82
河南	23 590	23 474	116	79 005	40 370	38 635	104. 49	78 444	40 210	38 234	561	160	401	3. 34
湖北	15 946	15 270	676	48 684	25 090	23 594	106. 34	46 089	23 490	22 599	2 595	1 600	994	3. 02
湖南	17 346	17 011	335	56 647	28 560	28 087	101. 68	54 555	27 678	26 878	2 092	882	1 209	3. 21
广东	30 143	28 166	1 977	91 922	48 859	43 063	113. 46	85 851	45 187	40 664	6 071	3 672	2 398	3. 05
广西	11 481	11 399	82	40 385	21 080	19 305	109. 20	39 992	20 866	19 126	393	215	178	3. 51
海南	2 138	2 065	73	7 640	4 002	3 638	110. 02	7 398	3 918	3 480	242	84	158	3. 58

续表

地区	户数(户)	家庭户	集体户	人口数(人)	男	女	性别比(女=100)	家庭户人口数(人)	男	女	集体户人口数(人)	男	女	平均家庭户规模(人/户)
重庆	9 099	9 044	55	25 337	12 641	12 696	99.57	25 142	12 553	12 589	196	89	107	2.78
四川	23 096	22 756	340	68 609	34 633	33 976	101.93	67 106	33 777	33 328	1 504	856	648	2.95
贵州	8 704	8 630	75	29 612	15 323	14 290	107.23	29 372	15 198	14 175	240	125	115	3.40
云南	11 090	10 831	259	39 709	20 564	19 145	107.41	38 260	19 661	18 599	1 449	902	547	3.53
西藏	695	686	9	2 797	1 404	1 393	100.85	2 735	1 370	1 365	62	34	28	3.98
陕西	10 090	9 813	277	31 649	15 615	16 034	97.38	30 310	15 407	14 903	1 339	207	1 132	3.09
甘肃	6 479	6 449	30	21 720	11 035	10 685	103.27	21 636	10 991	10 645	84	43	41	3.35
青海	1 471	1 459	11	4 939	2 541	2 399	105.93	4 908	2 518	2 390	31	22	9	3.36
宁夏	1 772	1 731	41	5 627	2 769	2 858	96.91	5 380	2 754	2 626	247	16	232	3.11
新疆	6 383	6 339	43	20 210	10 211	9 999	102.12	20 078	10 143	9 935	133	68	64	3.17

表11 分地区分性别、户口登记状况的人口(2017年)

本表是2017年全国人口变动情况抽样调查样本数据,抽样比为0.824‰。

单位:人

地区	人口数			住本乡、镇、街道,户口在本乡、镇、街道			住本乡、镇、街道,户口在外乡、镇、街道,离开户口登记均半年以上			住本乡、镇、街道,户口待定			居住在港澳台或国外,户口在本乡、镇、街道		
	合计	男	女	小计	男	女	小计	男	女	小计	男	女	小计	男	女
全国	1 145 246	586 072	559 174	916 678	469 345	447 334	219 571	112 117	107 454	7 217	3 607	3 610	1 779	1 003	776
北京	17 801	9 017	8 784	8 834	4 489	4 344	8 795	4 446	4 349	51	27	24	122	55	67
天津	12 778	6 725	6 053	8 560	4 368	4 191	4 181	2 342	1 840	26	9	16	11	5	6
河北	62 086	31 523	30 563	55 460	28 511	26 950	6 275	2 841	3 434	330	159	171	21	12	9
山西	30 550	15 887	14 664	24 546	12 696	11 850	5 837	3 104	2 733	165	83	82	3	3	
内蒙古	20 849	10 465	10 384	14 525	7 411	7 114	6 204	2 997	3 207	114	54	61	5	4	2
辽宁	35 969	17 996	17 973	29 527	15 016	14 511	6 184	2 851	3 334	82	39	43	176	90	86
吉林	22 424	11 346	11 078	17 485	8 933	8 551	4 747	2 308	2 440	56	26	30	136	79	57

续表

地区	人口数			住本乡、镇、街道，户口在本乡、镇、街道			住本乡、镇、街道，户口在外乡、镇、街道，离开户口登记均半年以上			住本乡、镇、街道，户口待定			居住在港澳台或国外，户口在本乡、镇、街道		
	合计	男	女	小计	男	女	小计	男	女	小计	男	女	小计	男	女
黑龙江	31 251	15 919	15 332	26 338	13 550	12 788	4 703	2 262	2 441	172	88	84	38	19	20
上海	19 826	10 085	9 740	9 116	4 578	4 538	10 465	5 387	5 078	76	39	37	168	81	87
江苏	66 100	33 542	32 558	51 463	25 862	25 601	14 090	7 373	6 717	376	190	186	172	117	55
浙江	46 573	24 550	22 023	31 407	15 939	15 467	14 741	8 389	6 352	245	129	116	180	92	88
安徽	51 658	26 449	25 209	44 314	22 720	21 594	6 796	3 446	3 350	525	269	256	23	14	9
福建	32 221	16 435	15 786	21 368	10 800	10 568	10 143	5 235	4 908	429	233	196	281	167	114
江西	38 163	19 840	18 323	35 150	18 315	16 835	2 776	1 401	1 375	230	121	109	7	3	4
山东	82 502	41 595	40 907	69 871	35 516	34 355	12 071	5 790	6 281	451	213	237	109	76	34
河南	79 005	40 370	38 635	72 881	37 375	35 506	5 705	2 761	2 944	372	195	177	47	39	9
湖北	48 S84	25 090	23 594	38 247	19 654	18 593	10 052	5 248	4 804	355	170	185	30	18	12
湖南	56 647	28 560	28 087	48 005	24 543	23 462	8 323	3 863	4 460	295	141	154	25	14	11
广东	91 922	48 859	43 063	58 041	29 985	28 056	32 898	18 386	14 513	889	449	441	93	40	53
广西	40 385	21 080	19 305	35 778	18 768	17 010	4 164	2 095	2 069	430	208	222	14	9	4
海南	7 640	4 002	3 638	5 958	3 202	2 756	1 595	753	842	81	45	36	7	3	4
重庆	25 337	12 641	12 696	18 779	9 433	9 346	6 399	3 126	3 273	149	79	70	10	3	7
四川	68 609	34 633	33 976	56 698	28 769	27 929	11 576	5 685	5 891	296	156	140	40	23	16
贵州	29 612	15 323	14 290	25 166	13 126	12 039	4 159	2 054	2 105	280	137	143	8	5	3
云南	39 709	20 564	19 145	35 559	18 342	17 217	3 900	2 111	1 789	238	103	135	12	8	4
西藏	2 797	1 404	1 393	2 694	1 346	1 349	73	40	33	29	19	11			
陕西	31 649	15 615	16 034	26 445	13 437	13 008	5 055	2 099	2956	145	76	69	5	3	2
甘肃	21 720	11 03S	10 685	19 515	9 963	9 552	2 070	1 007	1 063	123	58	65	12	7	5
青海	4 939	2 541	2 399	4 145	2 130	2 016	761	397	364	30	12	18	3	2	1
宁夏	5 627	2 769	2 858	4 256	2 170	2 086	1 346	586	761	22	12	11	2	2	
新疆	20 210	10 211	9 999	16 648	8 396	8 152	3 487	1 736	1 751	156	69	88	19	11	8

表 12 分地区人口年龄构成和抚养比（2017 年）

本表是 2017 年全国人口变动情况抽样调查样本数据,抽样比为 0.824‰。

地区	人口数（人）	0~14 岁	15~64 岁	65 岁及以上	总抚养比（%）	少年儿童抚养比	老年人口抚养比
全国	1 145 246	192 353	822 465	130 428	39.25	23.39	15.86
北京	17 801	1 942	13 633	2 225	30.57	14.25	16.32
天津	12 778	1 443	9 893	1 442	29.16	14.59	14.57
河北	62 086	11 152	43 608	7 326	42.37	25.57	16.80
山西	30 550	4 767	23 037	2 746	32.61	20.69	11.92
内蒙古	20 849	2 824	15 765	2 260	32.25	17.91	14.33
辽宁	35 969	3 650	27 257	5 063	31.96	13.39	18.57
吉林	22 424	2 790	16 900	2 735	32.69	16.51	16.18
黑龙江	31 251	3 108	24 350	3 793	28.34	12.76	15.58
上海	19 826	1 972	15 026	2 827	31.94	13.12	18.82
江苏	66 100	8 889	48 002	9 210	37.70	18.52	19.19
浙江	46 573	5 669	35 092	5 812	32.72	16.15	16.56
安徽	51 658	9 867	35 079	6 713	47.26	28.13	19.14
福建	32 221	5 956	23 196	3 069	38.91	25.67	13.23
江西	38 163	8 245	26 196	3 723	45.69	31.47	14.21
山东	82 502	14 588	57 242	10 672	44.13	25.49	18.64
河南	79 005	16 476	53 962	8 567	46.41	30.53	15.88
湖北	48 684	7 701	35 028	5 955	38.99	21.99	17.00
湖南	56 647	10 427	39 325	6 895	44.05	26.51	17.53
广东	91 922	15 472	69 329	7 121	32.59	22.32	10.27
广西	40 385	8 989	27 461	3 936	47.06	32.73	14.33
海南	7 640	1 514	5 500	626	38.90	27.52	11.38
重庆	25 337	4 154	17 566	3 618	44.24	23.65	20.60
四川	68 609	10 860	48 192	9 557	42.37	22.53	19.83
贵州	29 612	6 305	20 362	2 946	45.43	30.97	14.47
云南	39 709	7 518	28 855	3 336	37.62	26.06	11.56
西藏	2 797	671	1 965	162	42.36	34.14	8.22
陕西	31 649	4 948	23 190	3 512	36.48	21.34	15.14
甘肃	21 720	3 811	15 666	2 243	38.65	24.33	14.32
青海	4 939	990	3 559	390	38.76	27.80	10.96
宁夏	5 627	1 034	4 117	476	36.67	25.11	11.56
新疆	20 210	4 624	14 114	1 472	43.19	32.76	10.43

表13 分地区按性别和婚姻状况分的人口（2017年）

本表是2017年全国人口变动情况抽样调查样本数据，抽样比为0.824‰。

单位：人

地区	15岁及以上人口	男	女	未婚	男	女	有配偶	男	女	离婚	男	女	丧偶	男	女
全国	952 893	482 331	470 561	177 158	104 688	72 470	703 884	352 030	351 854	19 110	10 667	8 444	52 740	14 946	37 793
北京	15 858	7 998	7 860	3 599	1 979	1 620	11 335	5 746	5 589	323	128	194	602	145	456
天津	11 335	5 970	5 365	2 563	1 542	1 020	8 067	4 177	3 889	243	118	125	462	131	331
河北	50 934	25 489	25 444	7 519	4 236	3 284	39 823	19 883	19 940	810	517	293	2 781	853	1 928
山西	25 783	13 368	12 415	5 315	3 264	2 051	18 832	9 495	9 338	422	256	166	1 214	354	860
内蒙古	18 025	9 028	8 997	2 951	1 601	1 350	13 865	7 008	6 857	355	198	158	854	222	632
辽宁	32 320	16 076	16 244	5 385	2 945	2 441	23 868	11 970	11 898	1 180	614	566	1 887	547	1 340
吉林	19 634	9 859	9 775	2 665	1 567	1 097	15 126	7 596	7 530	729	386	343	1 115	310	805
黑龙江	28 144	14 256	13 888	4 258	2 476	1 782	21 168	10 700	10 469	1 147	641	506	1 570	439	1 131
上海	17 854	9 031	8 823	3 102	1 767	1 335	13 523	6 895	6 629	450	201	249	778	168	610
江苏	57 211	28 766	28 446	8 558	4 844	3 714	44 550	22 535	22 015	942	497	445	3 161	889	2 271
浙江	40 904	21 510	19 394	6 881	4 487	2 394	31 248	16 098	15 150	723	428	296	2 052	497	1 555
安徽	41 792	21 005	20 786	6 826	4 244	2 582	31 746	15 609	16 137	690	428	262	2 529	723	1 806
福建	26 265	13 206	13 060	4 594	2 688	1 906	19 863	9 960	9 903	436	234	202	1 373	323	1 049
江西	29 919	15 160	14 758	5 633	3 370	2 264	22 132	11 025	11 107	473	308	165	1 680	458	1 223
山东	67 914	33 725	34 188	9 779	5 625	4 154	53 300	26 425	26 875	818	483	335	4 017	1 192	2 825
河南	62 529	31 292	31 237	11 841	6 910	4 931	46 251	22 698	23 553	885	540	345	3 552	1 145	2 408
湖北	40 983	20 847	20 136	8 311	5 196	3 115	29 421	14 384	15 037	804	488	316	2 447	779	1 668
湖南	46 220	22 980	23 240	7 996	4 840	3 156	34 299	16 787	17 512	992	541	451	2 934	812	2 122
广东	76 450	40 422	36 028	19 202	11 386	7 816	53 147	27 802	25 345	1 063	509	554	3 038	726	2 313
广西	31 397	16 222	15 175	7 284	4 569	2 715	21 683	10 839	10 844	486	282	204	1 944	532	1 412
海南	6 126	3 170	2 956	1 621	961	660	4 166	2 099	2 067	68	44	24	272	66	206

续表

地区	15岁及以上人口	男	女	未婚	男	女	有配偶	男	女	离婚	男	女	丧偶	男	女
重庆	21 184	10 445	10 739	3 421	1 990	1 432	15 718	7 678	8 040	698	352	346	1 347	426	921
四川	57 749	28 912	28 837	10 809	6 514	4 296	41 562	20 368	21 194	1 505	874	631	3 874	1 157	2 717
贵州	23 307	11 905	11 402	5 254	3 163	2 091	16 022	7 961	8 061	608	348	260	1 422	433	990
云南	32 191	16 570	15 621	7 500	4 668	2 832	22 213	10 983	11 230	723	435	288	1 755	484	1 271
西藏	2 126	1 064	1 062	592	317	275	1 368	699	669	46	12	34	120	35	85
陕西	26 701	13 013	13 688	5 460	2 777	2 683	19 163	9 474	9 689	430	273	157	1 648	489	1 160
甘肃	17 909	8 960	8 949	3 526	2 099	1 427	13 021	6 384	6 637	264	156	108	1 098	321	777
青海	3 950	2 027	1 922	802	484	318	2 793	1 421	1 373	131	66	65	233	56	167
宁夏	4 593	2 218	2 375	1 037	481	556	3 265	1 638	1 627	98	51	46	194	48	147
新疆	15 586	7 838	7 748	2 874	1 697	1 178	11 347	5 695	5 652	569	259	310	795	188	608

表14　分地区按性别、受教育程度分的6岁及以上人口（2017年）

本表是2017年全国人口变动情况抽样调查样本数据，抽样比为0.824‰。

单位：人

地区	6岁及以上人口			未上过学			小学			初中			普通高中			中职			大学专科			大学本科			研究生		
	合计	男	女	小计	男	女	小计	男	女	小计	男	女	小计	男	女	小计	男	女	小计	男	女	小计	男	女	小计	男	女
全国	1 063 758	542 541	521 217	56 152	16 293	39 859	268 406	127 614	140 791	404 872	217 886	186 987	139 416	78 405	61 011	47 319	25 668	21 651	78 559	40 418	38 141	62 660	32 805	29 855	6 374	3 451	2 923
北京	16 734	8 450	8 283	252	60	192	1 520	676	843	3 768	1 992	1 777	2 130	1 089	1 042	1 096	546	550	2 324	1 155	1 169	3 961	2 008	1 954	1 682	925	757
天津	12 142	6 396	5 746	289	87	203	1 614	759	855	3 949	2 127	1 822	1 488	809	678	1 299	749	550	1 536	823	714	1 800	955	845	167	88	79
河北	57 431	29 039	28 392	2 380	735	1 645	13 450	6 349	7 107	25 999	13 716	12 282	7 739	4 137	3 601	2 128	1 184	943	3 470	1 850	1 620	2 130	1 000	1 130	136	66	70
山西	28 628	14 881	13 747	681	228	453	5 221	2 388	2 833	12 353	6 491	5 863	4 814	2 823	1 991	1 287	696	590	2 416	1 304	1 113	1 629	844	785	227	107	120
内蒙古	19 590	9 842	9 747	1 091	354	737	4 466	2 091	2 375	7 038	3 813	3 225	2 798	1 394	1 403	645	341	303	1 955	1 018	937	1 506	789	717	90	40	50
辽宁	34 534	17 292	17 242	723	244	480	6 541	3 061	3 479	15 209	7 905	7 304	4 601	2 311	2 290	1 472	755	717	2 904	1 453	1 451	2 770	1 410	1 360	314	152	162
吉林	21 350	10 783	10 567	844	276	567	4 731	2 306	2 425	8 754	4 535	4 220	3 069	1 615	1 454	788	418	370	1 473	765	708	1 574	814	760	117	55	62

续表

地区	6岁及以上人口			未上过学			小学			初中			普通高中			中职			大学专科			大学本科			研究生		
	合计	男	女	小计	男	女	小计	男	女	小计	男	女	小计	男	女	小计	男	女	小计	男	女	小计	男	女	小计	男	女
黑龙江	30 260	15 390	14 870	1 010	373	636	6 952	3 288	3 664	13 455	7 150	6 305	3 812	2 024	1 787	983	511	471	2 109	1 122	987	1 837	868	970	103	54	50
上海	18 860	9 579	9 281	497	125	373	2 238	988	1 251	5 674	2 975	2 699	2 790	1 498	1 292	1 241	664	577	2 430	1 254	1 176	3 323	1 703	1 620	665	372	293
江苏	62 123	31 410	30 713	3 920	966	2 954	13 433	6 118	7 315	23 092	12 484	10 608	7 716	4 469	3 248	3 223	1 811	1 411	6 225	3 042	3 183	4 152	2 318	1 833	362	202	160
浙江	43 977	23 165	20 813	2 632	706	1 926	11 975	5 789	6 186	15 863	8 891	6 972	4 980	2 931	2 048	1 676	995	682	3 322	1 799	1 523	3 317	1 941	1 377	211	112	99
安徽	47 478	24 152	23 265	3 389	1 003	2 384	13 465	6 210	7 254	19 196	10 317	8 878	5 259	3 110	2 149	1 595	972	623	2 623	1 422	1 201	1 768	1 040	728	124	77	48
福建	29 305	14 829	14 477	1 771	391	1 380	8 309	3 791	4 519	10 165	5 757	4 409	3 118	1 854	1 264	1 524	819	704	2 088	1 111	976	2 156	1 015	1 142	174	92	83
江西	35 029	18 080	16 948	1 637	473	1 165	10 917	5 155	5 762	13 316	7 251	6 065	5 034	2 948	2 087	1 170	605	564	1 897	1 034	857	1 010	581	428	53	33	20
山东	76 033	38 200	37 833	4 778	1 103	3 675	18 637	8 713	9 924	29 957	16 007	13 950	8 270	4 834	3 436	4 307	2 384	1 923	5 833	2 861	2 972	3 887	2 074	1 812	364	223	141
河南	72 645	36 884	35 761	3 841	1 142	2 700	17 886	8 913	8 974	31 332	16 319	15 013	11 110	6 251	4 859	2 185	1 141	1 044	3 972	1 889	2 084	2 115	1 130	985	203	100	103
湖北	45 344	23 253	22 091	2 673	708	1 965	11 070	5 220	5 850	16 182	8 680	7 503	5 946	3 461	2 485	2 126	1 148	978	3 291	1 711	1 580	3 854	2 209	1 644	201	116	86
湖南	52 384	26 302	26 081	1 897	609	1 289	12 956	6 041	6 914	19 232	9 723	9 508	9 702	5 373	4 328	2 409	1 168	1 241	3 568	1 870	1 698	2 423	1 408	1 015	197	110	87
广东	84 724	44 978	39 746	2 723	750	1 975	17 773	8 307	9 466	32 421	18 112	14 309	14 511	8 504	6 007	5 404	3 155	2 249	6 955	3 592	3 362	4 659	2 411	2 248	278	148	130
广西	36 659	19 062	17 598	1 558	524	1 034	10 502	4 976	5 526	16 127	8 915	7 212	4 034	2 285	1 749	1 633	893	740	1 823	965	858	906	459	447	77	45	32
海南	7 005	3 653	3 352	296	88	207	1 402	658	743	3 140	1 703	1 437	858	518	340	392	211	181	442	259	183	469	211	258	8	4	4
重庆	23 701	11 782	11 919	853	245	607	7 475	3 538	3 937	8 111	4 214	3 897	3 138	1 676	1 462	890	466	424	1 796	887	909	1 311	686	625	128	69	59
四川	64 419	32 454	31 965	4 658	1 301	3 358	21 122	10 340	10 782	22 131	11 929	10 202	7 078	3 953	3 125	2 543	1 302	1 241	4 561	2 392	2 169	2 182	1 157	1 025	143	81	63
贵州	26 997	13 887	13 110	2 670	796	1 875	9 012	4 496	4 516	9 478	5 400	4 078	2 431	1 404	1 027	822	425	397	1 319	688	631	1 245	667	578	20	12	8
云南	36 543	18 891	17 652	3 008	981	2 027	13 232	6 566	6 666	12 311	7 056	5 255	3 514	1 982	1 532	1 368	687	680	1 708	891	816	1 347	698	649	54	30	25
西藏	2 508	1 253	1 255	864	355	509	871	473	398	415	235	180	117	63	54	31	20	11	119	64	55	88	40	48	3	3	56
陕西	29 461	14 479	14 982	1 794	563	1 232	7 119	3 359	3 760	11 026	5 938	5 088	3 952	2 197	1 756	1 066	543	523	2 257	1 074	1 183	2 128	744	1 385	117	62	28
甘肃	20 151	10 181	9 970	1 913	566	1 347	6 216	3 005	3 211	6 066	3 332	2 733	2 452	1 393	1 060	702	366	336	1 471	795	676	1 277	699	578	53	26	4
青海	4 514	2 320	2 794	475	165	310	1 772	868	903	7 248	729	520	365	202	164	128	69	59	258	148	110	259	136	123	9	5	10
宁夏	5 211	2 544	2 668	374	109	266	1 343	642	700	1 769	976	793	727	319	408	179	95	84	452	216	235	346	175	170	21	10	36
新疆	1 063 758	9 131	8 949	658	269	388	5 187	2 529	2 658	6 093	3 213	2 880	1 864	979	884	1 009	527	482	1 968	963	1 005	1 231	615	617	71	35	2 923

表15　分地区按性别分的15岁及以上文盲人口（2017年）

本表是2017年全国人口变动情况抽样调查样本数据,抽样比为0.824‰。

地区	15岁及以上人口(人)			文盲人口(人)			文盲人口占15岁及以上人口的比重(%)		
		男	女		男	女		男	女
全国	952 893	402 331	470 561	46 221	11 668	34 554	4.85	2.42	7.34
北京	15 858	7 998	7 860	195	41	153	1.23	0.52	1.95
天津	11 335	5 970	5 365	217	51	167	1.92	0.85	3.11
河北	50 934	25 489	25 444	1 774	433	1 341	3.48	1.70	5.27
山西	25 783	13 368	12 415	459	116	343	1.78	0.86	2.77
内蒙古	18 025	9 028	8 997	869	254	614	4.82	2.82	6.83
辽宁	32 320	16 076	16 244	498	136	362	1.54	0.85	2.23
吉林	19 634	9 859	9 775	687	207	480	3.50	2.10	4.91
黑龙江	28 144	14 256	13 888	814	275	538	2.89	1.93	3.88
上海	17 854	9 031	8 823	408	77	332	2.29	0.85	3.76
江苏	57 211	28 766	28 446	3 405	727	2 677	5.95	2.53	9.41
浙江	40 904	21 510	19 394	2 208	557	1 651	5.40	2.59	8.51
安徽	41 792	21 005	20 786	2 843	782	2 062	6.80	3.72	9.92
福建	26 265	13 205	13 060	1 471	263	1 208	5.60	1.99	9.25
江西	29 919	15 160	14 758	1 304	306	998	4.36	2.02	6.76
山东	67 914	33 725	34 188	4 119	809	3 310	6.07	2.40	9.68
河南	62 529	31 292	31 237	3 128	794	2 334	5.00	2.54	7.47
湖北	40 983	20 847	20 136	2 333	567	1 767	5.69	2.72	8.77
湖南	46 220	22 980	23 240	1 447	408	1 038	3.13	1.78	4.47
广东	76 450	40 422	36 028	1 919	375	1 544	2.51	0.93	4.28
广西	31 397	16 222	15 175	1 037	250	786	3.30	1.54	5.18
海南	6 126	3 170	2 956	259	68	191	4.23	2.14	6.47
重庆	21 184	10 445	10 739	639	155	484	3.02	1.48	4.51
四川	57 749	28 912	28 837	4 071	1 019	3 052	7.05	3.52	10.58
贵州	23 307	11 905	11 402	2 356	638	1 718	10.11	5.36	15.07
云南	32 191	16 570	15 621	2 702	820	1 881	8.39	4.95	12.04
西藏	2 126	1 064	1 062	743	289	454	34.96	27.18	42.76
陕西	26 701	13 013	13 688	1 468	416	1 052	5.50	3.19	7.69
甘肃	17 909	8 960	8 949	1 642	444	1 198	9.17	4.96	13.38
青海	3 950	2 027	1 922	380	118	262	9.63	5.84	13.63
宁夏	4 593	2 218	2 375	330	88	242	7.19	3.98	10.18
新疆	15 586	7 838	7 748	497	182	315	3.19	2.32	4.06

注:本表“文盲人口”指15岁及15岁以上不识字及识字很少人口。

表 16 分地区按家庭户规模分的户数（2017 年）

本表是 2017 年全国人口变动情况抽样调查样本数据，抽样比为 0.824‰。 单位：户

地区	家庭户户数	一人户	二人户	三人户	四人户	五人户	六人户	七人户	八人户	九人户	十人及以上户
全国	367 273	57 226	100 061	90 883	62 853	32 866	15 854	4 533	1 688	678	629
北京	6 151	1 352	1 889	1 682	620	423	131	35	13	3	3
天津	4 162	591	1 313	1 375	550	230	82	12	6		2
河北	19 092	2 053	5 389	4 503	3 790	1 840	1 104	295	64	24	28
山西	10 104	1 429	2 731	2 667	2 132	769	305	49	14	6	2
内蒙古	7 644	968	2 682	2 520	990	356	104	20	3	1	1
辽宁	13 382	2 034	4 658	4 354	1 377	733	182	34	9	1	
吉林	8 426	1 253	3 054	2 544	902	469	162	32	9		
黑龙江	11 872	1 808	4 408	3 731	1 059	613	184	44	15	5	4
上海	7 729	1 742	2 578	2 095	742	436	112	17	8	1	
江苏	20 575	2 799	5 819	5 257	3 091	2 379	911	211	66	20	22
浙江	17 238	4 024	5 566	3 789	2 077	1 154	490	97	29	8	5
安徽	16 110	1 970	4 233	4 049	3 114	1 581	812	219	82	31	18
福建	10 142	1 955	2 615	2 125	1 686	913	586	160	49	25	27
江西	10 658	1 005	2 270	2 313	2 501	1 358	777	248	94	44	48
山东	28 862	4 142	9 043	7 792	5 143	1 693	888	119	24	12	7
河南	23 474	2 578	5 572	5 566	5 146	2 603	1 388	430	124	43	23
湖北	15 270	2 362	4 183	3 897	2 509	1 440	617	156	58	28	20
湖南	17 011	2 272	4 145	4 260	3 387	1 704	839	245	92	34	32
广东	28 166	7 489	6 142	4 939	4 202	2 571	1510	596	375	164	179
广西	11 399	1 540	2 288	2 427	2 473	1 403	662	307	132	78	89
海南	2 065	266	361	434	517	254	129	51	27	12	14
重庆	9 044	1 977	2 470	2 103	1 386	712	278	80	27	6	7
四川	22 756	4 083	6 221	5 326	3 779	2 172	838	236	66	25	10
贵州	8 630	1 093	1 811	1 912	1 925	1 010	548	208	77	25	21
云南	10 831	1 111	2 101	2 468	2 567	1 418	809	236	71	28	22
西藏	686	100	105	136	123	79	58	33	22	14	17
陕西	9 813	1 342	2 572	2 572	1 810	930	449	103	26	6	4
甘肃	6 449	688	1 539	1 656	1 223	696	438	132	52	18	6
青海	1 459	204	296	334	311	160	103	33	11	4	3
宁夏	1 731	190	469	474	339	150	73	23	10	2	1
新疆	6 339	804	1 539	1 583	1 380	617	285	74	33	10	14

主要统计指标解释

人口数：指一定时点、一定地区范围内有生命的个人总和。

年度统计的年末人口数指每年 12 月 31 日 24 时的人口数。年度统计的全国人口总数内未包括香港、澳门特别行政区和台湾省以及海外华侨人数。

城镇人口和乡村人口：城镇人口是指居住在城镇范围内的全部常住人口；乡村人口是除上述人口以外的全部人口。

出生率（又称粗出生率）：指在一定时期内（通常为一年）一定地区的出生人数与同期内平均人数（或期中人数）之比，用千分率表示。本资料中的出生率指年出生率，其计算公式为：

$$出生率 = \frac{年出生人数}{年平均人数} \times 1000‰$$

式中：出生人数指活产婴儿，即胎儿脱离母体时（不管怀孕月数），有过呼吸或其他生命现象。年平均人数指年初、年底人口数的平均数，也可用年中人口数代替。

死亡率（又称粗死亡率）：指在一定时期内（通常为一年）一定地区的死亡人数与同期内平均人数（或期中人数）之比，用千分率表示。本资料中的死亡率指年死亡率，其计算公式为：

$$死亡率 = \frac{年死亡人数}{年平均人数} \times 1000‰$$

人口自然增长率：指在一定时期内（通常为一年）人口自然增加数（出生人数减死亡人数）与该时期内平均人数（或期中人数）之比，用千分率表示。计算公式为：

$$人口自然增长率 = \frac{本年出生人数 - 本年死亡人数}{年平均人数} \times 1000‰ = 人口出生率 - 人口死亡率$$

总抚养比：也称总负担系数。指人口总体中非劳动年龄人口数与劳动年龄人口数之比。通常用百分比表示。说明每 100 名劳动年龄人口大致要负担多少名非劳动年龄人口。用于从人口角度反映人口与经济发展的基本关系。计算公式为：

$$GDR = \frac{P_{0-14} + P_{65^+}}{P_{15-64}} \times 100\%$$

其中：GDR 为总抚养比；

P_{0-14}为 0 ~ 14 岁少年儿童人口数；

P_{65^+}为 65 岁及 65 岁以上的老年人口数；

P_{15-64}为 15 ~ 64 岁劳动年龄人口数。

老年人口抚养比：也称老年人口抚养系数。指某一人口中老年人口数与劳动年龄人口数之比。通常用百分比表示。用以表明每 100 名劳动年龄人口要负担多少名老年人。老年人口抚养比是从经济角度反映人口老化社会后果的指标之一。计算公式为：

$$ODR = \frac{P_{65^+}}{P_{15-64}} \times 100\%$$

其中：ODR为老年人口抚养比；

P_{65^+}为65岁及65岁以上的老年人口数；

P_{15-64}为15～64岁的劳动年龄人口数。

少年儿童抚养比：也称少年儿童抚养系数。指某一人口中少年儿童人口数与劳动年龄人口数之比。通常用百分比表示。以反映每100名劳动年龄人口要负担多少名少年儿童。计算公式为：

$$CDR = \frac{P_{0-14}}{P_{15-64}} \times 100\%$$

其中：CDR为少年儿童抚养比；

P_{0-14}为0～14岁少年儿童人口数；

P_{15-64}为15～64岁劳动年龄人口数。

人户分离人口：是指居住地与户口登记地所在的乡镇街道不一致且离开户口登记地半年以上的人口。

流动人口：是指人户分离人口中不包括市辖区内人户分离的人口。市辖区内人户分离的人口是指一个直辖市或地级市所辖区内和区与区之间，居住地和户口登记地不在同一乡镇街道的人口。

（资料整理：党凌燕，国际欧亚科学院中国科学中心办公室副主任）

附录 5

中国城市基本数据(2016 年)

城市名称 Name of cities		行政级别 Admini-strative level	行政区域土地面积(平方公里) Total land area of city's administrative region(sq. km)	年末总人口(万人) Total population at year - end (10 000 persons)	六普常住人口(万人) Total residents of the Sixth National Population Census (10 000 persons)	建成区面积(平方公里) Area of built - up district (sq. km)	地区生产总值(万元) Gross regional product (10 000 yuan)	人均地区生产总值(元) Per capita gross regional product(yuan)	用水普及率(%) Water coverage rate(%)	污水处理率(%) Wastewater treatment rate(%)	人均公园绿地面积(平方米) Per capita public green space(sq. m)	生活垃圾处理率(%) Domestic garbage treatment rate(%)
北京市	Beijing	直辖市	16 411	1 363. 0	1 961. 24	1 420	25 6691 300	118 198	100. 00	90. 58	13. 70	99. 84
天津市	Tianjin	直辖市	11 917	1 044. 0	1 293. 87	1 008	17 8853 900	115 053	100. 00	92. 08	16. 01	94. 16
河北省	Hebei											
石家庄市	Shijiazhuang	地级市	13 056	1 038. 0	1 016. 38	278	59 277 293	55 177	100. 00	96. 12	15. 77	100. 00
唐山市	Tangshan	地级市	13 472	760. 0	757. 73	323	63 548 675	81 239	100. 00	97. 60	15. 28	100. 00
秦皇岛市	Qinhuangdao	地级市	7 802	298. 0	298. 76	131	13 493 526	45 280	100. 00	96. 60	19. 22	100. 00
邯郸市	Handan	地级市	12 065	1 055. 0	917. 47	172	33 370 903	35 265	100. 00	97. 71	18. 54	100. 00
邢台市	Xingtai	地级市	12 433	788. 0	710. 41	90	19 757 460	27 038	100. 00	96. 36	11. 57	100. 00
保定市	Baoding	地级市	22 185	1 207. 0	1 119. 44	187	34 771 269	29 992	96. 46	90. 54	10. 18	96. 48
张家口市	Zhangjiakou	地级市	36 797	470. 0	434. 55	100	14 659 911	33 142	100. 00	94. 67	11. 93	95. 54
承德市	Chengde	地级市	39 493	383. 0	347. 32	117	14 385 741	40 471	100. 00	92. 17	24. 58	99. 52
沧州市	Cangzhou	地级市	14 035	780. 0	713. 41	73	35 446 800	47 425	100. 00	99. 91	11. 00	100. 00
廊坊市	Langfang	地级市	6 382	470. 0	435. 88	68	27 063 015	58 972	100. 00	93. 03	13. 97	100. 00
衡水市	Hengshui	地级市	8 815	455. 0	434. 08	76	14 201 825	31 955	99. 63	88. 22	12. 97	63. 38
晋州市	Jinzhou	县级市	619	57. 2	53. 77	15	3 004 688	52 530	100. 00	97. 24	10. 01	94. 50
新乐市	Xinle	县级市	525	51. 7	48. 77	14	2 079 912	40 230	100. 00	96. 03	9. 57	100. 00
遵化市	Zunhua	县级市	1 513	76. 0	73. 70	26	5 122 370	67 400	98. 97	92. 33	11. 19	100. 00

续表

城市名称 Name of cities		行政级别 Admini-strative level	行政区域土地面积（平方公里）Total land area of city's administrative region（sq. km）	年末总人口（万人）Total population at year-end（10 000 persons）	六普常住人口（万人）Total residents of the Sixth National Population Census（10 000 persons）	建成区面积（平方公里）Area of built-up district（sq. km）	地区生产总值（万元）Gross regional product（10 000 yuan）	人均地区生产总值（元）Per capita gross regional product（yuan）	用水普及率（%）Water coverage rate（%）	污水处理率（%）Wastewater treatment rate（%）	人均公园绿地面积（平方米）Per capita public green space（sq. m）	生活垃圾处理率（%）Domestic garbage treatment rate（%）
迁安市	Qian'an	县级市	1 227	77.3	72.82	44	9 201 601	119 038	100.00	98.93	20.20	100.00
武安市	Wu'an	县级市	1 806	83.9	81.90	35	6 066 464	72 306	100.00	99.02	15.33	100.00
南宫市	Nangong	县级市	861	50.6	46.90	16	1 064 369	21 035	97.91	95.51	12.08	100.00
沙河市	Shahe	县级市	859	44.8	49.84	17	2 313 692	51 645	100.00	87.98	14.32	100.00
涿州市	Zhuozhou	县级市	751	69.2	60.35	34	2 852 423	41 220	100.00	95.95	10.70	100.00
安国市	Anguo	县级市	486	41.7	37.03	13	1 211 368	29 050	100.00	98.62	9.35	100.00
高碑店市	Gaobeidian	县级市	618	57.3	64.03	21	1 486 361	25 940	95.99	99.01	8.41	98.50
泊头市	Botou	县级市	1 009	63.5	58.43	20	2 157 759	33 980	100.00	98.01	11.13	100.00
任丘市	Renqiu	县级市	1 012	89.3	82.25	47	5 942 697	66 548	100.00	95.91	9.96	100.00
黄骅市	Huanghua	县级市	1 545	48.1	54.85	37	2 595 774	53 966	100.00	99.89	13.43	100.00
河间市	Hejian	县级市	1 322	89.1	81.03	21	2 872 111	32 235	100.00	99.00	13.03	100.00
霸州市	Bazhou	县级市	802	65.0	62.30	18	3 952 879	60 814	100.00	92.68	13.20	98.90
三河市	Sanhe	县级市	634	69.1	65.20	19	5 096 286	73 752	93.32	92.84	10.69	100.00
深州市	Shenzhou	县级市	1 245	57.7	56.61	20	1 501 796	26 028	100.00	93.13	9.19	99.50
定州市	Dingzhou	县级市	1 284	124.9	116.52	43	3 278 090	26 246	100.00	87.01	9.08	100.00
辛集市	Xinji	县级市	951	63.8	61.59	30	4 255 828	66 706	100.00	93.00	11.39	100.00
山西省	Shanxi											
太原市	Taiyuan	地级市	6 988	370.0	420.16	340	29 556 045	68 234	100.00	86.89	10.83	100.00
大同市	Datong	地级市	14 176	318.0	331.81	125	10 257 962	30 046	100.00	85.59	11.26	99.75
阳泉市	Yangquan	地级市	4 570	133.0	136.85	56	6 228 625	44 461	100.00	86.50	11.55	100.00
长治市	Changzhi	地级市	13 896	339.0	333.46	59	12 704 767	37 063	98.54	95.28	12.15	100.00
晋城市	Jincheng	地级市	9 425	220.0	227.91	46	10 493 400	45 271	98.98	94.99	12.08	100.00
朔州市	Shuozhou	地级市	10 625	163.0	171.49	42	9 180 640	52 010	99.12	97.97	14.14	100.00

续表

城市名称 Name of cities		行政级别 Administrative level	行政区域土地面积(平方公里) Total land area of city's administrative region(sq. km)	年末总人口(万人) Total population at year-end (10 000 persons)	六普常住人口(万人) Total residents of the Sixth National Population Census (10 000 persons)	建成区面积(平方公里) Area of built-up district (sq. km)	地区生产总值(万元) Gross regional product (10 000 yuan)	人均地区生产总值(元) Per capita gross regional product(yuan)	用水普及率(%) Water coverage rate(%)	污水处理率(%) Wastewater treatment rate(%)	人均公园绿地面积(平方米) Per capita public green space(sq. m)	生活垃圾处理率(%) Domestic garbage treatment rate(%)
晋中市	Jinzhong	地级市	16 444	332.0	324.94	77	10 911 041	32 646	100.00	96.96	17.45	100.00
运城市	Yuncheng	地级市	14 183	531.0	513.48	66	12 223 486	23 106	98.49	91.05	14.26	100.00
忻州市	Xinzhou	地级市	25 152	308.0	306.75	37	7 161 357	22 747	100.00	95.47	12.81	100.00
临汾市	Linfen	地级市	20 275	434.0	431.66	58	12 051 761	27 102	96.62	91.38	12.10	100.00
吕梁市	Lvliang	地级市	21 239	391.0	372.71	26	9 953 079	25 896	97.83	94.01	13.31	100.00
古交市	Gujiao	县级市	1 584	21.9	20.51	17	263 913	12 051	99.01	89.02	9.53	100.00
潞城市	Lucheng	县级市	630	22.7	22.69	11	905 406	39 886	99.24	83.00	8.24	100.00
高平市	Gaoping	县级市	980	48.4	48.49	18	2 002 904	41 382	99.53	95.55	13.38	100.00
介休市	Jiexiu	县级市	741	43.2	40.65	21	1 439 804	33 329	100.00	89.32	9.09	90.66
永济市	Yongji	县级市	1 208	44.7	44.47	23	1 340 707	29 993	99.01	91.02	14.16	100.00
河津市	Hejin	县级市	593	40.2	39.55	29	1 777 369	44 213	98.00	91.07	15.00	96.00
原平市	Yuanping	县级市	2571	48.9	49.12	15	1 168 137	23 888	100.00	95.76	10.03	100.00
侯马市	Houma	县级市	221	24.4	24.00	20	947 049	38 813	100.00	93.96	12.46	100.00
霍州市	Huozhou	县级市	764	31.0	28.29	15	708 396	22 851	98.00	91.02	9.04	100.00
孝义市	Xiaoyi	县级市	938	48.9	46.88	27	3 387 764	69 279	97.32	95.00	12.76	100.00
汾阳市	Fenyang	县级市	1 175	42.9	41.62	16	1 059 682	24 701	97.43	89.46	6.67	100.00
内蒙古自治区	Inner Mongolia											
呼和浩特市	Huhhot	地级市	17 453	241.0	286.66	260	31 735 900	103 235	99.96	94.64	19.69	100.00
包头市	Baotou	地级市	27 768	224.0	265.04	201	38 676 300	136 021	99.55	90.42	13.77	98.15
乌海市	Wuhai	地级市	1 669	44.0	53.29	62	5 722 261	102 725	100.00	96.50	20.06	98.60
赤峰市	Chifeng	地级市	90 021	463.0	434.12	106	19 332 792	44 936	98.60	93.78	17.37	100.00
通辽市	Tongliao	地级市	59 329	319.0	313.92	61	19 493 818	62 424	97.90	98.01	21.18	100.00
鄂尔多斯市	Ordos	地级市	86 752	159.0	194.07	117	44 179 341	215 488	99.82	97.27	33.84	97.70

续表

城市名称 Name of cities		行政级别 Administrative level	行政区域土地面积（平方公里）Total land area of city's administrative region (sq. km)	年末总人口（万人）Total population at year-end (10 000 persons)	六普常住人口（万人）Total residents of the Sixth National Population Census (10 000 persons)	建成区面积（平方公里）Area of built-up district (sq. km)	地区生产总值（万元）Gross regional product (10 000 yuan)	人均地区生产总值（元）Per capita gross regional product (yuan)	用水普及率（%）Water coverage rate (%)	污水处理率（%）Wastewater treatment rate (%)	人均公园绿地面积（平方米）Per capita public green space (sq. m)	生活垃圾处理率（%）Domestic garbage treatment rate (%)
呼伦贝尔市	Hulunbeier	地级市	252 777	259.0	254.93	93	16 208 500	64 140	97.52	99.34	20.30	100.00
巴彦淖尔市	Bayannur	地级市	66 277	175.0	166.99	51	9 153 800	54 480	97.49	98.72	22.56	100.00
乌兰察布市	Ulanqab	地级市	54 500	274.0	214.36	60	9 388 700	44 517	97.42	94.68	40.49	96.63
霍林郭勒市	Huolinguole	县级市	585	8.2	10.22	17	2 961 450	361 152	99.45	99.00	17.39	96.40
满洲里市	Manzhouli	县级市	735	17.2	24.95	27	2 415 531	140 438	98.96	92.17	12.89	94.56
牙克石市	Yakeshi	县级市	27 803	33.6	36.63	28	2 300 927	68 480	97.29	92.35	16.82	99.50
扎兰屯市	Zhalantun	县级市	16 785	41.2	35.22	19	1 879 193	45 611	97.16	92.76	14.50	100.00
额尔古纳市	Eerguna	县级市	28 958	8.1	11.04	10	477 728	58 979	95.38	94.24	16.03	100.00
根河市	Genhe	县级市	20 010	14.0	7.67	18	429 977	30 713	94.22	92.36	17.63	97.82
丰镇市	Fengzhen	县级市	2 722	31.7	24.56	25	1 462 225	46 127	95.10	95.25	29.84	93.80
乌兰浩特市	Wulanghaote	县级市	2 728	32.2	32.71	39	1 683 433	52 281	99.24	92.33	18.16	98.07
阿尔山市	Aershan	县级市	7 409	4.6	6.83	11	174 767	37 993	98.33	90.24	31.17	99.66
二连浩特市	Erlianhaote	县级市	4 015	3.2	7.42	27	1 096 575	342 680	99.32	97.11	21.50	100.00
锡林浩特市	Xilinhaote	县级市	14 780	18.7	24.59	43	2 281 409	122 000	98.10	86.57	17.70	100.00
辽宁省	Liaoning											
沈阳市	Shenyang	副省级市	12 860	734.0	810.62	588	55 464 498	66 893	99.91	94.92	11.52	100.00
大连市	Dalian	副省级市	12 574	596.0	669.04	396	68 101 998	97 470	99.76	94.73	11.02	100.00
鞍山市	Anshan	地级市	9 255	346.0	364.59	172	14 619 713	40 532	100.00	86.49	11.09	100.00
抚顺市	Fushun	地级市	11 272	215.0	213.81	139	8 650 721	41 741	98.62	98.21	10.71	100.00
本溪市	Benxi	地级市	8 411	150.0	170.95	109	7 667 098	44 745	99.56	97.08	10.75	86.21
丹东市	Dandong	地级市	14 967	238.0	244.47	77	7 512 352	31 223	100.00	87.65	11.07	100.00
锦州市	Jinzhou	地级市	10 047	302.0	312.65	112	10 328 139	33 692	100.00	89.79	13.55	100.00
营口市	Yingkou	地级市	5 242	233.0	242.85	189	11 562 477	47 358	100.00	81.59	11.75	71.39

续表

城市名称 Name of cities		行政级别 Administrative level	行政区域土地面积(平方公里) Total land area of city's administrative region(sq. km)	年末总人口(万人) Total population at year-end (10 000 persons)	六普常住人口(万人) Total residents of the Sixth National Population Census (10 000 persons)	建成区面积(平方公里) Area of built-up district (sq. km)	地区生产总值(万元) Gross regional product (10 000 yuan)	人均地区生产总值(元) Per capita gross regional product(yuan)	用水普及率(%) Water coverage rate(%)	污水处理率(%) Wastewater treatment rate(%)	人均公园绿地面积(平方米) Per capita public green space(sq. m)	生活垃圾处理率(%) Domestic garbage treatment rate(%)
阜新市	Fuxin	地级市	10 355	189. 0	181. 93	77	4 078 179	22 956	98. 94	98. 18	12. 93	100. 00
辽阳市	Liaoyang	地级市	4 788	179. 0	185. 88	105	6 541 758	35 476	100. 00	99. 68	10. 90	100. 00
盘锦市	Panjin	地级市	4 065	130. 0	139. 25	75	10 071 351	70 110	98. 58	97. 21	11. 56	71. 70
铁岭市	Tieling	地级市	12 985	300. 0	271. 77	57	5 880 423	22 178	99. 00	99. 81	11. 97	100. 00
朝阳市	Chaoyang	地级市	19 698	341. 0	304. 46	57	7 165 334	24 285	91. 65	99. 09	9. 82	100. 00
葫芦岛市	Huludao	地级市	10 414	280. 0	262. 35	93	6 473 518	25 347	100. 00	89. 99	14. 72	100. 00
新民市	Xinmin	县级市	3 318	68. 1	65. 78	26	2 310 973	33 935	90. 97	83. 43	9. 50	100. 00
瓦房店市	Wafangdian	县级市	3 643	99. 6	94. 22	36	9 019 748	90 560	100. 00	96. 03	13. 97	100. 00
庄河市	Zhuanghe	县级市	4 114	90. 4	84. 13	43	5 940 265	65 711	99. 83	93. 32	12. 75	100. 00
海城市	Haicheng	县级市	2 566	108. 0	129. 39	36	5 000 559	46 301	99. 45	95. 90	14. 80	100. 00
东港市	Donggang	县级市	2 399	60. 6	62. 75	22	2 238 841	36 945	100. 00	64. 33	12. 01	100. 00
凤城市	Fengcheng	县级市	5 515	56. 7	54. 39	21	1 697 856	29 945	93. 38	78. 32	10. 99	64. 54
凌海市	Linghai	县级市	2 585	51. 4	50. 81	21	1 523 981	29 649	100. 00	87. 16	11. 84	100. 00
北镇市	Beizhen	县级市	1 701	51. 6	51. 49	15	1 187 845	23 020	86. 30	97. 34	5. 27	100. 00
盖州市	Gaizhou	县级市	2 946	69. 8	69. 16	29	1 650 739	23 650	88. 97	86. 76	8. 78	94. 12
大石桥市	Dashiqiao	县级市	1 598	69. 8	70. 49	43	2 621 042	37 551	100. 00	48. 63	7. 47	100. 00
灯塔市	Dengta	县级市	1 170	44. 4	49. 61	14	1 198 961	27 004	98. 68	99. 29	16. 22	100. 00
调兵山市	Diaobingshan	县级市	262	23. 4	24. 14	19	872 155	37 272	97. 30	93. 19	8. 04	100. 00
开原市	Kaiyuan	县级市	2 838	57. 9	54. 56	28	933 055	16 115	100. 00	98. 45	7. 36	100. 00
北票市	Beipiao	县级市	4 419	57. 0	49. 62	18	1 093 851	19 190	92. 59	99. 50	8. 76	
凌源市	Lingyuan	县级市	3 282	65. 1	57. 07	25	1 372 126	21 077	94. 27	96. 30	7. 53	95. 89
兴城市	Xingcheng	县级市	2 102	54. 1	54. 62	30	1 043 842	19 295	97. 74	77. 72	13. 31	100. 00
吉林省	Jilin											

续表

城市名称 Name of cities		行政级别 Admini-strative level	行政区域土地面积（平方公里）Total land area of city's administrative region（sq. km）	年末总人口（万人）Total population at year - end（10 000 persons）	六普常住人口（万人）Total residents of the Sixth National Population Census（10 000 persons）	建成区面积（平方公里）Area of built - up district（sq. km）	地区生产总值（万元）Gross regional product（10 000 yuan）	人均地区生产总值（元）Per capita gross regional product（yuan）	用水普及率（%）Water coverage rate（%）	污水处理率（%）Wastewater treatment rate（%）	人均公园绿地面积（平方米）Per capita public green space（sq. m）	生活垃圾处理率（%）Domestic garbage treatment rate（%）
长春市	Changchun	副省级市	20 594	753. 0	767. 44	519	59 864 200	79 434	99. 81	93. 45	17. 78	90. 27
吉林市	Jilin	地级市	27 711	422. 0	441. 32	189	24 535 091	57 818	98. 57	96. 14	12. 05	100. 00
四平市	Siping	地级市	14 382	324. 0	338. 52	58	11 938 035	36 732	72. 21	97. 34	8. 41	91. 10
辽源市	Liaoyuan	地级市	5 140	120. 0	117. 62	46	7 652 485	63 480	95. 35	93. 89	9. 95	100. 00
通化市	Tonghua	地级市	15 612	220. 0	232. 44	54	9 475 914	42 979	94. 06	94. 73	14. 14	95. 48
白山市	Baishan	地级市	17 505	122. 0	129. 61	47	6 966 243	56 411	89. 24	86. 77	10. 21	99. 09
松原市	Songyuan	地级市	21 089	278. 0	288. 01	51	16 516 898	59 413	96. 06	96. 21	17. 79	96. 70
白城市	Baicheng	地级市	25 759	193. 0	203. 24	43	7 001 392	35 892	98. 51	80. 16	13. 00	96. 05
榆树市	Yushu	县级市	4 712	125. 5	116. 06	23	4 078 628	32 499	82. 43	99. 69	6. 44	100. 00
德惠市	Dehui	县级市	3 435	101. 0	74. 84	31	4 408 170	43 645	83. 33	65. 11	2. 50	100. 00
蛟河市	Jiaohe	县级市	6 370	43. 6	44. 72	20	2 045 764	46 921	95. 21	77. 16	21. 37	100. 00
桦甸市	Huadian	县级市	6 522	43. 4	44. 48	20	2 643 463	60 909	95. 68	90. 00	17. 95	100. 00
舒兰市	Shulan	县级市	4 557	62. 8	64. 57	25	2 037 229	32 440	84. 31	68. 68	11. 64	100. 00
磐石市	Panshi	县级市	3 861	52. 1	50. 58	24	2 559 683	49 130	91. 11	87. 02	9. 82	95. 00
公主岭市	Gongzhuling	县级市	4 141	104. 7	109. 29	33	4 647 818	44 392	92. 17	59. 65	6. 74	100. 00
双辽市	Shuangliao	县级市	3 121	37. 8	42. 07	22	1 687 649	44 647	79. 43	98. 92	7. 30	100. 00
梅河口市	Meihekou	县级市	2 179	60. 1	61. 52	25	3 557 017	59 185	98. 31	96. 46	10. 18	100. 00
集安市	Ji'an	县级市	3 341	21. 6	23. 23	9	1 100 277	50 939	98. 43	99. 45	10. 95	100. 00
临江市	Linjiang	县级市	3 009	16. 5	17. 50	10	1 019 022	61 759	95. 24	96. 88	21. 96	100. 00
扶余市	Fuyu	县级市	4 654	72. 2	71. 90	14	3 700 583	51 255	57. 23	95. 00	5. 19	79. 19
洮南市	Taonan	县级市	5 017	42. 0	43. 21	23	1 435 433	34 177	100. 00	90. 08	9. 08	100. 00
大安市	Daan	县级市	4 879	38. 9	43. 10	19	1 458 184	37 485	76. 39	92. 25	17. 51	71. 62
延吉市	Yanji	县级市	1 748	54. 5	56. 30	36	3 338 420	61 255	92. 51	90. 22	9. 14	99. 76

续表

城市名称 Name of cities		行政级别 Admini-strative level	行政区域土地面积(平方公里) Total land area of city's administrative region(sq. km)	年末总人口(万人) Total population at year-end (10 000 persons)	六普常住人口(万人) Total residents of the Sixth National Population Census (10 000 persons)	建成区面积(平方公里) Area of built-up district (sq. km)	地区生产总值(万元) Gross regional product (10 000 yuan)	人均地区生产总值(元) Per capita gross regional product(yuan)	用水普及率(%) Water coverage rate(%)	污水处理率(%) Wastewater treatment rate(%)	人均公园绿地面积(平方米) Per capita public green space(sq. m)	生活垃圾处理率(%) Domestic garbage treatment rate(%)
图们市	Tumen	县级市	1 143	11. 6	13. 45	11	457 408	39 432	85. 68	99. 55	11. 14	100. 00
敦化市	Dunhua	县级市	11 957	46. 7	48. 35	31	1 878 569	40 226	97. 10	88. 26	22. 07	100. 00
珲春市	Hunchun	县级市	5 184	27. 0	24. 18	18	1 510 078	55 929	82. 19	85. 98	9. 03	100. 00
龙井市	Longjing	县级市	2 208	16. 1	17. 72	12	410 618	25 504	82. 76	84. 00	10. 65	100. 00
和龙市	Helong	县级市	5 069	17. 0	18. 95	13	616 832	36 284	87. 63	97. 95	5. 32	100. 00
黑龙江省	Heilongjiang											
哈尔滨市	Harbin	副省级市	53 100	962. 0	1 063. 60	431	61 016 096	63 445	100. 00	92. 20	9. 21	91. 80
齐齐哈尔市	Qiqihar	地级市	42 496	544. 0	536. 70	140	13 253 110	25 690	98. 99	90. 93	10. 06	68. 32
鸡西市	Jixi	地级市	22 531	181. 0	186. 22	81	5 183 793	28 647	98. 52	74. 26	10. 82	87. 39
鹤岗市	Hegang	地级市	14 679	104. 0	105. 87	53	2 641 031	25 244	95. 78	72. 51	14. 98	100. 00
双鸭山市	Shuangyashan	地级市	22 681	145. 0	146. 26	58	4 373 971	29 959	98. 95	88. 37	14. 44	86. 25
大庆市	Daqing	地级市	21 219	276. 0	290. 45	245	26 100 031	94 690	95. 91	96. 08	14. 97	100. 00
伊春市	Yichun	地级市	32 800	118. 0	114. 81	157	2 512 167	21 043	86. 38	86. 38	23. 74	57. 38
佳木斯市	Jiamusi	地级市	32 704	238. 0	255. 21	97	8 450 332	36 878	96. 26	85. 00	14. 17	100. 00
七台河市	Qitaihe	地级市	6 221	80. 0	92. 05	68	2 166 414	26 500	98. 17	60. 84	12. 14	98. 21
牡丹江市	Mudanjiang	地级市	38 827	259. 0	279. 87	82	13 681 181	49 618	93. 66	100. 00	10. 61	100. 00
黑河市	Heihe	地级市	69 345	163. 0	167. 39	20	4 708 056	27 889	96. 97	92. 97	13. 36	100. 00
绥化市	Suihua	地级市	34 873	543. 0	541. 82	45	13 163 122	24 109	98. 64	88. 90	8. 53	100. 00
尚志市	Shangzhi	县级市	8 891	58. 0	58. 54	18	2 198 795	37 910	97. 25	98. 17	10. 95	100. 00
五常市	Wuchang	县级市	7 512	91. 8	88. 12	27	4 101 259	44 676	99. 64	99. 16	14. 46	100. 00
讷河市	Nehe	县级市	6 660	69. 9	62. 59	11	1 193 650	17 077	95. 01	100. 00	18. 14	100. 00
虎林市	Hulin	县级市	9 334	15. 4	31. 79	11	661 182	42 934	100. 00	100. 00	15. 20	100. 00
密山市	Mishan	县级市	7 731	34. 2	40. 75	19	942 073	27 546	75. 14	95. 00	9. 99	98. 38

续表

城市名称 Name of cities		行政级别 Admini-strative level	行政区域土地面积（平方公里）Total land area of city's administrative region (sq. km)	年末总人口（万人）Total population at year - end (10 000 persons)	六普常住人口（万人）Total residents of the Sixth National Population Census (10 000 persons)	建成区面积（平方公里）Area of built - up district (sq. km)	地区生产总值（万元）Gross regional product (10 000 yuan)	人均地区生产总值（元）Per capita gross regional product (yuan)	用水普及率（%）Water coverage rate (%)	污水处理率（%）Wastewater treatment rate (%)	人均公园绿地面积（平方米）Per capita public green space (sq. m)	生活垃圾处理率（%）Domestic garbage treatment rate (%)
铁力市	Tieli	县级市	6 443	35. 6	34. 94	17	730 488	20 519	90. 70	93. 26	15. 56	90. 32
同江市	Tongjiang	县级市	6 229	10. 9	17. 98	10	472 458	43 345	96. 38	100. 00	14. 57	100. 00
富锦市	Fujin	县级市	8 224	38. 0	43. 72	16	1 504 796	39 600	99. 19	100. 00	9. 50	100. 00
抚远市	Fuyuan	县级市	6 047	8. 4	12. 67	6	307 418	36 597	98. 82	83. 33	10. 52	
绥芬河市	Suifenhe	县级市	422	7. 1	13. 23	27	1 369 054	192 825	100. 00	100. 00	14. 16	100. 00
海林市	Hailin	县级市	8 816	37. 8	40. 09	17	2 128 774	56 317	99. 90	100. 00	13. 99	100. 00
宁安市	Ning'an	县级市	7 227	42. 2	43. 75	11	2 045 657	48 475	100. 00	100. 00	14. 99	100. 00
穆棱市	Muling	县级市	6 247	28. 4	29. 33	10	1 879 858	66 192	100. 00	100. 00	15. 72	100. 00
东宁市	Dongning	县级市	7 117	21. 0	20. 07	15	1 683 033	80 144	98. 66	100. 00	11. 11	100. 00
北安市	Bei'an	县级市	7 194	35. 0	43. 64	23	950 098	27 146	98. 04	100. 00	14. 48	100. 00
五大连池市	Wudalianchi	县级市	9 874	34. 3	32. 64	6	613 302	17 881	95. 38	100. 00	14. 68	99. 77
安达市	Anda	县级市	3 586	46. 7	47. 28	25	3 367 298	72 105	94. 98	100. 00	3. 73	100. 00
肇东市	Zhaodong	县级市	4 332	88. 0	90. 31	36	4 365 565	49 609	96. 19	90. 96	13. 22	98. 40
海伦市	Hailun	县级市	4 667	77. 4	76. 94	21	1 260 146	16 281	84. 14	83. 54	4. 75	
上海市	Shanghai	直辖市	6 341	1 450. 0	2 301. 92	999	281 786 500	116 562	100. 00	94. 29	7. 83	100. 00
江苏省	Jiangsu											
南京市	Nanjing	副省级市	6 587	663. 0	800. 37	774	105 030 200	127 264	100. 00	95. 98	15. 34	100. 00
无锡市	Wuxi	地级市	4 627	486. 0	637. 44	332	92 100 200	141 258	100. 00	97. 13	14. 91	100. 00
徐州市	Xuzhou	地级市	11 765	1 041. 0	857. 72	261	58 085 200	66 845	99. 81	93. 60	15. 74	100. 00
常州市	Changzhou	地级市	4 373	375. 0	459. 24	261	57 738 600	122 721	100. 00	96. 34	14. 45	100. 00
苏州市	Suzhou	地级市	8 657	678. 0	1 045. 99	461	154 750 900	145 556	100. 00	95. 16	14. 71	100. 00
南通市	Nantong	地级市	10 549	767. 0	728. 36	216	67 682 000	92 702	100. 00	94. 11	18. 47	100. 00
连云港市	Liangyungang	地级市	7 615	534. 0	439. 35	213	23 764 800	52 987	100. 00	87. 16	14. 66	100. 00

续表

城市名称 Name of cities		行政级别 Admini-strative level	行政区域土地面积（平方公里）Total land area of city's administrative region (sq. km)	年末总人口（万人）Total population at year-end (10 000 persons)	六普常住人口（万人）Total residents of the Sixth National Population Census (10 000 persons)	建成区面积（平方公里）Area of built-up district (sq. km)	地区生产总值（万元）Gross regional product (10 000 yuan)	人均地区生产总值（元）Per capita gross regional product (yuan)	用水普及率（%）Water coverage rate (%)	污水处理率（%）Wastewater treatment rate (%)	人均公园绿地面积（平方米）Per capita public green space (sq. m)	生活垃圾处理率（%）Domestic garbage treatment rate (%)
淮安市	Huai'an	地级市	10 030	568. 0	480. 17	179	30 480 000	62 446	100. 00	93. 20	14. 01	100. 00
盐城市	Yancheng	地级市	16 931	831. 0	726. 22	147	45 760 800	63 278	100. 00	90. 50	12. 75	100. 00
扬州市	Yangzhou	地级市	6 591	462. 0	446. 01	149	44 493 800	99 151	100. 00	94. 42	18. 58	100. 00
镇江市	Zhenjiang	地级市	3 840	272. 0	311. 41	139	38 338 400	120 603	100. 00	94. 51	18. 97	100. 00
泰州市	Taizhou	地级市	5 787	508. 0	461. 89	115	41 017 800	88 330	100. 00	91. 22	10. 69	100. 00
宿迁市	Suqian	地级市	8 524	592. 0	471. 92	86	23 511 200	48 311	100. 00	94. 53	15. 27	100. 00
江阴市	Jiangyin	县级市	987	124. 8	159. 51	125	30 832 600	247 056	100. 00	96. 30	14. 61	100. 00
宜兴市	Yixing	县级市	1 997	108. 3	123. 55	81	13 777 400	127 215	100. 00	95. 01	15. 14	100. 00
新沂市	Xinyi	县级市	1 592	113. 6	92. 06	36	5 620 600	49 477	93. 24	89. 76	10. 16	100. 00
邳州市	Pizhou	县级市	2 085	193. 9	145. 80	46	8 041 400	41 472	95. 44	90. 59	14. 00	100. 00
溧阳市	Liyang	县级市	1 535	80. 0	74. 95	29	8 012 600	100 158	100. 00	95. 94	12. 85	100. 00
常熟市	Changshu	县级市	1 276	106. 9	151. 05	98	21 123 900	197 604	100. 00	95. 01	19. 78	100. 00
张家港市	Zhangjiagang	县级市	987	92. 7	124. 68	51	23 172 500	249 973	100. 00	95. 02	14. 58	100. 00
昆山市	Kunshan	县级市	932	82. 4	164. 49	72	31 603 000	383 532	100. 00	95. 42	13. 51	100. 00
太仓市	Taicang	县级市	810	48. 3	71. 19	51	11 551 400	239 159	100. 00	95. 12	14. 09	100. 00
启东市	Qidong	县级市	1 715	112. 0	97. 25	30	8 818 500	78 737	100. 00	91. 16	10. 83	100. 00
如皋市	Rugao	县级市	1 576	143. 7	126. 71	39	9 042 700	62 928	100. 00	91. 33	13. 53	100. 00
海门市	Haimen	县级市	1 144	100. 1	90. 76	28	10 050 600	100 406	100. 00	93. 24	10. 57	100. 00
东台市	Dongtai	县级市	3 176	112. 5	99. 03	36	7 270 100	64 623	100. 00	87. 86	13. 08	100. 00
仪征市	Yizheng	县级市	902	56. 5	56. 40	39	5 571 100	98 604	100. 00	89. 61	10. 66	100. 00
高邮市	Gaoyou	县级市	1 922	81. 5	74. 47	27	5 375 000	65 951	100. 00	84. 73	10. 16	100. 00
丹阳市	Danyang	县级市	1 047	81. 2	96. 07	34	11 360 400	139 906	100. 00	89. 36	9. 92	100. 00
扬中市	Yangzhong	县级市	327	28. 2	33. 50	14	5 047 300	178 982	100. 00	91. 30	10. 33	100. 00

续表

城市名称 Name of cities		行政级别 Admini-strative level	行政区域土地面积（平方公里） Total land area of city's administrative region(sq. km)	年末总人口（万人） Total population at year-end (10 000 persons)	六普常住人口（万人） Total residents of the Sixth National Population Census (10 000 persons)	建成区面积（平方公里） Area of built-up district (sq. km)	地区生产总值（万元） Gross regional product (10 000 yuan)	人均地区生产总值（元） Per capita gross regional product(yuan)	用水普及率（%） Water coverage rate(%)	污水处理率（%） Wastewater treatment rate(%)	人均公园绿地面积（平方米） Per capita public green space(sq. m)	生活垃圾处理率（%） Domestic garbage treatment rate(%)
句容市	Jurong	县级市	1 378	59. 2	61. 77	27	4 932 100	83 313	100. 00	86. 40	12. 07	100. 00
兴化市	Xinghua	县级市	2 395	158. 3	125. 35	39	7 488 500	47 306	100. 00	89. 39	13. 45	100. 00
靖江市	Jingjiang	县级市	656	66. 7	68. 44	34	8 017 500	120 202	100. 00	92. 47	11. 43	100. 00
泰兴市	Taixing	县级市	1 170	119. 3	107. 39	29	8 329 100	69 816	100. 00	91. 36	11. 47	100. 00
浙江省	Zhejiang											
杭州市	Hangzhou	副省级市	16 596	736. 0	870. 04	541	113 137 223	124 286	100. 00	95. 07	14. 42	100. 00
宁波市	Ningbo	副省级市	9 816	591. 0	760. 57	331	86 864 911	110 656	100. 00	95. 41	11. 40	100. 00
温州市	Wenzhou	地级市	12 083	818. 0	912. 21	241	51 015 586	55 779	100. 00	92. 50	12. 73	100. 00
嘉兴市	Jiaxing	地级市	4 223	352. 0	450. 17	101	38 621 104	83 968	99. 27	88. 32	13. 36	100. 00
湖州市	Huzhou	地级市	5 820	265. 0	289. 35	106	22 843 743	77 110	100. 00	95. 43	16. 61	100. 00
绍兴市	Shaoxing	地级市	8 279	445. 0	491. 22	204	47 890 304	96 204	100. 00	94. 51	13. 51	100. 00
金华市	Jinhua	地级市	10 942	481. 0	536. 16	98	36 849 362	67 158	100. 00	94. 68	11. 74	100. 00
衢州市	Quzhou	地级市	8 845	257. 0	212. 27	71	12 515 883	58 281	100. 00	95. 76	14. 52	100. 00
舟山市	Zhoushan	地级市	1 456	97. 0	112. 13	63	12 411 989	107 463	100. 00	95. 35	13. 09	100. 00
台州市	Taizhou	地级市	9 411	600. 0	596. 88	140	38 986 594	64 287	100. 00	93. 40	12. 88	100. 00
丽水市	Lishui	地级市	17 298	268. 0	211. 70	35	12 102 414	56 238	100. 00	95. 20	11. 09	100. 00
建德市	Jiande	县级市	2 364	51. 1	43. 08	11	3 452 539	67 564	100. 00	95. 00	12. 57	100. 00
临安市	Lin'an	县级市	3 124	53. 2	56. 67	20	5 089 958	95 676	100. 00	90. 23	13. 09	100. 00
余姚市	Yuyao	县级市	1 501	83. 8	101. 07	51	9 047 535	107 966	100. 00	88. 01	11. 66	100. 00
慈溪市	Cixi	县级市	1 361	104. 9	146. 24	46	12 761 682	121 656	100. 00	91. 82	13. 20	100. 00
瑞安市	Rui'an	县级市	1 350	123. 5	142. 47	23	7 838 331	63 468	100. 00	89. 90	12. 71	100. 00
乐清市	Leqing	县级市	1 385	129. 6	138. 93	23	8 614 683	66 471	100. 00	90. 73	10. 55	100. 00
海宁市	Haining	县级市	863	68. 2	80. 70	51	7 679 202	112 598	100. 00	92. 49	16. 18	100. 00

续表

城市名称 Name of cities		行政级别 Admini-strative level	行政区域土地面积(平方公里) Total land area of city's administrative region(sq. km)	年末总人口(万人) Total population at year-end (10 000 persons)	六普常住人口(万人) Total residents of the Sixth National Population Census (10 000 persons)	建成区面积(平方公里) Area of built-up district (sq. km)	地区生产总值(万元) Gross regional product (10 000 yuan)	人均地区生产总值(元) Per capita gross regional product(yuan)	用水普及率(%) Water coverage rate(%)	污水处理率(%) Wastewater treatment rate(%)	人均公园绿地面积(平方米) Per capita public green space(sq. m)	生活垃圾处理率(%) Domestic garbage treatment rate(%)
平湖市	Pinghu	县级市	554	49. 4	67. 18	39	5 286 800	107 020	100. 00	91. 56	14. 37	100. 00
桐乡市	Tongxiang	县级市	727	69. 3	81. 58	49	7 179 464	103 600	100. 00	92. 59	14. 64	100. 00
诸暨市	Zhuji	县级市	2 311	108. 2	115. 79	44	11 200 520	103 517	100. 00	92. 82	12. 33	100. 00
嵊州市	Shengzhou	县级市	1 789	73. 0	67. 98	41	4 853 895	66 492	100. 00	92. 50	10. 66	100. 00
兰溪市	Lanxi	县级市	1 312	66. 5	56. 05	36	3 084 732	46 387	100. 00	91. 34	12. 64	100. 00
义乌市	Yiwu	县级市	1 105	78. 2	123. 40	103	11 318 016	144 732	100. 00	95. 62	13. 00	100. 00
东阳市	Dongyang	县级市	1 747	84. 0	80. 44	40	5 064 936	60 297	100. 00	95. 35	10. 99	100. 00
永康市	Yongkang	县级市	1 047	60. 2	72. 35	38	5 269 980	87 541	100. 00	87. 57	10. 71	100. 00
江山市	Jiangshan	县级市	2 019	61. 4	46. 79	18	2 738 799	44 606	100. 00	88. 23	12. 27	100. 00
温岭市	Wenling	县级市	836	121. 7	136. 68	35	8 991 382	73 882	100. 00	90. 20	13. 41	100. 00
临海市	Linhai	县级市	2 171	120. 0	102. 88	45	5 306 243	44 219	100. 00	92. 46	14. 86	100. 00
龙泉市	Longquan	县级市	3 059	29. 1	23. 46	15	1 188 037	40 826	100. 00	90. 21	13. 27	100. 00
安徽省	Anhui											
合肥市	Hefei	地级市	11 445	730. 0	570. 25	460	62 743 777	80 138	99. 25	99. 71	13. 50	100. 00
芜湖市	Wuhu	地级市	6 026	388. 0	226. 31	172	26 994 385	73 715	100. 00	93. 56	13. 42	100. 00
蚌埠市	Bengbu	地级市	5 951	380. 0	316. 45	145	13 858 228	41 855	100. 00	99. 51	13. 03	100. 00
淮南市	Huainan	地级市	5 532	389. 0	233. 39	110	9 638 395	27 990	99. 93	97. 47	12. 60	100. 00
马鞍山市	Maanshan	地级市	4 049	229. 0	136. 63	95	14 937 617	65 833	100. 00	99. 64	14. 98	100. 00
淮北市	Huaibei	地级市	2 741	217. 0	211. 43	85	7 990 337	36 427	99. 15	97. 97	16. 72	100. 00
铜陵市	Tongling	地级市	2 991	171. 0	72. 40	81	9 573 000	59 960	100. 00	93. 10	17. 67	100. 00
安庆市	Anqing	地级市	13 538	529. 0	531. 14	90	15 311 776	33 294	100. 00	97. 37	13. 96	100. 00
黄山市	Huangshan	地级市	9 678	148. 0	135. 90	67	5 768 174	41 905	100. 00	94. 54	14. 88	100. 00
滁州市	Chuzhou	地级市	13 516	454. 0	393. 79	85	14 228 257	35 301	100. 00	96. 71	14. 48	100. 00

续表

城市名称 Name of cities		行政级别 Administrative level	行政区域土地面积（平方公里）Total land area of city's administrative region (sq. km)	年末总人口（万人）Total population at year-end (10 000 persons)	六普常住人口（万人）Total residents of the Sixth National Population Census (10 000 persons)	建成区面积（平方公里）Area of built-up district (sq. km)	地区生产总值（万元）Gross regional product (10 000 yuan)	人均地区生产总值（元）Per capita gross regional product (yuan)	用水普及率（%）Water coverage rate (%)	污水处理率（%）Wastewater treatment rate (%)	人均公园绿地面积（平方米）Per capita public green space (sq. m)	生活垃圾处理率（%）Domestic garbage treatment rate (%)
阜阳市	Fuyang	地级市	10 118	1 062.0	759.99	124	14 018 589	17 642	95.55	94.09	13.95	100.00
宿州市	Suzhou	地级市	9 939	654.0	535.29	79	13 518 116	24 270	98.87	98.05	13.41	100.00
六安市	Lu'an	地级市	15 451	587.0	561.17	77	11 081 469	23 298	99.67	98.42	14.84	100.00
亳州市	Bozhou	地级市	8 521	647.0	485.07	62	10 461 044	20 611	98.83	94.09	13.39	100.00
池州市	Chizhou	地级市	8 399	162.0	140.25	37	5 890 196	40 919	99.51	93.90	17.08	100.00
宣城市	Xuancheng	地级市	12 313	280.0	253.29	55	10 578 243	40 740	99.50	93.94	14.10	100.00
巢湖市	Chaohu	县级市	2 046	85.8	78.07	48	2 686 592	31 312	100.00	94.10	13.21	100.00
桐城市	Tongcheng	县级市	1 546	75.6	66.45	27	2 440 014	32 275	93.73	85.05	13.30	100.00
天长市	Tianchang	县级市	1 753	63.6	60.28	30	3 183 306	50 052	94.00	95.95	14.96	100.00
明光市	Mingguang	县级市	2 350	64.5	53.27	25	1 305 516	20 241	96.55	94.97	17.01	100.00
界首市	Jieshou	县级市	667	81.7	56.20	21	1 614 037	19 756	98.60	94.91	10.17	94.68
宁国市	Ningguo	县级市	2 487	38.6	37.69	26	2 544 273	65 914	98.96	94.99	13.13	100.00
福建省	Fujian											
福州市	Fuzhou	地级市	12 675	687.0	711.54	265	61 976 395	82 251	99.99	93.21	14.07	99.00
厦门市	Xiamen	副省级市	1 699	221.0	353.13	335	37 842 662	97 282	99.81	93.63	11.47	97.75
莆田市	Putian	地级市	4 131	350.0	277.85	90	18 234 281	63 313	99.54	85.00	12.70	99.15
三明市	Sanming	地级市	23 095	287.0	250.34	39	18 608 197	73 261	99.86	87.01	14.76	98.60
泉州市	Quanzhou	地级市	11 015	730.0	812.85	231	66 466 294	77 784	99.11	95.00	14.20	98.68
漳州市	Zhangzhou	地级市	12 554	508.0	481.00	67	31 253 456	62 196	100.00	90.84	14.64	99.70
南平市	Nanping	地级市	26 280	321.0	264.55	41	14 577 378	55 009	100.00	86.90	13.11	95.28
龙岩市	Longyan	地级市	19 063	314.0	255.95	62	18 956 670	72 354	99.28	89.75	12.51	99.67
宁德市	Ningde	地级市	13 247	352.0	282.20	32	16 231 142	56 358	99.22	87.49	15.64	96.49
福清市	Fuqing	县级市	1 518	135.9	123.48	50	8 578 466	63 123	99.94	86.99	14.68	99.19

续表

城市名称 Name of cities		行政级别 Admini-strative level	行政区域土地面积(平方公里) Total land area of city's administrative region(sq. km)	年末总人口(万人) Total population at year-end (10 000 persons)	六普常住人口(万人) Total residents of the Sixth National Population Census (10 000 persons)	建成区面积(平方公里) Area of built-up district (sq. km)	地区生产总值(万元) Gross regional product (10 000 yuan)	人均地区生产总值(元) Per capita gross regional product(yuan)	用水普及率(%) Water coverage rate(%)	污水处理率(%) Wastewater treatment rate(%)	人均公园绿地面积(平方米) Per capita public green space(sq. m)	生活垃圾处理率(%) Domestic garbage treatment rate(%)
长乐市	Changle	县级市	664	72. 6	68. 26	23	6 266 843	86 320	99. 91	87. 54	14. 96	99. 94
永安市	Yong'an	县级市	2 931	33. 3	34. 70	25	3 372 370	101 272	98. 49	89. 81	12. 09	99. 04
石狮市	Shishi	县级市	178	33. 2	63. 67	38	7 036 800	211 952	99. 86	89. 17	13. 06	98. 60
晋江市	Jinjiang	县级市	744	113. 2	198. 64	38	17 442 420	154 085	99. 34	88. 70	11. 39	98. 62
南安市	Nan'an	县级市	2 036	161. 3	141. 85	35	8 981 384	55 681	93. 65	88. 87	12. 03	98. 57
龙海市	Longhai	县级市	1 337	87. 6	87. 78	23	7 232 400	82 562	100. 00	88. 70	15. 00	98. 60
邵武市	Shaowu	县级市	2 831	30. 9	27. 51	20	2 059 565	66 653	100. 00	90. 32	15. 87	98. 26
武夷山市	Wuyishan	县级市	2 803	24. 3	23. 36	10	1 503 313	61 865	99. 89	92. 10	13. 32	98. 26
建瓯市	Jian'ou	县级市	4 233	55. 5	45. 22	15	2 181 087	39 299	99. 64	88. 19	11. 23	98. 25
漳平市	Zhangping	县级市	2 976	29. 7	24. 02	15	2 037 559	68 605	96. 83	87. 33	11. 45	98. 83
福安市	Fu'an	县级市	1 880	67. 2	56. 36	15	3 789 536	56 392	99. 18	83. 31	13. 69	94. 50
福鼎市	Fuding	县级市	1 526	59. 9	52. 95	19	3 330 849	55 607	99. 03	85. 39	10. 40	95. 91
江西省	Jiangxi											
南昌市	Nanchang	地级市	7 402	523. 0	504. 26	317	43 549 927	81 598	98. 88	93. 50	11. 81	99. 99
景德镇市	Jingdezhen	地级市	5 261	169. 0	158. 75	79	8 401 484	50 989	98. 02	68. 16	17. 18	100. 00
萍乡市	Pingxiang	地级市	3 831	200. 0	185. 45	52	9 982 752	52 330	100. 00	90. 13	10. 62	100. 00
九江市	Jiujiang	地级市	19 798	520. 0	472. 88	107	20 961 347	43 338	99. 30	99. 47	17. 81	100. 00
新余市	Xinyu	地级市	3 178	124. 0	113. 89	78	10 361 912	88 548	100. 00	97. 06	18. 00	100. 00
鹰潭市	Yingtan	地级市	3 560	128. 0	112. 52	39	6 953 489	60 136	96. 11	97. 66	15. 29	100. 00
赣州市	Ganzhou	地级市	39 363	971. 0	836. 84	142	22 071 959	25 761	98. 38	85. 29	11. 45	100. 00
吉安市	Ji'an	地级市	25 373	535. 0	481. 03	56	14 613 721	29 772	94. 70	91. 98	17. 09	100. 00
宜春市	Yichun	地级市	18 669	602. 0	541. 96	70	17 819 520	32 269	96. 97	94. 61	15. 27	100. 00
抚州市	Fuzhou	地级市	18 799	401. 0	391. 23	60	12 109 070	30 259	99. 45	93. 00	14. 69	100. 00

续表

城市名称 Name of cities		行政级别 Admini-strative level	行政区域土地面积（平方公里）Total land area of city's administrative region(sq. km)	年末总人口（万人）Total population at year-end (10 000 persons)	六普常住人口（万人）Total residents of the Sixth National Population Census (10 000 persons)	建成区面积（平方公里）Area of built-up district (sq. km)	地区生产总值（万元）Gross regional product (10 000 yuan)	人均地区生产总值（元）Per capita gross regional product(yuan)	用水普及率（%）Water coverage rate(%)	污水处理率（%）Wastewater treatment rate(%)	人均公园绿地面积（平方米）Per capita public green space(sq. m)	生活垃圾处理率（%）Domestic garbage treatment rate(%)
上饶市	Shangrao	地级市	22 791	782. 0	657. 97	78	18 177 664	26 996	99. 76	78. 75	15. 49	100. 00
乐平市	Leping	县级市	1 980	94. 0	81. 04	25	2 898 747	30 838	97. 50	88. 76	18. 03	99. 97
瑞昌市	Ruichang	县级市	1 419	46. 5	41. 90	20	1 641 935	35 310	100. 00	80. 56	13. 21	100. 00
共青城市	Gongqingcheng	县级市	310	7. 3		15	974 909	133 549	79. 33	90. 32	21. 58	100. 00
庐山市	Lushan	县级市	641	28. 7	24. 55	11	1 057 365	36 842	94. 30	91. 01	14. 18	100. 00
贵溪市	Guixi	县级市	2 493	64. 5	55. 85	32	3 585 843	55 594	99. 30	82. 02	14. 08	100. 00
瑞金市	Ruijin	县级市	2 441	70. 4	61. 89	28	1 344 737	19 101	87. 51	87. 26	14. 89	100. 00
井冈山市	Jinggangshan	县级市	1 298	17. 0	15. 23	9	628 832	36 990	88. 48	91. 50	46. 88	100. 00
丰城市	Fengcheng	县级市	2 836	150. 2	133. 64	51	4 236 645	28 207	91. 92	86. 02	13. 10	100. 00
樟树市	Zhangshu	县级市	1 289	61. 1	55. 51	29	3 335 947	54 598	95. 70	84. 11	14. 59	100. 00
高安市	Gaoan	县级市	2 429	87. 6	81. 16	32	2 080 544	23 751	95. 29	70. 34	14. 63	100. 00
德兴市	Dexing	县级市	2 082	33. 8	29. 32	11	1 274 036	37 693	99. 55	72. 22	20. 18	99. 96
山东省	Shandong											
济南市	Jinan	副省级市	7 998	633. 0	681. 40	448	65 361 165	90 999	100. 00	97. 21	11. 31	100. 00
青岛市	Qingdao	副省级市	11 282	791. 0	871. 51	599	100 112 900	109 407	100. 00	96. 08	18. 55	100. 00
淄博市	Zibo	地级市	5 965	432. 0	453. 06	271	44 120 100	94 587	100. 00	96. 40	18. 74	100. 00
枣庄市	Zaozhuang	地级市	4 564	413. 0	372. 91	151	21 426 335	54 984	99. 44	95. 95	14. 98	100. 00
东营市	Dongying	地级市	8 243	193. 0	203. 53	151	34 796 000	164 024	100. 00	95. 89	22. 48	100. 00
烟台市	Yantai	地级市	13 852	655. 0	696. 82	330	69 256 587	98 388	97. 75	95. 84	20. 68	100. 00
潍坊市	Weifang	地级市	16 143	901. 0	908. 62	179	51 706 000	59 275	100. 00	95. 29	18. 07	100. 00
济宁市	Jining	地级市	11 311	876. 0	808. 19	199	43 018 200	51 662	100. 00	96. 10	14. 73	100. 00
泰安市	Tai'an	地级市	7 762	569. 0	549. 42	155	33 167 900	59 027	100. 00	96. 65	22. 77	100. 00
威海市	Weihai	地级市	5 798	256. 0	280. 48	193	32 122 000	114 220	100. 00	96. 08	26. 09	100. 00

续表

城市名称 Name of cities		行政级别 Administrative level	行政区域土地面积(平方公里) Total land area of city's administrative region(sq. km)	年末总人口(万人) Total population at year - end (10 000 persons)	六普常住人口(万人) Total residents of the Sixth National Population Census (10 000 persons)	建成区面积(平方公里) Area of built - up district (sq. km)	地区生产总值(万元) Gross regional product (10 000 yuan)	人均地区生产总值(元) Per capita gross regional product(yuan)	用水普及率(%) Water coverage rate(%)	污水处理率(%) Wastewater treatment rate(%)	人均公园绿地面积(平方米) Per capita public green space(sq. m)	生活垃圾处理率(%) Domestic garbage treatment rate(%)
日照市	Rizhao	地级市	5 359	300. 0	280. 10	104	18 024 900	62 357	100. 00	95. 85	21. 23	100. 00
莱芜市	Laiwu	地级市	2 246	129. 0	129. 85	120	7 027 600	51 533	100. 00	94. 18	22. 59	100. 00
临沂市	Linyi	地级市	17 191	1 141. 0	1 003. 94	208	40 267 500	38 803	100. 00	95. 35	19. 47	100. 00
德州市	Dezhou	地级市	10 358	593. 0	556. 82	154	29 329 900	50 856	100. 00	96. 71	24. 80	100. 00
聊城市	Liaocheng	地级市	8 984	633. 0	578. 99	101	28 591 800	47 624	99. 42	95. 19	12. 96	100. 00
滨州市	Binzhou	地级市	9 660	392. 0	374. 85	156	24 701 013	63 745	100. 00	95. 02	19. 53	100. 00
菏泽市	Heze	地级市	12 256	1 015. 0	828. 77	125	25 602 400	29 904	99. 34	96. 52	11. 21	100. 00
胶州市	Jiaozhou	县级市	1 324	83. 8	84. 31	56	10 359 032	123 616	100. 00	96. 99	15. 11	100. 00
即墨市	Jimo	县级市	1 921	115. 8	117. 72	60	11 846 830	102 304	100. 00	97. 00	13. 44	100. 00
平度市	Pingdu	县级市	3 176	139. 0	135. 74	62	8 127 293	58 470	100. 00	97. 01	12. 83	100. 00
莱西市	Laixi	县级市	1 568	74. 2	75. 02	34	5 603 339	75 517	100. 00	97. 01	14. 32	100. 00
滕州市	Tengzhou	县级市	1 495	171. 5	160. 37	57	10 648 010	62 088	100. 00	96. 11	13. 66	100. 00
龙口市	Longkou	县级市	901	63. 7	68. 83	43	11 109 892	174 410	99. 97	96. 97	14. 98	100. 00
莱阳市	Laiyang	县级市	1 731	91. 0	87. 86	42	3 505 900	38 526	98. 48	97. 01	13. 21	100. 00
莱州市	Laizhou	县级市	1 928	85. 0	88. 39	45	7 667 724	90 209	100. 00	97. 03	14. 66	100. 00
蓬莱市	Penglai	县级市	1 129	44. 9	45. 11	26	5 020 136	111 807	99. 32	92. 67	16. 45	100. 00
招远市	Zhaoyuan	县级市	1 432	56. 6	56. 62	33	6 872 553	121 423	100. 00	94. 61	17. 85	100. 00
栖霞市	Qixia	县级市	2 016	60. 8	58. 96	17	2 499 652	41 113	98. 76	97. 05	12. 11	100. 00
海阳市	Haiyang	县级市	1 910	64. 4	63. 87	34	3 025 781	46 984	99. 65	95. 86	14. 83	100. 00
青州市	Qingzhou	县级市	1 569	94. 4	94. 04	52	6 156 800	65 220	100. 00	96. 97	25. 60	100. 00
诸城市	Zhucheng	县级市	2 151	111. 0	108. 62	50	7 945 100	71 577	100. 00	97. 00	22. 60	100. 00
寿光市	Shouguang	县级市	1 990	108. 5	113. 95	40	8 568 000	78 968	100. 00	97. 02	24. 27	100. 00
安丘市	Anqiu	县级市	1 712	96. 2	92. 69	61	3 063 700	31 847	100. 00	96. 98	23. 99	100. 00

续表

城市名称 Name of cities		行政级别 Admini-strative level	行政区域土地面积（平方公里）Total land area of city's administrative region (sq. km)	年末总人口（万人）Total population at year-end (10 000 persons)	六普常住人口（万人）Total residents of the Sixth National Population Census (10 000 persons)	建成区面积（平方公里）Area of built-up district (sq. km)	地区生产总值（万元）Gross regional product (10 000 yuan)	人均地区生产总值（元）Per capita gross regional product (yuan)	用水普及率（%）Water coverage rate (%)	污水处理率（%）Wastewater treatment rate (%)	人均公园绿地面积（平方米）Per capita public green space (sq. m)	生活垃圾处理率（%）Domestic garbage treatment rate (%)
高密市	Gaomi	县级市	1 527	89. 3	89. 56	53	6 231 823	69 785	100. 00	97. 00	21. 73	100. 00
昌邑市	Changyi	县级市	1 628	58. 6	60. 35	25	3 995 033	68 175	100. 00	96. 98	20. 39	100. 00
曲阜市	Qufu	县级市	815	64. 7	64. 05	27	4 136 841	63 939	100. 00	96. 39	15. 00	100. 00
邹城市	Zoucheng	县级市	1 617	119. 6	111. 67	48	8 692 931	72 683	100. 00	96. 39	13. 75	100. 00
新泰市	Xintai	县级市	1 934	142. 8	131. 59	70	8 155 922	57 114	100. 00	97. 00	19. 47	100. 00
肥城市	Feicheng	县级市	1 277	99. 2	94. 66	40	7 300 360	73 592	100. 00	94. 45	19. 29	100. 00
荣成市	Rongcheng	县级市	1 526	66. 7	71. 44	53	10 780 240	161 623	100. 00	97. 00	26. 03	100. 00
乳山市	Rushan	县级市	1 665	55. 6	57. 25	34	5 121 200	92 108	100. 00	96. 99	18. 94	100. 00
乐陵市	Leling	县级市	1 173	71. 5	65. 24	33	2 385 201	33 359	100. 00	88. 38	13. 80	100. 00
禹城市	Yucheng	县级市	992	53. 8	49. 00	36	2 641 166	49 092	97. 88	96. 97	25. 49	100. 00
临清市	Linqing	县级市	950	82. 1	71. 96	29	3 896 813	47 464	99. 19	95. 02	13. 83	100. 00
河南省	Henan											
郑州市	Zhengzhou	地级市	7 446	827. 0	862. 71	457	81 139 666	84 114	100. 00	99. 82	8. 43	100. 00
开封市	Kaifeng	地级市	6 444	559. 0	467. 65	129	17 551 002	38 619	93. 33	93. 50	9. 30	100. 00
洛阳市	Luoyang	地级市	15 236	737. 0	654. 99	216	38 201 075	56 410	98. 51	99. 94	10. 46	95. 42
平顶山市	Pingdingshan	地级市	7 882	568. 0	490. 47	73	18 251 414	36 708	97. 90	99. 94	10. 32	100. 00
安阳市	Anyang	地级市	7 384	626. 0	517. 32	82	20 298 494	39 603	100. 00	97. 73	11. 03	100. 00
鹤壁市	Hebi	地级市	2 182	170. 0	156. 92	64	7 717 894	47 940	96. 65	92. 48	14. 57	100. 00
新乡市	Xinxiang	地级市	8 666	646. 0	570. 82	118	21 669 705	37 805	99. 22	92. 00	11. 00	100. 00
焦作市	Jiaozuo	地级市	4 071	374. 0	354. 01	113	20 950 796	59 183	99. 20	95. 00	13. 20	97. 50
濮阳市	Puyang	地级市	4 188	433. 0	359. 87	59	14 495 555	40 059	98. 18	93. 10	14. 32	99. 80
许昌市	Xuchang	地级市	4 997	510. 0	430. 75	108	23 777 133	54 522	98. 16	90. 53	12. 84	100. 00
漯河市	Luohe	地级市	2 617	269. 0	254. 43	67	10 819 257	41 138	88. 08	97. 59	14. 88	100. 00

续表

城市名称 Name of cities		行政级别 Admini-strative level	行政区域土地面积（平方公里）Total land area of city's administrative region (sq. km)	年末总人口（万人）Total population at year - end (10 000 persons)	六普常住人口（万人）Total residents of the Sixth National Population Census (10 000 persons)	建成区面积（平方公里）Area of built - up district (sq. km)	地区生产总值（万元）Gross regional product (10 000 yuan)	人均地区生产总值（元）Per capita gross regional product (yuan)	用水普及率（%）Water coverage rate (%)	污水处理率（%）Wastewater treatment rate (%)	人均公园绿地面积（平方米）Per capita public green space (sq. m)	生活垃圾处理率（%）Domestic garbage treatment rate (%)
三门峡市	Sanmenxia	地级市	10 496	229. 0	223. 40	49	13 258 631	58 894	93. 61	95. 80	12. 04	96. 74
南阳市	Nanyang	地级市	26 509	1 195. 0	1 026. 37	150	31 149 653	31 010	73. 81	98. 88	8. 04	96. 52
商丘市	Shangqiu	地级市	12 725	977. 0	736. 30	63	19 891 538	27 332	67. 10	78. 79	7. 33	100. 00
信阳市	Xinyang	地级市	18 787	908. 0	610. 91	94	20 378 010	31 733	98. 14	90. 07	14. 14	100. 00
周口市	Zhoukou	地级市	11 961	1 259. 0	895. 38	70	22 638 615	25 682	100. 00	93. 22	13. 56	99. 32
驻马店市	Zhumadian	地级市	15 087	949. 0	723. 12	80	19 729 881	28 305	93. 69	96. 66	11. 22	95. 46
巩义市	Gongyi	县级市	1 043	84. 1	80. 79	32	6 799 975	80 856	97. 31	95. 67	14. 91	100. 00
荥阳市	Xingyang	县级市	943	69. 4	61. 38	23	6 296 185	90 723	94. 20	95. 12	10. 96	100. 00
新密市	Xinmi	县级市	1 001	89. 3	79. 73	26	6 843 020	76 630	93. 17	96. 91	12. 67	100. 00
新郑市	Xinzheng	县级市	885	62. 3	75. 81	33	9 789 423	157 134	69. 62	90. 00	12. 27	100. 00
登封市	Dengfeng	县级市	1 217	72. 9	66. 86	24	5 719 747	78 460	81. 68	89. 67	11. 32	91. 32
偃师市	Yanshi	县级市	669	63. 2	66. 67	20	4 498 387	71 177	93. 76	92. 58	9. 00	100. 00
舞钢市	Wugang	县级市	641	34. 4	31. 38	16	1 265 211	36 779	97. 64	95. 41	12. 27	99. 96
汝州市	Ruzhou	县级市	1 573	116. 3	92. 79	37	3 961 518	34 063	43. 14	98. 99	14. 73	100. 00
林州市	Linzhou	县级市	2 046	114. 0	78. 97	24	4 917 412	43 135	98. 70	92. 59	10. 92	100. 00
卫辉市	Weihui	县级市	859	54. 4	49. 57	21	1 070 342	19 675	100. 00	98. 87	8. 31	100. 00
辉县市	Huixian	县级市	2 007	87. 9	74. 04	22	3 339 840	37 996	92. 58	89. 99	7. 09	98. 56
沁阳市	Qinyang	县级市	595	48. 6	44. 77	20	3 803 485	78 261	95. 35	56. 13	8. 19	100. 00
孟州市	Mengzhou	县级市	542	38. 4	36. 71	16	2 942 834	76 636	98. 23	94. 23	10. 84	92. 35
禹州市	Yuzhou	县级市	1 461	133. 0	113. 19	46	5 651 831	42 495	90. 49	99. 14	9. 67	100. 00
长葛市	Changge	县级市	650	78. 7	68. 71	26	5 529 341	70 258	88. 36	98. 09	14. 51	91. 77
义马市	Yima	县级市	112	16. 0	14. 48	18	1 275 287	79 705	89. 82	93. 30	11. 14	83. 78
灵宝市	Lingbao	县级市	3 011	75. 7	72. 10	23	4 868 386	64 312	98. 17	92. 15	10. 55	100. 00

续表

城市名称 Name of cities		行政级别 Administrative level	行政区域土地面积(平方公里) Total land area of city's administrative region(sq. km)	年末总人口(万人) Total population at year-end (10 000 persons)	六普常住人口(万人) Total residents of the Sixth National Population Census (10 000 persons)	建成区面积(平方公里) Area of built-up district (sq. km)	地区生产总值(万元) Gross regional product (10 000 yuan)	人均地区生产总值(元) Per capita gross regional product(yuan)	用水普及率(%) Water coverage rate(%)	污水处理率(%) Wastewater treatment rate(%)	人均公园绿地面积(平方米) Per capita public green space(sq. m)	生活垃圾处理率(%) Domestic garbage treatment rate(%)
邓州市	Dengzhou	县级市	2 369	178.0	146.82	33	3 738 293	21 002	87.59	89.39	7.73	92.65
永城市	Yongcheng	县级市	2 006	160.7	124.04	44	4 658 533	28 989	92.87	94.36	13.42	96.14
项城市	Xiangcheng	县级市	1 083	125.1	100.37	33	2 836 849	22 677	99.47	88.52	11.32	100.00
济源市	Jiyuan	县级市	1 899	72.0	67.58	55	5 389 108	74 849	99.94	97.10	12.02	100.00
湖北省	Hubei											
武汉市	Wuhan	副省级市	8 569	834.0	978.54	458	119 126 100	111 469	100.00	97.41	10.39	100.00
黄石市	Huangshi	地级市	4 583	270.0	242.93	79	13 055 500	53 033	100.00	92.69	11.85	100.00
十堰市	Shiyan	地级市	23 680	348.0	334.08	107	14 291 500	42 083	96.91	98.77	11.08	100.00
宜昌市	Yichang	地级市	21 230	394.0	405.97	167	37 093 600	89 978	100.00	93.69	14.59	100.00
襄阳市	Xiangyang	地级市	19 728	594.0	550.03	190	36 945 100	65 663	100.00	93.00	12.43	100.00
鄂州市	Ezhou	地级市	1 594	111.0	104.87	64	7 978 200	74 983	100.00	92.52	14.93	100.00
荆门市	Jingmen	地级市	12 404	300.0	287.37	63	15 210 000	52 470	100.00	96.14	11.83	100.00
孝感市	Xiaogan	地级市	8 910	523.0	481.45	79	15 766 900	32 236	100.00	95.90	9.60	100.00
荆州市	Jingzhou	地级市	14 243	646.0	569.17	86	17 267 500	30 305	99.81	92.01	10.45	100.00
黄冈市	Huanggang	地级市	17 457	747.0	616.21	53	17 261 700	27 373	100.00	97.80	13.90	99.15
咸宁市	Xianning	地级市	9 861	304.0	246.26	66	11 079 300	44 027	98.32	94.71	14.45	51.43
随州市	Suizhou	地级市	9 636	252.0	216.22	71	8 521 800	38 801	94.27	97.92	9.49	95.79
大冶市	Daye	县级市	1 566	98.0	90.97	32	5 404 900	55 152	99.97	89.71	9.15	
丹江口市	Danjiangkou	县级市	3 121	46.5	44.38	28	1 986 835	42 728	96.96	91.96	11.21	100.00
宜都市	Yidu	县级市	1 357	39.2	38.46	25	5 505 430	140 445	100.00	96.93	12.49	99.57
当阳市	Dangyang	县级市	2 159	47.2	46.83	23	4 741 277	100 451	99.29	90.06	9.40	100.00
枝江市	Zhijiang	县级市	1 310	47.9	49.60	23	4 724 317	98 629	100.00	91.50	10.98	100.00
老河口市	Laohekou	县级市	1 052	52.2	47.15	27	3 175 289	60 829	98.98	93.29	9.30	93.17

续表

城市名称 Name of cities		行政级别 Admini-strative level	行政区域土地面积(平方公里) Total land area of city's administrative region(sq. km)	年末总人口(万人) Total population at year-end (10 000 persons)	六普常住人口(万人) Total residents of the Sixth National Population Census (10 000 persons)	建成区面积(平方公里) Area of built-up district (sq. km)	地区生产总值(万元) Gross regional product (10 000 yuan)	人均地区生产总值(元) Per capita gross regional product(yuan)	用水普及率(%) Water coverage rate(%)	污水处理率(%) Wastewater treatment rate(%)	人均公园绿地面积(平方米) Per capita public green space(sq. m)	生活垃圾处理率(%) Domestic garbage treatment rate(%)
枣阳市	Zaoyang	县级市	3 276	114. 1	100. 47	49	5 624 052	49 291	93. 46	92. 88	14. 85	100. 00
宜城市	Yicheng	县级市	2 115	56. 5	51. 25	27	3 049 234	53 969	97. 83	92. 67	11. 99	100. 00
钟祥市	Zhongxiang	县级市	4 488	105. 9	102. 25	26	4 201 100	39 670	100. 00	89. 37	10. 89	100. 00
应城市	Yingcheng	县级市	1 103	66. 6	59. 38	17	2 598 326	39 014	96. 75	90. 58	12. 32	100. 00
安陆市	Anlu	县级市	1 355	62. 0	56. 86	20	1 880 698	30 334	99. 75	96. 15	9. 92	100. 00
汉川市	Hanchuan	县级市	1 659	110. 9	101. 55	27	4 541 423	40 951	97. 21	86. 59	6. 53	100. 00
石首市	Shishou	县级市	1 406	63. 0	57. 70	23	1 520 708	24 138	99. 93	93. 04	9. 58	100. 00
洪湖市	Honghu	县级市	2 444	93. 2	81. 94	24	2 131 001	22 865	96. 58	85. 22	4. 18	100. 00
松滋市	Songzi	县级市	2 177	84. 1	76. 59	17	2 438 273	28 993	98. 05	95. 03	11. 57	100. 00
麻城市	Macheng	县级市	3 747	117. 0	84. 91	36	2 662 700	22 758	99. 46	94. 19	11. 09	98. 00
武穴市	Wuxue	县级市	1 246	82. 3	64. 42	30	2 607 836	31 687	99. 66	93. 34	19. 32	56. 23
赤壁市	Chibi	县级市	1 723	53. 5	47. 84	27	3 602 200	67 331	98. 47	94. 01	9. 99	100. 00
广水市	Guangshui	县级市	2 647	93. 1	75. 59	32	2 652 400	28 490	96. 29	77. 34	11. 05	100. 00
恩施州	Enshi	县级市	3 967	80. 9	74. 96	36	1 878 648	23 222	100. 00	93. 00	9. 90	99. 96
利川市	Lichuan	县级市	4 606	92. 0	65. 41	19	1 072 735	11 660	83. 90	73. 24	7. 52	100. 00
仙桃市	Xiantao	县级市	2 538	156. 0	117. 51	51	6 475 500	41 510	100. 00	90. 01	9. 37	100. 00
潜江市	Qianjiang	县级市	2 004	102. 3	94. 63	50	6 021 934	58 865	100. 00	91. 80	9. 80	100. 00
天门市	Tianmen	县级市	2 622	163. 4	141. 89	31	4 712 629	28 841	100. 00	93. 07	8. 95	100. 00
湖南省	Hunan											
长沙市	Changsha	地级市	11 816	696. 0	704. 10	375	93 569 088	124 122	99. 85	96. 93	10. 75	100. 00
株洲市	Zhuzhou	地级市	11 307	404. 0	385. 71	142	24 884 543	62 081	100. 00	98. 02	12. 67	100. 00
湘潭市	Xiangtan	地级市	5 008	290. 0	275. 22	80	18 667 869	65 946	96. 12	95. 00	9. 34	100. 00
衡阳市	Hengyang	地级市	15 303	799. 0	714. 83	159	28 530 158	39 020	99. 82	92. 80	10. 17	100. 00

续表

城市名称 Name of cities		行政级别 Admini-strative level	行政区域土地面积（平方公里）Total land area of city's administrative region(sq. km)	年末总人口（万人）Total population at year-end (10 000 persons)	六普常住人口（万人）Total residents of the Sixth National Population Census (10 000 persons)	建成区面积（平方公里）Area of built-up district (sq. km)	地区生产总值（万元）Gross regional product (10 000 yuan)	人均地区生产总值（元）Per capita gross regional product(yuan)	用水普及率（%）Water coverage rate(%)	污水处理率（%）Wastewater treatment rate(%)	人均公园绿地面积（平方米）Per capita public green space(sq. m)	生活垃圾处理率（%）Domestic garbage treatment rate(%)
邵阳市	Shaoyang	地级市	20 830	830.0	707.17	72	15 302 577	20 987	95.22	88.81	12.41	98.01
岳阳市	Yueyang	地级市	14 858	571.0	547.61	100	31 008 720	54 832	100.00	94.56	9.45	100.00
常德市	Changde	地级市	18 190	611.0	571.46	93	29 538 202	50 543	96.34	93.98	13.63	100.00
张家界市	Zhangjiajie	地级市	9 534	171.0	147.81	34	4 930 990	32 300	98.03	87.12	9.22	100.00
益阳市	Yiyang	地级市	12 320	484.0	430.79	76	14 931 802	33 772	95.59	92.99	9.05	100.00
郴州市	Chenzhou	地级市	19 654	535.0	458.35	77	22 041 285	46 691	99.22	93.50	12.12	100.00
永州市	Yongzhou	地级市	22 260	645.0	519.43	64	15 658 072	28 744	98.78	90.32	11.10	100.00
怀化市	Huaihua	地级市	27 758	523.0	474.17	64	14 003 368	28 515	91.60	88.80	8.11	100.00
娄底市	Loudi	地级市	8 109	453.0	378.46	50	14 001 393	36 058	99.16	91.27	9.55	100.00
浏阳市	Liuyang	县级市	4 997	149.1	127.95	28	12 182 051	81 704	96.15	91.31	5.22	100.00
醴陵市	Liling	县级市	2 157	104.8	94.74	30	5 731 693	54 692	98.69	94.42	9.67	100.00
湘乡市	Xiangxiang	县级市	1 966	93.2	78.82	21	3 656 494	39 233	100.00	94.98	8.42	100.00
韶山市	Shaoshan	县级市	247	11.9	8.60	5	777 864	65 367	98.56	95.00	18.79	100.00
耒阳市	Leiyang	县级市	2 648	143.1	115.16	45	4 301 442	30 059	82.24	91.59	6.55	100.00
常宁市	Changning	县级市	2 048	97.0	81.04	15	2 966 707	30 585	91.67	95.45	7.08	100.00
武冈市	Wugang	县级市	1 539	84.6	73.49	20	1 322 395	15 631	79.25	91.07	7.85	100.00
汨罗市	Miluo	县级市	1 670	76.2	69.21	17	4 317 314	56 658	94.09	88.78	8.27	100.00
临湘市	Linxiang	县级市	1 719	54.3	49.83	16	2 331 699	42 941	93.09	95.93	14.11	100.00
津市市	Jinshi	县级市	556	24.0	25.09	17	1 336 743	55 698	98.52	90.02	9.70	100.00
沅江市	Yuanjiang	县级市	2 129	74.9	66.63	17	2 555 105	34 114	99.28	92.07	7.60	100.00
资兴市	Zixing	县级市	2 730	38.3	33.73	21	3 266 359	85 284	96.59	90.20	10.44	100.00
洪江市	Hongjiang	县级市	2 283	50.3	47.80	7	1 415 708	28 145	92.02	91.40	14.95	100.00
冷水江市	Lengshuijiang	县级市	438	37.2	32.71	24	2 881 191	77 451	92.81	88.01	11.97	96.72

续表

城市名称 Name of cities		行政级别 Administrative level	行政区域土地面积(平方公里) Total land area of city's administrative region(sq. km)	年末总人口(万人) Total population at year-end (10 000 persons)	六普常住人口(万人) Total residents of the Sixth National Population Census (10 000 persons)	建成区面积(平方公里) Area of built-up district (sq. km)	地区生产总值(万元) Gross regional product (10 000 yuan)	人均地区生产总值(元) Per capita gross regional product(yuan)	用水普及率(%) Water coverage rate(%)	污水处理率(%) Wastewater treatment rate(%)	人均公园绿地面积(平方米) Per capita public green space(sq. m)	生活垃圾处理率(%) Domestic garbage treatment rate(%)
涟源市	Lianyuan	县级市	1 912	118. 8	99. 55	15	2 637 235	22 199	92. 00	91. 44	8. 44	99. 71
吉首市	Jishou	县级市	1 078	30. 8	30. 21	38	1 365 130	44 322	87. 75	90. 02	22. 48	100. 00
广东省	Guangdong											
广州市	Guangzhou	副省级市	7 434	870. 0	1 270. 19	1 249	195 474 420	141 933	100. 00	94. 28	22. 09	100. 00
韶关市	Shaoguan	地级市	18 413	334. 0	282. 62	102	12 183 920	41 388	93. 75	87. 12	12. 52	100. 00
深圳市	Shenzhen	副省级市	1 997	385. 0	1 035. 84	923	194 926 012	167 411	100. 00	97. 62	16. 45	100. 00
珠海市	Zhuhai	地级市	1 732	115. 0	156. 25	141	22 263 708	134 546	100. 00	96. 29	19. 70	100. 00
汕头市	Shantou	地级市	2 199	559. 0	538. 93	258	20 809 729	37 390	100. 00	90. 32	15. 19	89. 83
佛山市	Foshan	地级市	3 798	400. 0	719. 74	159	86 300 002	115 891	98. 97	96. 69	13. 91	100. 00
江门市	Jiangmen	地级市	9 509	394. 0	445. 07	152	24 187 806	53 374	99. 50	92. 10	17. 78	100. 00
湛江市	Zhanjiang	地级市	13 263	835. 0	699. 48	111	25 844 327	35 612	93. 03	91. 12	13. 99	100. 00
茂名市	Maoming	地级市	11 429	799. 0	581. 75	128	26 367 435	43 211	100. 00	94. 33	16. 46	100. 00
肇庆市	Zhaoqing	地级市	14 891	444. 0	391. 65	120	20 840 190	51 178	98. 35	89. 49	20. 39	100. 00
惠州市	Huizhou	地级市	11 346	364. 0	459. 84	263	34 121 671	71 605	98. 52	97. 02	17. 85	100. 00
梅州市	Meizhou	地级市	15 865	551. 0	423. 85	58	10 455 668	24 032	92. 49	96. 58	17. 00	100. 00
汕尾市	Shanwei	地级市	4 865	362. 0	293. 55	22	8 284 882	27 351	97. 81	91. 21	14. 08	93. 75
河源市	Heyuan	地级市	15 654	373. 0	295. 02	38	8 987 162	29 205	100. 00	92. 52	12. 61	100. 00
阳江市	Yangjiang	地级市	7 956	296. 0	242. 17	64	12 707 564	50 431	100. 00	87. 90	12. 57	100. 00
清远市	Qingyuan	地级市	19 036	432. 0	369. 84	86	13 877 104	36 136	79. 98	81. 45	10. 00	80. 60
东莞市	Dongguan	地级市	2 460	201. 0	822. 02	957	68 276 868	82 682	100. 00	93. 49	22. 99	100. 00
中山市	Zhongshan	地级市	1 784	161. 0	312. 13	149	32 027 780	99 471	100. 00	96. 30	18. 41	100. 00
潮州市	Chaozhou	地级市	3 146	274. 0	266. 95	78	9 768 303	36 956	84. 89	80. 96	9. 70	100. 00
揭阳市	Jieyang	地级市	5 265	697. 0	588. 43	131	20 068 992	33 027	86. 54	78. 29	12. 10	96. 42

续表

城市名称 Name of cities		行政级别 Administrative level	行政区域土地面积（平方公里）Total land area of city's administrative region（sq. km）	年末总人口（万人）Total population at year-end（10 000 persons）	六普常住人口（万人）Total residents of the Sixth National Population Census（10 000 persons）	建成区面积（平方公里）Area of built-up district（sq. km）	地区生产总值（万元）Gross regional product（10 000 yuan）	人均地区生产总值（元）Per capita gross regional product（yuan）	用水普及率（%）Water coverage rate（%）	污水处理率（%）Wastewater treatment rate（%）	人均公园绿地面积（平方米）Per capita public green space（sq. m）	生活垃圾处理率（%）Domestic garbage treatment rate（%）
云浮市	Yunfu	地级市	7 787	301. 0	236. 72	29	7 783 051	31 502	99. 81	77. 87	19. 22	100. 00
乐昌市	Lechang	县级市	2 419	53. 0	39. 78	18	1 146 719	21 636	99. 24	99. 78	11. 51	99. 85
南雄市	Nanxiong	县级市	2 326	48. 6	31. 62	13	1 385 230	28 503	100. 00	100. 00	12. 19	98. 76
台山市	Taishan	县级市	3 286	97. 1	94. 11	31	3 567 209	36 737	94. 42	93. 99	19. 53	100. 00
开平市	Kaiping	县级市	1 659	68. 7	69. 92	33	3 108 586	45 249	94. 50	90. 02	14. 22	100. 00
鹤山市	Heshan	县级市	1 082	37. 2	49. 49	27	2 870 406	77 161	100. 00	91. 11	22. 79	100. 00
恩平市	Enping	县级市	1 698	49. 5	49. 28	38	1 632 628	32 982	98. 07	87. 56	17. 47	100. 00
廉江市	Lianjiang	县级市	2 867	182. 5	144. 31	46	4 708 243	25 799	71. 18	64. 08	14. 91	78. 09
雷州市	Leizhou	县级市	3 709	181. 0	142. 77	29	2 774 970	15 331	56. 01	91. 75	5. 88	83. 20
吴川市	Wuchuan	县级市	870	119. 8	92. 73	26	2 421 854	20 216	92. 42	65. 22	1. 11	100. 00
高州市	Gaozhou	县级市	3 276	181. 4	128. 87	33	5 016 326	27 653	100. 00	93. 12	16. 25	100. 00
化州市	Huazhou	县级市	2 357	174. 8	117. 88	35	4 365 131	24 972	100. 00	75. 99	3. 48	100. 00
信宜市	Xinyi	县级市	3 102	146. 8	91. 37	27	4 032 925	27 472	100. 00	91. 29	15. 02	100. 00
四会市	Sihui	县级市	1 263	46. 0	54. 29	28	5 742 785	124 843	99. 79	86. 96	12. 47	100. 00
兴宁市	Xingning	县级市	2 075	119. 4	96. 29	28	1 659 678	13 900	99. 61	90. 85	23. 89	100. 00
陆丰市	Lufeng	县级市	1 542	188. 9	135. 83	21	2 490 346	13 183	88. 72	70. 16	7. 57	79. 85
阳春市	Yangchun	县级市	4 054	120. 0	84. 95	25	3 721 841	31 015	99. 05	79. 81	11. 42	100. 00
英德市	Yingde	县级市	5 634	115. 5	94. 20	34	2 550 014	22 078	94. 07	98. 57	17. 80	99. 76
连州市	Lianzhou	县级市	2 668	54. 5	36. 76	17	1 366 657	25 076	96. 29	95. 01	13. 62	100. 00
普宁市	Puning	县级市	1 620	244. 1	205. 56	65	6 397 443	26 208	96. 97	75. 99	5. 52	94. 10
罗定市	Luoding	县级市	2 328	130. 1	95. 90	25	1 954 598	15 024	74. 52	85. 28	11. 15	100. 00
广西壮族自治区	Guangxi											
南宁市	Nanning	地级市	22 244	752. 0	665. 87	310	37 033 300	52 723	96. 14	89. 51	12. 07	99. 04

续表

城市名称 Name of cities		行政级别 Admini-strative level	行政区域土地面积(平方公里) Total land area of city's administrative region(sq. km)	年末总人口(万人) Total population at year-end (10 000 persons)	六普常住人口(万人) Total residents of the Sixth National Population Census (10 000 persons)	建成区面积(平方公里) Area of built-up district (sq. km)	地区生产总值(万元) Gross regional product (10 000 yuan)	人均地区生产总值(元) Per capita gross regional product(yuan)	用水普及率(%) Water coverage rate(%)	污水处理率(%) Wastewater treatment rate(%)	人均公园绿地面积(平方米) Per capita public green space(sq. m)	生活垃圾处理率(%) Domestic garbage treatment rate(%)
柳州市	Liuzhou	地级市	18 597	386. 0	375. 87	188	24 769 396	62 855	98. 36	95. 10	13. 46	100. 00
桂林市	Guilin	地级市	27 667	534. 0	474. 80	102	20 548 216	41 216	97. 17	90. 05	11. 91	100. 00
梧州市	Wuzhou	地级市	12 588	347. 0	288. 22	57	11 756 486	39 072	96. 17	90. 24	11. 14	100. 00
北海市	Beihai	地级市	3 337	174. 0	153. 93	76	10 066 500	61 580	97. 76	97. 20	10. 93	100. 00
防城港市	Fangchenggang	地级市	6 238	97. 0	86. 69	41	6 760 383	73 188	100. 00	87. 32	16. 01	100. 00
钦州市	Qinzhou	地级市	12 187	409. 0	307. 97	95	11 020 466	34 160	99. 92	95. 88	12. 75	100. 00
贵港市	Guigang	地级市	10 602	555. 0	411. 88	73	9 587 564	22 230	98. 29	99. 51	11. 78	100. 00
玉林市	Yulin	地级市	12 835	717. 0	548. 74	70	15 538 300	27 111	100. 00	99. 14	10. 23	100. 00
百色市	Baise	地级市	36 202	417. 0	346. 68	49	11 143 094	30 881	100. 00	87. 05	12. 15	100. 00
贺州市	Hezhou	地级市	11 753	243. 0	195. 41	66	5 181 900	25 499	99. 00	89. 16	8. 54	100. 00
河池市	Hechi	地级市	33 476	429. 0	336. 93	24	6 571 808	18 842	100. 00	93. 57	10. 30	100. 00
来宾市	Laibin	地级市	13 411	269. 0	209. 97	43	5 891 105	26 885	99. 93	87. 37	10. 33	100. 00
崇左市	Chongzuo	地级市	17 332	251. 0	199. 43	30	7 662 005	37 161	94. 87	34. 20	12. 92	62. 98
岑溪市	Cenxi	县级市	2 784	95. 5	77. 21	22	2 704 542	28 320	97. 90	96. 64	10. 96	99. 85
东兴市	Dongxing	县级市	589	14. 7	14. 47	12	929 897	63 258	99. 12	94. 84	10. 80	100. 00
桂平市	Guiping	县级市	4 071	201. 7	149. 69	36	3 227 486	16 001	99. 60	86. 98	5. 57	100. 00
北流市	Beiliu	县级市	2 457	149. 5	113. 22	25	2 985 919	19 973	100. 00	98. 39	10. 68	100. 00
靖西市	Jingxi	县级市	3 326	66. 1	49. 85	18	1 585 910	23 993	98. 88	79. 73	6. 16	100. 00
宜州市	Yizhou	县级市	3 857	66. 6	55. 86	17	1 156 695	17 368	100. 00	96. 24	10. 26	100. 00
合山市	Heshan	县级市	366	13. 8	11. 45	7	304 413	22 059	100. 00	85. 03	11. 00	90. 69
凭祥市	Pingxiang	县级市	645	11. 4	11. 22	12	653 655	57 338	82. 84	77. 44	21. 88	67. 20
海南省	Hainan											
海口市	Haikou	地级市	2 304	167. 0	204. 62	147	12 576 653	56 315	98. 46	94. 99	12. 10	100. 00

续表

城市名称 Name of cities		行政级别 Admini-strative level	行政区域土地面积(平方公里) Total land area of city's administrative region(sq. km)	年末总人口(万人) Total population at year - end (10 000 persons)	六普常住人口(万人) Total residents of the Sixth National Population Census (10 000 persons)	建成区面积(平方公里) Area of built - up district (sq. km)	地区生产总值(万元) Gross regional product (10 000 yuan)	人均地区生产总值(元) Per capita gross regional product(yuan)	用水普及率(%) Water coverage rate(%)	污水处理率(%) Wastewater treatment rate(%)	人均公园绿地面积(平方米) Per capita public green space(sq. m)	生活垃圾处理率(%) Domestic garbage treatment rate(%)
三亚市	Sanya	地级市	1 921	58.0	68.54	56	4 755 567	63 273	97.82	68.02	13.02	100.00
三沙市	Sansha	地级市	13	0.0		0.32			65.00	31.43	3.25	100.00
儋州市	Danzhou	地级市	3 400	95.0	93.24	35	2 577 835	28 770	99.77	93.94	13.71	100.00
五指山市	Wuzhishan	县级市	1 144	10.6	10.41	6	242 833	22 909	96.40	60.00	9.45	100.00
琼海市	Qionghai	县级市	1 710	51.3	48.32	27	2 197 368	42 834	93.26	47.33	9.82	100.00
文昌市	Wenchang	县级市	2 485	59.7	53.74	16	1 868 790	31 303	95.79	30.91	8.80	100.00
万宁市	Wanning	县级市	4 444	62.3	54.56	12	1 842 600	29 576	97.33	85.90	13.21	100.00
东方市	Dongfang	县级市	2 272	44.7	40.83	28	1 495 545	33 457	89.52	30.86	11.83	100.00
重庆市	Chongqing	直辖市	82 402	3 392.0	2 884.62	1 351	177 405 900	57 902	97.13	96.75	16.86	99.98
四川省	Sichuan											
成都市	Chengdu	副省级市	14 335	1399.0	1 404.76	837	121 702 335	76 960	94.95	94.30	14.23	100.00
自贡市	Zigong	地级市	4 381	327.0	267.89	116	12 345 637	44 481	77.10	94.82	10.18	100.00
攀枝花市	Panzhihua	地级市	7 401	111.0	121.41	76	10 146 839	82 221	83.56	93.26	11.01	100.00
泸州市	Luzhou	地级市	12 236	508.0	421.84	136	14 819 105	34 497	95.43	92.00	10.54	100.00
德阳市	Deyang	地级市	5 911	392.0	361.58	75	17 524 542	49 835	93.65	92.01	10.70	98.14
绵阳市	Mianyang	地级市	20 248	545.0	461.39	139	18 304 207	38 202	93.65	92.67	11.52	100.00
广元市	Guangyuan	地级市	16 319	305.0	248.41	60	6 600 100	25 072	98.16	98.69	11.87	97.13
遂宁市	Suining	地级市	5 322	378.0	325.26	79	10 084 521	30 615	99.14	99.11	10.23	100.00
内江市	Neijiang	地级市	5 385	420.0	370.28	76	12 976 712	34 667	93.37	90.02	10.63	100.00
乐山市	Leshan	地级市	12 723	355.0	323.58	76	14 065 848	43 110	97.10	87.77	7.33	99.53
南充市	Nanchong	地级市	12 477	741.0	627.86	120	16 514 004	25 871	98.33	88.00	12.34	100.00
眉山市	Meishan	地级市	7 140	350.0	295.05	64	11 172 317	37 227	96.95	85.53	12.17	100.00
宜宾市	Yibin	地级市	13 271	556.0	447.19	94	16 530 529	36 735	80.98	87.79	9.93	100.00

续表

城市名称 Name of cities		行政级别 Administrative level	行政区域土地面积(平方公里) Total land area of city's administrative region(sq. km)	年末总人口(万人) Total population at year-end (10 000 persons)	六普常住人口(万人) Total residents of the Sixth National Population Census (10 000 persons)	建成区面积(平方公里) Area of built-up district (sq. km)	地区生产总值(万元) Gross regional product (10 000 yuan)	人均地区生产总值(元) Per capita gross regional product(yuan)	用水普及率(%) Water coverage rate(%)	污水处理率(%) Wastewater treatment rate(%)	人均公园绿地面积(平方米) Per capita public green space(sq. m)	生活垃圾处理率(%) Domestic garbage treatment rate(%)
广安市	Guang'an	地级市	6 339	467.0	320.55	58	10 786 241	33 130	95.60	96.11	21.82	100.00
达州市	Dazhou	地级市	16 588	684.0	546.81	108	14 470 836	25 921	95.39	46.23	18.69	95.53
雅安市	Yaan	地级市	15 046	155.0	150.73	34	5 453 272	35 335	99.51	86.20	10.89	98.34
巴中市	Bazhong	地级市	12 293	375.0	328.31	48	5 446 605	16 415	85.59	87.23	12.08	98.00
资阳市	Ziyang	地级市	5 748	355.0	366.51	49	9 434 411	37 308	99.70	88.67	15.16	100.00
都江堰市	Dujiangyan	县级市	1 208	62.3	65.80	38	3 062 245	49 153	98.42	87.12	11.95	100.00
彭州市	Pengzhou	县级市	1 421	80.5	76.29	23	3 607 288	44 811	96.80	87.09	10.16	100.00
邛崃市	Qionglai	县级市	1 377	65.7	61.28	25	2 281 261	34 722	90.81	94.72	24.45	100.00
崇州市	Chongzhou	县级市	1 090	67.0	66.11	31	2 540 435	37 917	98.93	79.83	12.11	100.00
简阳市	Jianyang	县级市	2 213	149.9	107.12	33	3 827 838	25 536	97.77	85.82	14.19	100.00
广汉市	Guanghan	县级市	549	61.1	59.11	53	3 556 673	58 211	89.86	64.03	9.04	99.91
什邡市	Shifang	县级市	820	43.6	41.28	16	2 506 197	57 482	86.54	82.44	13.24	100.00
绵竹市	Mianzhu	县级市	1 246	50.5	47.79	13	2 377 654	47 082	83.68	91.57	10.39	99.99
江油市	Jiangyou	县级市	2 720	87.9	76.21	35	3 470 945	39 487	93.33	83.19	10.19	100.00
峨眉山市	Emeishan	县级市	1 181	43.3	43.71	21	2 411 977	55 704	90.66	98.60	15.04	100.00
阆中市	Langzhong	县级市	1 875	85.9	72.89	34	1 938 875	22 571	97.42	93.02	10.65	100.00
华蓥市	Huaying	县级市	464	36.3	27.84	14	1 432 162	39 453	97.52	89.48	9.65	100.00
万源市	Wanyuan	县级市	4 053	58.5	40.76	15	1 256 975	21 487	63.95	10.53	22.29	100.00
马尔康市	Maerkang	县级市	6 626	5.6	5.84	5	242 924	43 379	98.57	92.36	5.73	91.67
康定市	Kangding	县级市	11 486	11.2	13.01	4	550 841	49 182	84.69	68.20	3.08	96.51
西昌市	Xichang	县级市	2 657	66.3	71.24	43	4 572 006	68 959	75.48	60.51	11.40	100.00
贵州省	Guizhou											
贵阳市	Guiyang	地级市	8 043	401.0	432.26	249	31 577 001	67 772	98.83	97.56	16.18	96.00

续表

城市名称 Name of cities		行政级别 Admini-strative level	行政区域土地面积（平方公里） Total land area of city's administrative region(sq. km)	年末总人口（万人） Total population at year－end (10 000 persons)	六普常住人口（万人） Total residents of the Sixth National Population Census (10 000 persons)	建成区面积（平方公里） Area of built－up district (sq. km)	地区生产总值（万元） Gross regional product (10 000 yuan)	人均地区生产总值（元） Per capita gross regional product(yuan)	用水普及率（%） Water coverage rate(%)	污水处理率（%） Wastewater treatment rate(%)	人均公园绿地面积（平方米） Per capita public green space(sq. m)	生活垃圾处理率（%） Domestic garbage treatment rate(%)
六盘水市	Liupanshui	地级市	9 914	340. 0	285. 13	73	13 137 000	45 325	90. 92	72. 36	11. 11	95. 00
遵义市	Zunyi	地级市	30 762	802. 0	612. 71	120	24 039 400	38 709	94. 30	97. 13	17. 41	95. 26
安顺市	Anshun	地级市	9 267	300. 0	229. 76	68	7 013 500	30 216	99. 38	93. 42	20. 43	95. 14
毕节市	Bijie	地级市	26 849	917. 0	653. 75	55	16 257 900	24 544	97. 74	98. 65	21. 85	95. 00
铜仁市	Tongren	地级市	18 003	441. 0	309. 32	48	8 569 700	27 366	92. 43	86. 37	8. 33	92. 00
清镇市	Qingzhen	县级市	1 387	52. 3	46. 78	21	2 801 090	53 558	97. 28	95. 49	12. 09	90. 00
赤水市	Chishui	县级市	1 852	31. 6	23. 71	17	961 429	30 425	83. 33	97. 29	12. 67	94. 00
仁怀市	Renhuai	县级市	1 788	71. 0	54. 65	23	5 608 283	78 990	99. 80	93. 03	14. 11	95. 00
兴义市	Xingyi	县级市	2 908	87. 0	78. 31	44	3 668 973	42 172	85. 83	91. 67	7. 00	95. 00
凯里市	Kaili	县级市	1 570	57. 6	47. 90	67	2 433 862	42 255	96. 17	98. 44	13. 53	91. 00
都匀市	Duyun	县级市	2 285	49. 3	44. 37	32	1 905 754	38 656	96. 91	83. 55	8. 34	91. 00
福泉市	Fuquan	县级市	1 692	33. 4	28. 39	20	1 383 440	41 420	96. 49	64. 75	15. 12	86. 75
云南省	Yunnan											
昆明市	Kunming	地级市	21 026	560. 0	643. 22	436	43 000 780	64 156	98. 58	94. 07	11. 06	96. 98
曲靖市	Qujing	地级市	28 905	653. 0	585. 51	76	17 751 063	29 266	99. 53	92. 22	8. 93	99. 96
玉溪市	Yuxi	地级市	15 233	217. 0	230. 35	38	13 118 823	55 389	93. 31	93. 23	11. 18	100. 00
保山市	Baoshan	地级市	19 637	261. 0	250. 65	37	6 133 904	23 692	82. 64	85. 71	10. 07	90. 08
昭通市	Zhaotong	地级市	22 140	609. 0	521. 35	42	7 655 307	14 040	97. 13	81. 02	8. 02	100. 00
丽江市	Lijiang	地级市	20 680	122. 0	124. 48	24	3 092 899	24 116	98. 24	94. 13	24. 91	93. 06
普洱市	Pu'er	地级市	45 385	251. 0	254. 29	27	5 675 443	21 685	92. 59	90. 13	10. 54	98. 03
临沧市	Lincang	地级市	23 620	237. 0	242. 95	22	5 508 172	21 906	93. 50	92. 04	11. 91	80. 00
安宁市	Anning	县级市	1 301	27. 4	34. 13	35	2 728 745	99 589	100. 00	97. 07	15. 42	100. 00
宣威市	Xuanwei	县级市	6 053	152. 8	130. 29	37	2 488 842	16 288	99. 13	84. 09	9. 54	98. 00

续表

城市名称 Name of cities		行政级别 Admini-strative level	行政区域土地面积(平方公里) Total land area of city's administrative region(sq. km)	年末总人口(万人) Total population at year-end (10 000 persons)	六普常住人口(万人) Total residents of the Sixth National Population Census (10 000 persons)	建成区面积(平方公里) Area of built-up district (sq. km)	地区生产总值(万元) Gross regional product (10 000 yuan)	人均地区生产总值(元) Per capita gross regional product(yuan)	用水普及率(%) Water coverage rate(%)	污水处理率(%) Wastewater treatment rate(%)	人均公园绿地面积(平方米) Per capita public green space(sq. m)	生活垃圾处理率(%) Domestic garbage treatment rate(%)
腾冲市	Tengchong	县级市	5 845	67. 8	64. 48	26	1 601 177	23 616	84. 99	86. 50	11. 84	97. 40
楚雄市	Chuxiong	县级市	4 433	52. 6	58. 86	43	3 236 369	61 528	98. 14	98. 02	11. 97	90. 01
个旧市	Gejiu	县级市	1 587	38. 8	45. 98	13	2 247 213	57 918	98. 97	87. 90	10. 69	88. 00
开远市	Kaiyuan	县级市	1 957	28. 6	32. 27	21	1 679 983	58 741	94. 85	92. 13	14. 24	100. 00
蒙自市	Mengzi	县级市	2 228	40. 6	41. 72	32	1 643 145	40 472	95. 49	85. 73	11. 25	92. 00
弥勒市	Mile	县级市	4 004	54. 2	53. 97	22	2 720 029	50 185	86. 90	90. 22	14. 24	100. 00
文山市	Wenshan	县级市	2 959	49. 7	48. 15	35	2 084 738	41 946	100. 00	93. 00	8. 43	90. 00
景洪市	Jinghong	县级市	6 959	42. 0	51. 99	27	1 919 971	45 714	100. 00	81. 59	15. 36	100. 00
大理市	Dali	县级市	1 815	62. 5	65. 20	43	3 520 694	56 331	97. 50	91. 00	11. 21	100. 00
瑞丽市	Ruili	县级市	945	13. 4	18. 06	26	891 992	66 567	100. 00	80. 13	8. 16	91. 46
芒市	Mangshi	县级市	2 910	38. 9	38. 99	19	962 796	24 751	89. 02	90. 97	14. 22	100. 00
泸水市	Lushui	县级市	2 938	18. 1	18. 48	9	468 807	25 901	100. 00	75. 25	13. 82	72. 01
香格里拉市	Xianggelila	县级市	11 419	14. 9	17. 30	30	1 109 519	74 464	72. 29	91. 56	12. 30	100. 00
西藏自治区	Tibet											
拉萨市	Lasa	地级市	29 518	54. 0	55. 94	72	4 249 500	64 804	58. 46	89. 50	4. 70	91. 85
日喀则市	Xigaze	地级市	182 000	78. 0	70. 33	29	1 877 546	23 838	96. 56	84. 82	33. 25	87. 83
昌都市	Changdu	地级市	110 154	74. 0	65. 75	7			92. 59	53. 32	3. 33	90. 50
林芝市	Linzhi	地级市	116 175	19. 0	19. 51	13			100. 00	91. 82	9. 29	91. 19
山南市	Shannan	地级市	79 699	35. 0	32. 90	15	1 265 300	35 038	77. 78	93. 37	14. 02	91. 06
陕西省	Shaanxi											
西安市	Xi'an	副省级市	10 106	825. 0	846. 78	517	62 571 800	71 357	100. 00	92. 40	11. 87	99. 70
铜川市	Tongchuan	地级市	3 882	84. 0	83. 44	40	3 116 070	36 803	92. 94	91. 45	11. 84	90. 44
宝鸡市	Baoji	地级市	18 117	384. 0	371. 67	90	19 321 400	51 262	91. 73	91. 16	12. 34	99. 70

续表

城市名称 Name of cities		行政级别 Admini-strative level	行政区域土地面积(平方公里) Total land area of city's administrative region(sq. km)	年末总人口(万人) Total population at year - end (10 000 persons)	六普常住人口(万人) Total residents of the Sixth National Population Census (10 000 persons)	建成区面积(平方公里) Area of built - up district (sq. km)	地区生产总值(万元) Gross regional product (10 000 yuan)	人均地区生产总值(元) Per capita gross regional product(yuan)	用水普及率(%) Water coverage rate(%)	污水处理率(%) Wastewater treatment rate(%)	人均公园绿地面积(平方米) Per capita public green space(sq. m)	生活垃圾处理率(%) Domestic garbage treatment rate(%)
咸阳市	Xianyang	地级市	10 189	530. 0	509. 60	92	23 909 700	48 016	92. 72	92. 02	15. 37	96. 90
渭南市	Weinan	地级市	13 134	557. 0	528. 61	75	14 886 210	27 743	98. 62	88. 96	12. 77	95. 00
延安市	Yan'an	地级市	37 037	237. 0	218. 70	36	10 829 110	48 300	84. 94	90. 78	10. 65	96. 50
汉中市	Hanzhong	地级市	27 246	384. 0	341. 62	42	11 564 920	33 597	81. 45	91. 72	13. 37	98. 50
榆林市	Yulin	地级市	42 923	382. 0	335. 14	64	27 730 540	81 764	86. 66	89. 76	12. 37	93. 27
安康市	Ankang	地级市	23 536	304. 0	262. 99	45	8 428 616	31 770	95. 18	90. 26	13. 29	99. 70
商洛市	Shangluo	地级市	19 292	253. 0	234. 17	26	6 992 980	29 574	99. 75	81. 64	7. 06	96. 18
兴平市	Xingping	县级市	508	61. 4	54. 16	23	2 176 746	35 452	99. 13	79. 69	12. 81	97. 30
韩城市	Hancheng	县级市	1 621	40. 2	39. 12	18	3 203 839	79 697	100. 00	89. 22	9. 27	97. 31
华阴市	Huayin	县级市	817	25. 8	25. 81	18	700 225	27 141	98. 27	90. 33	9. 28	94. 76
甘肃省	Gansu											
兰州市	Lanzhou	地级市	13 086	324. 0	361. 62	247	22 642 318	61 207	97. 02	95. 44	12. 71	100. 00
嘉峪关市	Jiayuguan	地级市	2 935	21. 0	23. 19	70	1 534 089	62 641	100. 00	91. 19	36. 96	100. 00
金昌市	Jinchang	地级市	8 896	46. 0	46. 41	43	2 078 152	44 202	100. 00	95. 17	22. 86	100. 00
白银市	Baiyin	地级市	21 158	182. 0	170. 88	63	4 422 085	25 813	100. 00	94. 09	9. 51	95. 55
天水市	Tianshui	地级市	14 277	371. 0	326. 25	56	5 905 136	17 800	96. 77	95. 71	9. 89	100. 00
武威市	Wuwei	地级市	33 238	191. 0	181. 51	32	4 617 272	25 396	97. 32	99. 71	14. 96	99. 50
张掖市	Zhangye	地级市	41 924	131. 0	119. 95	64	3 999 436	32 729	100. 00	90. 61	45. 17	100. 00
平凉市	Pingliang	地级市	11 170	234. 0	206. 80	36	3 673 000	17 486	99. 73	90. 50	8. 35	100. 00
酒泉市	Jiuquan	地级市	193 974	112. 0	109. 59	55	5 779 341	51 721	100. 00	91. 56	11. 45	100. 00
庆阳市	Qingyang	地级市	27 119	270. 0	221. 12	25	5 978 324	26 734	100. 00	91. 53	7. 48	97. 40
定西市	Dingxi	地级市	19 609	303. 0	269. 86	25	3 310 768	11 892	98. 36	91. 12	16. 56	100. 00
陇南市	Longnan	地级市	27 839	288. 0	256. 77	14	3 398 884	13 805	95. 04	74. 74	5. 71	100. 00

续表

城市名称 Name of cities		行政级别 Administrative level	行政区域土地面积(平方公里) Total land area of city's administrative region(sq. km)	年末总人口(万人) Total population at year-end (10 000 persons)	六普常住人口(万人) Total residents of the Sixth National Population Census (10 000 persons)	建成区面积(平方公里) Area of built-up district (sq. km)	地区生产总值(万元) Gross regional product (10 000 yuan)	人均地区生产总值(元) Per capita gross regional product(yuan)	用水普及率(%) Water coverage rate(%)	污水处理率(%) Wastewater treatment rate(%)	人均公园绿地面积(平方米) Per capita public green space(sq. m)	生活垃圾处理率(%) Domestic garbage treatment rate(%)
玉门市	Yumen	县级市	13 496	16.0	15.98	11	1 190 244	74 390	100.00	85.15	23.01	100.00
敦煌市	Dunhuang	县级市	31 200	14.4	18.60	15	1 063 935	73 884	100.00	93.33	13.89	100.00
临夏市	Linxia	县级市	89	24.8	27.45	24	662 802	26 726	100.00	82.74	5.00	100.00
合作市	Hezuo	县级市	2 291	8.8	9.03	11	367 296	41 738	75.42	82.49	6.98	90.27
青海省	Qinghai											
西宁市	Xining	地级市	7 660	203.0	220.87	92	12 481 677	53 756	99.99	74.05	12.21	95.36
海东市	Haidong	地级市	13 161	171.0	139.68	34	4 227 986	28 999	99.49	78.05	5.78	98.50
玉树市	Yushu	县级市	15 412	11.1	12.04	14	197 692	17 810	85.65	98.29	9.66	98.00
格尔木市	Golmud	县级市	119 263	13.7	21.52	36	2 984 997	217 883	100.00	76.55	7.16	100.00
德令哈市	Delingha	县级市	27 358	7.7	7.82	22	621 717	80 742	100.00	95.92	10.92	90.77
宁夏回族自治区	Ningxia											
银川市	Yinchuan	地级市	9 025	184.0	199.31	171	16 177 071	74 288	92.22	95.21	16.64	97.00
石嘴山市	Shizuishan	地级市	5 310	75.0	72.55	103	5 135 744	64 880	99.79	95.72	23.27	97.72
吴忠市	Wuzhong	地级市	16 758	142.0	127.38	54	4 424 283	32 039	95.45	90.61	20.55	100.00
固原市	Guyuan	地级市	13 047	150.0	122.82	35	2 398 058	19 720	100.00	90.14	10.06	100.00
中卫市	Zhongwei	地级市	17 448	121.0	108.08	54	3 391 289	29 549	90.58	96.25	26.13	100.00
灵武市	Lingwu	县级市	3 846	24.7	26.17	15	3 846 221	155 717	96.24	93.01	26.35	100.00
青铜峡市	Qingtongxia	县级市	2 438	28.4	26.47	32	1 343 056	47 291	98.65	88.98	17.36	96.84
新疆维吾尔自治区	Xinjiang											
乌鲁木齐市	Urumqi	地级市	13 788	268.0	311.26	436	24 589 766	69 865	99.96	90.38	11.35	96.34
克拉玛依市	Karamay	地级市	7 735	30.0	39.10	75	6 209 989	137 307	100.00	95.32	11.62	99.08
吐鲁番市	Turpan	地级市	70 049	63.0	62.29	19	2 251 000	35 891	100.00	95.00	17.60	100.00
哈密市	Hami	地级市	138 919	56.0	57.24	41	4 036 800	65 298	99.95	86.13	13.26	100.00

续表

城市名称 Name of cities		行政级别 Administrative level	行政区域土地面积（平方公里）Total land area of city's administrative region(sq. km)	年末总人口（万人）Total population at year-end (10 000 persons)	六普常住人口（万人）Total residents of the Sixth National Population Census (10 000 persons)	建成区面积（平方公里）Area of built-up district (sq. km)	地区生产总值（万元）Gross regional product (10 000 yuan)	人均地区生产总值（元）Per capita gross regional product(yuan)	用水普及率（%）Water coverage rate(%)	污水处理率（%）Wastewater treatment rate(%)	人均公园绿地面积（平方米）Per capita public green space(sq. m)	生活垃圾处理率（%）Domestic garbage treatment rate(%)
昌吉市	Changji	县级市	8 215	37.8	42.63	62	3 847 598	101 788	99.42	97.22	12.14	98.00
阜康市	Fukang	县级市	8 529	16.7	16.50	22	1 432 737	85 793	99.90	97.67	19.89	95.00
博乐市	Bole	县级市	7 790	25.8	23.56	21	1 352 194	52 411	100.00	94.99	12.34	95.68
阿拉山口市	Alashankou	县级市	1 204	4.0		11	503 400	125 850	100.00	67.60	7.00	85.51
库尔勒市	Korla	县级市	7 267	46.0	54.93	76	5 237 026	113 848	99.98	95.02	14.51	95.32
阿克苏市	Akesu	县级市	15 033	51.3	53.57	47	1 601 946	31 227	96.22	99.00	11.08	91.94
阿图什市	Atus	县级市	16 151	27.2	24.04	15	435 643	16 016	100.00	75.80	8.17	92.16
喀什市	Kashi	县级市	1 059	62.8	50.66	70	1 601 800	25 506	99.88	97.02	23.80	98.05
和田市	Hetian	县级市	466	39.0	32.23	34	660 981	16 948	97.75	85.78	5.09	91.97
伊宁市	Yining	县级市	761	55.1	51.51	37	2 004 092	36 372	99.92	85.00	9.74	100.00
奎屯市	Kuitun	县级市	1 171	15.9	16.63	25	1 133 215	71 271	89.42	69.33	8.75	100.00
霍尔果斯市	Huoerguosi	县级市	1 909	6.5		18	390 490	60 075	66.67	55.29	9.00	98.54
塔城市	Tacheng	县级市	4 357	15.2	16.10	14	718 193	47 250	97.16	91.77	13.41	97.03
乌苏市	Wusu	县级市	14 394	22.3	29.89	23	1 225 830	54 970	95.03	81.93	11.09	97.00
阿勒泰市	Aletai	县级市	11 481	19.9	19.01	16	638 444	32 083	97.35	95.78	26.97	94.77
石河子市	Shihezi	县级市	460	40.8	38.01	48	3 196 407	78 343	100.00	100.00	10.07	100.00
阿拉尔市	Alar	县级市	5 898	23.0	15.86	11	2 796 114	121 570	100.00	95.10	12.88	100.00
图木舒克市	Tumushuke	县级市	2 003	17.0	13.57	13	743 100	43 712	69.06	100.00	33.90	98.73
五家渠市	Wujiaqu	县级市	740	9.3	9.64	17	1 436 382	154 450	100.00	100.00	12.50	96.66
北屯市	Beitun	县级市	911	5.2	7.63	24	353 143	67 912	87.23	94.34	12.10	92.44
铁门关市	Tiemenguan	县级市	563	2.2		5	159 850	58 384	90.91		18.00	
双河市	Shuanghe	县级市	742	5.0		14	429 000		100.00	97.26	13.24	
可克达拉市	Cocodala	县级市	980	7.5			1 575 300	67 300				
昆玉市	Kunyu	县级市	687	4.5		6	175 000	34 889	93.75	13.33	2.25	100.00

一、数据来源（Data Resources）

1. 行政级别（Administrative level）

2. 行政区域土地面积（Total land area of city's administrative region）

3. 年末总人口（Total population at year-end）

4. 建成区面积（Area of built-up district）

5. 地区生产总值（Gross regional product）

6. 城市人均地区生产总值（Per capita gross regional product）

以上数据来源：国家统计局城市社会经济调查司 编，《中国城市统计年鉴—2017》，北京：中国统计出版社，2017.12。

（注：该年鉴未发表2016年全国360个县级市的人均地区生产总值，本数据根据地区生产总值除以年末总人口得到。2004年1月6日国家统计局发布《关于改进和规范地区GDP核算的通知》（国统字〔2004〕4号），要求各省、区、市统一使用常住人口计算人均GDP，本统计得到的县级市人均地区生产总值并不一定确切反映城市的实际情况。）

7. 污水处理率（Wastewater treatment rate）

8. 生活垃圾处理率（Domestic garbage treatment rate）

9. 供水普及率（Water coverage rate）

10. 人均公园绿地面积（Per capita public green space）

以上数据来源：中华人民共和国住房和城乡建设部网站，《2016年城市建设统计年鉴》，http://www.mohurd.gov.cn/xytj/tjzljsxytjgb/jstjnj/w02018010521542516551482530.xls。

二、指标解释（Data Illumination）

1. 行政级别：按行政级别分组，全国657个城市分为：4个直辖市，15个副省级城市，278个地级市，360个县级市。

——《中国城市统计年鉴—2017》第3页

2. 行政区域土地面积：指辖区内的全部陆地面积和水域面积。

——《中国城市统计年鉴—2017》第397页

3. 年末总人口：是指本市每年12月31日24时的户籍登记情况统计的人口数。

——《中国城市统计年鉴—2017》第397页

4. 六普常住人口：以2010年11月1日零时为标准时点进行的第六次全国人口普查中的常住人口，包括居住在本乡镇街道、户口在本乡镇街道或户口待定的人；居住在本乡镇街道、离开户口登记地所在的乡镇街道半年以上的人；户口在本乡镇街道、外出不满半年或在境外工作学习的人。不包括常住在省内的境外人员。

——《第六次全国人口普查数据公报》

5. 建成区面积：指城市行政区内实际已成片开发建设、市政公用设施和公共设施基本具备的区域。

——《中国城市统计年鉴—2017》第397页

6. 地区生产总值：指按市场价格计算的一个地区所有常住单位在一定时期内生产活动的最终成果。

——《中国城市统计年鉴—2017》第398页

7. 供水普及率：指报告期末城区内用水人口与总人口的比率。计算公式：

供水普及率 = 城区用水人口（含暂住人口）/（城区人口 + 城区暂住人口）x 100%

——《城市（县城）和村镇建设统计报表》（国统制〔2015〕113号）

8. 污水处理率：指报告期内污水处理总量与污水排放总量的比率。计算公式：

污水处理率＝污水处理总量/污水排放总量 x100%

——《城市（县城）和村镇建设统计报表》（国统制〔2015〕113号）

9. 人均公园绿地面积：指报告期末城区内平均每人拥有的公园绿地面积。计算公式：

人均公园绿地面积＝城区公园绿地面积/（城区人口＋城区暂住人口）

——《城市（县城）和村镇建设统计报表》（国统制〔2015〕113号）

10. 生活垃圾处理率：指报告期内生活垃圾处理量与生活垃圾产生量的比率。计算公式：

生活垃圾处理率＝生活垃圾处理量/生活垃圾产生量 x100%

——《城市（县城）和村镇建设统计报表》（国统制〔2015〕113号）

注：

1. 2016年1月7日，国务院发布《国务院关于同意西藏自治区撤销山南地区设立地级山南市的批复》（国函〔2016〕8号），撤销山南地区和乃东县，设立地级山南市。在本次“2016年中国城市基本数据”的统计工作中，其六普常住人口取原山南地区的六普常住人口。

2. 2016年1月7日，国务院发布《国务院关于同意新疆维吾尔自治区撤销哈密地区设立地级哈密市的批复》（国函〔2016〕9号），撤销哈密地区和县级哈密市，设立地级哈密市。在本次“2016年中国城市基本数据”的统计工作中，其六普常住人口取原哈密地区的六普常住人口。

3. 2016年1月13日，民政部发布《民政部关于同意黑龙江省撤销抚远县设立县级抚远市的批复》（民函〔2016〕14号），经国务院批准，撤销抚远县，设立县级抚远市。在本次“2016年中国城市基本数据”的统计工作中，其六普常住人口取原抚远县的六普常住人口。

4. 2016年3月20日，国务院发布《国务院关于同意江西省调整九江市部分行政区划的批复》（国函〔2016〕58号），撤销星子县，设立县级庐山市。在本次“2016年中国城市基本数据”的统计工作中，其六普常住人口取原星子县的六普常住人口。

5. 2016年6月16日，民政部发布《民政部关于同意云南省撤销泸水县设立县级泸水市的批复》（民函〔2016〕176号），经国务院批准，撤销泸水县，设立县级泸水市。在本次“2016年中国城市基本数据”的统计工作中，其六普常住人口取原泸水县的六普常住人口。

6. 2016年6月8日，国务院发布《国务院关于同意河北省调整衡水市部分行政区划的批复》（国函〔2016〕103号），撤销县级冀州市，设立衡水市冀州区。原县级冀州市的六普常住人口为衡水市统计的一部分，故在本次“2016年中国城市基本数据”的统计工作中，不再重复计数衡水市的这一部分人口。

7. 2016年9月14日，国务院发布《国务院关于同意山东省调整济南市部分行政区划的批复》（国函〔2016〕155号），撤销县级章丘市，设立济南市章丘区。原县级章丘市的六普常住人口为济南市统计的一部分，故在本次“2016年中国城市基本数据”的统计工作中，不再重复计数济南市的这一部分人口。

8. 2016年9月14日，国务院发布《国务院关于同意浙江省调整宁波市部分行政区划的批复》（国函〔2016〕158号），撤销县级奉化市，设立宁波市奉化区。原县级奉化市的六普常住人口为宁波市统计的一部分，故在本次“2016年中国城市基本数据”的统计工作中，不再重复计数宁波市的这一部分人口。

9. 《中国城市统计年鉴—2017》未统计以下城市的行政区域土地面积：西藏自治区昌都市、林芝市和山南市，新疆维吾尔自治区吐鲁番市和哈密市。在本次“2016年中国城市基本数据”的统计工作中，上述数据取自中华人民共和国民政部全国行政区划信息查询平台。

10. 《中国城市统计年鉴—2017》未统计以下城市的建成区面积：山西省太原市，辽宁省沈阳市和丹东市，广东省河源市和潮州市，海南省三沙市和儋州市，西藏自治区日喀则市、昌都市、林芝市和山南市，青海省海东市，新疆维吾尔自治区吐鲁番市和哈密市，以及全部县级市。在本次“2016年中国城市基本数据”的统计工作中，上述数据取自《2016年城市建设统计年鉴》。

11.《中国城市统计年鉴—2017》未统计以下城市的地区生产总值和人均地区生产总值：海南省三沙市，西藏自治区昌都市、林芝市和山南市，新疆维吾尔自治区吐鲁番市和哈密市。在本次“2016年中国城市基本数据”的统计工作中，西藏自治区山南市数据取自《山南市2016年国民经济和社会发展统计公报》，新疆维吾尔自治区吐鲁番市数据取自《吐鲁番市2016年国民经济和社会发展统计公报》，哈密市数据取自《哈密市2016年国民经济和社会发展统计公报》。

12.《中国城市统计年鉴—2017》未统计新疆维吾尔自治区可克达拉市、昆玉市和双河市等新设城市数据。在本次“2016年中国城市基本数据”的统计工作中，其行政区域土地面积和年末总人口取自中华人民共和国民政部全国行政区划信息查询平台，可克达拉市地区生产总值和人均地区生产总值取自《新疆生产建设兵团第四师可克达拉市2016年国民经济和社会发展统计公报》，昆玉市地区生产总值和人均地区生产总值取自《第十四师昆玉市2016年国民经济和社会发展统计公报》，双河市地区生产总值取自《五师双河市2016年国民经济和社会发展计划执行情况及2017年国民经济和社会发展计划（草案）的报告》。

13.《中国城市统计年鉴—2017》统计的河北省秦皇岛市2016年全市人均地区生产总值（73 755元）高于该市当年市辖区人均地区生产总值（56 805元），并显著高于该市2015年全市人均地区生产总值（40 746元），可能存在统计错误。在本次“2016年中国城市基本数据”的统计工作中，秦皇岛市人均地区生产总值根据地区生产总值除以年末总人口得到（45 280元）。

14.《中国城市统计年鉴—2017》统计的新疆维吾尔自治区阿拉山口市2016年年末总人口（0.2万人）显著低于该市2015年年末总人口（4.0万人），可能存在统计错误。在本次“2016年中国城市基本数据”的统计工作中，阿拉山口市年末总人口取自中华人民共和国民政部全国行政区划信息查询平台（4.0万人）。

（数据收集整理：毛其智，清华大学教授，国际欧亚科学院院士；胡若函，自然资源部城乡规划管理中心助理研究员）

编后语

《中国城市发展报告2018/2019》坚持“城市编年史”基本定位，延续综论篇、论坛篇、观察篇、专题篇、案例篇、附录篇6个篇章的基本结构，在改革开放40周年和新中国成立70周年两大背景下，以“5G、人工智能、智慧城市”为主题，共组织编写了28篇回顾我国改革发展历程、记录城市最新进展、反映社会热点问题的文章。其主要看点聚焦在如下三个方面：

一是围绕改革开放40周年和新中国成立70周年两大背景，在“论坛篇”中组织了4篇具有一定标志性的文章，分别从国家改革开放、先锋城市——深圳、“一国两制”下的香港、澳门等不同角度，回顾总结了改革开放取得的伟大成就。

在庆祝改革开放40周年之际，96岁高龄的吴良镛院士以“人居环境科学的创建者”的贡献荣获国家“改革先锋”称号。他撰写的《在国家规划体系改革的过程中发展人居科学　共筑美好家园》，特别强调在具体的规划实践中，要有综合的观念，加强统筹协调，体现国家意志和国家规划的战略性，适应高质量发展和人民对美好生活的需求。借此机会，让我们向吴老先生表示衷心祝贺和崇高敬意！

作为改革开放先锋城市的探索者，83岁高龄的深圳市前市委书记厉有为同志，亲自撰写了《风口浪尖弄潮头——深圳改革开放四十年回顾》一文，简要回顾了深圳改革开放的艰难历程，总结了“方向、路线是根本”“拓荒牛精神万岁”“市场经济是法制经济”等重要经验，并就如何“建设世界级大湾区”提出了建议，既有宝贵的历史价值，又有深刻的现实意义。

作为香港的资深媒体人，凤凰卫视时事评论员杜平先生撰写了《香港的现状与未来》，从香港人的出行模式、生活空间、守成和自满等不同角度，观察了香港这个特区城市的发展现状，展现了香港的魅力所在，并对香港的未来充满期待。文章视角独特，观察细致入微，内容鲜活生动，又不乏理性思考，读后发人深省，给人以启迪。

作为澳门回归近20周年的亲历者，澳门大学原校长赵伟以《澳门回归和澳门大学改革发展》为题，介绍了在“一国两制”“澳人治澳”、高度自治的方针指引下，澳门大学的发展历程和取得的成就，从一个侧面反映了澳门回归后，社会安定、经济发展、居民安居乐业、多元文化发展的状况，澳门的前景令人鼓舞。

二是围绕“5G、人工智能、智慧城市”主题，特别邀请了3位著名专家为“论坛篇”撰写了3篇重要文章，分别介绍了我国现代信息技术在相关领域的发展状况，并聚焦于如何在促进城市发展中发挥作用，具有很强的针对性和指导意义。

在“中国正式进入5G商用元年”之际，航空航天大学党委书记曹淑敏教授撰写的《5G助力城市智慧化和高质量发展》，从移动通信1G、2G、3G、4G的发展历程和发展规律，到5G的概念、内涵、能力、产业进展和应用场景等方面进行了比较系统的阐述，对于认识5G、推动5G发展和在城市中的应用等都具有重要的启示意义。

中国工程院原副院长邬贺铨院士撰写的《信息技术赋能智慧城市》，以一些数据表现大城市病的影响，指出智慧城市建设正当其时。从信息技术推动城市数字化、网络化和智能化，论述智慧城市发展的技术基础，从绿色城市、健康城市、平安城市、宜居城市和创新城市等方面说明智慧城市的内涵。最后讨论了智慧城市发展的机遇与挑战，具有前瞻性和引领性。

中国科学院计算技术研究所李国杰院士撰写的《充分发挥人工智能在城市建设中的“头雁”作用》，就如何理性认识人工智能、如何发挥人工智能在城市建设中的“头雁”作用和如何让人工智能在智慧城市建设中落地等，发表了他个人独特而权威的观点，有助于澄清业内外一些模糊认识。文中提出的不做表面文章、重视开发智能产品、改变“头重脚轻”局面、充分发挥企业作用等推动人工智能落地的建议，具有很强的针对性。

三是围绕国家空间规划体系改革和“粤港澳大湾区”发展战略实施的最新进展，组织收集了关于国家规划领域的最新政策及其解读性文章，有助于读者全面正确理解有关政策的核心要义和丰富内涵，具有一定启发性和指导意义。

2019年5月23日中共中央、国务院发布了《建立国土空间规划体系并监督实施的若干意见》(以下简称《若干意见》)；5月27日国务院新闻办就《若干意见》召开了新闻发布会，自然资源部副部长赵龙等接受了媒体的采访；5月28日自然资源部下发了《关于全面开展国土空间规划工作的通知》。引起了政府部门、社会各界和专家学者的高度关注。报告“专题篇”收录了相关的政策文件及其解读文章，选登了陈为邦等8位专家的视点。本报告常务副主编毛其智院士专门为此写了“编者按”，介绍了《若干意见》出台的背景和文献收录情况。

2019年2月18日，中共中央、国务院印发了《粤港澳大湾区发展规划纲要》。广州市城市规划勘察设计研究院贺辉文、廖远涛撰写了《基于边界生产的〈粤港澳大湾区发展规划纲要〉解读》，从边界生产和再生产的概念出发，以“边界生产”的逻辑来解读规划纲要，提出以“边界思维”推动粤港澳大湾区的开放发展，对于读者理解“一个国家、两种体制、三个关税区”的特殊区域特征，具有一定的学术探讨价值。

而中国城市规划设计研究院深圳分院院长方煜教授撰写的《从“深圳特区”到“大湾区”的跨越》，则从深圳特区发展的视角观察问题，认为《粤港澳大湾区发展规划纲要》的发布实施，标志着以深圳特区为突破口的40年改革开放之后，大湾区将成为代表中国下一个现代化的崭新模板，这样的判断对于读者理解大湾区的价值和方向、回溯历史的“特区现象”也许有所启示。

另据新华社北京8月18日电，中共中央、国务院发布了《关于支持深圳建设中国特色社会主义先行示范区的意见》，有利于在更高起点、更高层次、更高目标上推进改革开放，形成全面深化改革、全面扩大开放新格局；有利于更好实施粤港澳大湾区战略，丰富“一国两制”事业发展新实践；有利于率先探索全面建设社会主义强国新路径，为实现中华民族伟大复兴的中国梦提供有力支撑。

最后，我谨向为本报告作序的国际欧亚科学院中国科学中心主席蒋正华先生、中国市长协会副会长齐骥先生，以及所有文章作者及编委会的同仁们表示衷心感谢！

邵益生

2019年8月24日